AFRICAN MASTERPIECES AND SELECTED WORKS FROM MUNICH: THE STAATLICHES MUSEUM FÜR VÖLKERKUNDE

AFRICAN MASTERPIECES AND SELECTED WORKS FROM MUNICH: THE STAATLICHES MUSEUM FÜR VÖLKERKUNDE

by Maria Kecskési

The Center for African Art, New York

Masterpieces from Munich is published in conjunction with an exhibition of the same title organized by The Center for African Art, New York, and shown at: the Madison Art Center; The Center for African Art and The Chrysler Museum. The exhibition has been made possible in part by grants from The National Endowment for the Arts and Lufthansa German Airlines.

Catalogue text: Dr. Maria Kecskesi
Editorial assistance: Hertha Menting
Drawing: Werner Engelmann
Layout: Swantje Autrum-Mulzer, Werner Engelmann
Translation: Dr. Otto Friedrich Raum, assisted by Carol Irmhof
Typography: David E. Seham Associates, Inc.
Copy Editor: Elizabeth Stillinger Guthman
Publication Coordinator: Susan Cohen
Cover photograph: Swantje Autrum-Mulzer
Cover design: Linda Florio
Cover illustrations: No.161, Nigeria, Benin commemorative head of a king, bronze.

Photography:

Swantje Autrum-Mulzer: 12, 14, 15, 17, 18, 19, 22, 25, 26, 27, 28, 29, 32, 33, 34, 35, 36, 37, 39, 41, 46, 47, 54, 55, 56, 57, 58, 59, 60, 61, 62, 63, 65, 68, 69, 70, 72, 74, 75, 78, 80, 83, 84 r., 85, 86, 87, 89, 90, 93, 94, 95, 96, 97, 98, 99, 101, 102, 103, 104, 105, 106, 107, 108, 109, 110, 111, 113, 118, 120, 121, 124, 125, 130, 132, 133, 134, 135, 138, 142, 144, 145, 146, 147, 152, 156, 157, 158, 159, 165 r., 166, 167, 168, 169 l., 171, 172, 173 l., 174, 175, 178, 179, 184, 185 l., 186, 188, 192, 196, 197, 201, 203, 205, 207, 208, 210, 211, 212 r., 213, 214, 215, 216 r., 217, 221, 226, 227, 228, 229, 230, 231 l., 233 l., r., 235, 240 r., 242, 243, 246, 247, 248, 249, 250, 251, 252, 253, 254, 255, 260, 262, 263, 265, 266, 267, 268, 269, 272, 273, 274, 275, 276, 280, 281, 282, 283, 284, 285, 286, 287, 288, 293, 297, 298, 301, 302, 303, 304, 305, 306, 307, 308, 311, 313, 314 m., r., 315, 316, 317, 318, 319, 320, 321, 322, 323, 326, 327 l., 328, 329, 330, 331, 332, 333, 334, 335, 336, 337, 338, 339, 340, 341, 342, 343, 344, 345, 346, 348, 350, 352, 353, 354, 355, 356, 357, 358, 359, 360, 361, 362, 363, 364, 366, 367, 368, 369, 370, 371, 372, 373, 374, 375, 376, 377, 378, 379, 380, 381, 382, 383 l., m., 384, 385, 386, 387, 388, 389, 391, 394 l., 396, 398, 399, 401 l., m., 405, 406, 407, 409, 410, 414, 415, 416, 417
Robert Braunmüller: 16, 20, 21, 23, 24, 30, 31, 45 o., 48, 49, 50, 51, 53, 64, 66, 67, 71, 76, 77, 79, 81, 82, 84, 114, 115, 116, 117, 122, 126, 127, 128, 129, 131, 136, 137, 139, 140, 143, 151, 153, 154, 155, 160, 161, 162, 163, 165, 169 r., 170, 173 r., 177, 180, 181, 183, 185 r., 187, 191, 193, 194, 198, 199, 200, 202, 204, 206, 209, 212, 216, 218, 219, 220, 223, 224, 225, 231 r., 232, 233 m., 234, 236, 237, 238, 239, 240 l., 244, 245, 258, 259, 261, 264, 270, 271, 289, 291, 292, 294, 295, 296, 299, 300, 309, 310, 312, 314, 325, 327 r., 349, 351, 365, 383 r., 392, 393, 394, 401 r., 402, 403, 404, 408, 411, 412, 413.
Sabine Linß: 195.

The Center for African Art,
54 East 68th Street, New York, NY 10021.
Library of Congress catalogue card no. 86-24497
Clothbound ISBN 0-9614587-3-9
Paperbound ISBN 0-9614587-5-5

Printed in Japan.

Foreword

This book and the accompanying exhibition show facets of African art seldom seen in this country. Not only the individual works, but the nature of this collection, and the intellectual approach of its curator are new to most Americans. Few American museums have collections as large as this one, over 20,000 objects from which the 450 here were culled—and few American collections have such a preponderance of material documented to the earliest days of collecting and before. Above all, few museums anywhere have had the energy and the resources to publish their African collections in so thorough a fashion.

The wealth of early material published here gives us a benchmark for African art against which we can measure objects that arrived in Europe later. Precious to scholar and connoisseur alike are the great series of nineteenth century works of art from the Kongo, the Luba, the Cross River area; the unparalleled Duala pieces, and those from Southern Africa. Complete with their original attachments, their surfaces unmarred by later polishing or cleaning, these resplendent works give us a rare image of art in pre-colonial Africa. Among them, the Kongo raffia plush cloth (No. 294), almost the only eighteenth century one to have survived, attests to the extraordinary quality of a craft that had disappeared among the Kongo peoples by the nineteenth century.

These early acquisitions also challenge the general assumption that the first works to arrive in Europe were authentic, that is, made for use by Africans, and actually used. While that is still obviously true, there are some startling exceptions here. Maria Kecskési's informative text describes gradations on the spectrum between old authentic objects and those made as souvenirs.

A longstanding willingness of African artists to experiment with unfamiliar modes is evident in the series of nineteenth century ivory tusks carved for Europeans (Nos. 295-297). The collection contains other early objects invented for foreigners such as the unsettling leather dolls made in South Africa before 1839, once in the collection of King Ludwig I (Nos. 447-451.) We also see new works made for foreigners in ancient forms such as the Ejagham headdress (No. 188). Still other works are a testament to the persistence of art forms and styles over centuries; a rare ivory horn (No. 187) collected in the late sixteenth century is similar in every respect to twentieth century horns from the Lower Niger River. And finally, the collection contains instances of innovations that affirm the vitality and survival of African art late in the twentieth century (No. 155).

The intellectual approach presented here will also be new to most Americans. Unlike current American and English scholarship, the German school focuses on a culture-historical analysis, seeking relationships between a people's art style and their social, political and ecological milieu. Continent-wide classifications such as "pole sculpture" and "round sculpture," for example, contrast sharply with the prevailing American tendency to closely focused studies of a single ethnic group or area. In its broader vision the German school seeks sources for motifs and stylistic elements wherever they may occur, often in ancient civilizations of the Mediterranean, in Europe, or in the Orient. This approach may seem old fashioned to us but is interesting to reexamine in the light of today's fuller knowledge of African history.

While the text includes all the relevant research in English, it is also based on publications rarely found in American bibliographies. Maria Kesckési's use of information unfamiliar to us—much of it in early travelers' reports and hard to find German ethnographies—enriches her text and distinguishes it from those recently published in this country.

There is much here for Americans to savor for the first time: masterpieces that have never before left Germany are here to enjoy, rare witnesses of Africa's past. Here too are new ideas, and unfamiliar approaches to ponder anew.

The Board of Directors and I wish to express our gratitude to the Staatliches Museum für Völkerkunde for their extraordinary generosity in lending one hundred masterpieces from their African collection to a traveling exhibition in the United States. We are particularly grateful to Dr. Maria Kecskési who oversaw the whole operation, to Dr. Walter Raunig who lent his unqualified support, and to Mrs. Carol Irmhof who collaborated on the translation and publication of this book.

We are happy to acknowledge the generous support of The National Endowment for the Arts and the gracious assistance of its Director for Museum Programs, Andrew Oliver. We thank Lufthansa German Airlines for their generous support.

At The Center for African Art, many people exhibited grace under pressure while contributing to the success of this project. Linda Florio and Elizabeth Stillinger respectively designed the cover, and copy edited the text of this book. Jeanne Mullin did additional copyreading which was most helpful. Coordination of a complex publication was efficiently handled by Susan Cohen; Melanie Forman, Petty Benitez and Pamela Bash deftly handled labels, lists, and pasteups for this publication and exhibition; Thomas G. B. Wheelock orchestrated the transfer of the works of art and served as registrar for this exhibition; Polly Nooter lent her many talents to all aspects of the publication and exhibition. The skill and humor of these and others on The Center's staff made this difficult task a pleasure. I thank them all.

Susan Vogel

Contents

Checklist of the Exhibition:

7. Door lock. Wood, iron. H.28 cm.
Mali, Dogon. Acquired 1914.

11 Ape mask. Wood, metal. H.31 cm.
Mali, Bamana, Nossombougou. Acquired 1933.

13 Headdress. Wood. H.51 cm.
Mali, Bamana, Bougouni. Acquired 1914.

17 Cloth. Resist-dyed cotton. 80 x 155 cm.
Mali, Bamana, Beledougou. Acquired 1915.

26 Pendant. Cast brass. H.5 cm.
Ivory Coast, Tusian. Acquired 1918.

28 Pendant. Cast brass. H.5.5 cm.
Ivory Coast, Tusian. Acquired 1918.

28 Pendant. Cast brass. H.5 cm.
Ivory Coast, Turka. Acquired 1918.

48 Mask with bird head. Wood, paint. H.43 cm.
Ivory Coast, Northern Guro, Mamnigi area. Acquired 1933.

55 Male figure. Wood. H.42 cm.
Ivory Coast, Aitu Baule. Acquired 1933.

83 Goldweight. Cast brass.
Ghana, Asante. Acquired 1911.

89 Goldweight. birds on a tree. Cast brass.
Ghana, Asante. Acquired 1896.

93 Goldweight: bird looking backwards. Cast brass.
Ghana, Asante. Acquired 1925.

94 Goldweight: bird trap. Cast brass.
Ghana, Asante. Acquired 1925.

96 Goldweight: monkey. Cast brass.
Ghana, Asante. Acquired 1911.

99 Goldweight: antelope. Cast brass.
Ghana, Asante. Acquired 1911.

106 Goldweight: woman. Cast brass.
Ghana, Asante. Acquired 1911.

107 Goldweight: man. Cast brass.
Ghana, Asante. Acquired 1911.

111 Goldweight: chair. Cast brass.
Ghana, Asante. Acquired 1911.

120 Vessel. Cast brass. H.17 cm.
Ghana, Asante, Koumasi. Acquired 1931.

133 Gelede mask. Wood, paint. H.22 cm.
Nigeria, Yoruba, Badagry(?). Acquired 1888.

136 Palace post. Wood, paint. H 182 cm.
Nigeria, Yoruba, Oke Igbira, Ekiti Province. Acquired 1972.

147 Lidded bowl. Wood. H.34 cm.
Nigeria, Yoruba, Ekiti, Abeokuta region. Acquired 1977.

150 Male twin figure. Wood, iron, beads. H.22 cm.
Nigeria, Yoruba. Acquired 1926.

155 Figure. Cast brass. H.12 cm.
Nigeria, Yoruba. Acquired 1959.

159 Lidded box in form of a hare. Wood. H.16 cm.
Nigeria, Yoruba. Acquired 1980.

160 Lidded calabash. D.25 cm.
Nigeria, Yoruba, Ife. Acquired 1918.

161 Head. Cast brass, iron. H.30 cm.
Nigeria, Kingdom of Benin, Edo. First half of the 18th century. Acquired 1898.

163 Head. Cast brass. H.48 cm.
Nigeria, Kingdom of Benin, Edo. 19th century. Acquired 1899.

164 Cock. Cast brass. H.53 cm.
Nigeria, Kingdom of Benin. Acquired 1898.

165 Figure group. Cast brass. H.27 cm., W.28 cm. Nigeria, Kingdom of Benin, Edo. Acquired 1898.

168 Relief plaque. Cast brass. H.46 cm. Nigeria, Kingdom of Benin, Edo. Acquired 1899.

169 Relief plaque. Cast brass. H.48 cm. Nigeria, Kingdom of Benin, Edo. Acquired 1899.

170 Relief plaque. Cast brass. H.30 cm. Nigeria, Kingdom of Benin, Edo. Acquired 1899.

171 Leopard figure. Cast brass, iron. L.60 cm. Nigeria, Kingdom of Benin, Edo. Acquired 1952.

174 Rectangular bell, brass. Nigeria, Kingdom of Benin, Edo. Acquired 1932.

175 Rectangular bell. Brass. Nigeria, Kingdom of Benin, Edo. Acquired 1933.

182 Elephant tusk with relief carving. Ivory. Nigeria, Kingdom of Benin, Edo. 18th century. Acquired 1899.

183 Bracelet. Ivory, metal. H.11 cm. Nigeria, Yoruba of Owo or Ijebu Ode. Acquired 1935.

186 Mask. Wood, paint. H.16 cm. Nigeria, Igbo, Nri-Awka. Acquired 1976.

187 Blowing horn with low reliefs. Ivory. Nigeria, Ejagham? Ibibio? coast of Calabar? Acquired 1926.

188 Headdress. Wood, leather, paint, basketry, and other materials. H.40 cm. Cameroon, Banyang (?), Obokum. Acquired 1928.

189 Headdress. Wood, leather, paint, basketry, and other materials. H.36 cm. Nigeria, Ejagham. Acquired 1905.

190 Headdress. Wood, leather, tin, paint, basketry, beads. H.24 cm. Cameroon, Banyang, Ossidinge District. Acquired 1917.

191 Janus helmet mask. Wood, leather, tin, iron. H.52.5 cm. Nigeria, Ejagham or Mbube? Acquired 1903.

192 Janus headdress. Wood, leather, paint, fur, and other materials. Nigeria, Ejagham or Anyang. Acquired 1905.

197 Headdress and costume. Wood, woven cotton, raffia. H.(mask) 20 cm., L.(costume) 195 cm. Nigeria-Cameroon border, Banyang? Acquired 1926.

199 Housepost. Wood. H.3 meters. Cameroon, Bangwa. Acquired 1905.

211 Stool. Wood. H.27.5 cm. Cameroon, Bamileke. Acquired 1905.

217 Royal tobacco pipe. Clay, wood, metal. H.151 cm. Cameroon, Bamileke, Bafut. Acquired 1915.

221 Tobacco pipe. Clay. H.21 cm. Cameroon, Bali. Acquired 1921.

224 Tobacco pipe. Cast brass. L.31 cm. Cameroon, Tikar. Acquired 1931.

228 Ox head. Cast brass. H.14.5 cm. Cameroon, Bamum? Acquired 1912.

233 Male figure. Wood, barkcloth, beads and other materials. H.50 cm.

Cameroon, Eastern Gbaja, Bogoto. Acquired 1915.

234 Male figure. Wood, barkcloth, beads and other materials. H.52 cm. Cameroon, Eastern Gbaja, Bogoto. Acquired 1917.

245 Mask. Wood, paint, iron. L.87 cm. Cameroon, Duala. Acquired 1973.

247 Horned mask. Wood, paint, fiber, iron. L.83 cm. Cameroon, Abo. Acquired 1888.

252 Male figure. Wood, fiber. H.22 cm. Cameroon, Balong. Acquired 1916.

254 Ritual object (?). Wood. H.44 cm. Cameroon, Kundu (?), Balong (?). Acquired 1894.

256 Carved panel. Wood, paint. H.182 cm. Cameroon, Bafo (?), Betsi (?). Acquired 1893.

258 a,b Two headdresses. Wood, ratan. H.65 and 48 cm. Cameroon, Bafo. Acquired 1894.

259 Female figure. Wood, glass beads. H.161 cm. Cameroon, Koko of Edea. Acquired 1895.

260 Male figure. Wood, glass beads. H.130.5 cm. Cameroon, Koko of Edea. Acquired 1895.

264-266 Three game chips (*abia*). Fruit pits. L.3.7—4.6 cm. Cameroon, Maka. Acquired before 1888.

269,272,273,277,282 Game chips (*abia*). Fruit pits. L.3-4.2 cm. Cameroon, Ewondo. Acquired 1942.

285 Mask (*ngel*). Wood, paint. H.35 cm. Gabon, Fang. Acquired 1914.

286 Female figure. Wood, metal, glass. H.46.5 cm. Gabon, Fang. Acquired 1929.

288 Male figure. Wood, metal, teeth. H.68 cm. South Cameroon, Fang. Acquired 1900.

290 Male figure. Wood, metal, glass. H.76 cm. Gabon, Fang. Acquired 1949.

291 Whisk handle. Wood, brass, beads, iron. H.22.5 cm. Cameroon or Gabon, Bane. Acquired 1940.

292 Staff with male figure. Wood. L.105 cm. Gabon, Bane. Acquired 1913.

298 Female figure. Ivory. H.8 cm. Zaire, Woyo. Acquired 1914.

299 Power figure. Wood, fur, cloth, glass, feathers and other materials. H.(without feathers) 34 cm. Zaire, Yombe. Acquired 1893.

301 Power figure. Wood, cloth, glass and other materials. H.41.5 cm. Zaire, Yombe. Acquired 1893.

304 Power figure. Wood, fur, cloth, glass and other materials. H.40 cm. Zaire, Yombe. Acquired 1893.

305 Power figure. Wood, leather, glass, clay and other materials. H.35.5 cm. Zaire, Yombe. Acquired 1893.

307 Power figure. Wood, glass, clay and other materials. H.19.5 cm. Zaire, Yombe. Acquired 1893.

309 Power figure. Wood, iron, clay and other materials. H.35 cm., L.74 cm. Zaire, Vili. Acquired 1957.

311 Female figure. Wood, glass, iron. H.16.5 cm. Zaire, Yombe. Acquired 1934.

314 Male figure. Wood, porcelain. H.26.5 cm. Congo, Bembe of Sibiti. Acquired 1928.

321 Mask (mbuya). Wood, paint, raffia. H. 28 cm. Zaire, West Pende. Acquired 1963.

323 Ceremonial staff (*muhango*). Wood. H.41 cm. Zaire, Mbuun. Acquired 1928.

326 Ceremonial staff (*mbweci*). Wood. H.59 cm.
Angola, Lwena or Chokwe. Acquired 1926.

327 Ceremonial staff (*mbweci*). H.60 cm.
Angola, Lwena or Chokwe. Acquired 1926.

328,329,330,331,332,333,334 Figures for divination. Wood. H.4.5-8 cm.
Angola, Chokwe. Acquired 1933.

336 Female figure for divination. Wood, brass wire. H.6.5 cm.
Angola, Lwena. Acquired 1933.

343 Palm wine beaker. Wood. H.22 cm.
Zaire, Kuba. Acquired 1918.

344 Palm wine beaker. Wood. H.18 cm.
Zaire, Shoowa, Butala. Acquired 1918.

349 Lidded container. Wood. H.18 cm.
Zaire, Kuba. Acquired 1915.

355 Lidded box. Wood. L.30.5 cm.
Zaire, Kuba. Acquired 1915.

356 Lidded box. Wood. L.18 cm.
Zaire, Kuba. Acquired 1915.

358 Lidded box. Wood. H.21 cm.
Zaire, Kuba, Ifuta. Acquired 1915.

362 Fabric. Length 156 cm. x 34 cm.
Zaire, Kuba. Acquired 1952.

364 Male figure (*mbulenga*). Wood, resin, reeds. H.21 cm.
Zaire, Luluwa. Acquired 1915.

369 Mask. Wood, paint. H.44 cm.
Zaire, Luba. Acquired 1905.

370 Mask. Wood, paint, fiber. H.40 cm., W.31 cm.
Zaire, Luba, Manyema. Acquired 1891.

373 Male figure. Wood, glass, tooth, and beads. H.47 cm.
Zaire, Luba-Hemba, Manyema. Acquired 1905.

374 Male figure. Wood, copper. H.48 cm.
Zaire, Luba-Hemba, Urua. Acquired 1913.

375 Female figure. Wood. H.62 cm.
Zaire, Luba-Hemba, Manyema. Acquired 1905.

378 Female figure.'Wood. H.27 cm.
Zaire, Luba, Manyema. Acquired 1913.

383 Caryatid stool. Wood. H.57.5 cm.
Zaire, Luba. Acquired 1913.

384 Caryatid stool. Wood. H.48 cm.
Zaire, Luba. Acquired 1925.

385 Caryatid stool. Wood. H.48.5 cm.
Zaire, Luba. Acquired 1911.

390 Amulet figure. Wood, beads, leather.
Zaire, Luba. Acquired 1911.

394 Amulet figure. Wood.
Zaire, Luba. Acquired 1913.

403 Ceremonial ax. Wood, metal. Length 38 cm., blade 28.5 cm.
Zaire, Luba. Acquired 1913.

406 Chief's staff. Wood, iron. H.82 cm.
Zaire, Luba-Hemba. Acquired 1913.

407 Bowstand. Wood. H.75 cm.
Zaire, Luba-Hemba. Acquired 1913.

408 Bowstand. Wood. H.122 cm.
Zaire, Luba-Hemba, Urua. Acquired 1913.

411 Chief's staff. Wood. H.169 cm.
Zaire, Luba-Hemba, Lake Kisale. Acquired 1911.

414 Half-figure. Wood, leather, medicine bundle. H.20 cm.
Zaire, Luba, Buli. Acquired 1911.

415 Male figure. Wood. H.14.5 cm.
Zaire, collected in the Luba area (Mambwe). Acquired 1913.

416 Whisk handle. Wood. H.27.5 cm.
Zaire, Buye. Acquired 1913.

418 Chief's staff. Wood, iron. H.154 cm.
Zaire, Holoholo. Acquired 1909.

420 Female figure. Wood, plant fiber, woven cotton. H.33.5 cm.
Zaire, Tabwa. Acquired 1905.

421 Male figure. Wood, plant fiber, woven cotton. H.36.5 cm.
Zaire, Tabwa. Acquired 1905.

425 Mask. Wood, paint, human teeth. H.26 cm.
Tanzania, Haya (Ziba). Acquired 1925.

427,428,430,431,432 Lids for gourd vessels. Plaited grasses. H.47-57 cm.
Tanzania, Rwanda and Uganda, Haya, Bukoba.
Acq. 1908,1908,1909,1913,1917.

433 Grave post. Wood. H.199 cm.
Kenya, Giryama. Acquired 1982.

434 Grave post. Wood. L.168 cm.
Kenya, Giryama. Acquired 1981.

436 Doll. Wood, human hair, beads. H.19 cm.
Tanzania, Zaramo. Acquired 1911.

438 Zither. Wood, beads. L.64 cm.
Tanzania, Makonde. Acquired 1917.

439 Mask. Wood, wax, paint. H.20.5 cm.
Tanzania, Makonde. Acquired 1917.

440 Mask. Wood, wax, paint. H.21 cm.
Tanzania, Makonde. Acquired 1919.

441 Mask. Wood. H.32 cm.
Tanzania, Makonde. Acquired 1928.

444 Staff. Wood. H.75.8 cm.
Tanzania, Pangwa (?). Acquired 1928.

445 Doll. Wood, leather, glass and shell beads. H.28 cm.
South Africa, Mangwato. Acquired 1883-1887.

449 Puppet. Leather stuffed with cotton, pins. H.32 cm.
South Africa, Khoikhoi. Acquired 1815-1830.

Introduction

In a period when the whole of Africa is experiencing profound changes in the social, economic, and spiritual arenas, one may well ask why African peoples are mainly represented by their art and, what is even more surprising, their traditional art. This publication should not present a limited perspective—on the contrary, ethnological museums document the cultures of the Third World in all their aspects. The large African collection of the Staatliches Museum für Völkerkunde, Munich, comprises some 20,000 objects representing the most varied aspects of African life from state organization to wedding customs, from religion to domestic labor. European art also deals with issues that, though often formulated by patrons, are in the last analysis posed by society itself. In Africa, art is an even more integral part of everyday life. Details of composition and structures of form are so deeply enmeshed in the texture of human existence that a work of art can be completely understood only when its function has been grasped. This is also true of unconventional representations that testify to the elan of strong artistic personalities capable of transcending a traditional framework. Consequently, this publication offers the reader a chance to gain insight into the culture and life of the peoples originally served by these art objects.

As far as possible the explanatory texts contain pertinent cultural-historical information. Many African peoples have no written historical documents and no detailed oral traditions that go back further than a few generations. So the comparative study of their cultures and their art is often the most productive method of unraveling their past. To sum up the results of such research in a single sentence: the peoples of Africa have never in any phase of their history led an isolated existence; they have always engaged in continuous spiritual and material exchange with one another and with non-African cultures. Our publication aims not only to show indigenous, specifically African, achievements, but also to reveal the interconnections between Africa and other parts of the world.

The overwhelming majority of the works exhibited fall into the category of traditional art, particularly the sculpture of West and Central Africa, regions that specialized in representational art. The applied arts from East and South Africa are represented by only a few remarkable pieces. Objects were selected on the basis of several criteria. Each art province was to be represented by both typical and outstanding pieces. Sometimes the decisive factor was an object's informative value if, for example, it illuminated ritual customs or was a very rare type. The oldest pieces were made in the sixteenth and seventeenth centuries, but most were created in the decades before 1930, the date when the tourist trade began to encourage mass production and falsification of African art (sometimes even in Europe and Asia). As is well known, the possibility of supplementing a collection with comparatively old pieces becomes more remote from year to year. There are still outstanding artists in Africa who strive consciously to perpetuate traditional styles, but their works, however worthy, differ in spiritual content and in execution from those of earlier artists, who worked under quite different technical, social, and spiritual conditions.

The present volume is a translated and revised version of *Kunst aus dem Alten Afrika,* which is itself a revised and enlarged version of the catalogue *Afrikanische Kunst* (Munich, 1976). Without the help of colleagues here and abroad who willingly contributed information and advice on incompletely documented pieces, this catalogue could not have appeared in its present form. Valuable and sometimes unpublished information was supplied by Professor Marie-Louise Bastin of Brussels, Dr. Herbert M. Cole of Santa Barbara, Professor Kenneth F. Campbell of Wisconsin, Dr. Henry J. Drewal of Cleveland, William Fagg of London, Dr. Eberhard Fischer of Zürich, Huguette van Geluwe of Tervuren in Belgium, Dr. Pierre Harter of Paris, Dr. Hans Joachim Koloss of Stuttgart, Nicolas de Kun of Brussels, Dr. Malcolm McLeod of London, Piet Meyer of Zürich, Professor Tamara Northern of Hanover, New Hampshire, Francine N'Diaye of Paris, Dr. Francois Neyt of Louvain, Dr. John Pemberton III of Amherst, Massachusetts, Dr. Manuel Laranjeria Rodrigues de Areia of Coimbra, Portugal, Professor Helmut Straube of Munich, Professor Johannes W. Raum of Munich, Dr. Ray Silverman of Washington D.C., Dr. Peter Valentin of Liestal, and Dr. Jan Vansina of Madison, Wisconsin. Ludvig Bretschneider placed his private library at my disposal, and Rosaritta Volke assisted with the translation of the Italian literature. To all of them I offer my heartfelt thanks.

The photographs, which combine painstaking care with a high degree of intuition, are for the most part the work of Swantje Autrum-Mulzer; the remainder are by Robert Braunmüller. Swantje Autrum-Mulzer and Werner Englemann collaborated on the layout and contributed numerous ideas and suggestions used in the catalogue. Nicola Rademacher and Franz Brandt are responsible for most of the technical photo work. Hertha Menting greatly assisted me in the editing, and Dr. Eva Gerhards, Carol Irmhof, Elisabeth Rittler and Renate Specht helped in preparing the manuscript and reading the proofs.

I extend special thanks to Professor Laszlo Vajda and Dr. Marit Kretschmar, who read the complete German text and suggested amendments and corrections. May I take this opportunity to express my gratitude to Dr. Walter Raunig, Director of the Staatliches Museum für Völkerkunde, Munich, for allowing me a free hand in the preparation of the catalogue.

The difficult task of translation for the English edition was well entrusted to Prof. Otto Friedrich Raum with supplementations by Carol Irmhof. The copy editing, done by Elizabeth Stillinger Guthman, was carried out with painstaking thoroughness. I am thankful to all three. My sincerest thanks as well to Susan Vogel and the staff of The Center for African Art, without whose enthusiastic assistance this English version could not have appeared.

The English text has been further supplemented and revised according to the latest results of research.

M.K. Munich

Catalogue of the Collection of the Staatliches Museum für Völkerkunde

Western Sudan

Since antiquity this savannah region, which forms a transition between the Sahara Desert and tropical rain forests, has been the stage for a lively exchange of both trade goods and cultural attitudes. The earliest empires of sacred kings were founded in this area, and Islamization occurred here earlier and with greater intensity than in most other parts of Africa. Several very ancient cultures have managed to remain intact here. Driven into regions untouched by the expansion of powerful states, the Bamana, Dogon, Kurumba, Bobo, Senufo, and others dwelling along the bend of the Niger have not only remained independent, but have been able to preserve their religious institutions and their cultural identity up to the present day. Until recently their political organization, in contrast to the hierarchical structures of the kingdoms was based on clan groups, whose affairs were settled by a council of elders. No political entity superseded the authority of the clans except the cult associations of the Bamana, Bobo, Senufo, and Ligbi. Traces of centralization existed only in the offices of the smith and of the "Lord of the Earth," who is genealogically linked with the first settler. The hereditary authority of these persons, acknowledged by all clans, extended to numerous sectors of economic, social, and religious life but never achieved tightly unified political leadership.

In spite of their great variety, the art traditions of ethnic groups of the Western Sudan are characterized by a number of common basic features. All accorded figurative wood sculpture great emphasis. The pole style dominates, with its tendency toward strict symmetry, geometric patterns, and reductionism. In such figures elongated human proportions very nearly correspond to the natural ratio. It would be erroneous to consider the pole style of the Western Sudan as a "primary" one, for the principle of abstraction underlying it is in no way spontaneous; the entire stylization is logically conceived. Certain peculiarities of this style may be attributable to the fact that the metal smiths, who frequently also acted as wood carvers, transferred the simplicity of their iron forms to their wooden ones.

Increasing interest in the clay sculpture of the Sudan was triggered by, among other things, important archaeological discoveries that revealed a quite unexpected early period during which clay sculpture flourished. The sites of discovery are mainly located in Mali along the Middle Niger, in northern Cameroon, and in Chad. The sculptures' pattern of distribution, as well as a presumed relationship with the archaeologically established art centers of Nigeria, suggest the culture-mediating influence of the ancient north-south trade route.

Lit.: H. Baumann 1940, pp.330-342; 1969, p.8ff.; E. Leuzinger 1970, p.15; A. Maesen in B. de Grunne 1980, p.VIf.; G. P. Murdock 1959, p.72f.; D. Westermann 1952, p.76f.

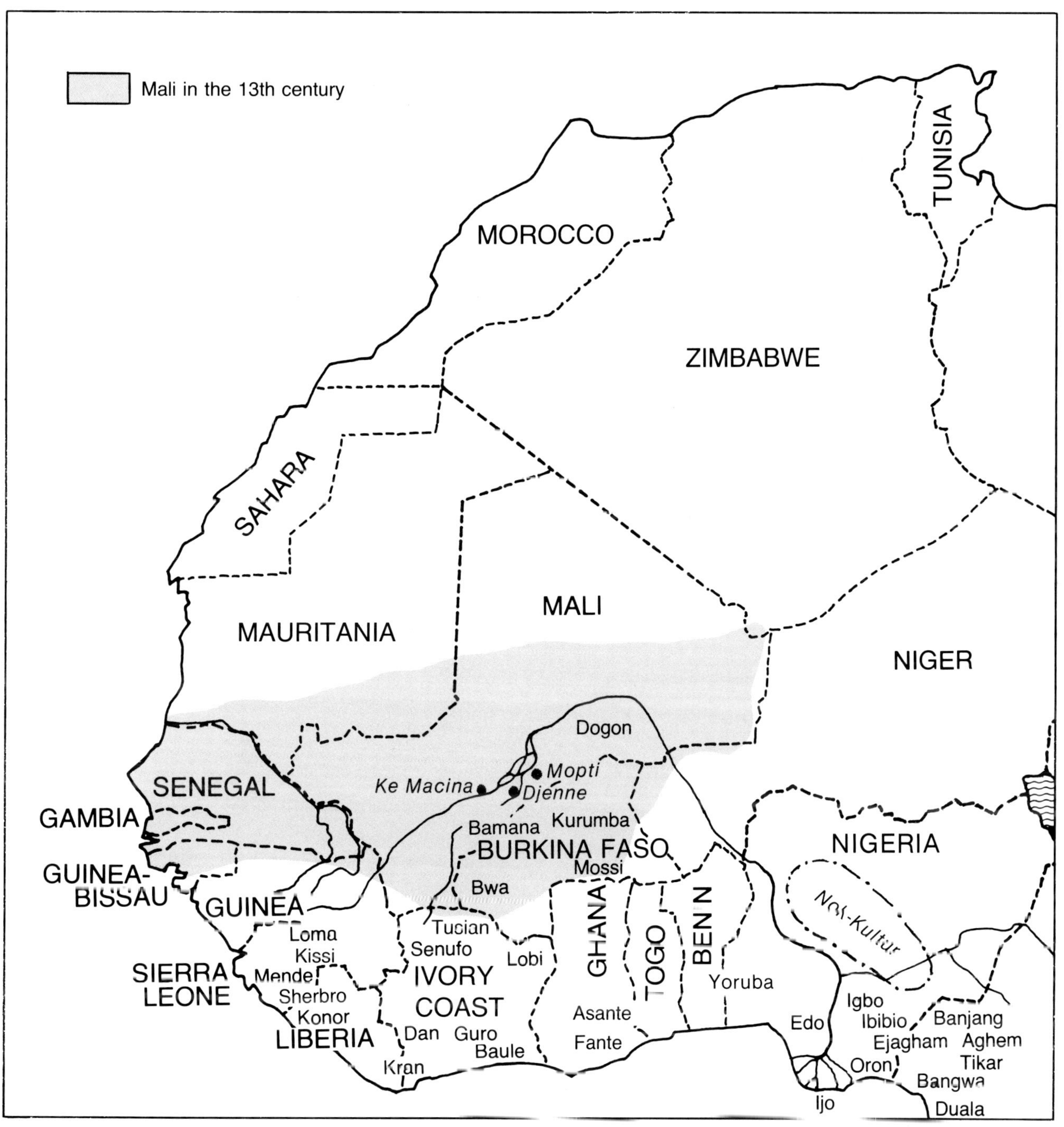
Mali in the 13th century
MOROCCO
TUNISIA
ZIMBABWE
SAHARA
MAURITANIA
MALI
NIGER
SENEGAL
GAMBIA
GUINEA-BISSAU
GUINEA
SIERRA LEONE
LIBERIA
IVORY COAST
BURKINA FASO
GHANA
TOGO
BENN
NIGERIA
Dogon
Mopti
Ke Macina
Djenne
Bamana
Kurumba
Mossi
Bwa
Loma
Kissi
Mende
Sherbro
Konor
Tucian
Senufo
Lobi
Dan
Guro
Baule
Kran
Asante
Fante
Yoruba
Edo
Igbo
Ibibio
Banjang
Ejagham
Aghem
Tikar
Oron
Bangwa
Ijo
Duala

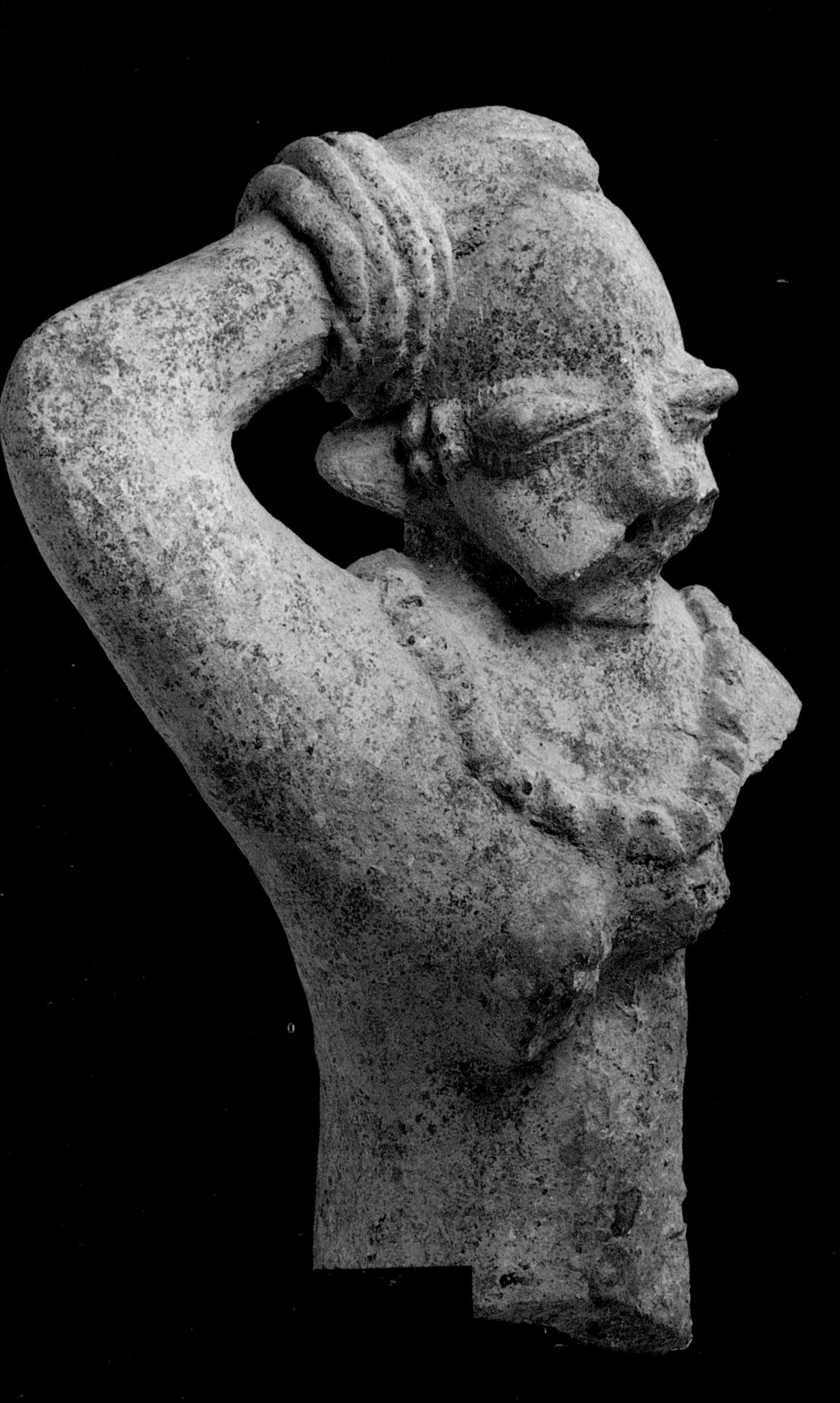

1

Djenne Terra-cottas (1-4)

Since the 1930's there have been numerous reports of fired-clay figures discovered during excavations in the present country of Mali, chiefly in the environs of the town of Djenne on the Middle Niger. Since most of these were accidental finds—scientific excavations began only in 1974—questions pertaining to their provenance and function have as yet scarcely been broached. According to radiocarbon and thermoluminescence tests, most of the figures were made in the fourteenth and fifteenth centuries. During that period important Islamic cultural centers were established in the ancient Mali Empire and in the Songhai Empire that succeeded it. In Djenne itself, for instance, a mosque was built as early as 1300. Apart from their aesthetic quality, the figures thus far discovered represent an unusual variety of themes that can be divided into several stylistic groups. The pieces shown in this exhibition represent the so-called Djenne or northern style, characterized by freedom of composition. Human figures are often forcefully dynamic, with protruding eyes that lend the face an unusual expressiveness. The very frequent snake representations are one of the important iconographic features of Djenne sculpture.

The original function of the figures has not yet been established with certainty. Those found near the foundation walls of old buildings may have served as building sacrifices to protect the houses against recurrent floods and other dangers. The figures may also have been used in burial rites or as portraits of mythical heroes.

Lit.: B. de Grunne 1980, pp. 1, 13, 19, 25-52; G. Guimont 1978, pp. 11-21; D. Mato in A. Stossel 1984, pp. 26-28; R. J. & S. K. McIntosh 1979, pp. 51-53.

1 Female figure fragment, terra-cotta.
Mali, Niger, Bani River area.

This figure, presumably originally seated, displays features typical of the Djenne style found throughout the triangle of Mopti, Ke-Macina, and Djenne north of the inland Niger delta: characteristic are the elongated bald head in a tilted position; large, precisely worked lozenge-shaped eyes with lashes indicated on the eyelids; prominent nose; protruding lips; and small projecting ears. Two rows of bold cicatrized tattoos ornament the temples. The shoulders are broad, the back is smooth, the torso somewhat full. The one preserved arm is raised high—an attitude extremely rare in West African art. The hand, placed on the head, has fingers of equal length cut off in a straight line at the tips. A woman of rank is suggested by the necklace of large beads and the broad, spiral shaped bracelet. The figure was dated to the fourteenth century by thermoluminescence.

Height 18 cm. 82-301 779
Acquired from M. v. Miller 1982

Lit.: B. de Grunne 1980, pp. 25, 48-50.

2 Head with snake, fragment, terra-cotta.
Mali, Niger, Bani River area.

Strongly modeled eyes with slightly hatched upper and lower lids lie under a bulbous forehead. Minute holes mark the nose. The body of a snake lying across the forehead ends in the fully sculptured mouth of the human figure.

Length 11 cm. 82-301 613
Acquired from F. Jahn 1982

3 Head fragment, terra-cotta.
Mali, Niger, Bani River area.

This round head with vague facial features rests on a powerful neck. Openings of the elongated ears and almost circular mouth are indicated in a sculptural manner.

Length 9 cm. 81-301 494
Acquired from F. Jahn 1981

2

3

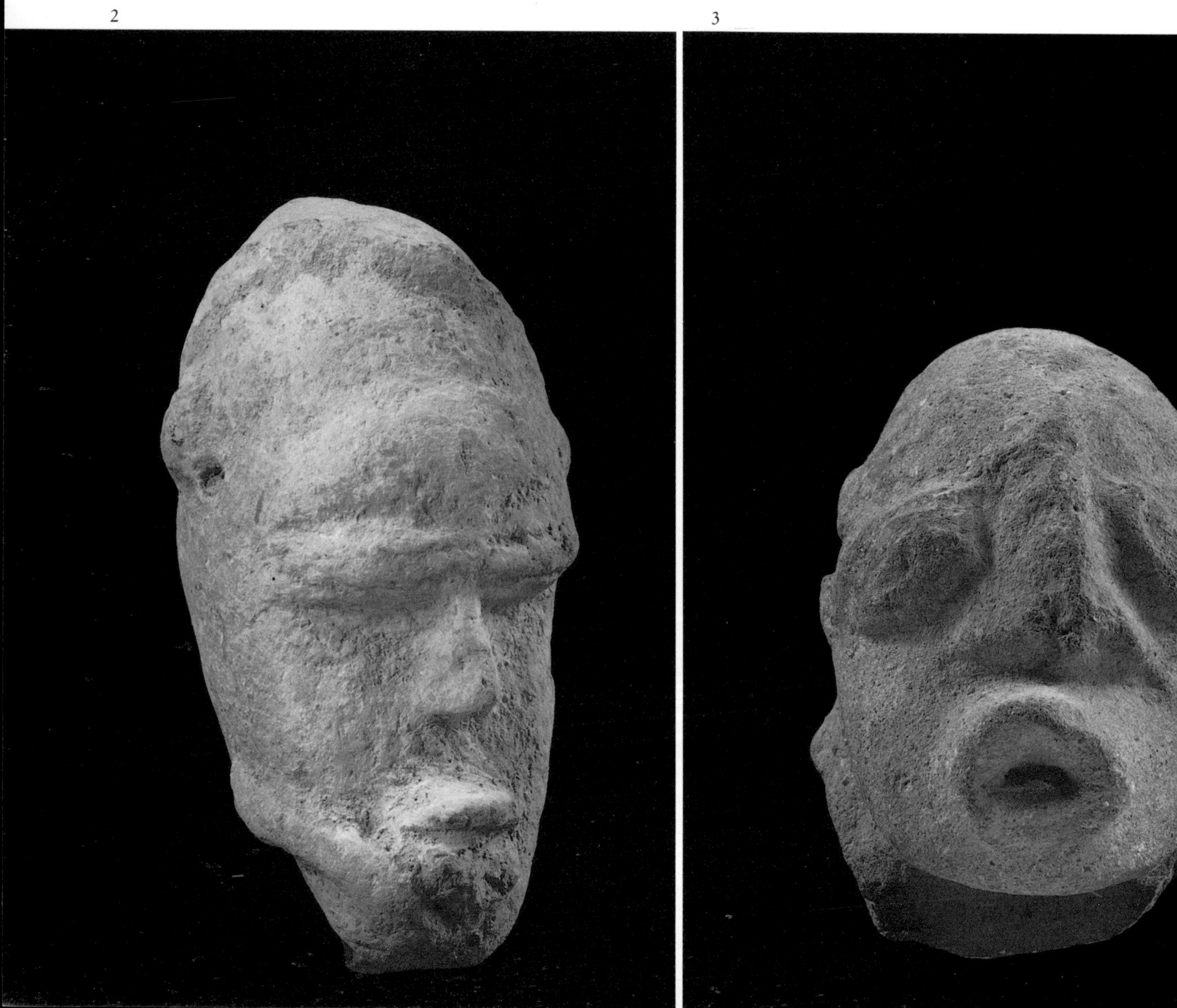

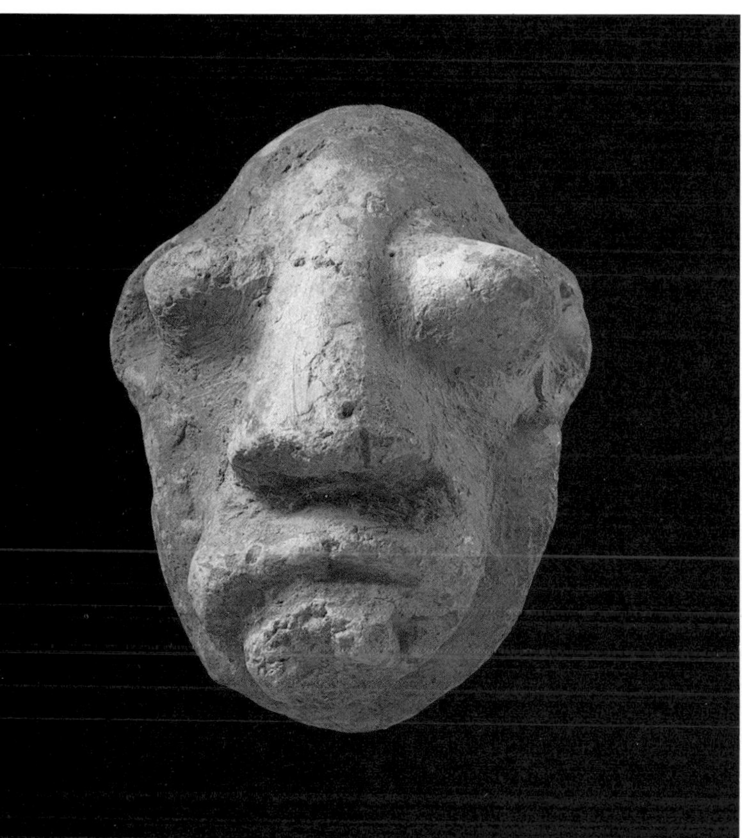

4

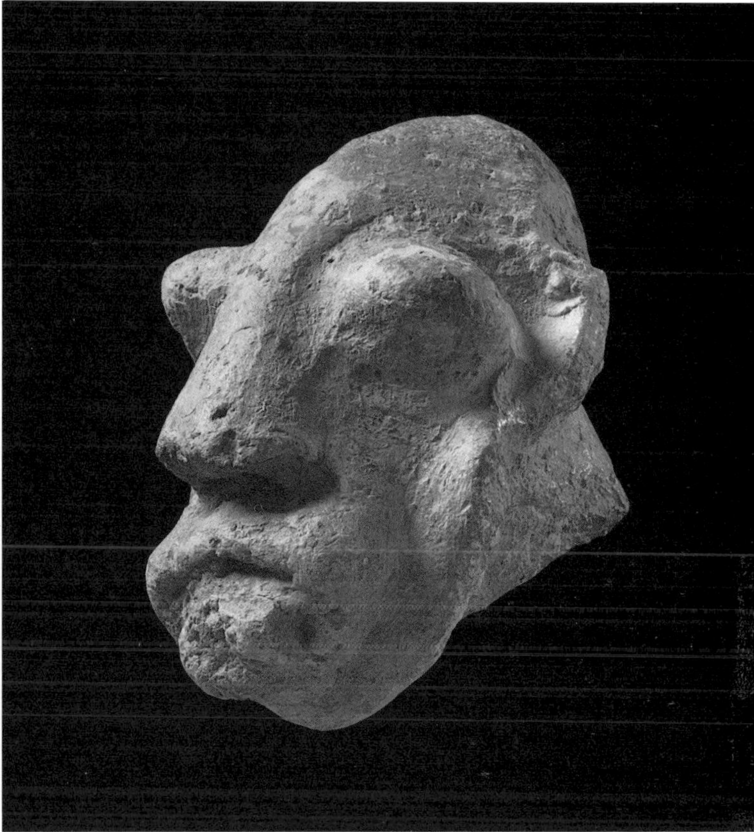

4

4 Head fragment, terra-cotta.
Mali, Niger, Bani River area.

Oversized eyes protrude from this expressive, robust head with wide, open mouth, funnel-shaped nose, fleshy ears, and powerful neck. A beard (or snake?) frames the face.

Height 10 cm. 82-301 612
Acquired from F. Jahn 1982

5 Pillar from a *toguna* building, wood.
Mali, Dogon.

This pillar was one of eight that supported the roof of a *toguna,* a rectangular building without side walls that stands in every Dogon village. There the council of elders reaches decisions and men pass much of their leisure time. Women may not enter the *toguna,* a prohibition that is still enforced although the sacred and social significance of such buildings is gradually declining as a consequence of Islamic and Western influences. *Toguna* are usually low-ceilinged (120-140 cm.), a fact that is explained by the Dogon in various ways; in the *toguna* no one should stand, for the truth is said sitting, nor should anyone quarrel there; the inside should be protected against the rays of the sun; under the low roof people are safe from the mounted warriors of aggressive neighbors; and so on. Possibly none of these explanations corresponds exactly to the original reason for the low construction of such buildings.

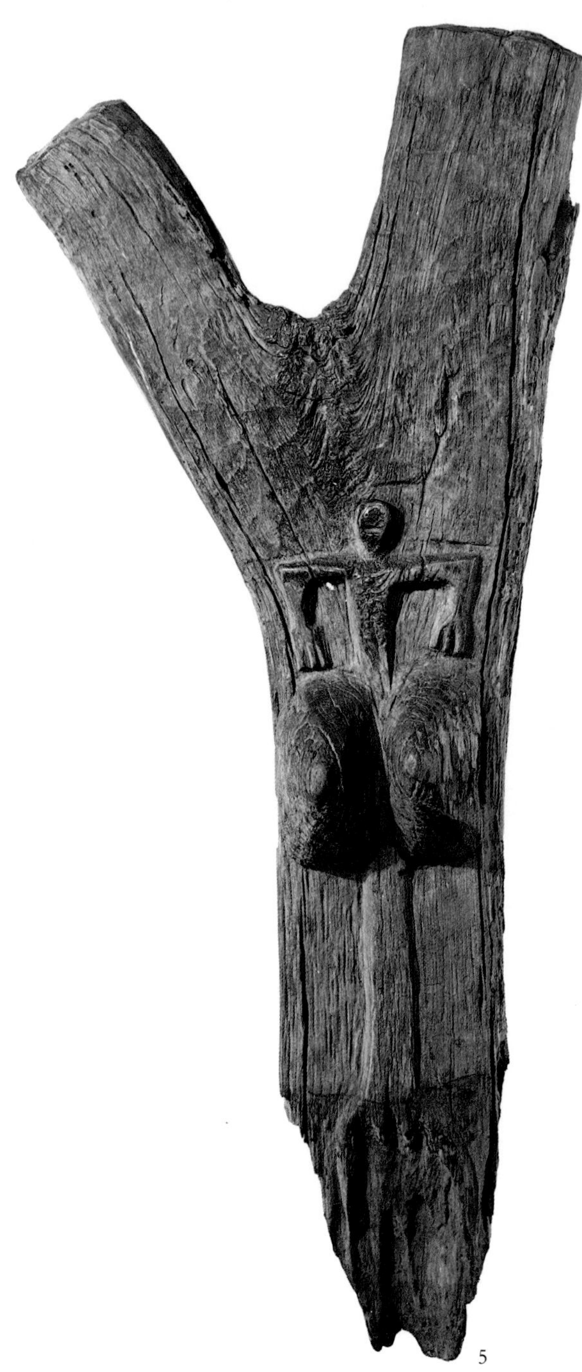
5

The comparatively high straw roof of the *toguna* is supported by pillars that consist of piled-up stones in the mountain villages, and of carved wood in villages on the plains. Trunks of a certain species of low-growing tree are used in compliance with traditional precepts. The customary number of eight pillars symbolizes the eight mythical forebears of the Dogon or the groups derived from them respectively, the eight cultivated plants that the ancestors received from God in primordial times, and so on. If the pillars are of wood, they are forked at the top and carved on the outside with mythical motifs and sexual symbols. This pillar is embellished with an abstract female figure whose exaggerated conical breasts, reminiscent of Bamana sculpture, are a symbol of fertility.

Height 140 cm., width 61 cm. 73-3-1
Acquired from L. Bretschneider 1973

Lit.: M. Griaule 1965, pp. 24, 31, 51; J. Laude 1973, Illus. 70-72; M. Palau Marti 1957, pp. 32-50; T. & S. Spini 1976, pp. 16-23.

6 Horseman, wood, iron.
Mali, Dogon.

This horse and rider form independent figures, a rare phenomenon in old African wood sculpture, possibly an indication of Western influence. A further remarkable feature of this piece is the artist's use of different proportions for the two figures. The rider's head is three times as large as his body, a comparative enlargement that is found in numerous human representations south of the Sahara. The exaggeration is further emphasized by the detailed facial features and the rather summarily depicted body. In contrast to the "ancient African" proportions of the rider, those of the stylized horse are almost naturalistic. The careful reality of the mane, combed to the left,

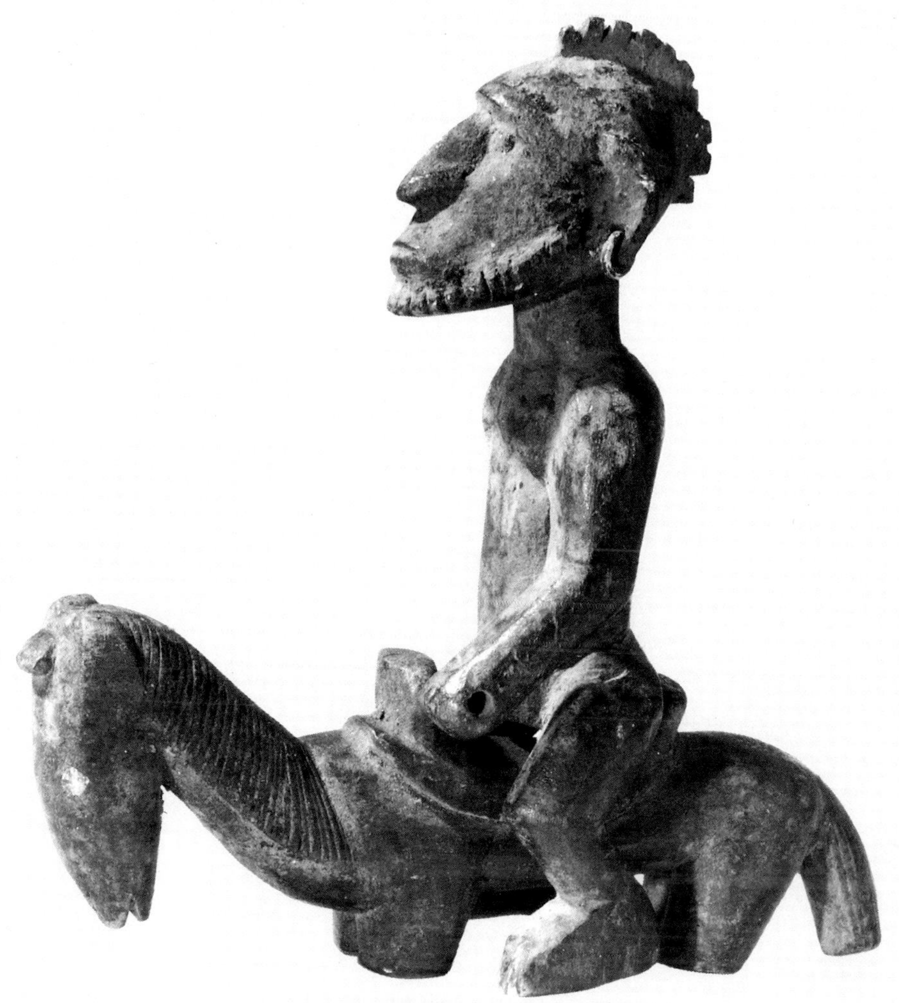

6

and of the tail and saddle is striking, but the legs are roughly shaped as if the hooves of the animal had been cut off. The rider's upper body is turned slightly to the right, and he appears to hold the reins in his left hand; a spear may originally have been in his right. Metal pins mark the eyes of both horse and rider. The figure probably represents the mythical primordial smith, usually depicted as a bearded man with cap mounted on a horse.

Height 16 cm. 81-301 488
Acquired from R. L. Stolper 1981

Lit.: M. Griaule 1965, pp. 42 46; J. Laude 1973, p. 42; M. Palau Marti 1957, pp. 25, 54ff.

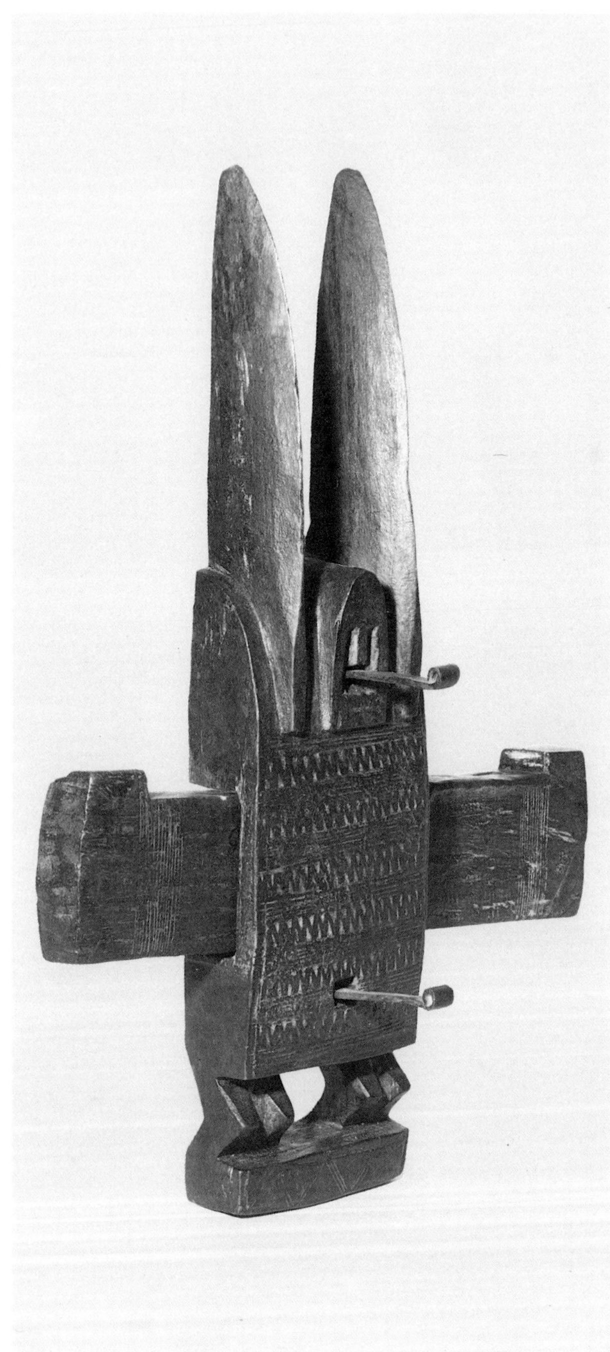

7

Dogon Door Locks (7/8)

Wooden locks with bolts were known in antiquity both in Asia Minor and southern Europe. Apparently they became familiar in sub-Saharan Africa only after the spread of Islam to various regions. In the western Sudan the Dogon and their neighbors, the Kurumba, Bamana, Bozo, Mossi, and Senufo, managed to transform the lock into a small work of art. The lock is conceived as part of the dwelling house or granary door and is provided with more or less elaborate carvings according to the social status of the owner. The motifs used are symbolic: bolt and lock stand for the generative act and are associated with the creation in primordial times. For this reason the figurative ornaments on the locks frequently relate to anthropomorphic and zoomorphic ancestors and primordial beings such as the sun lizard, all of which protect the entrances of buildings.

Lit.: J. Dieterlen 1970, pp. 7-28; P. J. Imperato 1972, p. 52ff.; 1978, pp. 54-57; F. von Luschan 1916, pp. 406,429; A. Schweeger-Hefel & W. Staude 1972, pp. 139-141; D. Zahan 1950, pp. 223-229.

7 Door lock, wood, iron.
Mali, Dogon.

The carving of this lock masterfully unifies form and function. The abstract male figure praying with arms uplifted for life-giving rain represents a Nommo, one of the eight mythical forebears. The surface of his rectangular torso is enlivened by zigzag lines, which in Dogon mystical symbolism indicate the primordial age. They symbolize the vibrations of the cosmos, of water, of light, and of the creative word, as well as the movements of the mythical snake and the descent of the heavenly ark. The movable parts, tongue (also considered a sexual symbol), and phallus contribute to the magical protection of the door lock through the defensive power ascribed them.

Height 28 cm., width 21 cm. 14-7-46
Acquired from the Museum für Völkerkunde Berlin 1914 (Collection L. Frobenius)

Lit.: P. J. Imperato 1974, p. 68; 1978, pp. 54-57; J. Laude 1973, pp. 68, 84.

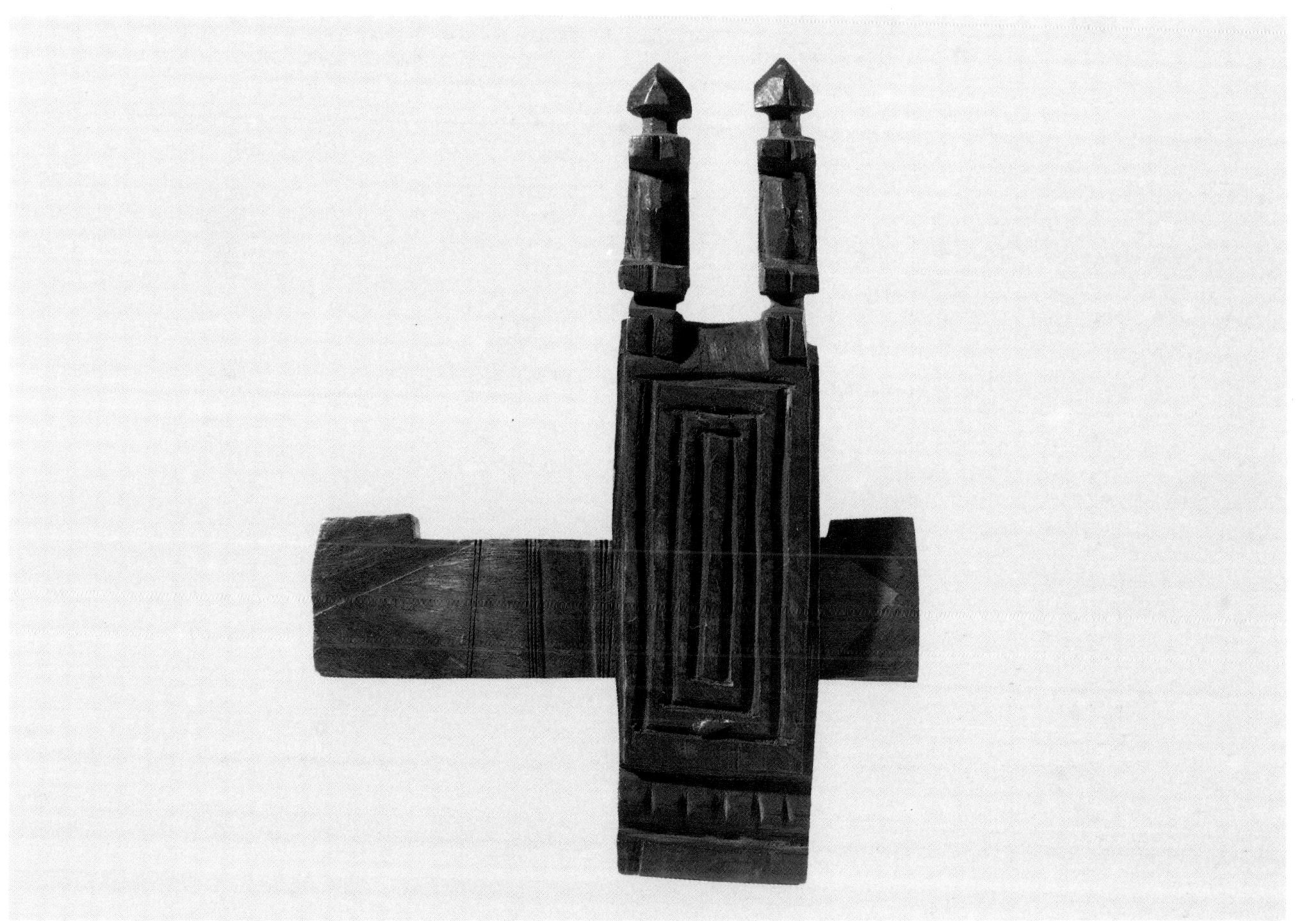

8

8 Door lock, wood, iron.
Mali, Dogon.

This lock consists of a crossbar and holding box with a pair of sculptured figures. As often occurs, the key that served to lift the lock pins is missing. Despite a distinct tendency toward schematization, the strictly symmetrical geometric configuration of the piece represents the classic Dogon style. Characteristic, among other things, are the figures' angular horizontal shoulders, the highly placed and sharply set-off chest, and a narrow, elongated torso with thin parallel arms. The figures represent a primordial pair of bisexual partners, fertilizing as well as child-bearing.

Height 25 cm. 21-11-25
Acquired from the Museum für Völkerkunde Berlin 1921

Lit.: G.J. Dieterlen 1970, pp. 7-28, M. Griaule 1965, p. 25; J. Laude 1973, Illus. 33.

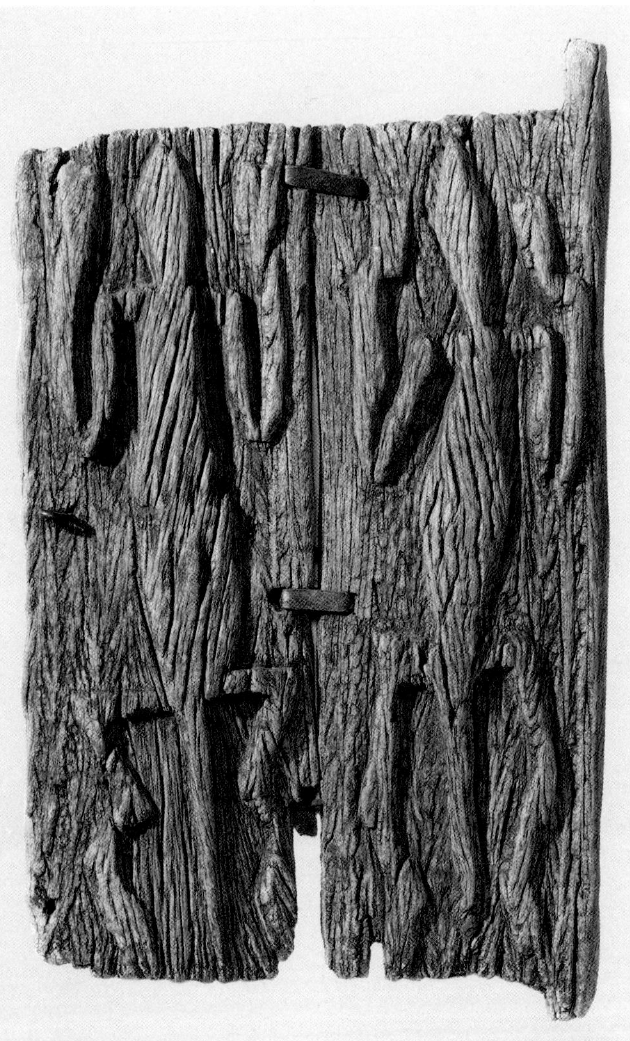

9

9 Granary door, wood, iron.
Mali, Dogon.

Hardwood is rare in the dry savannah, home of the Dogon, and for this reason doors are made of two panels held together by large iron staples to achieve the desired breadth. Dwellings as well as the vital granaries are placed under the protection of ancestors or mythical primordial beings. To the latter group belong the lizards rendered in low relief with human arms and legs; they are probably the so-called sun lizards which the Dogon consider a sexual symbol.

Height 60 cm. 64-13-1
Acquired from L. Bretschneider 1964

Lit.: M. Griaule 1965, pp. 22, 48, 127-28, 161; J. Laude 1973, Illus. 73/74.

10 Antelope headdress (*numtiri),* wood, paint.
Burkina Fasso, Kurumba, Belehede.

In contrast to the abstract planes of Bamana masks this antelope headdress of the Kurumba is sculptural and, despite stylization, tends toward a lifelike appearance. The pointillistic treatment of the surface does not imitate the animal's markings but, according to one theory, symbolizes the stars, whose appearance heralds the rites of sowing and harvesting. Another explanation interprets the painted dots as seeds of the cotton plant. The zigzag lines symbolize the heavenly ark of Dogon mythology in which the primordial hero descended to earth. Symbolism relating to agriculture and creation would seem to contradict the fact that the antelope headdress performs only at certain funerals; but according to Kurumba religion and that of other western Sudanese peoples, cosmic order, fertility of the fields, and the fate of the soul after death are connected in an essential way.

Kurumba headdresses are family property and individual headdress types are linked to specific family groups. For example, this antelope mask represents a type belonging to the Sawadugu family of Belehede. The masks are kept in a special mask house on the family homestead, hanging head downward and covered by a netted costume.

If an aged man or woman of the family dies, the masks appear at the conclusion of the funeral ceremonies and perform ritual dances. A family head who dies in old age is given his own mask. This represents an exceptional honor, and the mask serves as a dwelling place for the soul of the deceased, which returns at intervals. The mask, however, is not identified solely with the deceased or his spirit. It may temporarily accommodate the souls of other dead as well. The animal forms of the masks do not indicate a particular appearance for the soul. Rather, each mask is an independent being with a name of its own. When the wood decays, the mask is left to rot in the mask house, though it is often buried like a human being. Only the plant fiber costume is taken off and kept for a new mask. This may be carved at the death of an old chief or family head during the interval between his demise and the end of the funeral.

Each family has its own carver, who is himself a family member. He searches for the ritually prescribed wood and works for days in the bush—eleven days in one closely observed instance. During this time he is subject to various taboos and must, among other things, observe complete sexual abstinence. To prevent its being seen, the finished mask is covered and taken to the village at night. Generally, women may see the mask only in action. Another family member with exact knowledge of esoteric symbolism paints the mask, whose colors are refreshed before each appearance.

Height 109 cm. 64-4-1
Acquired from L. Bretschneider 1964

Lit.: A. Schweeger-Hefel 1966, pp. 240-247; A. Schweeger-Hefel and W. Staude 1972, pp. 184-191; A. Schweeger-Hefel 1980, pp. 16, 19, 27-28, 72, 89, 91, 144-45, 161, 164.

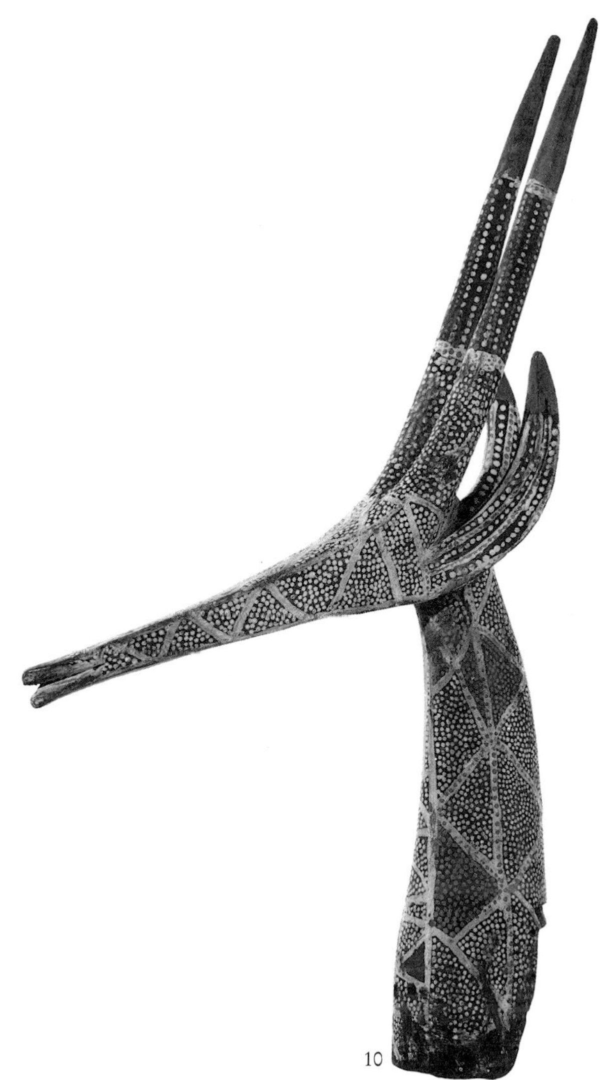

10

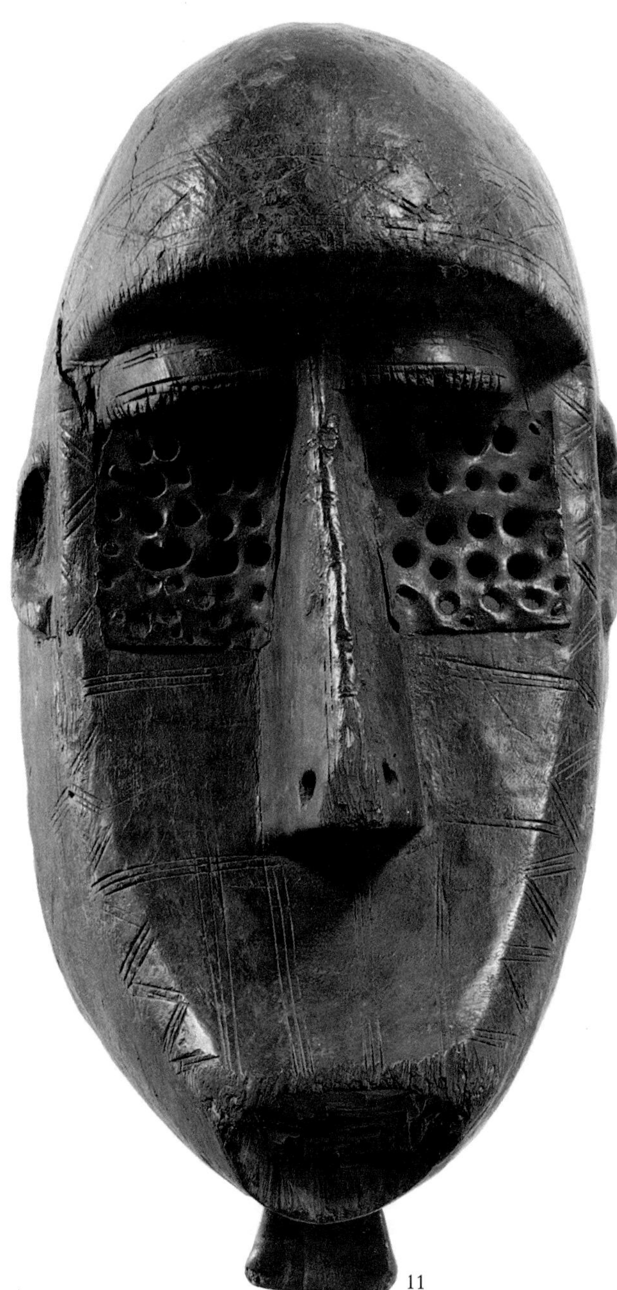

11

Bamana Masks

Within his lifetime every Bamana man who has not left the traditional rural community passes through a series of initiations. In the first of them, completed before circumcision, he is accepted into the lowest rank of the first initiation association. After about five years and four further stages, he becomes a member of the second association. There are six initiation associations in all, each subdivided into several stages. A man acquires new, partly secret, knowledge with every initiation, and upon reaching the highest grade is considered a bearer of the entire tribal tradition.

It is only within the last few decades that many components of the rich mask ritual associated with initiation and other festivities of various associations have spread to large parts of the Bamana area and beyond. Their sources lie in the Ouassoulou (Wassalu or Wassulu) District on the borders of the present nations of Mali and Guinea. Groups that migrated from that region introduced numerous masks to their new home.

Many masks represent composite beings. An animal—antelope, lion, hyena, ape, groundhog, or anteater, for example—may be given human features and ornaments (like the nose ring of the Bamana, although, with one exception, these ornaments have been removed from the masks in this exhibition). The choice of form corresponds to animal symbolism that relates to the individual stages of initiation. The masks are also stylistically distinct: while those used by the fifth association (characterized by their representations of antelope horns) are among the best developed examples of a gracefully abstract art, masks of other grades are distinguished by vigorous cubistic forms. How the mask is worn differs too: for certain initiations headdress masks are prescribed; for others, face masks. Masked dances, however, are not inseparably bound to the old initiation organizations of age groups. In towns, even in strongly Islamized regions, performances by professional dancers are extremely popular entertainment.

Lit.: P. J. Imperato 1981, pp. 31-42; D. Zahan 1974, pp. 15-24.

11 Monkey mask (*sula*), wood, metal.
Mali, Bamana, Nossombougou.

With its markedly geometric forehead and other facial features, this face mask represents the cubistic tendency in Bamana mask style. Finely incised geometric decoration and fittings of metal lamellae, possibly derived from leather applique work of the Sudan and North Africa, are frequently found in Bamana wood sculpture.

The name *sula* refers to the beautiful Colobus monkey, distinguished by long black fur, the symbolic animal of the highest grade of initiation reached only by elderly men. At their accession to this grade masked dancers appear, some wearing the monkey mask and moving like monkeys. According to Zahan, this is a reminder of the animality inherent in human beings that is overcome only upon entry into the *sulaw* grade.

Height 31 cm. 33-42-2
Acquired from C. Kjersmeier 1933

Lit.: F. H. Lemm 1949, p. 43; D. Zahan 1960, p. 200ff., 1974, p. 22-23.

12 Headdress (*sogoni koun, tyi wara*), wood, brass, iron.
Mali, Bamana, Minianka.

In this abstract representation of an equine antelope (*Hippotragus equinus*), the body is reduced to a rectangle and the dominant head rises from a spirited, curved neck with a stylized mane in which zigzag decoration appears (see No.7). The typically human ornaments—nose and earrings—should be noted.

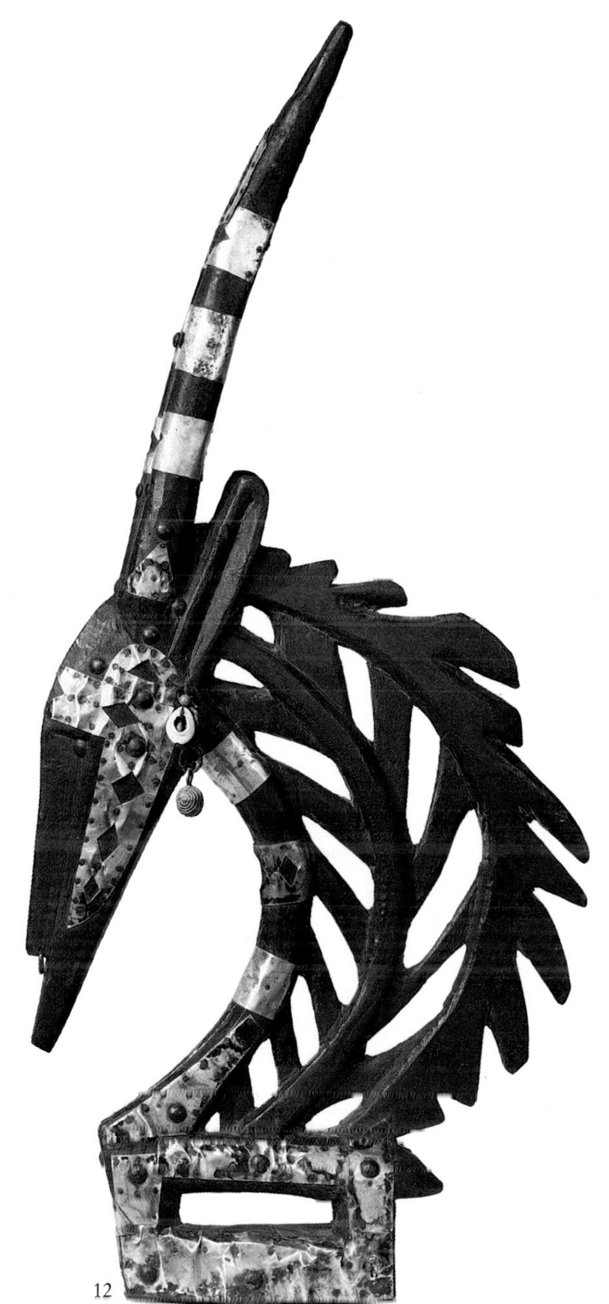

12

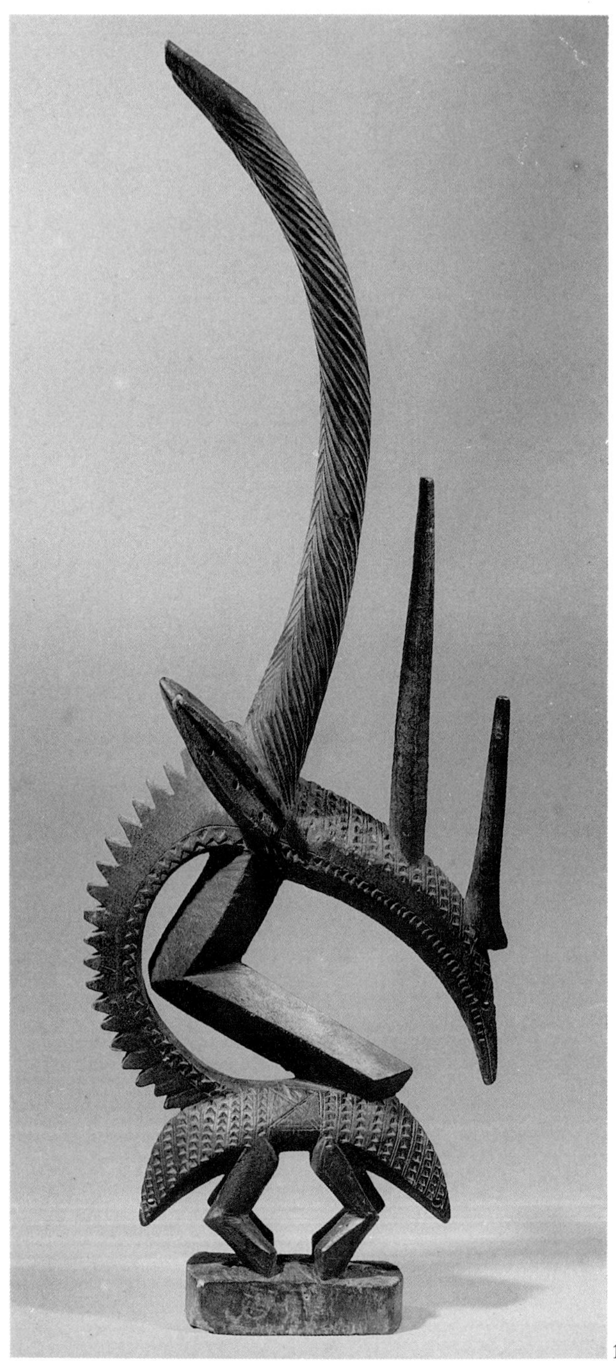

13

This headdress, like the two following, is associated with the *tyi wara* association, fifth among the above-mentioned initiation associations. In contrast to the others, it is open to women, though they may not participate in the secret initiation rites. Among the most important functions of the *tyi wara* is a ritual that increases the fertility of the fields, and in this connection the equine antelope has a special significance. According to the Bamana myth of primordial times, the water spirit Faro, in the shape of this animal, presented the first millet grains to man and taught him how to work the fields. Apart from this role of culture hero, the equine antelope also plays a part in the growing process. Each year a pair of *tyi wara* dancers inaugurates the most important agricultural work: clearing the ground, sowing, and harvesting. One partner wears an equine antelope headdress like this one representing the male, and the other wears a headdress depicting a female antelope with her offspring representing femaleness and the earth.

The headdress is fastened to the dancer's head by means of a plaited cap. The dancer himself is unrecognizable beneath a long fiber costume.

Height 84.5 cm. 57-15-1
Acquired from L. Bretschneider 1957

Lit.: P. J. Imperato 1970, pp. 8-13, 71-80; D. Zahan 1974, pp. 20, 30, 1980, pp. 49, 62ff., 68, 80ff., 91-92, 101. This piece is reproduced on Pl. 16, Fig. I M 45.

13 Headdress mask (*sogoni koun,tyi wara*), wood.
Mali, Bamana, Bougouni.

This type of Bamana mask, characterized by highly abstract and stylized forms, combines the properties of two species of animals: the equine antelope (see No.12) and the manis or pangolin (*Manis tricuspis*). According to Zahan, the latter animal symbolizes the earth and is conceived as female. The combination of its features with those of the male-solar antelope indicates the union of earth with the sun

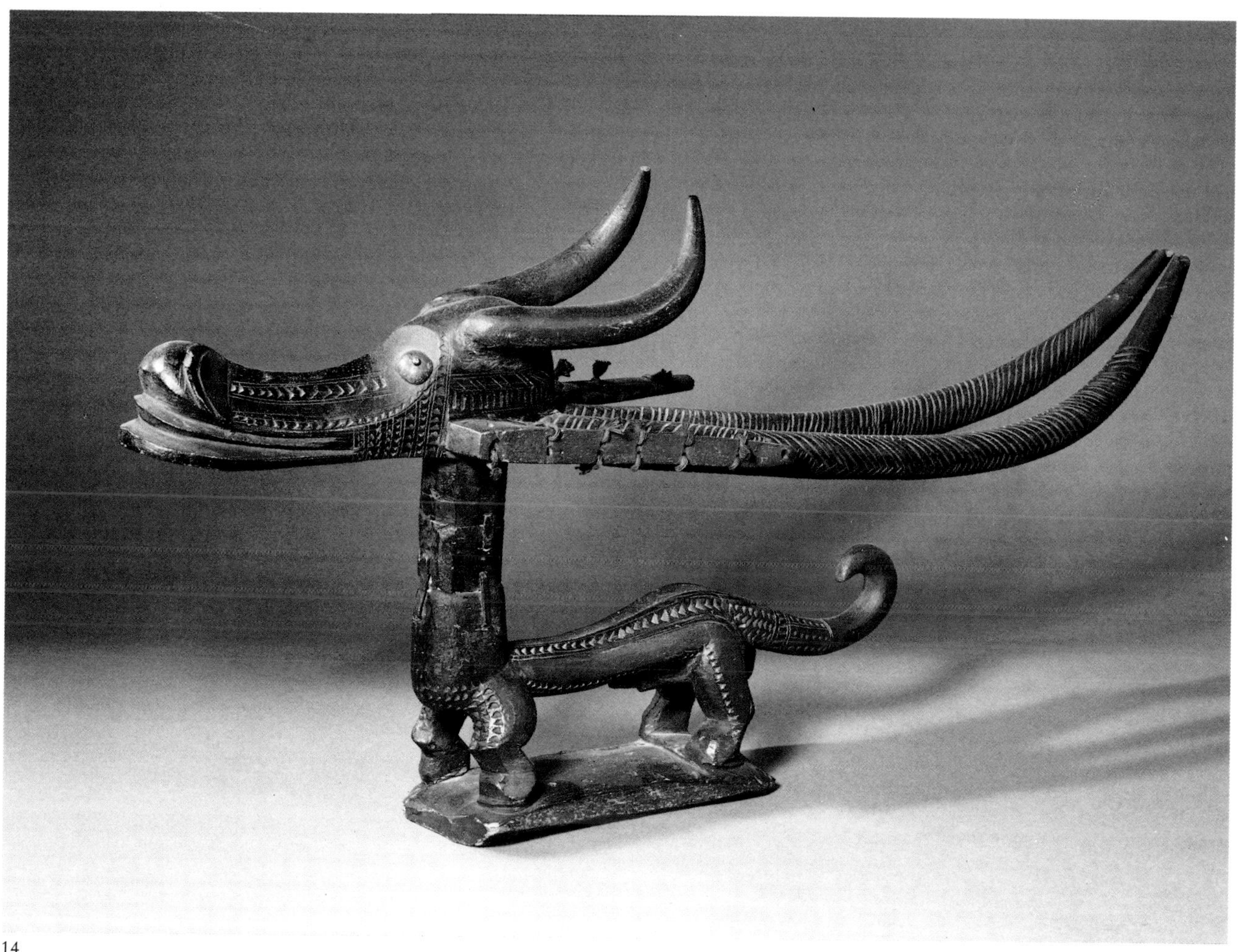

14

and forces like rain and wind: this union between sun and tilled field enables the growth of crops. Like the mask in No 12, this example is worn to initiate important agricultural tasks.

Height 51 cm. 14-7-6
Acquired from the Museum für Völkerkunde Berlin 1914 (Collection L. Frobenius)

Lit.: D. Zahan 1980, pp. 27-28, 36, 40f., 46, 70-71, 74ff., 79-80, 84. This piece is reproduced on Pl. 53, Fig. II 30.

14 Headdress mask (*sogoni koun, tyi wara*), wood, iron, brass, cotton. Mali, Bamana.

Like the last (No.13), this animal is a compound being. Formed of two pieces of wood joined at the neck by iron staples, this antelope headdress (the so-called horizontal type) is of a kind found chiefly in the Bamako district, which is the northwest area of the Bamana. Two of the four horns show the

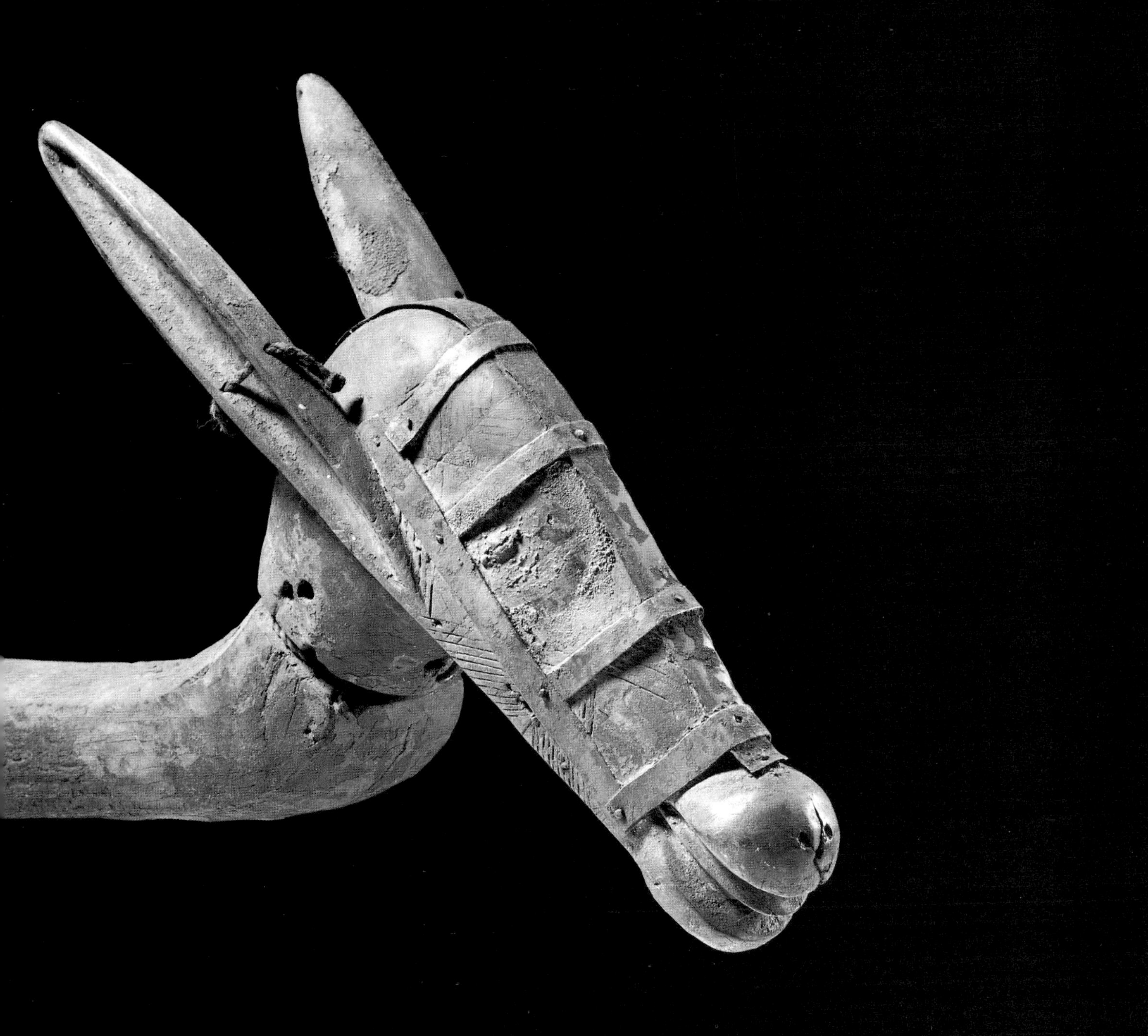

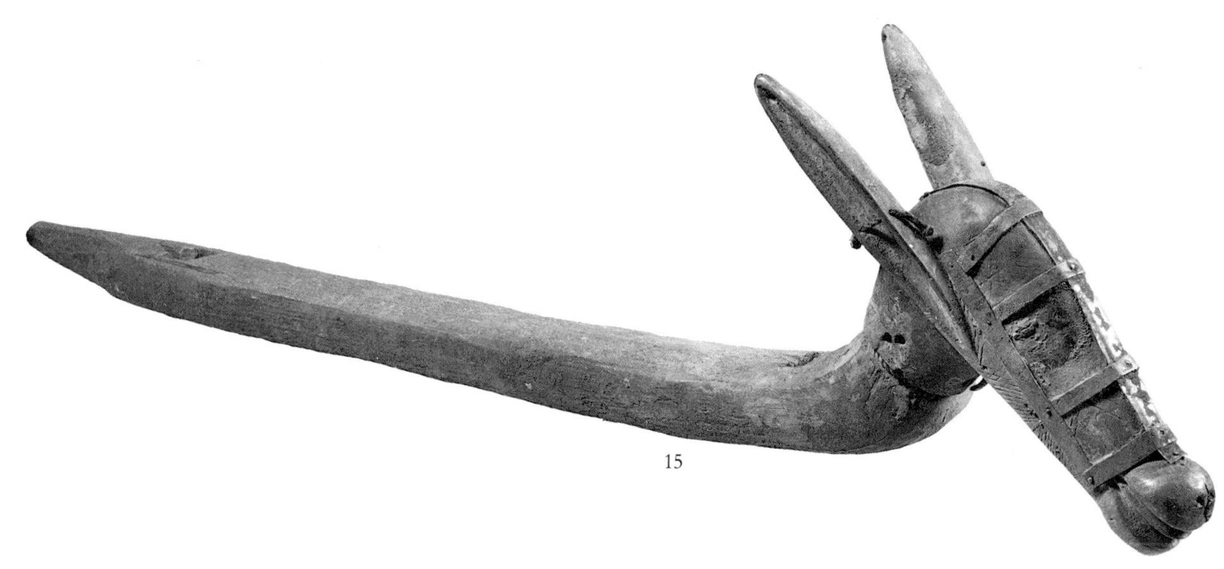

15

grooves characteristic of several species of antelope. A fringe of cotton threads ornaments one pair of ears; large studs form the eyes; and parts of the body and face are decorated with rows of triangles. The backbone is a deep, finely curved furrow. The two pairs of horns are to be viewed vertically, not horizontally; they are seemingly patterned after two distinct species of antelope (equine and oryx, *Oryx beisa*), and are combined with the head, body, and legs ascribed by Zahan to the aardvark (*Orycteropus afer*). The long tongue and prominent tail, presented here in stylized form, seem to support this identity. In the symbolism of the *tyi wara* association the aardvark, as symbol of the earth, assumes more or less the same function as the pangolin. The headdress was tied to a plaited cap that the dancer wore on his head.

Height 33.5 cm., length 72 cm. 82-301619
Acquired from L. Bretschneider 1982

Lit.: R. Goldwater 1960, pp. 16, 42f.; D. Zahan 1980, pp. 26ff., 39ff., 47, 69ff., 75ff., 83ff.

15 Marionette with animal head, wood, iron, brass, cotton.
Mali, Bamana.

Like the antelope headdress in No.14, this piece consists of two pieces fitted together. The finely worked animal head, with delicately incised decoration and brass fittings (halter), ends in the rounded base of the neck that has been bored through in several places; these holes held the cords that moved the head. The body, probably attached to the head later, is planklike with two square holes to admit the staffs on which the object was carried. This animal head is reminiscent of the pangolin type of Bamana headdress. Similar heads characterize the "hobbyhorses" that are one of the elements of the mask costume used in the rituals of the highest initiation association (*kore*). In the secret language of initiation the horse is designated by a name referring to the symbolism of the wind, of death, and of immortality.

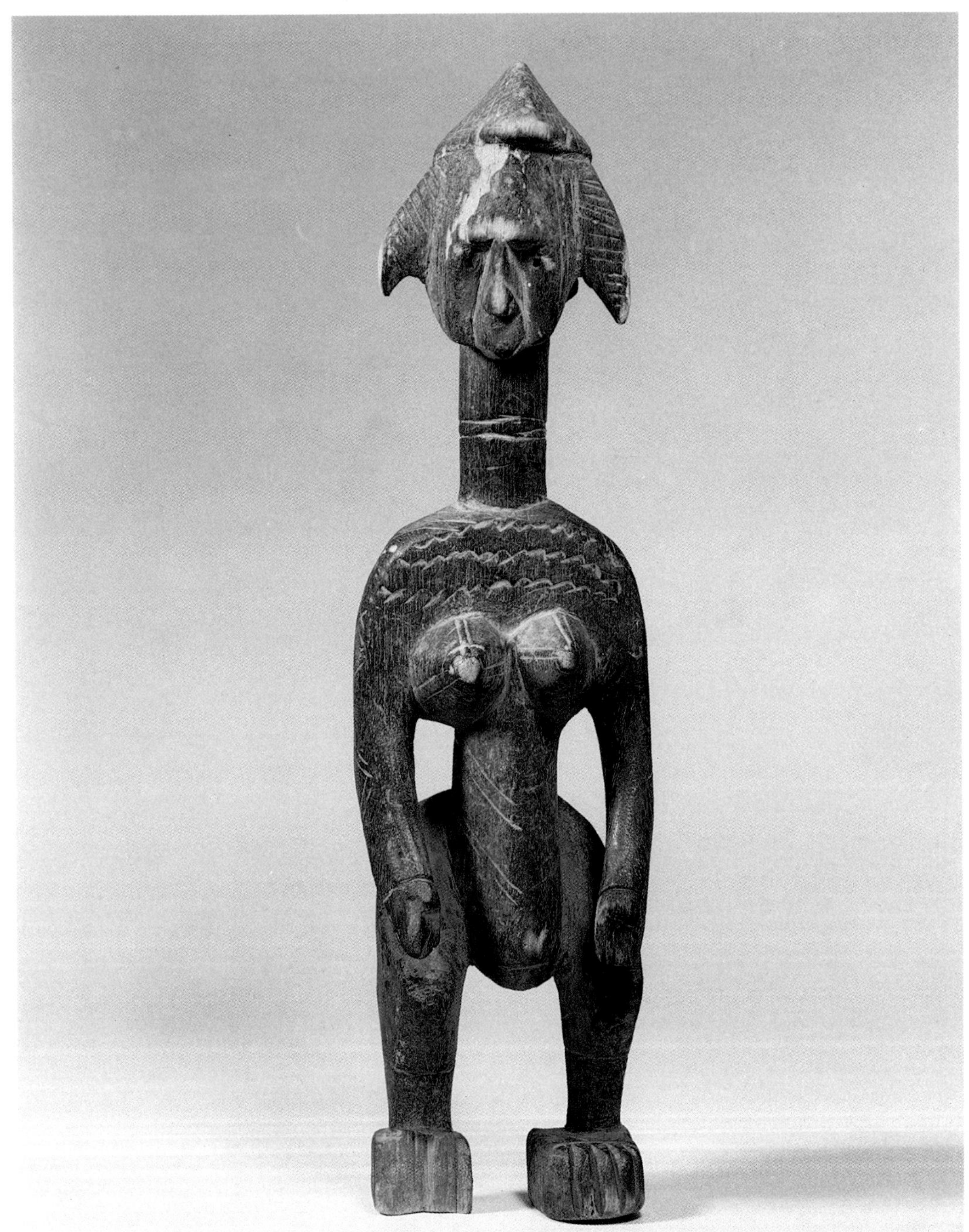

16

This piece represents a recent stage of development in Bamana art in which mythical beings are represented not only by the wearers of masks and headdresses but also by marionettes in public performances. The marionettes are made by the same artists who carve the masks. Many marionettes correspond exactly to the traditional mask costumes. The performances are prepared with the cooperation of the eldest initiated men and the dance of the marionettes, though no longer secret, not only entertains the onlookers but preserves much of the original sacred character as well.

Height 22 cm., length 83 cm. 82-301-621
Acquired from W. Ketterer 1982 (Collection K. F. Schädler)

Lit.: O. Darkowska-Nidzgorska & F. Ndiaye 1977, p.2; R. Pageard 1962, pp.17 20; D. Zahan 1960, pp.161ff., 175ff., 1980, p.22.

16 Female figure (*nunumani),* wood, iron.
Mali, Bamana, Suluba.

Many features of this figure are typical of the sculpture of the Bougouni District, stylistically one of the important Bamana provinces: the pillar-like torso and neck, the hanging arms (characteristic of pole art), the conical breasts, the coiffure with crest and plaits at the temples, and the block-shaped feet without base. The eyes are formed by metal nails. The nose ring is lacking. Simple incised linear decoration may be seen on coiffure and torso. The female figures of the Bamana are identified in the literature as fertility dolls or as representations of female ancestors. The large size of this piece may indicate that it belonged to the latter group. Literally, *nunumani* means "small man of the smith," a reference to the ironsmith who also manufactures wooden sculptures and dedicates them.

Height 45 cm. 33-42-3
Acquired from C. Kjersmeier 1933

Lit.: R. Goldwater 1960, p.17; C. Kjersmeier 1935, I.S. 14-15.

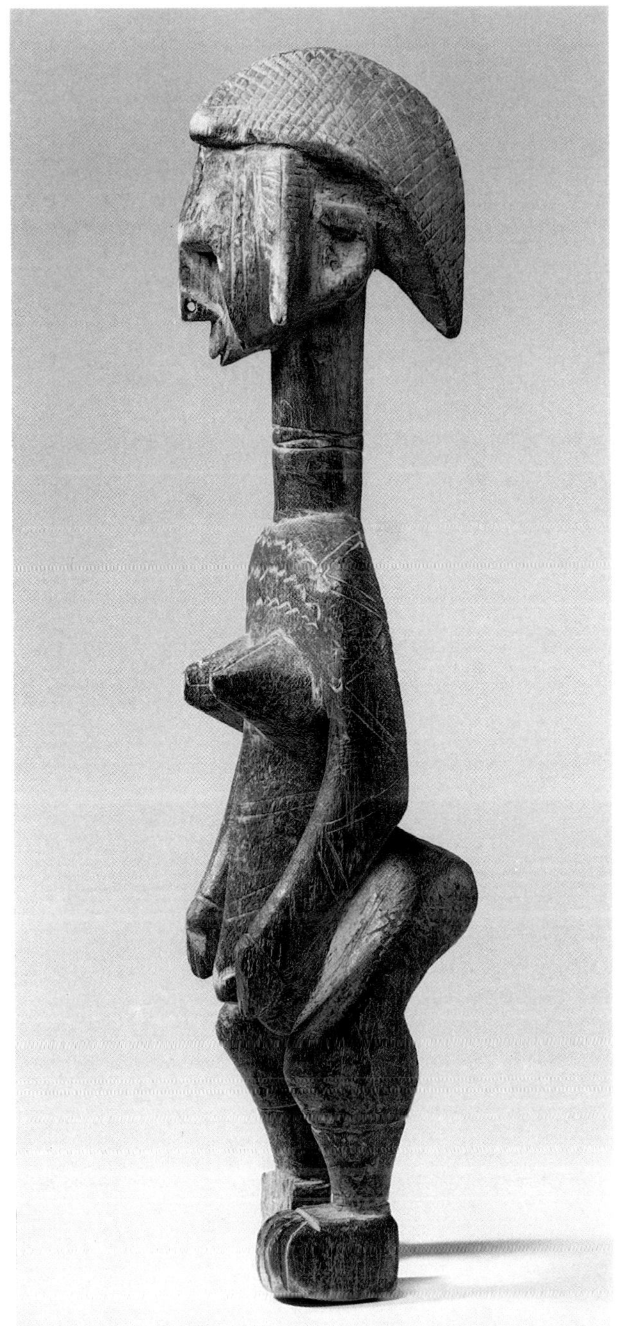

16

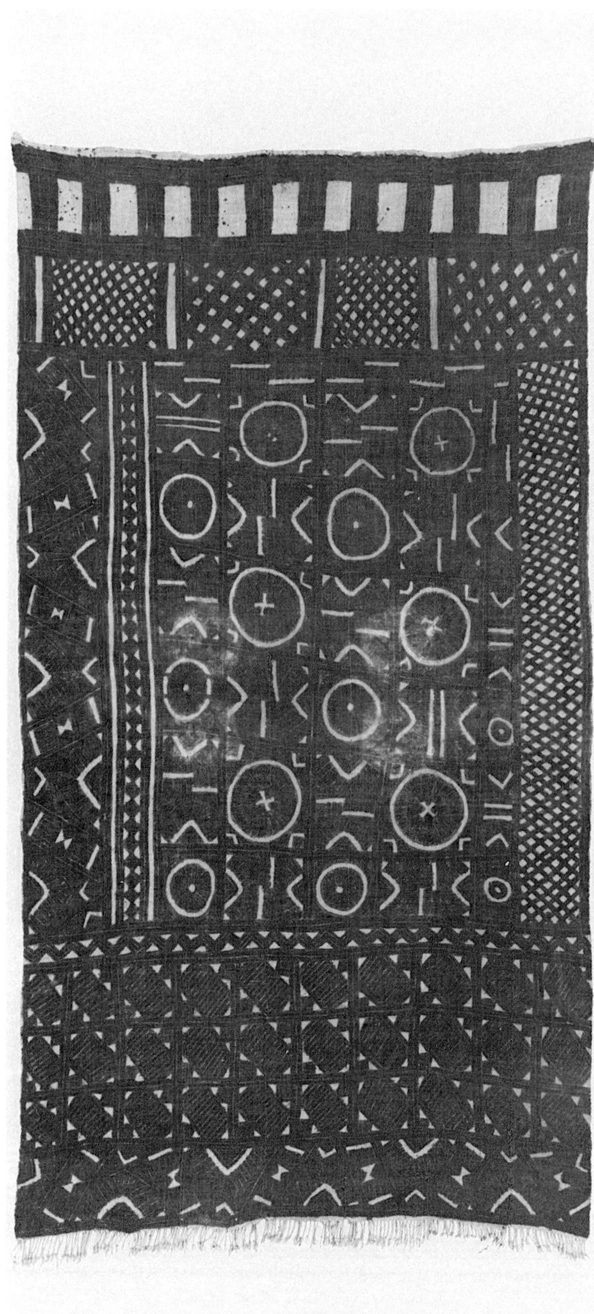

17

17 Resist Dyed fabric (*bokolanfini* or *finiknekele*), cotton.
Mali, Bamana, Beledougou.

Seven narrow bands woven on a treadle loom were sewn together to create this fabric, whose bright yellowish design (as negative pattern) stands out against a background that was originally dark grey or brown, but has paled with age. Such cloths, today a widely distributed trade item, were formerly commissioned with the desired decoration. Men wear them as short, sleeveless tunics, women as wraparound skirts. Hunters wear longer shirts with sleeves (perhaps as festive dress).

Making fabric is tedious work shared by two specialists: men weave, women do the dyeing and decorating. Dyeing commences when the cloth is dipped several times into an extract of leaves to give it a yellow color. The women then use spatulas to apply an outline of the design, using a ferruginous, dark, muddy substance taken from the middle of a dried-up pool. The outline is then filled in so that a yellow pattern is reserved on a dark ground. When the fabric is dry, it is dipped into water to rinse the mud out, but the blackish mud color around the yellow pattern remains. Generally the whole process—dipping, applying mud, rinsing—is repeated one or more times in order to intensify the dark color. The decoration is then usually etched in with a kind of mordant.

Present-day specialists maintain that the named decorative motifs they use reproduce schemata of everyday objects. But originally, decoration consisted of magical and symbolic signs.

Measurements 80 x 155 cm. 15-17-132
Acquired by the Museum für Völkerkunde Berlin 1915 (Collection L. Frobenius)

Lit.: R. Boser-Sarivaxévanis 1972, pp.36-38; P. J. Imperato & M. Shamir 1970, pp.32-41; B. Menzek 1972, II Illus. p.263.

18. Plank mask, wood, paint.
Burkina Fasso, Bwa (Bobo-Ule).

Long plank masks, carved of kapok wood and painted with variegated geometric patterns, occur only in a comparatively small area in Burkina Fasso and Mali among the Gurunsi, Bwa, Bobo, Mossi, Nyonyose, Kurumba, and Dogon, always along with other types of masks. The chief characteristics of plank masks are: the combination of a face mask with a large boardlike headdress; a broad-planed, essentially two-dimensional aspect; and a distinctive decoration composed of circles, zigzags, diamonds, and checks painted white, red, and black. The Bwa, also called the Bobo Ule, from whom this example came, do not manufacture plank masks themselves but obtain them from the carvers of a neighboring Gurunsi group.

Present-day Bwa do not know the significance of plank masks or their ornamentation. Presumably, the masks "transformed" their wearers into certain animals considered to be supernatural beings. Thus the circular face, eyes surrounded by concentric circles, long beaklike hooked nose, even the diamond-shaped mouth, are often interpreted by the Bwa as symbolic of certain birds such as owls and hornbills. In some cases the whole mask is interpreted as a stylized bird. According to Zwernemann, masks with a vertical row of hooks are said to symbolize the skeletons of snakes. Schweeger-Hefel and Staude see human figures in them and call them stele masks, believing that they are anthropomorphic grave stelae and are connected with the dead and ancestors. On the other hand Capron sees in all *do* masks, the group to which the plank masks belong, the incarnation of the creator god, *Do*.

In performances mask dancers dress in red-dyed fiber robes whose ritual importance is even greater than that of the wooden masks. Masks and robes, kept in the village mask house, are owned by the *do*

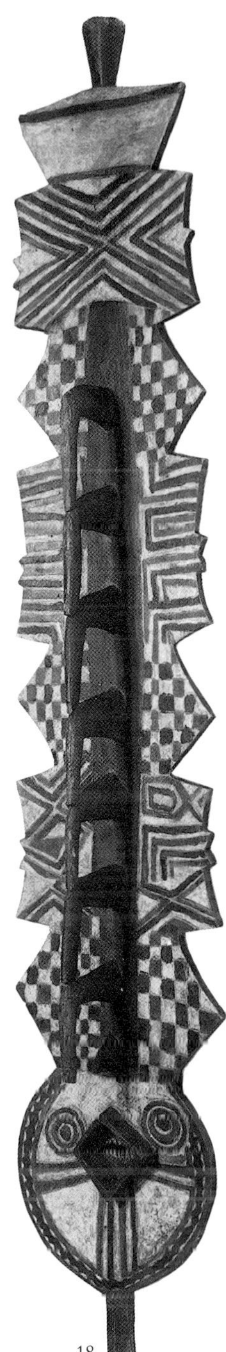

18

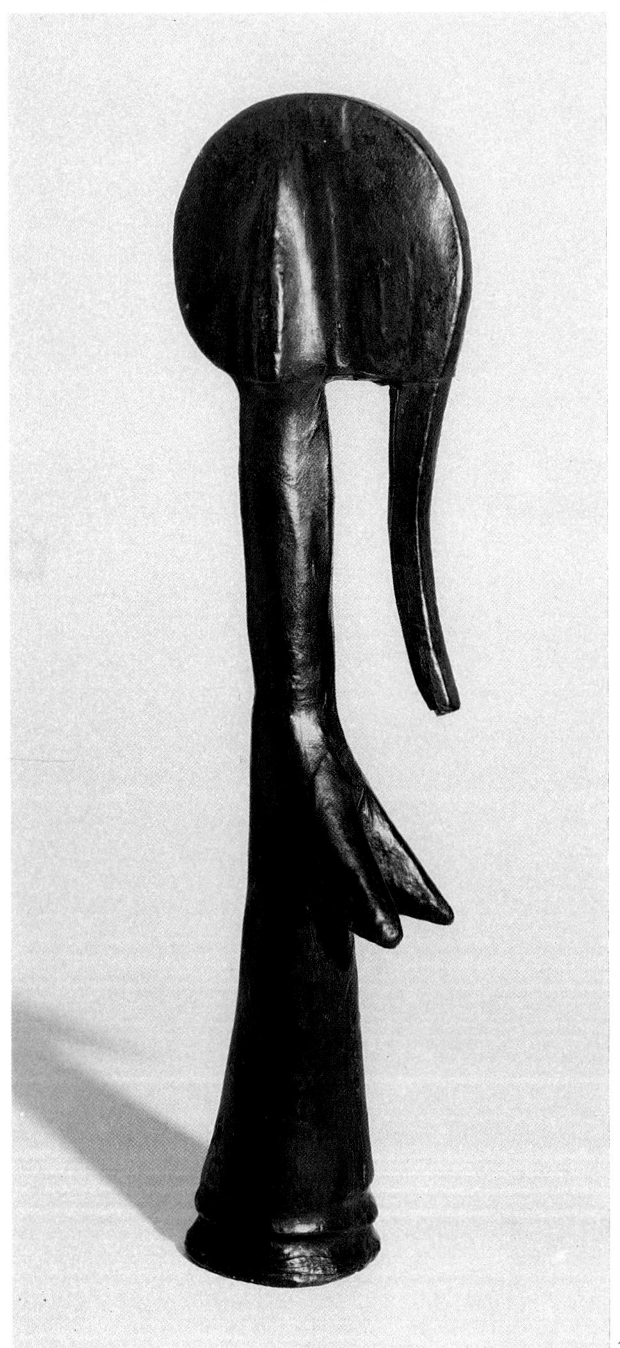

19

society, whose periodic dances promote the fertility of the fields and accompany human beings from one stage of life to the next. The appearance of the masks, including plank masks, is also linked with such agricultural events as the beginning of the rainy season, sowing, and harvesting, as well as with social events such as termination of adolescent initiation and funerals for *do* society members.

Height 190 cm. 76-5-1
Acquired from L. Bretschneider 1976

Lit.: J. Capron 1973, pp. 85, 251-260; K. Dittmer 1961, pp. 5-9; G. Le Moal 1980, p. 218ff.; A. Schweeger-Hefel & W. Staude 1972, pp. 191-194; J. Zwernemann 1978, pp. 50, 53, 56-57.

19 Fertility doll, wood, leather.
Burkina Fasso, Mossi.

Although the disk-like head of this female figure on a round base has no facial features, the stylized plaits at her temples are recognizable (see No. 16). Formerly, such an extremely large forehead plait was characteristic of unmarried Mossi girls. The elongated torso has neither shoulders nor limbs, but strongly accentuated longish breasts and a hip girdle. Whereas most Mossi dolls consist of wood only and are ornamented with incised lines, our piece belongs

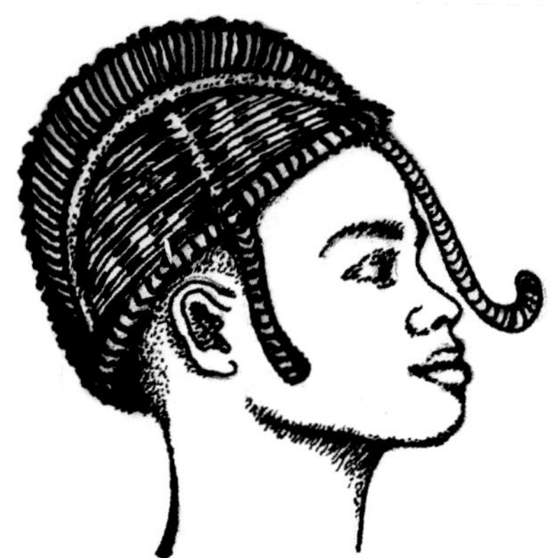

32

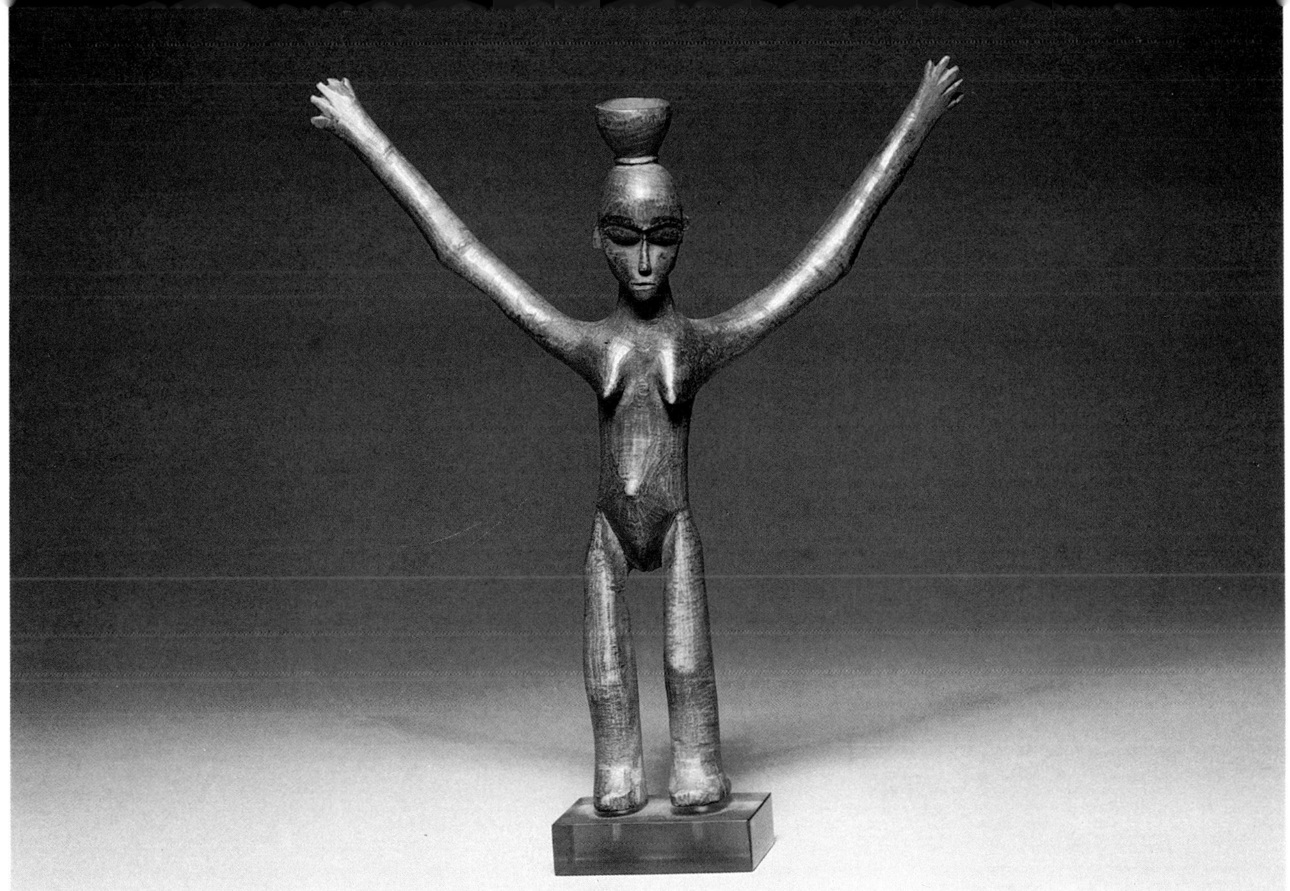

20

to a type recently introduced perhaps for reasons of prestige: these dolls are manufactured by the smith and are covered with thin leather by the shoemaker.

Stylistically comparable dolls are popular among such Mossi neighbors as the Bamana, Kurumba, and Dogon. Kafando considers them more developed variants of the simple maize cob dolls of the Western Sudan, whereas Segy sees formal resemblances to the ancient Egyptian and Coptic ankh sign and believes the dolls have phallic significance. Schweeger-Hefel feels they are general fertility symbols. According to Roy, dolls that were simply used as toys may be recognized by their soiled and battered surfaces; those with a shiny patina served to promote fertility.

Height 32.5 cm. 81-301-521
Acquired from W. Ketter 1981 (Collection K. F. Schädler)

Lit.: L. Meurer & E. Kafando 1964, pp.25-30; Ch. D. Roy 1981, pp.47-51; A. Schweeger-Hefel & W. Staude 1972, p.136; L. Segy 1972, p.33.

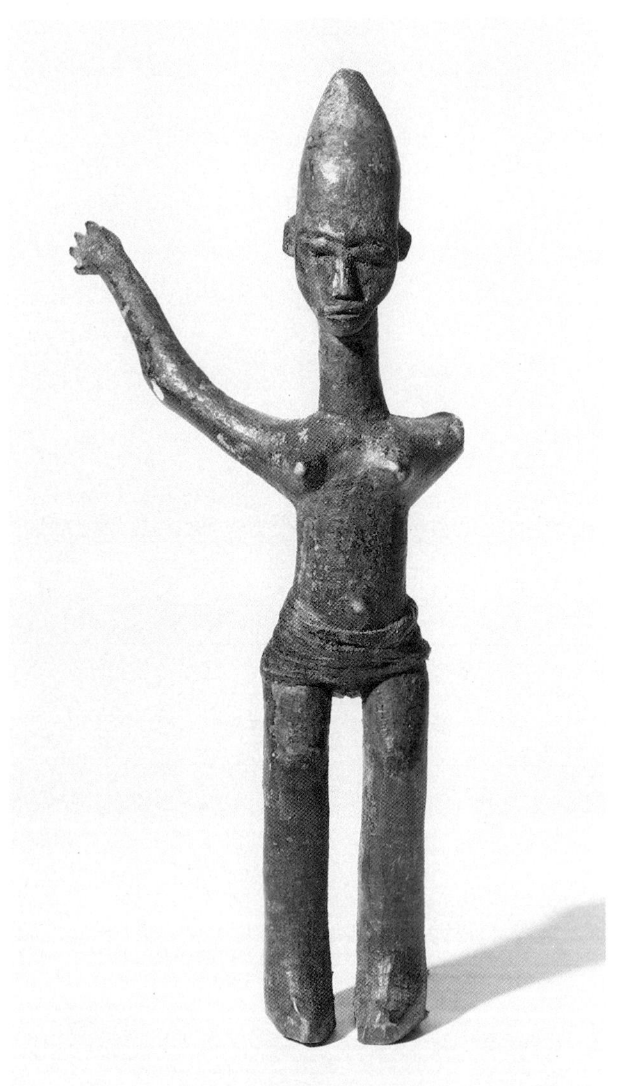

21

Lobi *bateba* Figures (20-23)

The designation *bateba* refers to human figures of wood, clay, and metal. These are looked upon as living beings charged with special power who move, fight against witches and sorcerers, and have intercourse with one another. After consultation with the diviner, a client commissions the manufacture of a figure. The Lobi believe that *bateba,* like bush spirits, are superior to humans but inferior to the tutelary spirits of the village *(thila).* This position in the hierarchy expresses itself, on the one hand, in their resemblance to human beings, and on the other in their dependence upon the *thila.* A *bateba* figure is first activated by being placed in the shrine of the *thila* or through some other association with *thila.* Of the *bateba's* several functions the most important are keeping sorcerers away and helping the *thila* ward off misfortune. They also play a role in the divination system.

Lit.: H. Labouret 1931, pp.180, 405, 407; P. Meyer 1981, pp.52-55, 57.

20 Female figure (*bateba),* wood.
Burkina Fasso, Lobi.

This young woman with small pointed breasts, vaulted abdomen with convex navel, and well sculptured backbone and buttocks, carries a vessel on a raffia ring upon her shaven and slightly inclined head. Her eyebrows are blackened by a heated knife, her nose and mouth are crisply carved. Slender, elongated arms end in widely spread fingers without a suggestion of wrist or palm, and the carelessly formed legs are short and stumpy with rounded calves and massive block feet.

The posture with upheld arms is rarely seen in African art and the Lobi believe that this stance can magically ward off witches and sorcerers. For this reason such figures serve as guardians of the house and protect it from invisible intruders. The Lobi consider these figures, called *ti puo,* more powerful in the struggle against witchcraft than the usual *bateba.* On the side of the figure is written in ink: *Oliva yao. Viamo do* (or *Alica yao Tiamio do).*

Height 17 cm. 80-301-344.
Acquired from L. Bretschneider 1980

Lit.: P. Meyer 1981, pp.56, 88.

21 Female figure (*bateba),* wood, plant fibers.
Burkina Fasso, Lobi.

Like the figure in No.20, this belongs to the group of *ti puo* figures considered to have special magical powers. They are recognized by the warding-off pose, with one or both hands held high. The upward elongation of this figure's head may have resulted from careless formation of the high padded coiffure or of the shaven edges of the forehead. Its surface is dark grey with a dull patina, a belt of plant fibres is arranged around its hips, and one arm is broken off.

Height 19.5 cm. 81-301 493
Acquired from F. Jahn 1981

22/23 Pair of figures (*bateba*), wood.
Burkina Fasso, Lobi.

Probably the work of the woodcarver Biniathe Kabire from Tiamne, these figures resemble each other greatly. They belong to the category of "ordinary *bateba,*" and should probably be considered twins rather than a married couple. Characteristic features include their composed attitude, rounded forms, elongated heads without suggestion of coiffure or head covering, and heart-shaped faces with large coffee-bean eyes. A skin fold connects the breasts, the sexual organs are only faintly indicated, and the abdomen (with convex navel) and the buttocks are rounded. Tapering arms hang freely, and long legs become thicker as they descend. Neither fingers nor toes are indicated.

Height 54, width 46 cm. 82-301 622/23
Acquired from F. Jahn 1982

Lit.: H. Himmelheber 1966, p.82f.; P. Meyer 1981, pp.54, 74; Illus. 45.

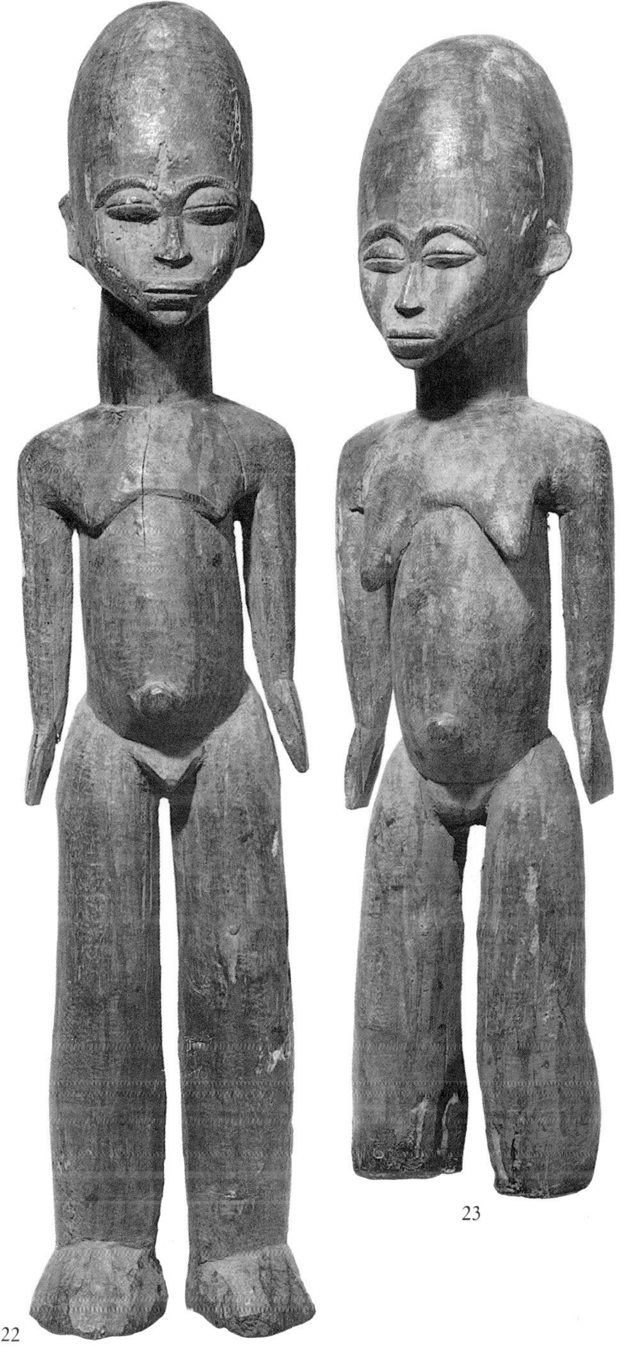

23

22

24 Heddle pulley with bird's head, wood.
Ivory Coast, Senufo.

Part of the treadle loom widely used in West Africa is the heddle pulley, which is here missing its spool.

As the weaver's personal property, it is often an heirloom. The carved bird's head serves not only as ornament but also as magical protection for the weaver's work (see also p.76 for a discussion of the heddle pulleys of the Baule and Guro). The beak suggests that of a hornbill and the coiffure, which corresponds to the customary hairdo of Senufo women, is said to symbolize this bird (see No. 30).

Height 17 cm. 36-26-8
Acquired from L. Segy 1932

Lit.: H. Himmelheber 1960, p.98; D. Mato 1979, p. 8-11, Illus. 15.

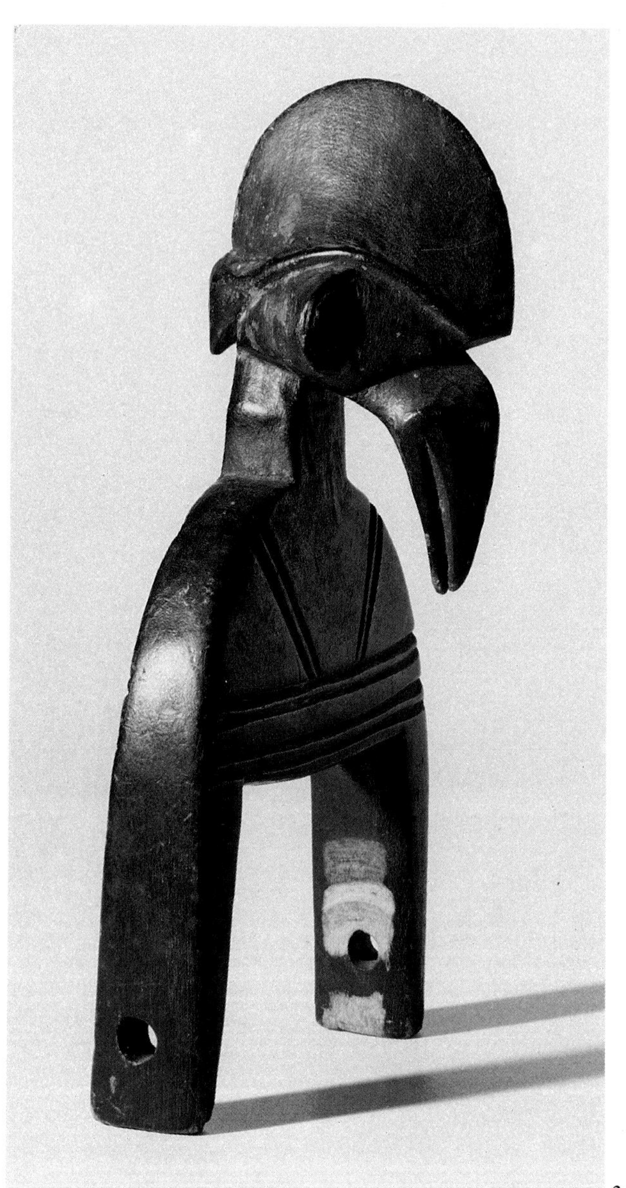

24

25 Male figure, wood.
Ivory Coast, Senufo.

This small, boldly abstracted figure is an impressive work of Senufo wood carving. It clearly demonstrates the ability, so aptly described by Fagg, of imbuing small sculptures with a monumental quality. Remarkable features include the high combed coiffure, circular ears, small stylized triangular face with a strong forward thrust, and slender torso with neck and legs of almost equal length. Bulky oversized hands rest on the hips, while the feet are merely flat ovals raised only slightly above the base. Originally the figure was light colored, but is now stained black and polished.

Figures such as this, used mostly in pairs, represent the diviner's ancestors, who help her in casting and interpreting the divination tools. The diviner is highly esteemed in Senufo society and leads the women's *lo*-cult association which exists in every village.

Height 34 cm. 28-31-2
Acquired from F. Fénéon 1928

Lit.: W. Fagg 1970a, p.20; R. Goldwater 1964, p.23; H. Himmelheber 1960, p.110, 1967, p.256.

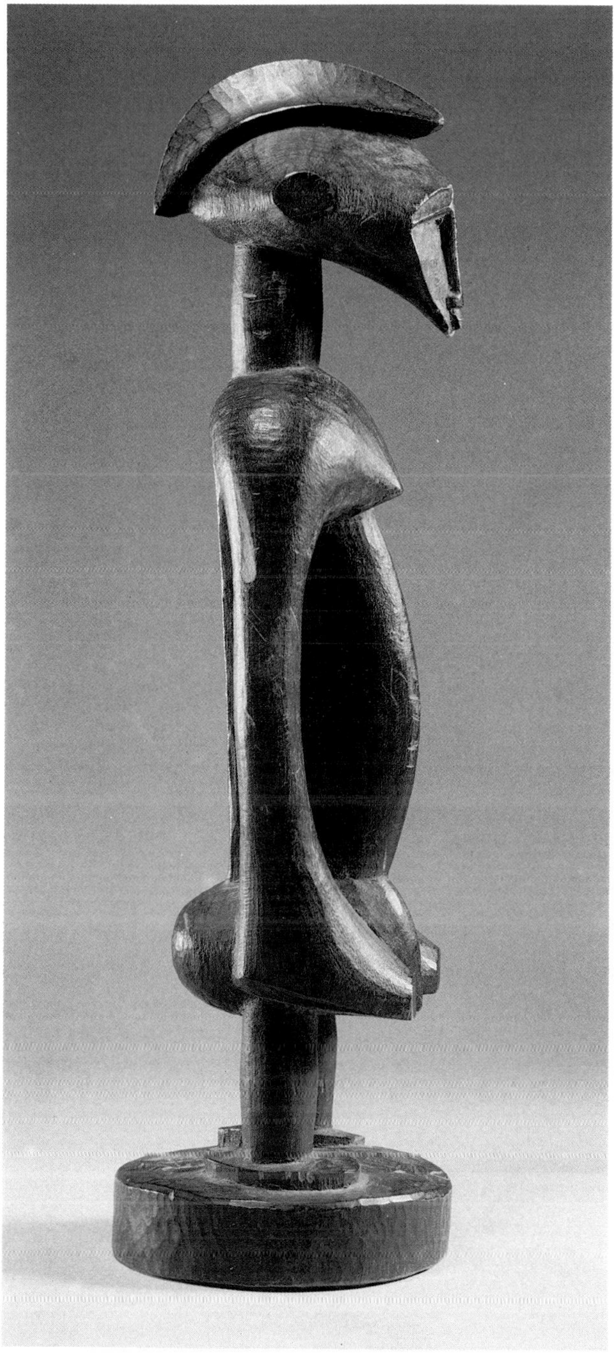

25

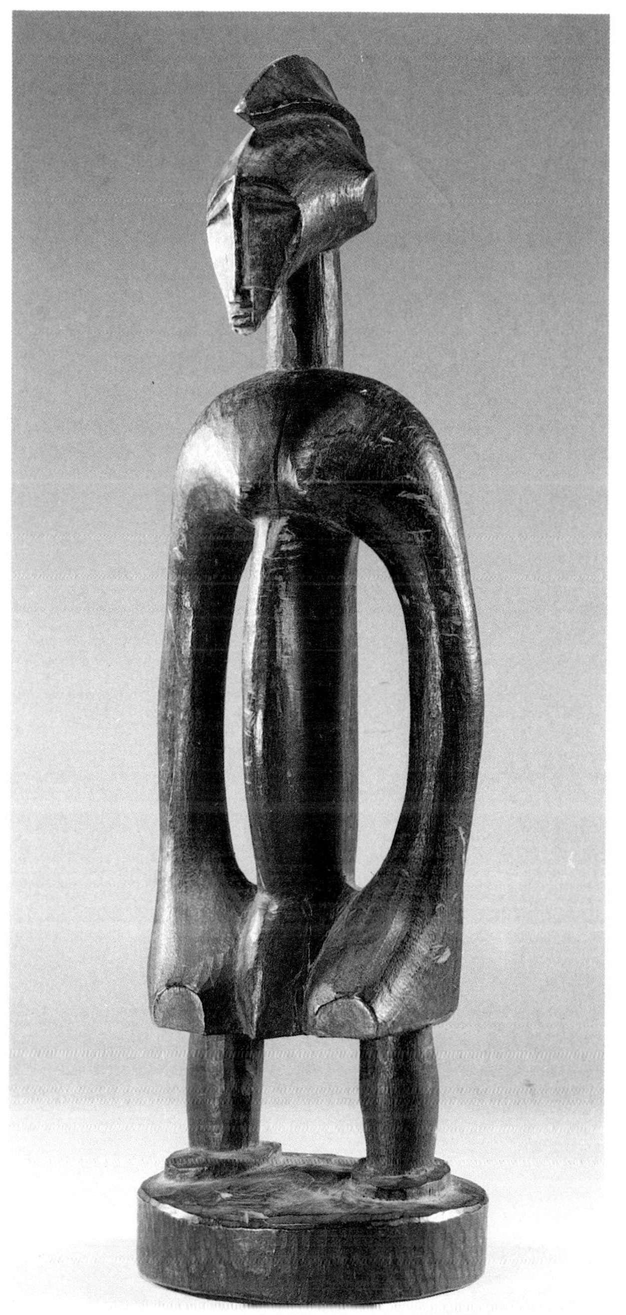

25

Cast Brass Pendants and Finger Rings (26-30)

Among the Senufo and their neighbors (the Turka, Tusian, Bwa, and others), people who are ill or feel themselves persecuted by misfortune have small cast brass amulets made in the form of pendants and finger rings, according to the instructions of diviners. When the misfortune has passed, the amulet can be resold to another person. Finger rings are usually worn by men, and pendants by women, as neck or belt ornaments. Both kinds of amulets are decorated with small sculptures, the most usual being of the first animals of creation, twins, and anthropomorphic forest spirits.

The material used is a kind of brass, an alloy of copper and zinc, sometimes with pewter or lead added as well. This easily melted alloy is well suited to the lost-wax process generally used in West Africa.

For small sculptures or decorations such as spirals, braiding, zigzag lines, or band decoration, wax threads are set onto a wax model. For larger objects, the wax shape is formed around a core of clay, and the whole—clay core and detailed wax object—is then covered with a thick coating of clay and dried. When the object is heated in an oven the wax melts and runs out through channels cut in the clay, leaving a hollow in the shape of the model. The liquid alloy is then poured in through those same channels and when it cools and hardens the surrounding coat of clay is broken away. Any defects are retouched and the surface is polished. Since the clay mold is always destroyed in the lost wax method, serial production is not possible; each piece is, therefore, unique.

Lit.: A. Glaze 1978, pp.63-71; H. Himmelheber 1967, pp.248-250; B. Menzel 1968, pp.23-35.

26/27 Pairs of anthropomorphic figures, brass.
Ivory Coast, Tusian.

This type of amulet pendant is interpreted as a representation of twins. The Senufo, like many other West African peoples (see No.137ff.), believe that twins are bearers of special mystical powers that can do harm as well as good but that, above all, are dangerous for people around them. This supernatural power is effective not only within the twins' lifetime but increases greatly after their death. Spirits of dead twins, *ng'aabele,* are especially angered by unequal treatment. The principle of equality finds its expression in the matching of pendants worn by immediately threatened relatives.

Wooden sculptures such as that seen in No.25 served as models for these designs. The narrow elongated triangular faces are markedly stylized; the facial features have become indistinct through frequent use. Shoulders are rounded, arms lengthened, and the hands resting on hips are of the same size as the feet. The slender torso is hardly longer than the neck or legs.

Height 5 cm, 5.5 cm. 18-7-3/18-7-7
Acquired from L. Frobenius 1918

Lit.: A. Glaze 1975, p.65f.; H. Himmelheber 1967, p.250.

28 Anthropomorphic pendant, brass.
Ivory Coast, Turka.

Although its style resembles that of the figure pairs seen in Nos. 26 and 27, this figure is said to represent one of the many bush spirits, *madebele.* These spirits are believed to resemble human beings not only externally but also in their way of life: they have their own villages, cult associations, music, dances, and

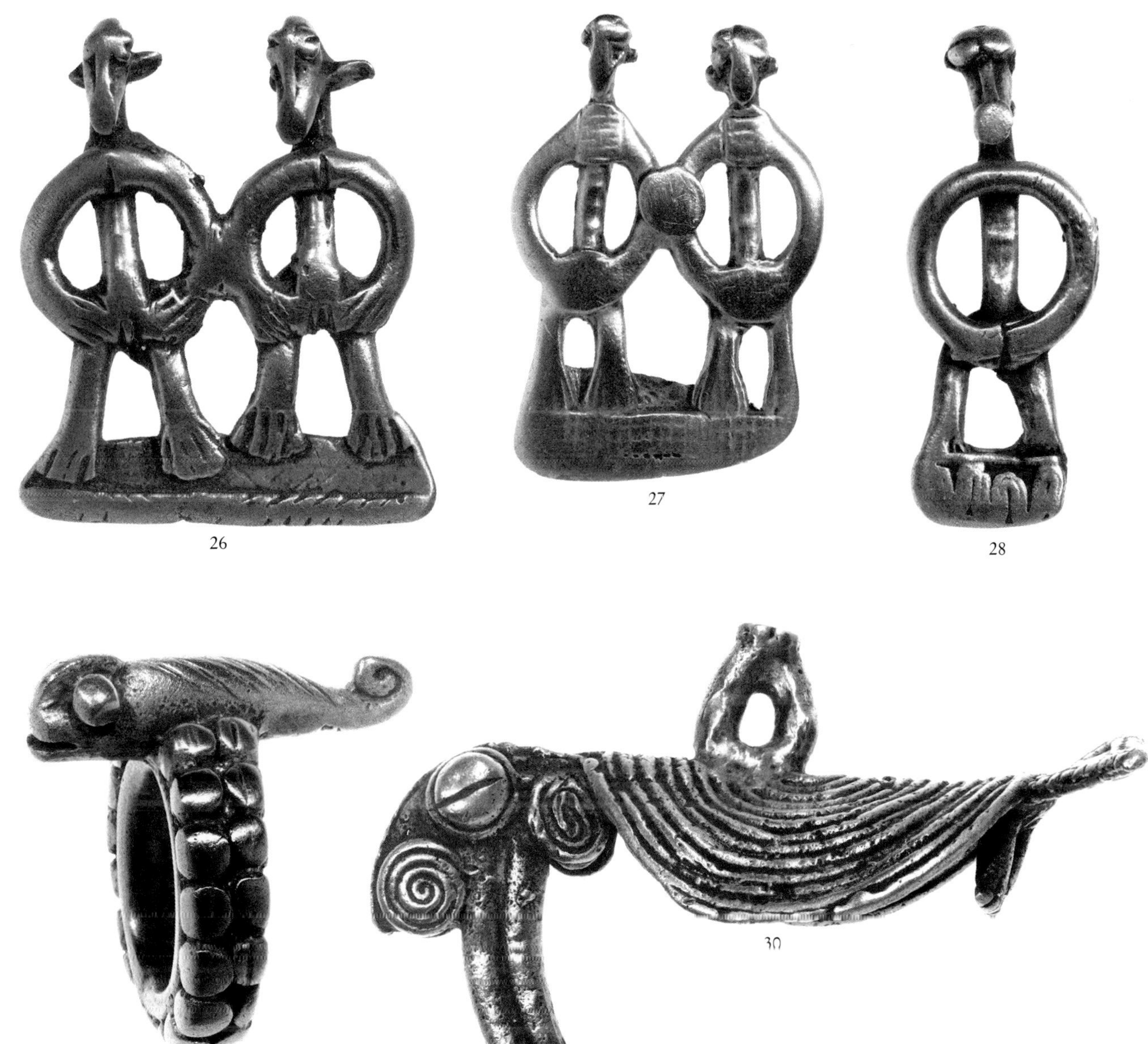

26 27 28

29 30

so on. When neglected by the inhabitants of their district or provoked by them—even unintentionally—these spirits cause serious trouble such as illness. In their affliction people consult diviners who, in turn, are inspired by the bush spirits. These spirits are thus the source of the diviner's powers and the cause of those very problems people hope to solve with his help.

Height 5 cm. 18-7-11
Acquired from L. Frobenius 1918

Lit.: A. Glaze 1978, p.65; H. Himmelheber 1967, p.250.

29 Finger ring: chameleon, brass.
Collected in southern Togo, Senufo?

The chameleon is one of the five primordial beings (see No.30). Its groping gait recalls the soft, mudlike state of the earth after creation. According to some tales, this animal cheated man of immortality by its slowness in transmitting a message from God. Apart from its primordial role, the chameleon is feared in daily life as an uncanny being, commanding dangerous forces. If it is killed, for instance, the killer or his children may die. Amulet rings and pendants are frequently furnished with protective figures of the chameleon.

Diameter 3.8 cm. 18-7-31
Acquired from L. Frobenius 1918

Lit.: A. Glaze 1978, p.67; H. Himmelheber 1967, p.249f.; B. Holas 1960, p.57f.

30 Pendant: hornbill, brass.
Ivory Coast, Turka.

Many peoples of the Guinea coast produce representations of the hornbill (Bucorvus abyssinicus), for the bird occupies an important place in mythology. Along with the chameleon, python, tortoise, and crocodile, the Senufo consider it to be one of the five primordial animals that organized the universe. Like the other four primordial creatures, the hornbill has further mythical and ritual functions, carrying the dead into the Great Beyond, for instance. Its belly, which appears swollen, alludes to pregnancy, while its long beak is associated with the phallus.

Length 8 cm. 18-7-22
Acquired from L. Frobenius 1918

Lit.: B. Holas 1960, p.57f.; D. F. McCall 1975, pp.272, 274, 279, 301.

31 Hand painted shawl (*filafani* or *flafani*), cotton.
Ivory Coast, Senufo, Fakaha.

This cloth was manufactured in 1978 by the farmer Secon Secongo of Fakaha. It consists of thirteen narrow bands sewn together and painted with a dark brown geometric decoration. This pattern, first applied to the cloth as a bright yellow positive design, is afterwards traced in with dark mud.

The Bamana make similar cloths but by a different method: they dip the fabric into a yellow colored dye and then paint over the spaces between the design outlines with dark mud so that the patterm is reserved in the ground color (see No.17).

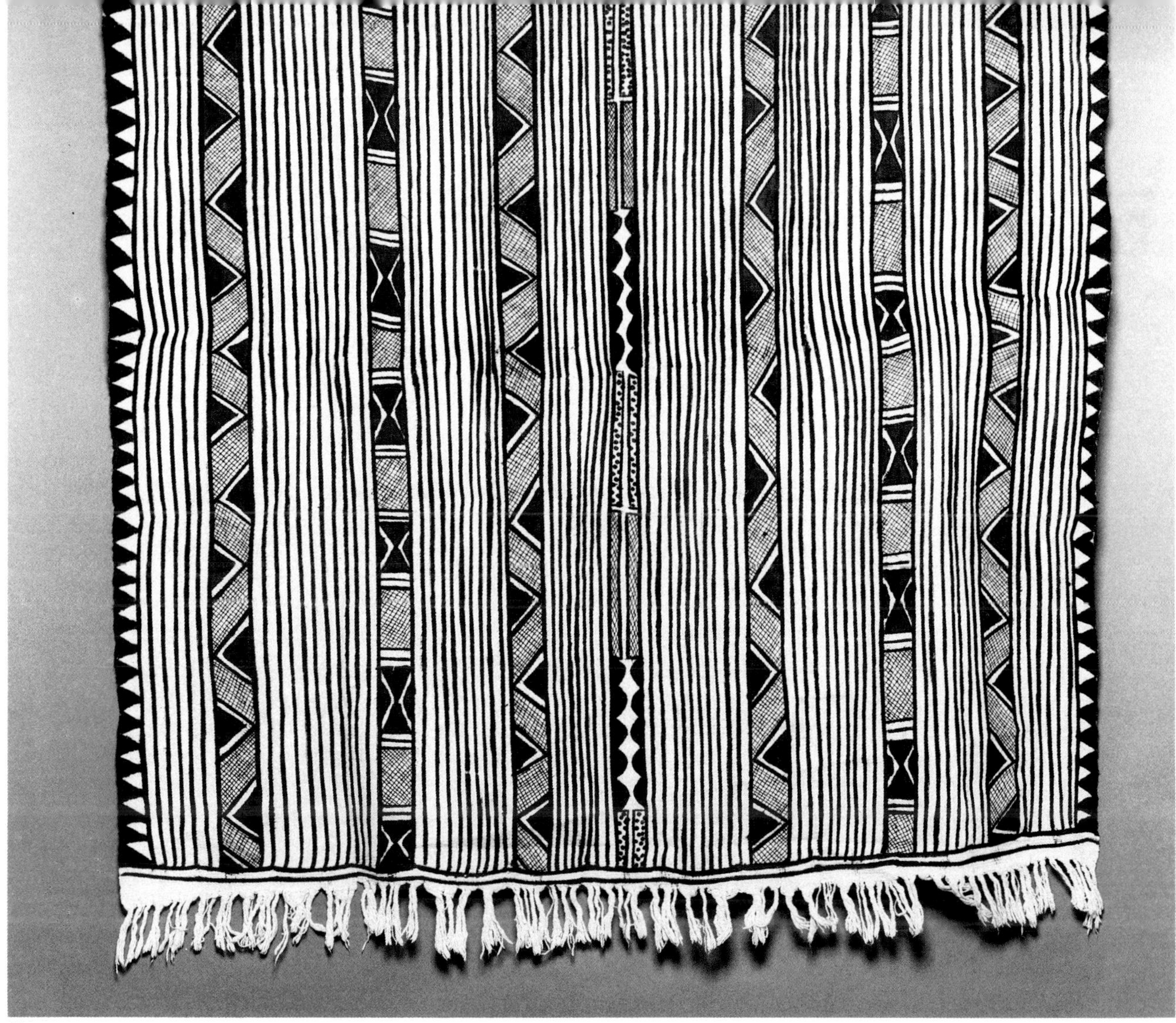

31

Like the finger rings and pendants previously mentioned, such cloths are prescribed to clients by a diviner, who dictates precisely when and for how long the cloths must be worn. Although the motifs may be freely improvised, the frequent snake motif, suggested here by an abstract zig- zag line, seems to have symbolic significance. Among the Senufo the snake serves as a mediator between spirits and diviner. The decoration is not the work of a craftsman but of a gifted villager. The finished wrapper or, in more recent times, the shirt cut from the cloth, is charged with magical force to cure and protect by means of sacrifices and incantations recited at the diviner's shrine.

Measurements 120 x 200 cm. 81-301-453
Acquired from K. H. Krieg 1981

Lit.: R. Gardi 1969, p.234ff.; A. Glaze 1978, p.70f.; K. H. Krieg 1980.

The Guinea Coast

Two different forms of traditional political organization and cultural life exist within the Guinea Coast. Small, loose political units, often consisting of a single village, characterize the modern states of Guinea, Sierra Leone, Liberia, and the western part of the Ivory Coast as well as the Cross River region (the boundary districts between Nigeria and Cameroon). In the Ivory Coast, present-day Ghana, the Republic of Benin (named Dahomey before 1975), and large parts of Nigeria, well-organized states have existed for centuries. They did not achieve the territorial extent of the empires of the western Sudan, but equaled them in political and social organization and in court activities.

In the small local communities of the Guinea Coast and the Cross River region, life was directed by a council of elders and by rather powerless chiefs. In the centralized states, however, power lay in the hands of omnipotent kings whose authority was supported by religious institutions (see the discussion of sacred kingdoms on p. 112). Thus the religious life and the art of the forest peoples were mainly determined by cults of clan ancestors, bush spirits, and so on, while in the kingdoms the religious cults, often conducted by priestly associations, were largely integrated into state activities. There, clan ancestors were often overshadowed by royal ancestors. These differences in social and cultural development may be attributed to the influence of ancient Near Eastern and Mediterranean cultures, which affected the eastern half of the Guinea Coast more strongly than the western. These foreign influences reached the Guinea Coast as a result of vigorous trading policies of the empires of the western Sudan. The latter fell under the influences of Islam in the Middle Ages, while the sacred kingdoms of the Guinea Coast states—those of the Akan (such as the Asante and the Bono), Yoruba, and Bini—maintained their institutions more or less intact until a few decades ago.

In contrast to the western Sudan, where sculpture is determined by the stylistic tradition of pole sculpture, Guinea Coast art is distinguished by the round style. Nevertheless, the art of the forest cultures and that of the forest kingdoms differ notably from each other. The royal courts with their wealth and precisely established court procedures, the hierarchically structured bureaucracy with its many signs of office, the strong need for representation among rulers and notables—all these influenced the art of the kingdoms. Most artists and/or craftsmen were organized in guildlike groups and were chiefly employed by the court. Their works were expected not only to satisfy aesthetic and religious needs but also to make visible the wealth and power of the court. In the villages and more remote districts of the kingdoms where a folk art thrived, however, the few professional artists kept to traditional models.

Lit.: H. Baumann 1940, S. 289-299; 1969, 10-17

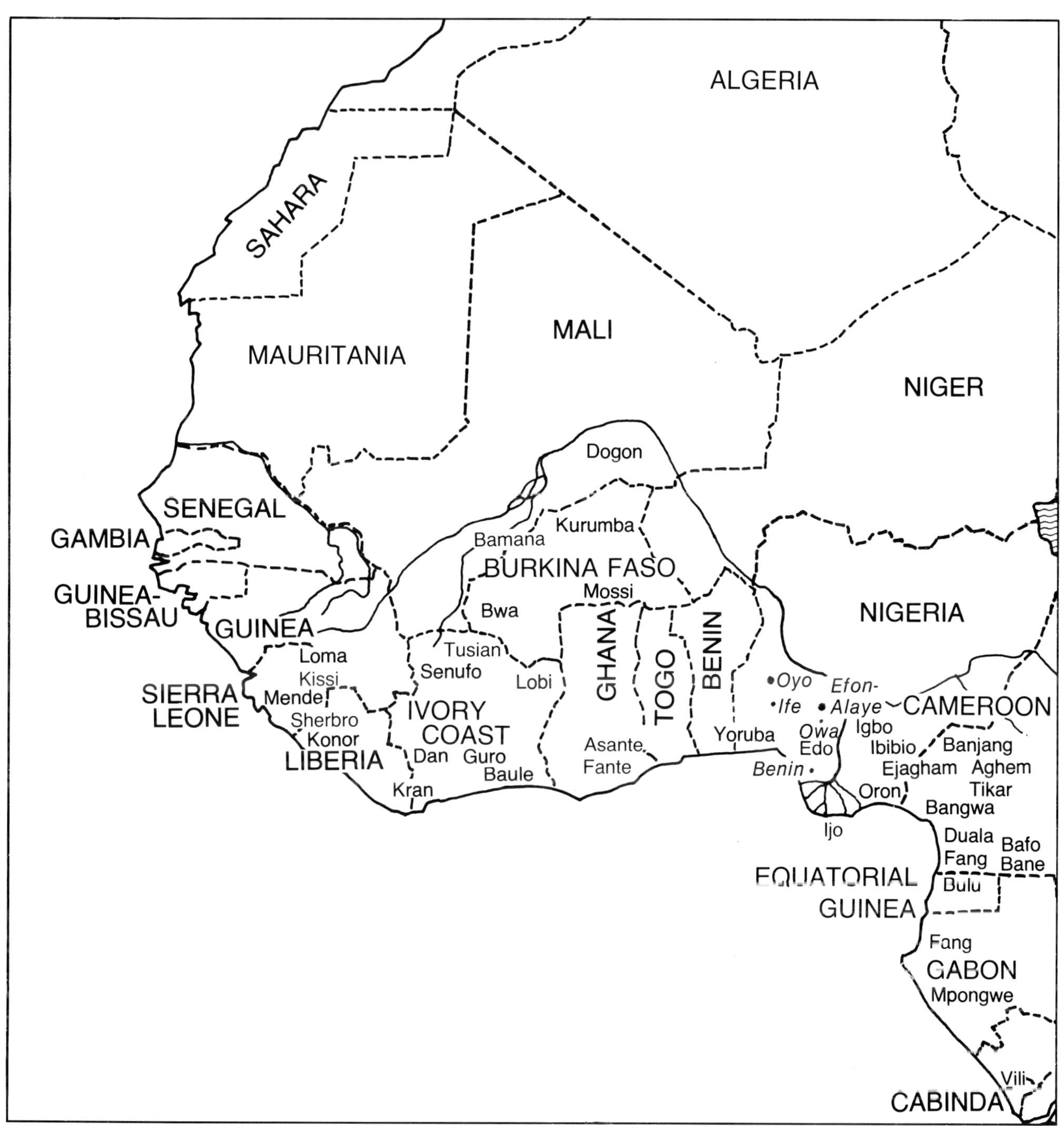
ALGERIA
SAHARA
MALI
MAURITANIA
NIGER
Dogon
SENEGAL
GAMBIA
Kurumba
Bamana
BURKINA FASO
Mossi
GUINEA-
BISSAU
GUINEA
Bwa
NIGERIA
Loma
Tusian
Kissi
Senufo
Lobi
GHANA
TOGO
BENIN
Oyo
Efon-
Alaye
Ife
CAMEROON
SIERRA
LEONE
Mende
Sherbro
Konor
IVORY
COAST
Owa
Igbo
Yoruba
Edo
Asante
Fante
Ibibio
Banjang
LIBERIA
Dan
Guro
Baule
Benin
Ejagham
Aghem
Kran
Oron
Tikar
Bangwa
Ijo
Duala
Bafo
Fang
Bane
EQUATORIAL
GUINEA
Bulu
Fang
GABON
Mpongwe
Vili
CABINDA

Stone Figures and Afro-Portuguese Ivories from Guinea and Sierrra Leone

At least six hundred years ago, a style of figurative stone sculpture developed within the comparatively limited area of the dense rain forests of Guinea and Sierra Leone. The small stone figures that the present-day inhabitants of the area know by the Kissi word *pomdo* or the Mende word *nomoli* probably served as ancestral or grave statuettes among the former upper strata of the Bulom people. The figures are of special interest in African art because they reveal, among other things, the continuity and transformation of a cultural tradition over several centuries. The oldest pieces, which were probably made in the thirteenth and fourteenth centuries, display characteristics that can also be observed in examples made during the period of decline in the seventeenth and eighteenth centuries. They thus adhere to tradition while showing a tendency to innovation. There are, of course, motifs and stylistic properties characteristic of certain periods only. For instance, military and political events in the middle of the sixteenth century were seminal in the introduction of the equestrian motif. Troops of mounted warriors from the Mandingo of the Sudan penetrated the area and established themselves as a ruling elite. Although the tropical climate soon forced them to abandon cavalry, the figure of the horseman long remained a symbol of prestige and power.

The Kissi continued to produce their art, but it rapidly deteriorated and finally ended in mass production of articles for the tourist trade. Even the original function of their ancestral and grave sculpture has been forgotten. Old stone figures accidentally found in the bush or in the ground by present-day inhabitants are considered magical objects with the power to promote fertility, or to be the abodes of tutelary spirits that prevent theft, insure a good harvest, and serve as oracles. Cult associations prefer to establish their meeting places around such a figure.

Pomdo and *nomoli* may be dated by reference to ivory figures made for the most part in the late fifteenth and the sixteenth centuries by the Sherbo and Bulom. These ivory carvings are known as "Afro-Portuguese" because they were made for Portuguese customers and therefore conform to European Renaissance models. But the technique and style of the figurative details correspond entirely to old African artistic traditions known to us from stone ancestral and grave figures. Thus, for instance, some human faces on Afro-Portuguese ivory cups correspond in style to the bulging-eye style of figures that represent a late phase of the stone sculptures.

Lit.: T. J. Alldridge 1901, pp.163, 64, 1910, pp. 286-89; K. Dittmer 1967, p. 183ff.; W. Fagg 1959.

32 Horn: crocodile head, ivory.
Sierra Leone, Sherbro, Bulom, Temne.

This fluted form may be traced to foreign models, for such horns were known in European and Islamic countries in the Middle Ages. Even the animal head at the tapered end of the horn is characteristic of the European ivory-horn tradition. The subject of a crocodile head, and the placement of the blowing hole on the concave side, however, are typically African. Only a few comparable pieces are known (in Vienna, Paris, London, and Copenhagen).

This side-blown horn comes from the "curiosity cabinet" of the Jesuit Father Ferdinand Orban Ingolstadt (1657-1732), who considered it an ancient Benin work and whose collection of curiosities was among the most famous sights of Bavaria in the eighteenth century. According to Müller, "The establishment and turbulent history of the collection, as well as the kind of objects collected, made it characteristic of the bourgeois cabinets of the day. As a

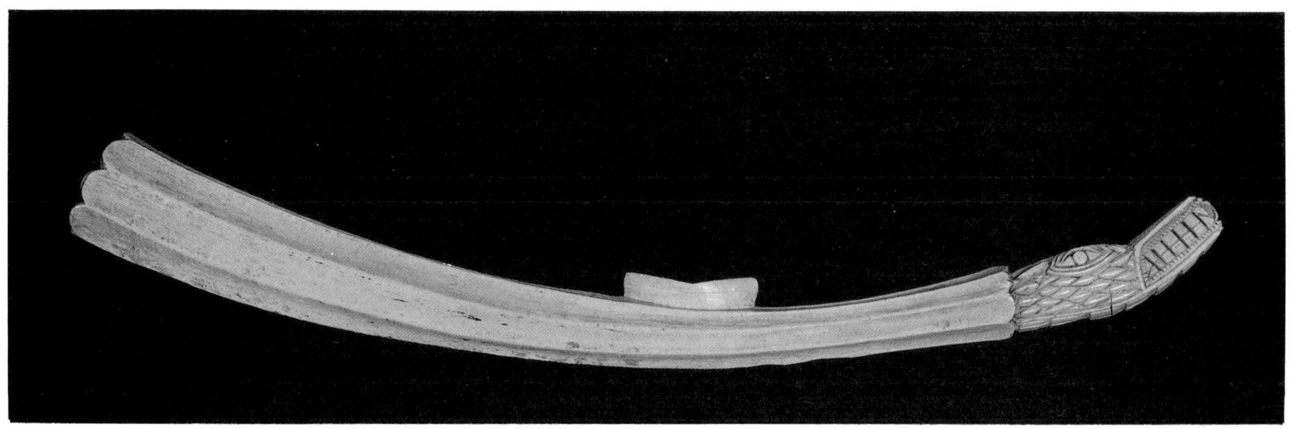

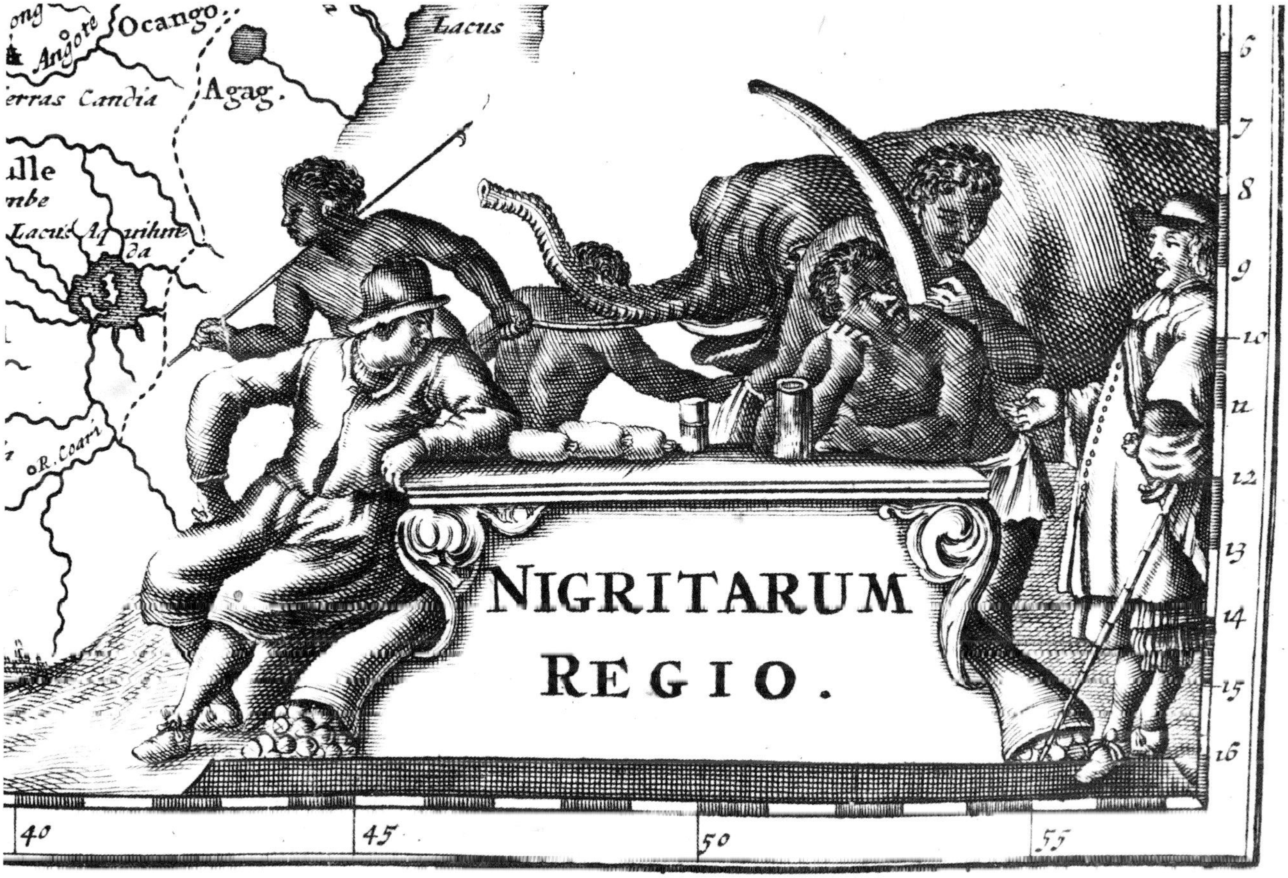

From O. Dapper, *Umbstandliche und eigentliche Beschreibung von Afrika . . .*, 1670.

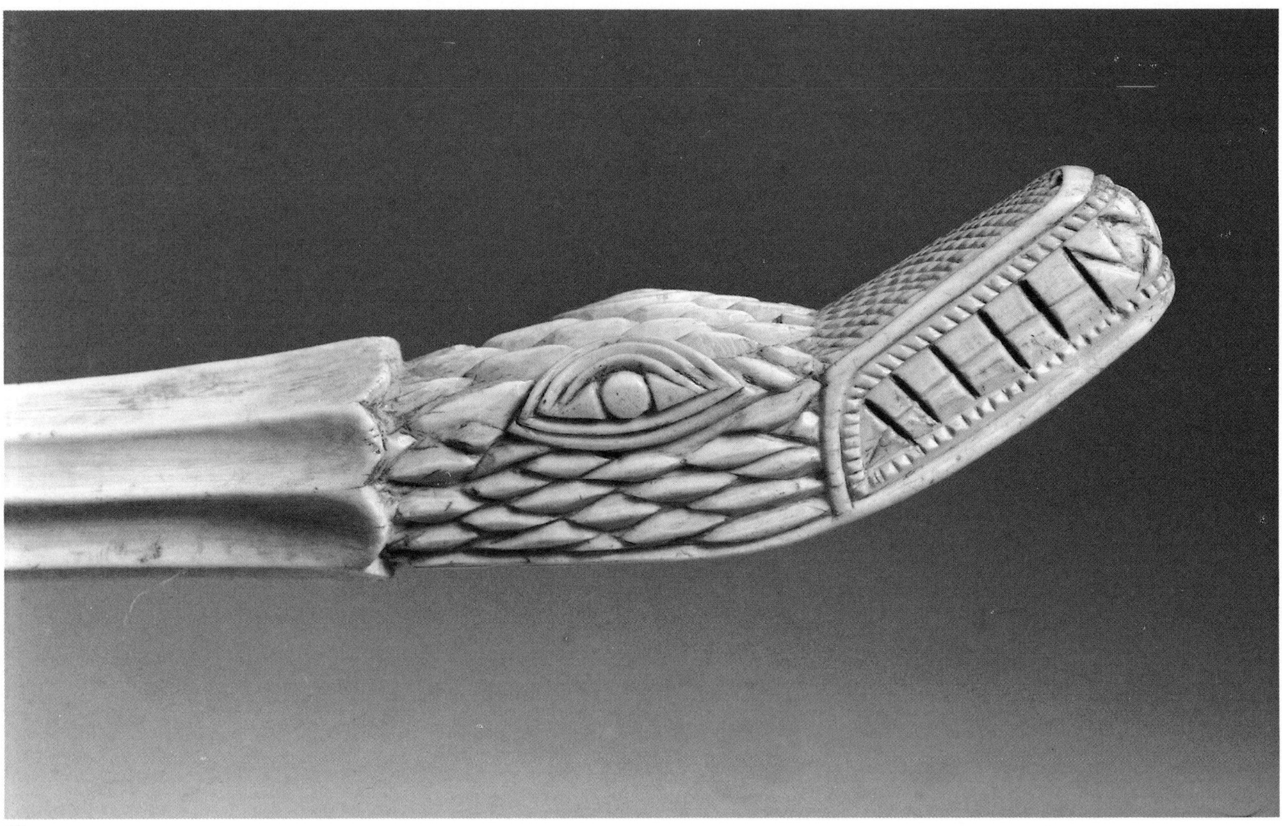

32

much traveled scholar especially conversant with the natural sciences, Orban became a teacher at several universities. Perhaps even more significant was the fact that this highly educated Jesuit was employed as preacher at the courts of several German principalities. These connections enabled him to lay systematically the foundation of a considerable collection."

Length 53.5 cm. Orb. 20
Acquired from Ingolstadt University 1881

Lit.: E. B. Dam-Mikkelsen & T. Lundback 1980, p. 49; W. Fagg 1959, p. XI; F. Heger 1899, p. 103; C. C. Müller 1980, p.16; Ed. Tardy 1977, pp. 83, 130-31, 399, 425, 26, 432, 33.

33 Spoon, ivory.
Sierra Leone, Sherbro, Bulom, Temne.

Benin, the provenance recorded for this spoon in the old inventory, is incorrect. An example of the hybrid Afro-Portuguese style, this piece probably comes from Sierra Leone—an assumption based on a customs list from 1504-5 showing that Portuguese seafarers took home great numbers of inexpensively purchased ivory carvings, mainly spoons and saltcellars from Sierra Leone. A sturdy midrib strengthens the undersurface of the bowl of the spoon. The handle, a masterly piece of carving, is in the form of an openwork double knot and is therefore movable. The double knot, a symbol of kingship in West Africa, is here in the form of a vertical eight, echoed

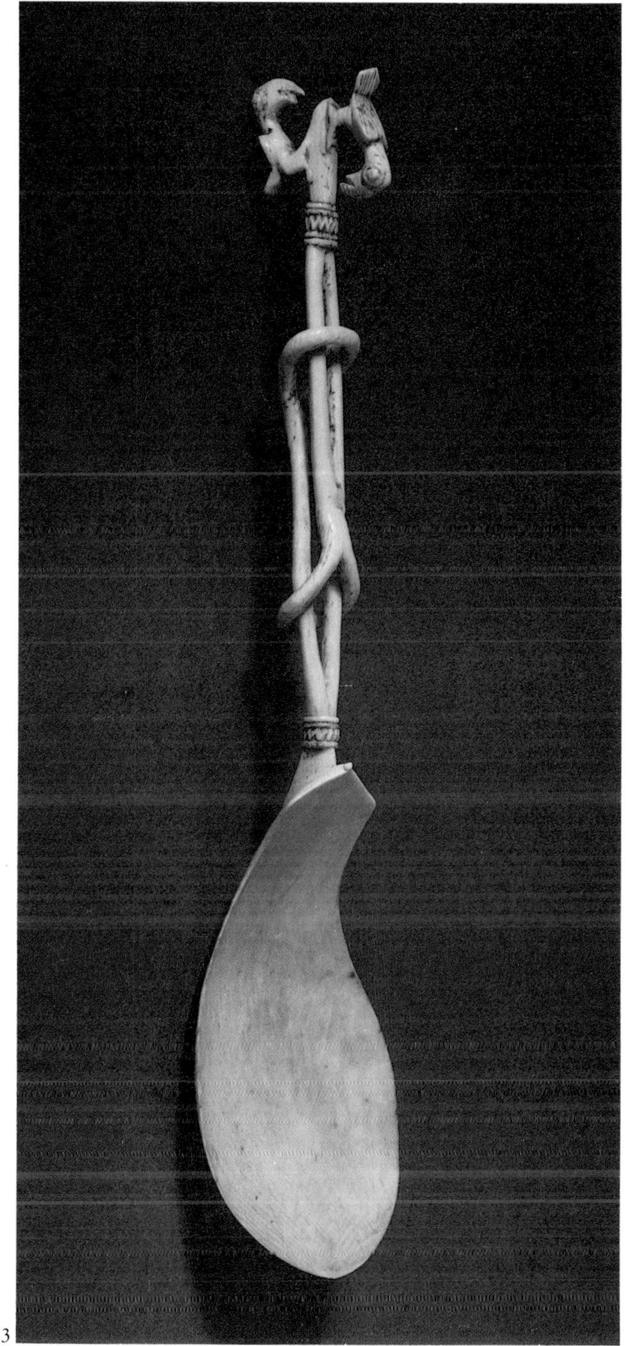
33

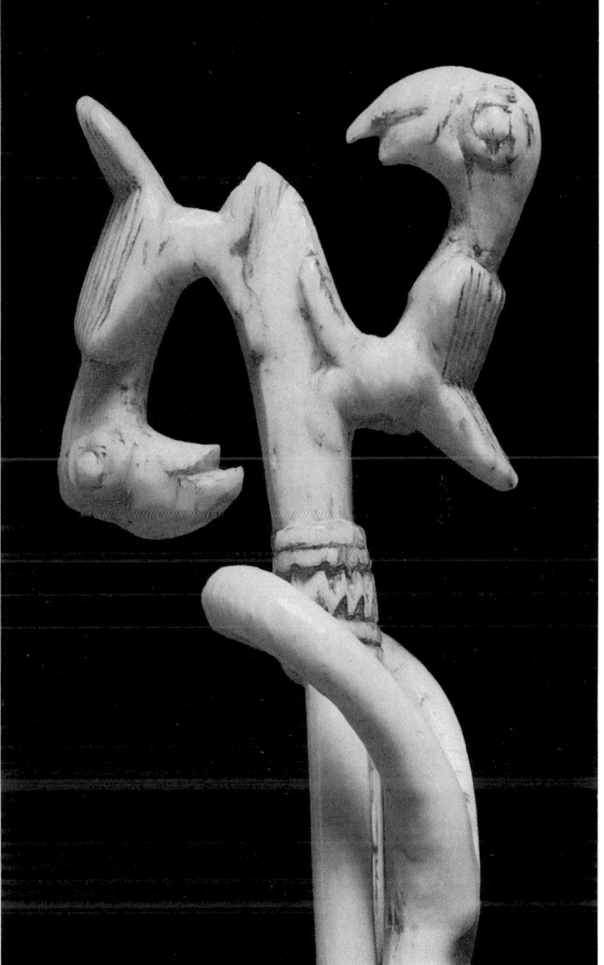
33

in the horizontal eight produced by the bird figures (parrots or hornbills?) at the tip of the handle.

Length 20.5 cm. (drawn out), 18.5 cm. (drawn together) 26-N-129
Acquired from the Bayerische Nationalmuseum 1926 (probably from the Bavarian Royal Household)

Lit.: W. Fagg 1959, pp. XIII; A. F. C. Ryder 1964, pp. 363-65.

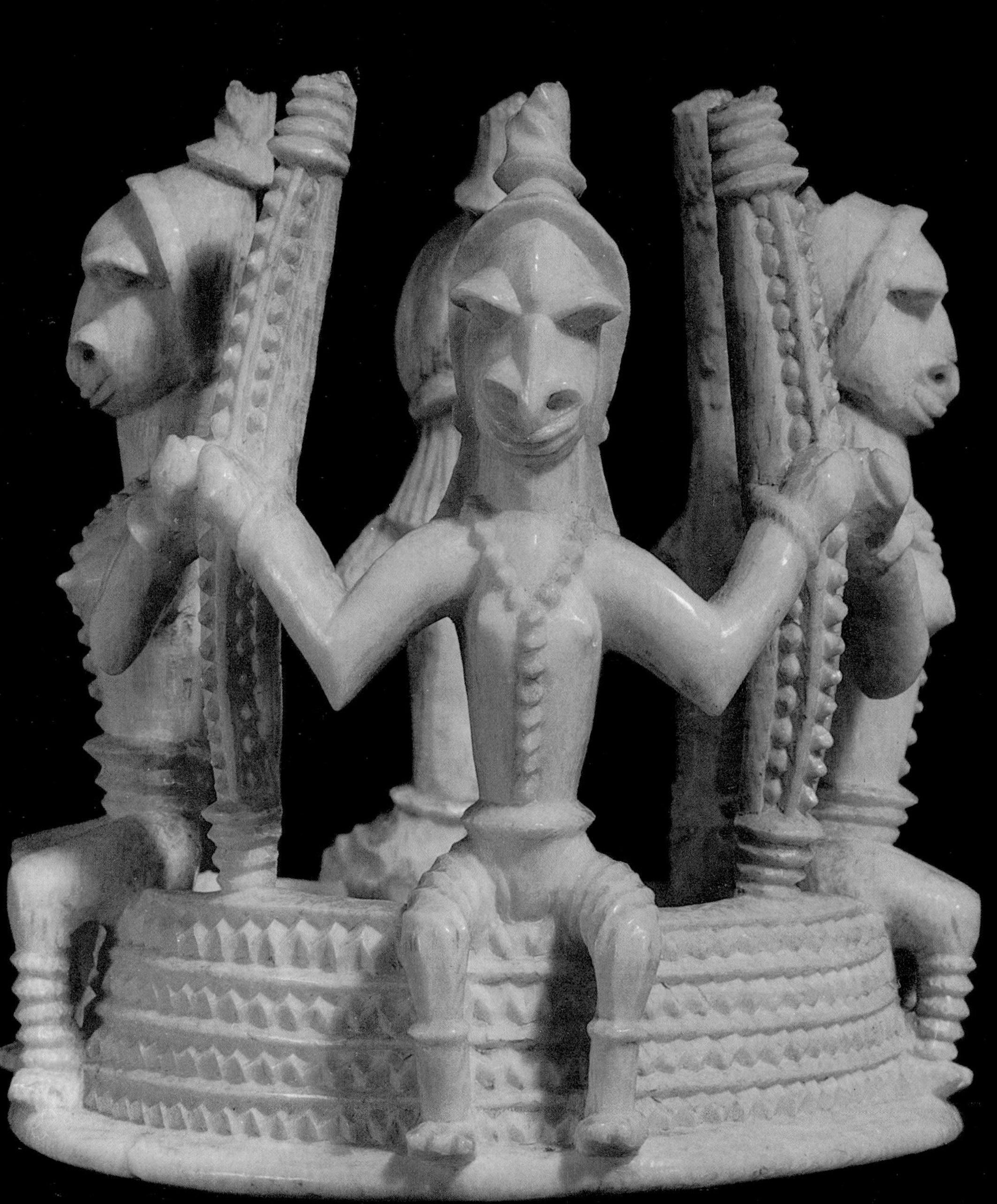

34

34 Lower part of a pedestal cup, ivory.
Sierra Leone, Sherbro, Bulom, Temne.

This sixteenth century Afro-Portuguese work is probably one of the oldest pieces in Munich's African collection. A chalice or spherical bowl—possibly of delicate Renaissance form, judging from comparable examples—once rested on this base. In contrast, the artist gave the faces African features he considered "classical," known to us from the carved stone human figures seen in Nos. 35 and 37. These two figures may be placed in the "middle *nomoli* stylistic phase," characterized by such details as large head with strong, sharp features, vertical forehead scar, eyes half hidden by markedly protruding lids, broad nose with distended nostrils, and wide mouth. Dress and body ornaments are also those of West Africa.

The sculptured ivory cups, spoons, forks, and hunting horns supplied by craftsmen of the Sherbro-Bulom empire and often praised by European travelers of the sixteenth century may, in a certain sense, be described as an early variety of tourist art. These early commissioned objects were, however, distinguished by the use of especially valuable materials and by their outstanding craftsmanship. Of the surviving pieces, the majority—some hundred objects—are in the British Museum, London, and are also well represented in the collections of Berlin, Bologna, and Rome.

Height 9.2 cm., diameter 9 cm. 5380
Acquired from the Bavarian Royal Household 1881

Lit.: E. Bassani 1977a, pp. 38, 39; W. Fagg 1959, pp. XI, XII; V. L. Grotanelli 1975, pp. 14-23; A. C. Ryder 1964, pp. 363, 65.

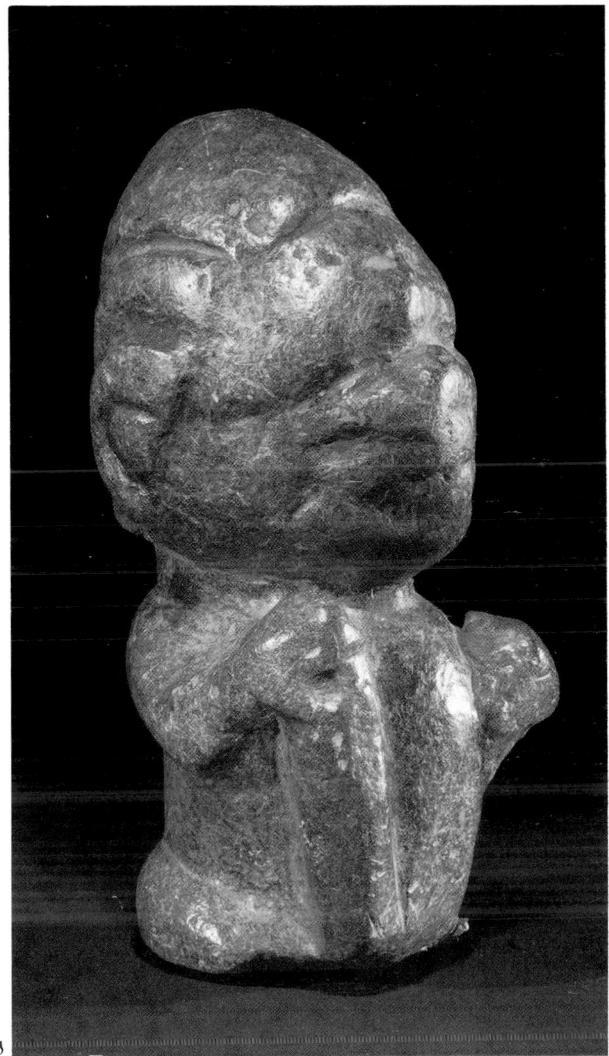
35

35 Figure *(pomdo)*, steatite.
Sierra Leone, collected among the Mende.

Features typical of the Kissi style are apparent in this warrior with shield and spear. Ratio of body to head

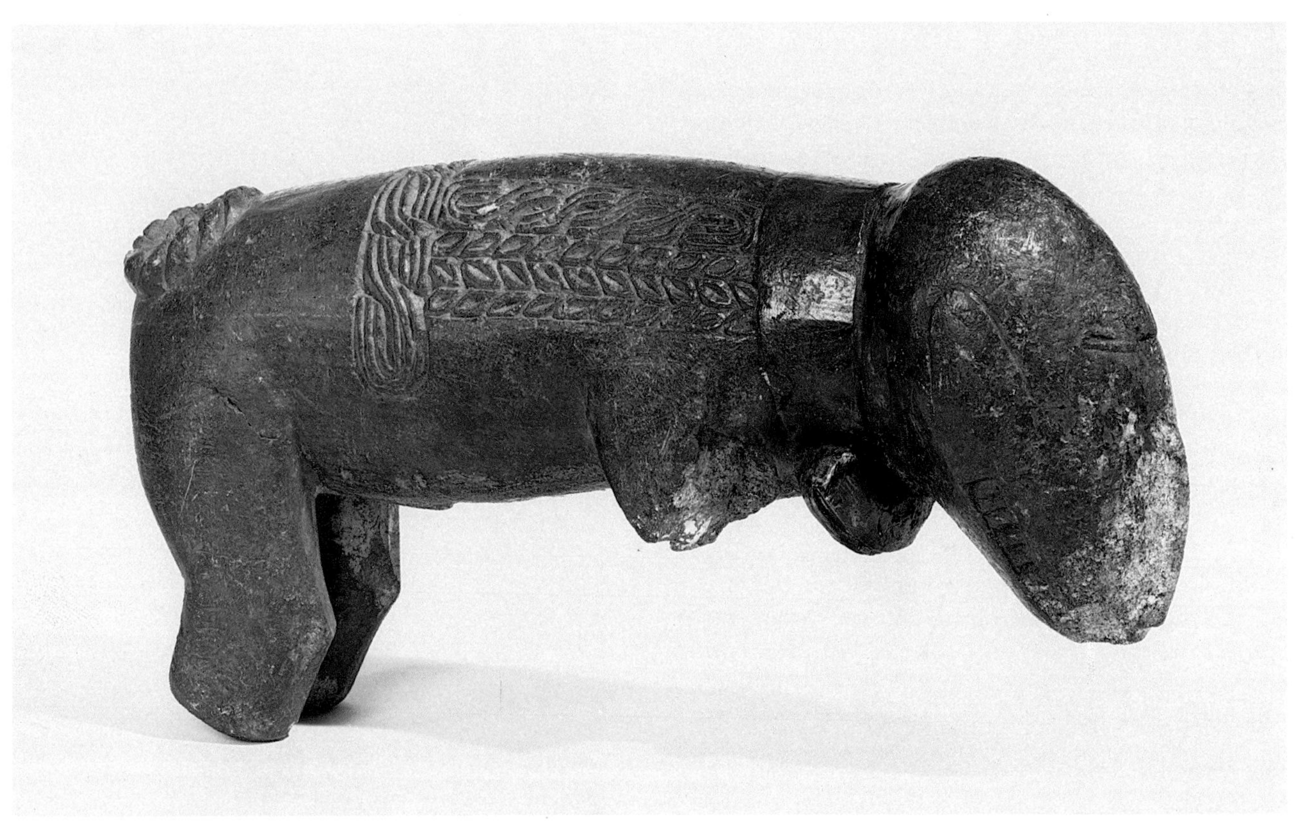

36

is one to one; the torso is rudimentary, shoulder blades and thighs form a roll each, and the dominating head has a coiffure with several partings. Small slit eyes are formed by one continuous notch; the nostrils of the wide nose are distended, the lips broadly everted, the chin pointed, and the large ears stylized. This small, presumably seventeenth century statue does show a certain deterioration of style, probably owing to frequent repetition of the theme.

Height 9 cm. 11.399
Acquired from O. W. Oldman 1911 (collected by T. J. Alldridge 1890, 1901)

Lit.: K. Dittmer 1967, p. 188.

36 Animal figure *(pomdo)*, steatite.
Sierra Leone or Guinea, collected among the Kissi.

This animal with caparison, neckband with bell, and coiled tail is so far the only figure known of its kind. The careful treatment of these details suggests an early origin. The rounded blocklike shape of the animal's body shows a strong tendency toward geometrization and reduction. Details are partly incised, partly sculptured. The incised S-knot and leaf-motif decoration on the back recalls the ornamented shoulder straps of Mandingo warriors. The carving probably belongs to that style of stone sculpture in which human beings are represented by wide grinning mouths, bared teeth, thin straight noses, and narow slit eyes.

Length 31 cm. 66-5-1
Acquired from L. Bretschneider 1966

Lit.: K. Dittmer 1967, pp. 189, 212; A. Tagliaferri 1974, n.p.

37 Equestrian figure *(pomdo)*, steatite.
Sierra Leone, collected among the Mende.

Only the framed lancet-shape eyes, the parted lips, and broad nose stand out from the tattooed face of this mounted warrior with spear and round shield. The horse, only barely recognizable, indicates the Mandingo conqueror of the sixteenth century. This piece is probably considerably later, possibly seventeenth or eighteenth century. It could be a copy of an older figure.

Height 18 cm. 11.400
Acquired from O. W. Oldman 1911 (collected by T. J. Alldridge 1890-1901)

Lit.: K. Dittmer 1967, p. 210.

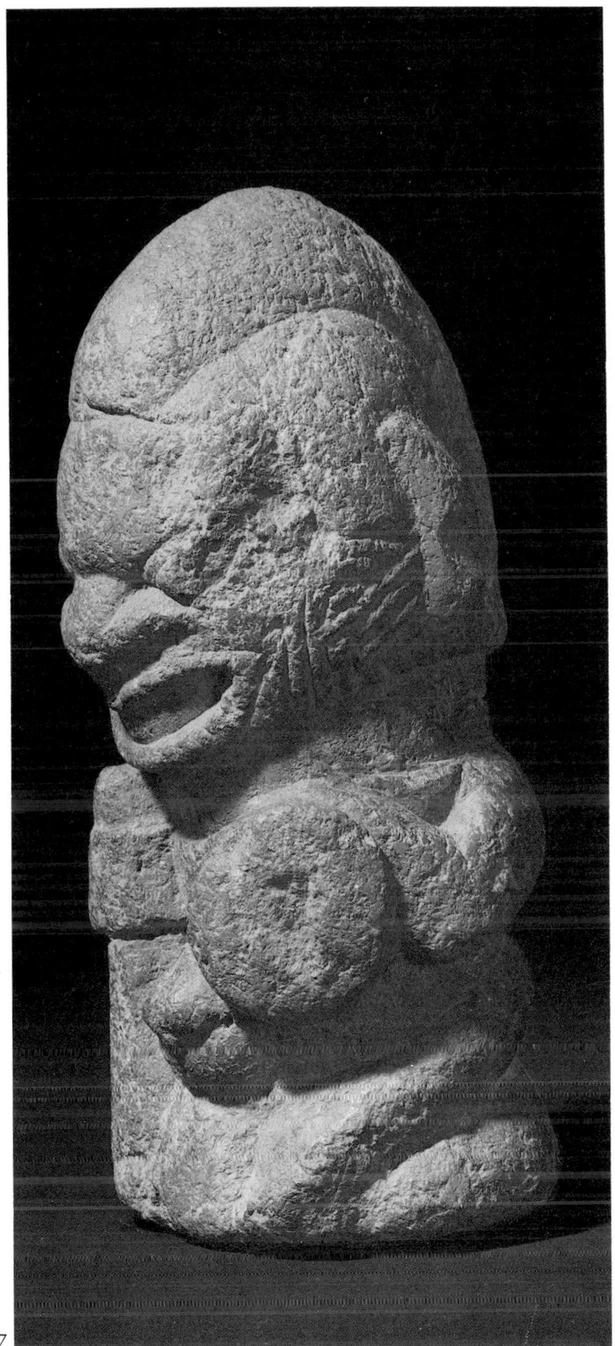

37

Masks of the Dan and Their Neighbors (38-43)

A fairly unified style of mask sculpture is found throughout the extensive area that reaches from Guinea across Sierra Leone and Liberia to the central Ivory Coast. In the western half of this area the masks are associated with the activities of the influential *poro* cult association or secret society. In the eastern half, among the Dan and other groups, a presumably more ancient tradition of mask ritual has been preserved, one that has not been adopted by supraregional associations.

According to Himmelheber and Fischer, Dan masks chiefly represent bush spirits, who, in mythical tradition, were the earliest prehuman owners of the land. It is thought that they originally permitted the founders of each village to clear the forests and establish settlements. Descendants of the founders were, and still are, convinced that they are under the control of bush spirits. The most important social implication of this belief is that it has preserved the authority of the council of elders, who are believed to be ruled by bush spirits. The elders arbitrate legal disputes and make other binding decisions. In a society with no central government, the expression of the will of the bush spirits is for the most part accepted without question and serves as a highly effective regulatory force.

The bush spirits' authority is continually strengthened by the masked figures through which they reveal themselves. There are different ways to gain possession of such a mask. A bush spirit can appear to someone in a dream, for instance, and direct him to have a mask made to represent the spirit and communicate its wishes to the villagers. The care of masks whose spirits are worshiped by whole villages or peoples may be the responsibility of individuals found worthy of the honor. Privileged families inherit the right to provide caretakers for such masks. The number of spirits and the masks representing them is unlimited. The rather frequent feuds of former times often resulted in the victors' confiscating masks and assigning their spirits new functions that benefited the conquering group. For this reason the exact function of a mask cannot be established with certainty on the sole basis of its external appearance.

Most of the masks exhibited here represent the classical Dan style, with predominantly quiet, well-distinguished forms and gentle convexities. The harmonious distribution of the planes along the longitudinal and lateral axes is likewise characteristic.

Lit.: E. Fischer & H. Himmelheber 1976, pp. 6-12; E. Fischer 1980, pp. 81-88; G. W. Harley 1950, p. 7; W. C. Siegmann 1980, pp. 89-95.

38 Mask (*dea* or *deaboa),* wood.
Ivory Coast, southern Dan.

The female spirit portrayed here endowed barren women with fertility, protected the newborn, and presented them to the community. However, the same mask played a role in the ceremonies of sacrifice to the ancestors, performed at sowing time, and, strangely enough, also assumed the role of guardian of the boys' bush school, chasing away the uninitiated and settling quarrels among the students.

The concept of beauty prevalent among the southern Dan is apparent in this idealized female face. Characteristics are the high forehead, slit eyes within sharply tapered ovals set between deeply notched horizontal grooves, tatoos near the eyes, broad nose, and full lips. The light-colored wood underlines the realism of the representation.

Height 24 cm. 51-3-14
Acquired from L. Kegel 1951

Lit.: G. W. Harley 1950, pp. 26, 36; H. Himmelheber 1960, p. 156; R. F. Thompson 1974, pp. 160-6.

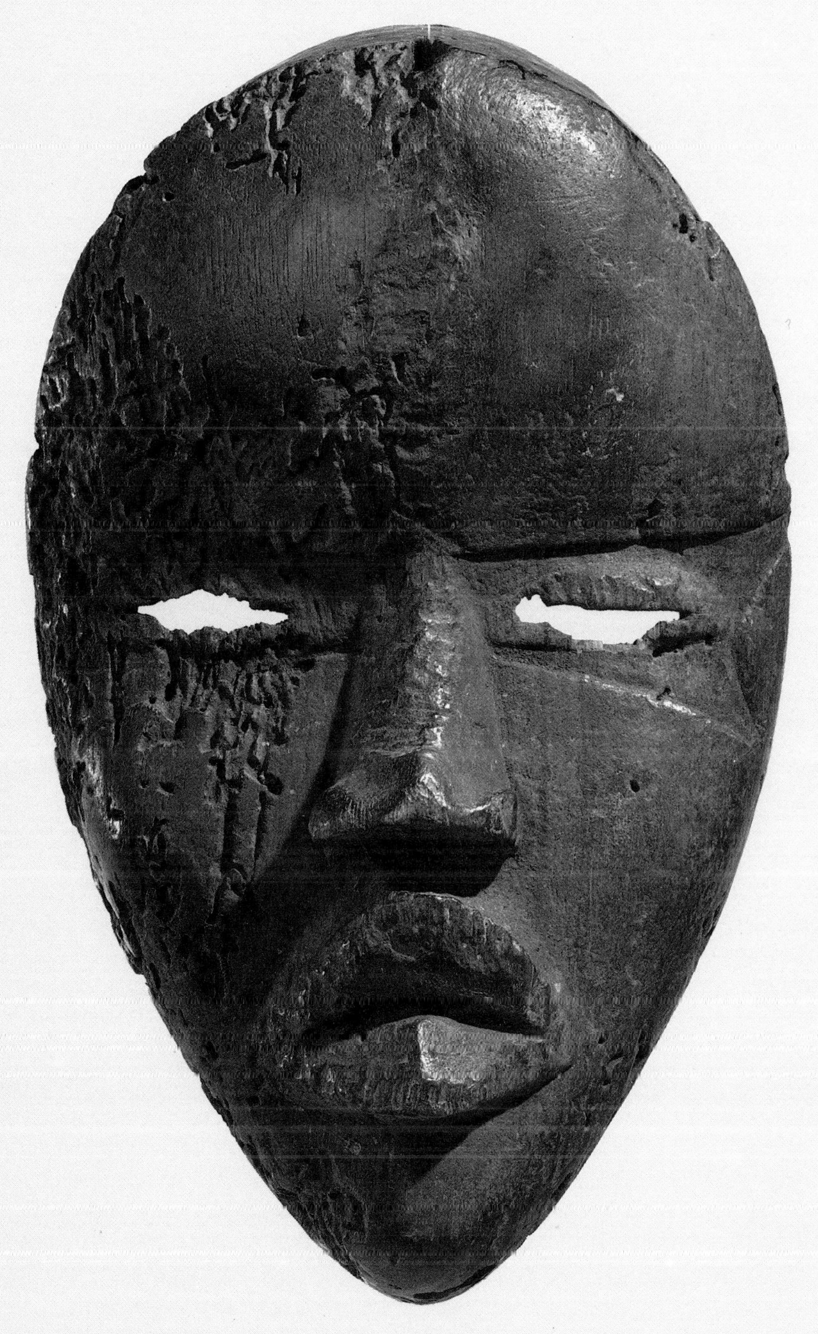

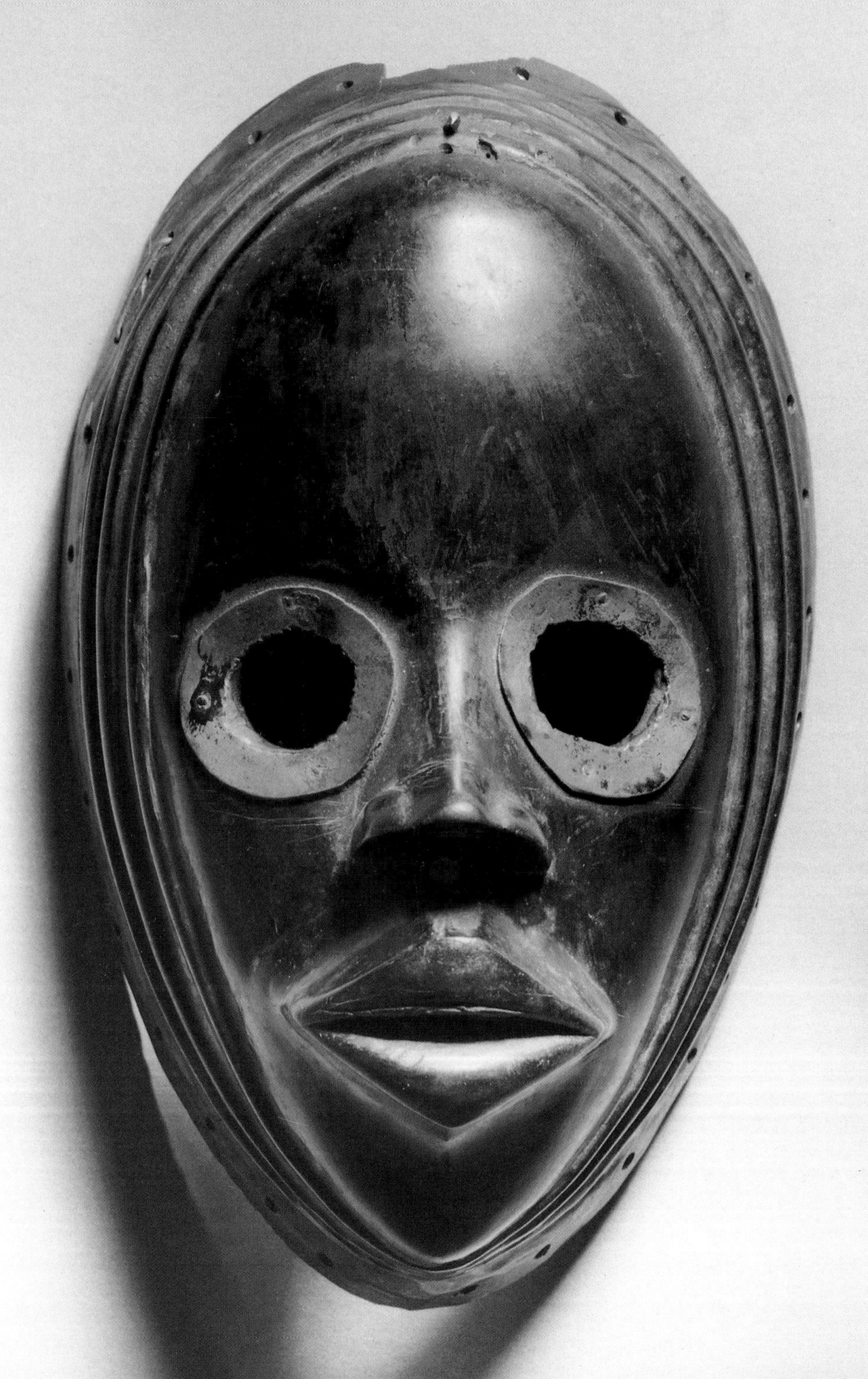

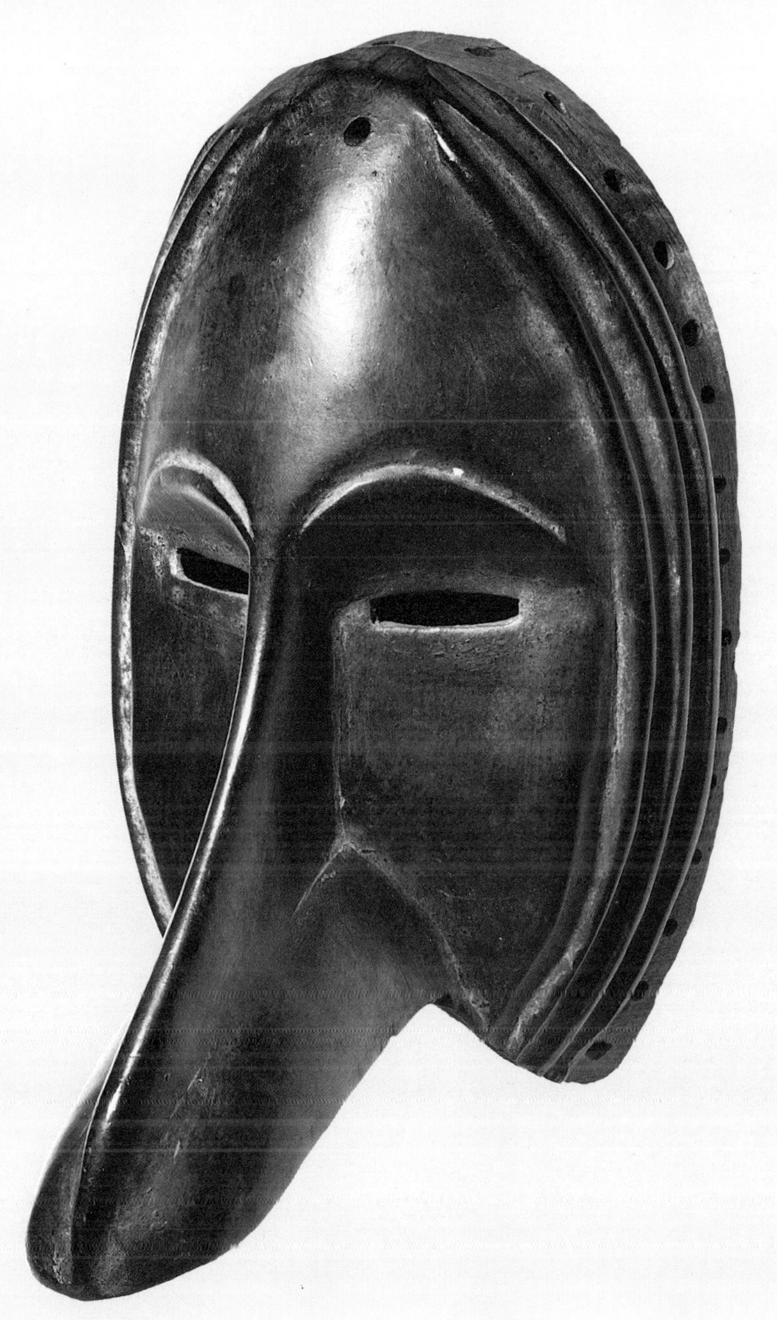

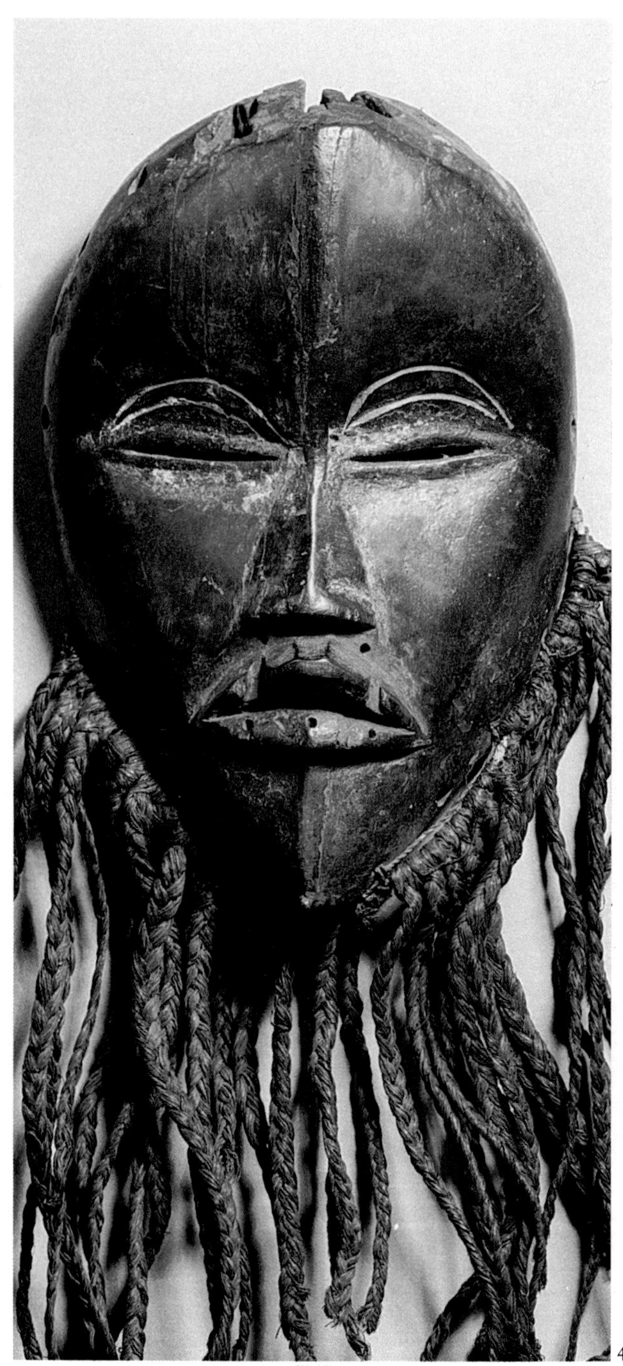

41

39 Mask, wood, brass.
Ivory Coast, northern Dan.

Chief characteristics of this typical northern Dan mask are its oval form, tattooed facial outline, high shaved hairline, circular eyes, full lips, and brilliant black surface achieved by oiling and rubbing the sap of liana leaves and tree latex into the wood.

The three parallel lines that frame this female face correspond to the tattoos of neighboring Mandingo princesses. This is probably a fire-messenger mask. In the savanna area, where the northern Dan settlements lie, the danger of fire is especially great. The fastest runner of a village is selected in a contest and given the task of reporting fires to people working in the fields. This same man must see that the women extinguish their hearth fires in the dry season. Masked, he undertakes his round of inspection, and the spirit he represents punishes careless women by upsetting their cooking pots and taking a utensil or ornament as pawn.

Height 22 cm. 32-24-9
Acquired from H. Himmelheber 1932

Lit.: H. Himmelheber 1972a, pp. 77-84; E. Fischer & H. Himmelheber 1976, p. 20.

40 Beaked mask *(gagon)*, wood.
Ivory Coast, northern Dan.

This mask may once have had an important ritual function. Harley suggests that the combination of human and animal properties alone indicates its spiritual power, for in myths similar to those of the Senufo the hornbill, represented by the wearer of the mask, is among the beings linked with the creation of the earth. He is also a culture hero who gave humans the oil palm. In recent decades, however,

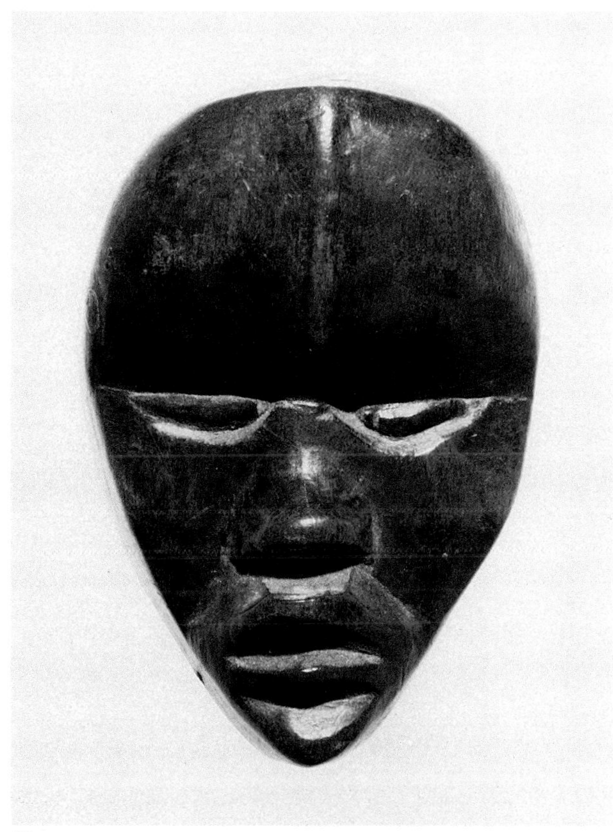

42

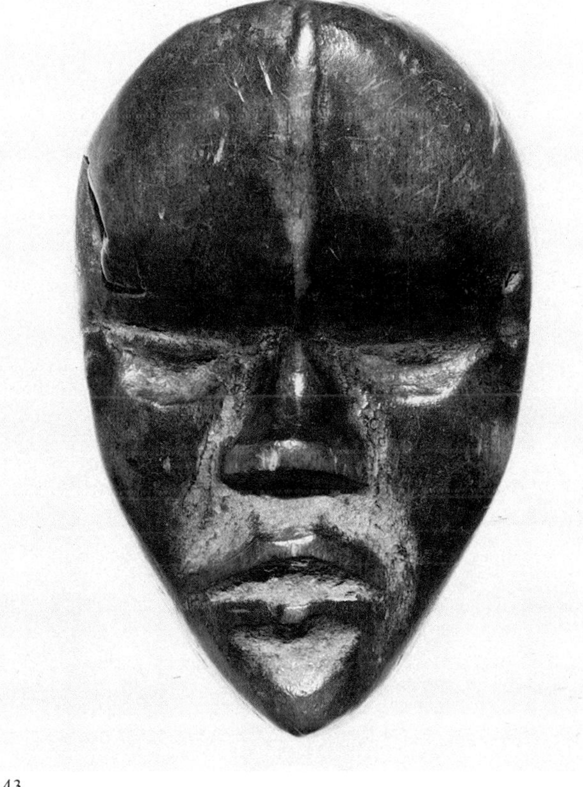

43

the mask's function has been simply to entertain: the masked man imitates the hornbill, addresses mainly women (a remnant of erotic fertility rites), and relates the hornbill's mythical deeds.

Gagon, the usual name for this type of mask, actually denotes the masked male figure that appears in the company of a female companion. The mask type represented by our piece does not assume this role, however. Nor does the name express the bird-like quality conveyed by the mask's elongated nose and its wearer's behavior. This type of mask, found solely among the northern Dan, originally came from alien neighboring peoples, the Konor, among whom it is the most esteemed mask of the cult association.

This typical hornbill *(calao)* mask displays such anthropomorphic features as narrow eyes with eyebrows and the tattooed facial outline of northern Dan masks. The movable lower jaw that originally belonged to this piece is missing.

Height 22 cm. 28-22-5
Acquired from P. Guillaume

Lit.: E. Fischer & H. Himmelheber 1976, pp. 23-40, 119-23, G. H. Harley 1950, p. 35; H. Himmelheber 1972a, pp. 123-25, D. F. McCall 1975, p. 272.

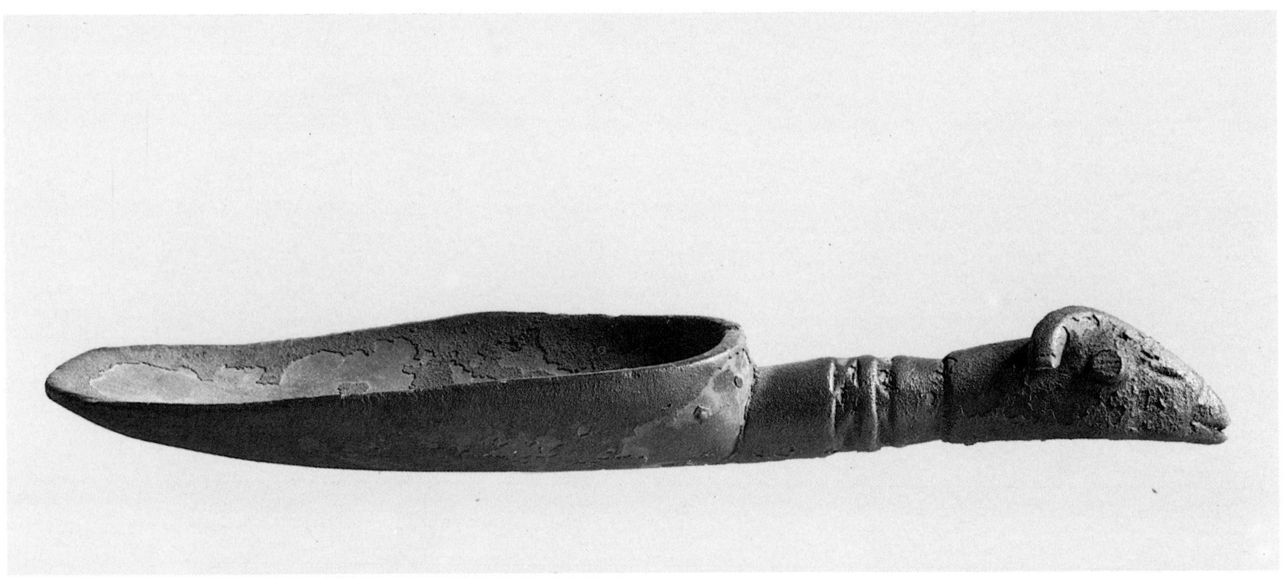

44

41 Mask, wood, plant fibers.
Ivory Coast, southern Dan.

This second example of a southern Dan mask exhibits the characteristic narrow eyes and pointed chin seen in No. 38 as well as a central forehead scar and a black surface with dull luster. Metal teeth, once inserted in the half-open mouth, are now missing. The beard may suggest the ceremonial use of an artificial beard, a mark of dignity.

Height 21 cm. 28-22-11
Acquired from P. Guillaume 1928

42,43 Two miniature masks, wood, sacrificial patina.
Ivory Coast, southern Dan.

Miniature masks are exact imitations of large ones, in this case *dea masks* like No. 38. Persons assigned religious functions, or families that possess masks, commission such miniatures and carry them as talismans while working in the fields or traveling. They are also used for divination. The small mask, substituting for the larger one and representing its spirit, may receive sacrifices or be entreated for aid. To maintain the mask's power the Dan offer food sacrifices and smear small portions of food over its mouth—rice mixed with palm oil, for instance. Miniature masks are often worn on a string around the neck as pendants. Women may possess small masks but never large ones.

Height 6.5 cm., 7 cm. 51-3-15/16
Acquired from L. Kegel 1951

Lit.: E. Donner 1940, pp.91, 92; E. Fischer & H. Himmelheber 1976, p. 139; H. Himmelheber 1960, pp. 161, 62.

44 Ceremonial spoon: ram's head (*minatu*), wood.
Liberia, Kran.

Among the Dan and the Kran, large ceremonial spoons, often up to eighty centimeters long, are emblems of distinction for the most hospitable woman, or *wunkirle,* of a village quarter. Only a woman married into these groups from outside may qualify for the *wunkirle* office. She must be efficient and generous enough to receive guests and to regale them especially at a beef-slaughter feast. She leads the women in festival dances, carrying the ceremonial spoon and using it to distribute rice. Her dance corresponds in some respects to the men's masked performances, and her ceremonial spoon is said to represent a bush spirit, as do the masks. Among the ways the power of the spoon expresses itself is that any person who carelessly touches it as it hangs on the wall must pay for a public feast. An orchestra accompanies the *wunkirle,* and she sings a melody reserved for her alone.

Handles are often artistically carved. Among popular motifs are geometric forms, heads of women or of animals (most often the ram and the duiker, a small African antelope), and bent human legs. The handle of this spoon is carved into what is presumably a ram's head (now missing its left horn).

Length 41 cm. 51-3-13
Acquired from L. Kegel 1951

Lit.: E. Donner 1940, pp. 88, 89; E. Fischer & H. Himmelheber, 1976, pp. 157-59; H. Himmelheber 1960, pp. 164-66, 1965, pp. 171-81.

45 Miniature mask: monkey, wood.
Sierra Leone, Konor.

Despite its size, this piece is still classified as a miniature (see Nos. 42 and 43). Among the Dan the original full size specimens of this mask type, representing the chimpanzee or the mangabe monkey, are the symbol of a predominately aggressive mythical being. During the mask's appearance it throws forked branches at the audience and attacks some members, supposedly making all of them "hot," or wild.

In his systematic cubistic rendering of anatomic details, the artist has stressed particularly: the short

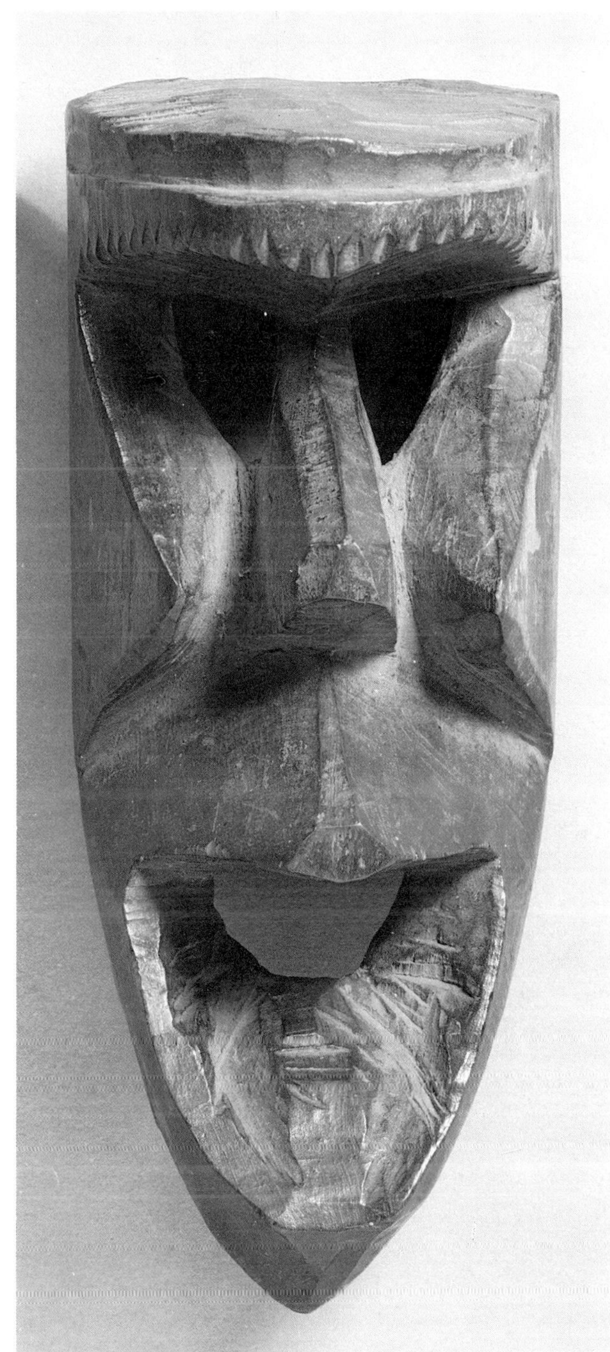

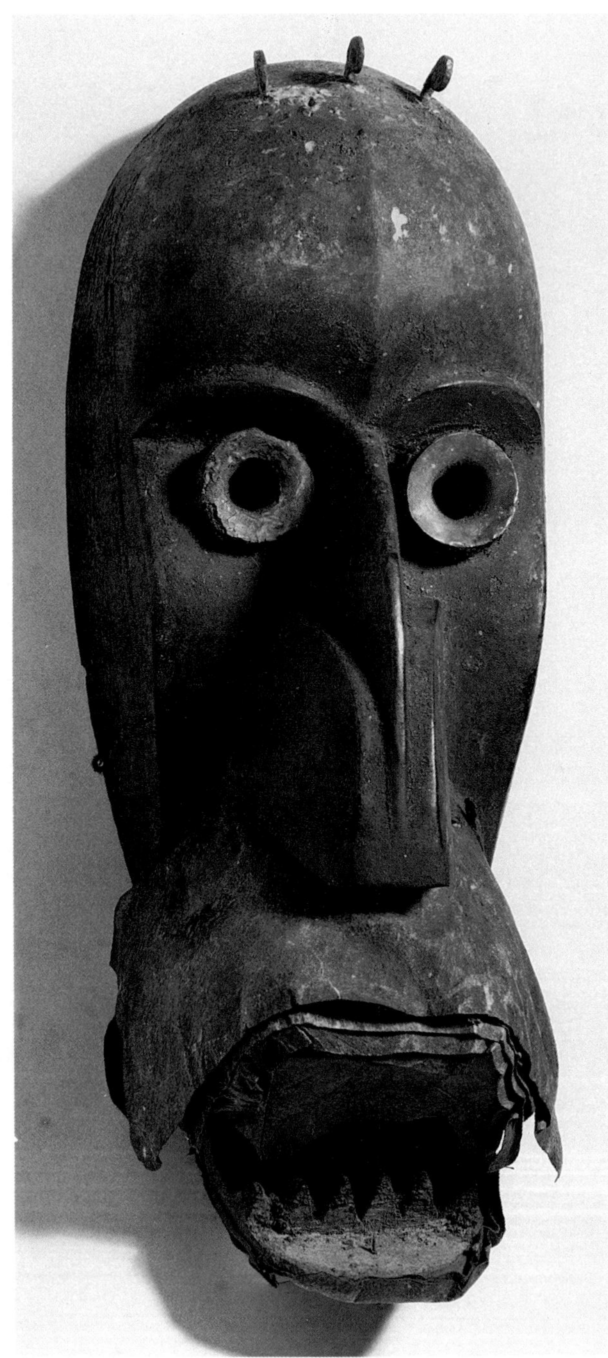

bulbous forehead above deep-set triangular eye sockets, the angular pyramid-shape facial muscles, and the jaw with open, lipless mouth. The antelope or gazelle horns originally attached to such masks to heighten their efficacy are here signified by the zigzag line on the forehead.

Length 15.5 cm. 51-3-17
Acquired from L. Kegel 1951

Lit.: E. Donner 1940, pp. 91, 92; E. Fischer & H. Himmelheber 1976, pp. 104-10, 139; H. Himmelheber 1960, pp. 161, 62; P. S. Wingert 1954, p. 69.

46 Mask, wood, leather, metal.
Liberia and Sierra Leone, Loma (Toma).

These masks were probably adopted by the peoples of northeastern Liberia (Komo, Kpelle, Mano, and others) under the influence of their eastern neighbors, the Loma. The precise function of this mask among the Loma is unknown. A similar one appears as companion to and herald of the grim judge's mask, feared because of its stern administration of justice in village affairs.

Human and animal features blend in this patinated mask. It exemplifies a style dominated by a cubistic and expressionistic treatment of the face: the sinuous ornamental line on the cheeks, the forehead scar, the tubular eyes with metal rings, the beaklike hooked nose, the pronounced prognathism, the movable lower jaw, and the three small iron hooks (horns) above the forehead.

Length 32 cm., width 13.5 cm. 16-8-13
Acquired from L. Frobenius 1916

Lit.: E. Donner 1940, pp. 103, 4; E. Fischer & H. Himmelheber 1976, pp. 40, 120, 135.

See page 30
Cat. No. 17

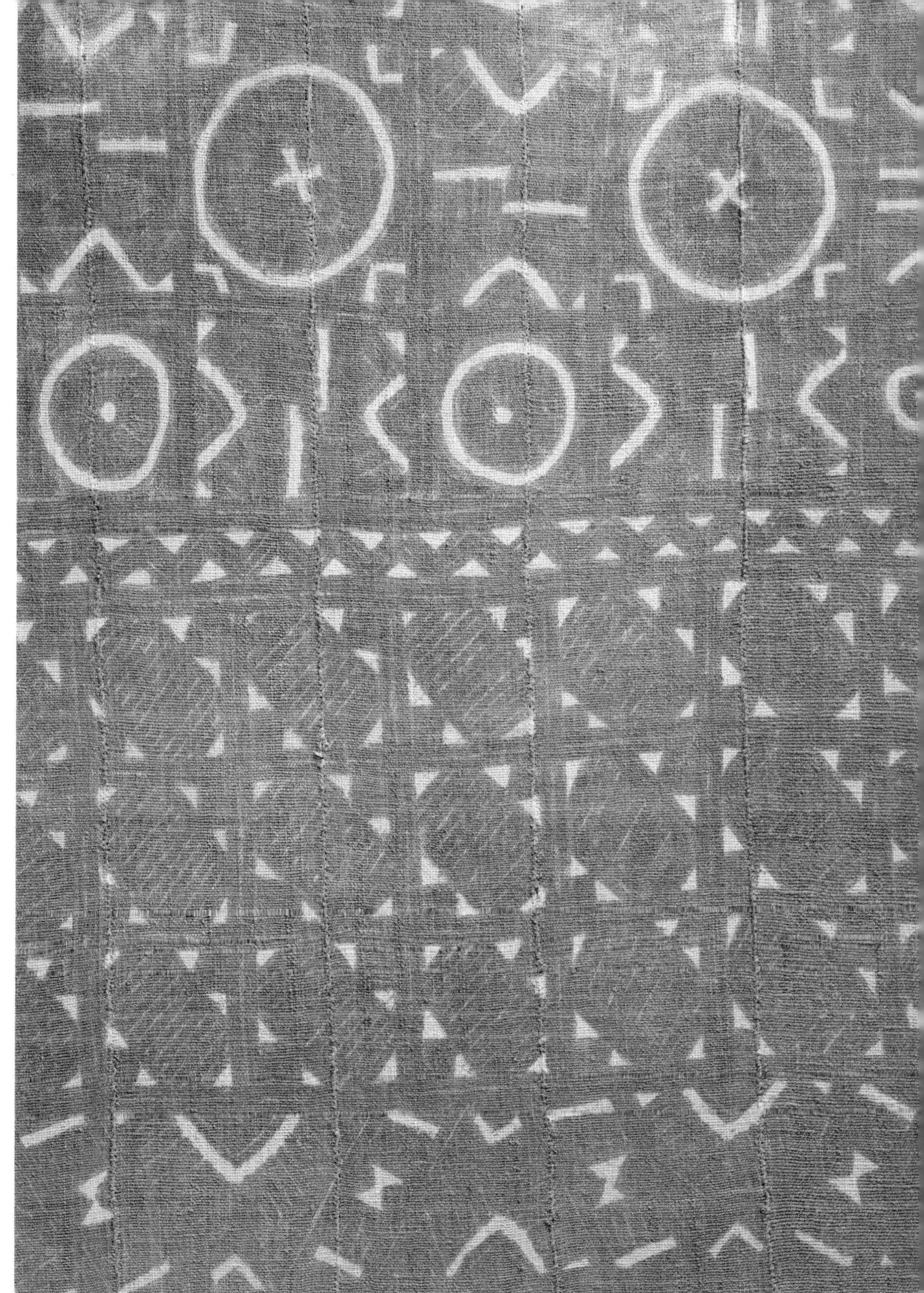

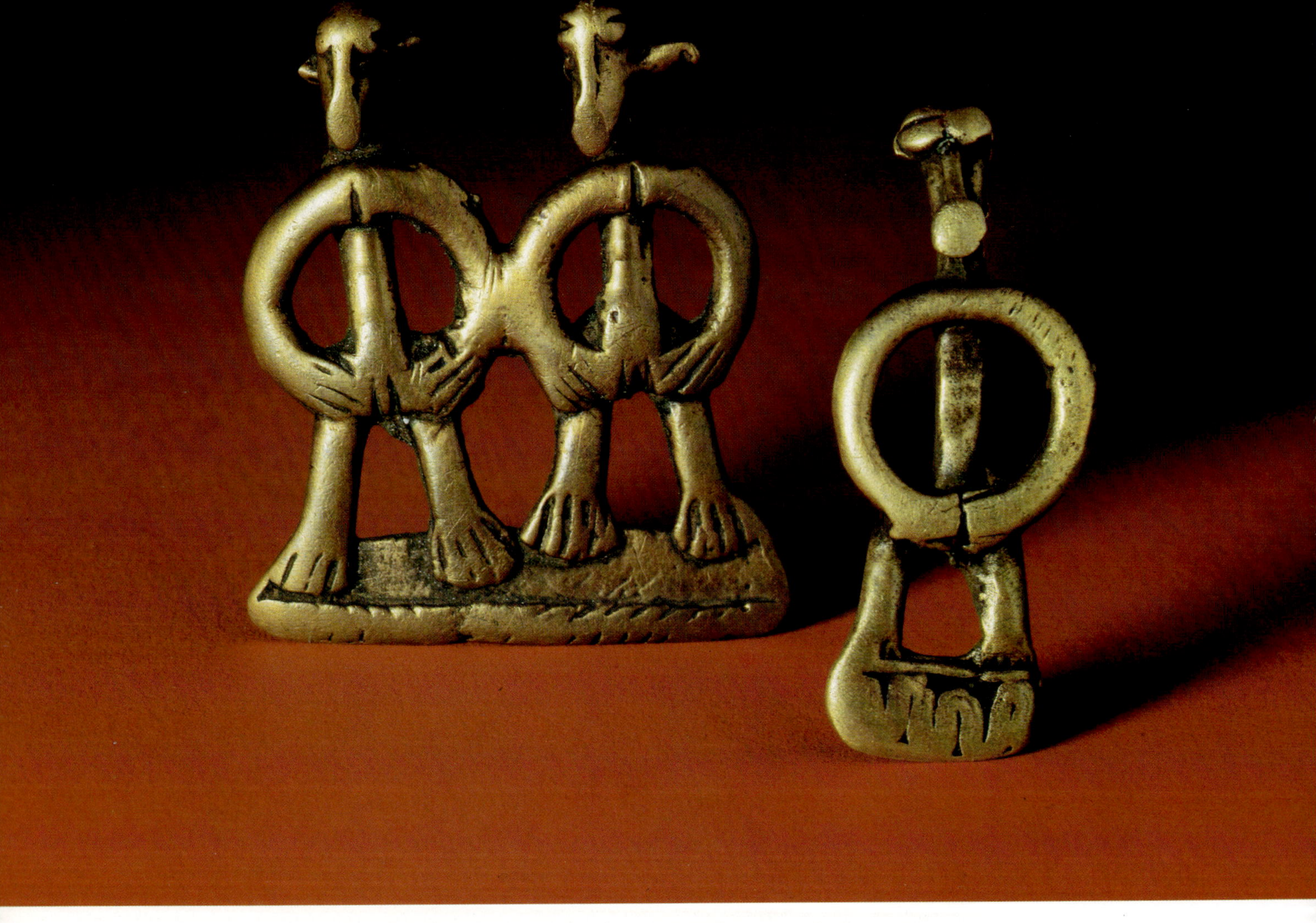

See pages 38-40
Cat. Nos. 26 and 28

See page 75
Cat. No. 48

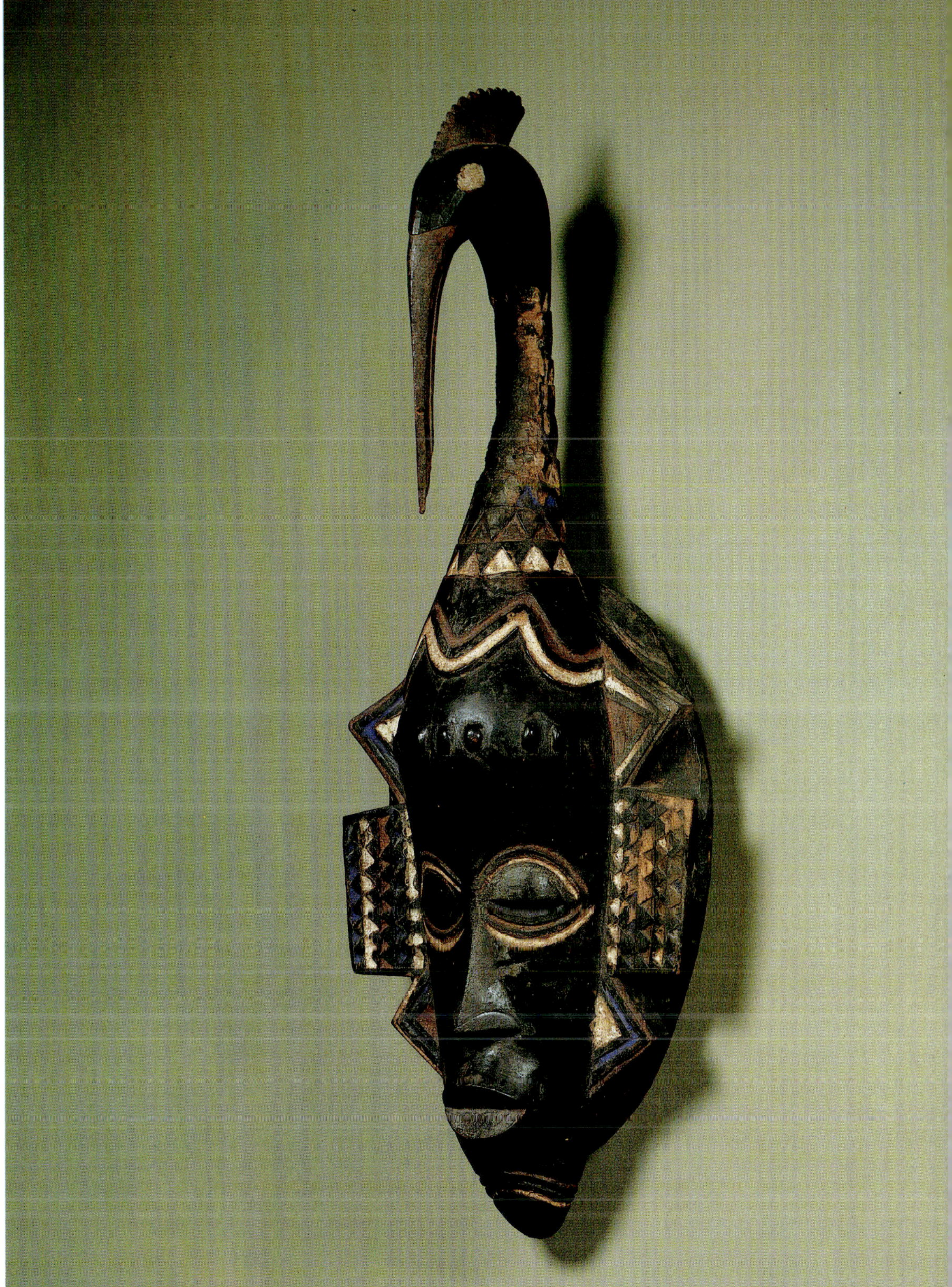

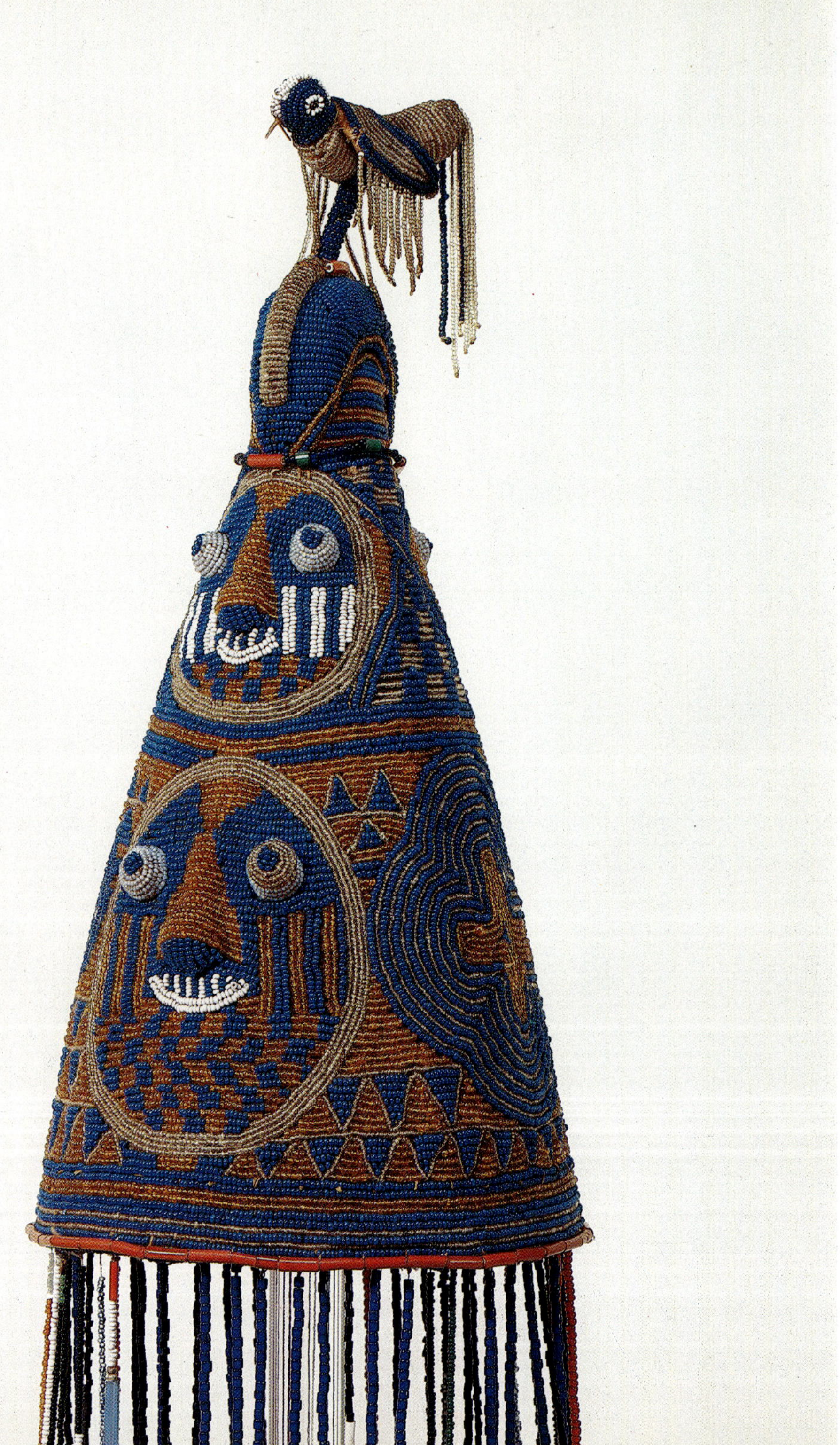

See page 114
Cat. No. 129

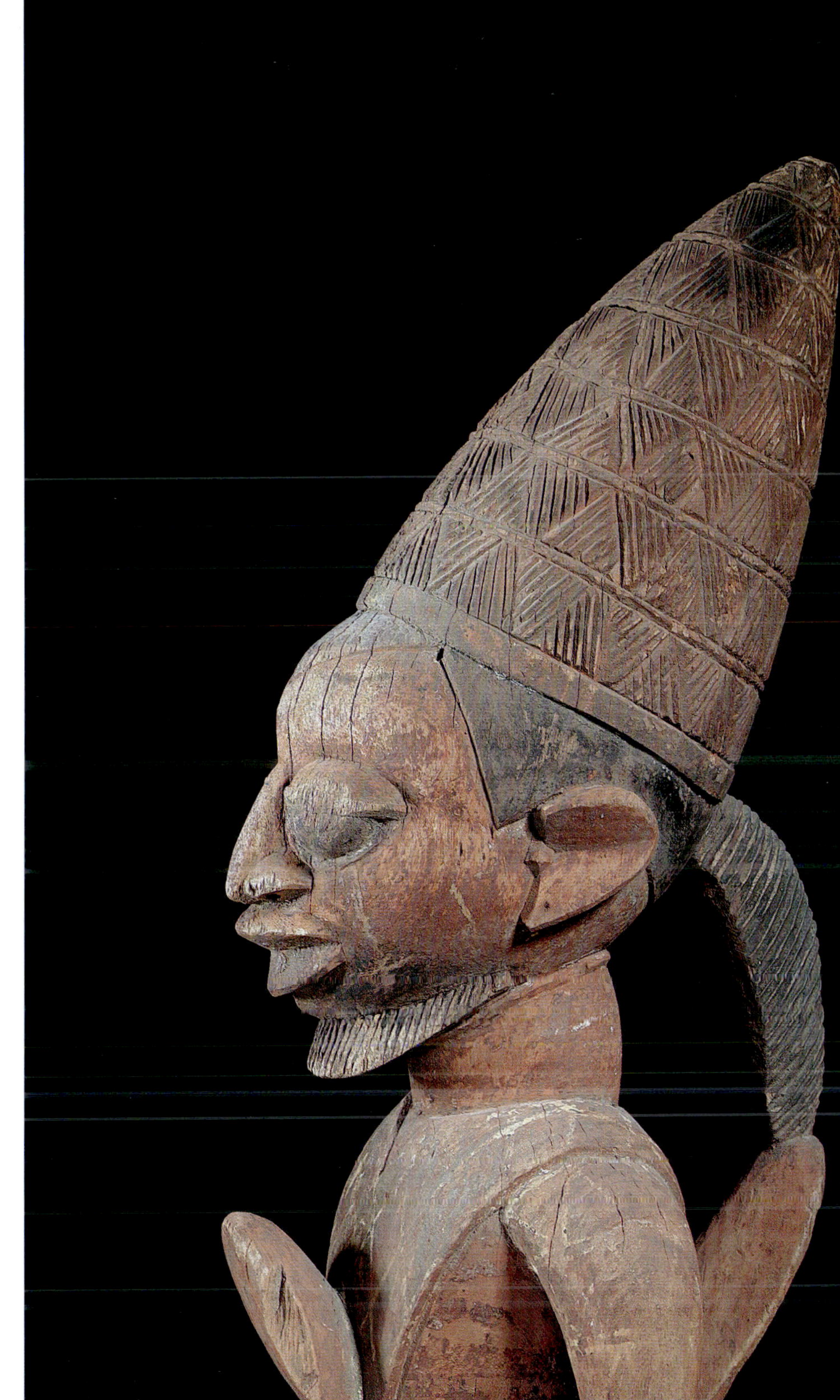

See page 117
Cat. No. 130

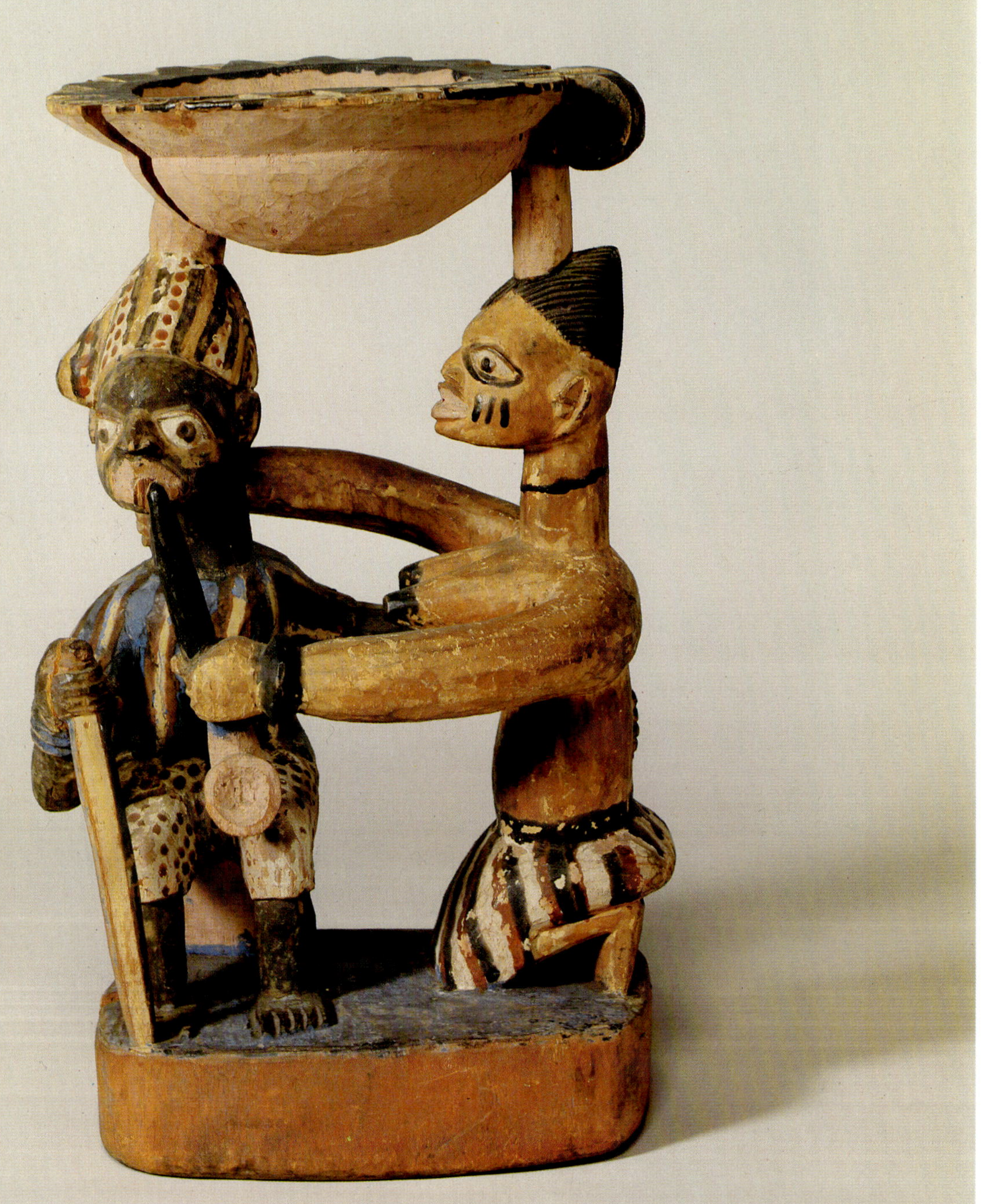

See page 131
Cat. No. 144

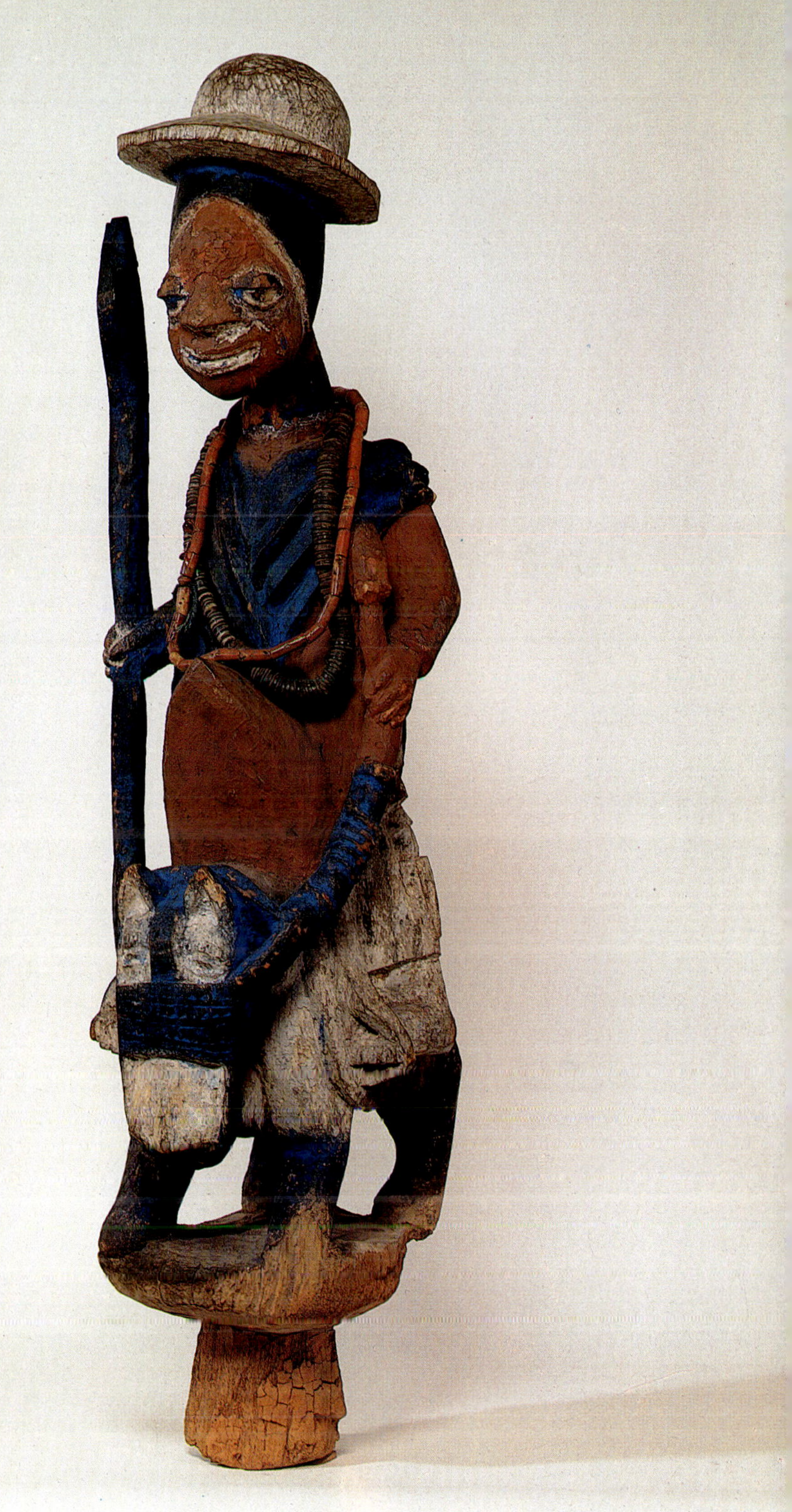

See page 126
Cat. No. 138

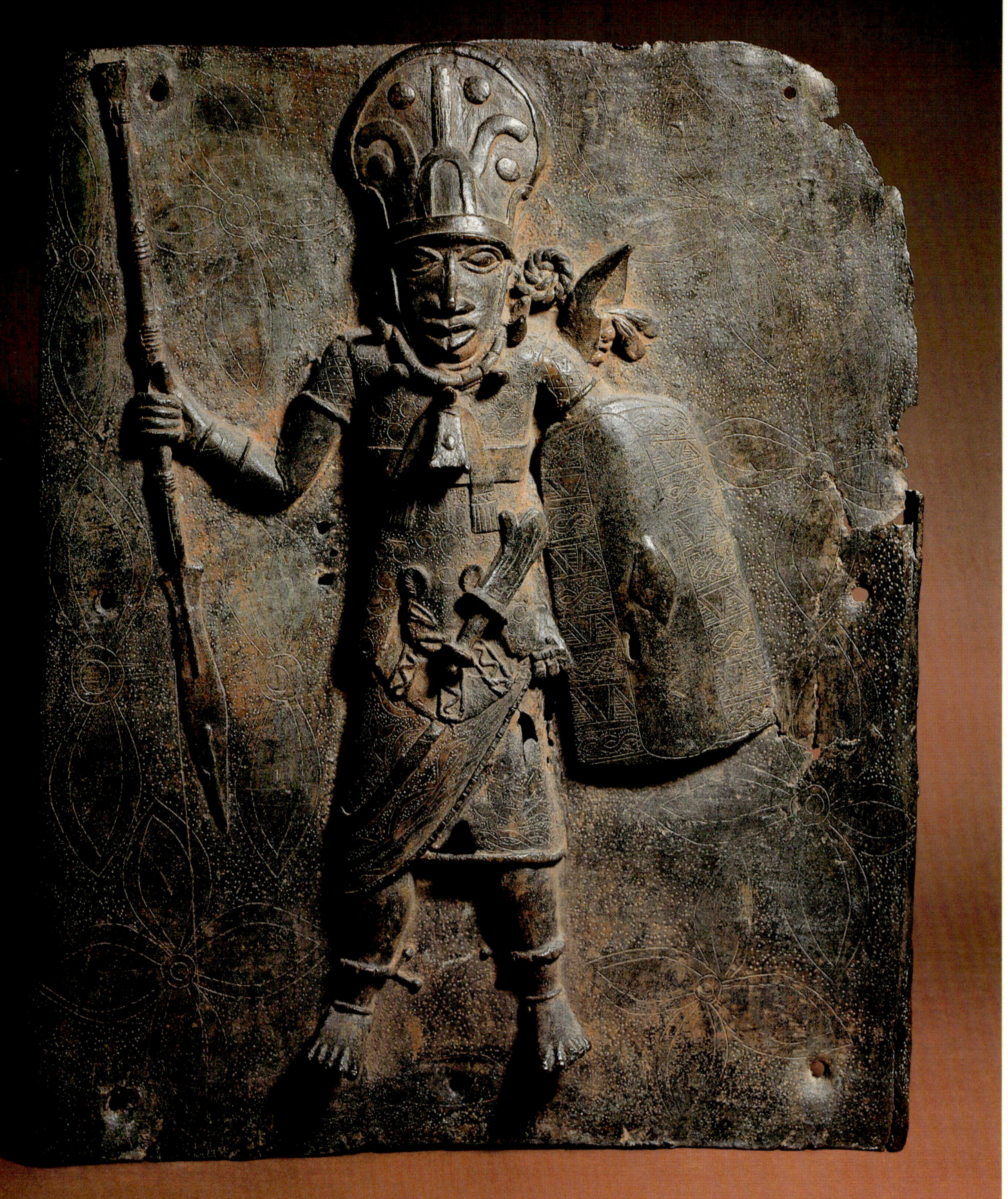

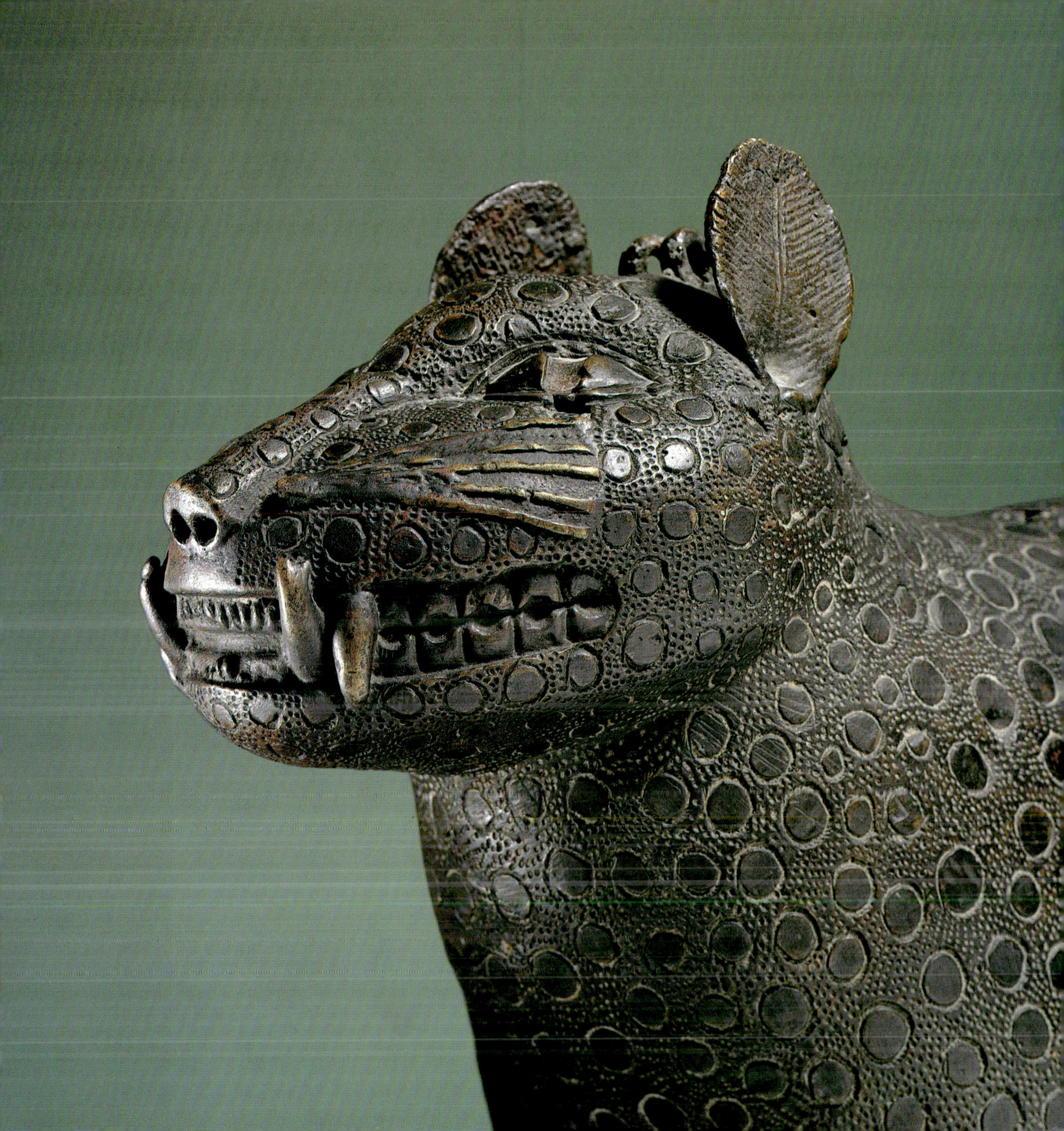

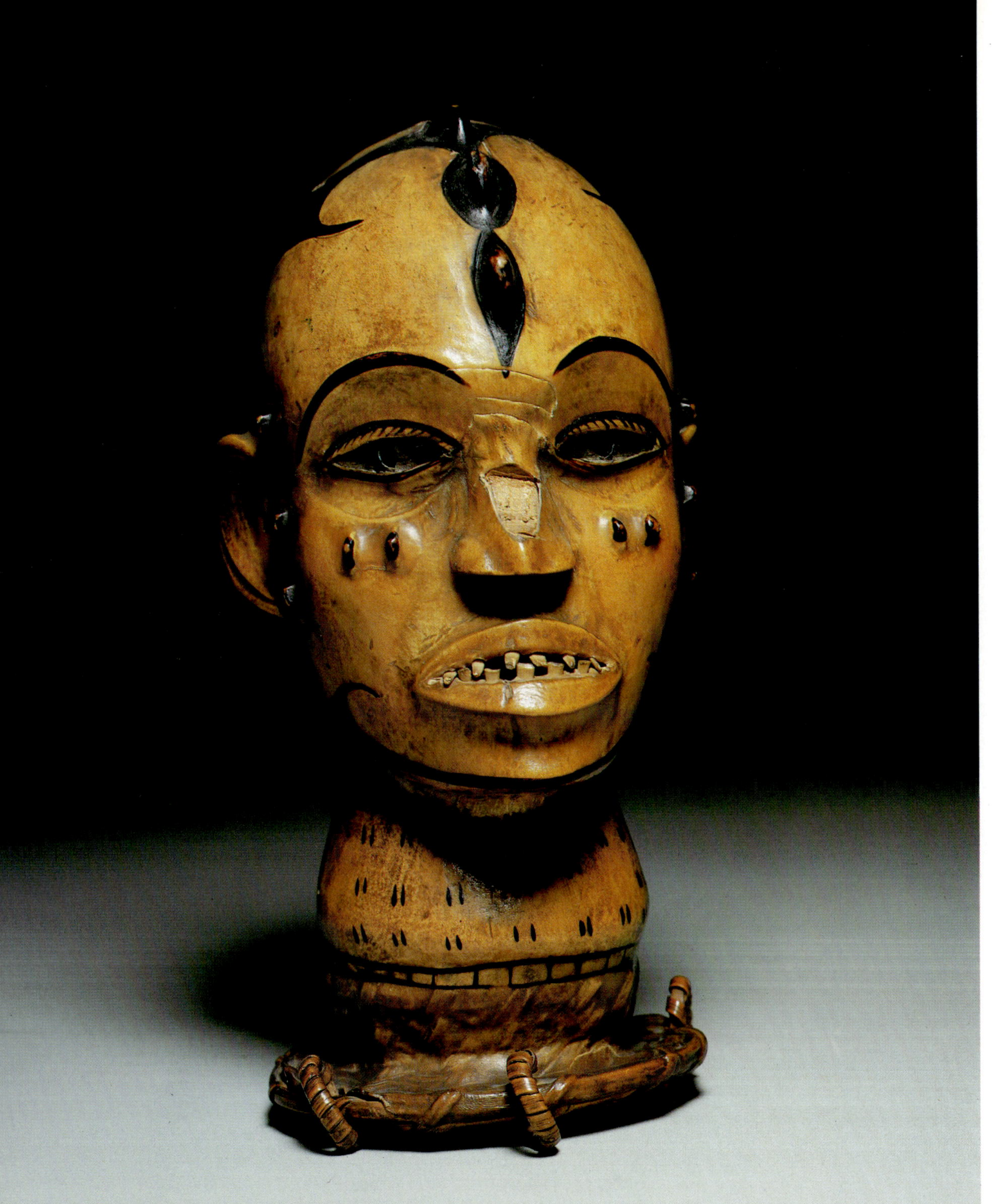

See page 181
Cat. No. 190

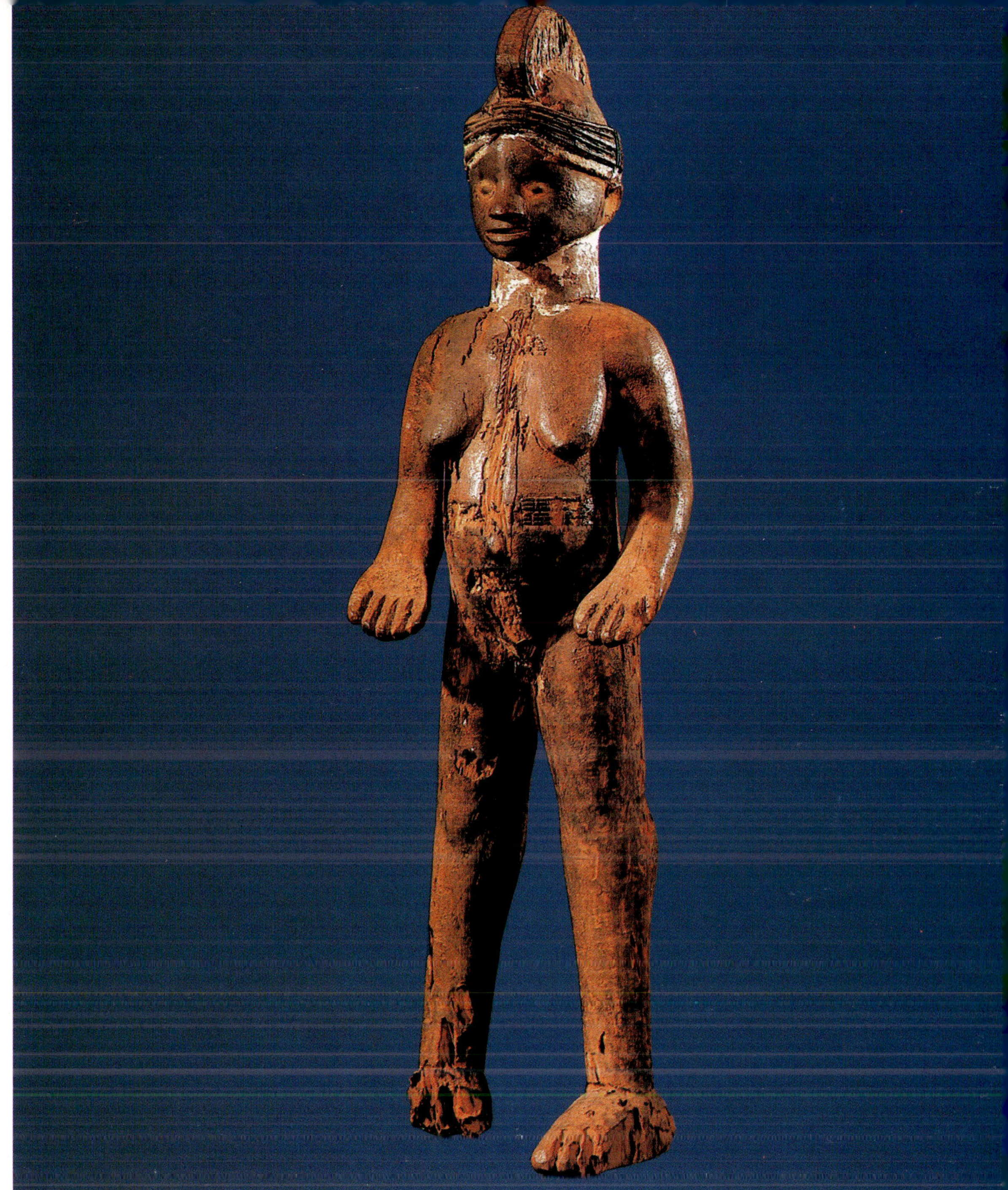

Page 71:
See page 176
Cat. No. 184

Page 72:
See pages 238-239
Cat. No. 256

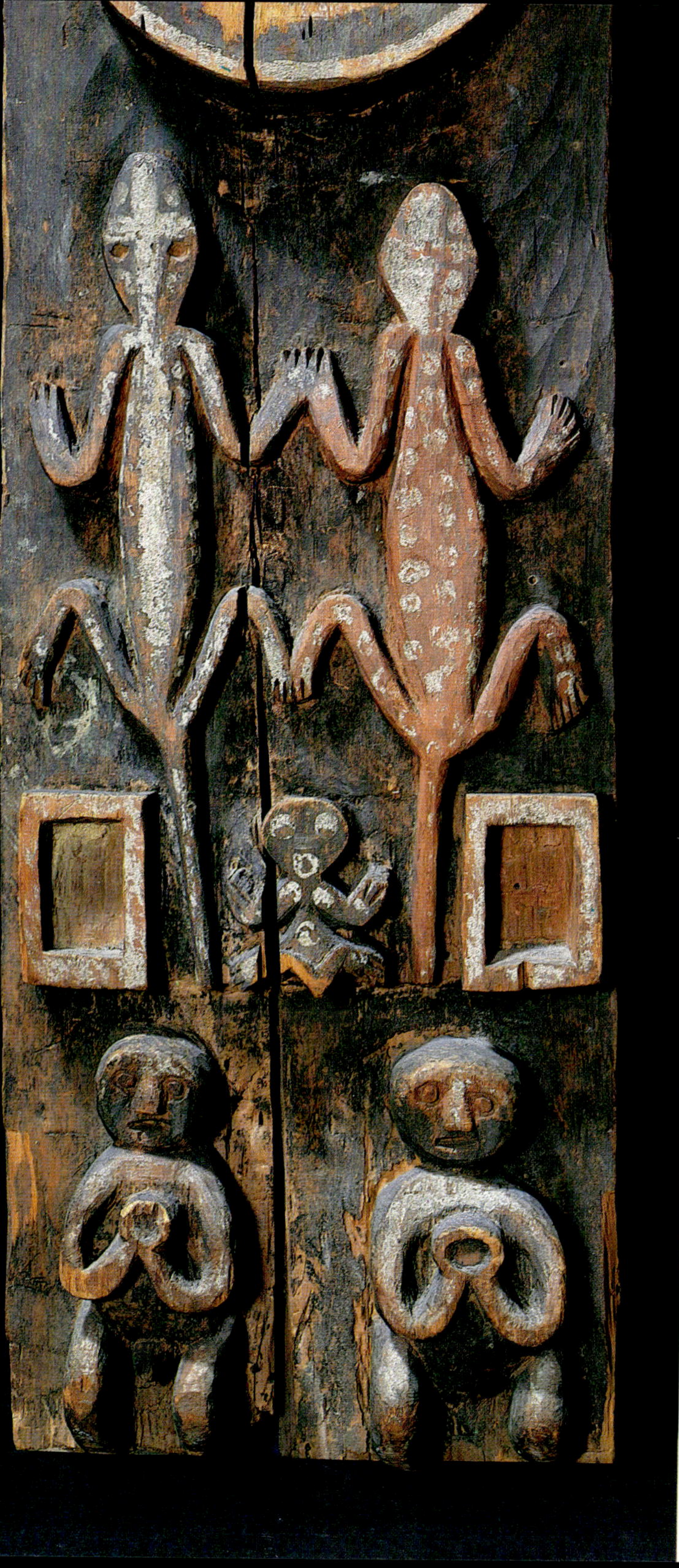

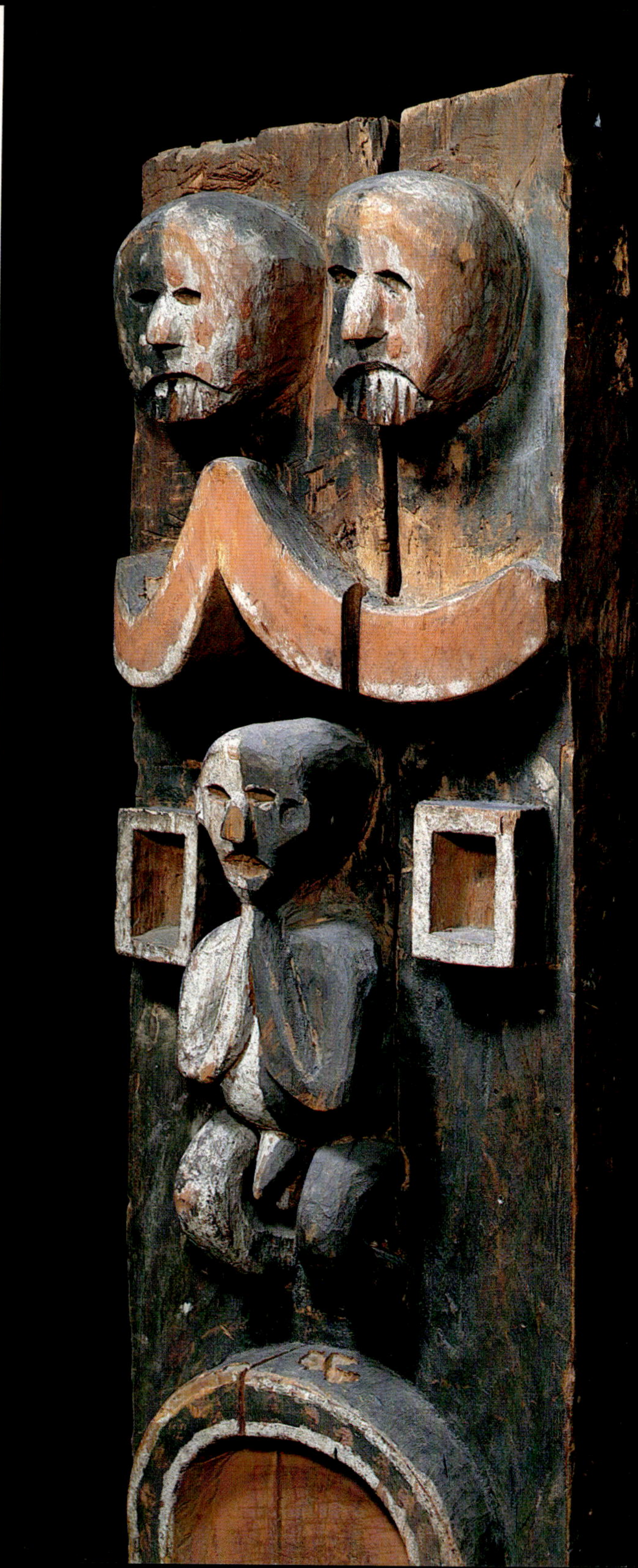

The Guro and the Baule

The art of the Guro and Baule peoples of the Ivory Coast displays so many common traits that for purposes of research they are often treated as a unit, even though their languages and cultures are quite different in other respects. The Bandama River separates them, providing both a physical boundary between forest and savanna and a psychological boundary between two originally quite distinct cultures. The Guro are related to the Dan, We, and other forest peoples who live in clan or village groupings without central governing institutions. The Baule represent the people of the open savanna, for whom state organization and sacred kingdoms were typical.

The Baule were originally part of the Asante empire (in present-day Ghana), but in 1730, as a consequence of succession disputes, they founded their own realm in the present Baule country, combining Asante traditions with new ones. The applied arts of the Asante were highly developed, created for the royal court, particularly in the areas of brass casting and goldsmithing, but not in that of wood carving. In their new domicile, however, the Baule (particularly the western Aitu group) were introduced to another art tradition by the Guro: the western Sudanese mask style of the Senufo (distinguished by narrow elongated and sometimes heart-shape faces) and possibly also figure carving. Both these forms of artistic expression are thus relatively recent phenomena among the Baule and have really been completely adopted only by the Aitu. Their art has been especially treasured by European collectors for over half a century, and this has certainly been a factor in the development of their wood carving. With the exception of wood sculpture from the Fang of Gabon and the Luba of Zaire, Baule sculpture conforms to traditional European aesthetic preferences to a considerably greater degree than other African art. It is not yet clear how much the European demand has influenced the style of Baule artists.

Lit.: W. Fagg 1968, Illus. 82; H. Himmelheber 1960, pp. 198-202.

Two Guro Masks

Several ethnic groups of the Ivory Coast have cult associations with mask rituals reported under similar names, among them *do* and *du*. This can be confusing, for different associations may sometimes bear the same name, and their ceremonies seem to be subject to rapid transformations. Several of these associations are indigenous to the very people who have been adherents of Islam for centuries, for instance the Mande Dyoula and Ligbi, while some non-Islamized groups are said to have adopted these associations and their masks very recently under Islamic influence. Though their original forms and functions are unknown, the masks doubtless came into being during a pre-Islamic period. In the characteristic *do* masks animal traits such as buffalo, bushbuck, or antelope horns on a human head perhaps point to an original association with wood and bush spirits.

Performances of *do* masks, unless already fully integrated into the annual Islamic festival program, are reserved for nighttime. Apart from participating in burials of deceased association members, the *do*'s chief task seems to be that of pursuing sorcerers ("soul eaters"). Certain types of these masks have been used in entertainments in more recent times, and at competitions among dancers.

Lit.: R. A. Bravmann 1974, pp. 147-72; E. Fischer & L. Homberger 1985, pp. 17, 18, 75, 76., H. Himmelheber 1935, p. 42; 1972, pp. 21-24, 48, 49, 55, 56; B. Holas 1948, pp. 5, 6; L. Tauxier 1921, pp. 295, 1924, pp. 202, 219, 253ff.

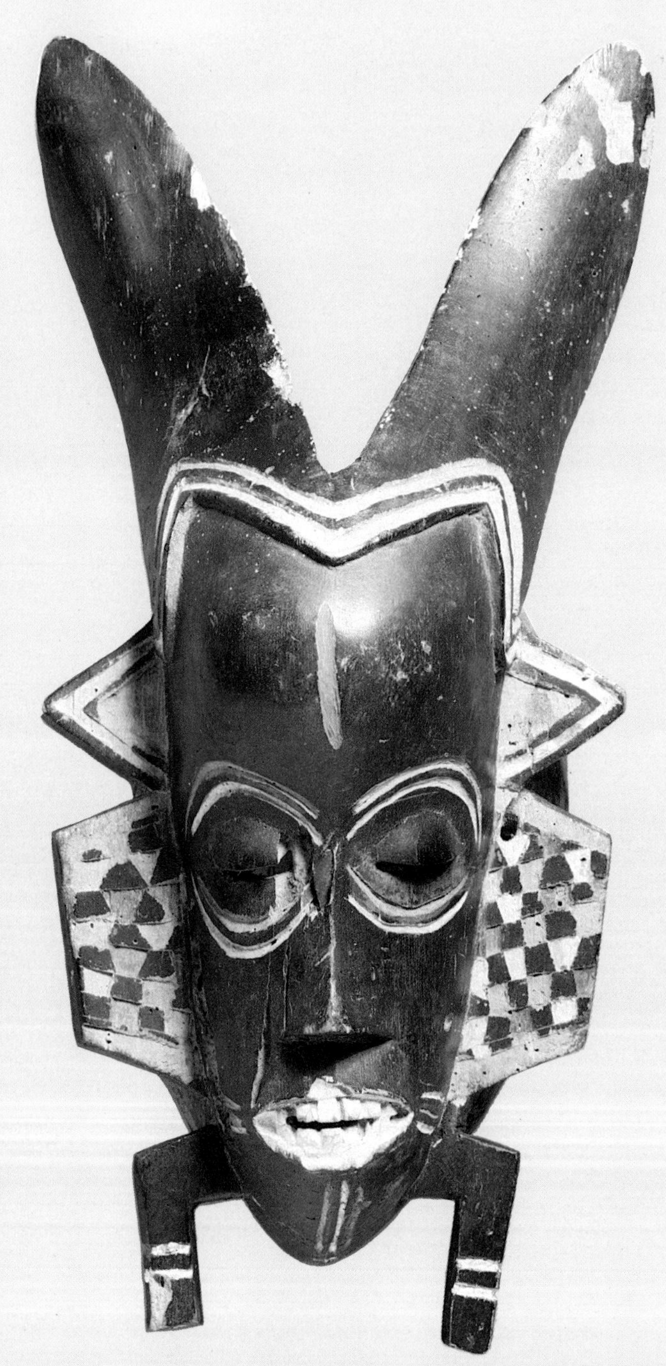

47 Horned mask, wood, paint.
Ivory Coast, Guro.

Typical of northern Guro style, this mask is also related to the *kpelie* type mask of the Senufo. The bulbous forehead with scalloped hairline, pointed nose, deep set almond-shape eyes, and the brilliant black surface with colored patterns reveal on the one hand an inclination to surface decoration, and on the other a striving toward three-dimensionality. The unique projections at the mask's edge can be traced to the bird motifs on Senufo masks and large sculptures. The triangles and trapezoids indicate plumage, while the angular appendages are to be understood as the bird's legs. The bird's head is replaced by horns, for which the traditional *do* mask probably provided the model. This is an entertainment mask, attributed to the artist known to us as the Master of the Duonu.

Height 34 cm. 33-34-10
Acquired from H. Himmelheber 1933

Lit.: E. Fischer & L. Homberger 1985, pp. 44ff., 213, 220.

48 Mask with bird's head, wood, paint.
Ivory Coast, northern Guro, from Mamnigi.

Like No. 47, this piece exemplifies the extent of Senufo influence and the superior skill with which the Guro artist, probably the Master of the Duonu, incorporated it into his own artistic tradition. The mask can be read as an attempt to represent a bird with outspread wings.

Height 43 cm. 33-34-9
Acquired from H. Himmelheber 1933

Lit.: E. Fischer & L. Homberger 1985, pp. 44, 45., 75, 76, 213, 217, 220.

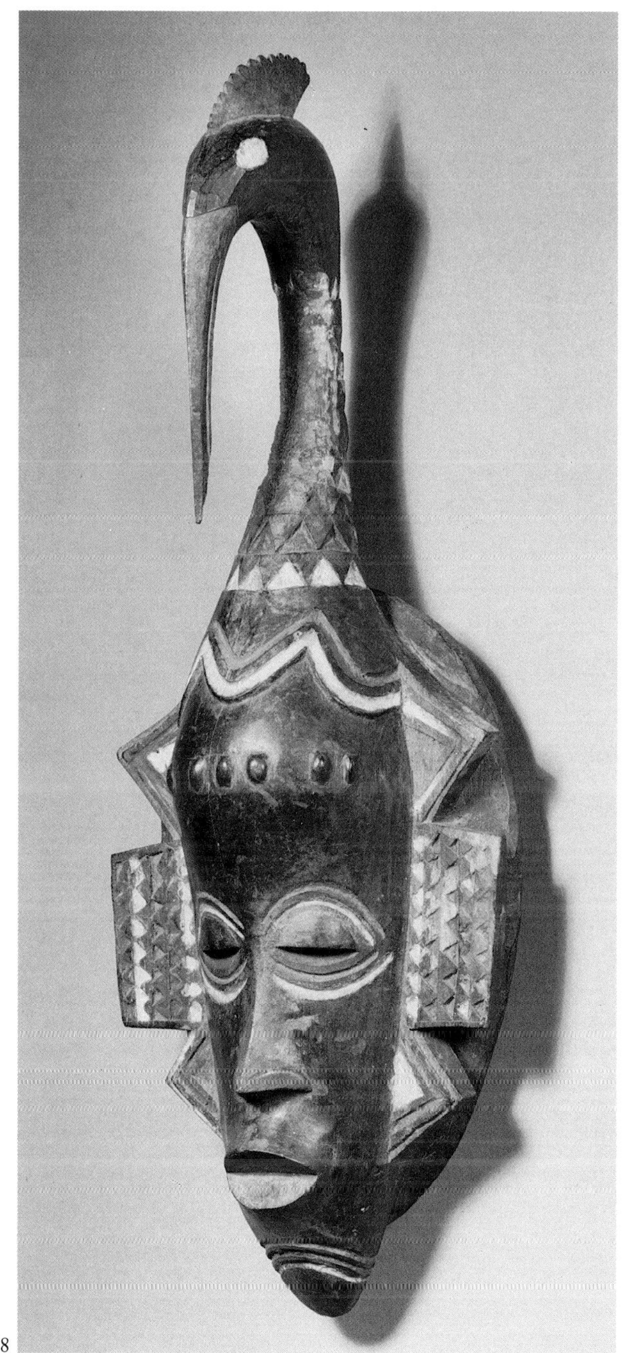

48

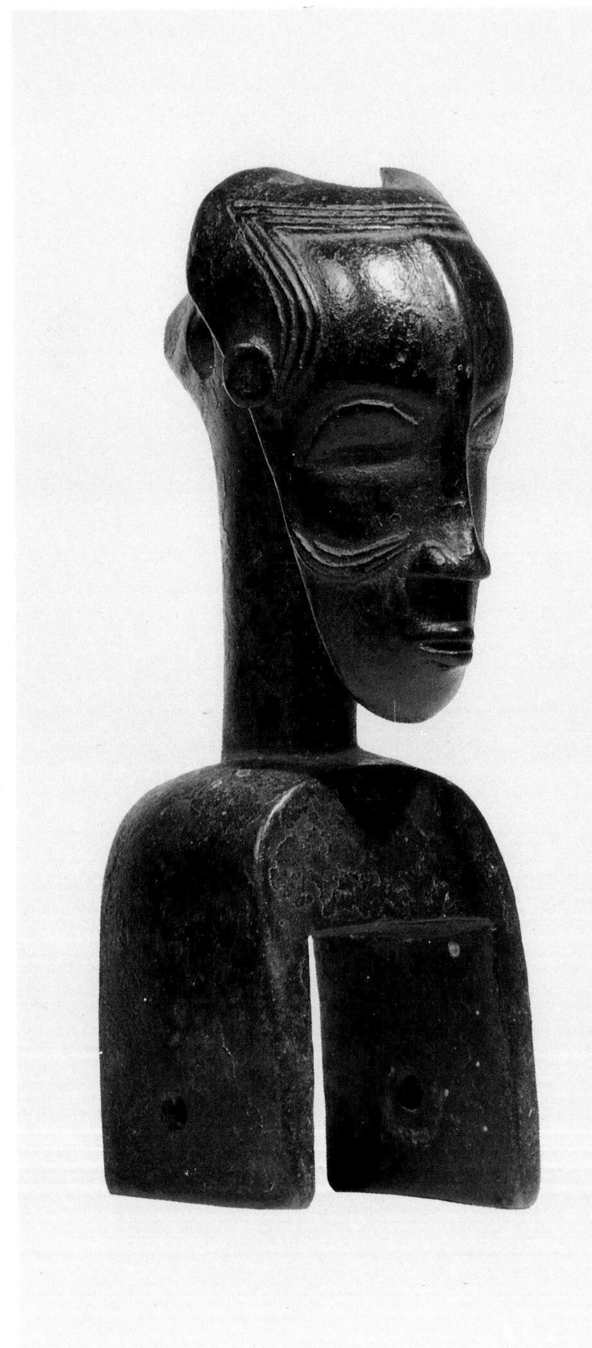

49

Guro and Baule Heddle Pulleys (49-52)

Pulleys are part of the weaving looms common to all of West Africa. They hold the spool through which passes the string connecting two heddles, allowing the weaver to raise and lower the warp threads.

The heddle pulley has become a popular object for artistic treatment among many peoples of Ghana and the Ivory Coast. These pulleys carved with human or animal heads, or with miniature replicas of the most important masks, occur among the Dyoula, Senufo, Samo, Asante, and others, but those of the Guro and Baule are superior to all others in variety and execution. Guro artists are especially successful in creating a formal unity of head, neck, and frame. The profile view is often as aesthetically significant as the front.

Lit.: E. Fischer & L. Homberger 1985, pp.237, 38; B. Menzel 1972, I. Illus. pp. 270-303

49 Heddle pulley: horned mask, wood.
Ivory Coast, Guro.

This face mask, set off sharply from the neck with its composed, spiritualized effect, is of the highest artistic quality. The broken-off ram's horns that crown the head indicate that the artist used a horned mask characteristic of the *do* association as a model. The artist even captured the three-dimensionality of Guro masks (see Nos. 47 and 48).

Height 17.5 cm. 33-34-33
Acquired from H. Himmelheber 1933

50 Heddle pulley: horned mask, wood, tack.
Ivory Coast, Guro.

This pulley retains its spool and has a finely carved head reminiscent of *do* masks with ram's horns.

Height 14.8 cm. 28-22-8
Acquired from P. Guillaume 1928

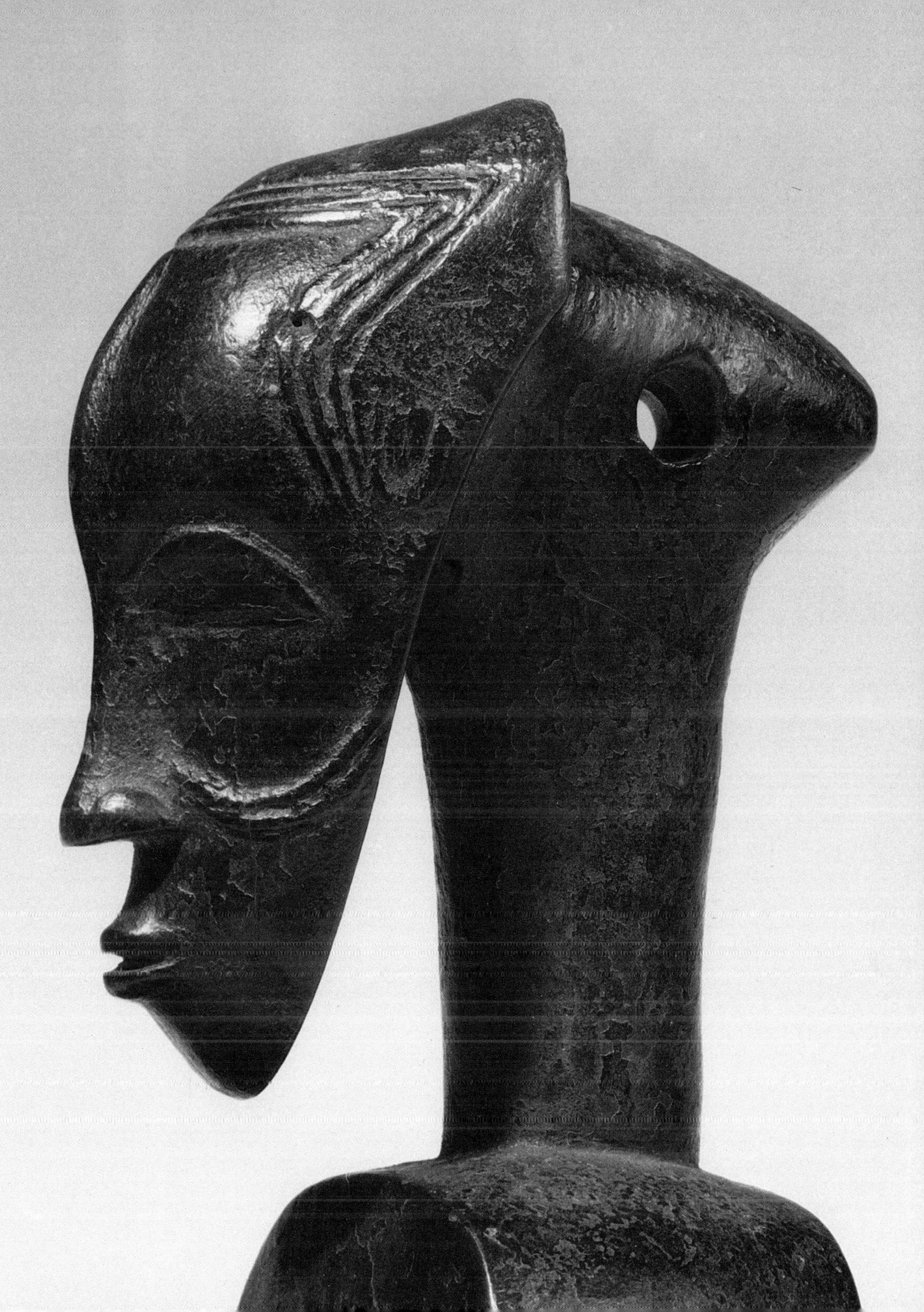

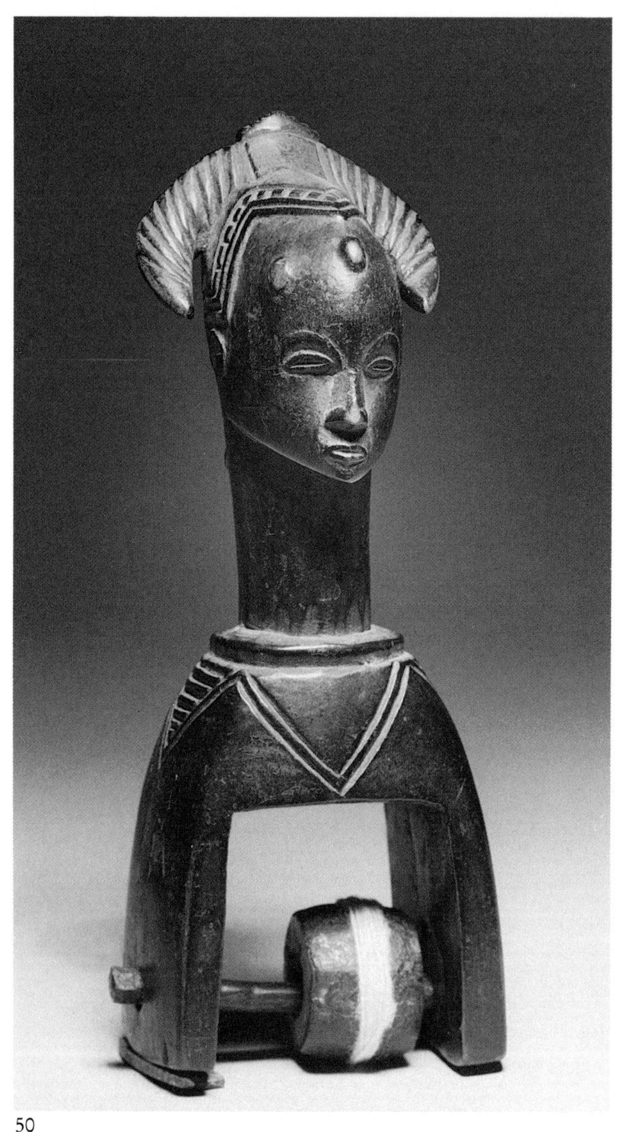

50

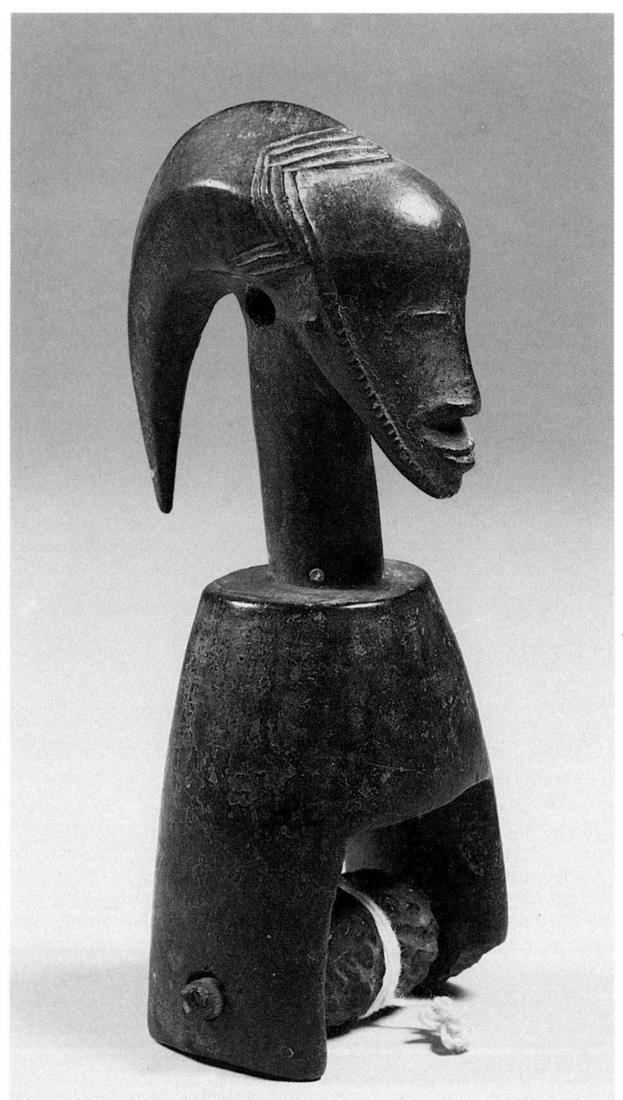

51

51 Heddle pulley: male head, wood.
Ivory Coast, Guro.

Since a beard and hornlike braid coiffure are considered signs of high social status, this piece may well represent a dignitary.

Height 13.5 cm. 33-34-17
Acquired from H. Himmelheber 1933

52 Heddle pulley: male head, wood, iron hook.
Ivory Coast, Aitu Baule.

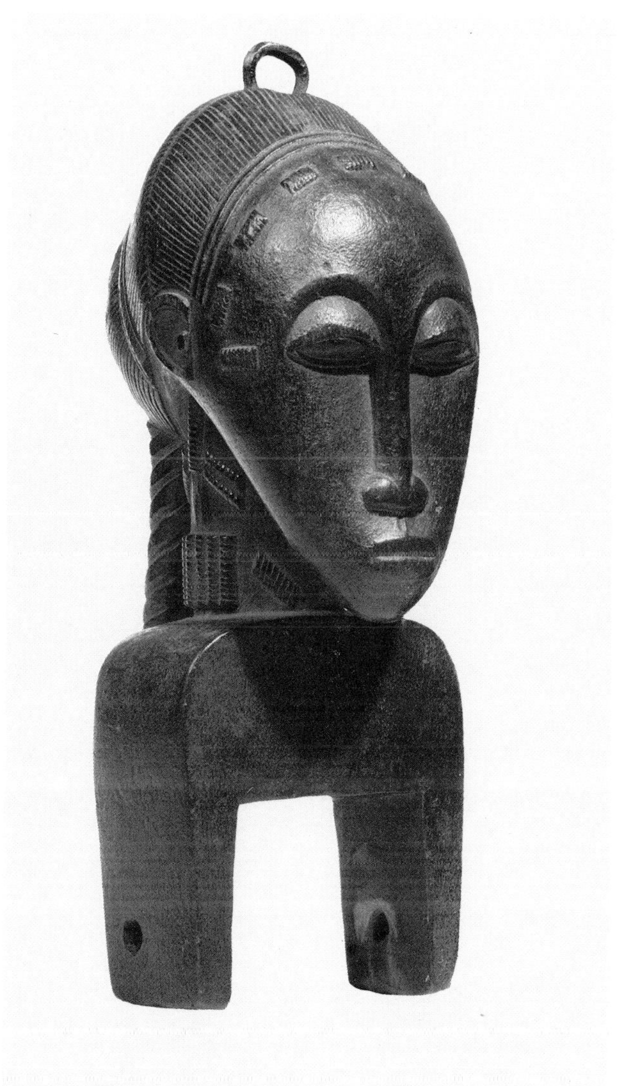

52

In this case, too, the heddle pulley is ornamented with the head of a ruler or dignitary whose artistic coiffure, ending in a braid, is represented in minute detail. The style and expression of the broad face, flat and two-dimensional in effect, are reminiscent of Baule masks, for heart-shape faces, though widespread in African art, are especially common in Baule

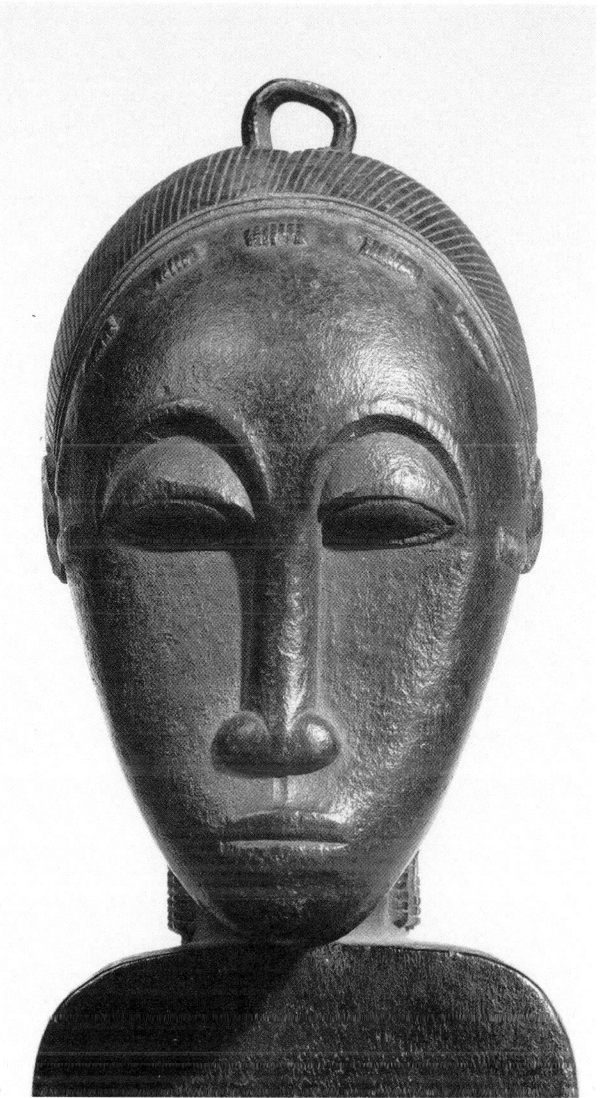

52

sculpture. The lines of the eyebrows almost unnoticeably extend to the mouth. Only eyes, nose, and mouth interrupt the plane of the face.

Height 17.5 cm. 39-1-4
Acquired from H. Heinrich 1939

Lit.: E. G. Bay, in D. F. McCall and E. G. Bay 1975, pp. 253, 54.

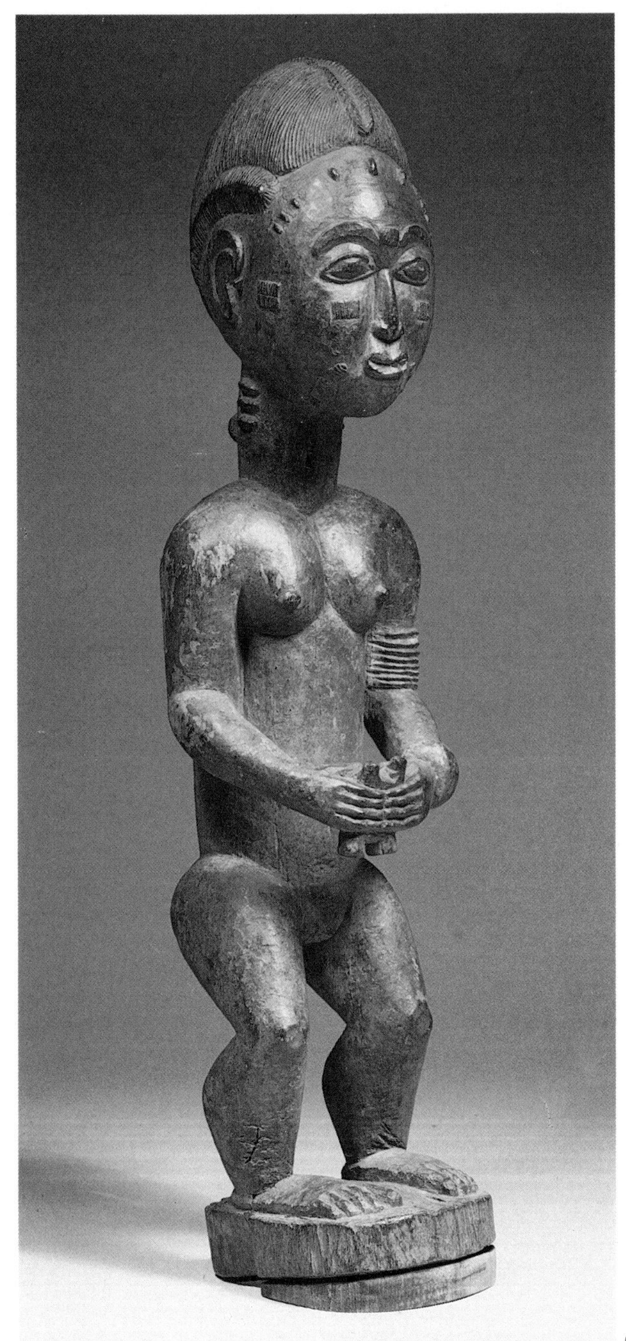
53

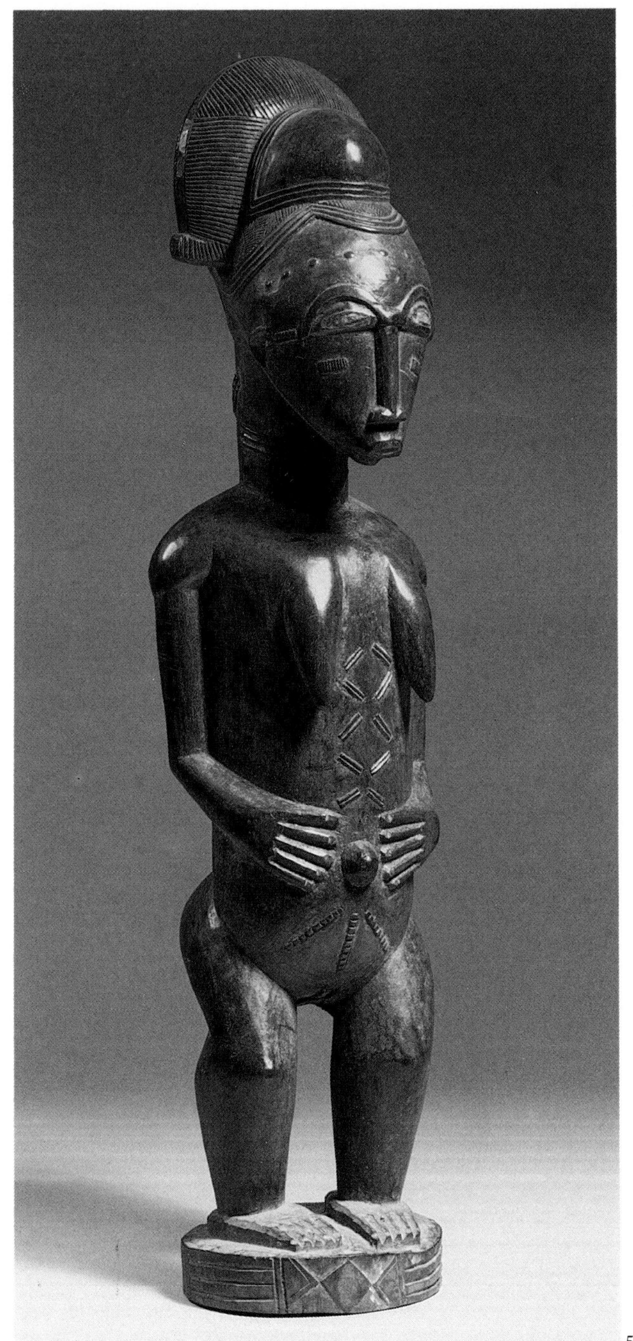
54

Baule Figures (53-57)

The carved wood figures of the Baule are usually only twenty to fifty centimeters high, with a few reaching about one meter. Face, coiffure, and tattooing of the often markedly stylized figures are very carefully executed. Most Baule figures are viewed as embodiments of "spirit spouses." Before birth every man is said to have a female spirit spouse (*blolo bla)* in the other world (*blolo),* just as every woman has a male spirit spouse (*blolo bian).* Illness, misfortune, and a failure to marry are explained as being due to the neglect felt by this spirit. To conciliate the spirit a person has a figure carved in accordance with the diviner's instructions, offers sacrifices, and devotes one night of each week to dreaming of this spirit only.

Lit.: M. Delafosse 1900, pp. 501, 537, 567; H. Himmelheber 1935, pp. 38, 39; B. Holas 1969, pp. 90, 196; L. Meurer 1980, pp. 53, 60; S. M. Vogel 1973, pp. 23, 26, 1980, p. 3.

53 Male spirit spouse: *blolo bian,* wood.
Ivory Coast, Baule.

The softly curving lines of the body and the portraitlike facial features of this figure show a tendency toward realistic representation rare in Baule sculpture. Other traits unusual in Baule figures include the small magical horns the figure holds in his hands, his spiral arm bangle, and his wrist bracelet. The bracelet—of ivory—is characteristic of the less well-known figure sculpture of the Guro, according to Siroto, but also occasionally occurs in Baule art. More recent studies also support an attribution to the Baule rather than the Guro, so the undeniable deviations from the predominating Baule style perhaps derive from an older tradition. Fagg believes that the rounded calves and detached arms are more characteristic of older pieces. This example may well be the product of a workshop not yet precisely identified.

Height 53.5 cm 39-1 2
Acquired from H. Heinrich 1939

Lit.: W. Fagg 1968, Illus. 82, 83; E. Fischer & L. Homberger 1985, pp. 227-35; L. Siroto 1953, p. 18; S. M. Vogel 1980, p. 11.

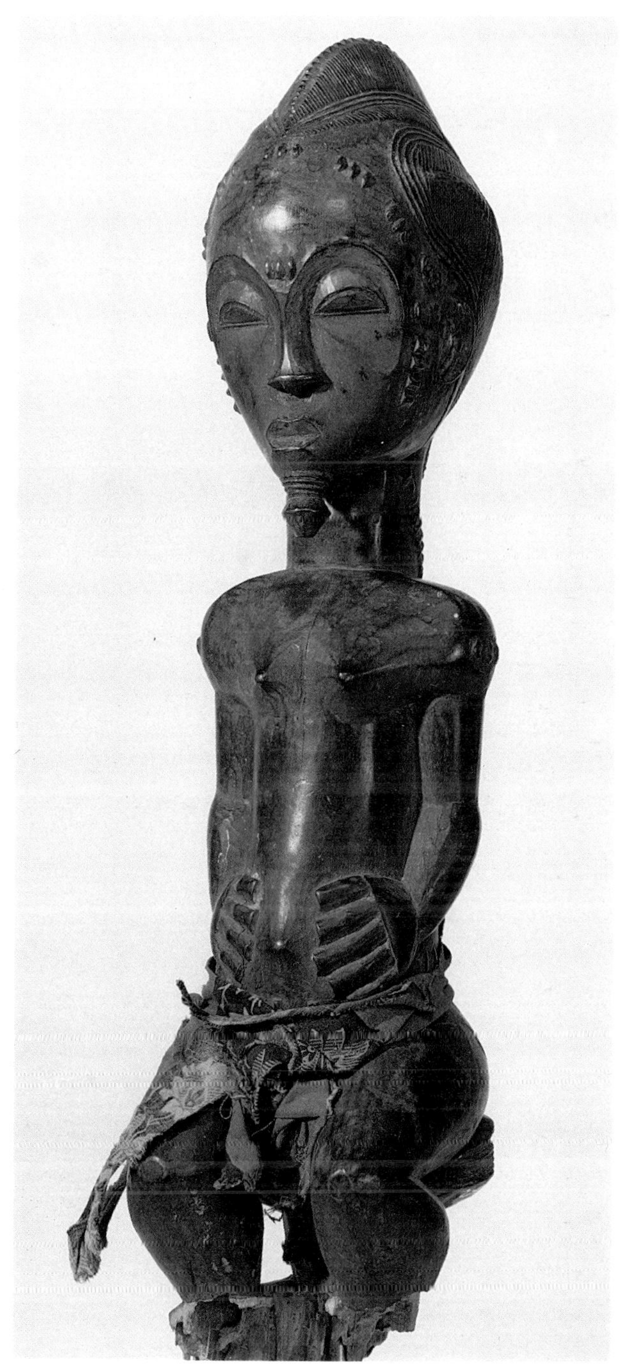

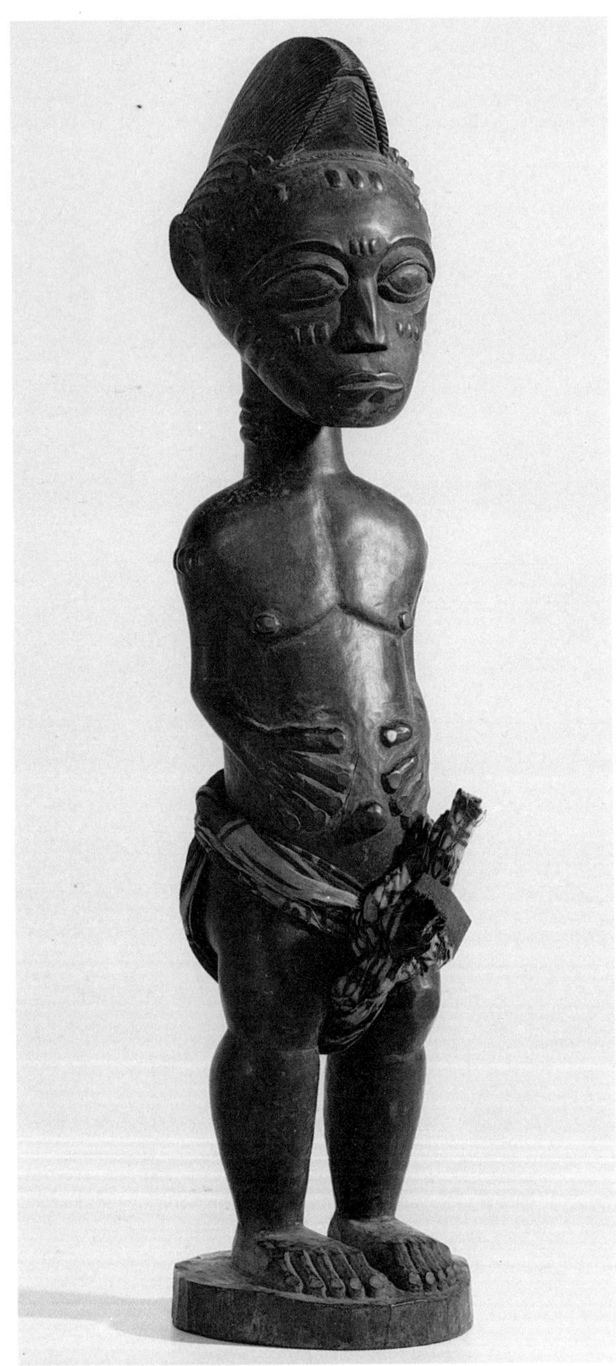

56

54 Female spirit spouse: *blolo bla,* wood.
Ivory Coast, Baule.

Baule sculptors often strive to refine form without loss of expressiveness. Here the artist has concentrated on the head, with its delicately stylized heart-shape face and superb coiffure. The overly angular torso with thin arms pressed against it appears rigid by contrast. Neck, torso, and back tattoos are depicted in low relief.

Height 53.5 cm. 39-1-1
Acquired from H. Heinrich 1939

55 Male spirit spouse: *blolo bian,* wood, cloth.
Ivory Coast, Aitu Baule.

The carver of this piece worked in the same style as that of No. 54 but surpassed him in quality. Head and torso form a harmonious unity, and facial details, coiffure, and beard are carefully executed. The goatee is a mark of chiefly office. All prominent members of the extended family are granted the right to use a stool such as the one this figure sits on; it is placed at the ancestral shrine after its owner's death to serve the spirit of the deceased as a temporary abode. The researcher who acquired this figure reported that it is the "portrait" of a great chief's corpse, which was set upon a stool.

Height 42 cm. 33-34-12
Acquired from H. Himmelheber 1933

56 Male spirit spouse: *blolo bian,* wood, cloth.
Ivory Coast, Baule.

In many respects this figure resembles the female figure No. 57, but it is less well balanced. Whereas face, coiffure, chest, and hands with large round fingernails are most carefully executed, the legs and the unnaturally short and closely attached arms appear rigid. Vogel states that the lifelike proportions of the legs are typical of more recent work (compare by contrast the strongly rounded calves of Nos. 53 and 57). The loincloth is probably a later addition.

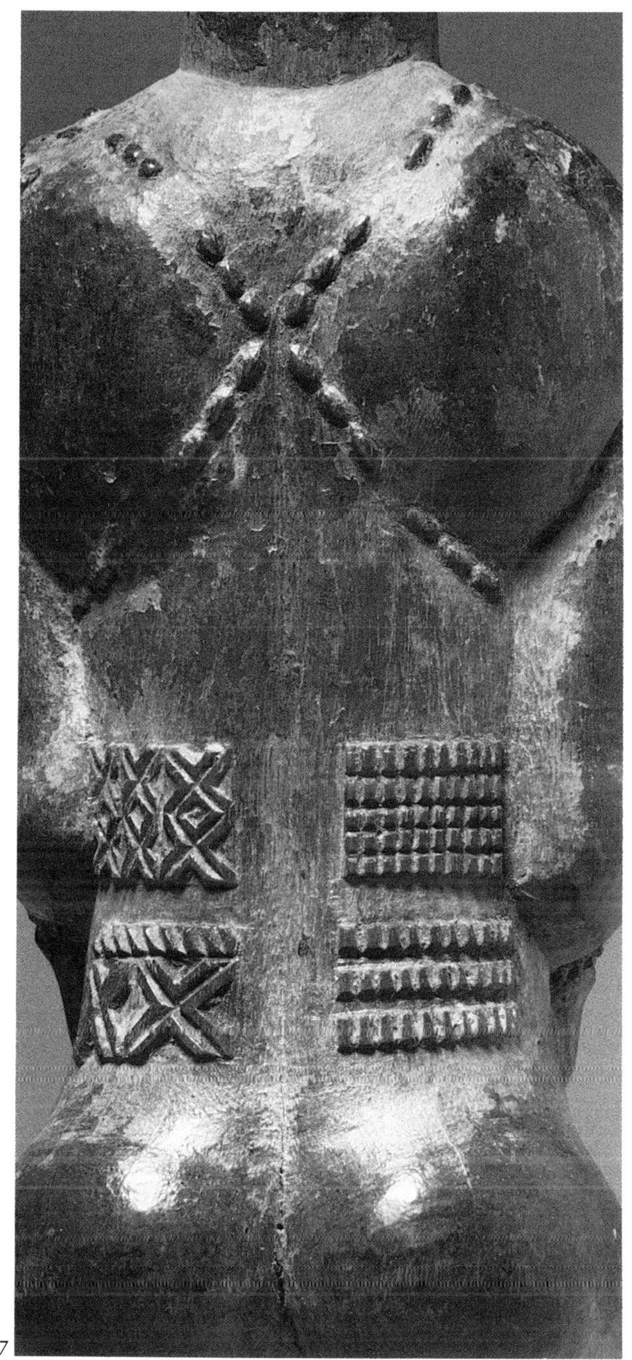

57

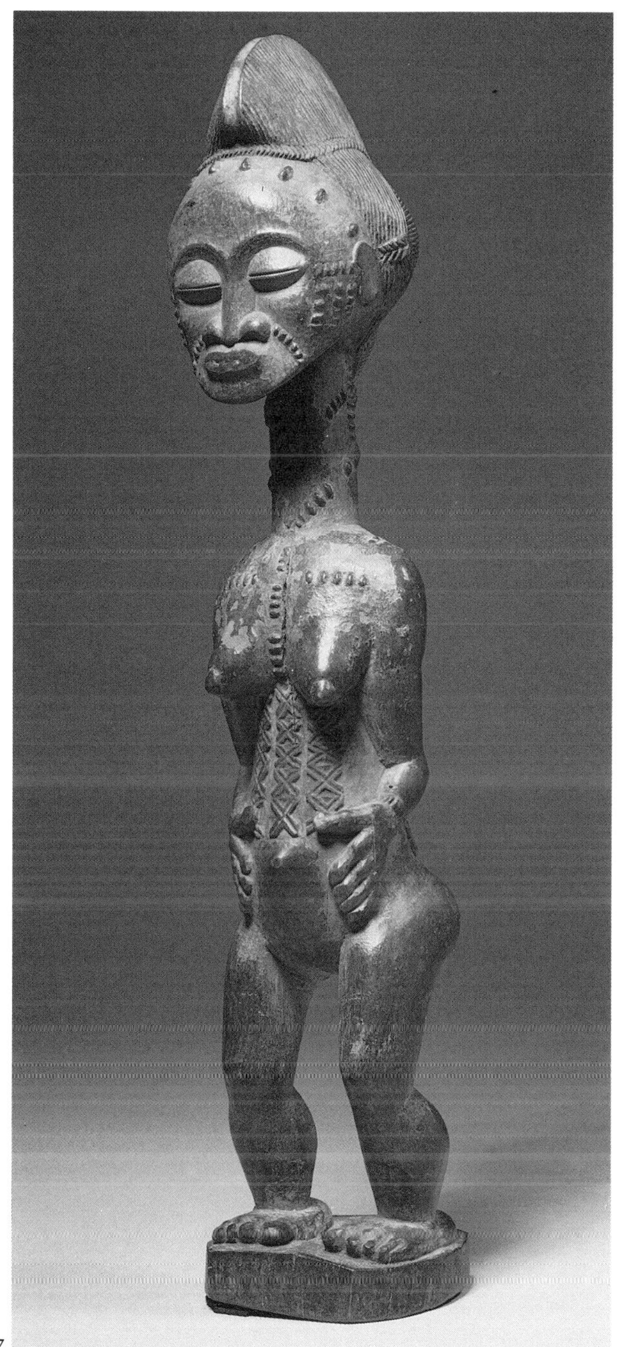

57

58

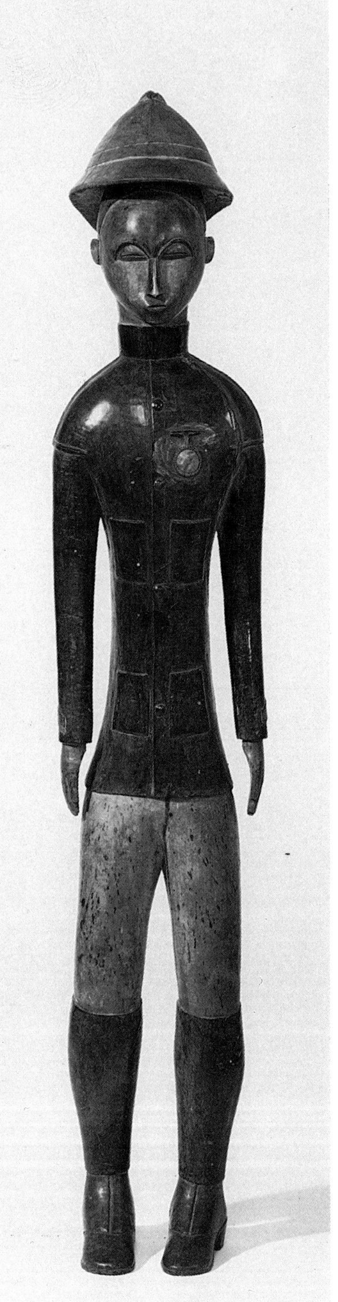

59

Height 38.5 cm. 39-14-1
Acquired from H. Heinrich 1938

Lit.: S. M. Vogel 1980, p. 11.

57 Female spirit spouse: *blolo bla,* wood.
Ivory Coast, Aitu Baule.

The high quality of Baule wood carving, with all details carefully executed, is apparent in this figure. We might expect the expressive face, artistic coiffure, and ornamental scars in high relief, but it is striking that details ordinarily neglected (backbone, shoulder blades, and buttocks) are carefully modeled. Fingers, toenails, and even the knuckles are dexterously formed. Arms and legs with strongly rounded calves are muscular. The long neck not only corresponds to the Baule ideal of beauty but also is valued as a sign of outstanding character and of social prominence. In contrast to most Baule statues, this figure is not stained black but is a reddish color.

Height 37 cm. 33-34-44
Acquired from H. Himmelheber 1933

Lit.: S. M. Vogel 1980, p. 10.

Baule Representations of Europeans (58,59)

58,59 Figures of colonial officers, wood, paint.
Ivory Coast, Aitu Baule.

Unusually large in comparison with most Baule sculptures, these figures were probably carved at the turn of the century. They offer a good example of how the traditional artist approached a novel task. The composition of the figures deviates from that of cult sculptures. The heads are not enlarged, the thin arms run parallel to the elongated torso, and the legs, rigid in appearance, stand free without a base. These features recall the pole sculpture tradition (see p. 42), whose characteristics are not seen in Baule cult figures. The Europeans' heart-shape faces cor-

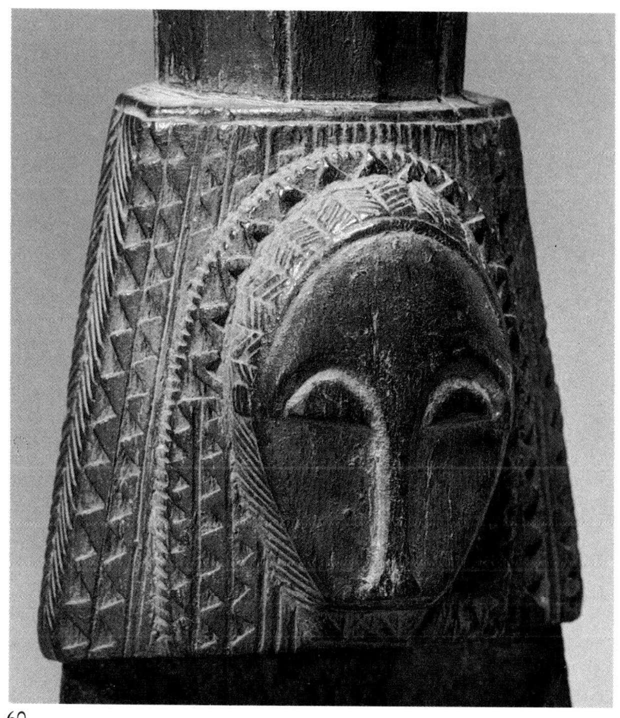

60

respond to those of classical Baule figures, however. Also typically African is the detailed representation of essential or characteristic traits—here the tropical helmet, uniform jacket with medal of distinction, and footwear.

Height 140 cm., 149 cm. 59-19-1/2
Acquired from L. Bretschneider 1959

Lit.: F. Kramer, in J. Jahn (ed.) 1983, p. 207; J. Lips 1937, pp. 73-96

60 Ceremonial knife, wood, iron, leather.
Ivory Coast, Aitu Baule.

This handle is carved with a frog in relief on one side and a human-face mask on the other.

Length 34 cm. 33-34-28
Acquired from H. Himmelheber 1933

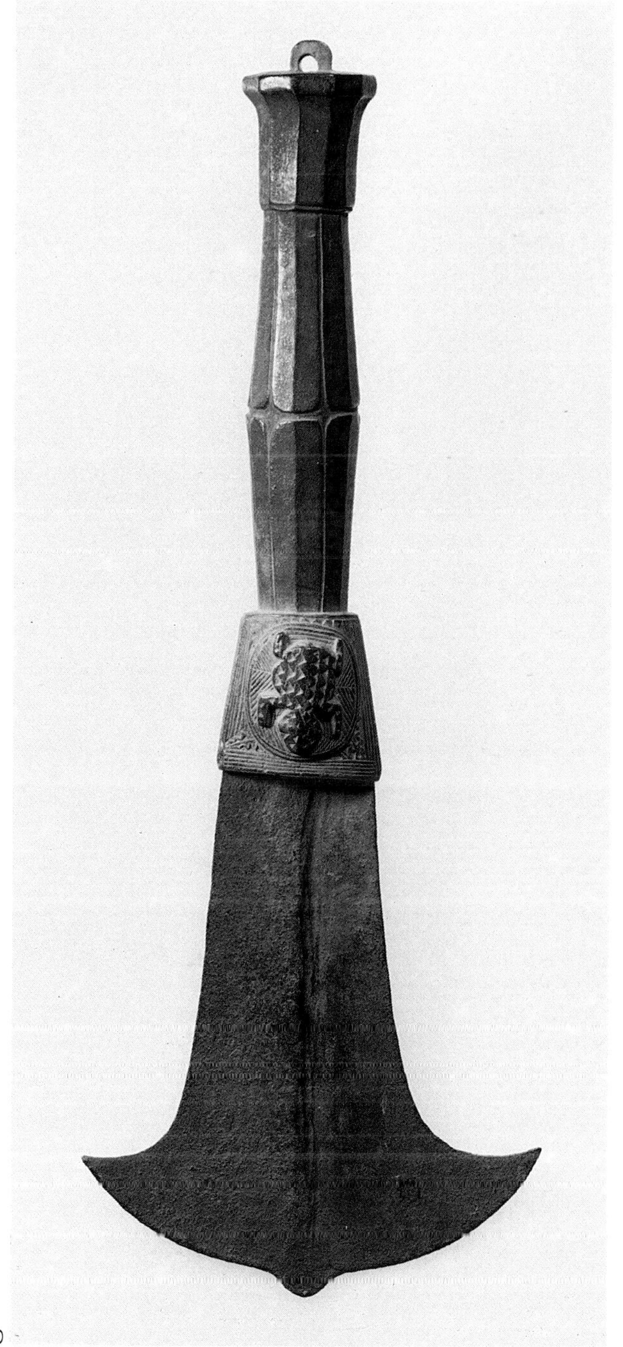

60

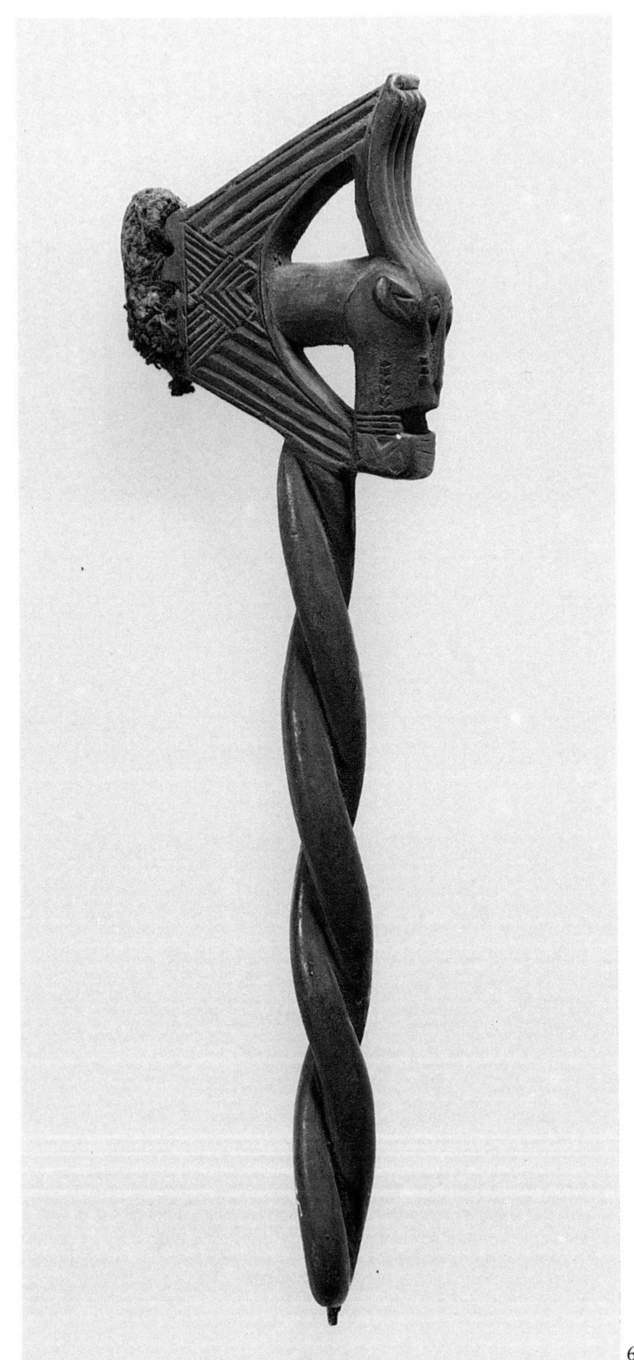

61

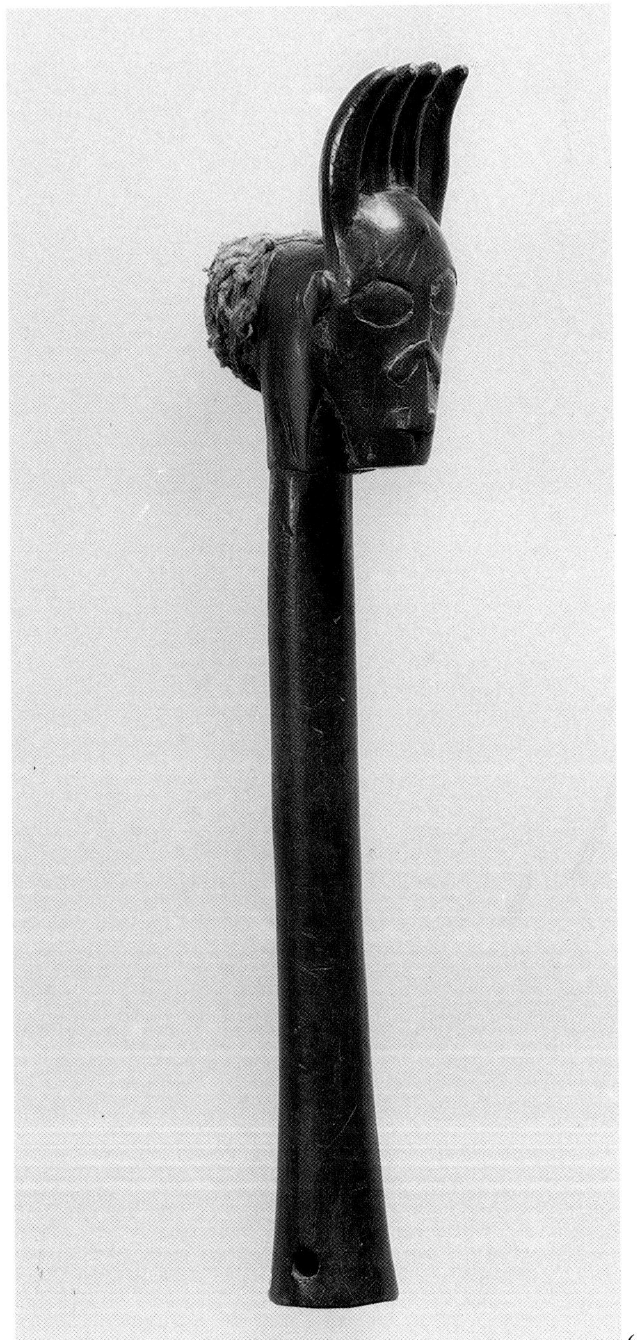

62

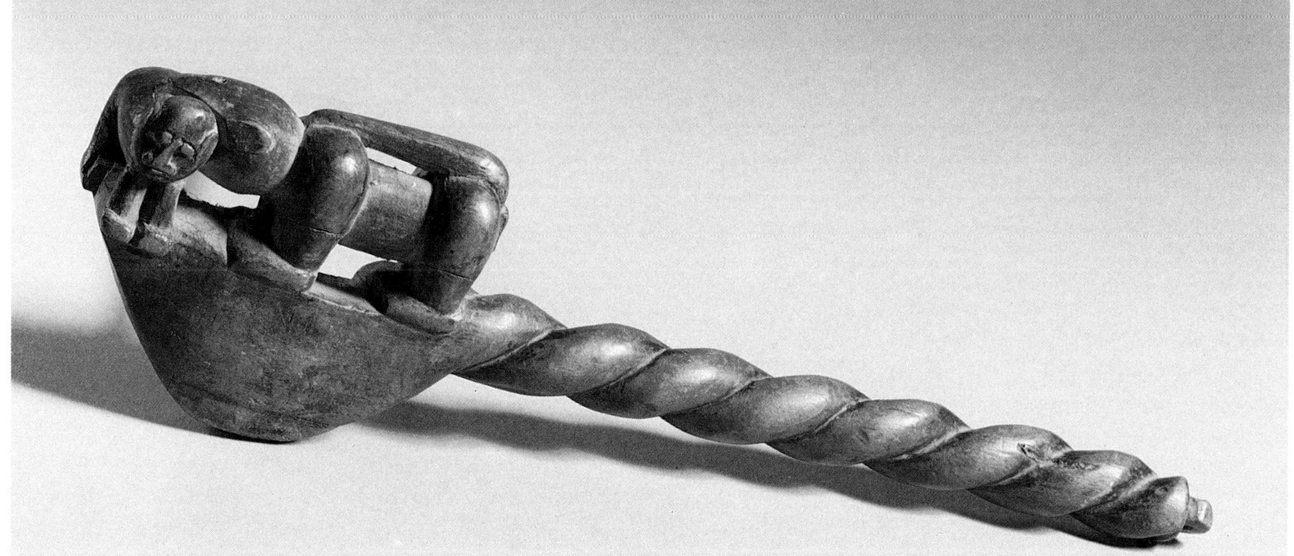
63

61,62 Two gong beaters, wood, cotton pad.
Ivory Coast, Aitu Baule.

The bell-shape gong used in the *do* cult (see No. 64) is sounded with special beaters whose clang is supposed to drive away evil spirits. The motifs carved on them relate to the *do* religion: these handles end in antelope masks with four horns whose model may well have been a horned mask of the *do* cult.

Length 26.5 cm., 24 cm. 33-34-35/36
Acquired from H. Himmelheber 1933

Lit.: B. Holas 1969, p. 156.

63 Gong beater, wood.
Ivory Coast, Baule.

The ornamental sculpture on this beater depicts a leopard carrying a cub in its mouth. The small cotton pad that served to deaden the sound has been lost.

Length 27.5 cm. 78-300-394
Acquired from K. Zeller 1978

Wooden Objects Prepared for Gold Plating (64-67)

The application of hammered gold leaf to wood is an old tradition among the Baule. In Asante, the former home of the Baule, all objects representative of king and chiefs, from sandal buttons to the tips of chiefly umbrellas, were covered with gold leaf. Among the Baule, too, dignitaries appeared for official events with richly gilded regalia. Thus the handles of fly whisks and swords, the carefully carved tips of staffs and umbrellas, and a variety of ornamental chains, bangles, and forehead fillets are covered with gold leaf.

This technique is employed today by members of the Aitu group especially in two villages—Assabonu and Kongonu. (A third such center, Ngatadolikro, does not work with gold leaf but produces objects cast in a gold alloy.) The gold was formerly panned in river beds, but today it is obtained through trade. In most cases, gold leafing is a family industry with division of labor: one member carves, another gilds. In order to make the gold leaf adhere to the wood effectively, handles, points, and other objects to be gilded are carved with allover geometric decorations around figurative motifs. Softened resin is put into the grooves, and the gold leaf is pressed into them with an ivory knife.

Recently, Aitu craftsmen have been manufacturing such objects not only for Baule chiefs but also for foreign rulers and dignitaries who have learned to enhance their prestige by wearing these valuable objects, which serve no other purpose than to represent high office.

Lit.: E. Fischer & H. Himmelheber 1975, p. 9; H. Himmelheber 1968, pp. 83-90.

64 Imitation of a metal gong, wood.
Ivory Coast, Aitu Baule.

The fine surface incisions indicate that this piece was to be covered with gold leaf. Metal gongs and beaters (see Nos. 61 and 62) were used by spirit mediums who performed divinations while in a trance.

Height 17 cm. 33-34-30
Acquired from H. Himmelheber 1933

65 Fly whisk handle in form of a flower, wood.
Ivory Coast, Aitu Baule.

This piece, originally designed to be covered with gold leaf, shows the care with which Aitu craftsmen undertook the decoration of small surfaces. Among the Baule, as in most parts of Africa, the fly whisk is a badge of office. It also has ritual functions: it wards off evil spirits and harmful mystical powers just as it does flies. The corpse of a chief lying in state, for example, is protected from evil by fly whisks. After the object lost its significance as a privilege of rulers and courtiers it became, among other things, a guarantee that a defendant ceded to a plaintiff as pawn until commencement of a legal case. This whisk is said to have been such a guarantee. Precious fly whisks were often made even more valuable by the addition of the hair or tails of certain particularly esteemed species of animals. The Baule imported horsetails from the western Sudan for this purpose.

Length 30 cm. 33-34-40
Acquired from H. Himmelheber 1933

Lit.: E. Fischer & H. Himmelheber 1975, p. 15; H. Himmelheber 1972b, p. 186.

66 Fly whisk handle, wood.
Ivory Coast, Aitu Baule.

The artist ornamented the functionally necessary thickening of the central knob of this whisk handle with masklike faces, two of which can be seen upright only when the fly whisk is raised. The fine striation and crosshatching of the entire surface show that this piece was intended to be covered with gold leaf.

Length 33 cm. 33-34-47
Acquired from H. Himmelheber 1933

Lit.: E. Fischer & H. Himmelheber 1975, p. 15.

67 Necklace, wood, cotton twine.
Ivory Coast, Aitu Baule.

Finely carved diamonds, chevrons, and zigzags on the back and partly on the front side of these pendants ornamented with flattened human faces indicate that this piece was to be covered with gold leaf.

Length 30 cm. 33-34-43
Acquired from H. Himmelheber 1933

68 Pendant of a mask, gold alloy.
Ivory Coast, Baule.
(not illustrated)

Chiefs, and other prominent persons among the Baule and Asante were privileged to wear golden ornaments. Small gold masks cast in the lost-wax process were tied to the swords of kings and chiefs as substitutes for trophies of slain enemies. On these masks are to be found traces of the coiffure with

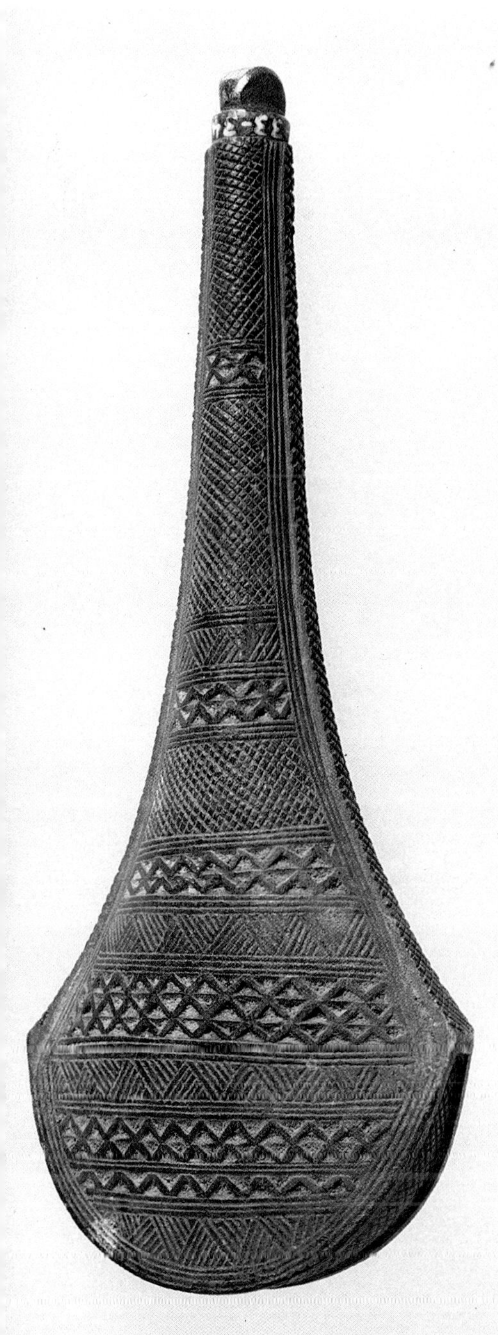
64

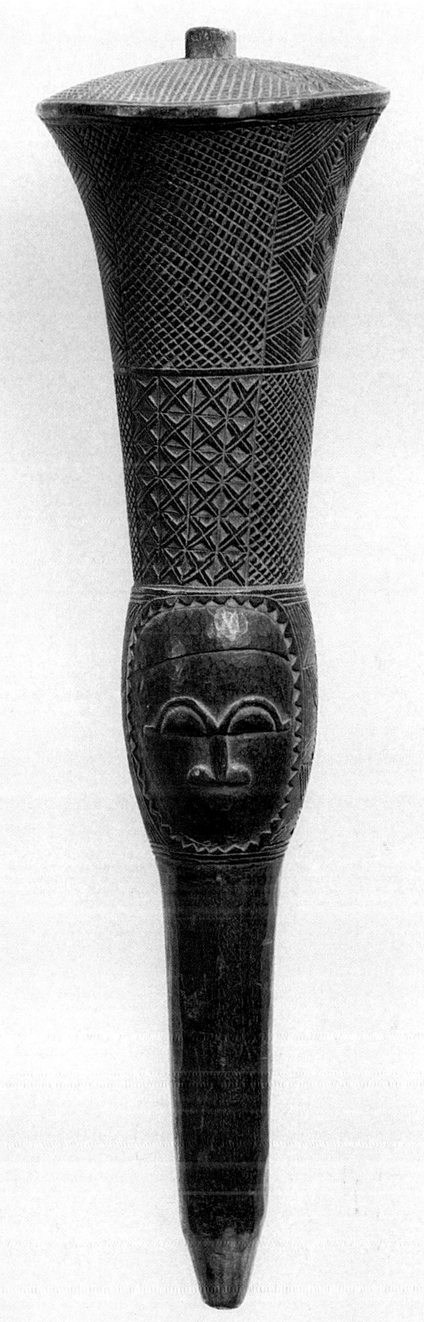
65

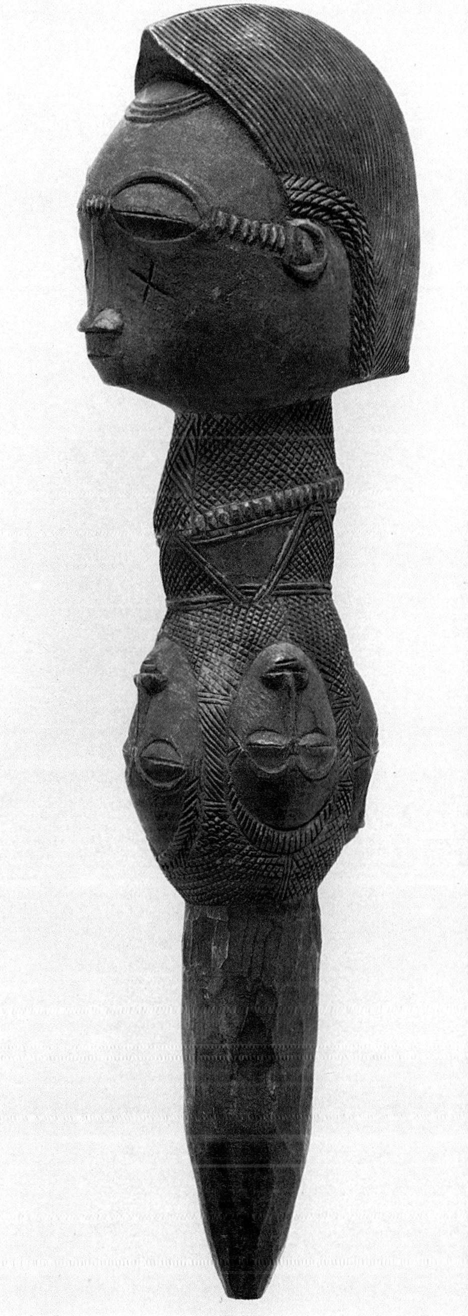
66

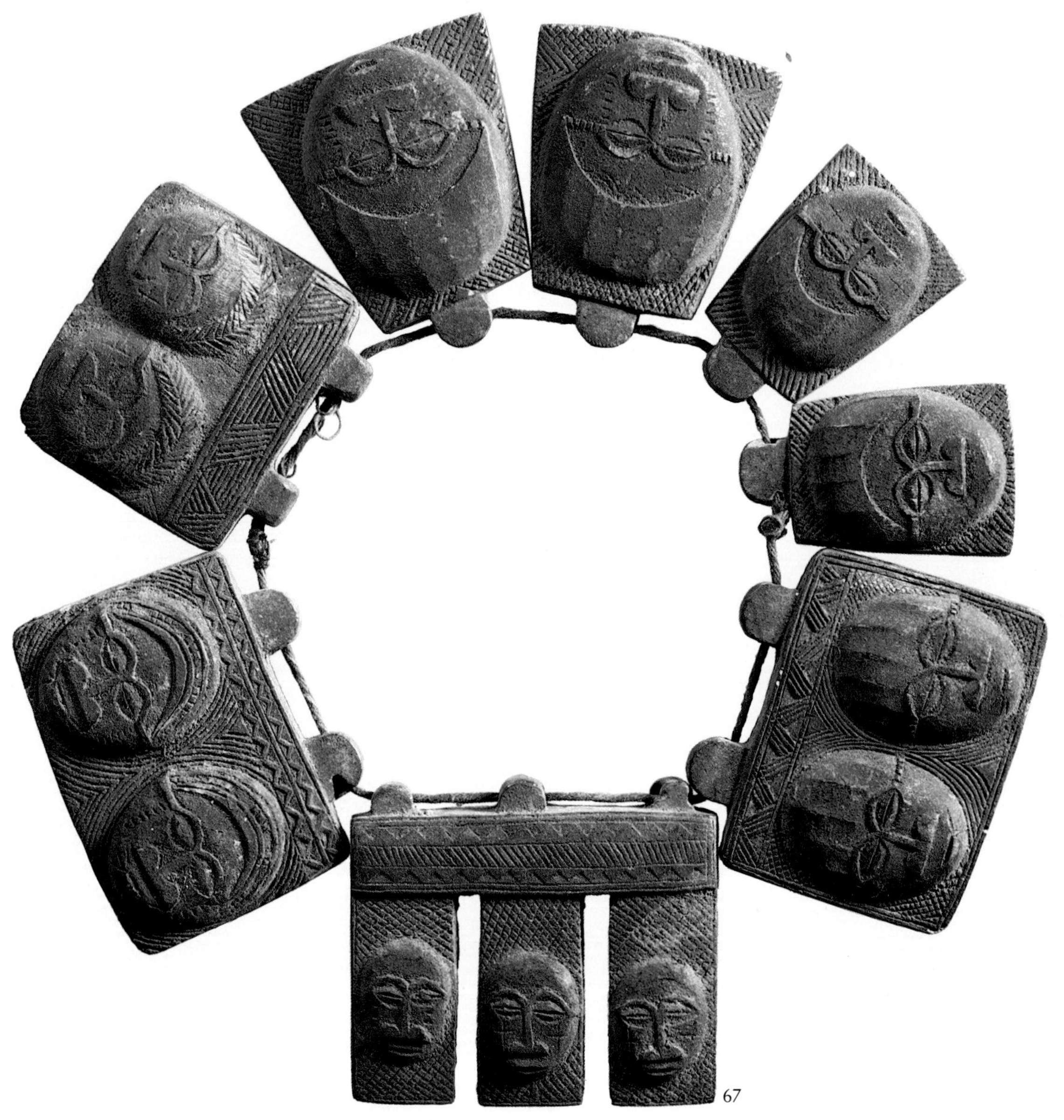

67

upright hornlike projections that in former times marked a warrior.

Height 10 cm. 75-18-1
Acquired from L. Bretschneider 1975

Lit.: E. Fischer & H. Himmelheber 1975, pp. 8, 26, 27; B. Holas 1969, pp. 53-57, 208-14; C. Ratton 1951, pp. 136-55.

The Gold Trade in the History of West Africa: Asante Gold Weights

It is said that gold from the western Sudan was known to the Romans. It long remained impossible, however, to establish a workable trade network between the North African provinces and the gold sources far to the south. We know that this was not due to insurmountable transport difficulties, for regular caravan traffic across the Sahara would have been technically possible by the first century A.D. at the latest. The use of dromedaries as beasts of burden was certainly known in the north at that time. Nevertheless, it was probably not until the seventh century that the development of the trans-Sahara trade (and thereby the gold trade) first took place. The most important factor was the rise of the great Sudanic empires, for which trade with North Africa was vitally important. This empire was powerful enough to control the traffic of goods between the gold regions of the far south (in Upper Senegal, around the Niger headwaters, and in the Ghana of today) and the markets lying north of the Sahara.

The earliest large state recorded in the history of the region was the ancient kingdom of Ghana, which arose in the area of what is today Mali (and therefore not a predecessor of modern Ghana). This realm, founded by forebears of the Soninke in the seventh century A.D. at the latest, is described in contemporary Arabic sources as the "gold land" because it was the center of the northbound gold export trade. For the next few centuries this trade continued unhampered despite the Islamization of the western Sudan and the political changes that occurred early in the thirteenth century. The Mali empire, founded in the eleventh century by forebears of the Mandingo or Malinke, conquered ancient Ghana and by the fourteenth century ruled the entire western Sudan. Like Ghana before it, the empire promoted the export of gold.

Until the seventeenth century, West Africa remained the most important gold source for both Islamic and Christian lands. An important goal of fifteenth century Portuguese sailors was to discover a direct sea route to the legendary gold lands so as to avoid the caravan routes, which were blocked by Islamic states to the north. When this direct route was discovered, a turning point in the gold trade occurred. Caravans no longer traveled across the Sahara but sought contact with European traders on the west coast.

The center of gold production and trade then shifted to the coast of present-day Ghana (the "Gold Coast" of colonial times), where the Portuguese had founded a fortified trading settlement by 1481. Firearms and gunpowder were important among the wares they traded African chiefs for gold. This continuous delivery of weapons helped the Akan groups, living in the richest gold areas, to achieve considerable military power and successful conquests. In the seventeenth century the most important of these groups was the Asante kingdom, in whose life gold played an especially important role both as a trading item and as a ceremonial and cult medium. Gold used extravagantly for representational and religious purposes was the chief characteristic of the Asante realm. Obtaining gold for status symbols covered with gold leaf and for body ornaments presented no technical difficulties. Since the gold veins were usually near the earth's surface, it could be collected either by panning or by making simple vertical shaft mines; sometimes a heavy rainfall even brought gold to the surface. The king took the largest share: all gold nuggets had to be turned over to the court in return for a compensation corresponding to one-third of their trading value.

Gold dust, however, was free of levy. It served as legal tender up to the present century, so anyone wishing to buy or sell had to use a scale and weights. This practice was based on Mediterranean models, but the weights in West Africa were not standardized, so that each time they traded buyer and seller were forced to compare their weights. Goldsmiths, whose guilds enjoyed a privileged position among artisans, cast the weights of brass with a percentage of zinc, using the lost-wax method.

The thousands of gold-dust weights in safekeeping in museums and other collections show an astounding diversity of form. The earliest types are predominantly geometric with ornamentation reminiscent of Islamic (and thus, indirectly, of Roman) monetary weights that were presumably introduced by Mande-speaking traders from the western Sudan. From about the seventeenth century on, figurative weights—representations of human beings, animals, and household utensils—became more and more common. These miniature sculptures are accorded special significance in African art history for several reasons. First, we are dealing with a rare occurrence in ancient Africa, products of a secular art; the simple but lively figures express the ordinary themes of everyday life. Second, the figures achieve movement and show that asymmetry, the depiction of groups, and narrative configurations were in no way unfamiliar to the artists. Many of these figures illustrate proverbs, fables, and anecdotes. Garrard has informed us that figural gold weights were in use not only in the famous Asante kingdom, as was formerly assumed, but also among various other Akan peoples. However, it is not yet possible to localize individual forms.

Lit.: T. F. Garrard 1980, pp.1-36; N. Levtzion 1973, pp. 3-5, 7-12, 124-35, 153-57; B. Menzel 1968, pp. 11-14, 18, 21-24, 36-38, 71; R. S. Rattray 1923, pp. 300-13.

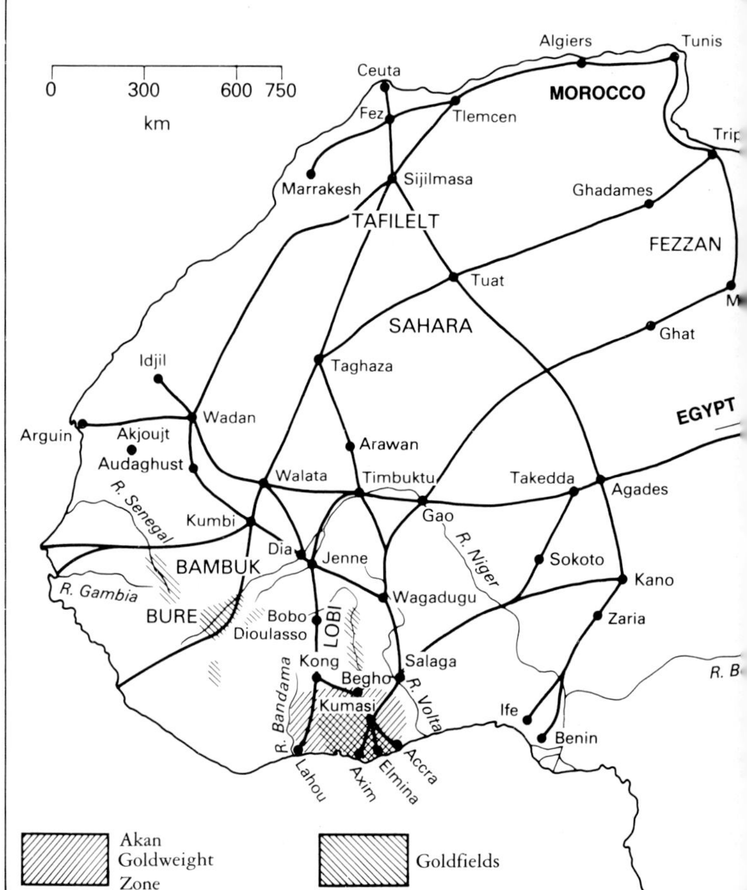

Principal trade routes from North Africa to the Guinea Coast (after Garrard 1980)

69,70 Two *saawa* spoons, sheet brass.
Ghana, Asante.

These spoons, decorated with engraved and repoussé ornaments, were used in the gold trade. They prevented the trader from handling the gold dust and picking up any under his fingernails.

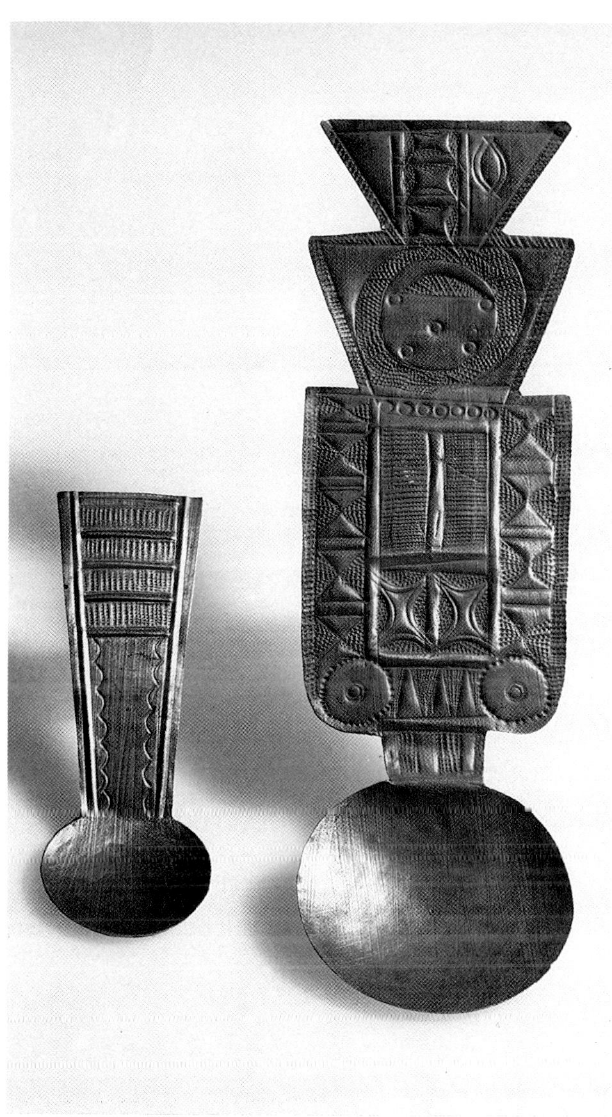

69 70

71

Length 8.4 cm., 16.4 cm. 79-301, 087/088
Acquired from S. Gidal 1979

Lit.: M. McLeod 1981, p. 131; B. Menzel 1968, pp. 83, 84.

71 Equal-armed crossbar scale *(nsania),* sheet brass, cotton cords.
Ghana, Asante.

Such scales for the weighing of gold dust were manufactured by indigenous goldsmiths, who patterned them after foreign coin or jewel scales. Their suspension system and circular decoration were borrowed from the same source.

Length of beam 13.5 cm., diameter of scales 6.5 cm. 79-300 920
Acquired from J. Bolt von Vay 1979

Lit.: B. Menzel 1968, pp. 82, 83.

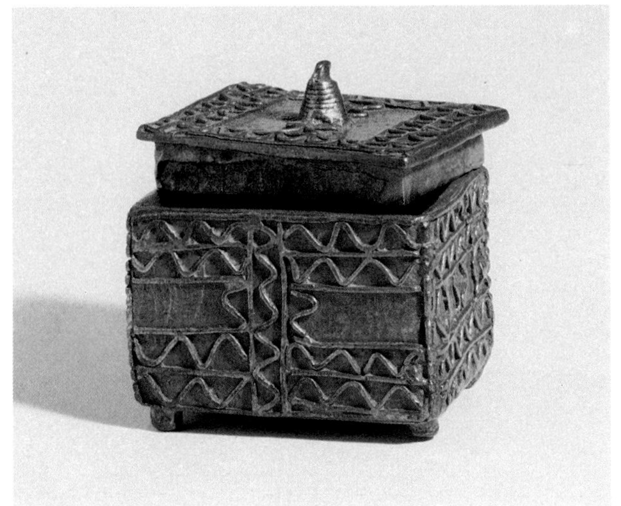
72

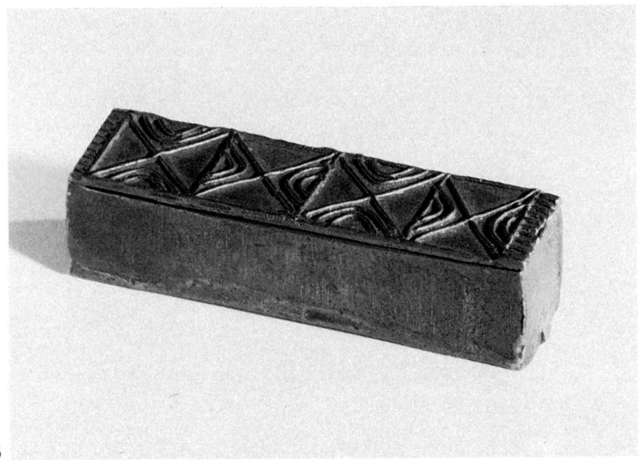
73

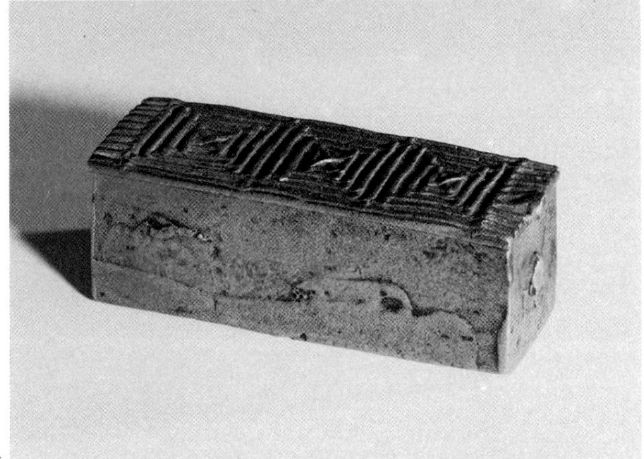
74

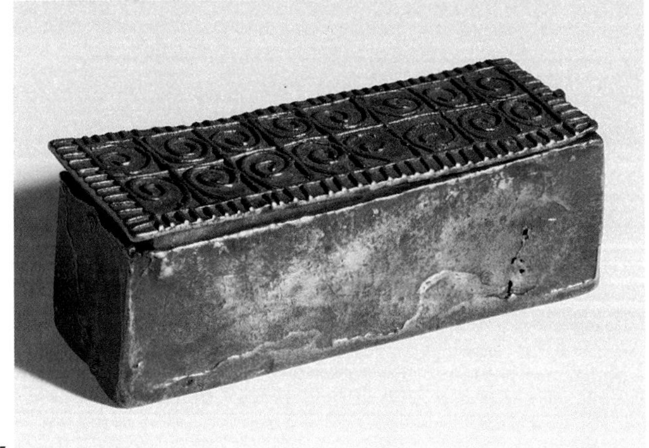
75

72-75 Gold-dust boxes, brass.
Ghana, Asante.

These small, rectangular, receptacles with fitted lids, decorated by means of the wax-thread technique were used to store gold dust. They are similar to the gold weights seen in Nos. 108-19 both in casting technique and in that they are miniature depictions of larger objects, in particular chests, boxes, and wooden cases with iron fittings. European trading partners gave the large containers to Asante rulers, who used them to hold larger amounts of gold dust. The smaller receptacles served the same purpose for the ordinary citizen.

Height 1.5–3.3 cm., length 3.4–6.7 cm.
10.362, 11.12, 11.16, 11.332
Acquired from L. v. Schaky 1910, M. Neubauer 1911, O.W. Oldman, 1911.

Lit.: B. Menzel 1968, pp. 65, 86.

76-84 Geometric weights, brass.
Ghana, Asante.

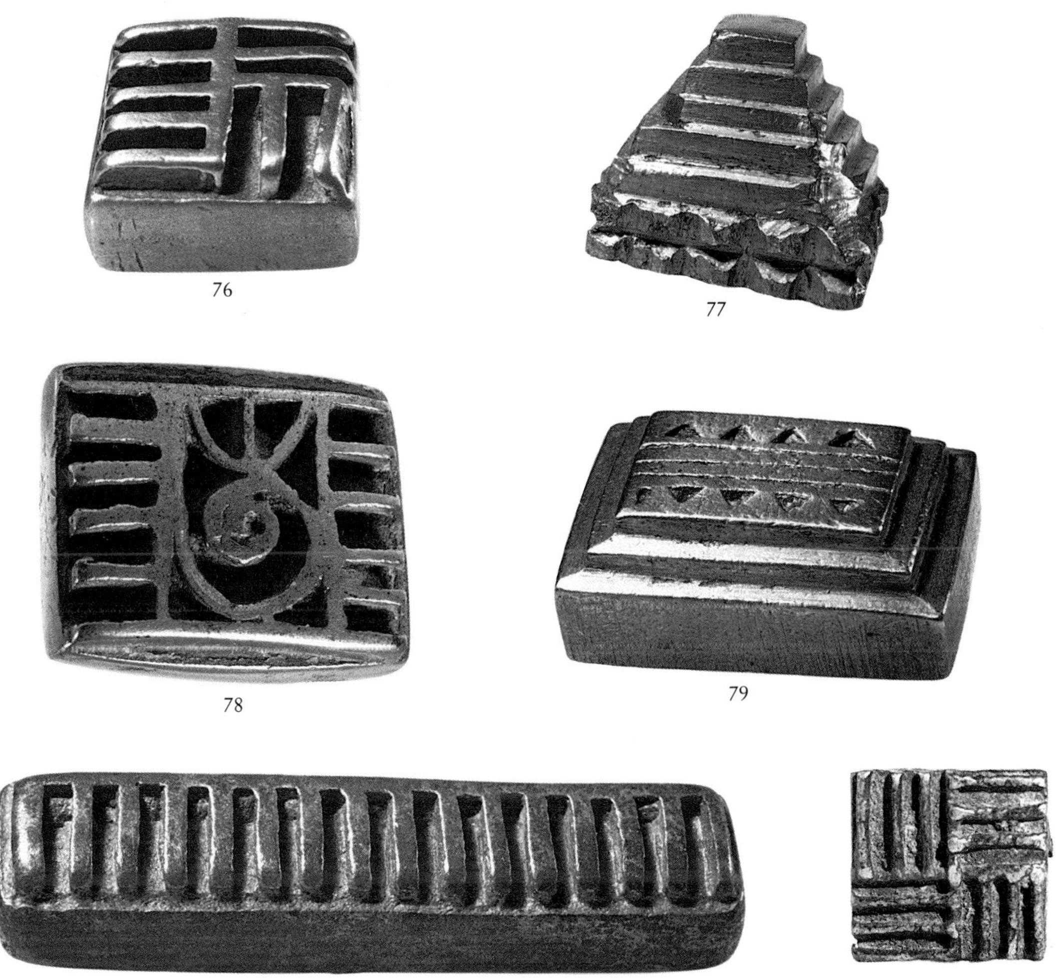

76 77 78 79 80 81

The oldest weights are geometric in form with stamped or incised decoration and were for the most part larger than later types (see Nos. 79 and 82-84). The manufacture of geometric forms did not cease after figurative weights became popular but decoration of the more recent geometric pieces was done with wax thread integral to the lost wax casting. Some of the waves, zigzag or straight lines, spirals, and swastikas have symbolic significance among the Asante, although in the case of the weights they seem only to have identified owners.

The weight in the shape of a fish (No. 83) corresponds technically and in size to the oldest of the geometric types. The fish's semi-circular outline is also reminiscent of earlier types.

Length 1.3, 5.7 cm. 11.297, 96.184, 11.305, 96.185, 11.30, 11.32, 11.302, 11.299, 11.270

Acquired from M. Riggauer 1896, M. Neubauer 1911, O. W. Oldman 1911
(Reproduced twice actual size)

Lit.: T. F. Garrard 1980, pp. 257, 87; B. Menzel 1968, pp. 36, 37.

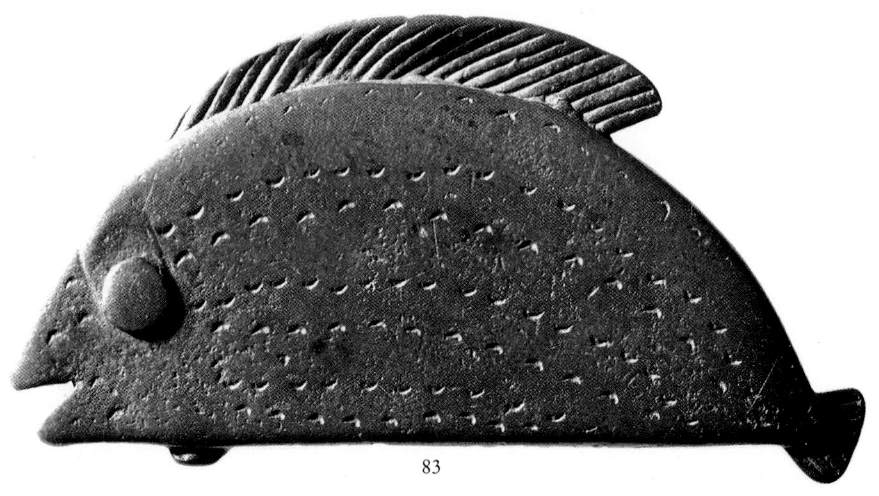
83

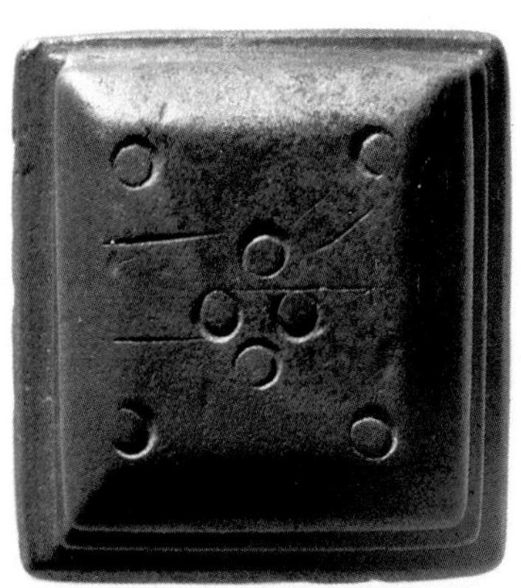
82

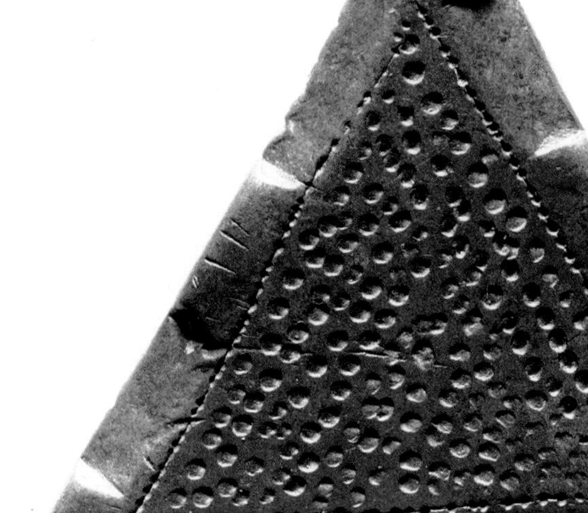
84

Asante Figurative Weights Cast from Nature (85-88)

The earliest reports from the sixteenth century mention the use of weights but never refer to figurative ones, though the latter seem to have emerged by the seventeenth century.

In creating figurative weights by means of the lost-wax technique (see p. 38), a suitable natural object—the body of a crab or insect, seeds, or fruits with a hard shell—is sometimes used instead of a wax model. In casting "from nature," the craftsman surrounds the object with a clay coat and fires it; the object is reduced to ashes and the molten metal poured into its place.

85 Crab's claw.

Proverb: "Eat the claws of a crab without breaking them! Crabs are feared because of their claws." If, in colonial times, the Asante king sent the British a crab-claw model (gold-dust weight?), this was tantamount to a declaration that he would rather fight than submit. 11.268

86 Peanut (groundnut).

Proverb: "Marriage is like a groundnut; you must break it to see what is in it. Plant groundnut for me and not maize." The moral is that the new social bonds (that is, those between bridegroom and parents-in-law) should remain as firm as tough groundnut roots.

Length 4 cm. 11.266
Acquired from O.W. Oldman 1911

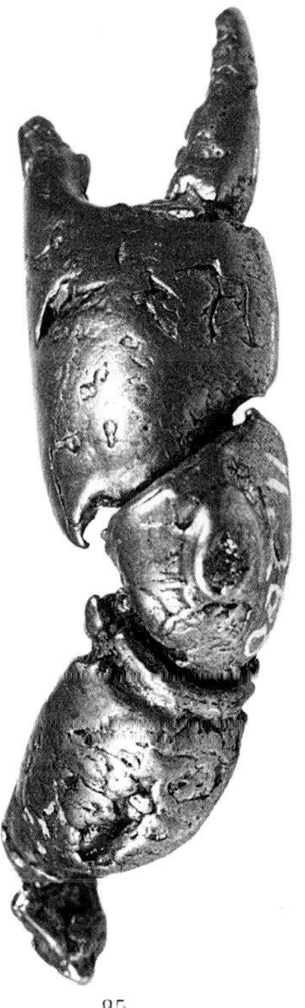

85

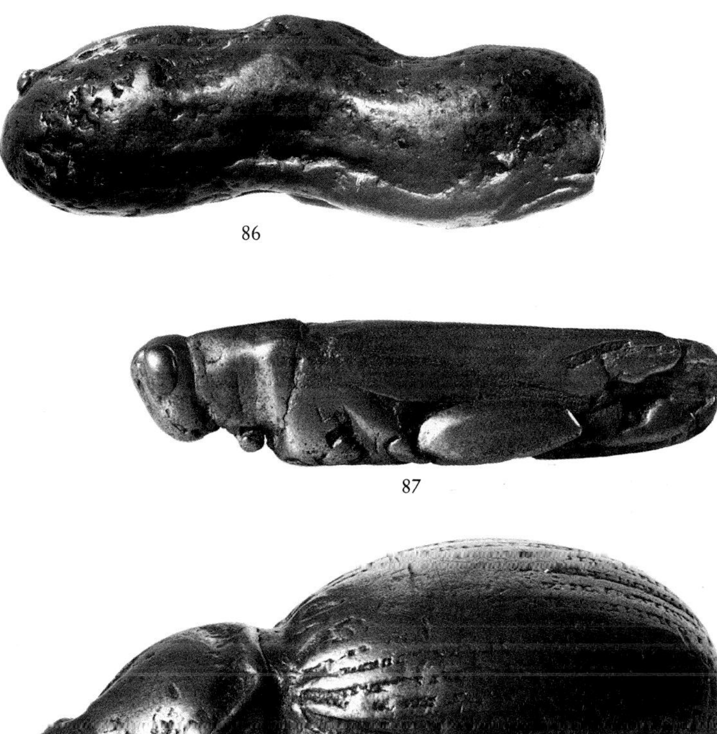

86

87

88

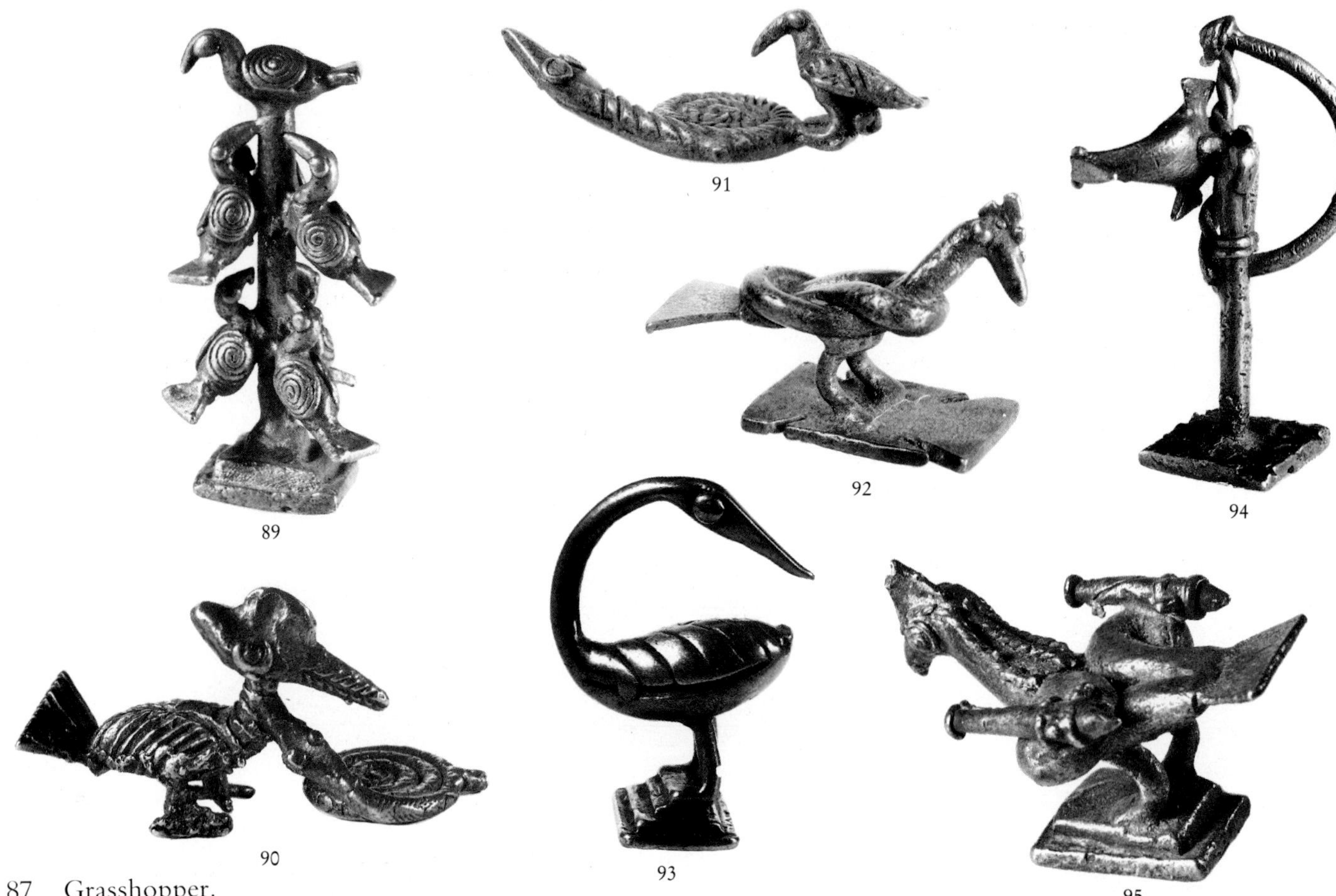

89 90 91 92 93 94 95

87 Grasshopper.
Length 4.8 cm. 11.89
Acquired from M. Neubauer 1911

88 Beetle.
Length 3 cm.
Acquired by Richter 1925 25-44-6

Lit.: P. Appiah 1979, p. 66; B. Menzel 1968, pp. 175, 178.

Weights in the Shape of Birds, Brass. Ghana, Asante (89-95)

89 Birds on a tree.
Proverb: "Ensee birds always want a tree to die so that they can peck holes in it."

90 Hornbill and snake.
Proverb: "Although the viper cannot fly, it caught the hornbill."

91 Snake and bird.
The combined snake-and bird motif originated in the ancient Near East and was usually interpreted there in an astral-mythological sense (as the struggle between light and darkness, for example). In West Africa it was given a new, popular significance, expressed in the proverb in No.90.

92 Bird with knotted body.
This symbolizes the wise man who is able to tie and untie knots of wisdom.

93 Bird looking backward.
Proverb: "Beware of what is happening behind you as well!" The watchful, circumspect chief is symbolized here.

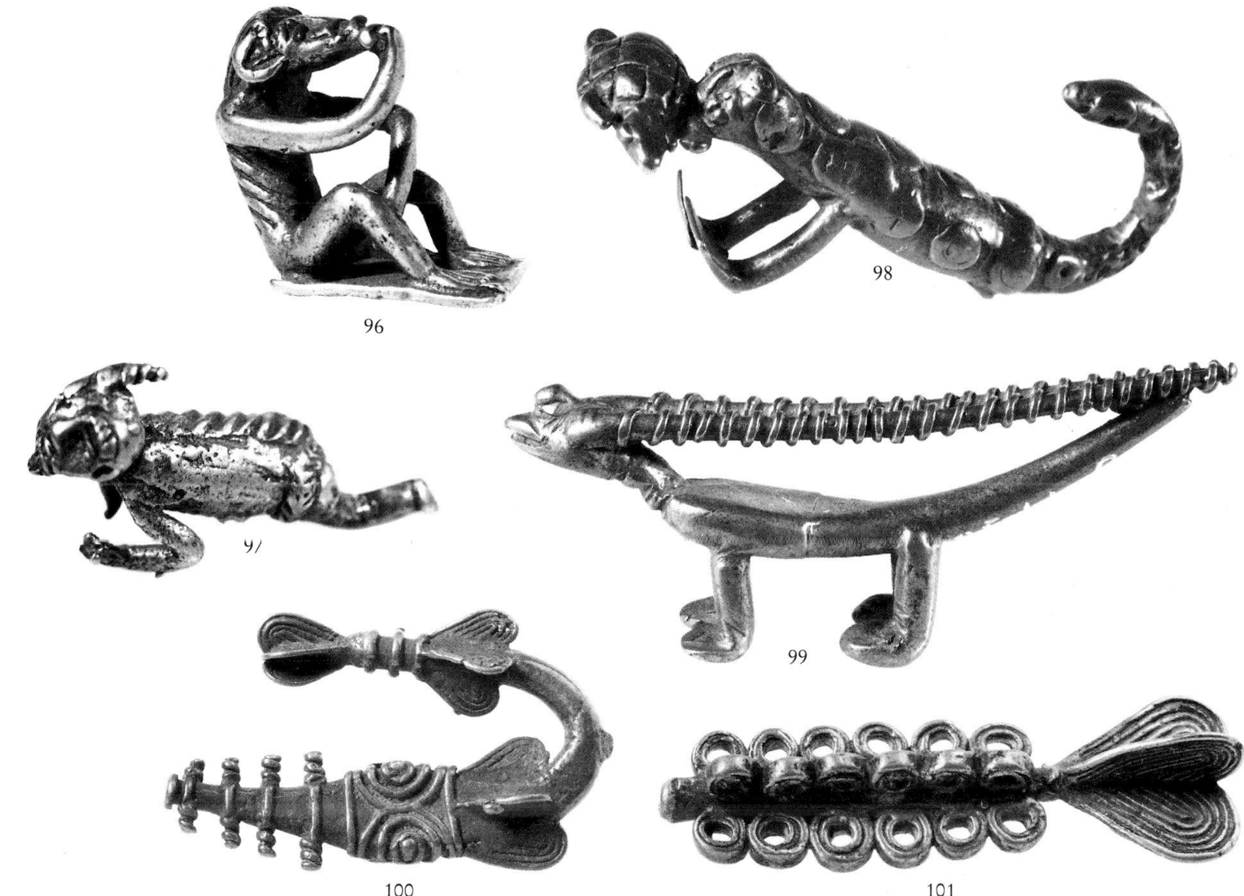

96 98 97 99 100 101

94 Bird in spring pole trap.

Proverb: "The bird's cry in the trap is different" (from the cry he gives in freedom).

95 Bird supporting a cannon.

Proverb: "The wild bird of Commenda is protected by its cannon." This is the emblem of Commenda fortress.

Length Nos. 89-95: 1-4.5 cm., height 1.5-4 cm. 96.169; 10.383; 11.361; 11.337; 25-44-13; 25-44-11; 10.372.
Acquired from Riggauer, O.W. Oldman, Richter, L. v. Schaky

Lit.: P. Appiah 1979, pp. 64, 65; B. Menzel 1968, pp. 59, 190, 91. 195, 96.

Weights in the Shape of Animals, Brass. Ghana, Asante (96-101)

Among these forms there are also figures of fabulous animals (No. 101), compound beings (No.97), indigenous animals, and those that could have been known to the Asante only through distant travels or hearsay, for example the oryx and the sawfish.

96 Monkey.

Proverb: "Evil wishes alone do no harm."

97 Compound being, half human, half antelope.

98 Leopard with tortoise in its mouth.

Proverb: "A hungry leopard will try to eat any animal."

99 Oryx.

Proverb: "In the end it is always said, had I only known that beforehand."

100 Sawfish.

101 Fabulous animal with stylized fishtail and ornamental rings.

Length Nos.96-101: 2-8 cm.

11.277, 11.294, 11.333, 11.282, 11.327, 25-44-8
Acquired by O.W. Oldman 1911, Richter 1925
Lit.: P. Appiah 1979, p. 67; B. Menzel 1968, pp. 199, 203.

Anthropomorphic Weights, Brass. Ghana, Asante (102-107)

Weights in human form often display antiquated features and clothes such as simple loincloths. Prototypes of these representations may have been made as early as the seventeenth century, before the large togalike *kente* cloth came into general use. The coiffures seen in these weights served as status symbols: A tuft of hair on the crown of the head as in No.104 indicated that the father of that person was still alive. A shaved head (No.102) implied mourning.

In spite of these archaic elements most weights may well be comparatively recent. Only Nos. 104 and 106 reveal great age through their patinas and well-worn surfaces. These two objects surpass the others both in size and in artistic quality, and are probably the oldest figurative weights in this collection.

102 Man with crossbow.

The crossbow was introduced to Africa by Portuguese sailors in the sixteenth century.

103 Flutist.
104 Standing drummer.

105 Priest sacrificing a fowl.

On the forked post is a bowl for blood.

106 Woman with child and agricultural tools.

107 Man collecting tree bark.

Proverb: "If a man tries to collect bark by himself, his efforts are in vain!"

Height 3.7-7 cm.
11.350, 11.352, 11.351, 11.346, 11.342, 11.349
Acquired by O.W. Oldman 1911

Gold Weights in the Shape of Various Objects, Brass. Ghana, Asante (108-113)

There is scarcely an article of Asante material culture that was not duplicated in a diminutive weight.

108 Blowing horn with shoulder strap.

The lower jaws attached to this horn represent war trophies.

109 Gong in the shape of a double bell.

110 Board game.

Originally derived from the Orient, this game is widespread on the African continent.

111 Chair.

This type of chair, introduced to Africa from Europe in the sixteenth century, was a status symbol.

112 Drum.

Like the horn in No. 108, this instrument is adorned with lower jaws.

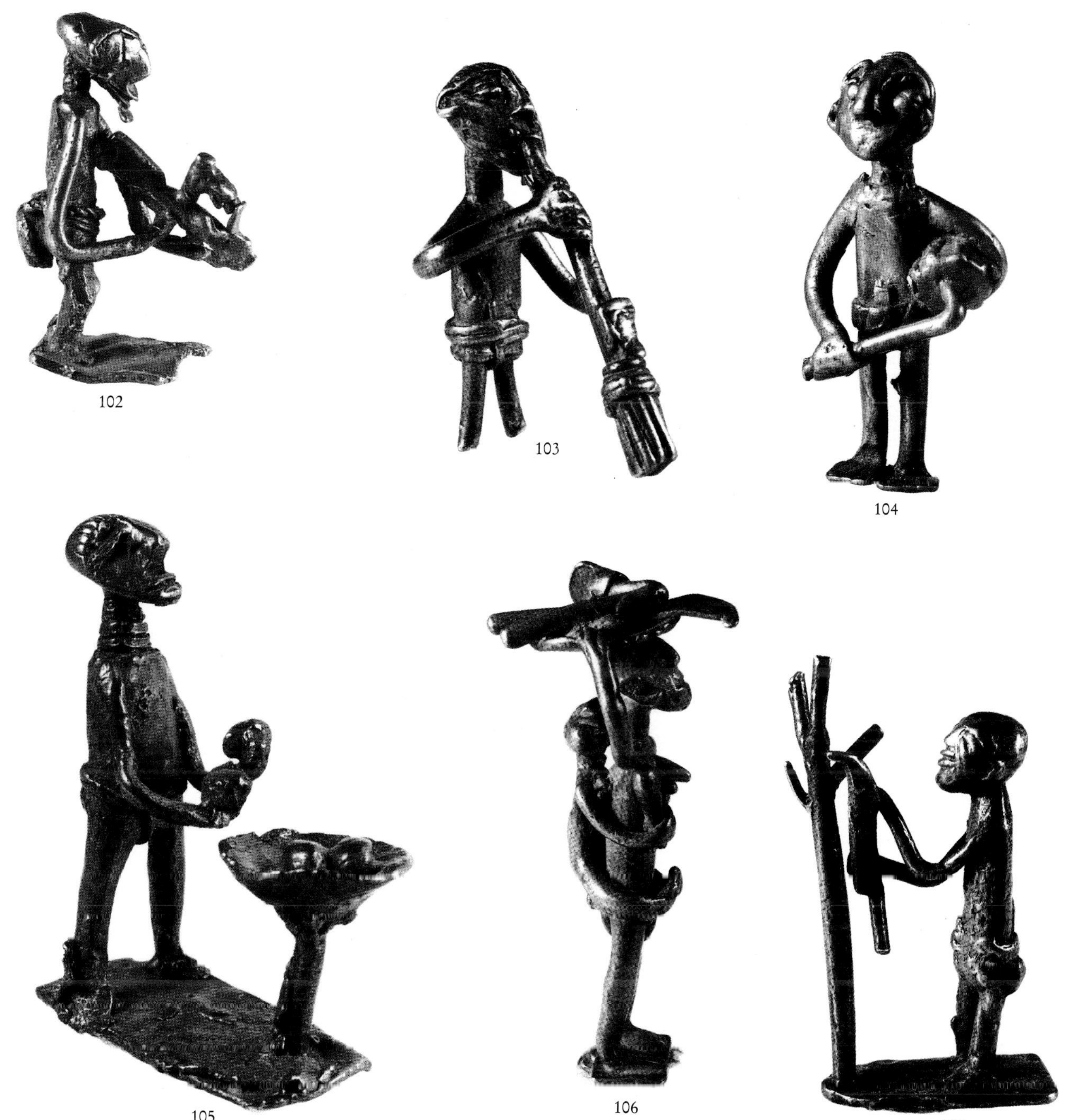

102

103

104

105

106

107

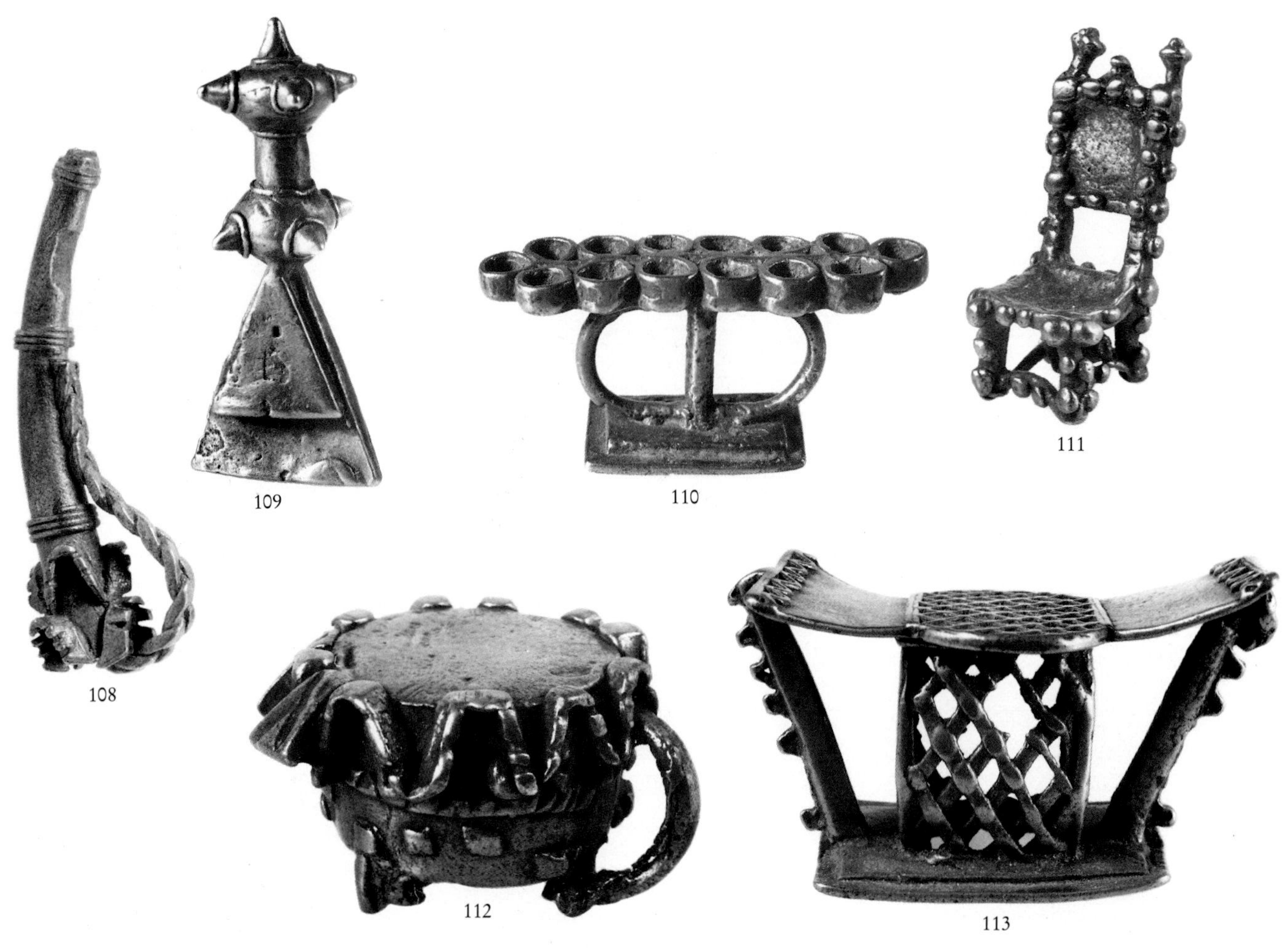

113 Stool.

This type of stool is among the most important cultural symbols of the Akan people. It not only served as an object of daily use but also occupied an important place in religious life as an ancestral altar. A golden stool of this type, to which a divine origin is ascribed, is valued as a sacred symbol of the power of Asante kings.

Length 3.7-5.7 cm.
11.329, 11.53, 11.54, 11.335, 25-44-22, 11.300.
Acquired by M. Neubauer 1911, O. W. Oldman 1911, Richter 1925.

Lit.: B. Menzel 1968, p. 47; S. F. Patton 1979, p. 74.

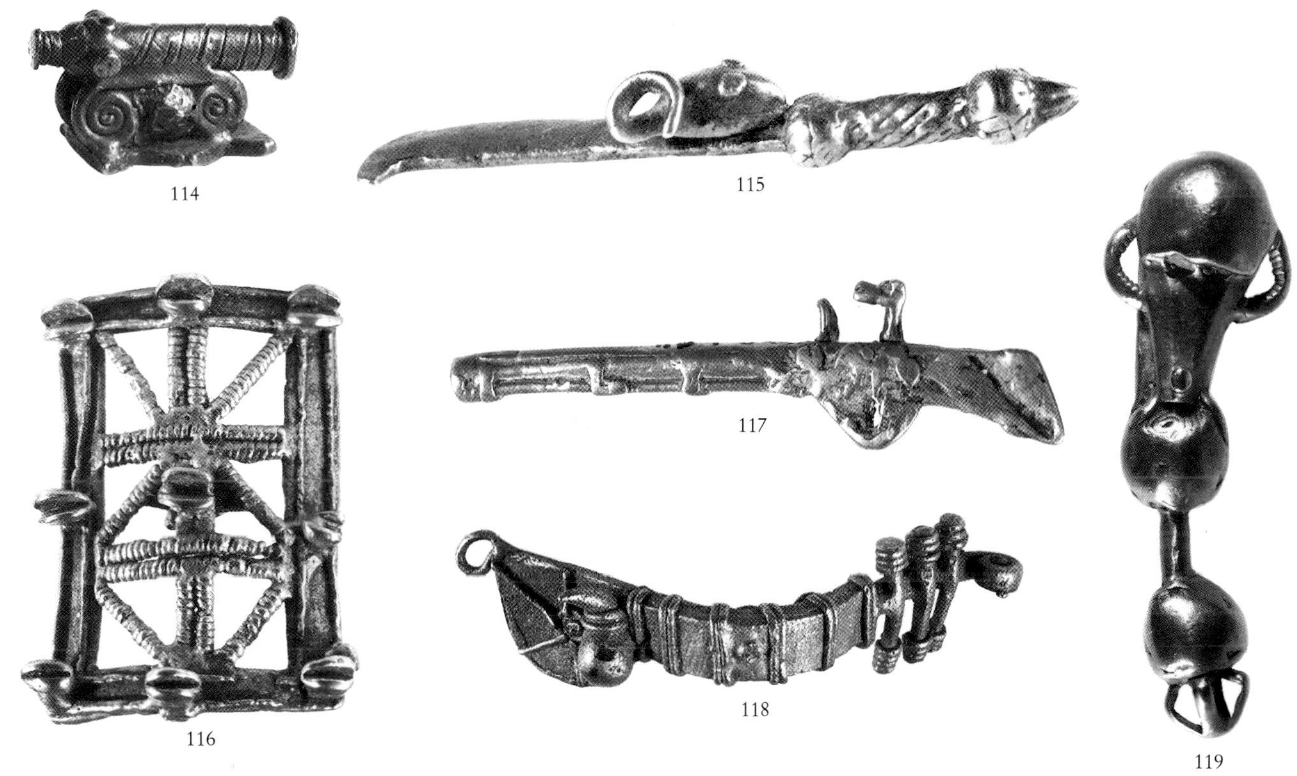

114

115

116

117

118

119

Gold Weights in the Shape of Weapons, Brass. Ghana, Asante (114-119)

The weapons shown were imported in large quantities from Europe for gold and played an important role in the victorious campaigns of the Asante. Several of the showpieces and cannons, however, served as items of prestige rather than as instruments of war.

114 Cannon.

115 Ceremonial sword with animal emblem (ram's head).

116 Frame of a shield.

Proverb: "When a shield is worn out the frame remains."

117 Flintlock gun.

118 Cartridge belt.

119 Ceremonial sword with animal emblem (monkey skull).

Length 3-6 cm. 11.46; 11.371; 11.286; 10.401; 25-44-30; 25-44-23

Acquired from L. v. Schaky 1910, M. Neubauer 1911, O. W. Oldman 1911, Richter 1925.

Lit.: B. Menzel 1968, pp.51, 59, 223.

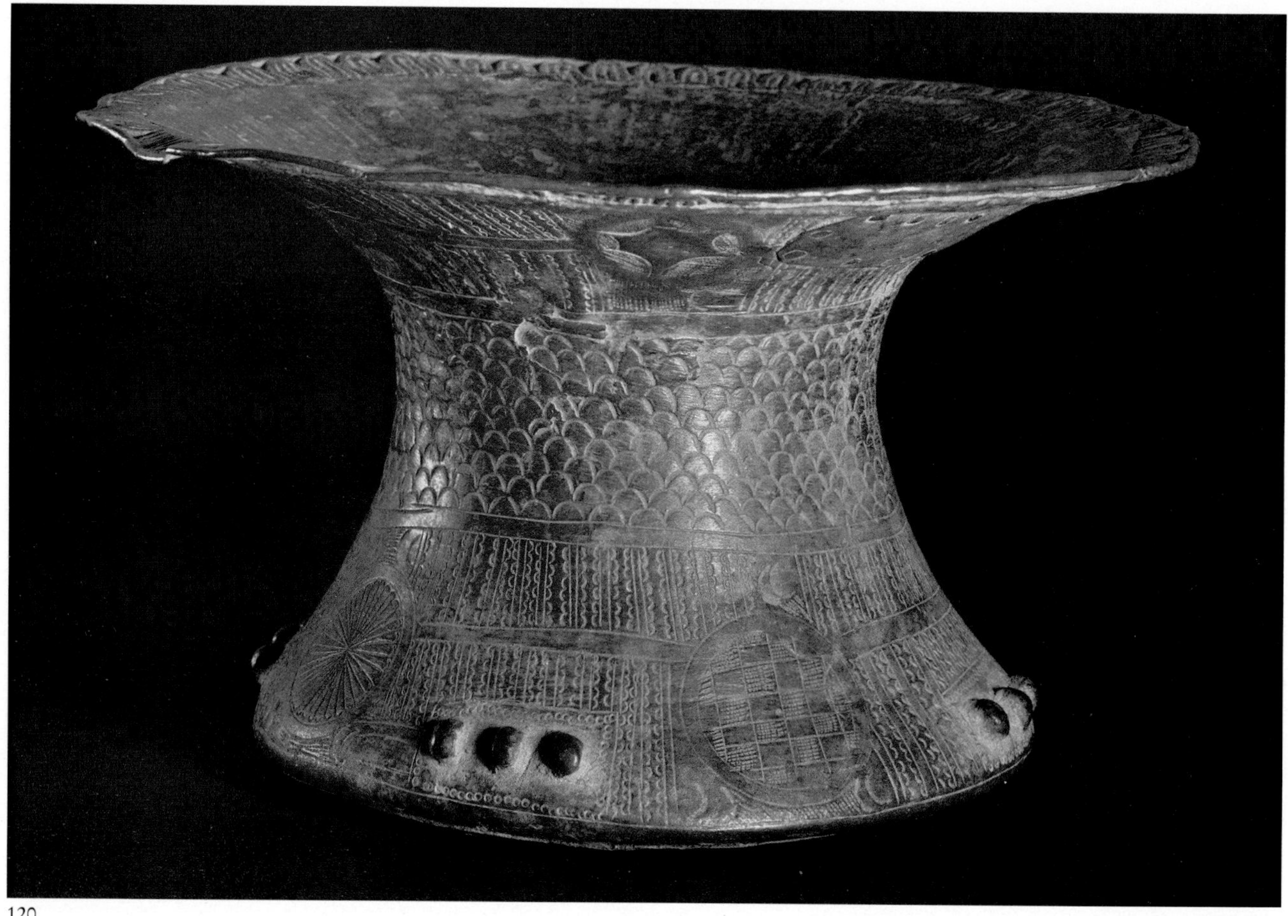
120

Akan Metal *kuduo* Vessels (120-123)

Models for *kuduo* were thin-walled vessels of copper and brass that came partly from North African workshops and partly from workshops of the western and central Sudan. Around the fourteenth century they were introduced to the Akan by traders from Timbuktu and Djenne. The artistically cast vessels were so appreciated that they were incorporated into the myths of origin despite their alien provenance: the founding ancestors of several Akan ethnic groups are supposed to have descended from heaven in such vessels. Akan craftsmen soon learned to produce similar vessels from imported metals. This indigenous production grew rapidly in the sixteenth century when European trading ships increased the supply of the necessary metals from the coast.

Vessels manufactured by Akan casters were, at first, merely imitations of pieces imported from North Africa and the Sudan. In the course of time, however, new forms and decorations evolved. Hinges, fastenings, and chased ornament were simplified or omitted and the lidded vessels were provided with base rings, which Silverman suggests were copied from African pottery stands. They were also adorned with small sculptural figures strongly reminiscent of figural gold weights.

The *kuduo* was used for storing gold dust and precious beads or sacrificial food, drink, and blood. The scarcity of old examples is largely due to the fact that it was customary to place them with their contents in the grave at the death of their owner. The question of age, however, remains to be clarified. Among those shown here, No.120, probably dating from the sixteenth century, is thought to be the earliest.

Lit.: R. Bravmann 1973, p.13; T. F. Garrard 1979, pp.36-39; B. Menzel 1968, p.88; R.S. Rattray 1923, pp.51f., 313-315; (personal communication R. A. Silverman)

120 *Kuduo* bowl with projecting rim, cast brass.
Ghana, Asante, Kumasi.

Both shape and surface engravings recall the Islamic metal vessels after which the *kuduo* was modeled. The purely geometric decoration of the outside is divided into horizontal bands filled either with a scaly pattern formed of semicircles, or with vertical lines and rows of minute arches. Below the rim and just above the base are four symmetrically spaced circles filled alternately with rosettes and checkerboard patterns. The lip of the comparatively thick-walled vessel is decorated with double arches. The bowl is much worn and has been repeatedly repaired with thin hammered metal sheet and copper rivets. The inside is encrusted.

Height 11 cm., diameter 20 cm. 10.357
Acquired from L. v. Schaky 1910

Lit.: T.F. Garrard 1979, p.42.

121 Vessel (*kuduo*), cast brass
Ghana, Asante, Kumasi.

Silverman believes that this is the second oldest vessel in our collection, having been made sometime be-

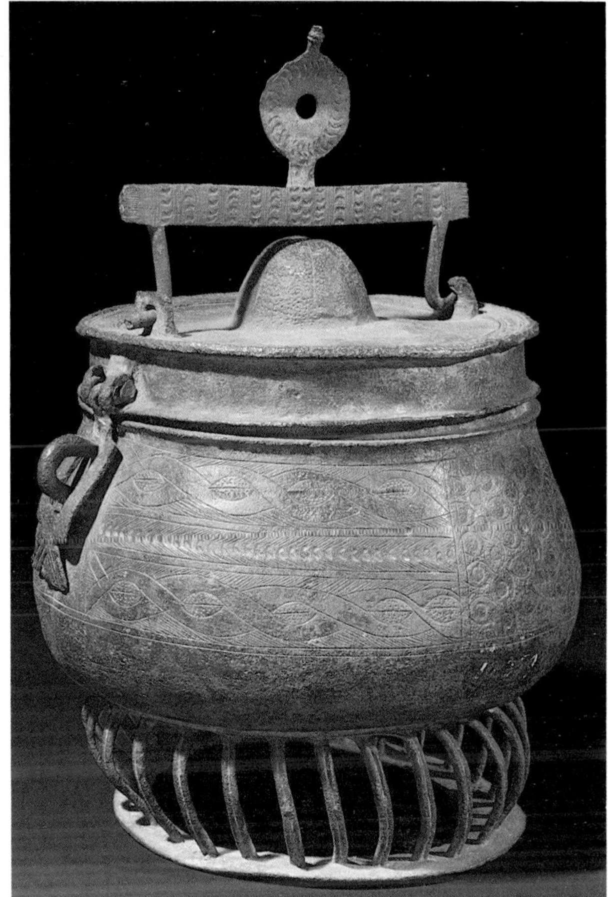

121

tween the sixteenth and eighteenth centuries. It has a convex shape with circular openwork base and fitted lid. Many features—hinge and lid fastening, handle, and finely engraved outer surface divided into horizontal and vertical fields, ornamented chiefly with entwined bands and circles—suggest North African-Sudanese models. The inside contains verdigris and encrustations.

Height 11 cm., diameter 11.5 cm. 10.359
Acquired from L. v. Schaky 1910

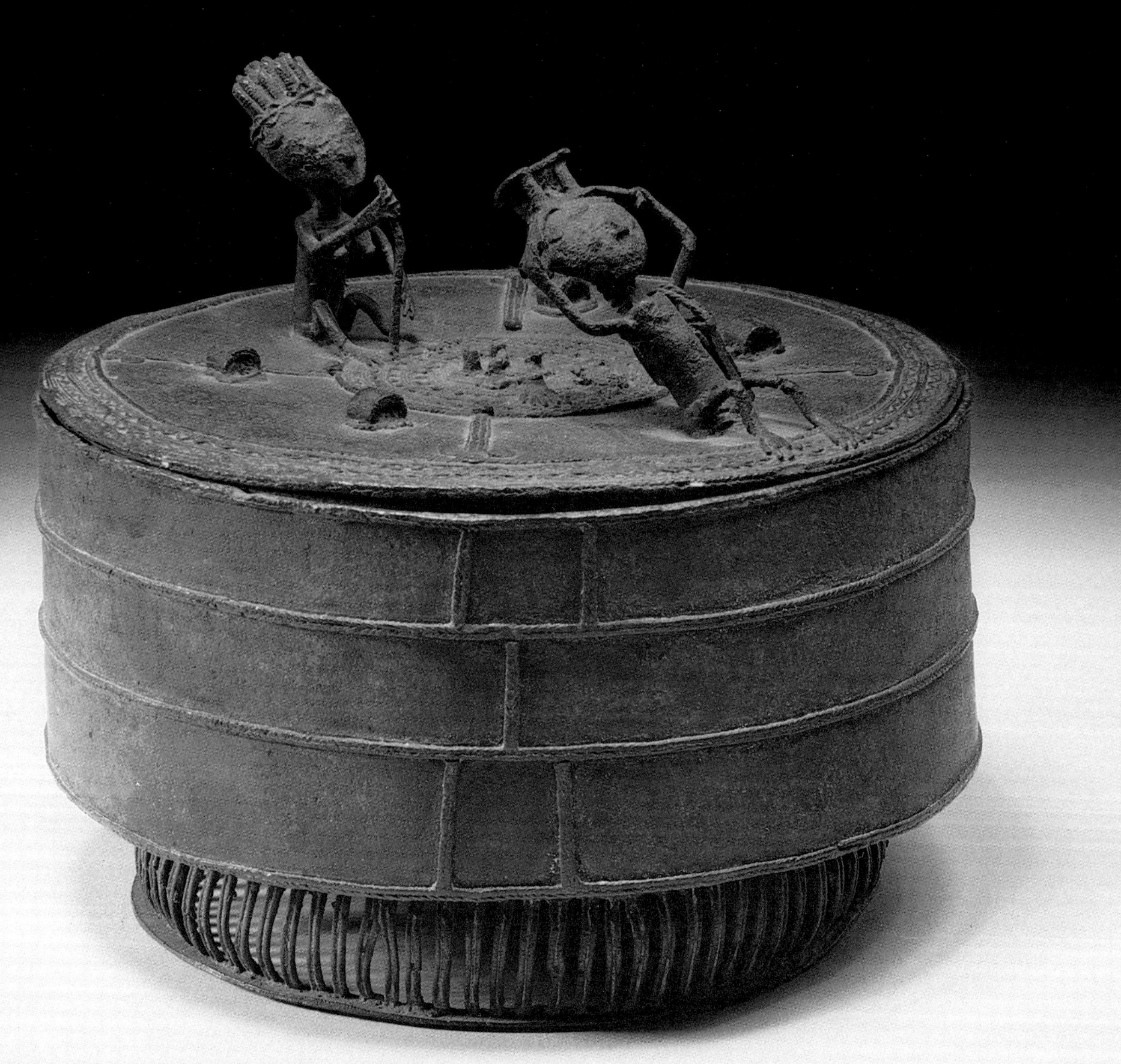

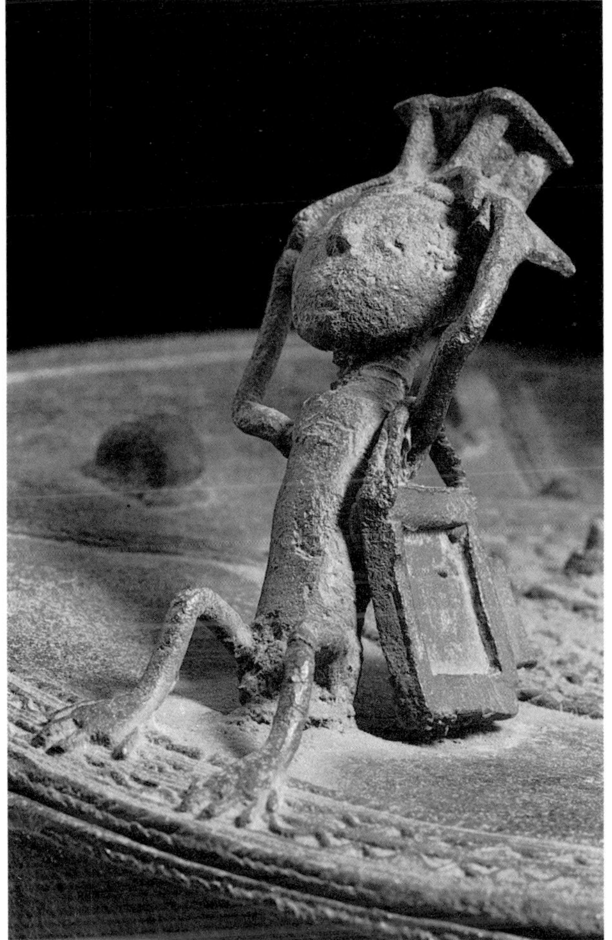

122

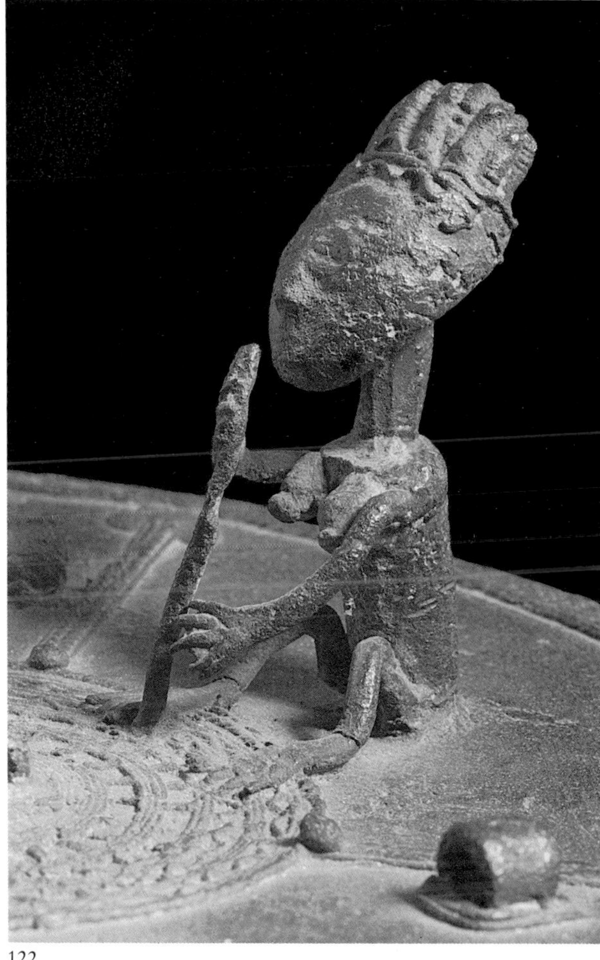

122

122 *Kuduo* vessel, brass.
Ghana, Asante.

According to McLeod and Silverman, this cylindrical object with an openwork base, a fitted lid with fine linear decoration, and a dark patina dates from the eighteenth century. A group of figures (originally three) adorns the lid. The missing central figure of which only the bare feet remain was presumably a dignitary seated on his stool and not a king, since a king would scarcely be barefoot. The two remaining figures represent a man (probably the carrier of the ancestral stool and bag containing the gold weights), and a noble woman with an artistically braided coiffure holding a staff in her hand. These two are also depicted without sandals. The detailed modeling of the female figure (coiffure, long neck, breasts with nipples, asymmetrically disposed hands, long slender feet) is noteworthy.

Height 17 cm., diameter 18 cm. 31-24-3
Acquired from O. W. Oldmann 1931

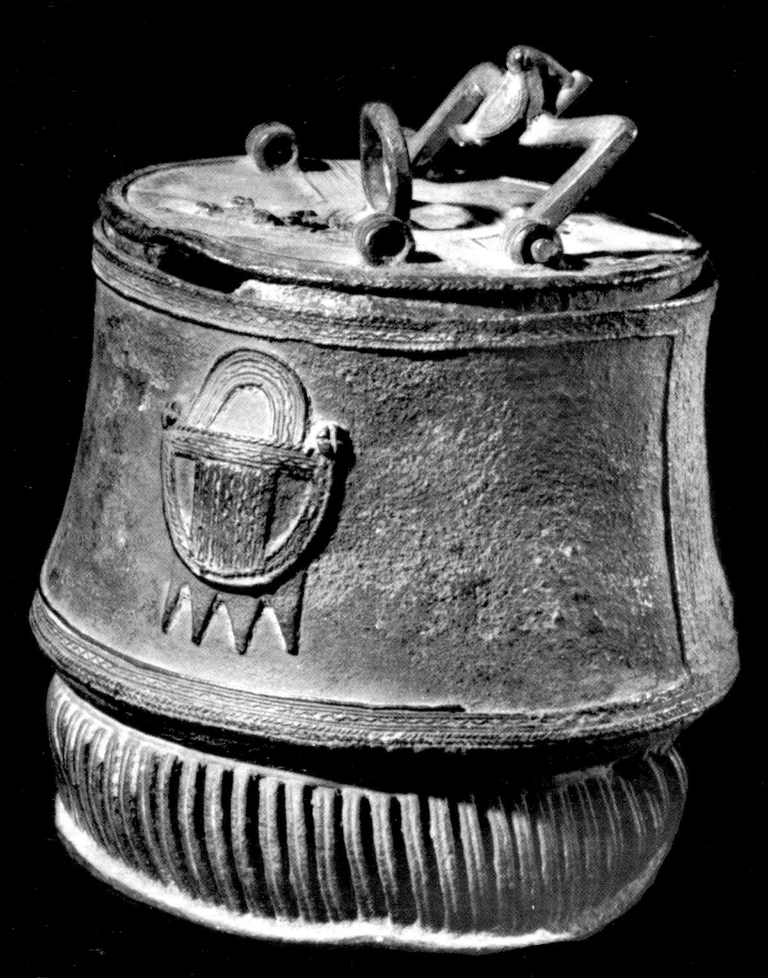

123 *Kuduo* vessel, cast brass.
Ghana, Asante, Kumasi.

This piece has a wall drawn gradually inward toward the rim, a circular base in openwork, and a fitted lid. One of the handles is missing; the remaining one is decorated with a small bird figure. The reliefs on either side of the vessel's wall represent leather bags for the storing of gold weights and balance. The fine band decoration was achieved by means of thin wax threads applied to the model. The inside shows verdigris.

Height 11 cm., diameter 9 cm. 10.358
Acquired from L. v. Schaky 1910

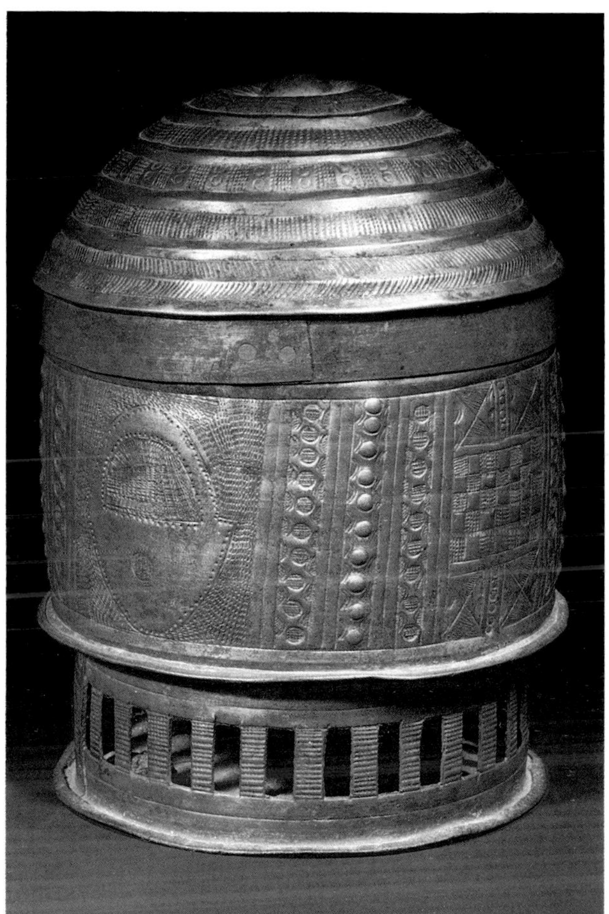

124

124 *Forowa* vessel, brass, copper.
Ghana, Fanti.

Forowa jars were used to contain such diverse substances as sheabutter (a vegetable fat used nutritionally, cosmetically, or as fuel), herbs, pearls, gold dust, and cowries. They were designed for profane use, but because of their high prestige they sometimes played a role in burial rites as well.

Such jars are made of several individually cut brass plates—ours is of six—forged together. The plates are decorated with engraved geometric and figural motifs before being joined. Among figural designs the combination of bird and padlock is particularly favored and is usually arranged in two panels placed on opposite sides of the jar. The lock is a symbol of power and authority, while the bird with head turned backward symbolizes the watchful, prudent chief (see proverb, No.93). It is not known just exactly how long these jars have been used in Ghana, but one account maintains that they appeared as early as the end of the seventeenth century (Cole and Ross), while another places them after 1850 (Ross).

Height 13 cm., diameter 10.5 cm. 78-300 389
Acquired from S. Gidal 1978.

Lit.: H. M. Cole & D. H. Ross 1977, pp.64-66; D. H. Ross 1974, pp.40-49.

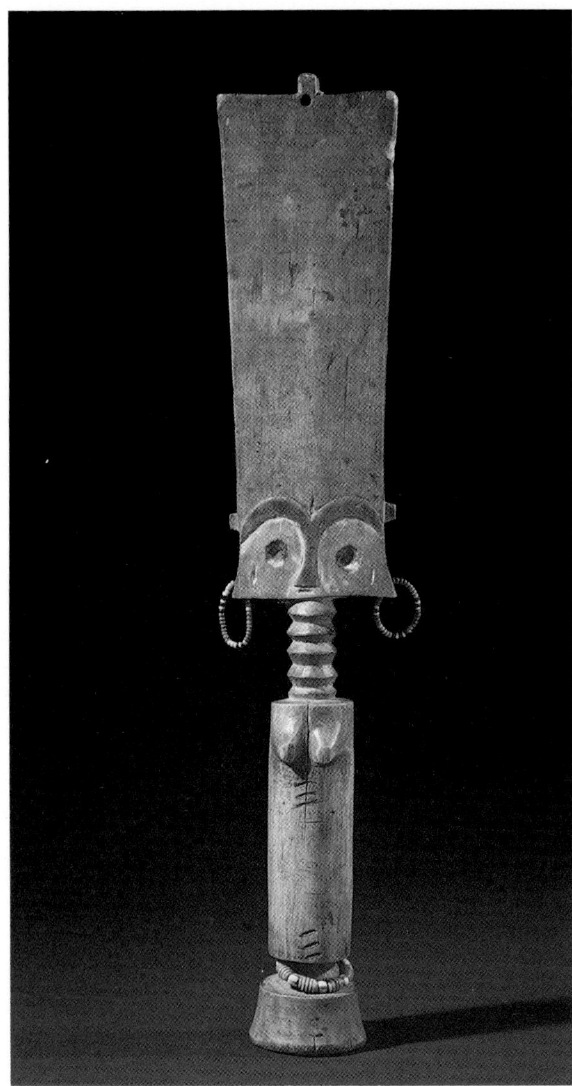
125

Asante and Fanti *akua ba* "Fertility Dolls" (125, 126)

The best-known wood sculptures of the Asante and Fanti, both Akan peoples, are small stylized figures dominated by large, flat heads. Among the Asante the head is given the form of a disk (see No.126); among the Fanti a rectangular form (see No.125). All the figures have a long ringed neck. Older examples have neither arms nor legs—only since the turn of the century have artists rendered the figures with limbs, often merely suggested though sometimes naturally formed.

Information about the function of these figures is contradictory. According to several reports, especially those who are barren or pregnant, carry them like dolls. They are said to secure the birth of many children and, moreover, to promote the birth of a child with well-shaped head and long neck with rings of fat signifying health and prosperity — a combination that produces the Asante ideal of beauty. (In order to promote this ideal the head of the newborn is assiduously shaped with hot cloths). The dolls acquire their power from the deity to which they are dedicated, and after a child's birth they are placed at the shrine of this god.

According to other information the dolls are not used by married women but by girls, and serve as toys or as a means of learning the duties of motherhood. The differing testimonies neither exclude one another nor are they entirely satisfactory. There is no explanation, for instance, of why the dolls are predominately female. Other, purely hypothetical, interpretations suggest, for instance, a comparison with the ancient Egyptian and Coptic *ankh,* a symbol of life.

Lit.: B. Benzing 1970, pp. 75-77; H. M. Cole, H. D. Ross 1977, pp.103–105; R. S. Rattray 1927, pp.54, 281; L. Segy 1963, pp.853, 859–866.

125 Doll (*akua ba*), wood, beads.
Ghana, Fanti.

The rectangular head of this piece has hollowed eye sockets and mouth, while eyebrows and nose are swooping fire-blackened arches that stand out against the light ground color. The back of the head is dec-

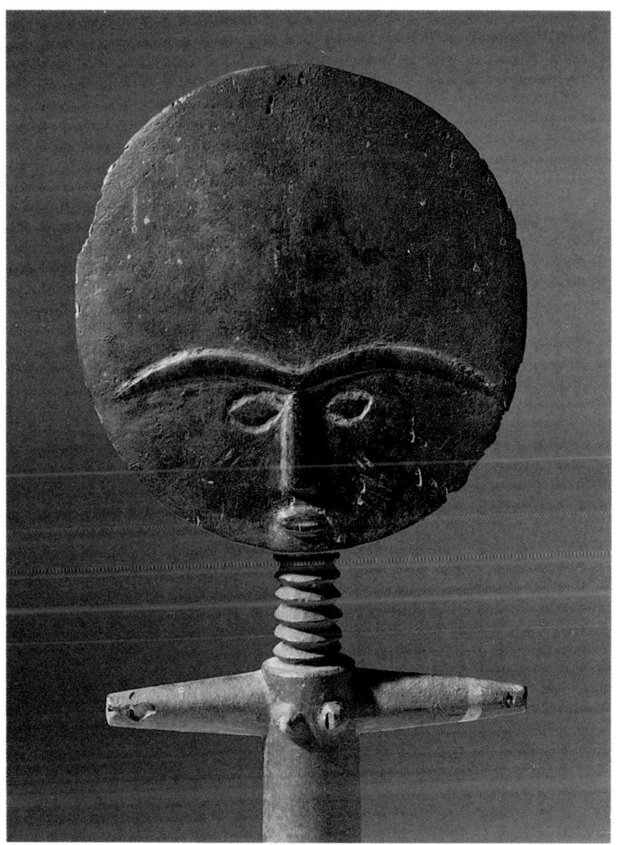

126

orated with geometric patterns divided into panels. Small holes have been drilled in the upper edge of the head to accomodate tufts of hair now missing. The survival of the dainty beaded earrings indicate how lovingly the doll was treated.

Height 27.5 cm. I1318
Acquisition date unknown

126 Doll (*akua ba*), wood.
Ghana, Asante.

On the disk-shape head of this doll the eye outlines are incised and traced with chalk. Eyebrows, nose, and mouth are raised above the plane of the face,

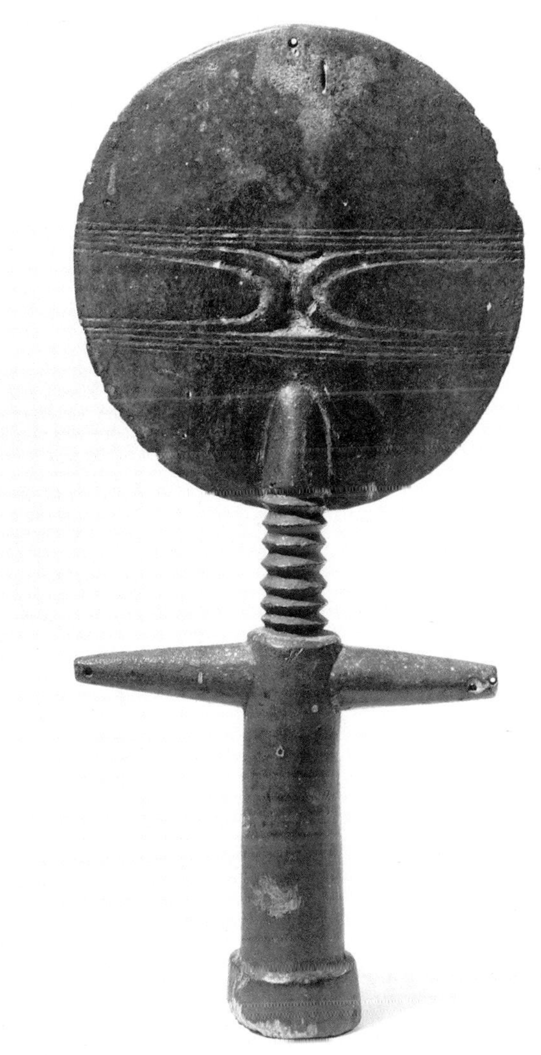

126

and the back of the head is adorned with incised lines filled with chalk (to ward off evil).

Height 29.5 cm. 82-301 620
Acquired from W. Ketterer 1982 (Former collection K. F. Schadler)

Yoruba Art and Culture

The German researcher Frobenius was the first European to identify the Yoruba as the bearers of an ancient high culture. The Yoruba, whose population of about fifteen million makes them one of the largest African ethnic groups south of the Sahara, exhibit an imposing richness of ideas and forms in their traditional culture. In many of its manifestations—mythology, poetry, symbolism—their culture is marked by a high degree of organization.

In precolonial times the Yoruba were already subdivided into numerous small states. The widely respected religious authority of the sacred city of Ile-Ife created a common spiritual bond and a consciousness of Yoruba solidarity, although the individual kingdoms were politically independent. As in other sacred kingdoms of West Africa, each of the old Yoruba towns was the seat of a ruler who also performed priestly functions. The ruler's most important religious function was to maintain the cults of local tutelary gods.

A striking feature of Yoruba religion is the existence of a hierarchically ordered pantheon. In spite of considerable differences between various regions and even between individuals, the basic structure can be recognized everywhere—pronounced in some places, barely recognizable in others. After the high god come sixteen principal deities, each with power over a distinct domain such as heaven, earth, thunderstorms, agriculture, metal forging, war, and so on.

Some sources maintain that the sixteen gods are part of the *orisha* system of deities, but it is more generally believed that only the divinities of the stage below belong in this category. Some reports state that the number of *orisha* is unknown, others that there are 401 such deities, corresponding to the number of old Yoruba clans, each of which derives from one *orisha*. Presumably the lesser deities were originally ancestral spirits—mountain, river, tree spirits, and so forth—and were only secondarily incorporated into the system of Yoruba theology.

Many works of Yoruba art relate to the *orisha* cult, and without a thorough knowledge of the myths about these lesser deities, many sculptures would remain unintelligible to us. The painting of sculptures, too, rare in other parts of Africa, may be associated with color symbolism rooted in mythology. Masks serve religious purposes, but the widespread mask cult societies (Egungun, Epa, Gelede) are principally concerned with celebrating outstanding ancestors, historical heroes, and socially significant persons. Many ancient ideas and rites have been retained within these masking systems of worship that are in considerable contrast to *orisha* worship. The Yoruba also make entirely nonreligious items for domestic use which depict themes from everyday life.

Since so little historical data is available to the student of African art, Yoruba sculpture offers a rare opportunity to investigate a particularly rich artistic tradition over time. Human representations including those in the work of living artists follow distinct formulas, for instance the body proportions that enlarge the head up to one third of the total body height in symmetrical and static compositions. These stylistic principles can be seen in the terra-cotta figures of Ife (1000-1200 A.D.) and in the sculptures of the Nok culture of Nigeria (400 B.C. to 300 A.D.).

In contrast to the predominantly anonymous art of most African provinces, a number of outstanding Yoruba artists have been identified in the last few decades. An analysis of their work shows clearly how new elements are fused with faithfully retained traditions.

Lit.: A. B. Ellis 1894, pp.85–89; E. Eyo 1977, pp.23, 25; C. D. Forde 1962, p.29f.; L. Frobenius 1926, pp.68–89, 119–196; S. Johnson 1921, pp.26–29, 244–246; F. Willet 1967, pp.119–121, 183–201.

127,128 Ritual staff (*opa orisha Oko*), iron, wood, and sheath, (*ewu orisha Oko*) beaded leather. Nigeria, Yoruba.

This solid iron staff is forged in two parts and variously subdivided; the two ends fit into sockets in the central wooden piece and are secured with nails. Along with relatively simple examples like this one, there exist finely executed staffs richly adorned with engraved designs. Characteristic of all such staffs is the square middle section with chiseled pattern consisting of a cross and four marks.

These staffs are sacred symbols of the deity (*orisha*) Oko, whose cult center and pilgrimage place is the village of Irawo in the northwest Oyo Province. Irawo smiths produce the cult staffs from hoe blades taken there by both male and female devotees of Oko. Upon arriving home, the pilgrims keep the staffs in their dwellings, standing upright against the wall. Because the staff must not touch the ground it is placed in a sheath of cloth or leather covered with beads and small crownlike cap is placed upon the top.

Information about the nature of Orisha Oko and the origin of the iron staff varies. According to some tales, Oko was a very old man who presented his elect with rich yam harvests but was himself so weak that he could not walk without the help of a staff. At his death his corpse miraculously disappeared and his staff was preserved as a relic. This cult legend associates the deity with the fertility of yam plantations, which produce the staple food of the Yoruba, This version is supported by cult practices; the cult staff is made from hoe blades, and at the yam harvest first-fruit sacrifices are made to Orisha Oko on the cult staff.

In other versions Oko is portrayed as a childless young woman condemned to death on the strength of false evidence. After her innocence was proven by ordeal she had a cult staff forged and gave birth to children. This tradition associates Oko with jurisprudence and the granting of children to her devotees. A further aspect of the deity is her link with

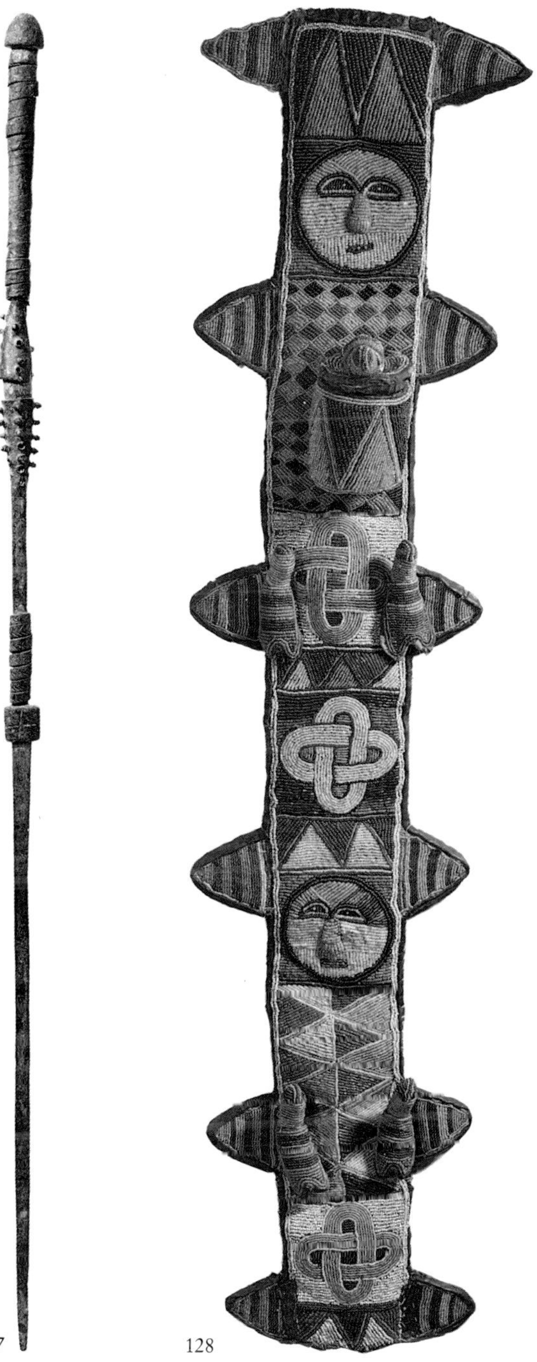

127

128

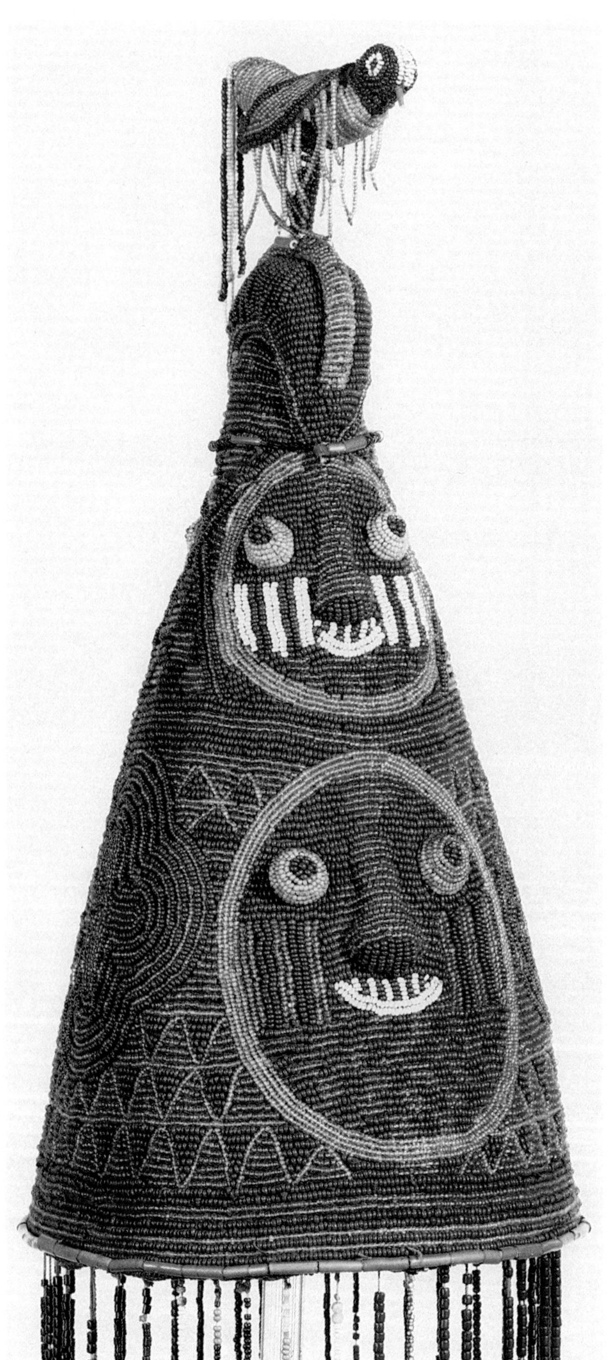

129

royalty and its symbolism. The crown and the beaded designs on the leather sheath recall those found on objects used by royal persons (see No. 129).

The multiple associations relating to Orisha Oko may have originated in several independent traditions preserved in myths and customs that were gradually combined into a common tradition.

Length of staff 124 cm. 81-301 515a,b Length of sheath 118 cm.

Acquired from G. and M. Stoll 1981

Lit.: W. Fagg & J. Pemberton 3rd 1980, pp.16–23; S. Farrow 1926, p.3f; L. Frobenius 1926, pp.146–156; S. Johnson 1921, 37f.; G. J. A. Oyo 1966, p.169; J. Picton in S. M. Vogel 1981, p.96; R. F. Thompson 1971b, Ch. 10/1-5.

129 Crown *(ade),* basketry, cotton cloth, beads. Nigeria, Yoruba, Idowa (?), Ijebu Province (see color plate p.64)

The wearing of beaded ornaments was originally a privilege reserved for kings, certain priests and priestesses, and specialists in medicinal herbs and divination. Beaded headdresses in the shape of a fillet or a flat cap served as royal insignia in Ile-Ife in the twelfth and thirteenth centuries (the cap form was also adopted by the Obas of Benin). The cone-shaped crown did not appear until the eighteenth and nineteenth centuries. The high conical crown with its beaded fringe, frontal faces, and bird figures is worn only by a limited number of kings who can trace their descent to Oduduwa, the first king at Ile-Ife and founder of the Yoruba people. Other petty rulers wear simpler crowns.

The bead industry thrived in the sacred city of Ile-Ife as early as the tenth to fourteenth century and later in several Yoruba towns. Beads of red stone such as carnelian and jasper and later of imported coral were shaped by specialized craftsmen. Recently, imported glass beads have been used extensively.

Renowned for its carvers, the Adeshina family in Efon Alaye, Ekiti Province, is equally famous for its beadwork, especially the making of crowns. Over the years, Efon Alaye has been one of the great Yoruba wood carving centers (see Nos. 130 and 136).

The features of this crown refer to the institution of kingship. The beaded fringe hides the wearer's face, for it would be dangerous for bystanders to see the ruler's face during festivals, the face of one in whom supernatural powers are at work. The frontal faces indicate the presence of the first king, Oduduwa, who was sent from heaven and is said to have introduced the beaded crown as a royal insignia and to have presented each of his sixteen sons with one. The doubling of the faces expresses the omniscience of the ruler, one who can look into the past and the future as well as the omnipotence of one who possesses both terrestrial and heavenly supremacy. The bird on the peak of the crown may symbolize his link with heaven. The cross and zigzag (sign of lightning) also represent supernatural power. Red and white are associated with Shango, the god of thunder, and Obatala, the god of creation, respectively, and blue with Oshun, the god of medicinal waters.

Before the crown is used, magical substances are placed in its tip to protect the king's head as carrier of his fate. The Yoruba believe that divine presence is concentrated in the tip of the crown and in the heads of certain dignitaries (including the royal messenger, *ilari*, see Nos. 151 and 152) and even in the gables of houses.

Height 45 cm. 7-9-1
Acquired from J. Konietzko 1967

Lit.: M. T. Drewal 1977, pp.43,49; W. Fagg & J. Pemberton 3rd 1980, pp.10f.,12,40,50, O. Ogunba 1964, pp.249-261; R. F. Thompson in D. Fraser & H. M. Cole 1972, pp.227-256.

Epa Helmet Masks (130,131)

At different times, from different directions, strong cultural influences were felt by the northeastern Yoruba province and were reflected in their ceremonies. The Epa festival, which takes place every two years,

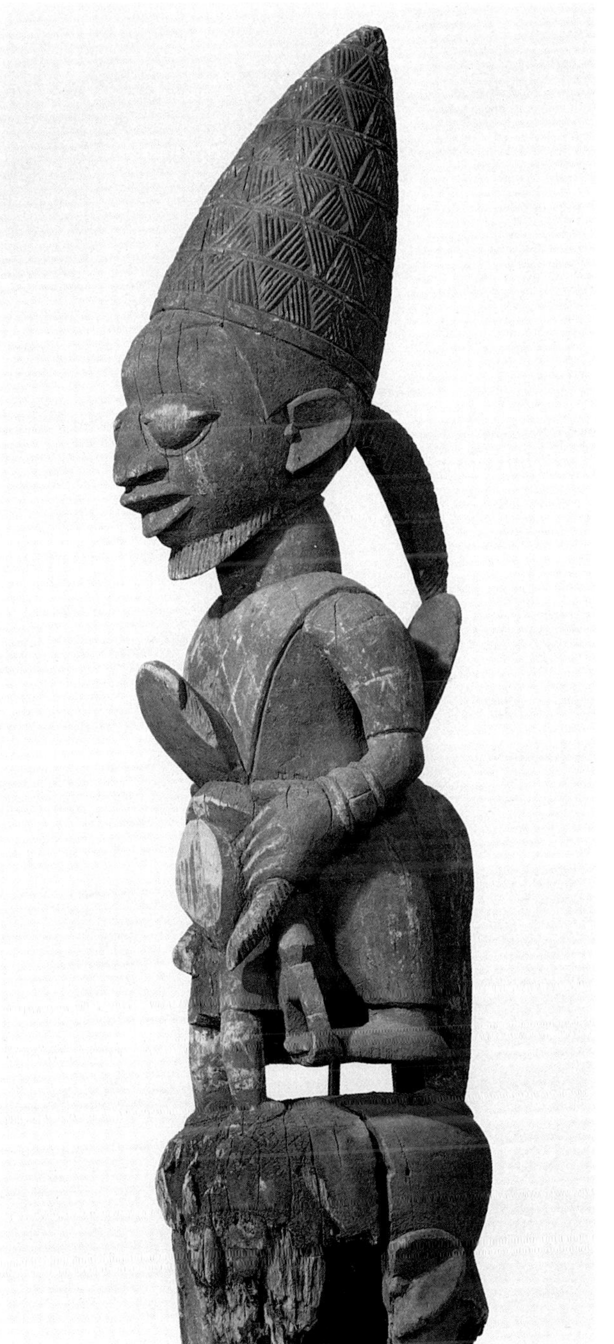

130

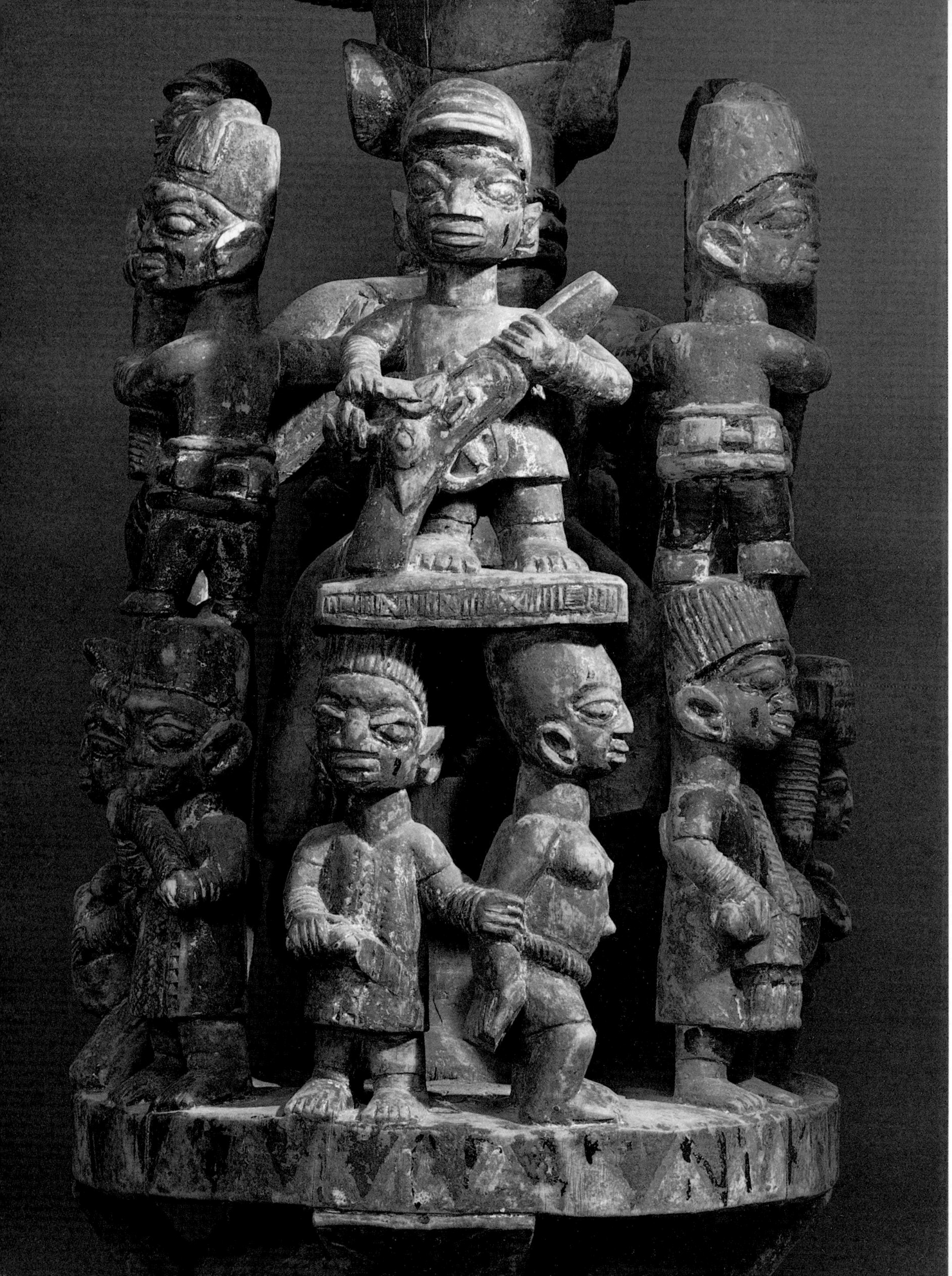

is a kind of agricultural festival with a military aspect in which defensive powers are mobilized against destructive magic. Even today, tests of strength between young men take place during this celebration as they perform dances and leaps wearing masks that weigh more than twenty kilos.

The grotesque stereotyped faces of the helmet masks recall the late period wood and cast brass heads of the royal ancestors of neighboring Benin (see Nos. 161-63 and No. 167), just as the Epa cult corresponds to the Ekpo cult of Benin. The superstructures of the masks, however, display the typically realistic round Yoruba style and are often shaped in an individualistic manner. The masks No. 130 and 131 demonstrate how very differently the same subject has been handled by two famous Yoruba artists.

Lit.: J. D. Clarke 1944, 1ff., H. J. Drewal 1980, p.88f.; W. Fagg 1961, cat.no.117; W. Fagg & J. Pemberton 3rd. 1982, pp.20-22, 41f., 72, 132, 200; R. F. Thompson 1971b, Ch.9/1-6; pp.102-4, 191-8; M. Vander Heyden 1977, pp. 14-21.

130 Helmet mask *(aguru epa)*, wood, paint. Nigeria, Yoruba, Efon Alaye in Ekiti. (see color plate p.65)

This mask, carved around 1910, is the work of the well-known sculptor Agbonbiofe (d.1945) or one of his pupils from the Adeshina family of carvers in Efon Alaye. According to Drewal, the chief characteristics of Adeshina family carvings are massivity; a trend toward cubistic rendering of chest, torso, robes, and lower extremities, the short legs and flat feet in particular; and clear separation of elements—for example, the sharp boundaries between head and neck or face and coiffure

A mounted former ruler or war hero is the subject of this mask—a man who victoriously repulsed an attack on the town of Efon Alaye in 1880. Heroism is expressed in the equestrian pose and in the extreme proportions (one to one) of body to head. No superfluities distract from the dominance of the figure. The large, beautifully shaped hands are par-

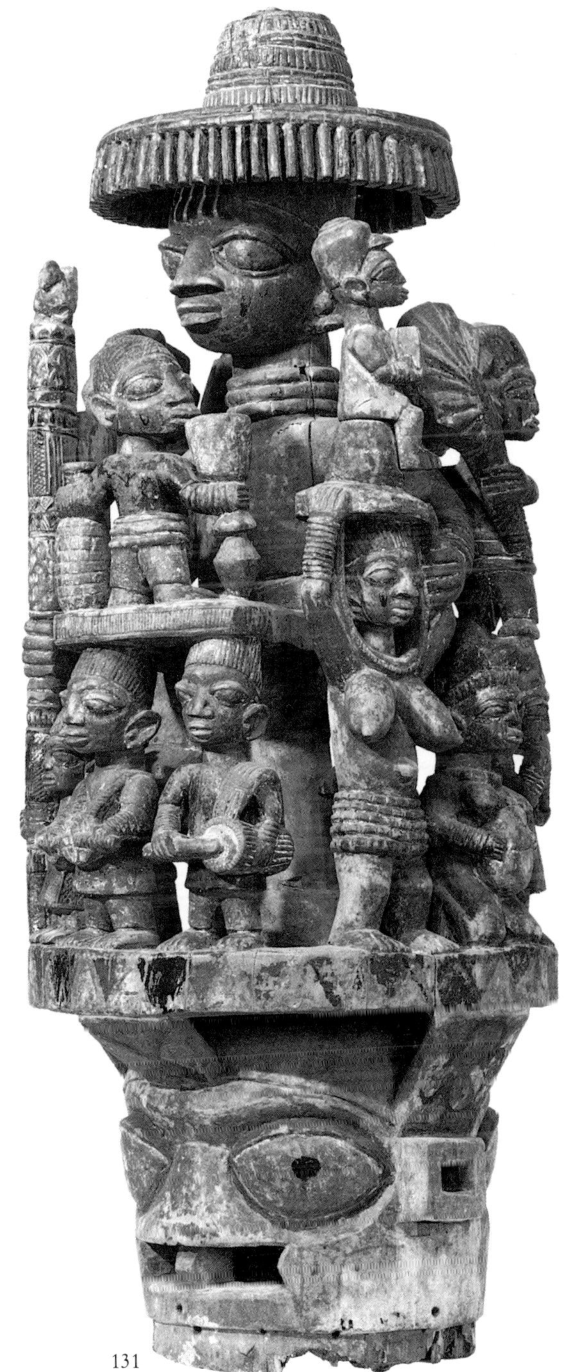
131

ticularly noteworthy, and the hairstyle may be that of the hunter warrior. (The horse's head is missing.)

Height 120 cm. 59-1-1
Acquired from L. Bretschneider 1959

Lit.: L. K. Carroll 1967, p.84f.; H. J. Drewal 1980, p.88f.

131 Helmet mask *(aguru epa),* wood, paint. Nigeria, Yoruba, Osi, Ekiti Province.

The lower part of this sculpture, that is, the actual mask, is janus-faced and provided with eyeslits on one side. During performances the helmet mask is supported by poles inserted in lateral openings, held by the dancer's companions.

The superstructure, unlike the previous one, No. 130, depicts a scene composed of numerous figures: a king surrounded by family members and courtiers. Although the king would normally be shown riding a horse, here, oddly enough, he is seated astride a plank and is holding a ceremonial staff decorated with the figure of a bird.

To his left one of his wives wearing ceremonial ornaments holds over her head her son, a fully clothed mission pupil with a book in his hand. The

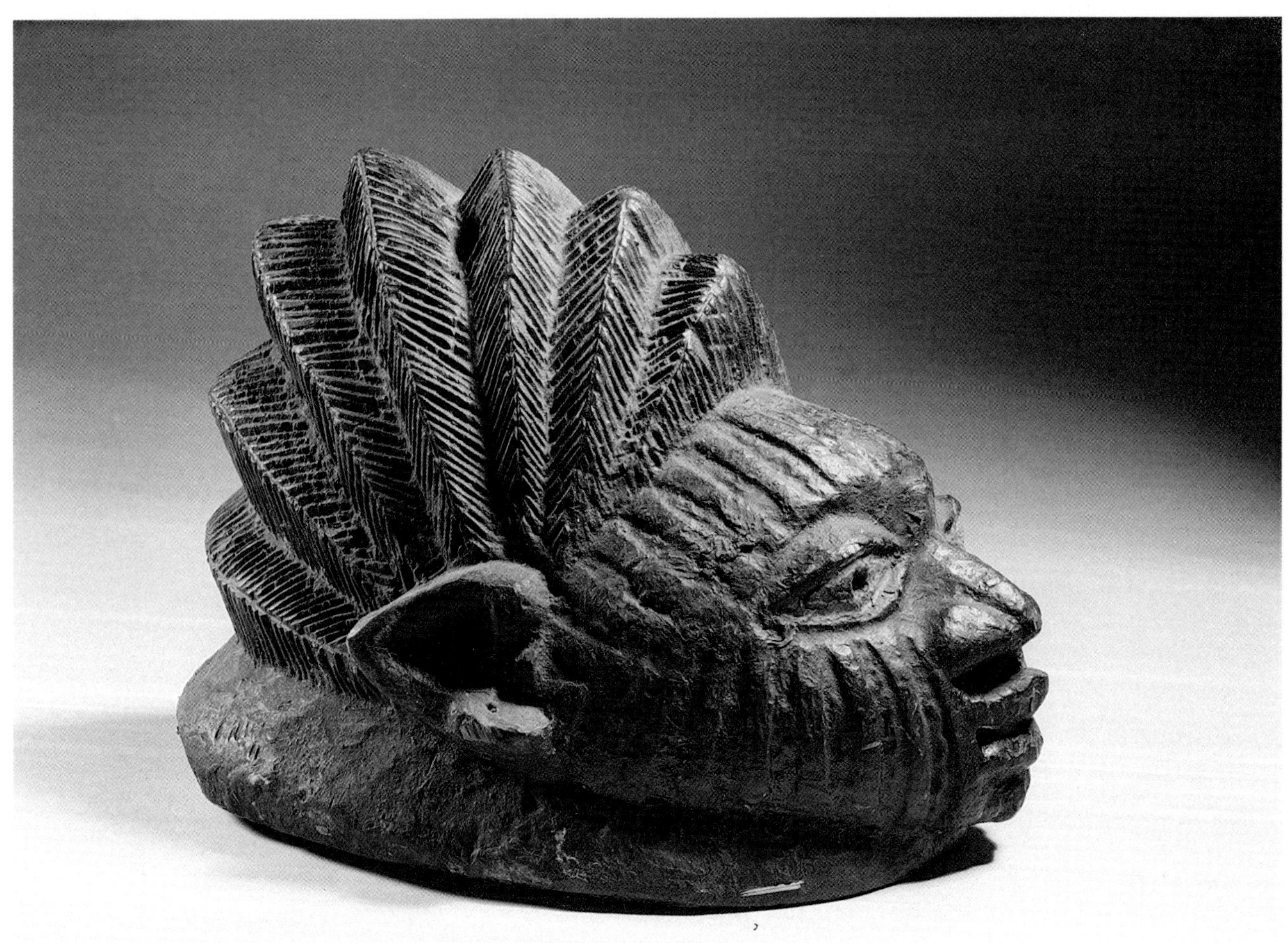

132

remaining figures are shown partly in traditional, partly in modern clothing and coiffure, and some hold weapons. Among the figures are three drummers, a kneeling priestess with divination vessel, two servants with fans, and an armed soldier leading away a prisoner.

The mask was carved about 1930 by the artist Areogun (1880-1954) who lived in Osi, Ekiti Province. Areogun invented special tools, which he had made by a smith, but, like other artists, he polished his masks with abrasive leaves, painted them with a solution of red ochre and waterproofed them with the milky sap of a cactus. Traces of oil paint applied by a later owner are still visible on this example.

Height 130 cm. 5-19-1
Acquired from G. and M. Stoll 1975

Lit.: L. K. Carroll 1967, p.84f.

The Egungun Cult

The Egungun cult is the most extensive Yoruba association inside as well as outside their borders. It fosters in particular the ancestor cult and worship of the local *orishas*. At funerals of cult members, mask wearers, representing the dead, work themselves into a trance state and transmit messages from the ancestors to the living.

Lit.: H. J. Drewal 1978, 18f.; W. Fagg 1968, No.111; G. J. A. Ojo 1966, p.17f.

132 Mask *(ere Egungun)*, wood.
Nigeria, Yoruba.

This represents a special style of Egungun mask found in the area between Ibadan and Ife. Notched carving in parallel grooves and zigzag ornaments cover the whole of the darkly stained surface.

Height 20 cm., width 21 cm. 6-3-23
Acquired from O. W. Oldman 1926

Lit.: H. J. Drewal 1980, p.84.

The Gelede Society (132,133)

Gelede cult associations distributed throughout the western Yoruba provinces, hold public performances during the cultivation of the fields and at the funerals of deceased members. The supernatural powers ascribed to the society are also invoked during crises, such as natural catastrophes. Gelede activities are based upon the special relationship between the society and the mother goddess Iya Nla (also called Yewajobi or Yemoja). This primordial mother, who is mentioned in the Odu texts of Ifa divination (see p.129f.), obtained mystical powers *(aje, ase)* from the creator god, Olodumare. Since that time all women have special powers, though usually only in latent form. The Gelede rituals are thus directed not only to Iya Nla and certain *orisha* closely associated with her, but also to living and dead women, especially in their role as mothers. The *ase* power of women is ambivalent. It can act destructively, causing trouble, but can also act creatively, reducing social tension and chanelling useful knowledge or capabilities. Gelede's ritual activities aim at orienting this power in a direction favorable to society in general.

Most Gelede masks represent women; their wearers—all of them men—wear female apparel and often body masks with artificial breasts. Masks are worn on top of the head and the dancer's face is covered by a pierced cloth or net. Performances mirror the hierarchy of the cult: men of lower rank dance in the afternoon and the whole event has the character of a popular festival; the higher ranking members make their appearance at night wearing the more important masks.

Lit.: U. Beier 1958, pp.5-18; H. J. Drewal 1974a, p.26, 58f.; B. Lawal 1978, pp.65-70; R.F. Thompson 1971b, Ch.14/1-2.

133 Mask *(ere Gelede)*, wood, paint. Nigeria, Yoruba, Badagry (?).

One of the earliest acquisitions in the African collection, this mask has been in the museum since 1888, when it was acquired in Lagos along with two similar masks. None of the three shows traces of use. The gaudy imported European oil paints (reddish brown, red, blue, and white) remind us that age does not presuppose quality.

Apart from its coloring, this mask is a typical traditional cult mask produced for the Gelede society (see No. 134). The face is compressed and drawn forward, eyes are rimmed, nose and mouth are equally broad, upturned lips are slightly parted, and forehead and cheeks show ornamental scarifications. Distinguishing features of this mask are the slight asymmetry of the face and the ornamental hair combs. According to a letter from Frobenius, dated 23 March 1918, "this kind of mask was made in the territory of French Dahomey (Republic of Benin), particularly at Badagry; at some time this was taken to Lagos to be sold there".

Height 22 cm., width 33 cm. 88.160
Acquired from F. A. Schran 1888

Lit.: H. J. Drewal 1974b, pp. 8-12; W. Fagg 1968, Illus. 109/110; R. F. Thompson 1971b, Ch. 14/1-7.

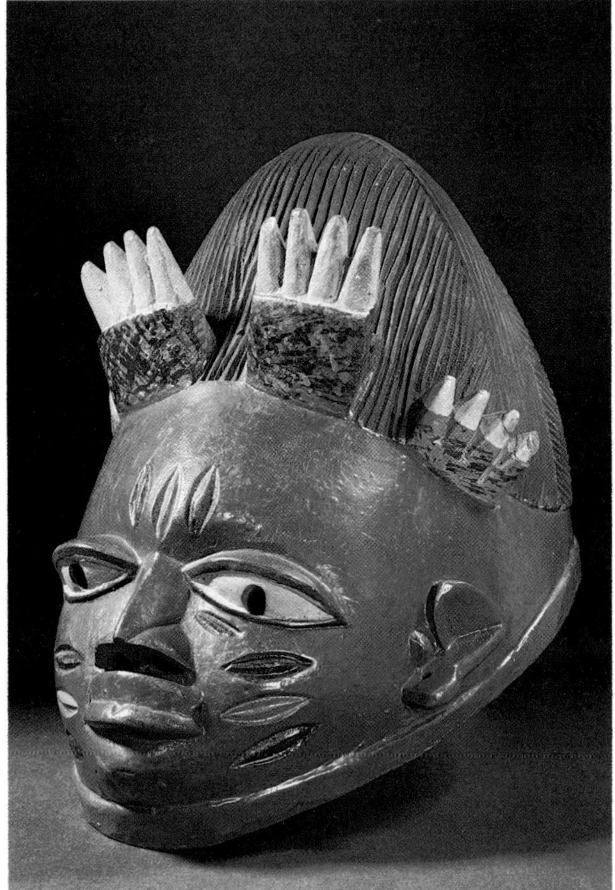

133

134 Mask *(ere Gelede)*, wood, paint. Republic of Benin, Yoruba.

This mask resembles No. 133, but is more expressive and is painted with the traditional Yoruba colors of white, blue, and black. Masks with representations of snakes occur mainly in the border area between Nigeria and the Republic of Benin, where the snake cult of the neighboring Fon, who dwell in the coastal area near Abomey, exercises a strong influence.

Height 33 cm., width 23 cm. 39-1-5
Acquired from E. Heinrich 1939

Lit.: W. Fagg 1968, Illus. 109.

135 Mask, brass. Yoruba caster from Nigeria, now living in Togo.

The itinerant craftsman Ali Amonikoyi, from a clan of brass casters in Ilorin, made this mask. From 1907 to 1909 Amonikoyi lived in Kete Kratchi, the former German government station in Togo, producing ornaments for the inhabitants of the area. He also made figural brass casts on commission from and

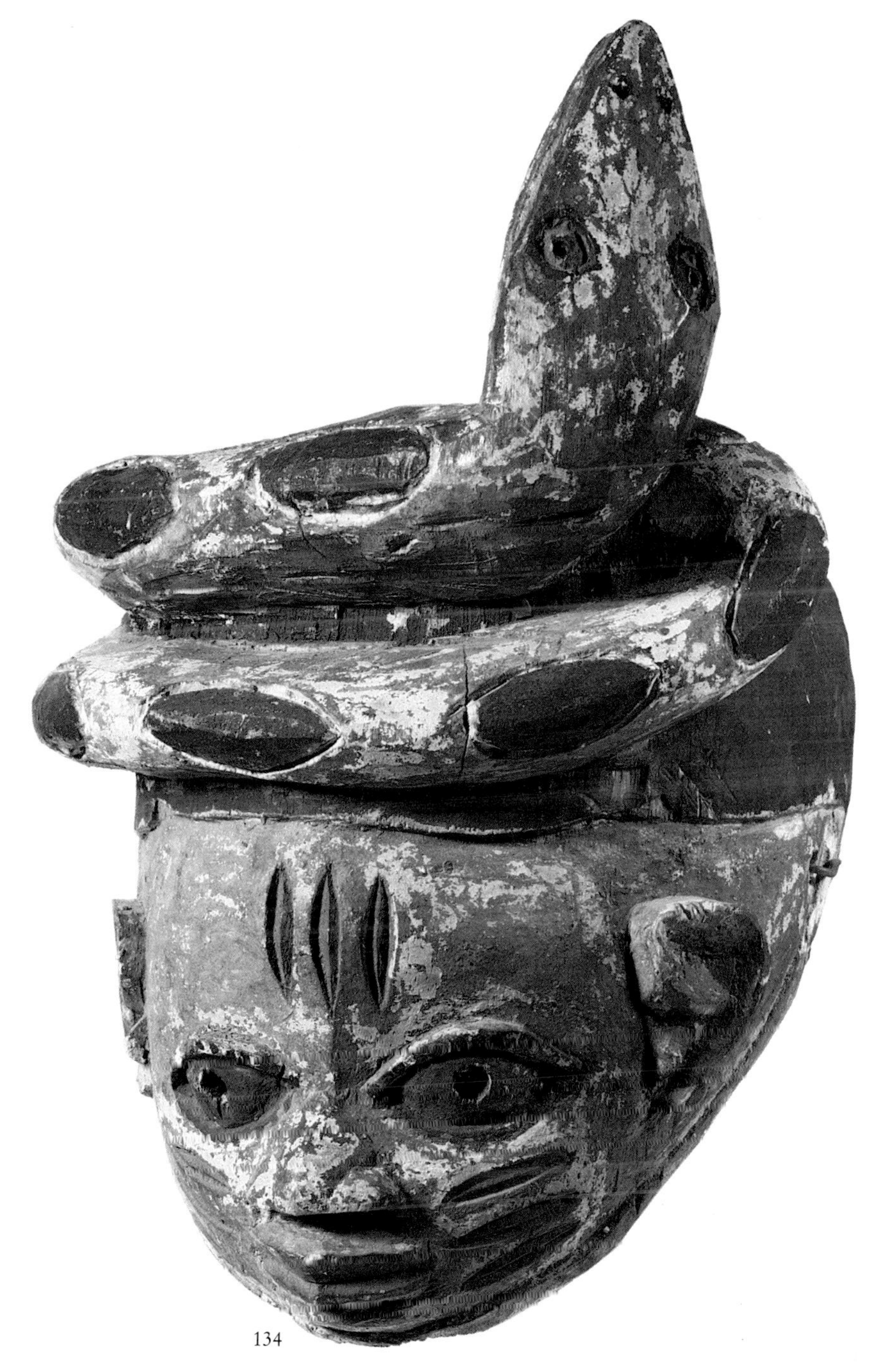

134

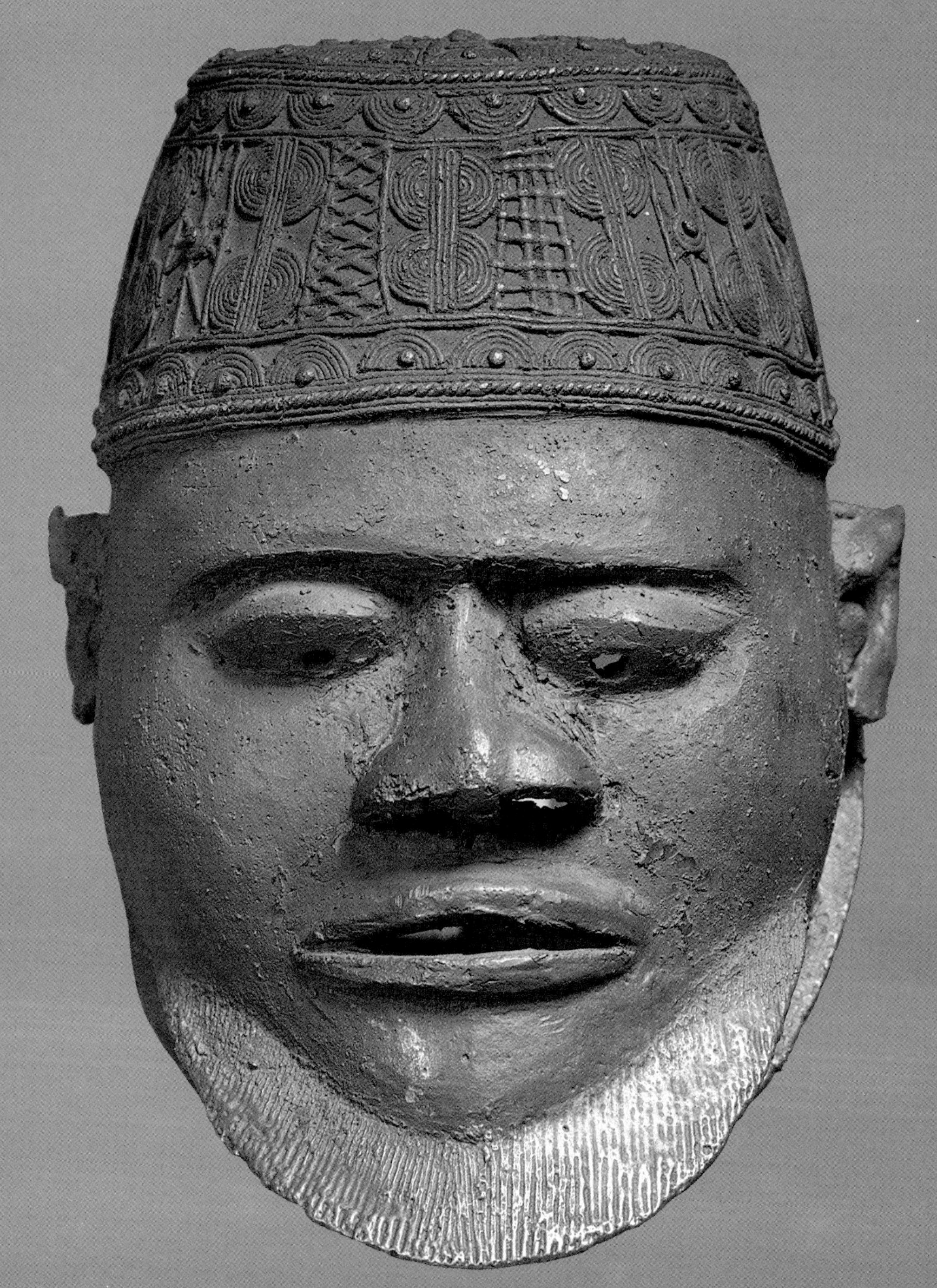

even with specifications provided by Mischlich, chief official of the station and an ethnographical researcher. It is not known just why Mischlich promoted this gifted artist. His aim does not seem to have been financial gain but unfortunately he propogated incorrect information concerning the alleged traditional functions of the objects he encouraged Amonikoyi to produce. The brass masks, for instance, he claimed were worn as face masks and/or placed into or on top of the graves of chiefs. Several of Amonikoyi's works recall Benin objects; Drost observes that Mischlich stimulated Amoniloyi's imagination, perhaps by telling him about Benin art (which fascinated experts in those years), or by showing him pictures. In spite of this, Amonikoyi's works are unique artistic creations neither imitative nor dependent upon the dictates of foreigners .

Apart from the examples published here these curious brass masks are represented in the Munich collection by others acquired, not by Mischlich but by Count Zech, in 1915. Judging from their style they must also be the work of Amonikoyi. All resemble the wooden masks of the Yoruba Gelede society. Most include a cap, characteristic of Islamized groups. A great number of Amonikoyi's works found their way into the museums of Stuttgart and Leipzig and, in smaller numbers into other German, Swiss, and British museums.

Height 33 cm., width 23 cm. 15-1-145
Acquired from J. Zech 1915

Lit.: D. Drost 1975, pp.41-44, 65-67; E. Fischer 1966, p 89.

135

136 Palace veranda pillar *(opo)*, wood, paint. Nigeria, Yoruba, Oke Igbira, Ekiti Province.

Artfully carved pillars often support the roofs bordering the courtyards of sacred buildings, royal palaces, and dwelling houses of priests or high dignitaries. We can distinguish two main types—those that consist of a single human figure (see No. 137), and those composed of several individual figures or groups of small figures standing one above the other, as in this example. Although variously expressed, royal power is the theme in both types of pillar. Here the importance of ruler and priests is shown by their size in relation to their accompanying warriors and dignitaries. Below, the king appears as war hero on horseback with his insignia: full beard, head covering, fly whisk, and spear. Above him is a high priest (or king in priestly role) with a rattle staff ornamented with the head of the god Eshu. The priest's beaded crown with four birds is a symbol of rank among less important rulers. The upper end of the post forms an unadorned cube, on which human faces alternate with birds. According to Thompson, these allude to conquered enemies, beheaded criminals, sorcerers, or witches. The latter are said to change into birds at night and tear the heads of the slain to pieces. Among the figures on the back of the richly carved pillar is a monkey nibbling on a maize cob, held to be the manifestation of certain departed spirits.

The paint colors—black, white, yellow, and reddish brown—have traditional symbolic significance: white, for instance, is the color of the god of heaven; black belongs to the trickster god Eshu-Elegba. Other details, such as the priest's rattle staff ornamented with Eshu's head, indicate that its owner belonged to the Eshu cult.

This post probably comes from the workshop of the famous carver Agunna (d.1930) in Oke Igbira and shows to perfection his ascetic style—the antithesis, as it were, of the full massive style of the

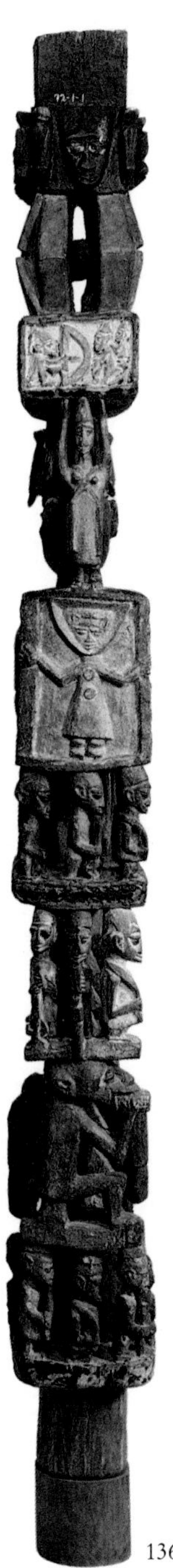
136

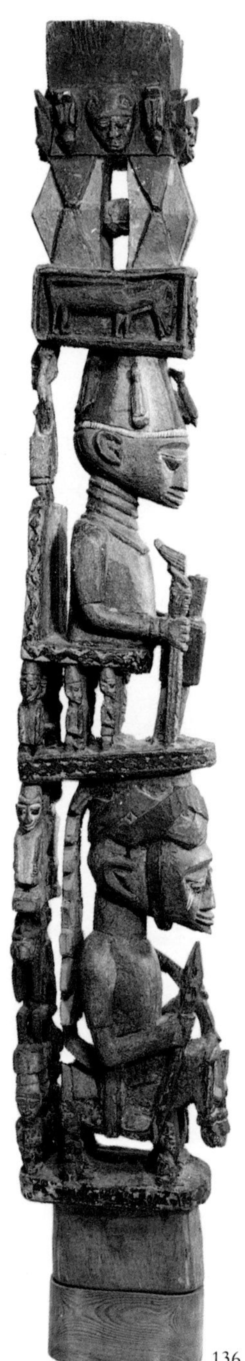
136

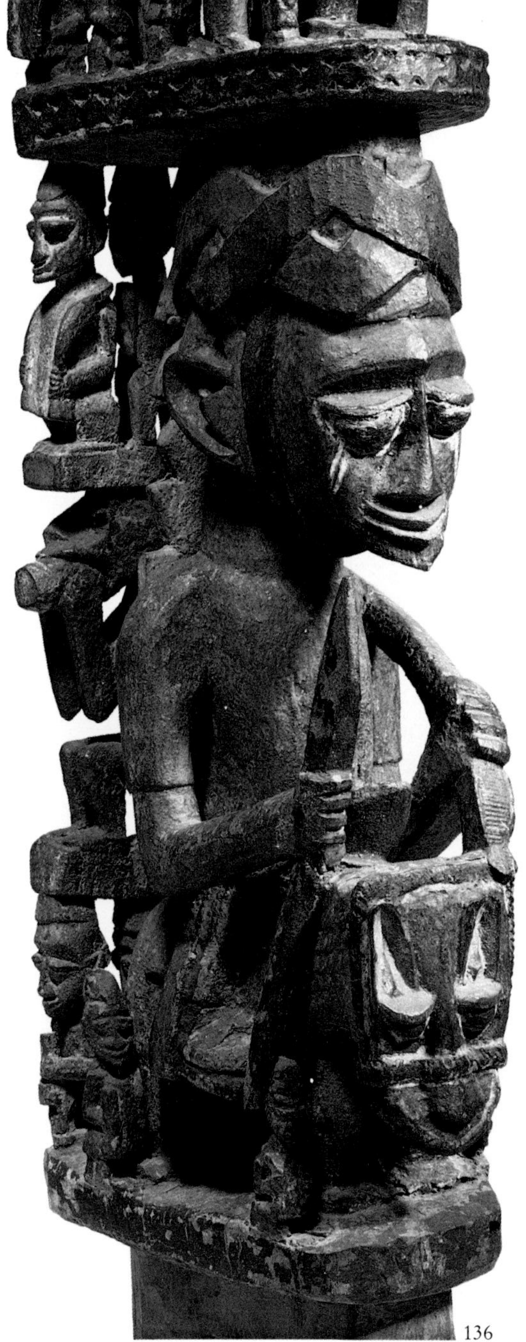
136

equally important Agbonbiofe (see No. 130). The rather awkward figure of the horse here seems incongruous when the quality of the sculpture as a whole is considered. But since horses are rare in the tropics, kept only in small numbers and almost exclusively for purposes of royal representation, the artist may have had little opportunity to study the animal in the flesh.

Height 182 cm. 72-1-1
Acquired from Rosen 1972 (in the Rosen family since 1920)

Lit.: W. Fagg & M. Plass 1966, p.93; G. J. A. Oyo 1966, p.167; R. F. Thompson in D. Fraser & H. M. Cole 1972, pp.243, 252.

137 Veranda pillar *(opo),* wood.
Nigeria, Yoruba, Efon Alaye.

In contrast to No. 136, this carved pillar features a single figure. She is a priestess of the thundergod, Shango, a fact indicated by the stole that is a part of her official dress. She is shown wearing a carefully worked shawl with seam, belt with fringe and ornament, and necklace with amulet. Stylistically, this piece belongs to the sculptures of the Adeshina family, but the proportions of head and body are more balanced than those of No. 130. The finely shaped feet are comparatively small, the hands are large and strong, and the lower arm wears a broad bracelet. Further characteristics include a high finely grooved coiffure, domed forehead, large eyes with half-closed lids, flat ears, finely shaped breasts, slightly protruding abdomen, and nose and mouth of equal width. The small roll between neck and head also appears in No. 130.

Height 120 cm. 57-9-1
Acquired from L. Bretschneider 1957

Lit.: W. Fagg 1961, Illus. No. 160.

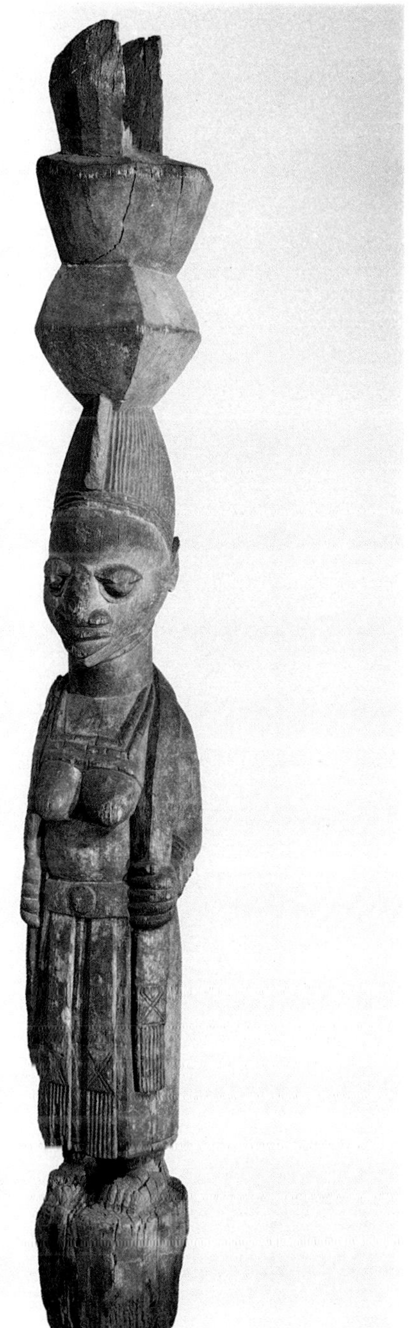

137

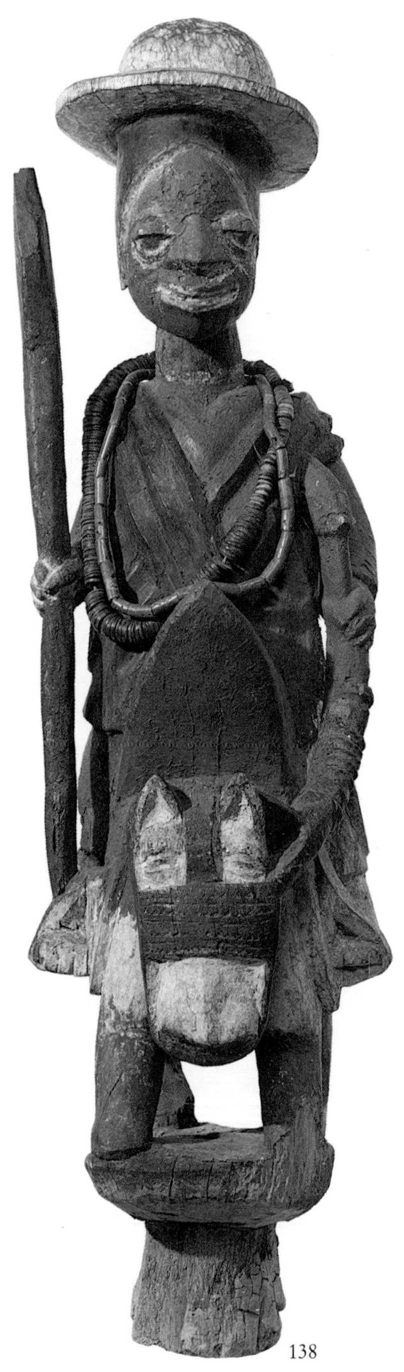
138

138 Figure of a horseman, wood, paint, stone beads.
Nigeria, Yoruba, Ekiti Province. (see color plate p.65)

A ruler or warrior chief with pith helmet rather than beaded crown, perhaps even Shango, the god of thunder and war, is represented here. Despite the nobility implied by his mount he appears not as an idealized potentate but pensive, even melancholy. The composition is highly idiosyncratic; asymmetry, rather than strict frontality, results from a minute turning of the upper body and head. The hands are very small, the eyelids lowered. The artist concentrated wholly on the human figure, so except for its saddle, the horse is rendered rather perfunctorily.

Height 131 cm. 76-2-1
Acquired from G. and M. Stoll 1976

139 Cult staff *(opa Osanyin* or *opa Erinle),* iron.
Nigeria, Yoruba, Oyo Province.

This type of wrought iron staff crowned with birds served as an emblem for herbalists—those healers or "medicine men" with a profound knowledge of medicinal plants. These staffs are also the symbol of the god of medicine, Osanyin, who is worshiped as the owner of curative plants. (Occasionally the staffs are associated with the river or hunting god, Erinle, Eyinle, or Enjille.) The staff's ornamental top shows a large central bird carrying two beings in human shape and surrounded by sixteen smaller birds. One of the many largely hypothetical interpretations of this rather frequent figure grouping alludes to the myth of creation. Fagg gives us the version in which a hen and her chicks scraped the bottom of the primordial ocean, and molded the earth. Thompson, however, proposes that the bird figures indicate those witches in bird shape who must be tamed by a greater power—that is, the large bird in the middle.

Height 74 cm. 73-3-3
Acquired from L. Bretschneider 1973

Lit.: H. J. Drewal 1980, p.34f.; A. B. Ellis 1894, p.79; W. Fagg 1968, Illus.138; L. Frobenius 1926, pp.109-111, 164f.; R. F. Thompson 1971b, Ch.11/1-3.

140 Top of a cult staff *(opa Oshun)*, iron.
Nigeria, Yoruba.

This comparatively recent small sculpture, (about1930), depicts an execution. In an animated scene a horseman, possibly the legendary war hero Orangun or Jagunjagun, raises his sword against a prisoner. The latter's arms are tied behind him with a rope originally attached to the bridle of the horse but now partly broken off.

Wrought iron staffs of this type are kept in the shrine of the river goddess, Oshun—hence the designation "Oshun's staff."

Height 62 cm. 59-1-2
Acquired from L. Bretschneider 1959

Lit.: R. F. Thompson in D. Fraser & H. M. Cole 1972, p.246.

141 Ritual staff, iron.
Nigeria, Yoruba, Efon Alaye.

This staff with two birds (herons?) in a nest probably belonged to an herbalist-healer and Ifa priest. According to Thompson, the small cones represent the leaves of a medicinal plant and are usually fitted with clappers that produce a rattling sound that drives away evil powers each time the staff is thrust into the earth. The staff normally stands in the personal shrine of an Ifa priest to guard him while he sleeps. It must remain upright, for its fall would mean the death of the priest; at its owner's death the staff is broken.

Height 55.5 cm. 70-2-1
Acquired from L. Bretschneider 1970

Lit.: W. Bascom 1969, p.84; R. F. Thompson 1971b, Ch. 11/1-3.

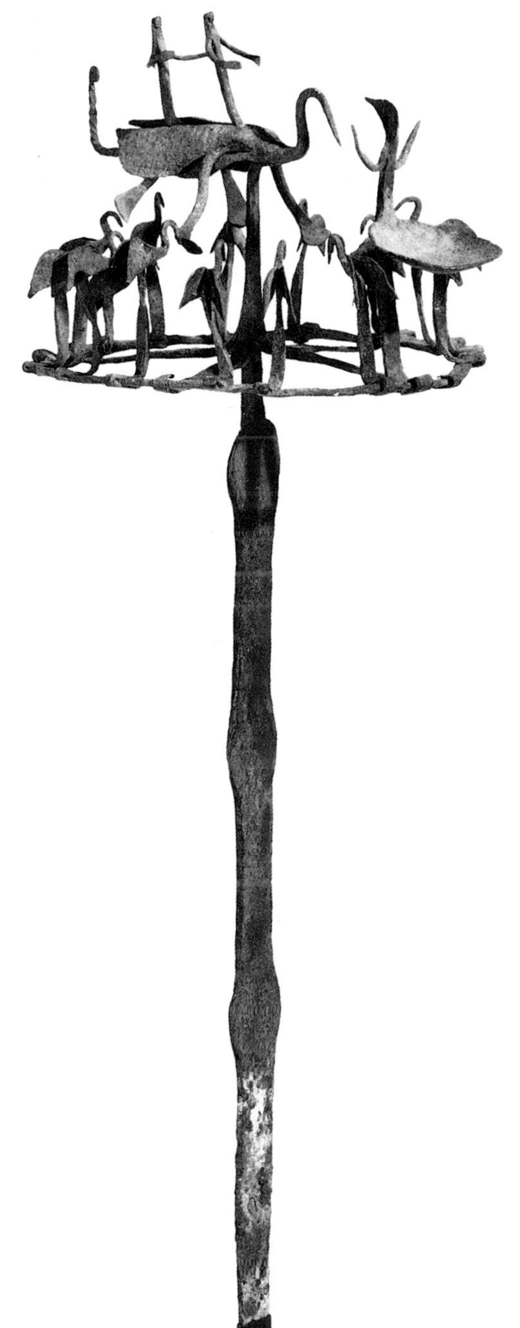

139

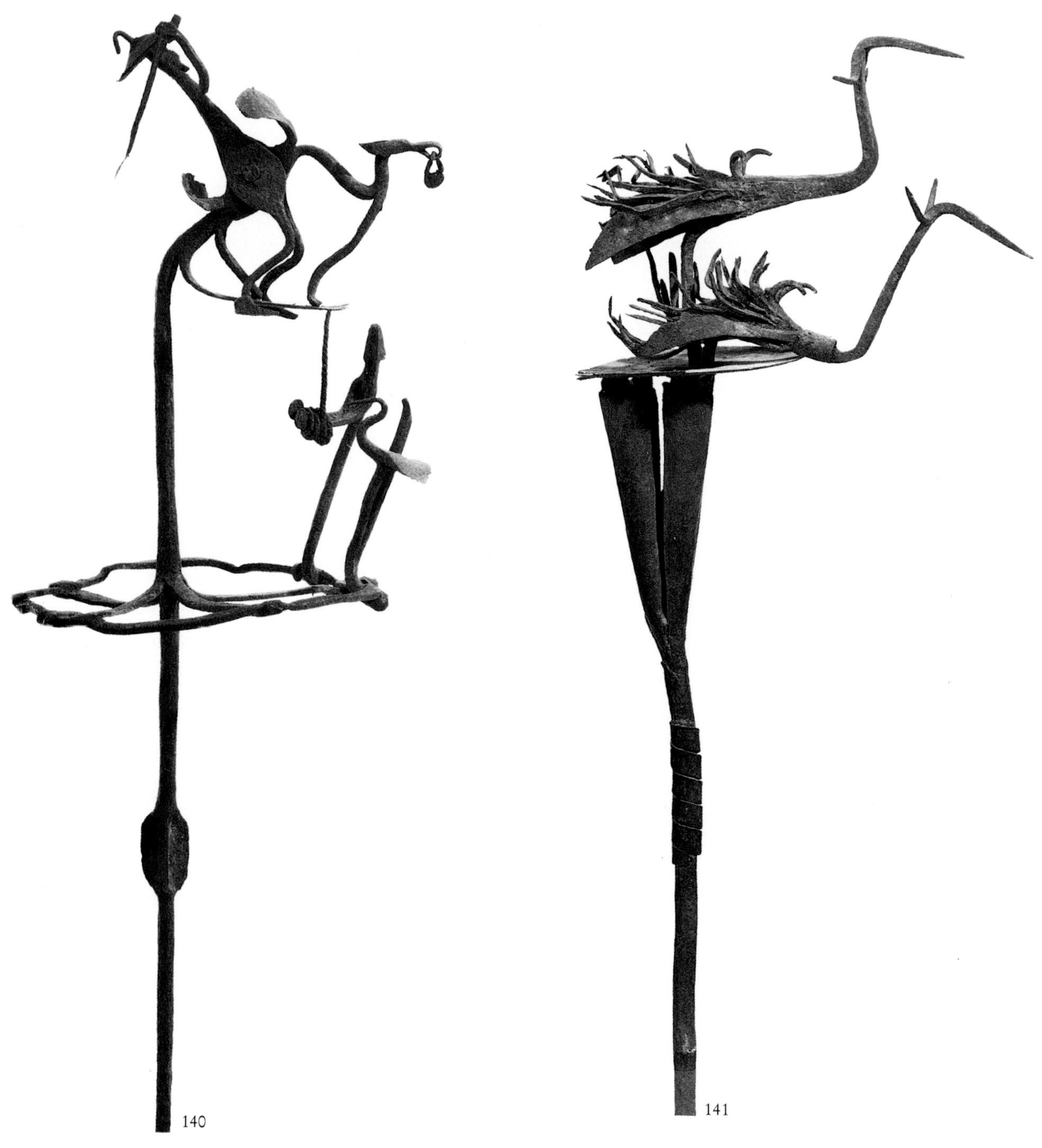

140

141

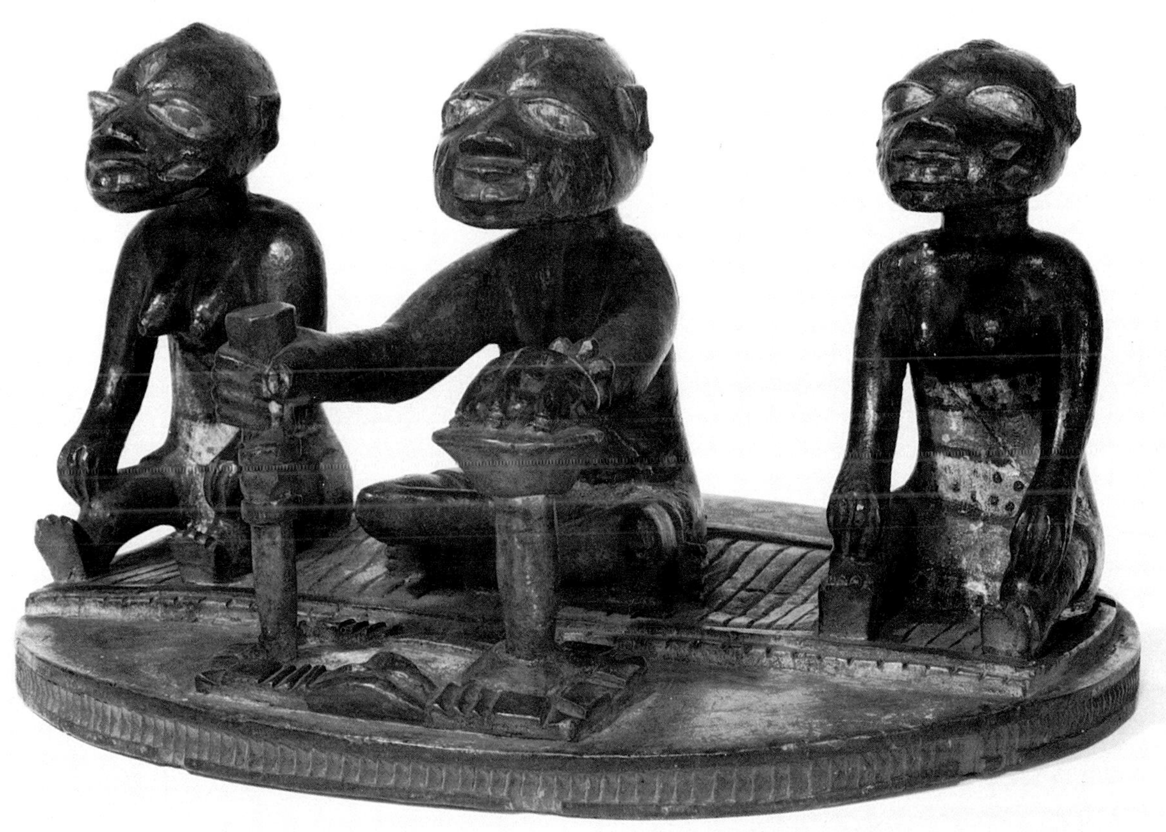

142

Ifa Divination (142–147)

The ancient process of Ifa is the most renowned divining method practiced in West Africa. It is used in much of southern Nigeria, throughout the Republic of Benin, and in Togo. Slaves of Yoruba origin even introduced it into Cuba and Brazil. Mankind is thought to have obtained it from Ifa, the god of wisdom, or from Eshu, the trickster god in the sacred Yoruba city of Ile-Ife.

Palm nuts are one of the most important instruments in Ifa consultation. Holding many nuts in his right hand, the Ifa priest (*babalawo*) attempts to grasp as many as possible with his left, leaving only one or two nuts. He may also throw them into the air with his right hand and try to catch them with his left. His divination is based on whether he catches an odd or an even number of nuts. With his fingers the priest then draws short vertical lines on the flour-strewn divination board before him (see Nos. 145 and 146). If only one nut remains in his right hand or if he has caught an odd number he draws two

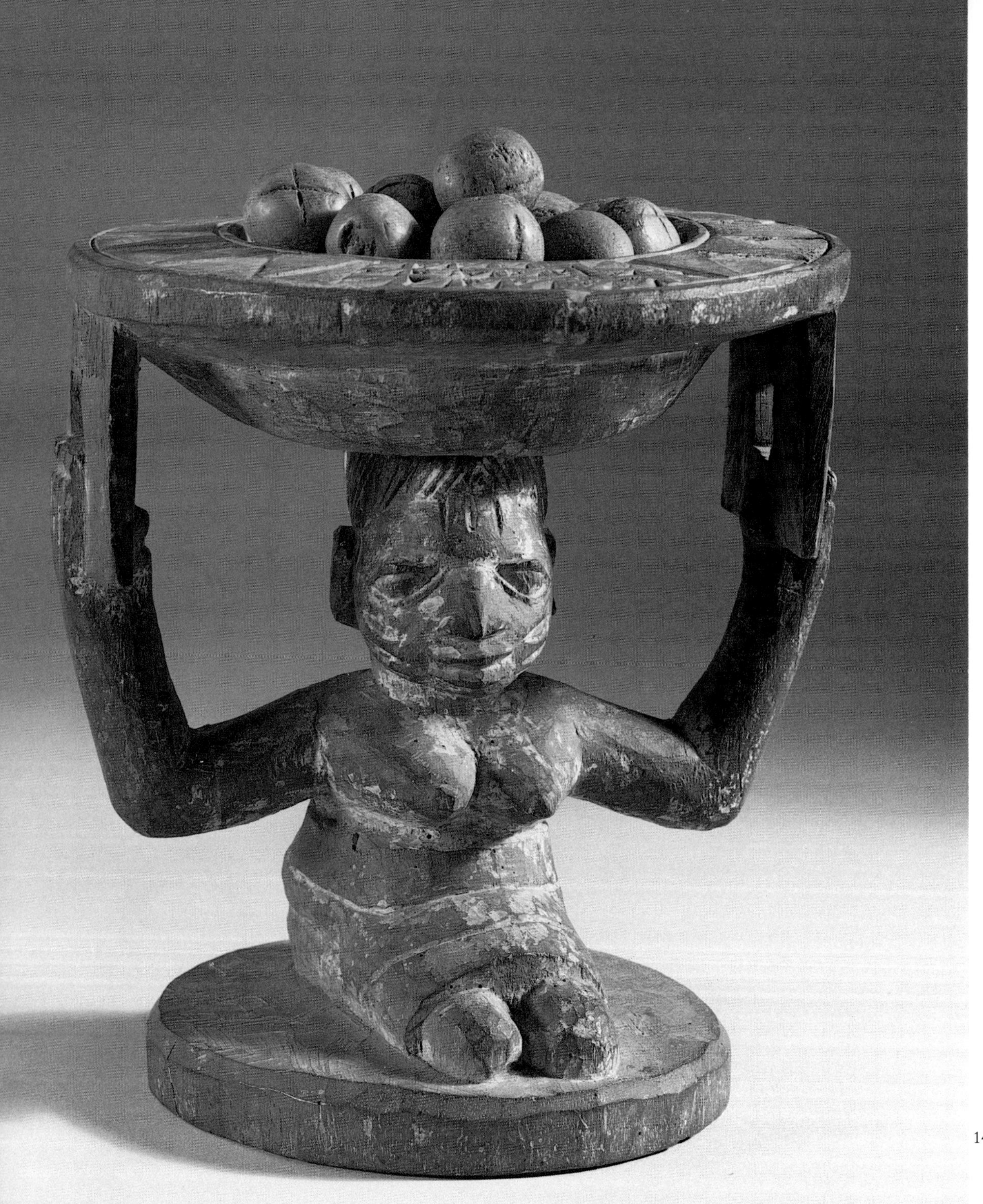

lines; if he catches an even number he draws only one line. This procedure is repeated eight times until a combination of lines *(odu)* appears on the divination board. There are in all 256 possible combinations (sixteen times sixteen), each of which corresponds to part of the thousands of verses in the ritual texts. An Ifa priest is expected to know at least 1,000 verses by heart, since the divination is based on his interpretation of the verses determined by the lines.

142 Fragment (base) of an Ifa bowl *(agere Ifa)*, wood.
Republic of Benin, Yoruba.

The diviner keeps the sixteen palm kernels used for Ifa divination in a wooden bowl that is frequently supported by fully sculptured figures. On this fragment—the bowl is missing—the divination scene itself is depicted. The diviner sits on a mat with his two assistants (wives of Ifa). In front of him is the Ifa equipment: the rectangular board with Eshu's face (see Nos. 145,146), tappers for calling the god, and a footed bowl containing palm kernels, which can be seen between the priest's fingers. The strongly compressed projecting faces recall Gelede masks (see Nos. 133,134).

Height 14 cm. 28-12-2
Acquired from C. Ratton 1928

143 Ifa bowl *(agere Ifa)*, wood, palm kernels.
Nigeria, northern Yoruba.

This kneeling female figure probably represents an Ifa priestess. The carver concentrated on modeling the head and breasts, leaving the long simplified arms to terminate in large hands with fingers of equal length that are cut off in a straight line at the tips.

Height 20 cm. 15-17-143
Acquired from the Museum für Völkerkunde Berlin 1915

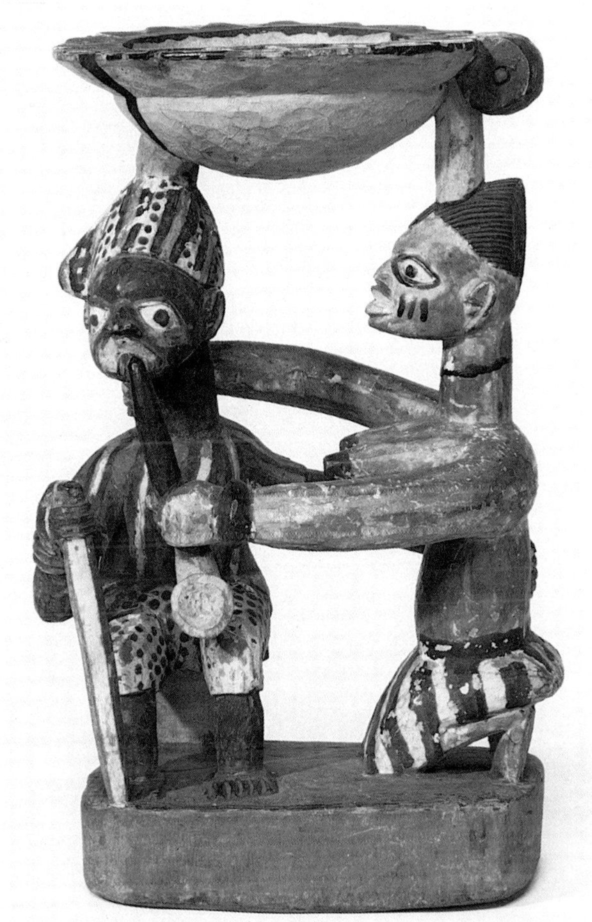

144

144 Ifa bowl *(agere Ifa)*, wood.
Republic of Benin, Yoruba.
(see color plate p. 66)

The subjects depicted in divination bowl supports are not always associated with Ifa divination. Here, for instance, a kneeling woman hands a pipe to a seated man in a domestic scene.

Height 33.5 cm. 16-16-4
Acquired from L. Frobenius 1916

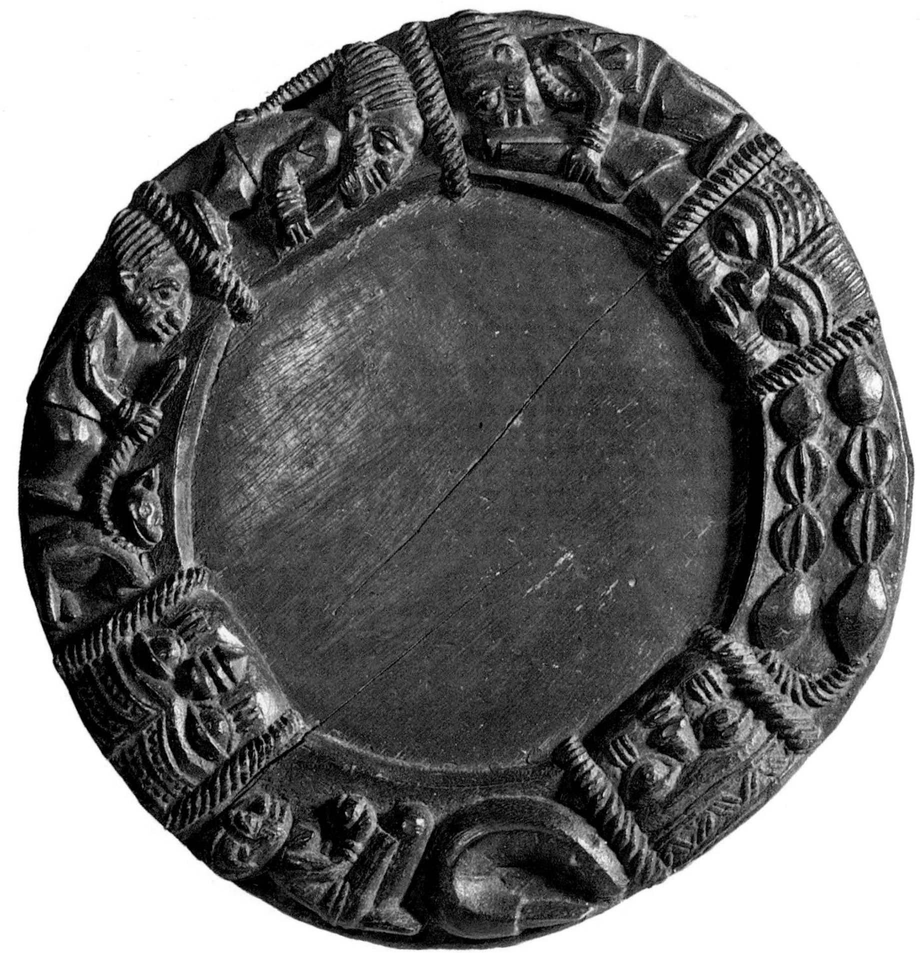

145

145 Divination board (*opon Ifa*), wood.
Nigeria, Yoruba, Ife.

During divination the Ifa priest records the results of repeated throws of palm kernels or cowries, or brass chains upon the surface of a divination board dusted with flour. The rim of a divination board is ornamented with carvings whose themes derive from the myth of Eshu and the divination process. Eshu appears repeatedly on this board, sometimes only as a face, sometimes as an entire figure with bow, flute, or sacrificial dog. A kneeling priestess with divination bowl and row of cowries refers to the consultation itself.

The coiled mudfish at the bottom here may symbolize fertility and royal power, as in ancient Benin art. Since the decorated rim is divided into four parts, it is possible that the tray is a symbol of the cosmos.

Diameter 30 cm. 18-22-14
Acquired from L. Frobenius 1918

Lit.: W. Bascom 1969, pp. 29, 40f.; B. Frank 1965, p. 71f.; H. Witte 1984, p.19.

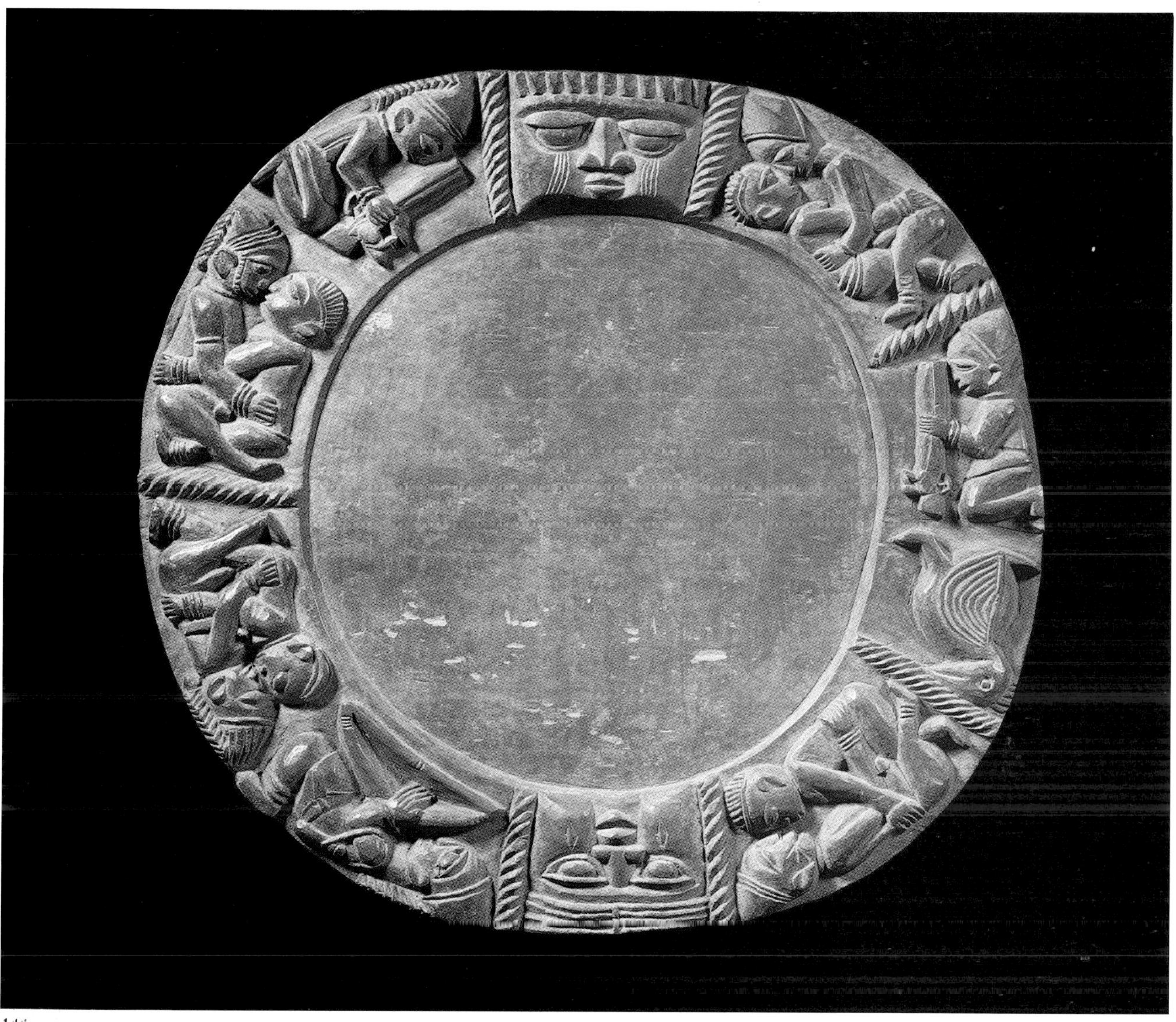

146

146 Divination board *(opon Ifa),* wood.
Nigeria, Yoruba.

Relief carvings on the rim of this board show the face or figure of Eshu, recognized by his plaited coiffure, pointed cap, and war paint. A bird—possibly a representation of the mythical hen whose scratching created solid ground from the primordial ocean mud (see No.137)—interrupts the symmetrical disposition of motifs.

Diameter 42 cm. 16-8-1
Acquired from L. Frobenius 1916

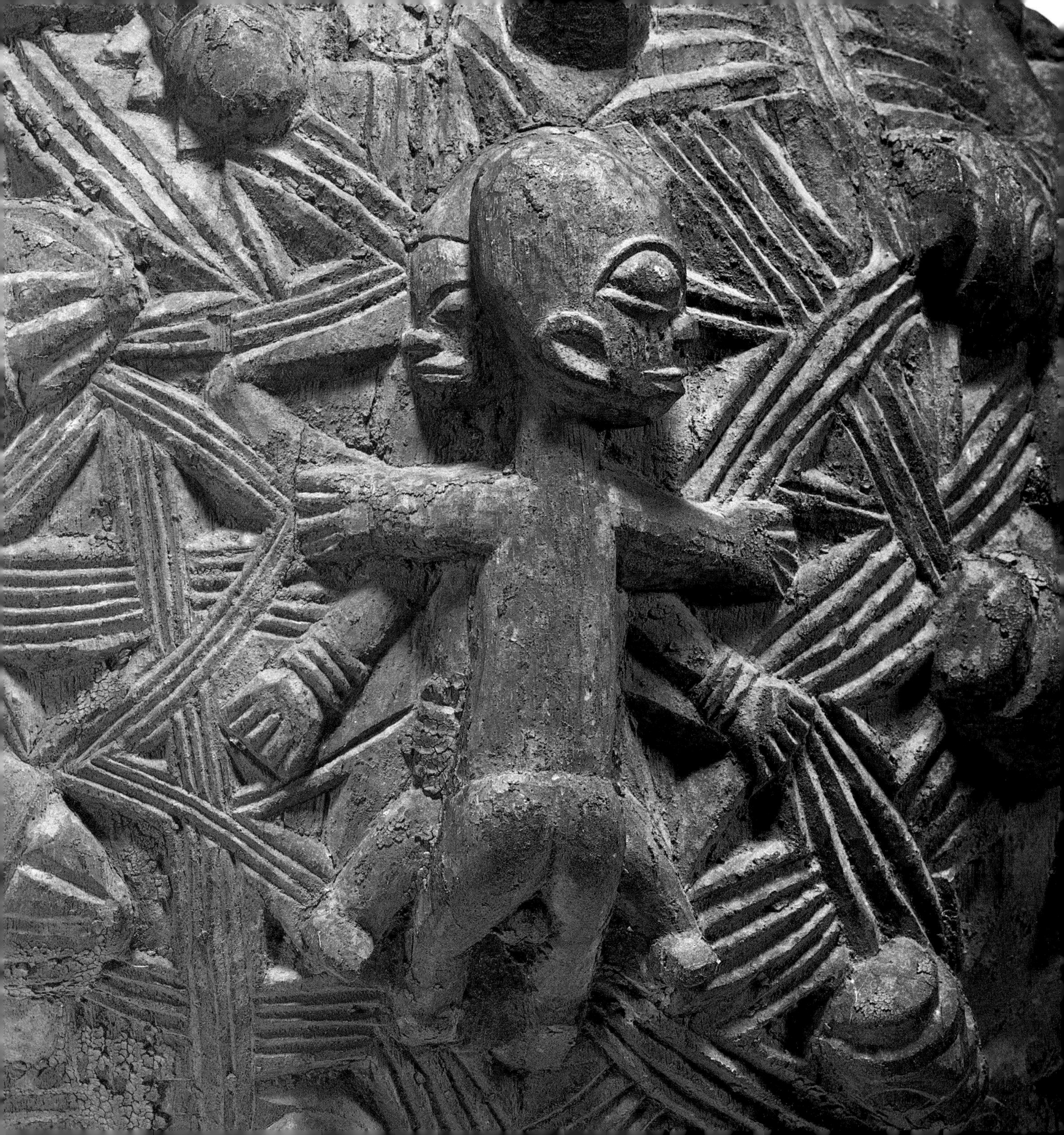

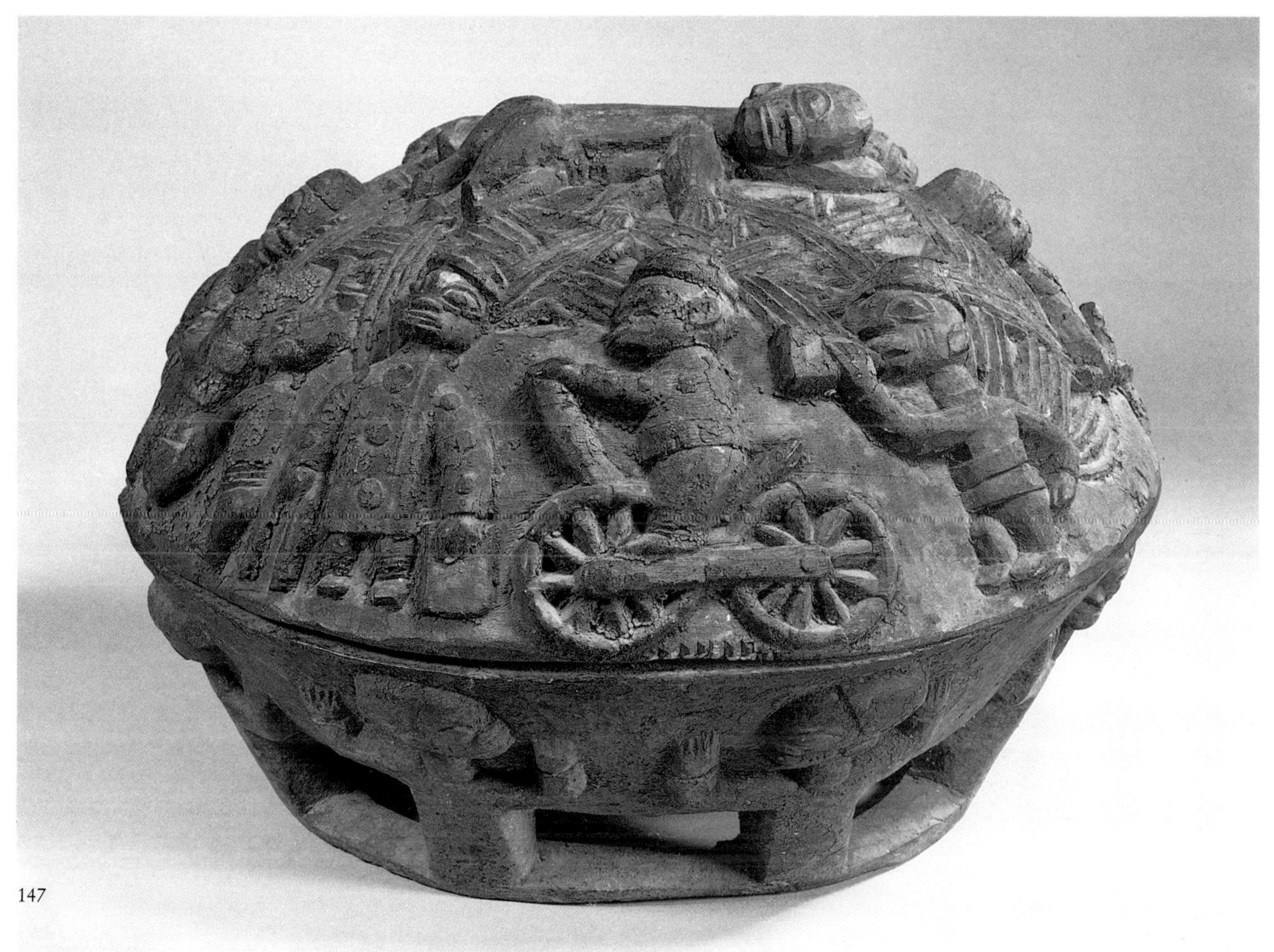

147

147 Lidded bowl for divination equipment, wood.
Nigeria, Yoruba, Ekiti, Abeokuta.

Eight male figures on the lower part of this bowl appear to support the lid, which is ornamented with a variety of motifs in relief. A seated diviner wearing a hat, sixteen divination pieces, chains, and a sacrificial dog relate to the bowl's use in divination. The copulation scene on top of the lid recalls Eshu's role as giver of fertility. The conventional representation of a king on horseback is surrounded by scenes from everyday life, such as women pounding yams in mortars. Some figures are shown with objects that document European influence, such as foreign costume, a bicycle, and a liquor flask. The textured background pattern for the figures suggests that this piece may have been made by the famous Yoruba artist Areogun (see No. 131).

Height 34 cm., diameter 50 cm. 77-4-1
Acquired from G. and M. Stoll 1977

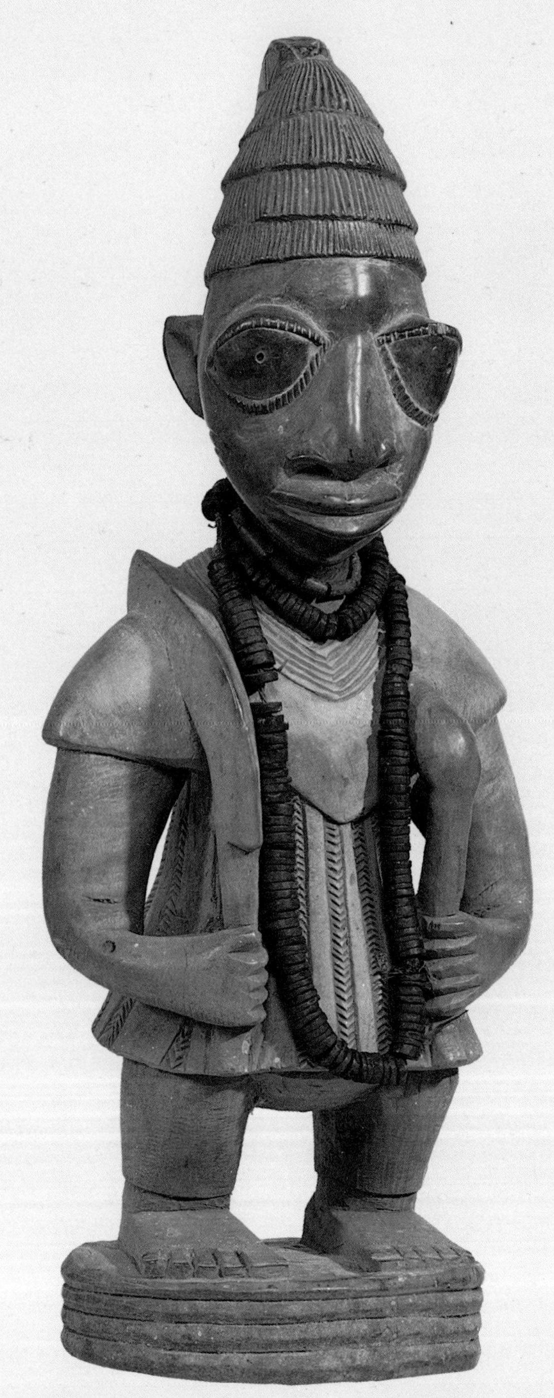

148

Eshu, the Trickster God (148,149)

One of the most fascinating figures in the religion of the Yoruba and their neighbors is Eshu or Elegba (Elegabara). His cult is widespread: among the eastern Ewe (Republic of Benin) he is known as Legba, among the Edo as Esu, and among the Ibo as Agu. The immensity of the area these peoples occupy explains the regional peculiarities of ideas and customs associated with Eshu. For instance, Eshu's erotic traits are emphasized mainly by the southwestern Yoruba. Eshu is not an idealized deity but represents an extreme, sometimes antisocial individualism. Because of his devious pranks he is counted among the trickster gods and mythical rogues. He is full of contradictions: he enjoys provoking quarrels between people but is also thought of as a peacemaker. He causes misfortune but can also make a person rich and happy. He may be as dignified as a king or as simple as a child or an old man. He sometimes appears unexpectedly in the street or the marketplace performing a wild frenzied dance. He is the adversary of the gods (Christians and Moslems identify him with the devil) but serves as their messenger. Eshu's anarchical nature and immoderate sexuality are manifestations of the enormous power given him by Olodumare, creator and maintainer of the world, which enabled him to promote change and growth. An equally strong determinant of his character is Eshu's association with the god of divination, Ifa. Ritual equipment of Ifa depicts Eshu, usually as a man, alone or with a female companion, but sometimes as a hermaphrodite. His characteristic attributes are a long tuft of hair (often interpreted as a phallus) or a pointed cap, a flute, and a calabash filled with magical ingredients.

Lit.: A. Leurquin-Tefnin 1980, pp. 26-37; J. Pemberton 1975, pp. 20-27, 66; J. Wescott 1962, pp. 336-53.

148 Figure from Eshu shrine (*Ogo Elegba*), wood.
Nigeria, Yoruba, Ilobu-Oshogbo, Oyo province.

This expressive figure, probably from the workshop of the master carver Igbuke of Oyo, exemplifies the round style and typifies Yoruba carving. Head and body are in a proportion of one to three. Frequent washing has lightened the body and dress, and frequent oiling has given a patina to the carefully modeled head. Facial features are clearly set off from one another. The dominating eyes are overly stylized, the tip of the broad funnel-shape nose is drawn downward, the narrow protruding lips are cut off vertically at the corners of the mouth, and the tipped-back ears are stressed. Eshu, whom we know by his pointed cap, further displays such dignitaries' insignia as the fly whisk, dancing club, and full ceremonial dress.

Height 58 cm. 75-3-1
Acquired from G. and A. Stoll 1975

149 Eshu head (*ela* or *irin Ifa*), bone.
Nigeria, Yoruba.

In divination services sometimes an Eshu head, recognizable by its pointed cap, is placed beside the Ifa board. This example has particularly intense facial features and ornamental cicatrices. Its open mouth (rare in Yoruba art) reveals a row of upper teeth with a triangular gap between the two front incisors.

Height 6 cm. 16-8-5
Acquired from L. Frobenius 1916

Lit.: W. Bascom 1969, p. 28; D. Forde 1962, p. 27; L. Frobenius 1912, pp. 256-58.

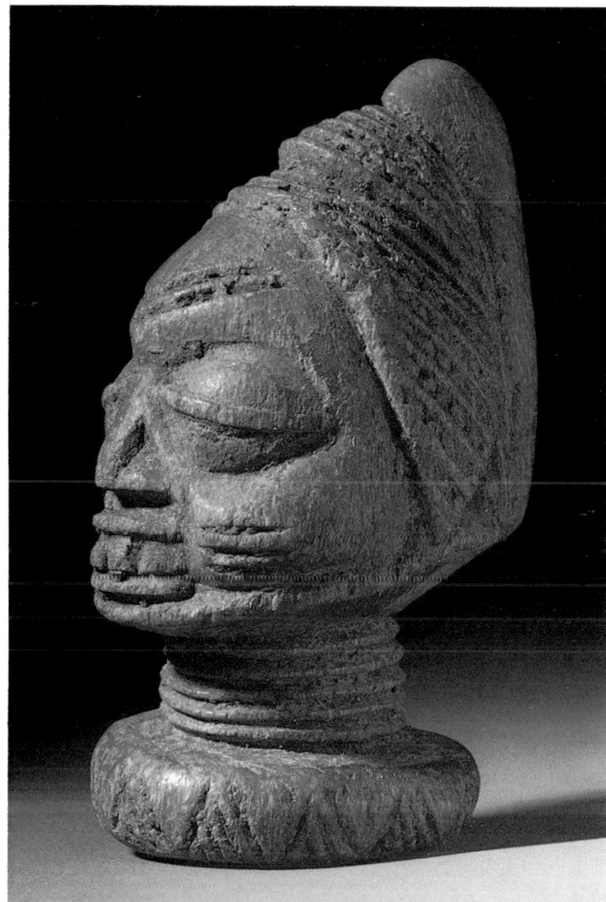
149

Twin Figures (150-154)

Many African peoples consider the birth of twins a mysterious event brought about by supernatural forces. Local tradition determines whether these births are to be celebrated as a sign of luck and wealth or are to be considered an omen of misfortune. In some areas twins were accordingly respected for their supernatural capacities, while in others they were feared and, in a few places, killed at birth. Early reports described the Yoruba as having a negative interpretation of twins, but while this attitude was prevalent in the eastern (Igbo) part of the country until relatively recently, about a century ago a decisive change took place among the west and central Yoruba, who since then have joyfully celebrated twin births, which enhance the family's social standing.

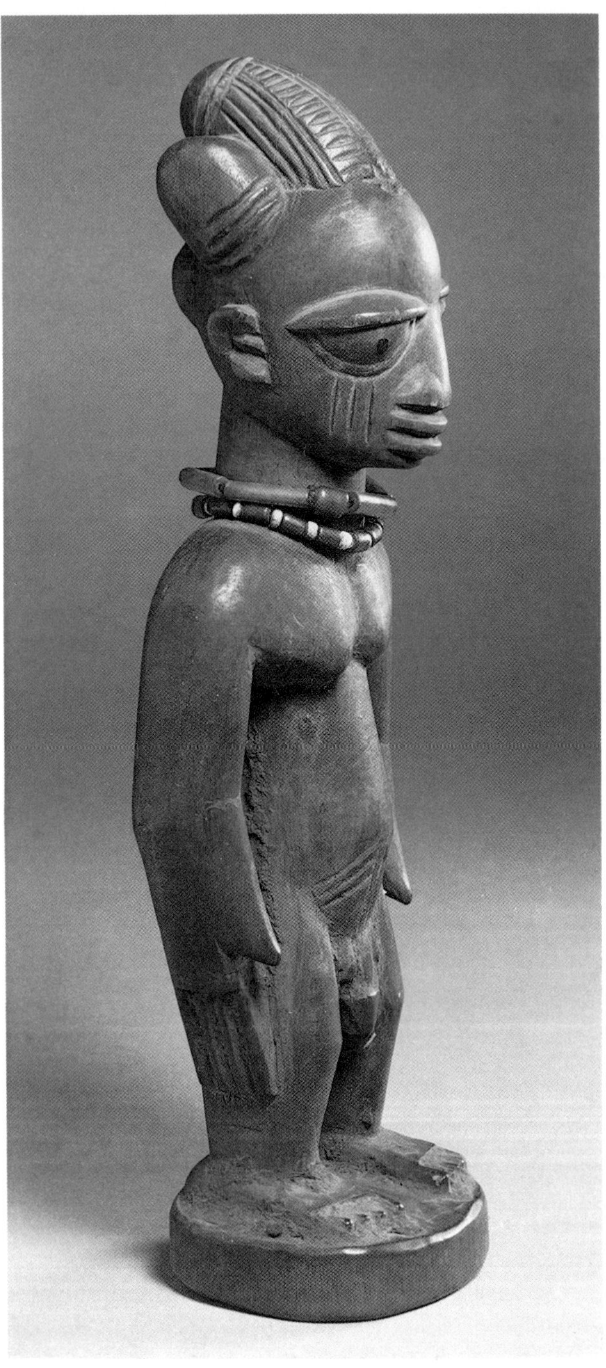

150

This new attitude found expression not only in social and religious life but also in art. Small twin *ibeji* figures began to be commissioned from professional artists. Carved mostly in pairs, the figures are kept in the family shrine and regularly supplied with food offerings, particularly black beans. The ideas associated with these figures are by no means uniform. In some instances they represent twins who died in infancy. In others they are votive gifts offered to the twin god *orisha ibeji* after a twin birth. The desire for twins may lead a couple to commission such figures. The idea that twins possess a common soul provides a further motive: if one sibling dies, his part of the soul must be housed in an appropriate figure so that the other twin can live on. The mother cares for the wooden figure as if it were a living child. She carries it about in her wrapper as women carry children and washes, anoints, clothes, caresses, and symbolically feeds it. A diviner determines whether the deceased twin desires an *ibeji* figure or not. He also sees to it that the soul of a dead twin settles in the figure. After their mother's death deceased twins state through the diviner whether the *ibeji* figures are to be buried with her or put in charge of another relative.

The figures themselves are not meant to be portraits; they do not even represent children, though they are always of the same sex as the twin they represent. The figures are carefully carved in detail, with the usual one-to-three proportion of head to body. The faces almost always show the effects of wear from frequent washings and anointings, and traces of red camwood paste are often found in the grooves.

Lit.: H. J. Drewal 1980, p. 50; S. Farrow 1926, p. 58; M. H. Houlberg 1973, p. 20; S. Lagerkrantz 1941, pp.42-6; T. Mobolade 1971, pp. 14-15; L. Segy 1970, pp. 107, 110; G. & M. Stoll 1980, pp. 36-44; R. F. Thompson 1971a, pp. 8ff.

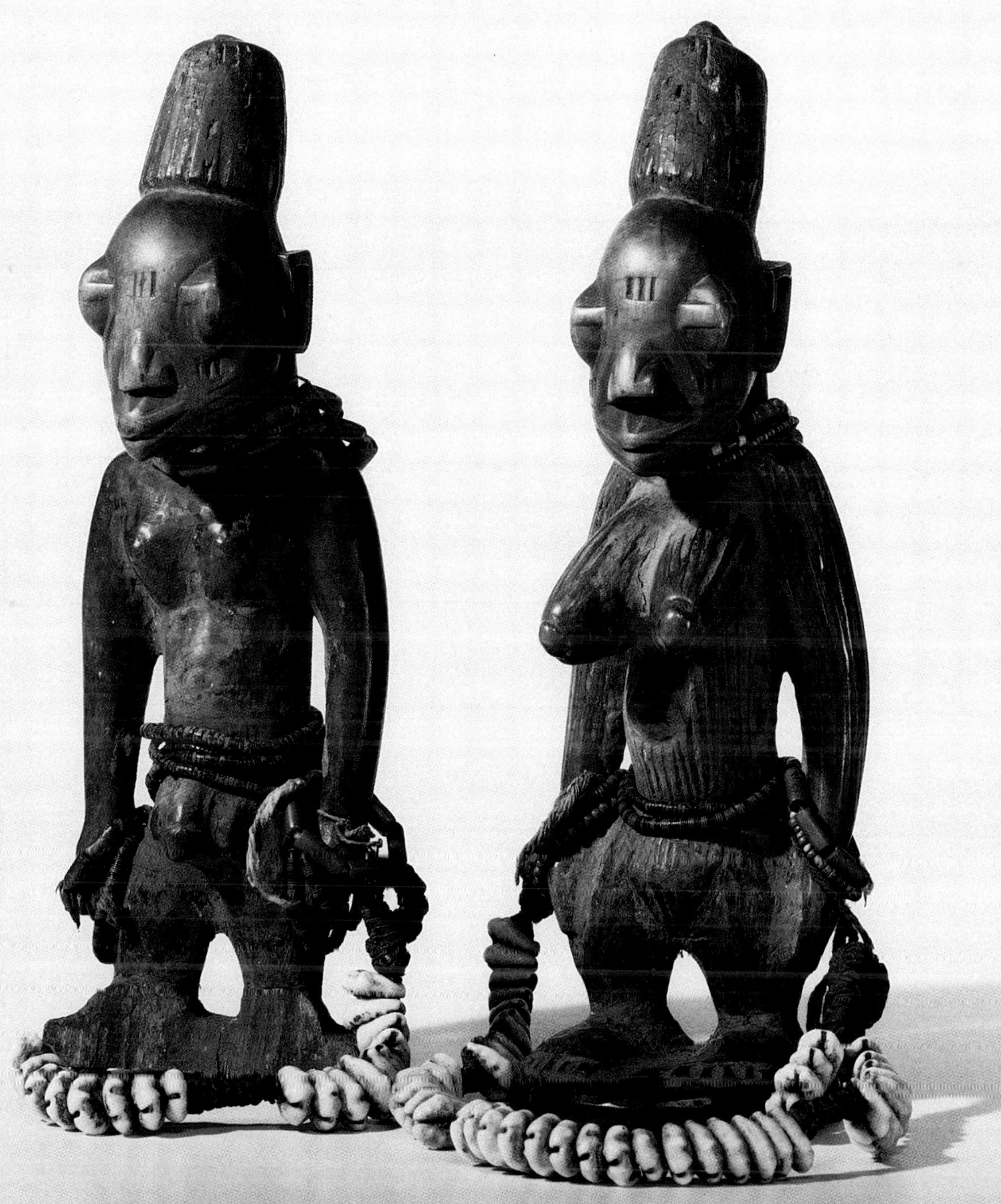

151/152

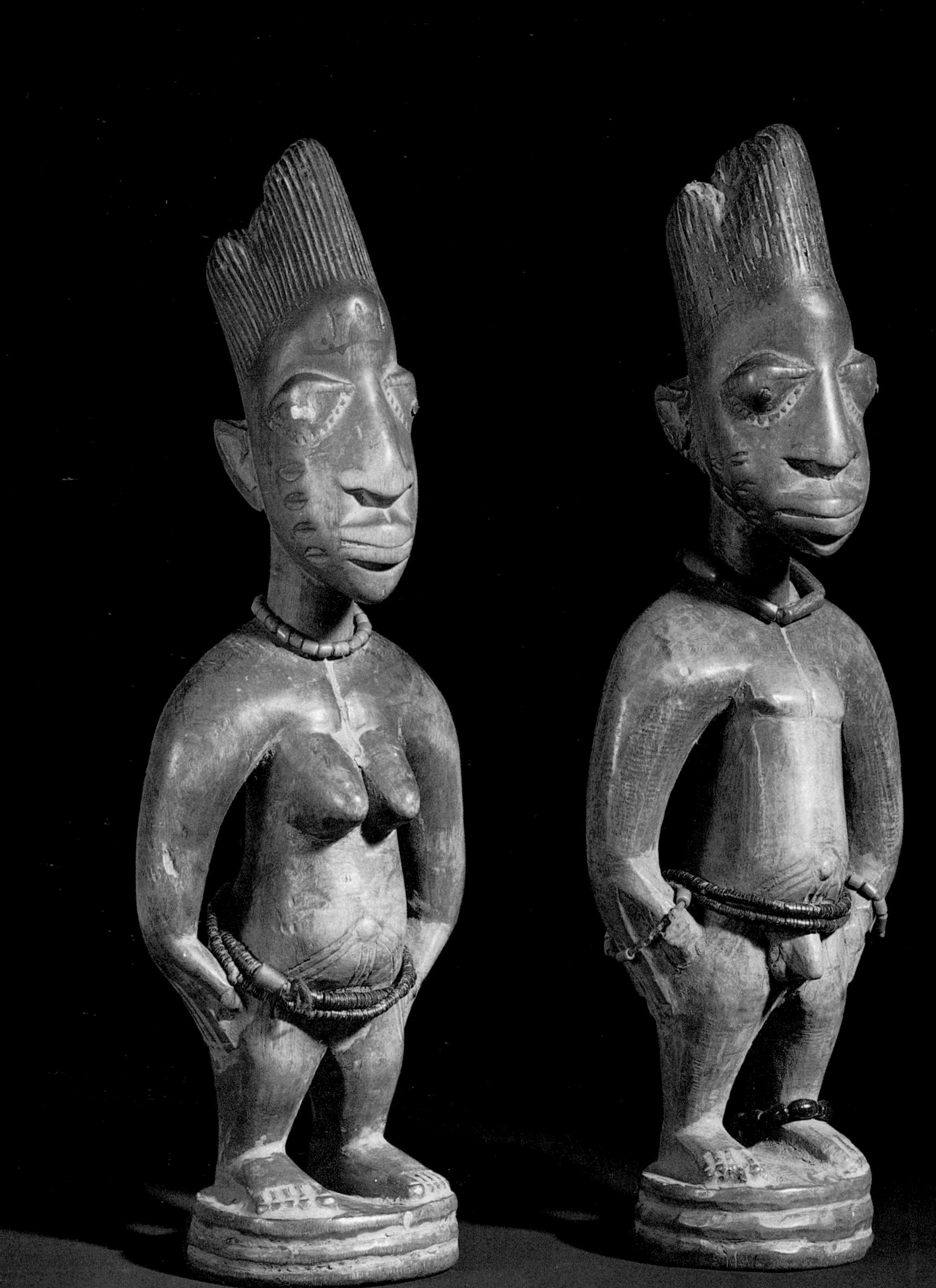

153/154

150 Male twin figure (*ere ibeji*), wood, iron, beads.
Nigeria, Yoruba.

This, the oldest *ibeji* figure in our collection, was brought to Europe in 1981. It represents an especially fine, rare type. Noteworthy are the delicate outline, the careful treatment of details such as spinal column and shoulder blades, and a tendency to naturalism. Lips and upper eyelids protrude markedly; ears are small and close to the head, in contrast to other *ibeji* types. The face is tattooed, and the slightly pointed abdomen has three parallel lines radiating from navel to sexual organ, which is more naturalistic than those in other figures. Such tattooing is typical for *ibeji* figures from Oyo and Egba provinces. The base is adorned. This early *ibeji* sculpture is in many respects similar to more recent figures produced in the traditional manner by the Igbuke carving family of Oyo (see Nos. 148, 153, and 154).

Height 22 cm. 26-36-3
Acquired from G. von Max 1926 (Collection H. Pohl)

Lit.: H. J. Drewal 1980, p. 57; G. & M. Stoll 1980, pp. 107, 131, 158.

151,152 Twin figures (*ibeji),* wood, glass, shell, metal, cowries.
Nigeria, Yoruba.

In contrast to the balanced quietude of the oldest *ibeji* figure (No. 150) and of the figures of the Igbuke school (Nos. 153 and 154), this pair of twins is decidedly dynamic. Significant features include roundish head with high shaved forehead, large protruding eyes with half-closed lids, pointed protruding lips with upper-lip groove, short nose, linear facial cicatrices, angular ears, and short, strong neck with forwardly inclined accentuated nape. Long arms ending in clumsy hands contrast with short sturdy legs ending in feet with clearly indicated toes. The female figure has full, high breasts with large nipples, and her body is vigorously ornamented with linear tattooing. The towering conical coiffure is characteristic of royal messengers (*ilari)* of Oyo, as well as of priests and priestesses of the river goddess Oshun. Presumably the figures were commissioned by a family who were either dedicated to the river goddess or who held the office of royal messenger. According to Drewal, the coiffure is a sign of the divine presence that, apart from kings and members of the Egungun society, manifests itself especially in priests and royal messengers. The cowrie string attached to each figure indicates both the wealth of the family and respect for the deceased.
Fagg located a similar *ibeji* in the area of Ila-Orangun, Oke Onigbin (Igbomina province). The Stolls classify these relatively rare figures as of the Igbomina type.

Height 26.5 cm., 27.5 cm. 57-13-1/2
Acquired from L. Bretschneider 1957

Lit.: M. T. Drewal 1977, pp. 43-44; W. Fagg 1961, No. 148; G. & M. Stoll 1980, pp. 289, 320.

153,154 Twin figures (*ere ibeji),* wood, iron, bead and shell chains. Nigeria, Yoruba, Oyo.

The balanced structure and strongly sculptural front and profile views of these two figures are typical of the style attributed to the Igbuke brothers, artists who work in the town of Oyo. The name Igbuke was famous during the artists' lifetime, and their style is still imitated by their descendants and other carvers. Among the chief characteristics of the *ibeji* of this school are a towering, finely grooved coiffure in four sections colored with indigo or laundry bluing (as in this case), which blends smoothly into the forehead; eyes with upper lids, eyelashes indicated by incised lines, and pupils marked by iron tacks; and forehead, cheeks, and abdomen lined with tattoo marks. The protruding, grooved upper lip almost touches the tip of the wide, flattened nose. The ears are angular, the neck is straight and relatively long, and the sloping shoulders end in powerful arms akimbo. The large hands rest on the thighs. The rounded abdomen has a flat navel, the buttocks project, and a thin line indicates the spinal column. Short stumpy legs and feet with carefully carved toes stand on round grooved bases.

Height 30, 30.5 cm. 67-1-2 (male)
57-13-3 (female)

Acquired from L. Bretschneider 1957, 1967

Lit. H. J. Drewal 1980, p. 59; G. & M. Stoll 1980, pp. 156-58.

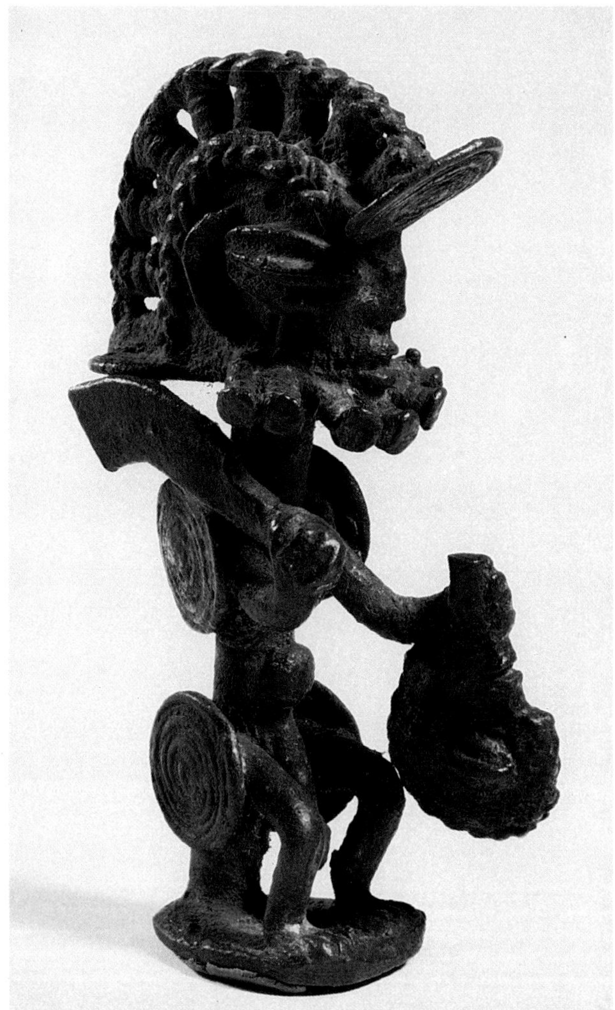

155

The Yoruba Shango Cult (155-157)

Shango, god of war and thunder, is worshiped faithfully in Oyo province, where the annual Shango festival assumes the character of a state celebration. According to Yoruba tradition Shango reigned as third ruler of Oyo, once the most powerful Yoruba kingdom. In the course of time his cult spread to areas outside Yoruba territory—as far as the Ivory Coast, Ghana, and Togo.

Legends describe King Shango as a feared and irascible tyrant who was an energetic ruler and a successful warlord. His magical power, which expressed itself in his extraordinary vitality, enabled him to secure the rain necessary for his country. According to one version of the myth, Shango's very knowledge of the magic of thunder and lightning led to his doom when, by accident, he destroyed his own palace and with it his wives and children. He then hanged himself in the forest, becoming deified after death. Most researchers do not subscribe to this view and consider Shango to have been a god from the beginning. At any rate, he belongs to the ritually venerated deities *(orisha),* of the Yoruba. He is, alone or together with his wife, Oya, among the most popular figures in Yoruba art. Many of his characteristics and many details of his iconography (for instance his essential attributes of thunderbolt and double-bladed ax) recall the storm deities of ancient Mediterranean cultures.

Lit.: L. Frobenius 1912, I, pp. 238–45; G. J. A. Oyo 1966, p. 172; R. F. Thompson 1971b, Chapter 12/1-6.

155 Votive figure, brass.
Nigeria, Yoruba.

A seated king or the god Shango, fully cast in the lost-wax process, holds a machete and a severed human head. This small figure is of recent date but reflects the spirit of traditional sculpture in an artistically convincing manner.

Height 12 cm. 59-1-3
Acquired from L. Bretschneider 1959

156 Kneeling female figure, wood.
Republic of Benin, Yoruba.

This small figure is provided with symbols of the thunder god: a double-bladed ax rests on her head, and zigzag lines that stand for lightning decorate the base. The character represented is either Shango's chief wife, Oya—associated in mythology with water and fertility—or a woman wearing the stole characteristic of devotees of the Shango cult. She is kneeling, a sign of reverence, dependence, or salutation.

Height 17 cm. 28-12-1
Acquired from C. Ratton 1928

Lit.: C. Odugbesan, in M. Douglas 1959, p. 207; R. F. Thompson, 1974, p. 80.

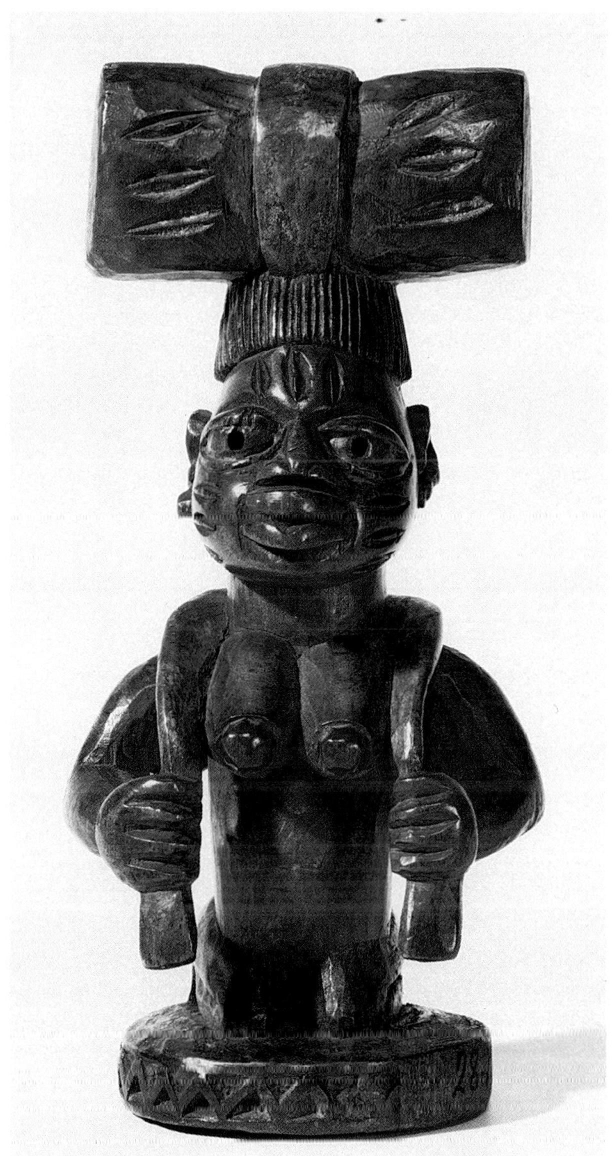

156

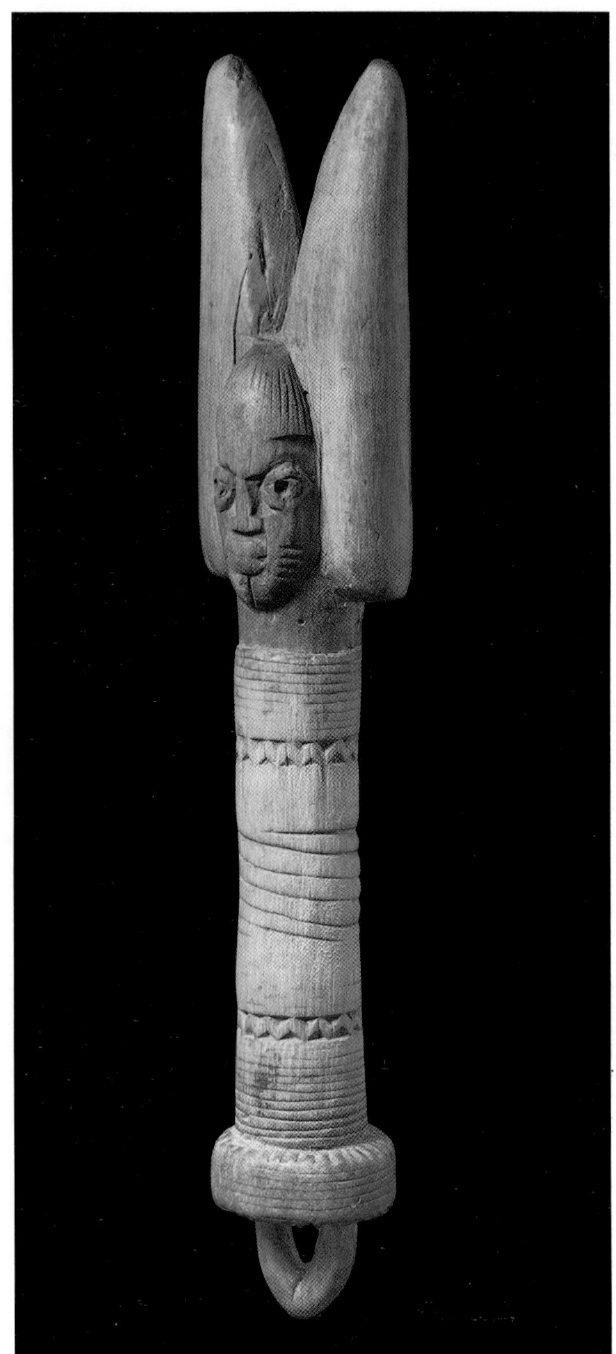

157

157 Dancing staff (*oshe Shango),* wood, iron. Nigeria, Yoruba, Offa.

In the course of the Shango festival the high priest is possessed by the god and in a trancelike state takes a dance staff like the one shown here, then dances while prophesying. The iconography from the altar of these dance staffs deals with the relationship of Shango to thunderstorms: the zigzag lines on the handle symbolize lightning. On the upper part of the staff are the most important Shango symbols: the double-bladed ax and the thunderbolt. The female face represents either Shango's chief wife, the powerful river goddess Oya, or a priestess or devotee of the cult expecting or acknowledging the gift of fertility from the god.

This is probably the work of Amos Lafia or his workshop at Idi Aro. The long, slender shape of the double-bladed ax, and the chip-carved decoration, consisting of alternating bands of horizontal and slanting lines, and of zigzag ornaments, are characteristic elements of his style.

Height 24 cm. 16-8-7
Acquired from L. Frobenius 1916

Lit.: H. J. Drewal 1980, p. 30; L. Frobenius 1912, I, pp. 240-42; C. Odugbesan in M. Douglas 1969, p. 207; R. F. Thompson 1971b, Chapters 12/1-6, 13/57.

158 Bell (*omo*), brass.
Nigeria, Yoruba.

Yoruba bead crowns (see No. 129) and bells with faces are related in style and content, for the faces on both types of object represent ancestors with whom contact is established by means of the bell. Only chiefs of the royal line may possess such bells; they wear them on the left hip during public festivals.

Height 15 cm. 32-36-2
Acquired from H. Meyer 1932

Lit.: R. F. Thompson, in D. Fraser & H. M. Cole 1972, p. 244.

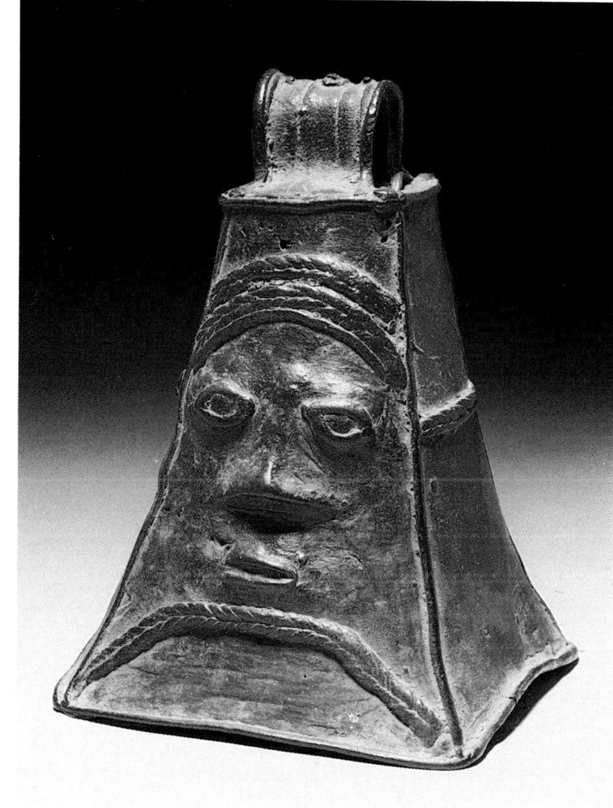

158

159 Container, wood.
Nigeria, Yoruba.

In Yoruba animal symbolism the hare is a nocturnal animal associated with the world of witches, but in animal fables the hare appears as a sly hero whose role corresponds approximately to that of the fox in European folklore. Animal-shape containers were used mainly for storing ornaments, offering cola nuts to guests, and—filled with cola nuts—as precious gifts.

This figure of a hare is greatly simplified but still clearly recognizable. Decorative bands of fine incised triangles encircle the animal's body in a technique that may be borrowed from calabash decoration (see No. 160). Inside, the lower part of the container is divided into two sections.

Height 16 cm., length 40 cm. 80-301-255
Acquired from L. Bretschneider 1980

Lit.: W. Fagg 1968, Illus. 137, R. F. Thompson 1971b, Chapter 15/2.

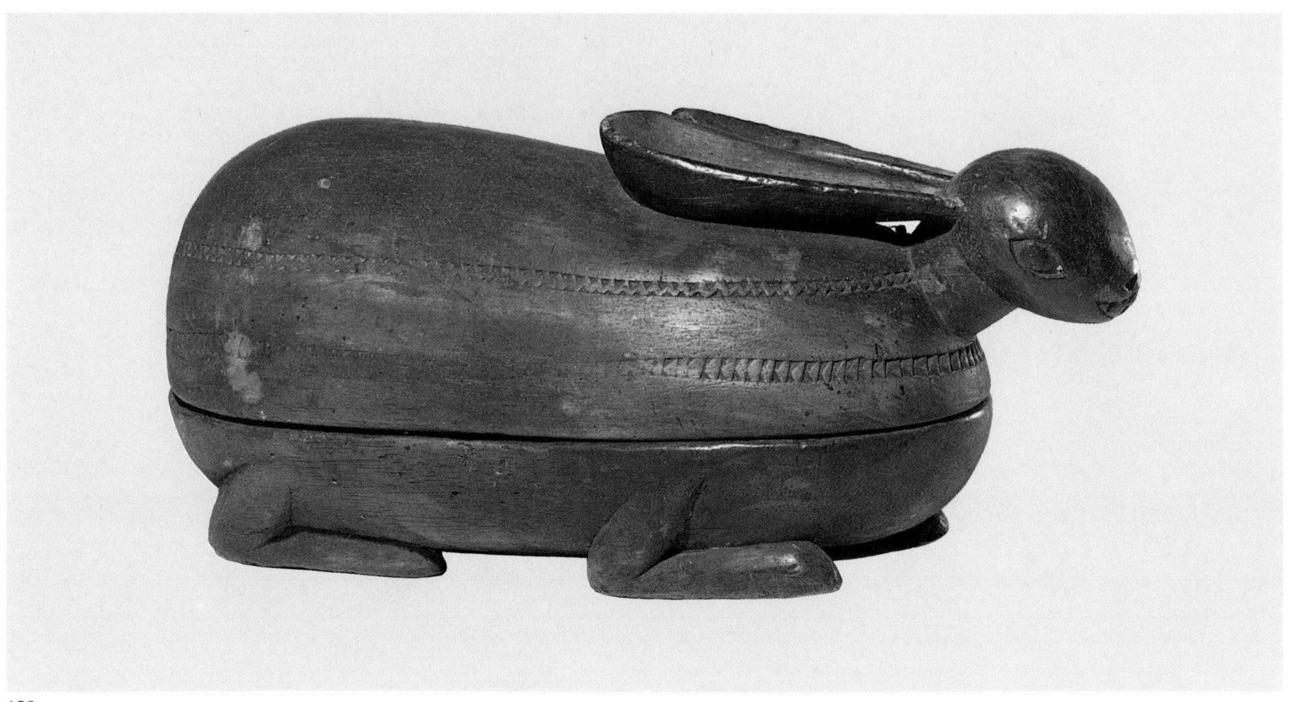

159

160 Calabash vessel with lid.
Nigeria, Yoruba, Ife.

To make a calabash vessel, a fresh green gourd is cut in half crosswise and scraped out; the outer skin is removed, the shell dried and then carved in flat relief or openwork. Among the Yoruba such vessels are used mainly in northern regions where gourds thrive.

The most artistic examples come from Oyo province, where, used as containers (see also No. 159), they are considered prestige objects; they are also used for ritual purposes in sacrifices to the gods, and in divination. Gourd vessel and lid also symbolize the pair of gods Obatala (heaven) and Oduduwa (earth).

On this vessel from the royal household, the so-called Solomon's knot and entwined band, both associated with royalty in West Africa, dominate the decoration. The precisely divided surface also contains several bird figures and a snake attacking a bird (not visible here), a common theme in Asia Minor and the Mediterranean (see Nos. 235 and 236).

Diameter 25 cm. 18-22-15
Acquired from L. Frobenius 1918

Lit.: G. J. A. Ojo 1966, pp. 182, 246-48.

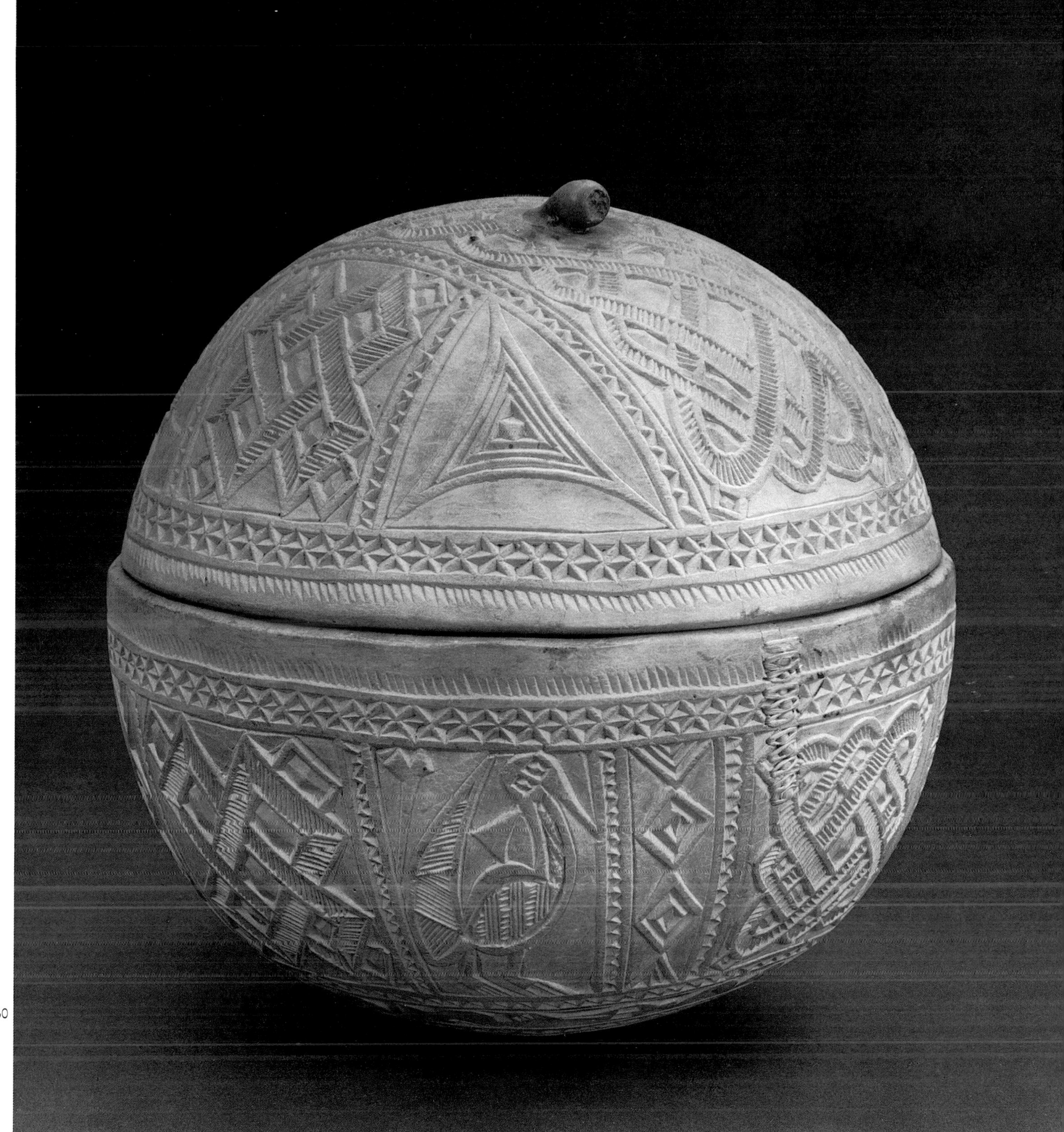

Ancient Benin: History and Art of a Kingdom

Nothing definite is known about the early days of the Benin kingdom and its people, the Edo (Bini). Oral tradition suggests that in this part of present-day Nigeria only small chiefdoms existed up to the end of the thirteenth century. The Edo are said to have lived under the rule of kings about whom we know nothing but their proud title, *ogiso,* "ruler of heaven." The last *ogiso* was driven out in an insurrection, and the people requested the king of Ile-Ife, the sacred Yoruba center, to send one of his sons to rule Benin. The reign of the dynasty that rules to this day began with the accession of the Yoruba prince Oranmiyan toward the end of the thirteenth or beginning of the fourteenth century. Its real founder, however, is considered to be Oranmiyan's son and successor, Eweka. Along with other institutions, he introduced the ruler's title, *oba,* that has become traditional.

Because of the successful economic and military policies of energetic *oba,* Benin developed into a powerful state. Most of the small Edo principalities were conquered, and trade grew with Ile-Ife and the other Yoruba towns as well as with the areas east of the Niger (Igala, Igbo) and with Islamic cities far to the north. Various foreign goods came into the country (cowries, copper, tin, and zinc, for example) by way of distant trade routes. Portuguese seafarers, who reached Benin for the first time between 1470 and 1486 and afterward visited it regularly, reported a rich art tradition that seemed to be associated almost exclusively with the royal court. Entire guilds of craftsmen, including metal casters, ivory and wood carvers, weavers, and tanners, were constantly occupied in carrying out the king's commissions. The establishment of trade relations with the Portuguese also stimulated art. European weapons, armor, ornaments, illustrated books, and pictures; Indian ivory carvings; and allegedly even Chinese textiles reached Benin through the Portuguese. Such imports led to more than simple imitation: the art of Benin offers impressive examples of work by indigenous artists that integrated and elaborated on foreign impulses.

The art of casting metal in the lost-wax technique (see p. 38) is older than the first Portuguese contact. According to tradition, it was introduced by Igue-Igha, a craftsman from Ile-Ife. Another tradition speaks of a "white stranger," Ahamangiwa—a light-skinned Hausa (?) from the Niger-Benue confluence—as the one who taught the Edo brass casting and bronze working. At our present stage of research, this important question in West African cultural history cannot be satisfactorily answered.

Although Portuguese authors had repeatedly described the splendors of the royal court, Benin art was forgotten in Europe during the eighteenth and nineteenth centuries. It was rediscovered in 1897 when a British punitive expedition occupying the capital uncovered vast treasures in the palace of the *oba.* Thousands of works of art in metal, ivory, and terra-cotta reached England as war spoils and from there entered the international art trade.

But the catastrophe of 1897 did not destroy the kingdom. The next *oba* had the palace and the ancestral altars rebuilt and many cult sculptures recast. The modern Edo consider themselves and their king to be both citizens of Nigeria and preservers of a great and ancient tradition, exclusively theirs. The time-honored art of casting continues, although there is a noticeable loss in artistic quality. Brass objects are no longer made only for the court but for the art market.

Lit.: P. Ben-Amos 1980, pp. 5,13-14, 24-25; P. J. C. Dark 1973, pp. 14; P. J. C. Dark and W. & B. Forman 1960, p. 9-10; W. Schmalenbach 1961, pp. 86-88; I. L. Tunis 1979, p. 2; D. Williams 1974, pp. 188-210.

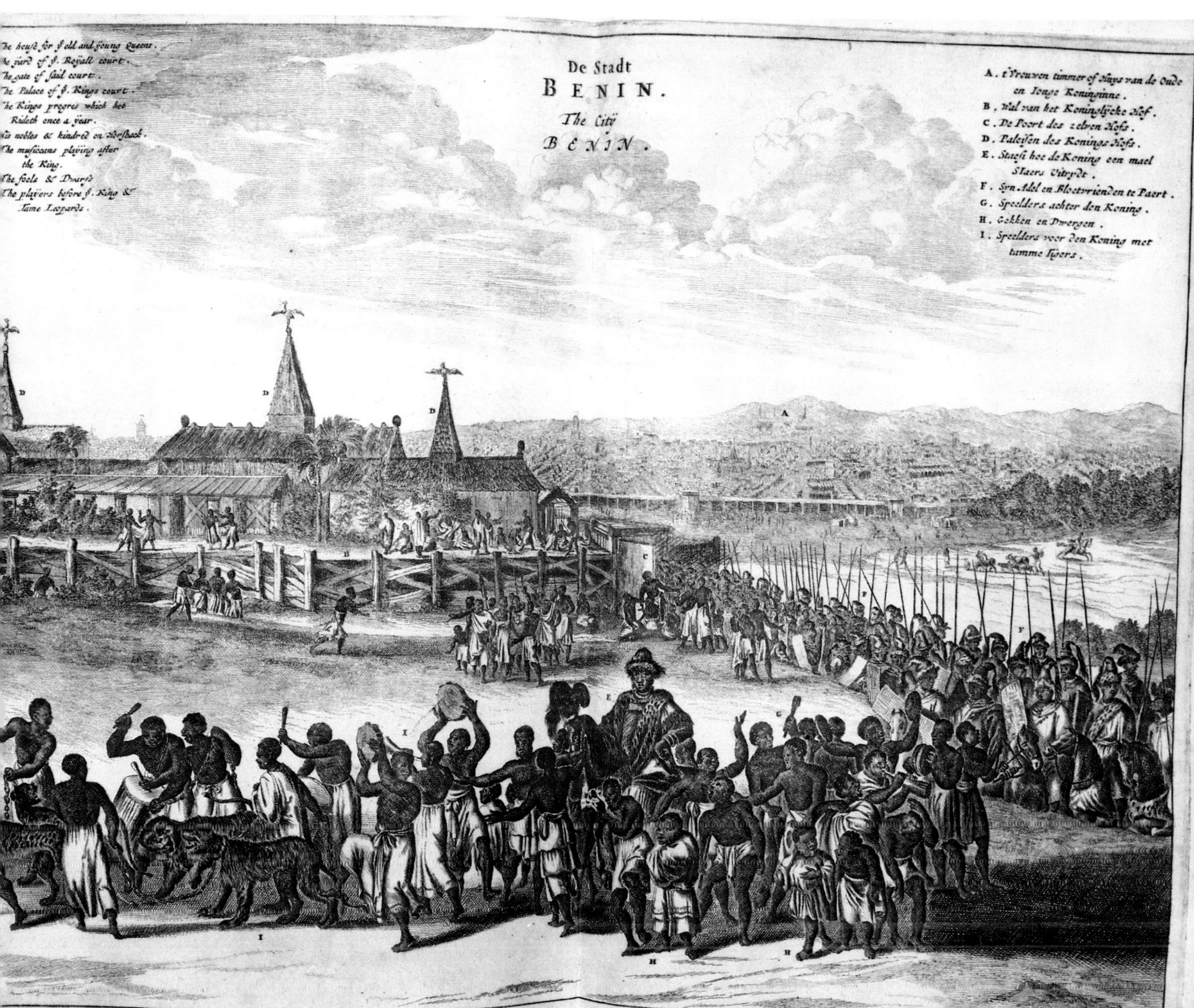

The Palace of Benin, from O. Dapper, *Umbstandliche und eigentliche Beschreibung von Afrika . . .*, 1670.

Brass Heads of Royal Ancestors (161-163)

The idea of the head as the place where one's vitality and soul reside found an especially dignified expression in the art of Benin (and that of the Yoruba kingdoms of Ife and Owo). Instead of preserving his skull, the Edo commemorated the deceased by placing a wooden or terra-cotta image of his head on the ancestral altar. From about the fourteenth century to the middle of the nineteenth only the *oba* and his kinsfolk were honored with metal commemorative heads. These were conceived as representations of individuals, although they were idealized or stylized with no great effort made to achieve a realistic likeness.

The approximately one hundred sixty preserved heads have been divided by Fagg and Dark into five stylistic periods that fall between the years 1325 and 1933. This system is now in need of revision, however, for it rests on the unproved assumption that, in metal casting, the Edo were docile pupils of their Ife masters: that those pieces stylistically close to Ife style must be the oldest. Although this may not be the case, one thing is certain—the Benin heads span a long period of time. A number of the heads, among them those presumed to be the oldest, are strikingly light and thin walled. These pieces probably originated during times when copper, zinc, and tin, the metals traded from afar, were in short supply. Only during the Portuguese trading period, when metals were plentiful, did the heads become larger and heavier, the walls thicker. The heads then also acquired an additional function, that of serving as bases for carved elephant tusks on altars.

Benin metal art is often described incorrectly as "bronze sculpture." Chemical analyses have shown that most of the pieces are copper with zinc, lead, and tin as the main alloys.

Lit.: W. P. Bauer 1975, p. 31; P. Ben-Amos 1980, pp. 14-16, 24, 63-64; P. J. C. Dark 1973, pp. 9-12; J. U. Egharevba 1934, p. 11; W. Fagg 1963, pp. 32-38; T. Shaw 1978, pp. 172-84; O. Werner 1970, pp. 71, 135-37.

161 Royal head of a king (*uhumnw-elao*), brass, iron.
Nigeria, Edo, kingdom of Benin, first half of the 18th century.

This head, which is encrusted with a reddish-brown substance, displays insignia of the *oba*: the high collar of coral beads, the flat cap with spiked cinquefoil rosettes, the large cylindrical agate beads, and the bead strings with globular ends. The two parallel iron grooves on the forehead are for sacrificial blood, added from time to time to renew the power that dwells in the head. Characteristic features include ornamental forehead scars, and on the flat projecting base, leopard and bovine skulls in high relief; fish, including mudfish; and an elephant trunk ending in a human hand with trefoil.

Most significant among the insignia shown are the coral beads, which could be worn only by the king, the queens, and certain high officials. Coral, obtained from traders, came from the Balearic Islands, and according to tradition was ground into beads in the Yoruba town of Ilorin. A myth explains the importance of coral beads in court ceremonies: Oba Ewuare (mid-fifteenth century) is said to have stolen the first coral beads from the palace of the ocean god Olokun. In commemoration of this mythical feat all the coral ornaments were cleansed in sacrificial blood once a year to renew their magical power.

Height 30 cm., diameter 28 cm. 98.40
Acquired from A. Maschmann 1898

Lit.: P. Ben-Amos 1980, pp. 64, 68, 75; P. J. C. Dark 1973, pp. 11-12, 95-96.; W. Fagg 1980, p. 10; F. v. Luschan 1919, p. 353-54.

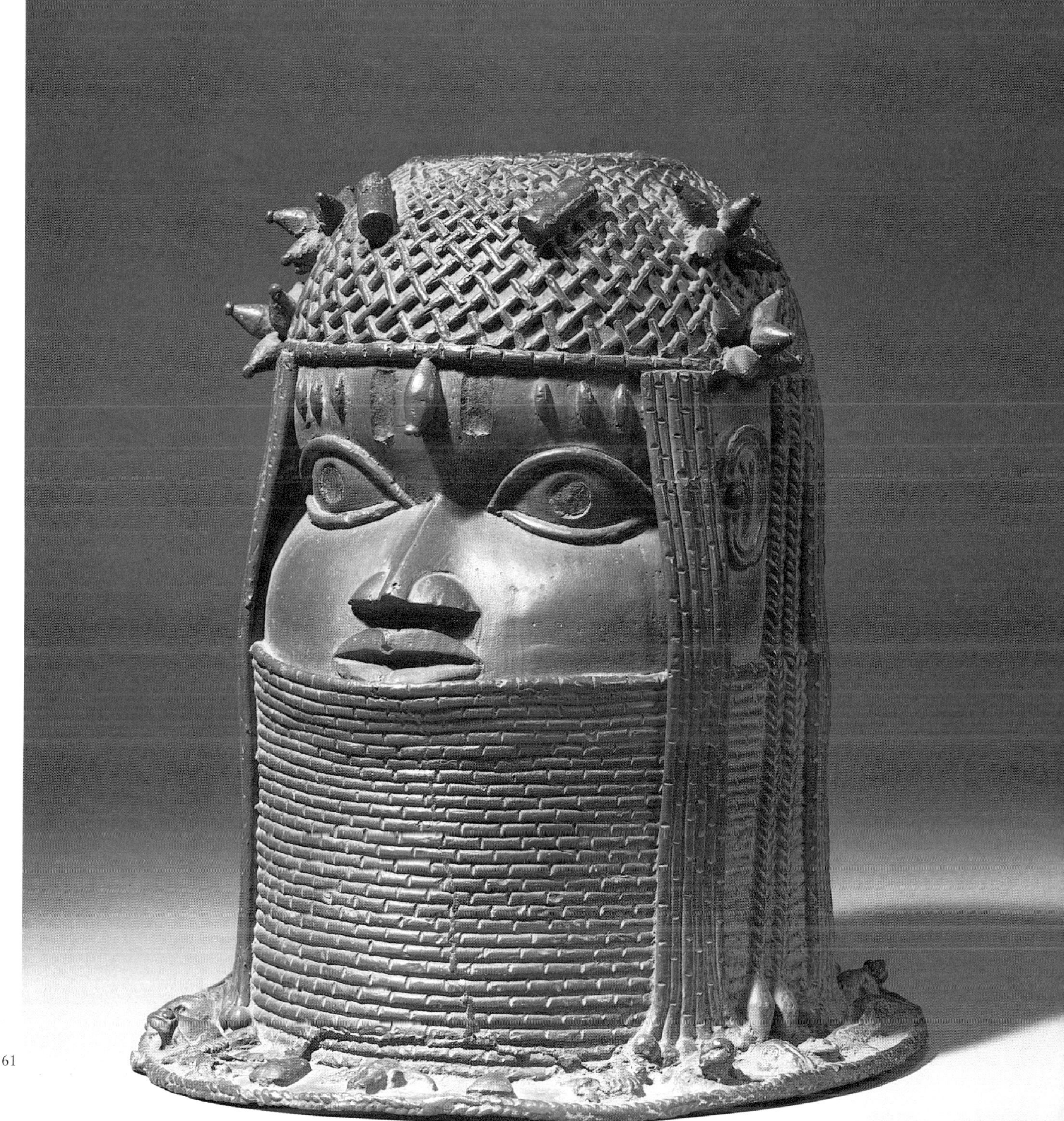

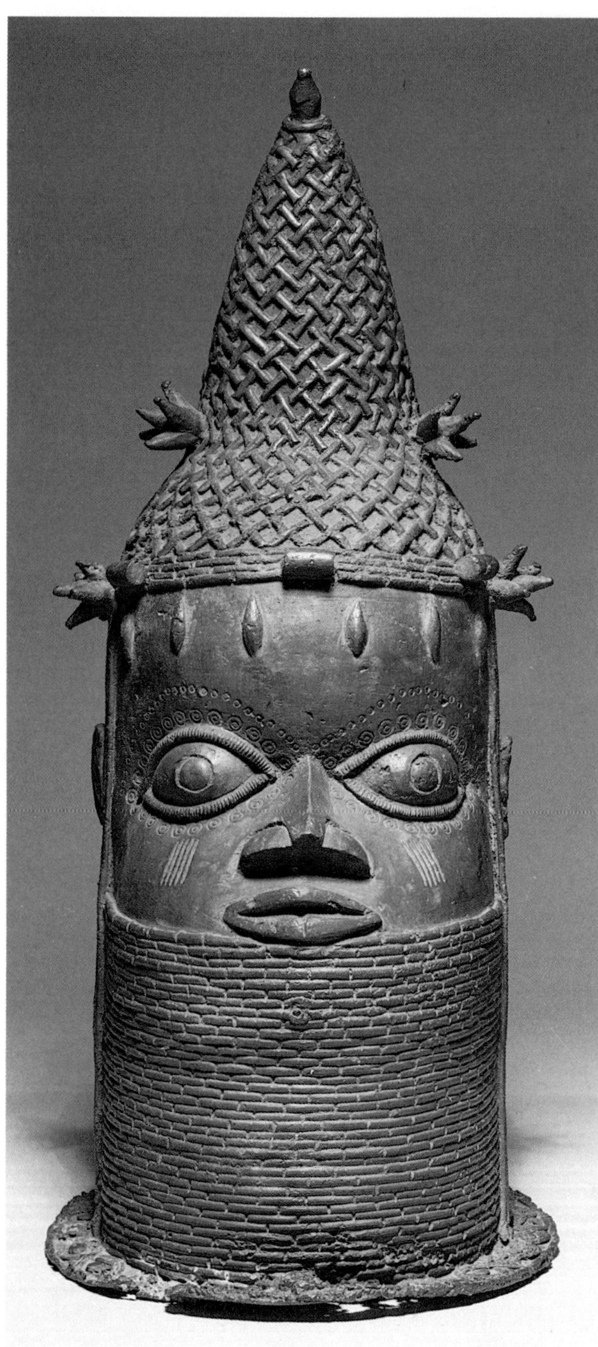

162

162 Head of a queen mother (*uhumnw-elao),* brass.
Nigeria, kingdom of Benin, Edo. End of the 18th century (thermoluminescence date of core).

From the sixteenth century on, the *iye oba,* natural mother of the king, occupied a very high place in court life. After death she was given an altar of her own equipped with a brass head dedicated to her memory. The pointed headdress of coral beads served as the unmistakable badge of her office. Later the coiffure was decorated with spiked rosettes, long strings of beads, and large cylindrical agate beads.

Among this head's characteristics are a rigid facial expression barely relieved by the rich chased ornament around the eyes; ornamental forehead scars; thick walls; and omission of the iron forehead lines. Behind the cap is a hole for the wooden peg onto which the elephant tusk was fixed (see No. 161). A guilloche band, symbol of power, ornaments the projecting base.

Height 49.5 cm., diameter c. 23 cm. 98.41
Acquired from A. Maschmann 1898

Lit.: P. Ben-Amos 1980, p. 25; P. J. C. Dark 1973, pp. 12, 95; F. v. Luschan 1919, pp. 350-53.

163 Royal head (*uhumnw-elao*), brass.
Nigeria, kingdom of Benin, Edo. 19th century.

The shape of this royal headdress with lateral "wings," introduced by Oba Osemwese (1816-1848), marks this as a nineteenth century piece. Other characteristics support this date: enlarged dimensions, thick walls, highly stylized rigid face, chased eyebrows and lids, arcs of punched circle-and-point ornaments, ornamental forehead scars, absence of iron forehead grooves, and the high broad collar of coral-bead strings. On the projecting base the guilloche band is partly hidden by high-relief three-dimensional leopards, bovine skulls, frogs,

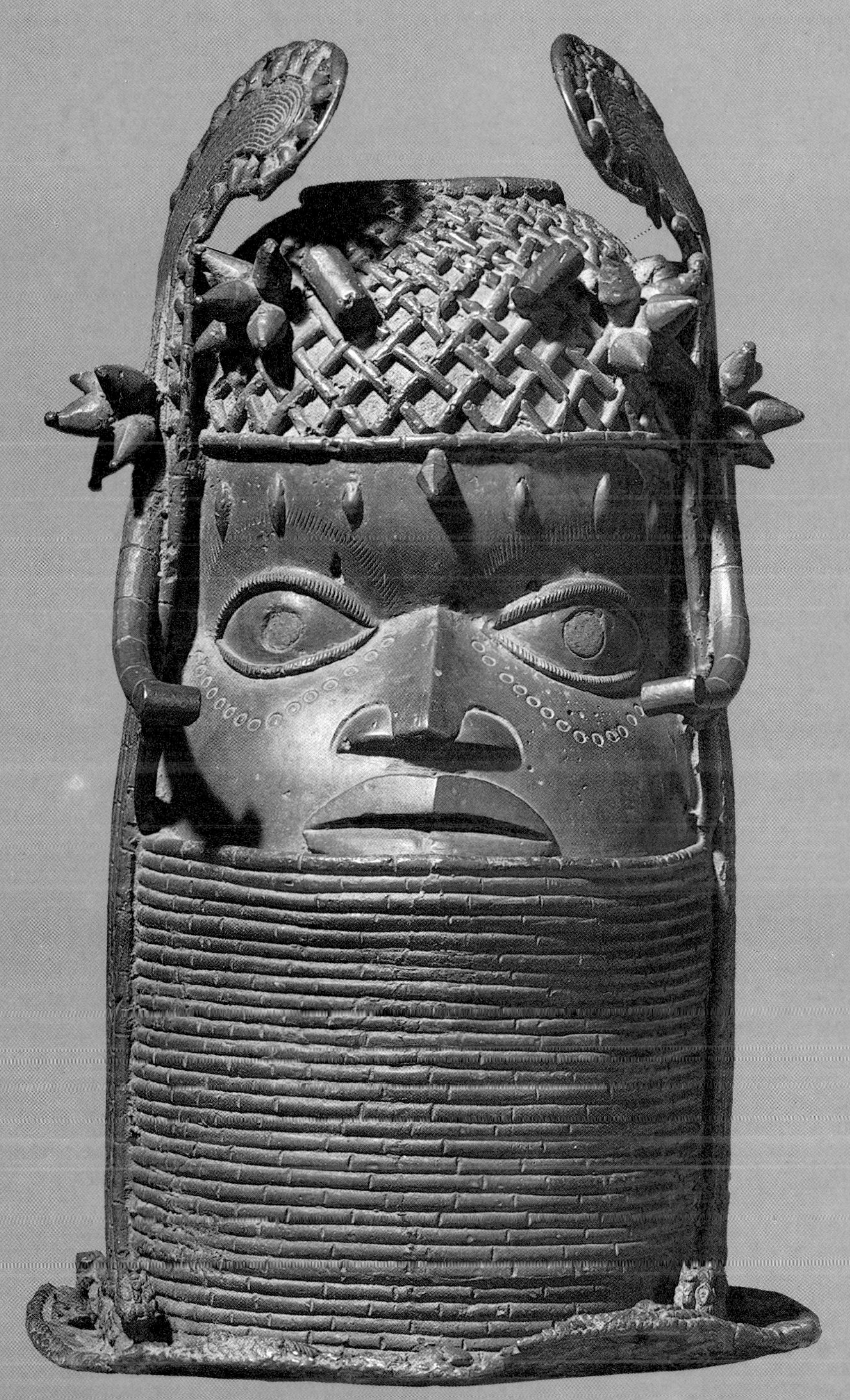

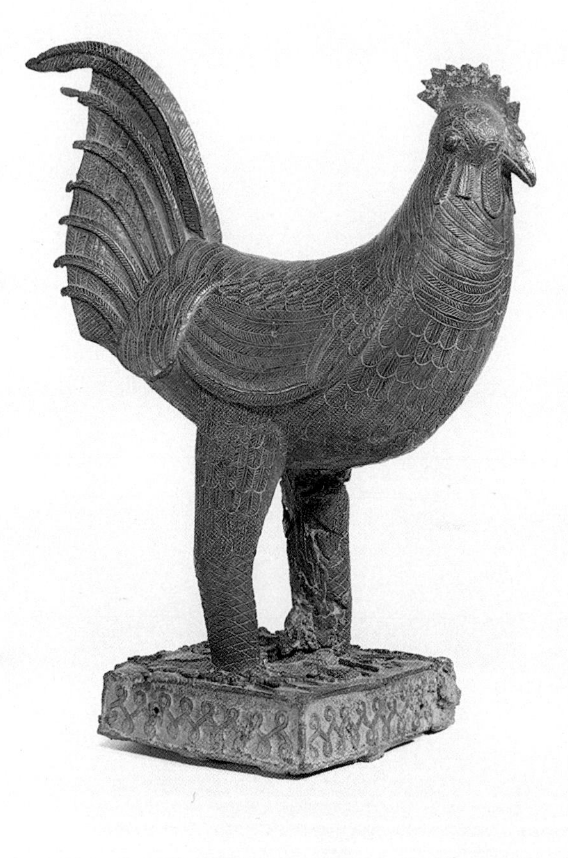

164

mudfish, and "thunderbolts" (stone celts that were found in the earth and were considered to be magically charged). On the rim of the back of the cap is a miniature bronze ax that perhaps serves as an amulet.

Height 48 cm., diameter 30 cm. 99.2
Acquired from the Museum für Völkerkunde Berlin 1899

Lit.: P. J. C. Dark 1973, pp. 12, 95; F. v. Luschan 1919, pp. 343-47.

164 Rooster, brass.
Nigeria, kingdom of Benin, Edo. 16th century.

The stylized plumage, partly sculptural and partly engraved, of this life-size thick-walled piece is precisely executed. On the base is a human arm in relief holding a trefoil, and near it a 3.5 cm. hole that serves as a receptacle for sacrificial gifts such as cola nuts. Casting faults appear on the base, which is surrounded by a guilloche band less carefully worked than the plumage. There are over thirty rooster figures among known Benin art works, all of which seem to date from the sixteenth century. What scant information we have on the symbolic significance of the rooster is contradictory. According to one tradition, the rooster was a protective spirit and a kind of spy for the archaic Ogiso dynasty (see p. 148). Later reports identify the cock as the sacrificial animal of the paternal ancestors of the *oba*. This conflicts with a recent report that the altars of deceased queen mothers were provided with rooster figures.

Height 53 cm., base 21 x 18 cm. 98.39
Acquired from A. Maschmann 1898

Lit.: P. Ben-Amos, in S. Vogel (ed.) 1981, p. 134; P. J. C. Dark 1973, p. 30; P. J. C. Dark & W. & B. Forman 1960, p. 40; F. v. Luschan 1919, pp. 337-39; T. Shaw 1978, p. 181.

165 Queen mother with retinue, brass.
Nigeria, kingdom of Benin, Edo. 18th century.

Presumably, this group once stood upon the commemorative altar of a dead queen mother. This piece reflects the high position of the queen mother in Benin and also displays the splendid dress and weapons of her courtiers. From the sixteenth century onward she ruled over her own establishment, which lay outside the capital. The female figures' rich ornaments and the men's rufflike collars actually consisted of threaded coral beads (see for example No. 161). Figures are shown in wrappers made from

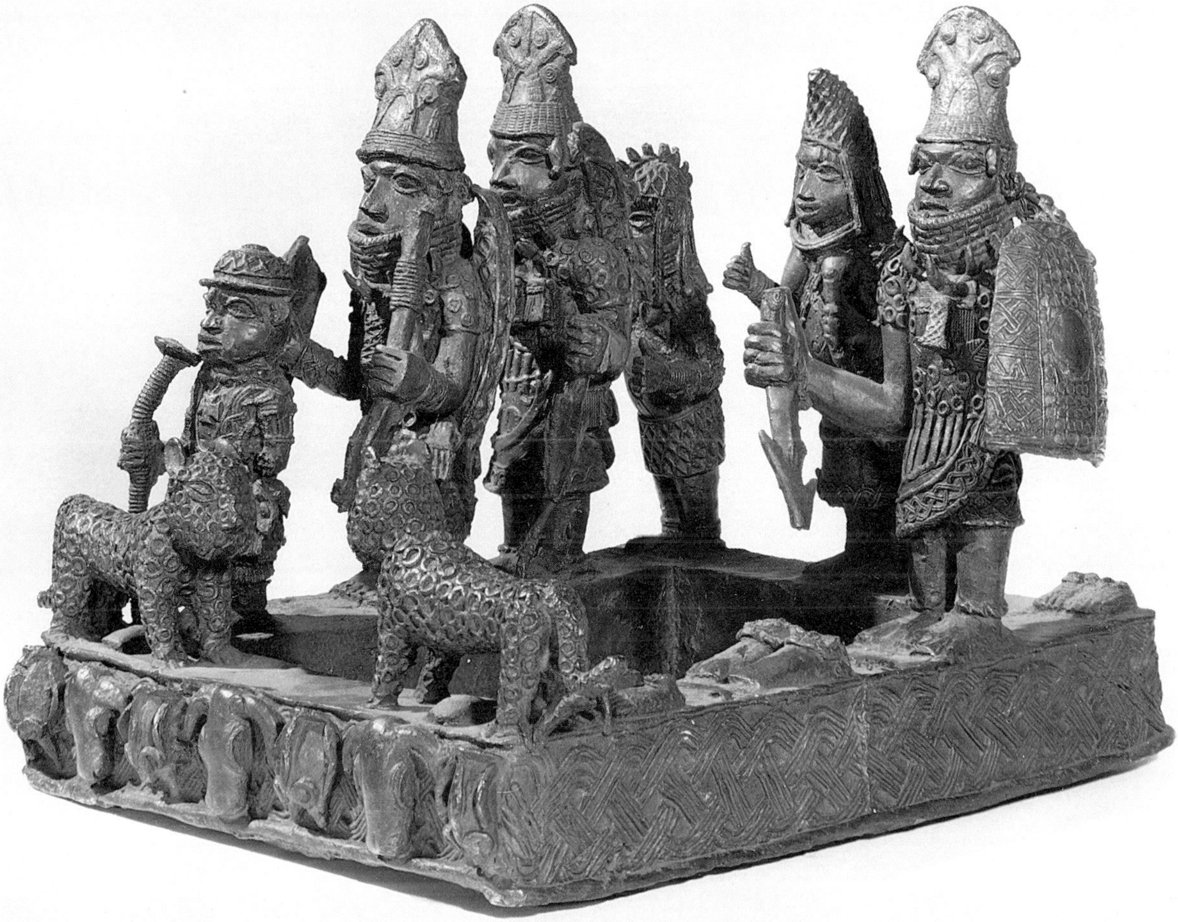

165

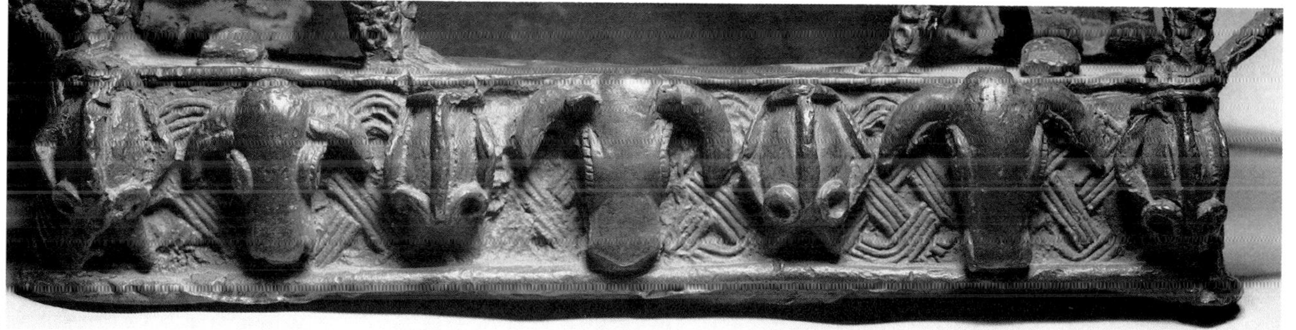

165

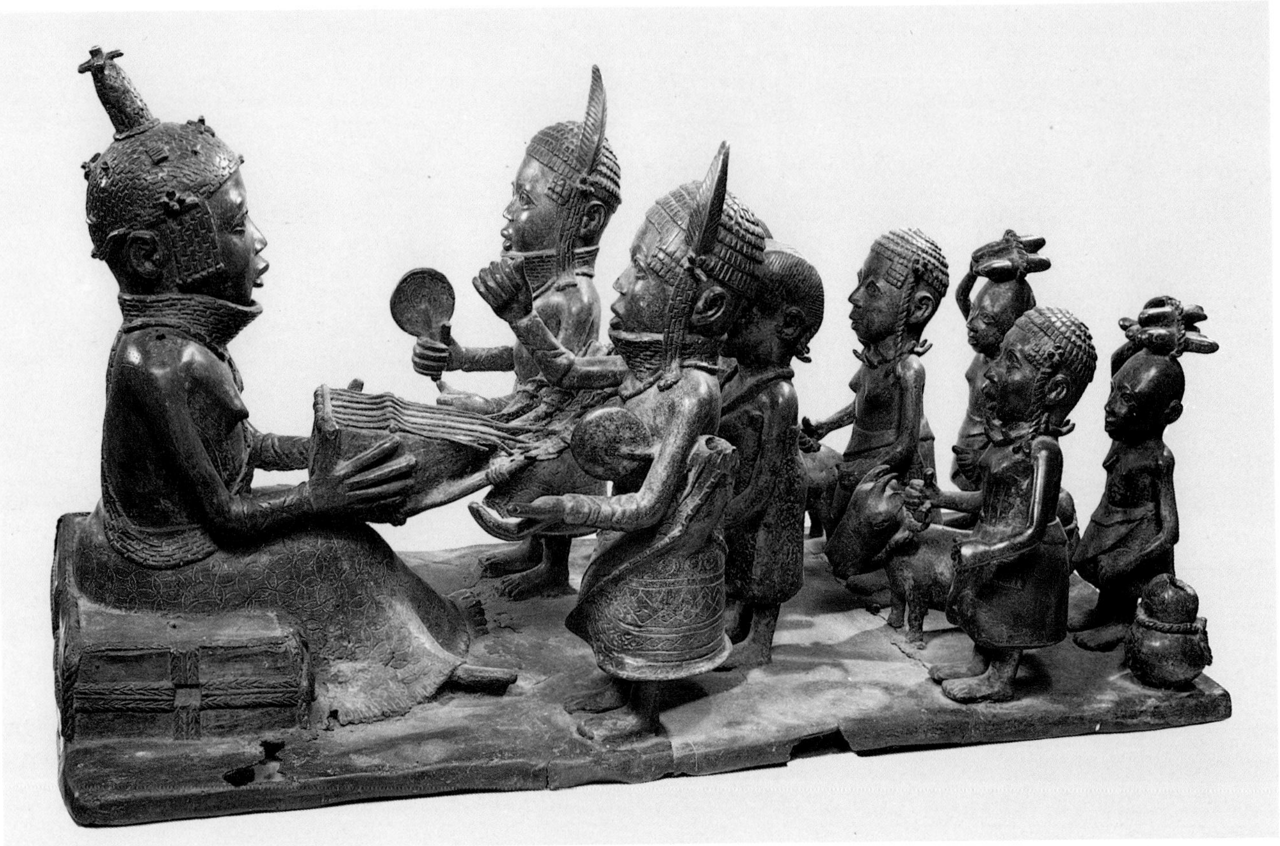

166

narrow bands of imported North African sheep's wool sewn together and embroidered with figurative and geometrical decorations. They are further ornamented by a stiffened border with a guilloche motif, which can be seen projecting above the left shoulders of the large figures.

Here the queen mother *(iye oba)* is shown accompanied by high dignitaries, dwarflike men carrying messenger staffs, and musicians with a box-shape instrument (see also No. 182). Two leopards face one another in the foreground. Three figures are missing—those of a dignitary, a musician, and a messenger. Guilloche bands decorate the sides of the base, while high-relief skulls of four leopards and three cows enrich its front. Cola nuts and other sacrificial gifts could be left in the hollow in the middle of the base. The figures are solid cast; the base is hollow.

Measurements 34 × 28 × 27 cm. 11.2
Acquired from A. Maschmann 1911

Lit.: P. J. C. Dark 1973, pp. 66-68; F. v. Luschan 1919, pp. 310-19; S. Wolf 1970, p. 202.

166 Harvest ceremonial before the king, brass. Nigeria, kingdom of Benin, Edo. Early 20th century.

This is one of the largest group compositions in metal from all of Africa south of the Sahara and has the greatest number of figures. An example of the survival of the brass-casting tradition for sacred purposes, it was probably made for the royal court in the 1930s. The base plate is formed of three parts, and the figures, except for the main one, were separately cast and sodered on.

Although this scene has not been found in any other work of art, it depicts a well-known ritual from the Guinea coast. Its subject is the offering of the first ripe yam tubers of the year to the king so that he, in turn, may make the first-fruit offerings to his forebears. This event, the greatest ancestral feast of the year, has the character of a state festival. In many parts of West Africa it initiated the new year. After the king's sacrifice the people could harvest, offer sacrifices, and consume the new yams.

The king, with a bow harp in his hand, is receiving a group that includes two dignitaries with fans, one in the attitude of reverence with the fan under his arm; two women, chief wives of the king, or priestesses, in wrappers that cover their breasts; two other dignitaries with sacrificial goats; and two young men carrying yam tubers on their heads; beside the last are two large calabash vessels that hold palm wine for the libation.

In comparison with the eighteenth-century altar group of figures (No. 165), the king, dignitaries, and women here wear much simpler regalia. But the traditional wrappers with embroidered borders, the head coverings, the high rufflike collar of coral beads, and even the neck ornament of lion claws have survived. The king no longer wears the ceremonial dress of coral beads here, although it is still in use today. A further peculiarity is that the king holds a bow harp and sits opposite the group. In earlier groups of this kind the king always sits or stands facing in the same direction as the other figures.

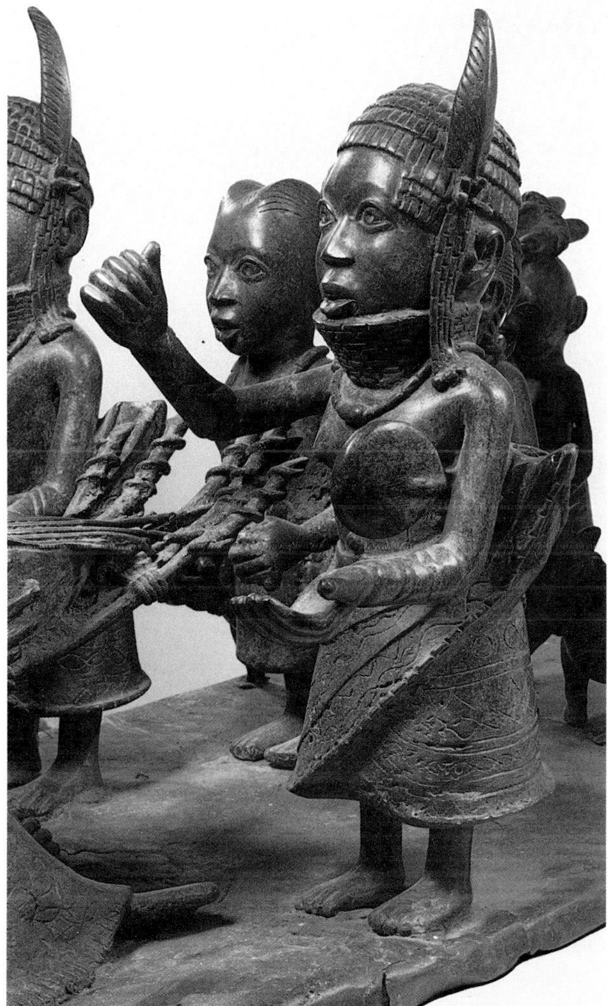

166

Nothing is known of the function of a royal musical instrument at the yam festival, though the musician with harp is a popular subject in twentieth-century Benin art.

Measurements 82 x 42 x 42 cm. 79-300-875
Acquired from G. and M. Stoll 1979

Lit.: P. J. C. Dark 1973, Illus. 124-5, Illus. 145-6; F. v. Luschan 1919, pp. 310-19; H. Melzian 1955, pp. 92, 98-100.

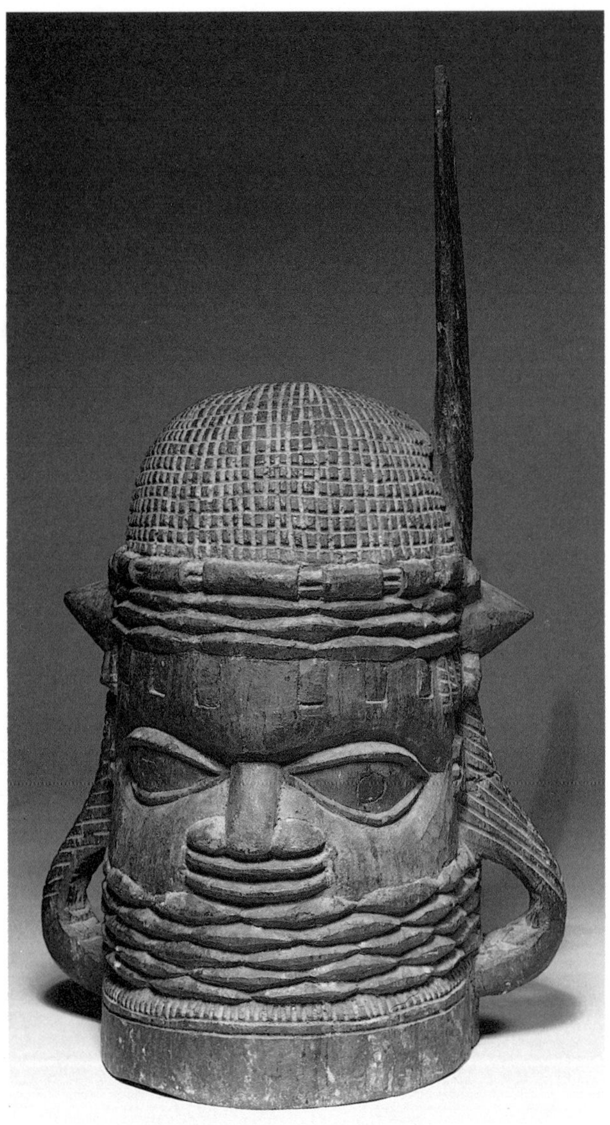

167

167 Ancestral head (*uhunmw elao*), wood. Nigeria, kingdom of Benin, Edo. About 1900.

Chiefs as well as kings commissioned head sculptures for their departed forefathers, but theirs were wood: only heads destined for the royal altars were of metal. Wooden heads were modeled on royal metal heads and occasionally had a thin covering of brass sheet, although this piece does not have one. Like the royal heads, they had high, broad, rufflike collars and no bases. A feather at the left temple announced the wooden subject's chiefly office. The hole in the crown of the head and the long slit at the back held the head to the altar by means of a post.

Darker wood was used for the pupils of the eyes and the forehead marks on this example, which dates to about 1900. The ears are small, geometric, and stylized. More detail is apparent on the front of the sculpture than on the back.

Height 64 cm. 81-301-484
Acquired from R. L. Stolper 1981

Lit.: P. Ben-Amos 1980, p. 63; P. J. C. Dark 1973, pp. 101-3; F. v. Luschan 1919, pp. 495-96.; F. Willet & J. Picton 1967, pp. 62-70.

Brass *Ama* Relief Plaques (168–170)

The first relief plaques were probably cast in the middle of the sixteenth century, during the period of upsurging power in the Benin kingdom. Dark and others have dated the latest examples of this type of court art to the early eighteenth century.

More recent research in Berlin, however, based on thermoluminescence, metal analysis and other testing, has led Irwin Tunis (1983) to conclude that the relief plaques were made during a period of only fifty years. About nine hundred plaques have been preserved from this short period. They decorated the posts of the royal palace, recalling former *obas*, army leaders, and warriors, as well as Portuguese visitors. Emblems of royal power, Portuguese heads (see No. 169), or busts frequently appear in the corners of the plaques.

The custom of providing the palace with such commemorative plaques may be very old. According to Dark, metal reliefs replaced the clay ones of

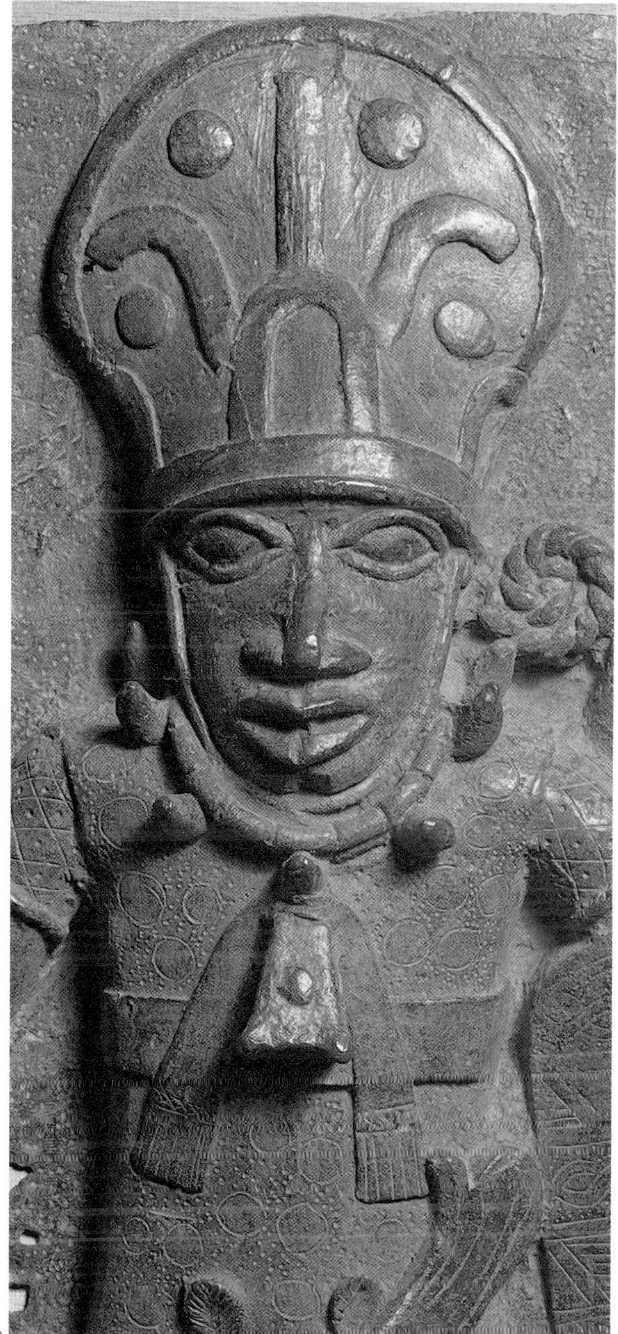

168

earlier times. The abundance of forms seen on the plaques, however, seems to be the result of stimuli from European medieval art, known through woodcuts, book illustrations, and so on. For instance, the engraved background ornaments of the plaques—the wheel with cross and the four-petaled (more rarely, two and three-petaled) flowers—are of foreign inspiration. Presumably, these originated in European or Islamic art and in the course of time were smoothly incorporated into indigenous tradition. The blossoms are related to certain water plants used by the Ogun cult. The characteristic quartering of both ornaments easily acquires symbolic value in a culture in which the theory of life and chronology are subject to the number four (four compass points, four-day week, four times of the day, and so on).

Dark distinguishes three stylistic periods in these relief plaques. The oldest plaques, some twenty in number, consist of two halves, separately cast and furnished with simply ornamented elongated figures in low relief; their backgrounds are ornamented with circle-and-cross motifs. Those of the middle period also display elongated figures (see Nos. 168 and 170) but exhibit as well a trend toward three-dimensionality (see No. 169), which is fully developed in the third epoch. In both the middle and the last period most backgrounds are decorated with engraved flowers.

Williams distinguishes, according to cultural-historical considerations, two short periods of plaque art—the first beginning in the sixteenth century with the "Portuguese Period," followed by the "Hieratic Period."

Lit.: P. Ben-Amos 1980, pp. 28-29; P. J. C. Dark 1973, pp. 3-4; W. Fagg 1963, p. 34; I.L. Tunis 1979, pp. 62-65, 1983, pp. 45-53; D. Williams 1974, pp. 149-78; S. Wolf 1970, p. 209.

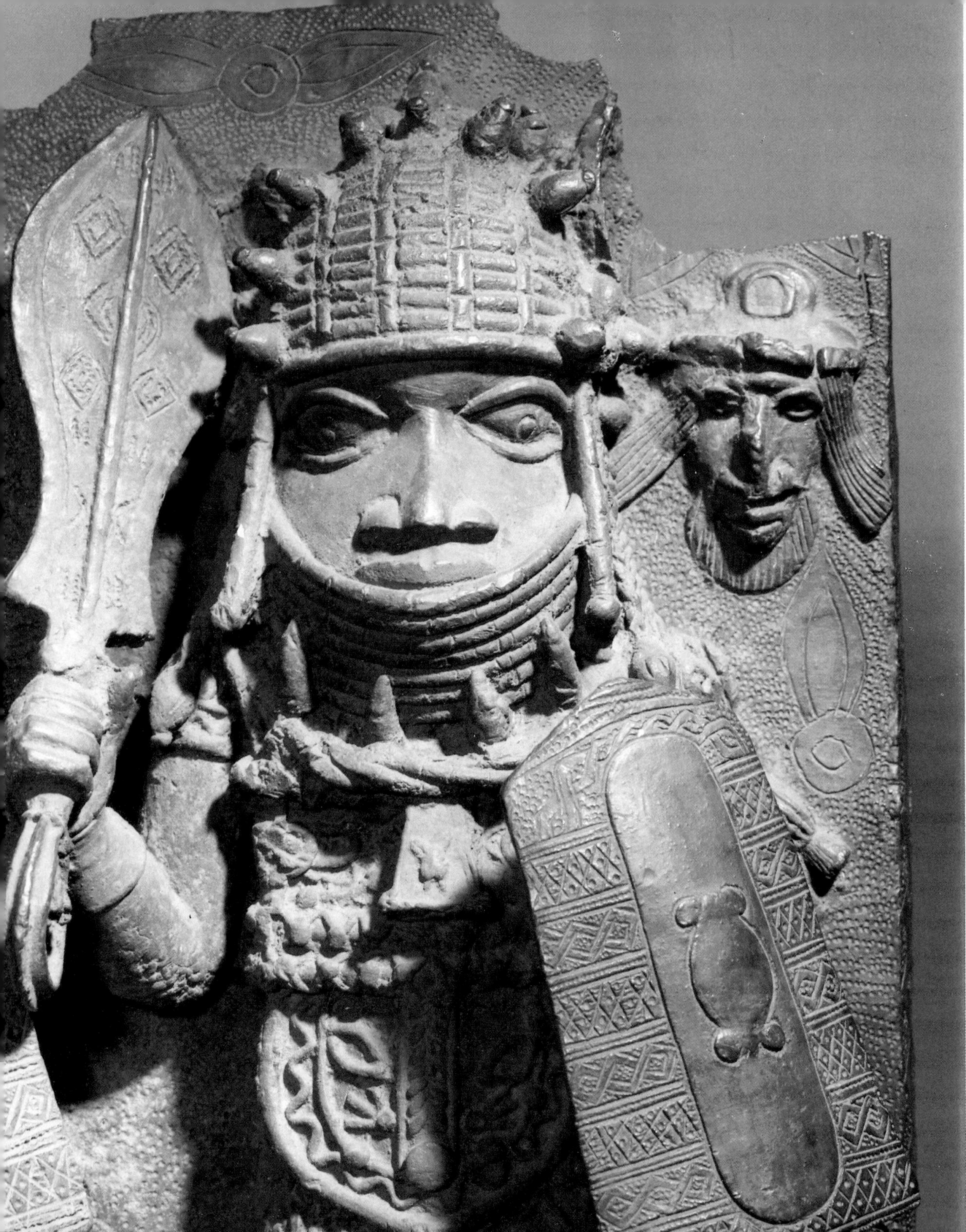

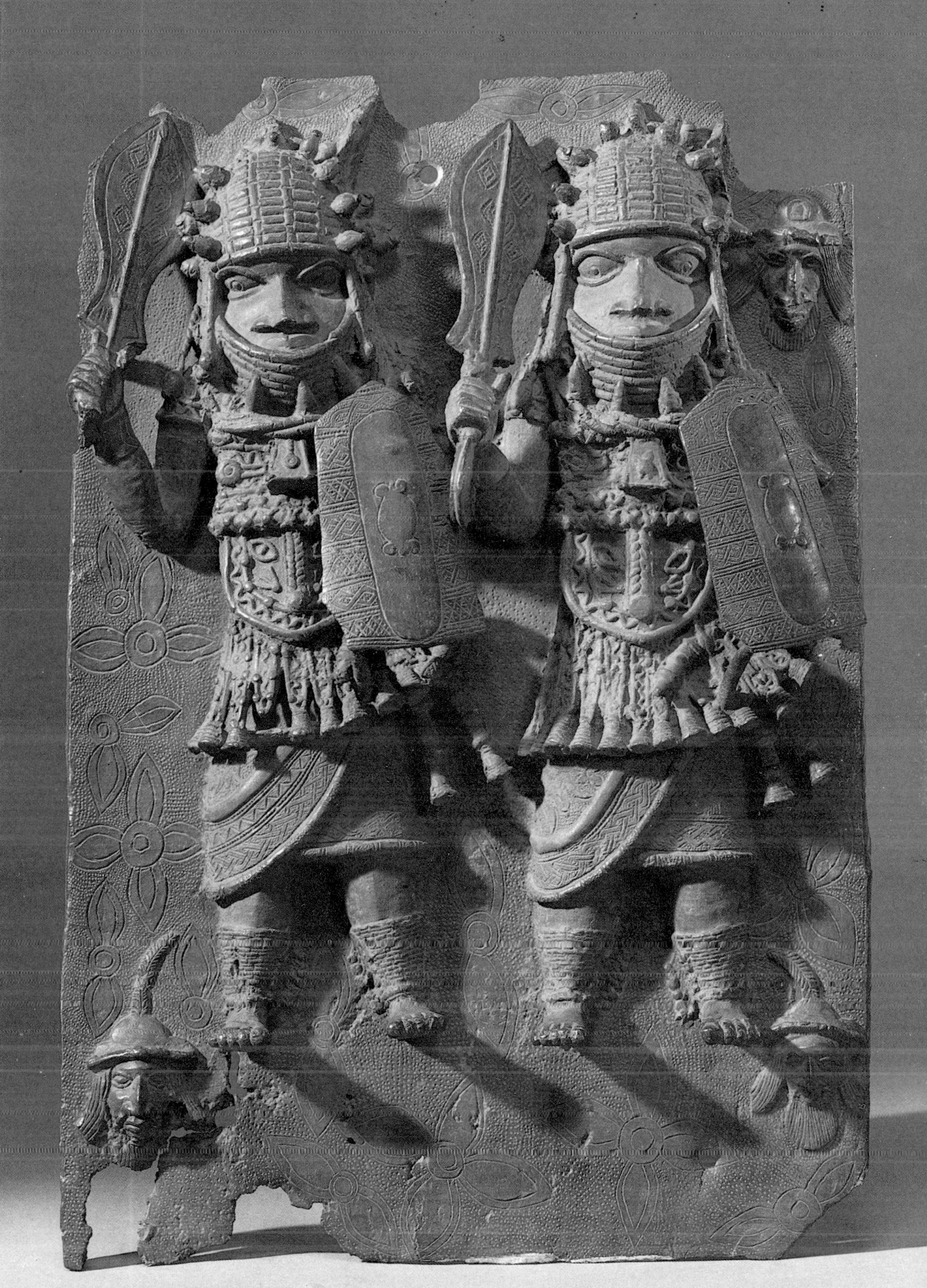

169

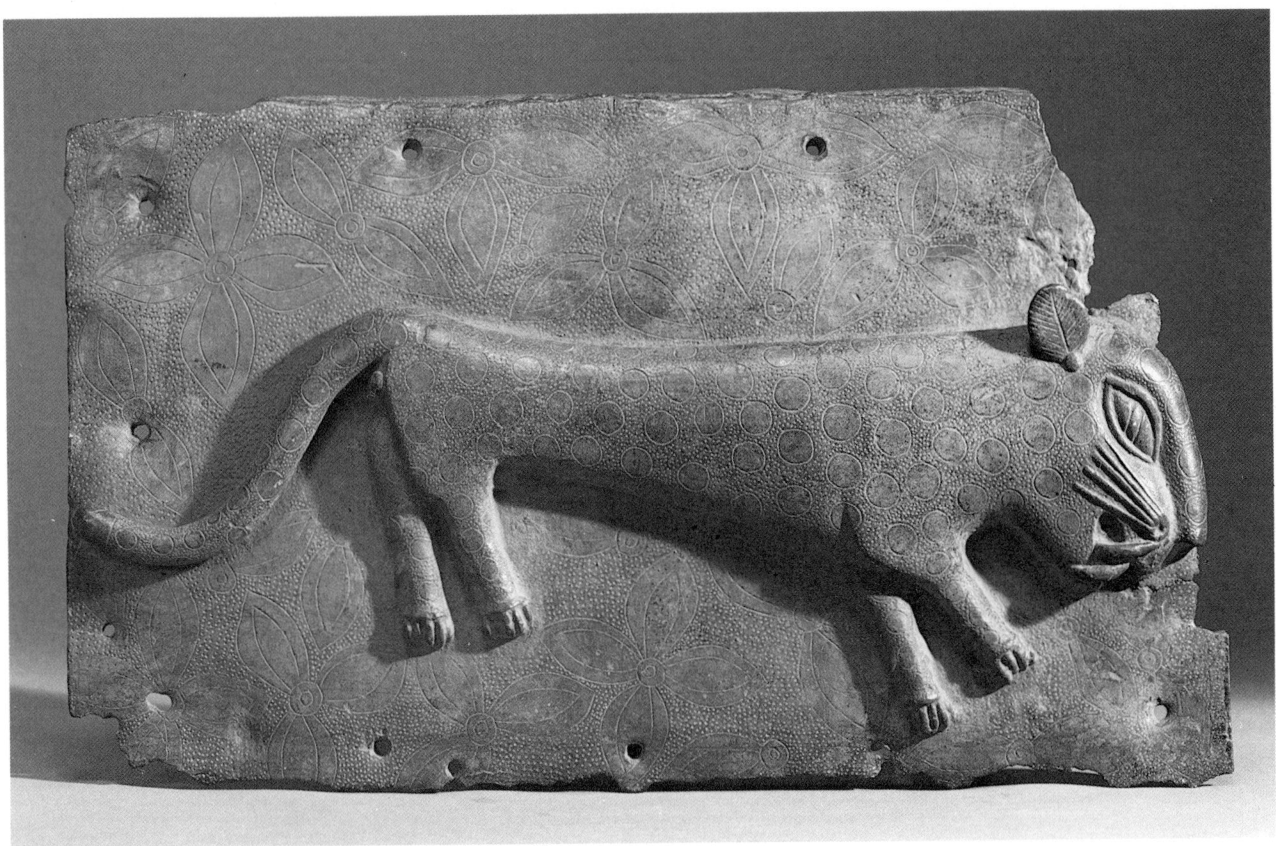

170

168 Relief plaque (*ama*), brass.
Nigeria, kingdom of Benin, Edo.
(see color plate, p. 68)

This armed military leader or *oba*'s spear carrier appears in the full dress with shirt and wrapper that only important dignitaries were allowed to wear. Further symbols of this figure's high rank are his leopard-skin cloak, necklace of coral beads and leopard claws, rectangular bell, broad bracelet, anklets, miter-shape hat, and patterned wrapper.

Height 46 cm., width 38 cm. 99.7
Acquired from the Webster Collection 1899

169 Relief plaque (*ama*), brass.
Nigeria, kingdom of Benin, Edo.

Two dignitaries, each with a ritual sword (*eben*), coral-bead cap, and collar so high that it covers the chin, can be seen here. Portuguese heads decorate the corners of this example from the last period of plaque art, in which the figures have become three-dimensional. They are also squatter and sturdier with more splendid dress and ornaments.

Height 48 cm., width 33 cm. 99.6
Acquired from the Webster Collection 1899

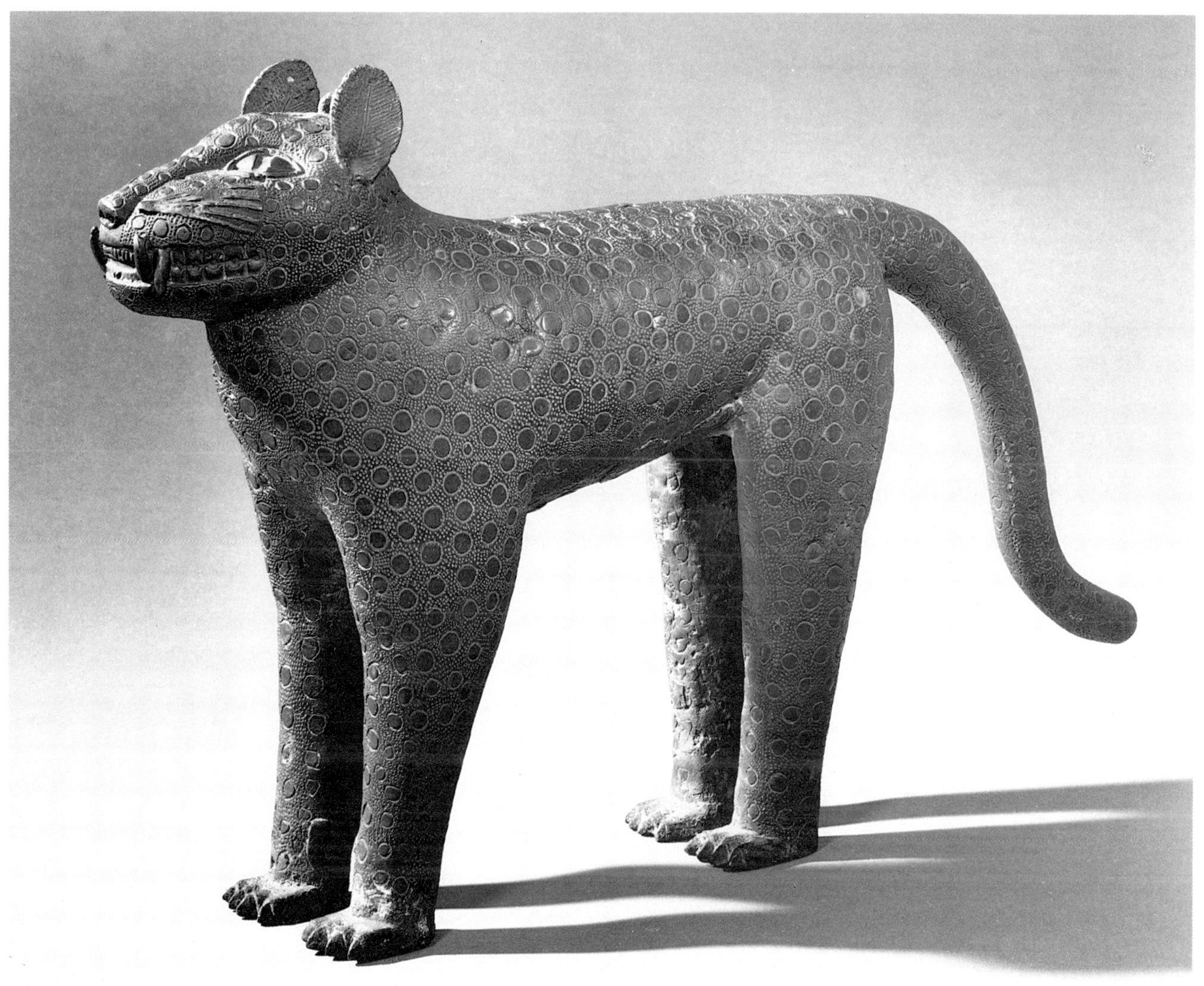

171

170 Relief plaque *(ama)*, brass.
Nigeria, kingdom of Benin, Edo.

Animals appear on a number of reliefs from the second phase of plaque art. The leopard in particular displays artistic conventions—such as stylized spots indicated by circles and points, and ears that resemble ribbed leaves—that many experts believe were obsolete by the eighteenth century. Sculpture in the round developed similarly (No. 171).

The animals depicted are of species that have symbolic or mythological significance. One of the most important of these is the leopard, respected throughout Africa not only because of his ferocity but also as a bearer of magical powers—as a sorcerer transformed or as the reincarnation of certain dead persons. In Benin these beliefs were associated with royalty. On the one hand, the leopard was considered a symbol of the *oba*'s legitimate authority and power. On the other, as king of the wilderness, it represented the antithesis of the king of the human realm.

A group of professional leopard hunters lived at court, and the *oba* claimed all leopards. Captured or slain animals were turned over to him, and he distributed skin and claws as signs of office. Captured leopard cubs were trained for hunting purposes. At the annual *igue* festival, held to renew the king's magical powers, a leopard was killed and its blood daubed on the *oba* and his insignia.

Height 30 cm., width 51 cm. 99.8
Acquired from the Webster Collection 1899

Lit.: H. Baumann 1950, pp. 192,207; P. Ben-Amos 1976, pp. 246-48, 1980, pp. 76, 82, 85, 88; P. J. C. Dark 1973, p. 91.

171 Leopard figure, brass, iron.
Nigeria, Kingdom of Benin, Edo.
(see color plate p. 69)

In the Middle Ages, European animal-shape metal vessels called aquamaniles, based on Islamic models, were used to pour water for priests or guests to wash their hands at the table. The Portuguese introduced such vessels into Benin, which stimulated Edo casters to make zoomorphic water containers, though their form and function were modified in the spirit of indigenous tradition.

Leopard-shape vessels are the most common among the pieces that have been preserved. According to von Luschan, nine specimens are known. The vessels were always made and used in pairs, and the pendant to this one, believed to have been made in the seventeenth or early eighteenth century, is in the Minneapolis Institute of Arts. Before casting, the artist transferred the carefully drawn skin pattern to the wax model. As in several of the Benin head sculptures, the eyes have an iron lining. During the annual *egie erha oba* festival celebrating the royal ancestors, water was poured over the *oba*'s hands through the animal's nostrils. Perhaps the leopard vessel was chosen for this ceremony because of its symbolic connection with royalty (see No. 170).

Height 43 cm., length 60 cm. 52-7-1
Acquired from L. Bretschneider 1952 (The complete pair was a present of Consul E. Schmidt to Emperor Wilhelm II).

Lit.: P. Ben-Amos 1976, pp. 246-48, 1980, pp. 76, 82, 85, 88; P. J. C. Dark 1973, p. 91; A. Lommel 1953, pp. 178-79; F. v. Luschan 1919, pp. 335-37; W. Robbins 1966, Illus. 176.

172 Fragment of a scepter, brass.
Nigeria, Kingdom of Benin, Edo. Late 18th century.

Here the *oba* appears in ceremonial dress with loincloth, coral-bead cap, high collar, and coral-bead strands crossed over his chest. In his hands are a carved wooden ancestral staff and a stone ax (thunderbolt), symbols of power. In many parts of Africa the ax is thought to convey magical power.

Height 9 cm. 98.47
Acquired from Captain A. Maschmann 1898

Lit.: P. J. C. Dark & B. Forman 1960, p. 53; L. F. Pitt-Rivers 1900, p. 22.

173 Figure of a sword bearer, brass.
Nigeria, Kingdom of Benin, Edo.

This is a late work in the Edo casting tradition, probably from the nineteenth century. This subject is known mainly from relief plaques such as that seen in No. 169. The dignitary here carries the state sword, or *eben,* seen in the earlier piece, but the rich ornamentation and ceremonial dress of that example are missing here.

Height 17.5 cm. 13-73-4
Acquired from v. Christ 1913

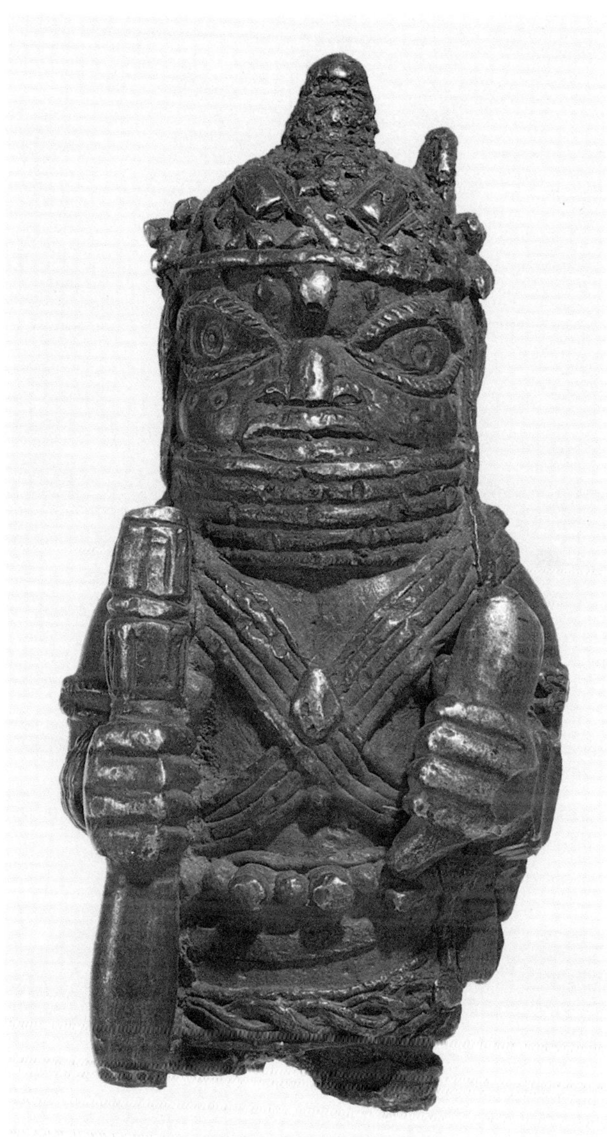
172

174 Rectangular bell, brass.
Nigeria, Kingdom of Benin, Edo.

All outer surfaces of this bell are covered with a point-and-circle decoration similar to that used to represent leopard skin (see Nos. 170 and 171). In

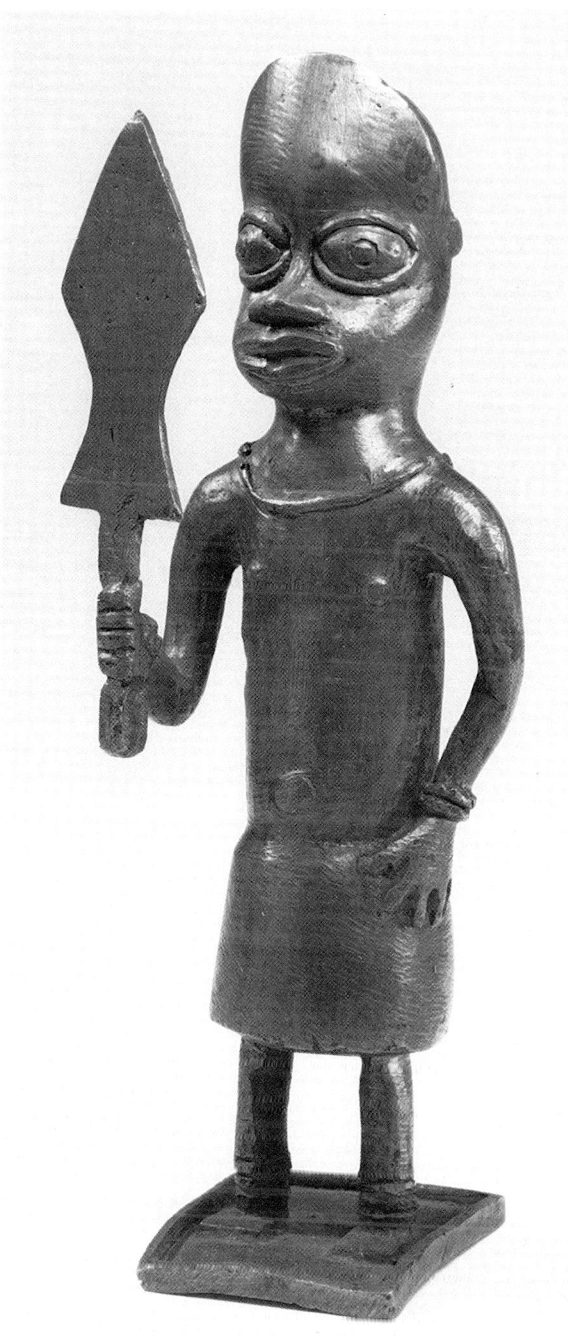
173

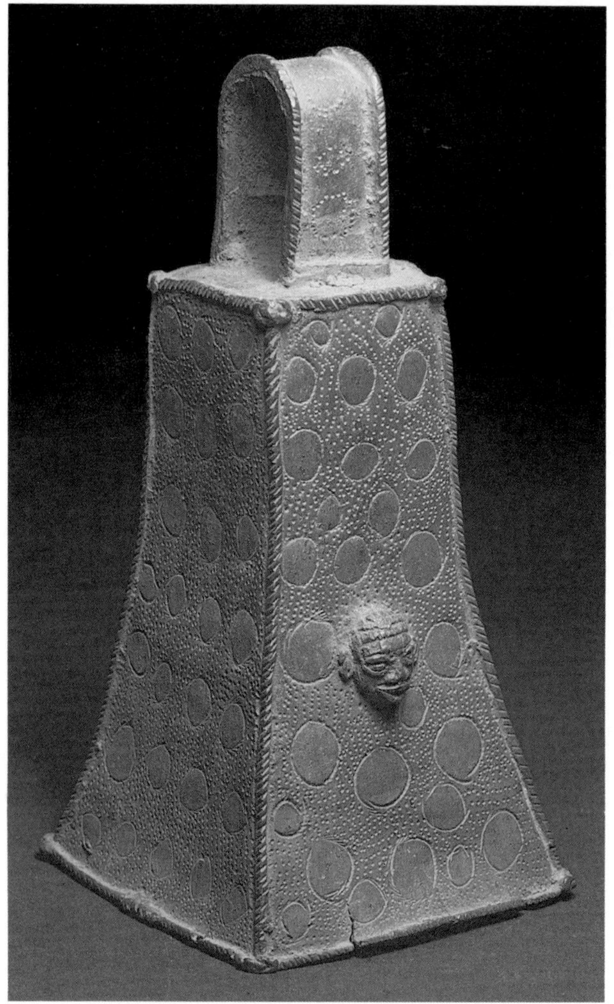

174

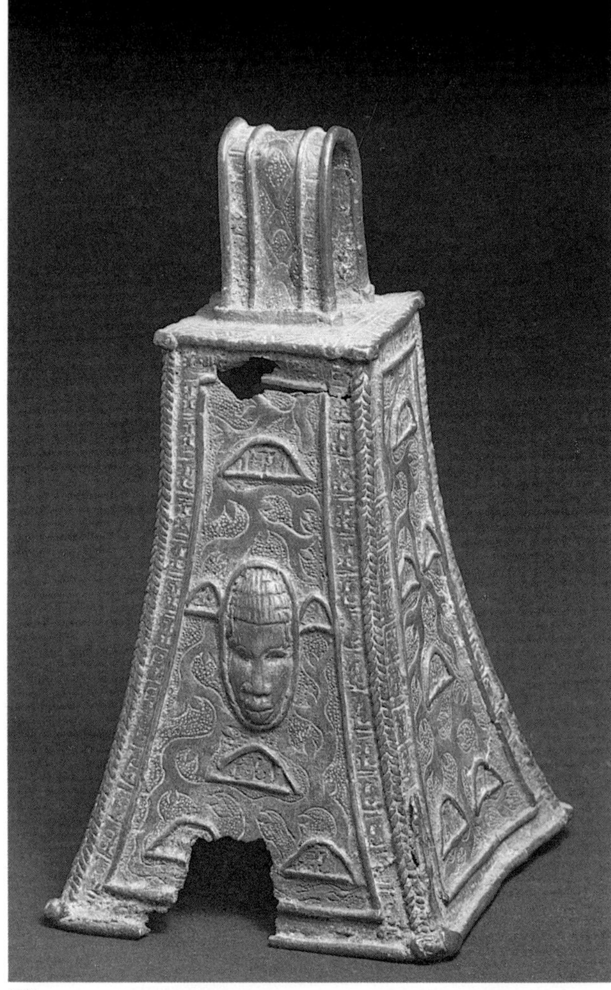

175

addition, a human head with graduated coiffure—a type known chiefly from metal and terra-cotta commemorative plaques and from ivory masks—is to one side. Such bells had numerous uses: worn round the neck, they served as a sign of office; rung, they could call ancestors; placed on an ancestral altar, they served religious purposes. Warriors as well as rulers could use them.

Height 16 cm. 32-36-3
Acquired from H. Meyer 1932

Lit.: W. Froehlich 1966, p. 283; S. Wolf 1972, Illus. 22,3 and p. 35.

175 Rectangular bell, brass.
Nigeria, kingdom of Benin, Edo.

This bell is more finely executed than that in No. 174. Aside from the cast ornament, the background of all four walls consists of stylized creepers meandering on a field of tiny dots.

Height 18 cm. 32-36-1
Acquired from H. Meyer 1933

Lit.: P. J. C. Dark 1973, p. 73.

176 Messenger staff, brass.
Nigeria, kingdom of Benin, Edo.
C. 18th century.

Messengers of the *oba* carried such staffs on assignments to settlements outside the capital. According to local tradition, these journeys were usually undertaken to collect animals from the villages for royal sacrificial feasts. As with most objects made for ruler and court, messenger staffs were artistically formed of valuable materials. The lower part of this staff is a narrow blunt blade engraved with a simplified tendril ornament (see also No. 175). Sculptured figures ornament the upper part. The top figures hold the ceremonial sword, or *eben,* carried only by the *oba* and certain chiefs. Lower figures hold the bird-shape percussion instrument *ahianwen-oro,* a power symbol well known to relate to the ruler. The messenger staff thus not only legitimizes the bearer but also serves as a reminder of royal power and a warning to subjects not to disregard the order the messenger delivers.

Height 100 cm. 98.42
Acquired from Captain A. Maschmann 1898

Lit.: P. Ben-Amos 1980, p. 70; P. J. C. Dark 1973, p. 73; P. J. C. Dark & B. Forman 1960, pl. 2, p. 30; S. Wolf 1963, p. 135.

177 Bracelet, brass.
Nigeria, kingdom of Benin, Edo.

An openwork guilloche band ornament provides a decorative contrast to the two faces with strong linear tattooing—Yoruba rather than Edo portraits. As recently as 1958 the royal retinue walked or danced in the procession at the annual feast of the *oba* wearing such bracelets. As the bracelet was held in a hand raised vertically, one face looked forward, the other backward (symbolizing the *oba*'s ability to look both into the past and into the future?).

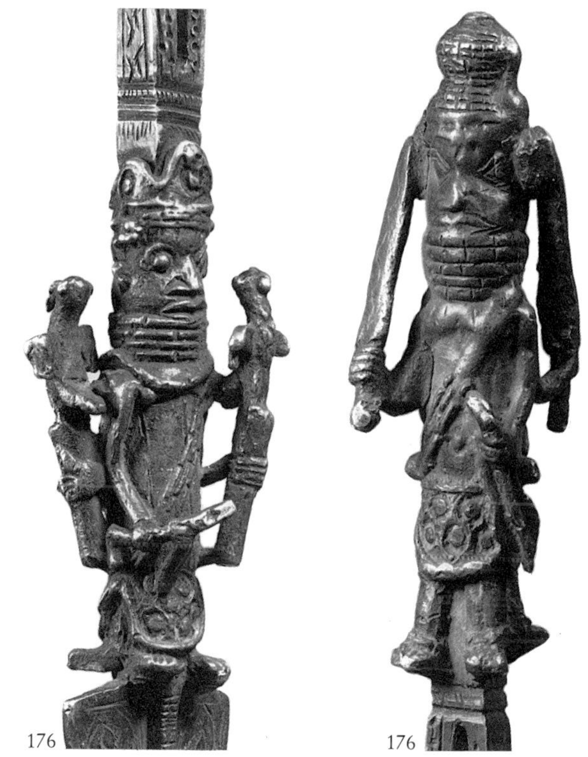

176 176

Diameter 8 cm. 98.50
Acquired from Captain A. Maschmann 1898

Lit.: W. Fagg 1968, Illus. 147.

178 Bracelet, brass.
Nigeria, kingdom of Benin, Edo

The *oba* and his highest dignitaries wore cufflike bracelets like this, one on each arm, at festivals (see No. 166). Our piece, a late work that is possibly a copy of an earlier one, is provided with human figures alternately upside down and right side up. These can be recognized as schematic representations of

Europeans, presumably Portuguese, important trading partners of the kingdom depicted in Benin art from the sixteenth century onward. The figures are rendered in part respectfully, in part critically, and occasionally as caricatures. An almost identical piece is in the Museum für Völkerkunde in Hamburg.

Height 13 cm. 98.43
Acquired from Captain A. Maschmann 1898

Lit.: S. Wolf 1972, Illus. 26,27.

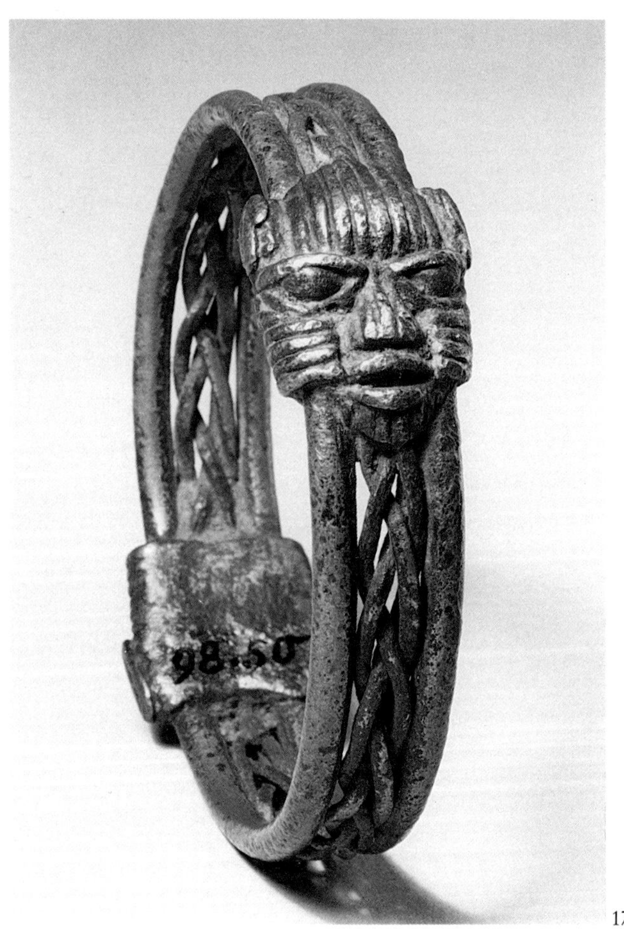

177

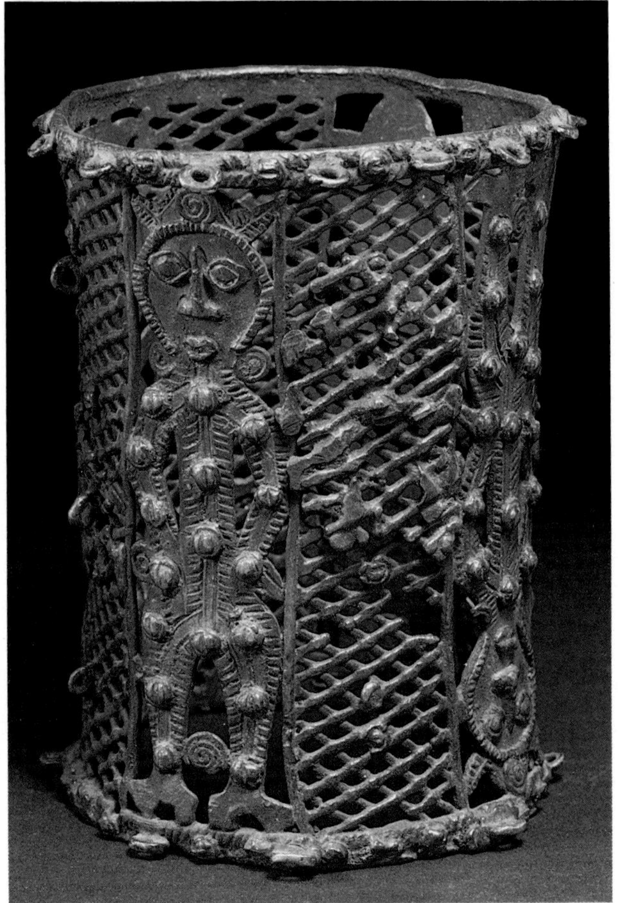

178

179 Fragment of a pendant, brass.
Nigeria, kingdom of Benin, Edo.
Beginning of the 18th century.

This originally shield-shape piece, worn as a pendant at waist level, accompanied the court dress. The queen is represented here as bell beater, in a ceremonial dress of coral beads, conical bonnet, collar, and pectoral cross (see also the queen in the group of figures in No. 165).

Representations of women became more frequent in Benin art only after the sixteenth century, as women's importance in social and ritual life increased. This may well have been due to the flourishing of the Olokun cult and the prestige of Olokun priestesses.

This object, known to have been gilded in Benin, is one of the few examples of African use of this technique, which was probably practiced as a result of foreign influence.

Height 8.5 cm. 11.1
Acquired from M. Maschmann 1911

Lit.: S. Wolf 1968, p. 108, 1970, pp. 208, 213, 221-23.

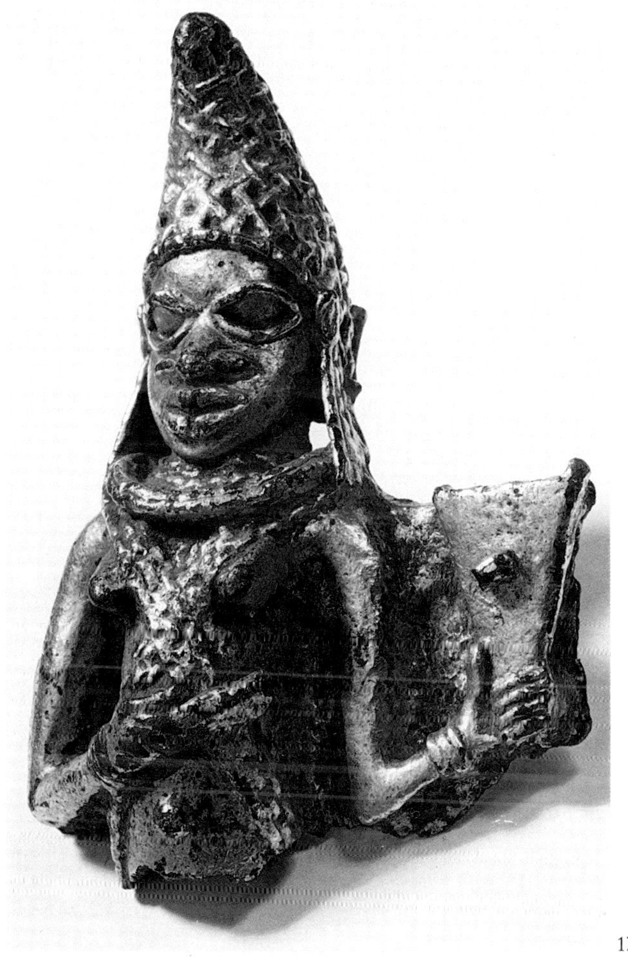

179

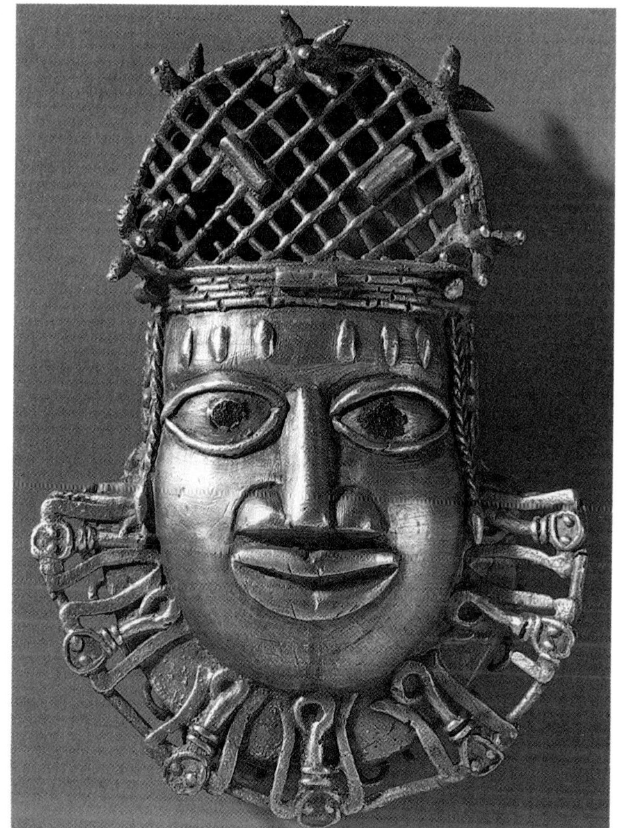

180

180 Masklike pendant, brass, iron.
Nigeria, kingdom of Benin, Edo.

The *oba* is seen here with coral cap and neck ruff with a design of stylized mudfish. Sixteenth-century Portuguese frilled collars were very likely the source of African neck ruffs. This face is rigid, recalling the most recent of the ancestral heads. Numerous such pendants, worn as belt ornaments on the left hip, have been preserved from various centuries.

Height 17.5 cm. 12-62-1
Acquired by L. Glenk (Heppner) 1912

Lit.: P. J. C. Dark 1973, pp. 95-96; W. Froelich 1966, p. 265; F. v. Luschan 1919, pp. 374ff.

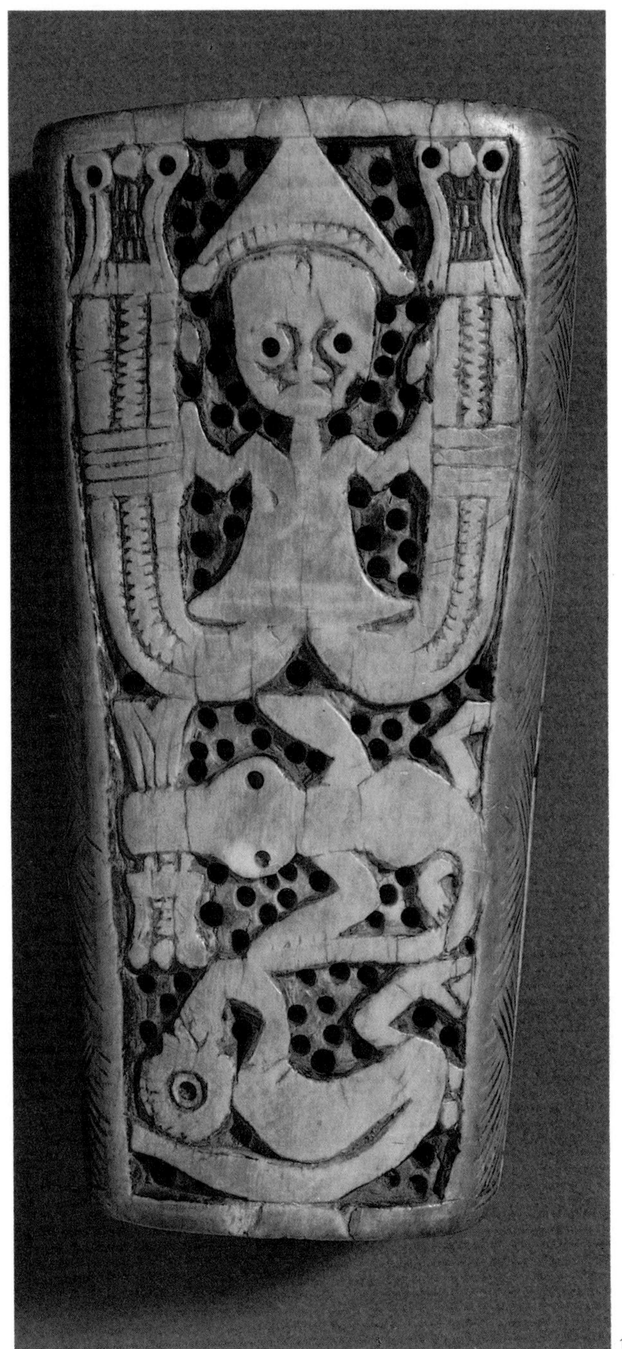
181

Ivory Carving

181 Lidded box, ivory.
Nigeria, Yoruba, Owo,
commissioned by Edo.

This lidded box is an independent, unconventional work without counterpart among the few preserved examples of the form. Its figurative decoration is more freely composed than most, without the more usual overly rich ornament. The figures cut out in flat relief are the god Olokun (a human shape with fish legs), his companion the crocodile, and a monkey eating a maize cob (this motif is known in Yoruba art; see No. 136). The box was originally stained reddish brown with palm oil; now its worn surface is covered with a beautiful patina, suggesting great age. Filled with cola nuts, the box may have served as a precious gift.

The asymmetrical arrangement and the combination of low-relief designs with an openwork background are typical of the work of Yoruba carvers of Owo, which was for a time under the rule of Benin. The box probably originated there but was obviously commissioned by an Edo citizen, for some of the motifs are characteristic of traditional Benin art.

Length 16 cm. 24-24-4
Acquired from W. Carl 1924

Lit.: D. Fraser 1972, pp. 261-94; L. v. Luschan 1919, p. 486; R. Poynor 1976, pp. 40, 42.

182 Elephant tusk with relief carving.
Nigeria, kingdom of Benin, Edo. 18th
century.

Elephant tusks are among the symbols of royalty in many parts of Africa, and kings frequently claimed all tusks. In Benin the tusks were placed on the royal ancestors' altars as a tribute. The majority of the high-relief figures carved on the front of this piece are

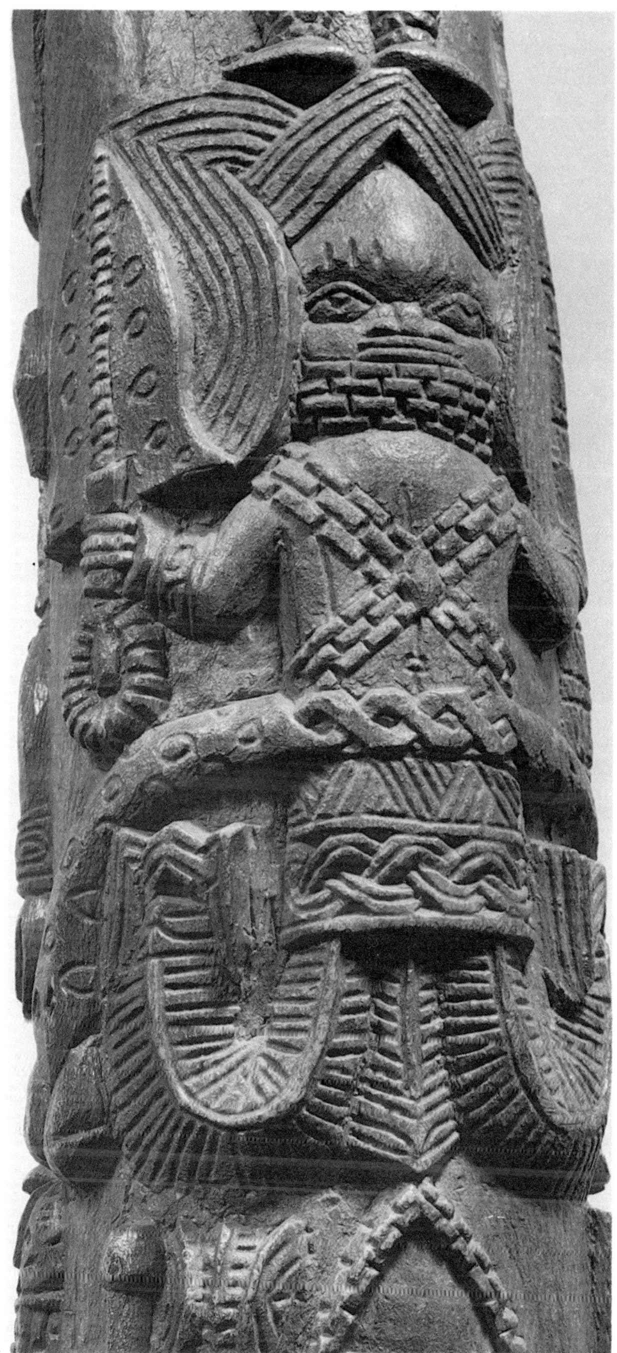

182

probably to be understood as dead rulers. Except for those on the lower part, the figures display royal insignia, suggesting that this tusk represents members of a dynasty. Set off from the remaining figures by his size and central position, Oba Ohen appears in the shape of the god Olokun (see also No. 181). Two curving mudfish form his legs, the mudfish's barbel his hair, and he carries the state sword and the ancestral staff. Snakes biting tortoises emerge from his belt. Olokun was considered god of the waters, including the ocean; of wealth; and of the abundance of children. After the establishment of regular trade with the Portuguese in the sixteenth century, Olokun's cult began to flourish. The Edo are said to have ascribed the arrival of the foreign merchants with heavily laden ships to Olokun's influence. Just why he was represented as fish-legged is as unclear as why he was made a mixed being in the first place. Some scholars consider him to be indigenous, while others believe he derived from Mediterranean mythology (that is, from Triton) or from pre-Islamic Asia Minor. Others see in him an echo of European ship figureheads of the Renaissance period. But not all fish-legged figures represent Olokun: the legendary Benin king Ohen (fourteenth century) is similarly represented. Fusion of the images of Olokun and Oba Ohen is explained by the facts that Ohen introduced the Olokun cult to Benin and is said to have been lame.

Other fish-legged figures swing crocodiles or catfish in their hands, an iconography that refers to variants of the "lord of the animals" swinging lions or leopards and originated in Oriental antiquity. Deonna has also recorded its occurrence in Benin. The figures on our tusk probably refer to the mythical lord of aquatic animals or to the king's ancestors, heroized after death. The lower parts of the tusk show a number of remarkable figures that seem to have no thematic connection: a monkey covering its eyes with its paws, an unusual motif in Benin art; a man being swallowed by a python, a mythical scene frequently depicted, especially among the Yo-

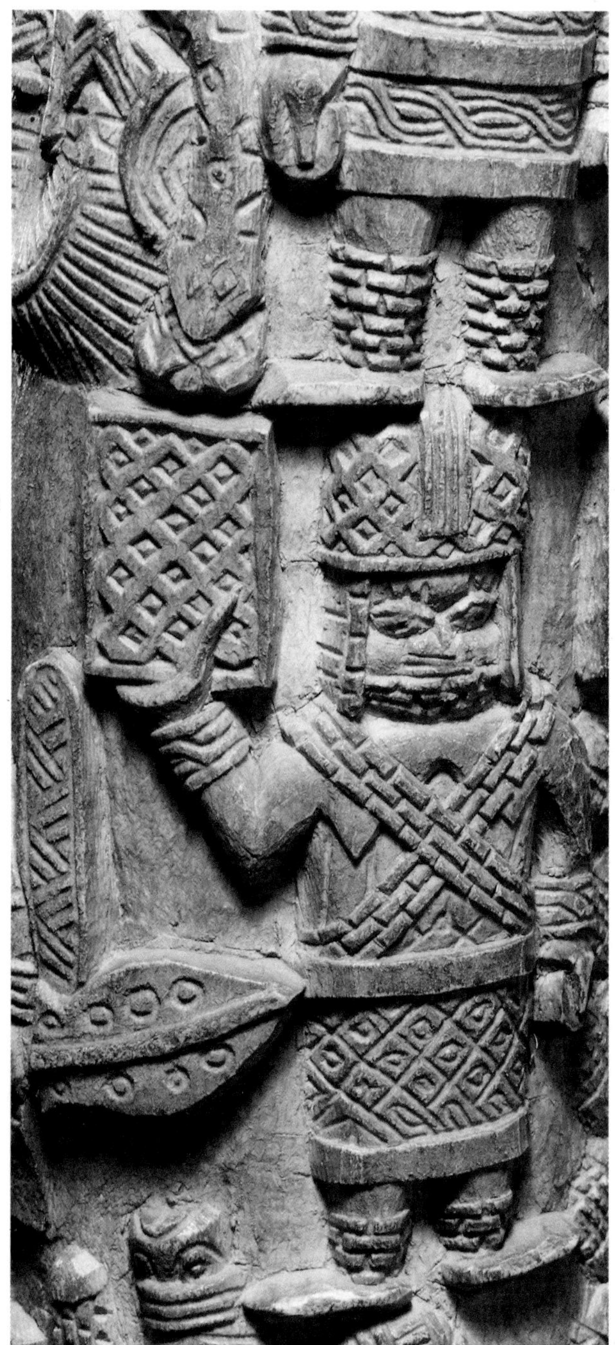
182

ruba of Owo; the messenger of a neighboring people with tatooed mouth corners and a pectoral cross (no Christian emblem!) accompanied by two Portuguese; the *oba*, supported by his subjects according to royal custom and flanked by two female musicians with boxlike instruments (see also the group of figures in No. 165). In the interstices between larger figures are cult and power symbols: mudfish, leopard, snake, and bird, and an elephant trunk ending in a hand. A guilloche ornament runs around the base of the tusk. The cult use of elephant tusks is an indigenous tradition in Benin, as in other parts of West Africa. The rich relief carving over the entire surface seems to have become customary only in the course of contacts with the Portuguese, however. Dating the large relief-decorated tusks is based on stylistic criteria and the dress and ornaments of the figures. The date of our piece can be no earlier than the seventeenth century, when high, broad coral-bead collars were first introduced, but the generalized and schematized figures place the tusk in the late phase of Benin art. Thus this carving was probably made in the eighteenth century.

Length 154 cm. 99.4
Acquired from the Webster Collection 1899

Lit.: P. J. C. Dark 1973, p. 88; W. Deonna 1949, p. 371; D. Fraser 1972, pp. 261-94; A. Lopasic 1965, n.p.; S. Wolf 1970, pp. 215-16.

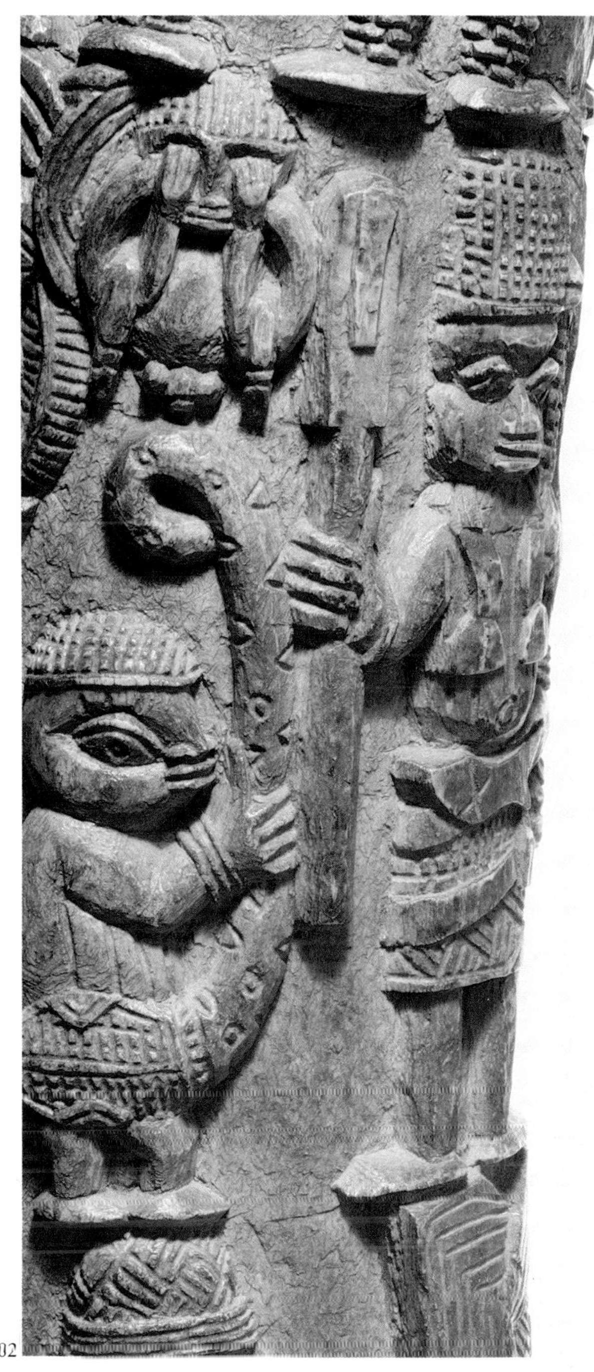
182

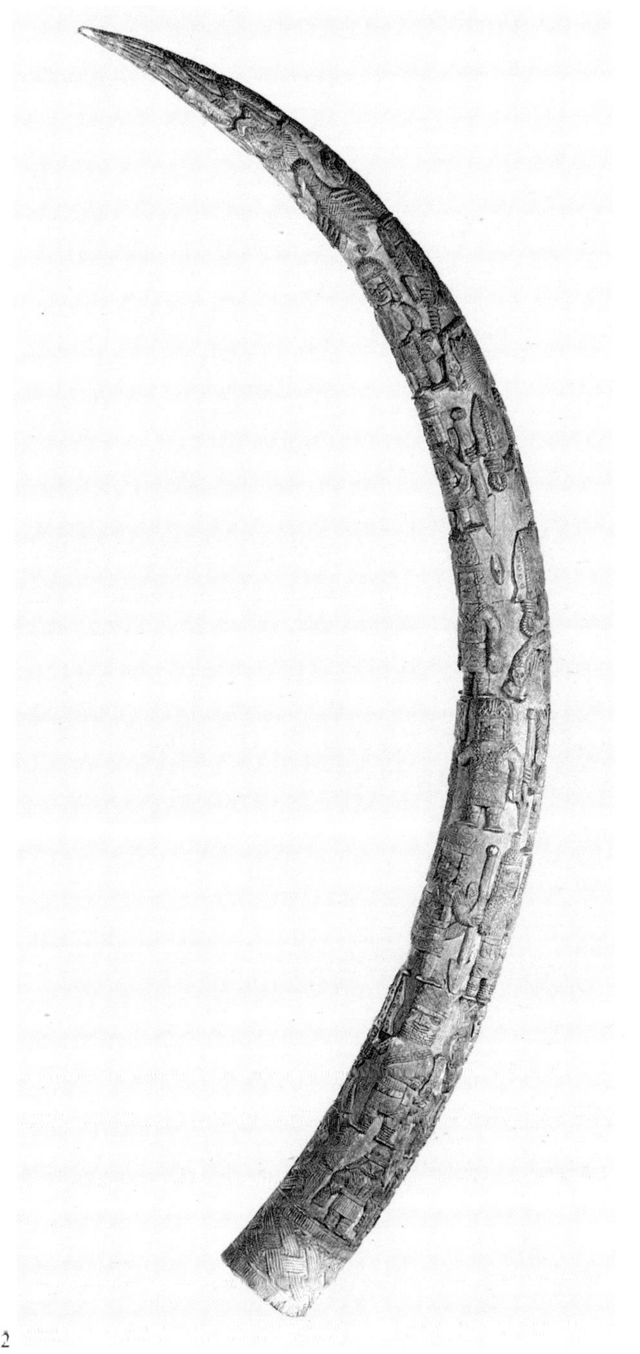
182

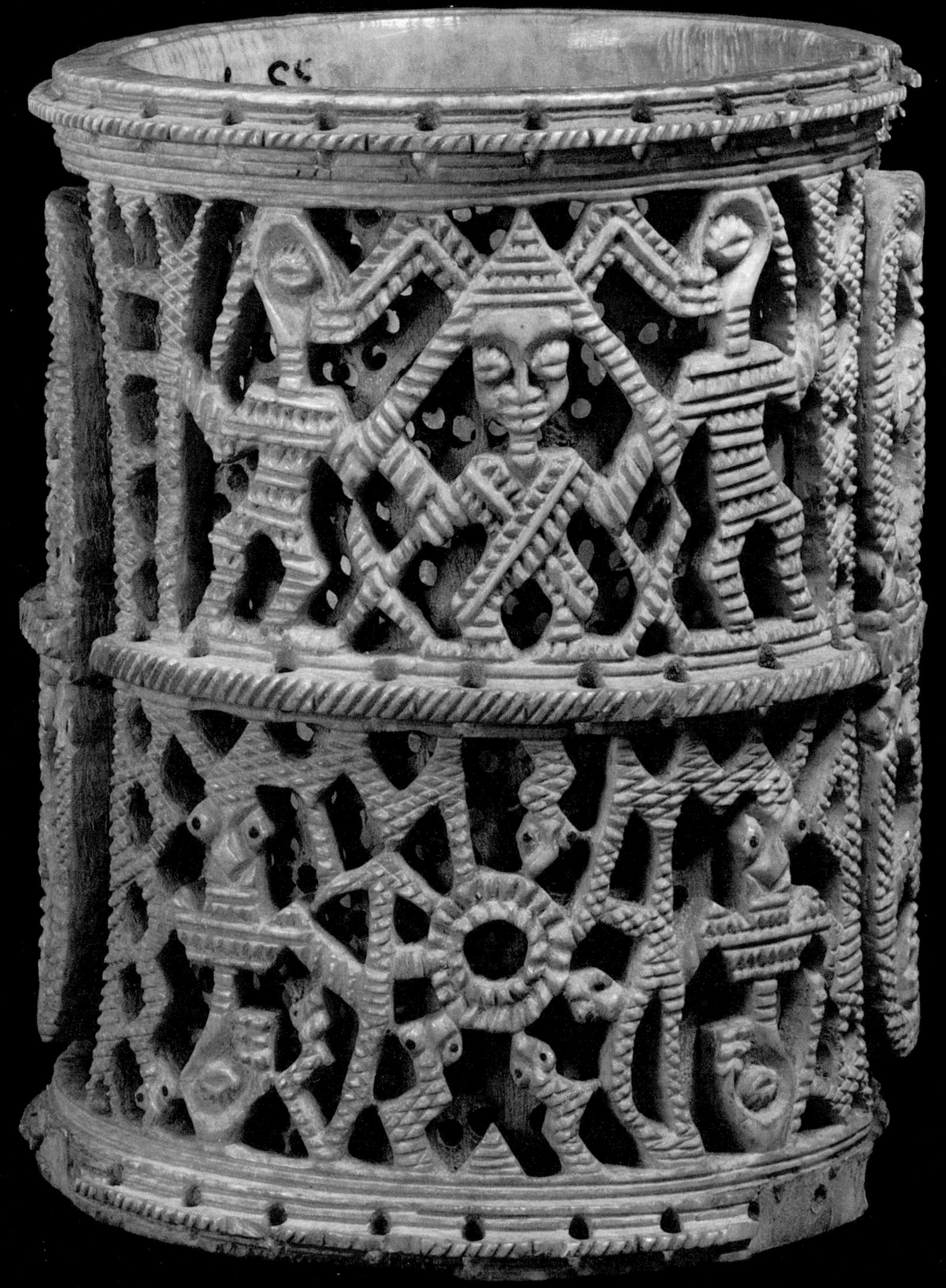

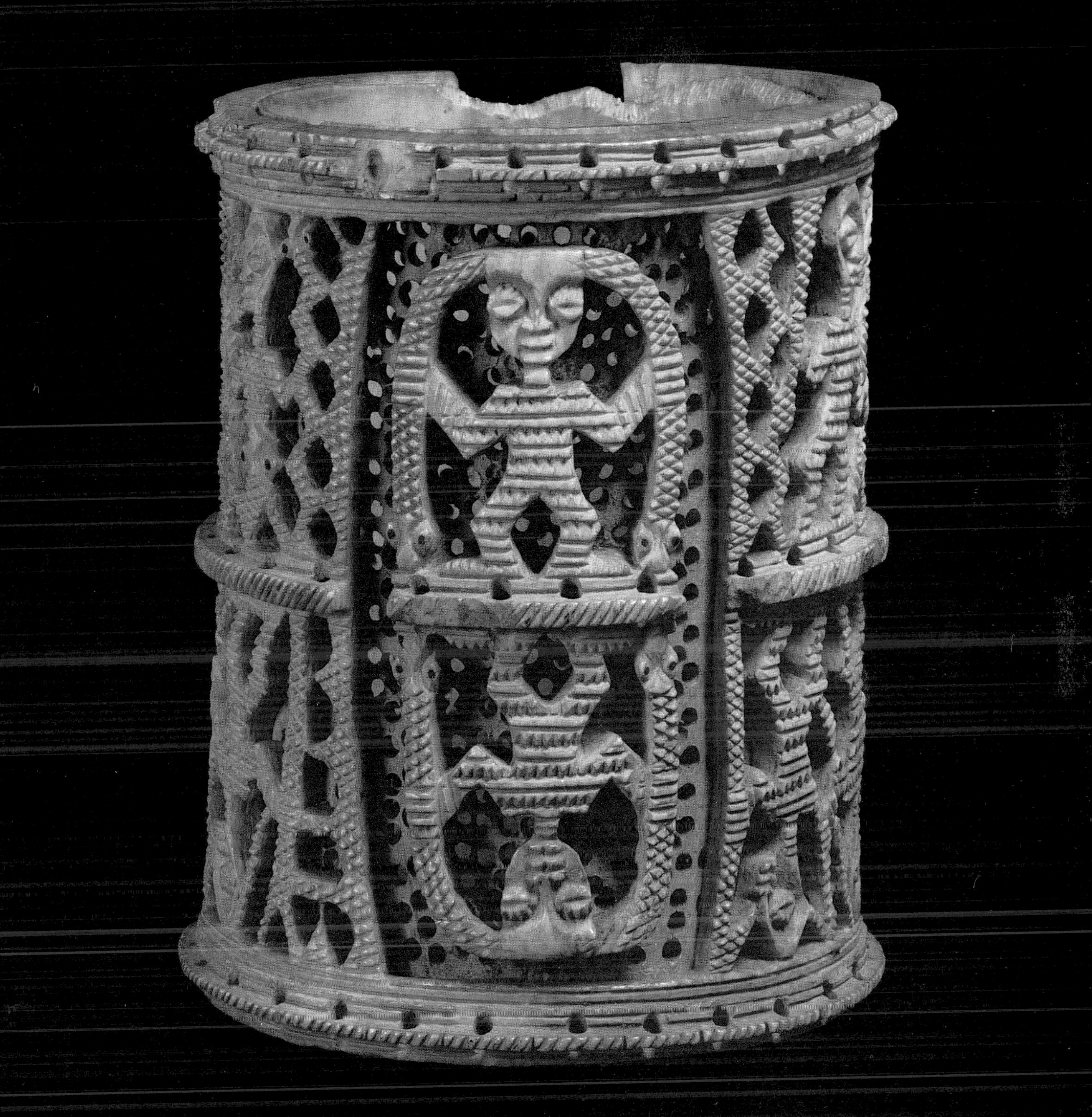

183 Armlet (*iroko),* ivory.
Nigeria, Yoruba, Owo or Ijebu Ode.
(Illus. pp. 174, 175)

This bracelet with an outer openwork wall resembles two cylinders, one inserted into the other; the walls are, however, firmly attached in the middle. On one side of the outer cylinder are two human figures, one reflecting the other. They hold snakes that arise from their heads, a motif characteristic of late Benin art. It replaced the fish-legged ocean god that was the most important figure on bracelets of the seventeenth and eighteenth centuries. On the top row of the other side the king is supported by two companions; below him is a scene with snakes flanked by mirror-image designs symbolizing a recurring mythical event—a snake swallowing a human (see also No. 182). Small metal bells originally decorated the edges of this piece.

The king wore broad ivory or metal bracelets on both forearms while leading the ritual dance at certain festivals. Ivory carvers worked in Benin itself and also among the Yoruba of Owo and Ijebo Ode: the *oba* commissioned our piece from the Yoruba.

Height 11 cm., diameter 8 cm. 35-4-8
Acquired from H. Meyer 1935

Lit.: P. Ben-Amos 1980, pp. 82-83, 86-87; P. J. C. Dark 1973, p. 89; F. v. Luschan 1919, p. 400; F. Willet 1967, p. 167; S. Wolf 1972, Illus. 26.

Igbo Wood Sculpture (184–186)

The traditional art of the Igbo, also called Ibo, who dwell in the area between the Cross and Niger Rivers, displays considerable regional variation in round sculpture and in masks. Apparently these differences evolved as a result of contrasting forms of political organization—whereas most Igbo groups lived without central authority like the Cross River cultures, there were also some kingdoms ruled by sacred kings, particularly in the Yoruba-influenced western provinces of Awka and Onitsha. As in most parts of West Africa, the royal court exercised a strong stimulus on artistic activity, and a style of wood sculpture developed in the kingdoms that was not to be found among other Igbo groups. This school of sculpture was characterized by comparatively large idealized figures (see No. 184) comparable to those of the neighboring Yoruba and Edo.

184 Standing female figure, wood.
Nigeria, North Igbo, south of Awka.
(see color plate p. 71)

This hardwood figure, which Cole believes was carved by a professional artist from the Agulu Adaziani area, displays characteristics typical of northern-Igbo sculpture in the round: almost natural proportions, arms hanging freely, upturned palms, and stiff legs ending in pigeon-toed block-shape feet. The face is idealized, the coiffure is helmetlike, and the scarifications *mbubu* on chest and abdomen are of cross shape. The figure, which probably represents the daughter of a local tutelary deity, was repainted with redwood powder and white chalk after each cult event. It was only recently established that such cult figures comprise family members (father, mother, and children).

Height 94 cm. 73-12-1
Acquired from L. Bretschneider 1973

Lit.: H. M. Cole 1969, pp. 39-41–and personal communication; H. M. Cole & C. C. Aniakor 1984, pp. 89-93.

185 Pair of figures, wood, human hair.
Nigeria, Igbo-Ibibio.

Moving figures are rare in African sculpture, so this dynamic and rhythmic composition is remarkable. The stylized heart-shape faces reflect the influence of Cameroon forest culture, but nothing further is known of the origins of this piece. The form of the

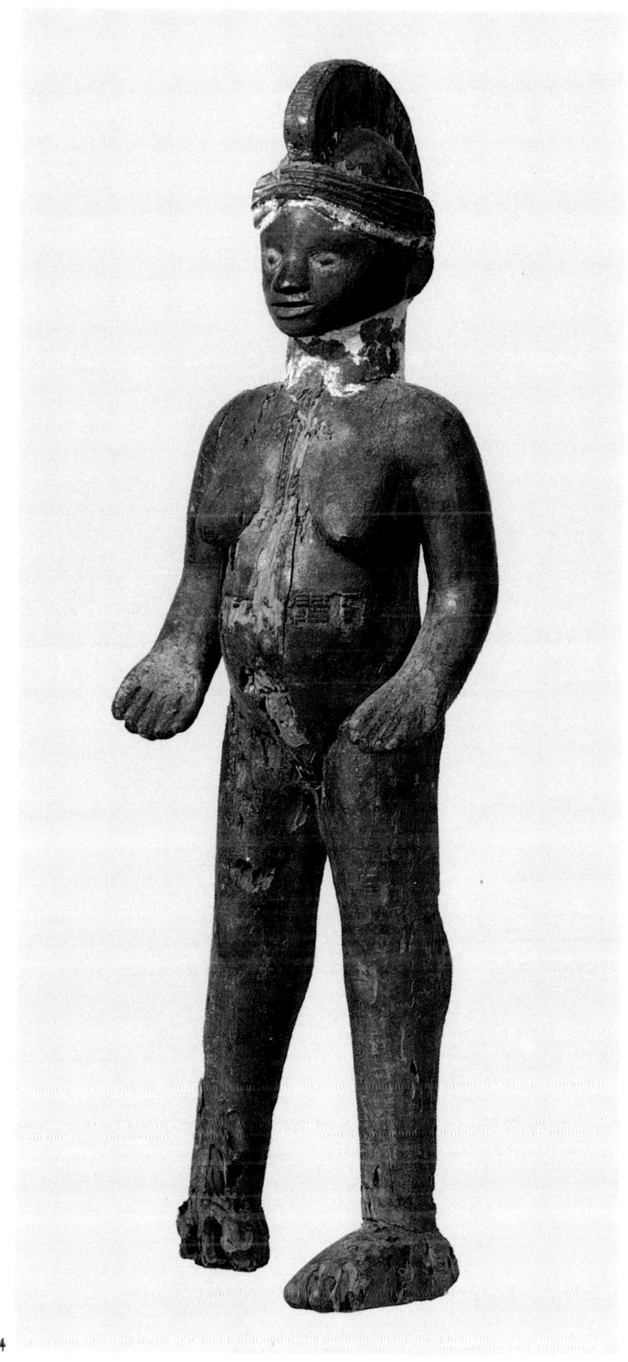
184

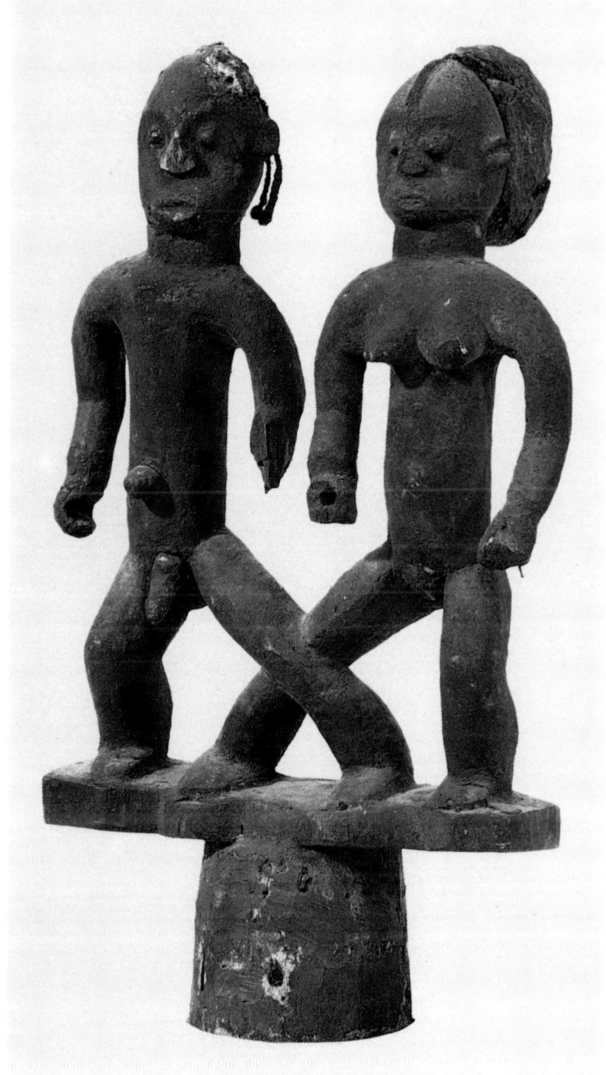
185

base suggests that it might have been part of a head-dress mask. This depiction of legs crossed probably signifies a marriage custom.

Height 44 cm. 75-11-1
Acquired from L. Bretschneider 1975

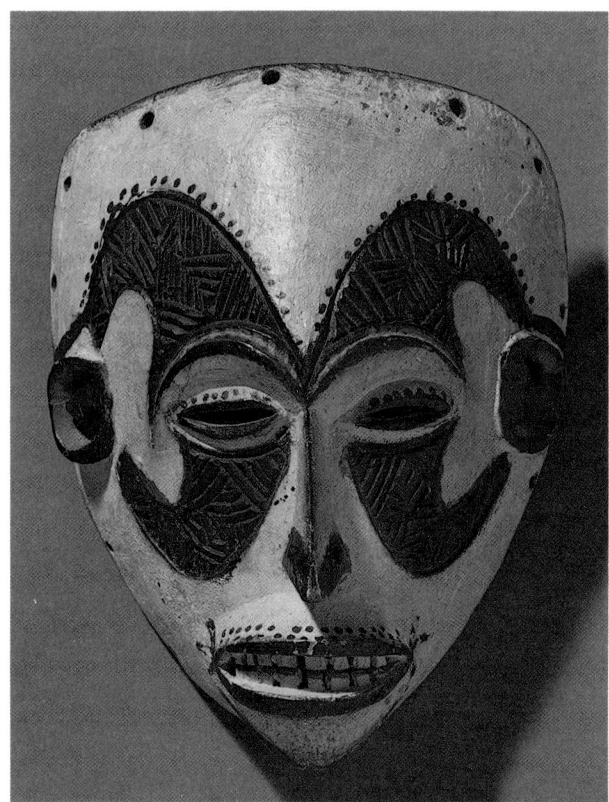

186

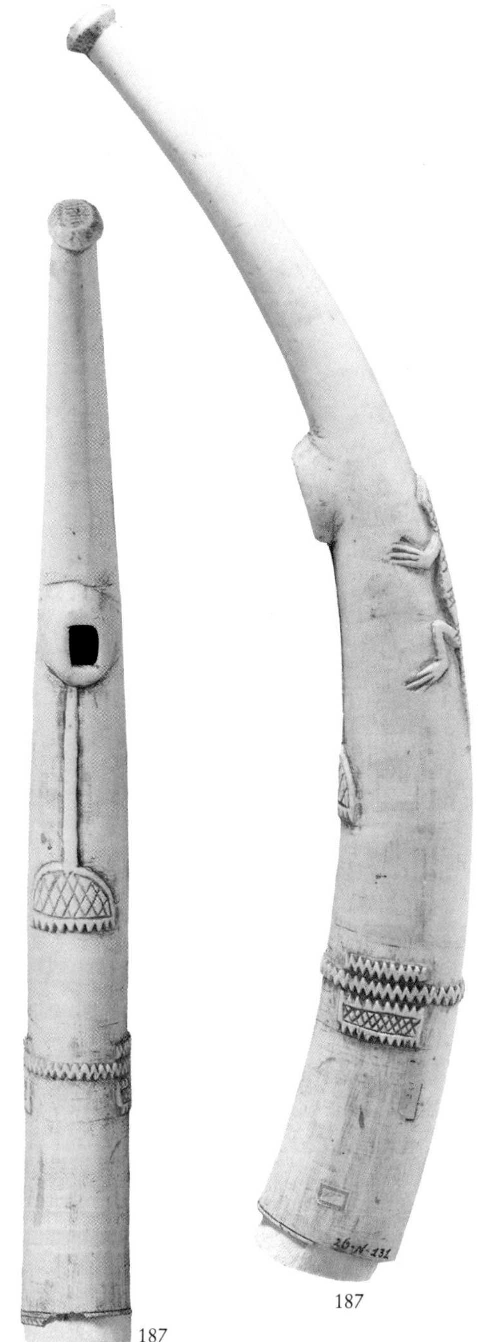

187

187

186 Mask, wood, paint.
Nigeria, Igbo, Nri-Awka.

Black and white paint heightens the expressiveness of this strikingly small, light, and thin-walled face mask, as do the narrow slightly hooked nose and the open mouth revealing a row of teeth. Despite its size, this mask, representing a female spirit of the dead (*mmo*), is wearable. Its chin covers the nose of the dancer, who can see through the eye and ear openings. This type of mask, usual among the northern Igbo, was formerly furnished with a carved wooden headdress, which was later replaced by a complicated and varied arrangement of fabric, tassels, mirrors, small bells, and other ornaments.

Height 16 cm. 76-9-1
Acquired from L. Bretschneider 1976

Lit.: J. S. Boston 1969, pp. 55, 60.

187 Blowing horn with low reliefs, ivory.
Nigeria, Ejagham? Ibibio? coast of Calabar?

Ivory horns of this type, measuring from forty-six to eighty centimeters in length, are preserved in collections in Brunswick, Florence, Copenhagen, Paris, Ravenna, Rome, and Vienna. They have not only the lateral hole characteristic of such African horns but also a hole at the tip—sometimes only an imitation—and are occasionally even found complete with the original metal mouthpiece. There is often a lizard or crocodile image carved in flat relief and decorated with incised ornament on the convex side. The reptile's head usually faces the mouth of the instrument; its reversed position on our piece is rare, The concave side of such horns is most often ornamented with a fanlike geometric motif. One to four zigzag bands are carved in relief near the mouths of the instruments, as they are here.

Horns of this kind are strikingly similar, probably because they were made in the same area at about the same time—presumably in the sixteenth century. The majority of museum-owned pieces are very old, perhaps having reached Europe via Amsterdam. Our piece, third oldest among the datable examples, is listed in the inventory of the art treasures of the dukes of Wittelsbach in 1598. Nothing is known of the horns' original use, or of the meaning of the decoration.

Length 56 cm. 26-N-131
Taken over from the Bavarian National Museum (Royal Estate) 1926

Lit.: E. Bassani 1977c, pp. 187-96; W. Fagg 1959, p. IX; E. Tardy 1977, p. 400.

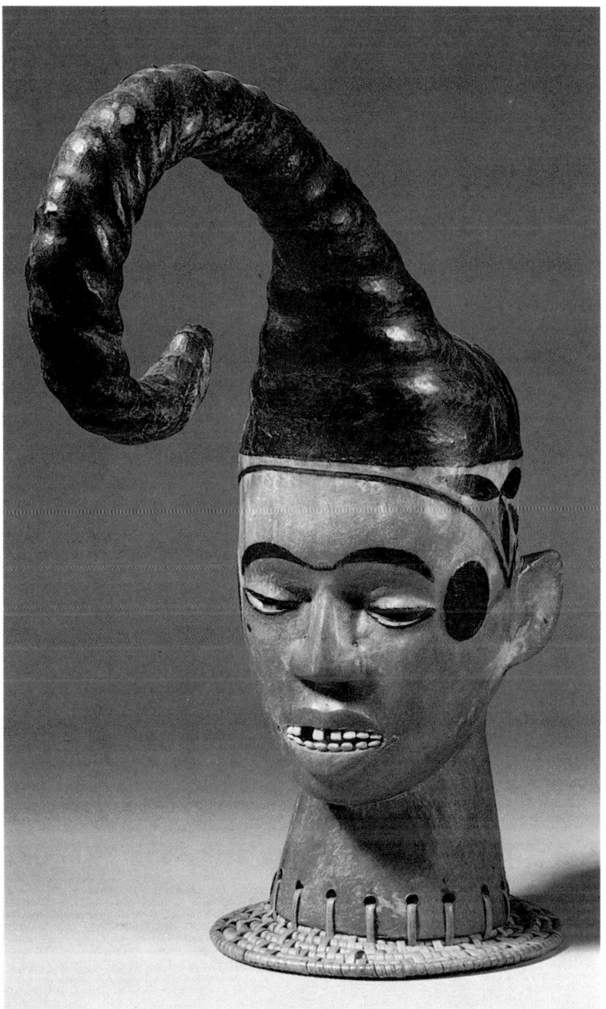

188

Skin-Covered Headdress of the Cross River Region (188-192)

The semi-Bantu peoples in the densely forested boundary region between Cameroon and Nigeria are in many respects typical of the woodland style of life. Their small settlements were essentially autonomous, with no centrally governed states and with social life controlled in part by the clan organization

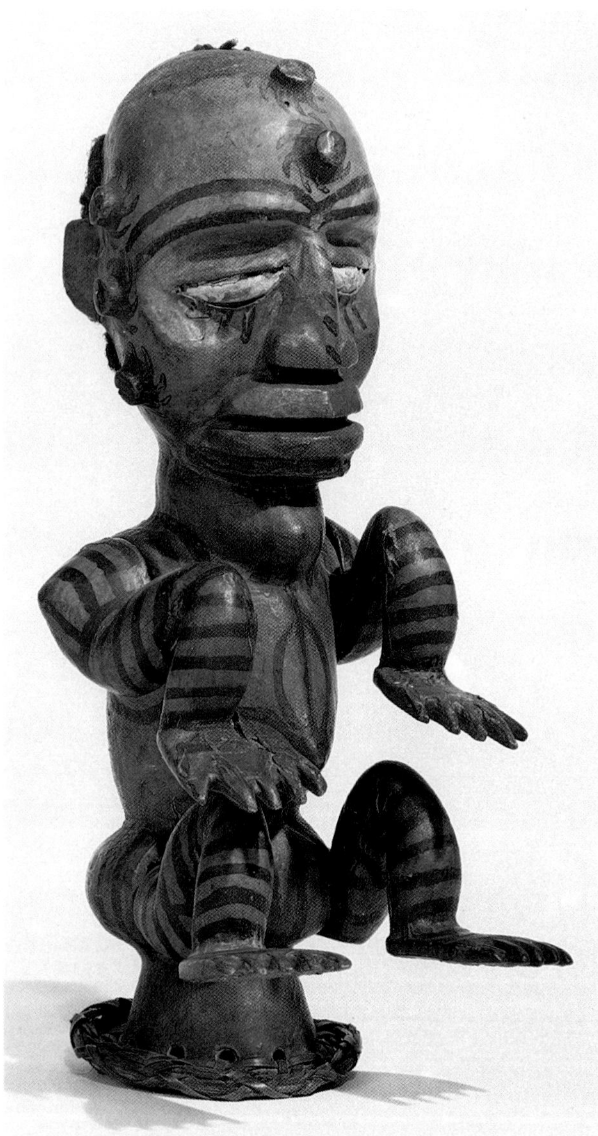

189

and community, in part by age groups and cult societies. Of the latter, the Leopard association (*ngbe, ekpe*) and the *ekpo* cult, particularly, strove to maintain social order, even interregionally. Women enjoyed a high status in family life and ran their own ranked societies.

In spite of sharing many cultural features in the region as a whole, almost every tribe displays artistic specialties. This is strikingly evident in mask art, which displays a wealth of forms—face masks, two-headed helmet masks, and headdress masks—and an unusual range of variations in style from naturalistic to abstract. By far the most original group is that of the headdress and helmet masks, carved of wood in the form of almost life-size to oversize human heads. Their realism is heightened by a covering of antelope skin scraped thin and often dyed. Naturalistic hair and occasionally beards, often of human hair; tin-sheet insertions for whites of eyes; and brilliant white bone or wood teeth increase their expressiveness. Details were considered essential and were for the most part precisely executed—the shaved foreheads, deformed teeth, and facial cicatrices and painted symbols are examples.

It is not known what inspired the Cross River tribes to make skin-covered headdress masks. Some scholars surmise that the masks once served as substitutes for head trophies, others that they represent important dead persons. This latter theory is supported by the many surviving female representations and takes into account the respect accorded women both before and after death, when they take their place among the revered ancestors. Skin-covered masks are used chiefly at *ekpo* and *ngbe* festivals. By the turn of the century, however, they were already being produced for sale to Europeans.

Lit.: H. Baumann 1940, p. 286; P. Dark 1973, p. 3; W. Fagg 1964, p. 60; A. Mansfeld 1908, pp. 56-57, 59; K. Nicklin 1974, pp. 8-9; A. Tunis 1985, pp. 501ff.

188 Headdress mask, wood, mixed media. Cameroon, western Ejagham(?), collected in Obokum.

Plastically modeled facial muscles and eyes formed of tin sheet with nails to indicate pupils heighten the realism of this female face. The horned coiffure is part of the festive dress of nubile girls, whose hair is shaved over the forehead and above the temples except for the reserved trefoil design. The large keloid disc in front of the ears is a typical example of western-Ejagham style. Hidden by hair and a skin covering on the back of the head is a depression for magical substances (see also No. 190). This headpiece shows no traces of use, and according to a personal communication from Campbell is probably one of the pieces being manufactured for European collectors by about 1900.

Height 40 cm. 28-55-4
Acquired from J. Konietzko 1928

Lit.: A. Mansfeld 1908, pp. 56-57, 60.

189 Headdress mask, wood, mixed media.
Nigeria, Anyang.

Among some Cross River groups, the artistically composed parallel lines generally painted on the bodies of women, such as those here, both satisfy the aesthetic sense and provide protection against misfortune of all kinds. Pinwheel designs surround facial scarification, and a four-leaf motif is painted around the navel (see also Nos. 166 and 168-70).

Height 36 cm. 05.299
Acquired from Berke 1905

Lit.: A. Mansfeld 1908, p. 59; K. Nicklin 1974, p. 13; R. F. Thompson 1974, p. 180.

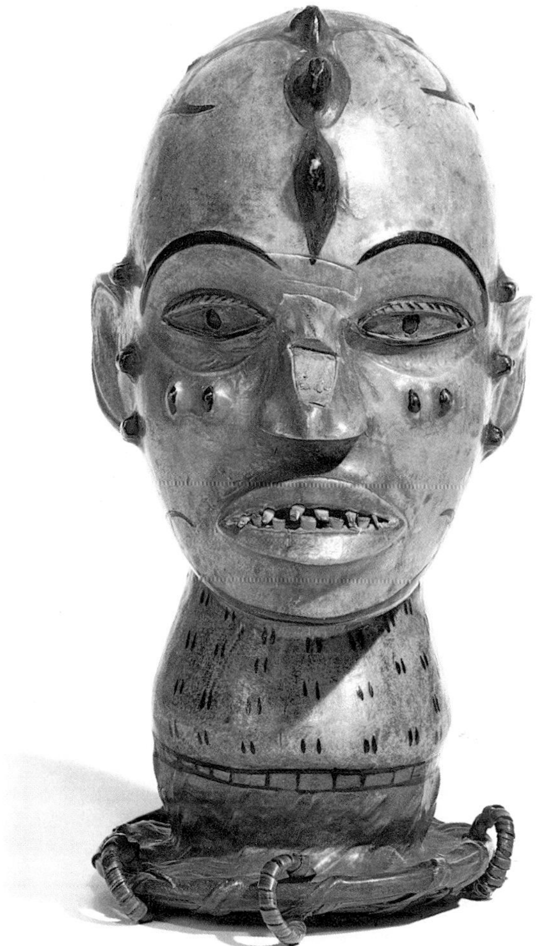

190

190 Headdress mask, wood, mixed media.
Cameroon, Ossidinge District, collected in eastern Ejagham.
(see color plate p. 70)

This shaved female head is ornamented with rich cicatrization and curvilinear painting on forehead, eyebrows, and chin. At the back of the head is a hollow for magical substances (see also No. 188). The collector informs us that when German troops occupied the cult house the "fetish man" intentionally damaged the nose, presumably to destroy the mask's magical power so that the strangers could not use it.

Height 24 cm. 17-7-21
Acquired from E. Hinz 1917

Lit.: A. Mansfeld 1908, p. 59.

191 Janus-face helmet mask, wood, leather, paint, and other materials.
Nigeria, Anyang or Keaka.

This mask combines a light female face with a dark male face. Its generous dimensions recall those of Cameroon Grasslands masks, but local tradition has dictated a realistic representation here. Except for the tin-sheet eyes and the empty eye sockets of the male face, which indicate blindness, all other details correspond to reality. Tooth chipping, for example, is indicated by obliquely ground upper incisors. The painted ornaments on the female face are pseudo *nsibidi* marks, whose significance was once generally known among members. Through facial painting renewed daily, women indicated which experiences (such as love, reconciliation, birth, and death) occupied them at the moment. *Nsibidi* symbols are to be found even on the stone monuments erected to ancestors dating back to the sixteenth century.

Present-day inhabitants of the Cross River region have long since forgotten the original meaning of the Janus-face symbolism. Attempts have been made to link it with the Mediterranean Janus, to explain it as an iconographic expression of divine omniscience, or as a representation of the god of heaven and goddess of earth, and so on. The contrasts expressed in the mask (light/dark, sight/blindness, female/male) might also be intended to symbolize light (day and night, sun and moon). No known mythical traditions confirm such interpretations, however. It is an established fact that the masks belonged to the *ntsebe* society and were worn after military victories, and at burials of society members. They are still used today at such burials.

There are occasional recent attempts to provide new explanations for traditional objects that are no longer understood. The explanation of an Ejagham chief, recorded in 1969, provides an example: "The mask represents Tata Agbo and his wife. Tata Agbo was born during a war. All his brothers and sisters had been killed in the conflict. Only he and his wife survived. Each time he went to battle his wife followed him. When he had fired his gun, she reloaded it until he was victorious. After his death this mask was made in commemoration, for while the man faced the battlefield his wife faced backward while reloading the gun."

Height 52.5 cm. 03.25
Acquired from M. v. Stefenelli 1903

Lit.: K. Nicklin 1974, pp. 8-11, 67; E. v. Sydow 1932, pp. 14-27; P. A. Talbot 1912, p. 12; R. F. Thompson 1974, pp. 175, 180-81

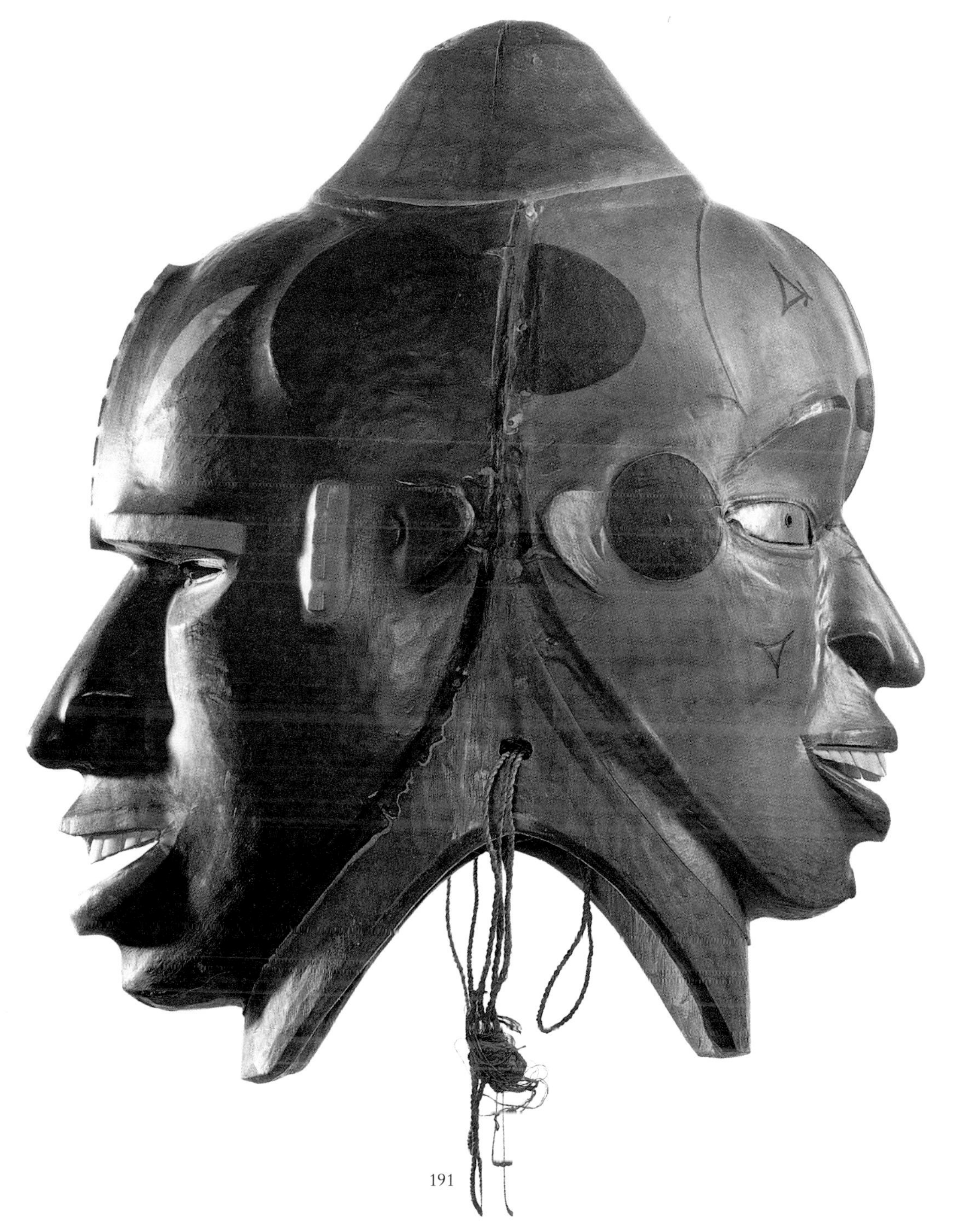

191

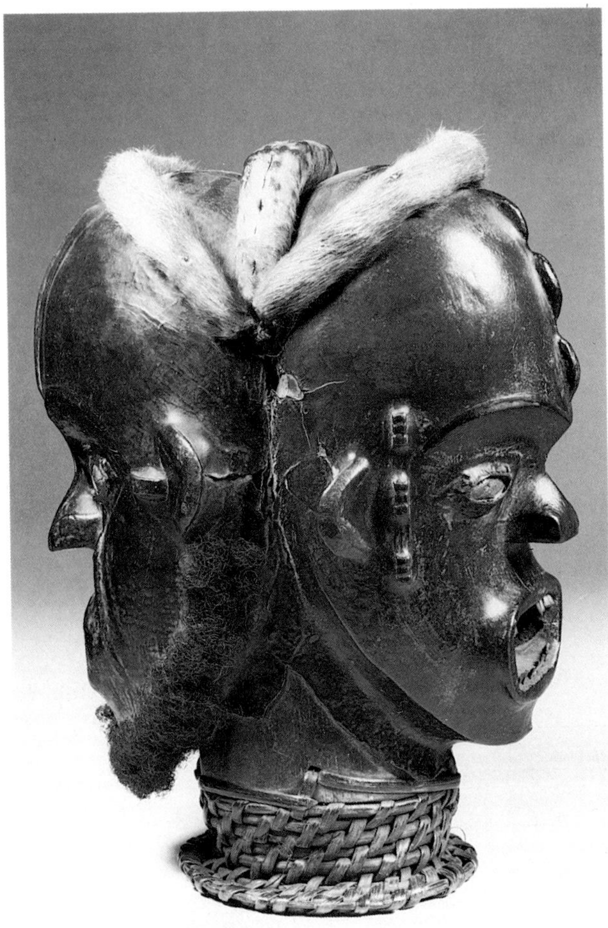

192

192 Janus-face headdress, wood, leather, paint, fur, and other materials.
Nigeria, Ejagham or Anyang.

Both faces of this mask are male, stained dark brown like most male masks of the Cross River region, but with contrasting cicatrizations. Both faces have beards, one indicated by incised lines, the other naturalistically rendered with real hair. Fur rolls above the foreheads represent the upturned brims of the plaited caps worn during hunts and at festivals. The open square mouths reveal rows of teeth. In a personal communication Campbell proposed that these masks originated in the eastern Ejagham or Anyang areas.

Height 28.5 cm. 05.297
Acquired from Berke 1905

Lit.: A. Mansfeld 1908, pp. 58, 70, and pl. 55; K. Nicklin 1974, p. 14; E. v. Sydow 1932, pp. 17, 25.

193 Face mask, wood.
Nigeria, Ibibio, Eket.

Originally furnished with a movable lower jaw, this mask was painted black and white. Characteristic of this type of Ibibio mask is the vigorously expressive geometric style, sharply demarcated facial parts, and a horizontal emphasis. The exaggerated raised decorative scars are signs of various age grades, as is the black disk in the middle of the forehead, which depicts concentric circles of body paint. On the mask's upper edge is a head fillet worn by hunters and warriors (see also No. 192). This is a mask of the *ekpo* society, which makes its most important appearance during the yam-harvest festival.

Height 22 cm., width 20 cm. 04.64
Acquired from M. v. Stefenelli 1904

Lit.: P. A. Talbot 1923, pp. 183, 188-89, 215.

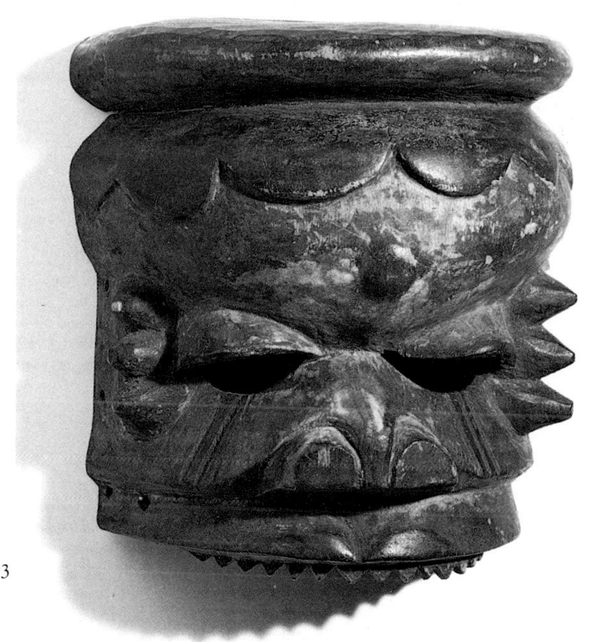

193

194 Globular headdress with figures, wood. Nigeria, Oron.

Despite incorporation of foreign elements (flagpole, pipe, and hat shape), the artist remained faithful to traditional style. The figures are small and abstract, yet essentially typical of Oron ancestral sculpture, complete with horned and bulbous coiffures. The small latticework chest cages represent simplified arms and the pendulous pointed beards of ancestral figures. Although the Oron gave up carving about 1920, their traditions have been maintained by artists of the kindred Ibibio people, one of whom may have designed this bold composition.

Height 79 cm. 73-13-1
Acquired from L. Bretschneider 1973

Lit.: W. Fagg 1964, p. 56; F. Neyt 1979, pp.144-45, illus. 56; P. O. Nsugbe 1961, pp. 357-65.

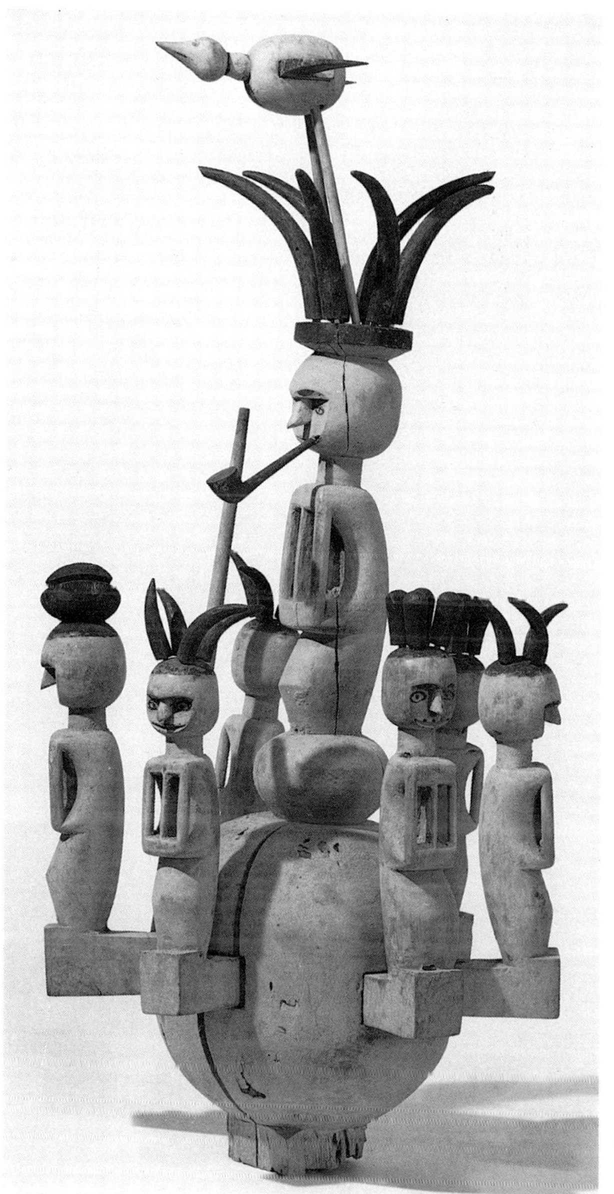

194

195 Headdress, wood, raffia fiber.
Nigeria, Ijo.

This large mask designed in the form of a sawfish was worn horizontally on the head. The fish body is cut of one block, to which teeth and fins have been added. The fish is represented with half-open mouth, its sword is about one-third of its body length, its eyes are red rimmed, its frontal and lacrimal bones protrude, and its blowholes are colored red. On the underside are well-developed ventral fins and four gill apertures on each side. The dorsal fin has been set into the elongated tail portion. Most of these anatomical details are evidence of exact observation.

The Ijo and their neighbors live in the Niger Delta region where rivers and the sea play a determining role in their lives. It is understandable that aquatic creatures such as hippopotamuses, crocodiles, and fish are important in their myths and worship. Among the few masks so far known, representations of these animals predominate. They personify water spirits that determine the yields of fishing and agriculture. The masks' most important appearance is at a festival that lasts several days, held either at the beginning of the year or during the floods. In the course of the festival the river spirits—that is, the masks—visit the villages to free them of the past year's evil influences. The Ijo borrowed this custom from the neighboring Abua, whose artists make the masks.

Length 125 cm. 81-301-490
Acquired from R. L. Stolper 1981

Lit.: E. Eyo 1974, pp. 52-55.

196 Headdress, wood, wickerwork.
Nigeria, Ijo.

This starkly stylized bird mask is composed of geometric and abstract forms that create the effect of a silhouette. The midsection of the larger central angular arc has been broken off. Nothing is known of the mask's function, or of the bird's species or meaning. Structurally, the piece represents a rare variant of technique, for the joining of several parts

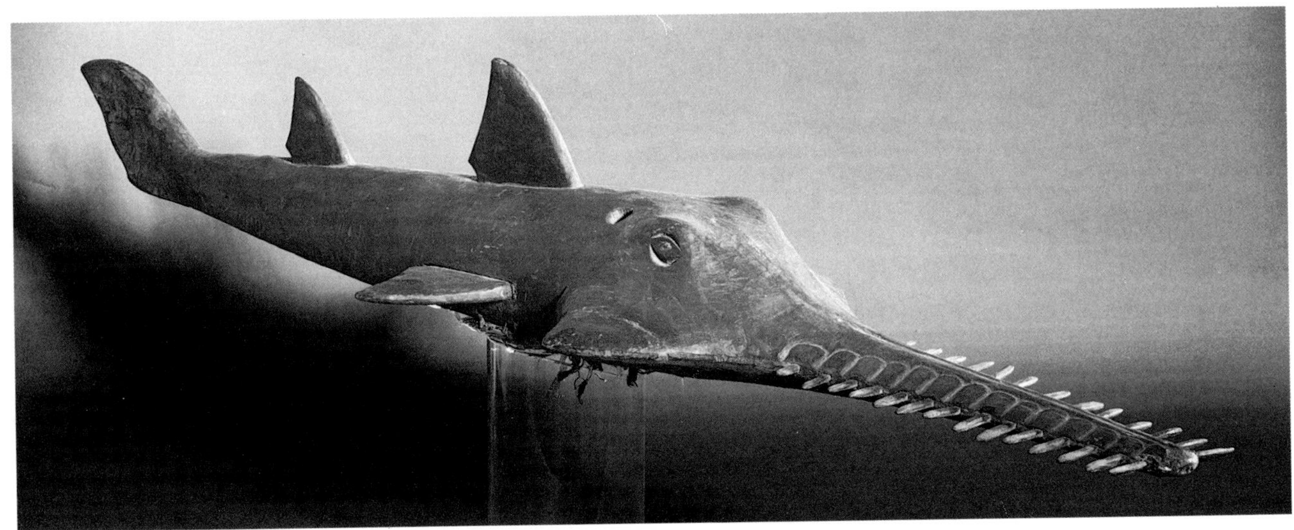

195

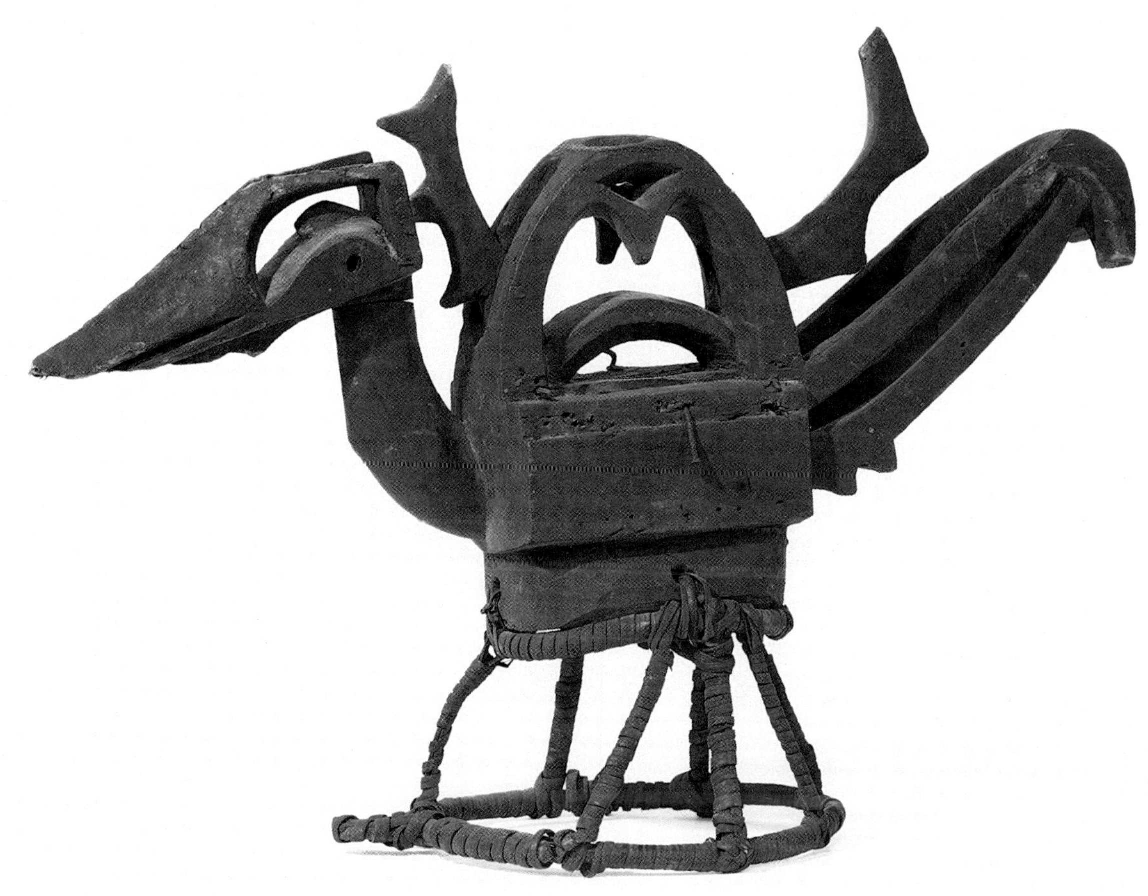

196

was foreign to ancient African sculpture. North African and/or European influence probably accounts for its occurrence in West Africa. Himmelheber illustrates a counterpart to our piece.

Height 37 cm., length 75 cm. 75-5-1
Acquired from L. Bretschneider 1975

Lit.: H. Himmelheber 1960, p. 278.

197 Mask and costume (*obasinjom*), wood, cotton, raffia, mixed media.
Nigeria-Cameroon border, Banyang?

The mask atop this costume is in the form of a stylized crocodile head, with metal-set mirror eyes, upright ears, and mouth open to reveal a protruding tongue. The throat, hollowed to the back of the head, is stuffed with pressed herbs. Encrusted traces

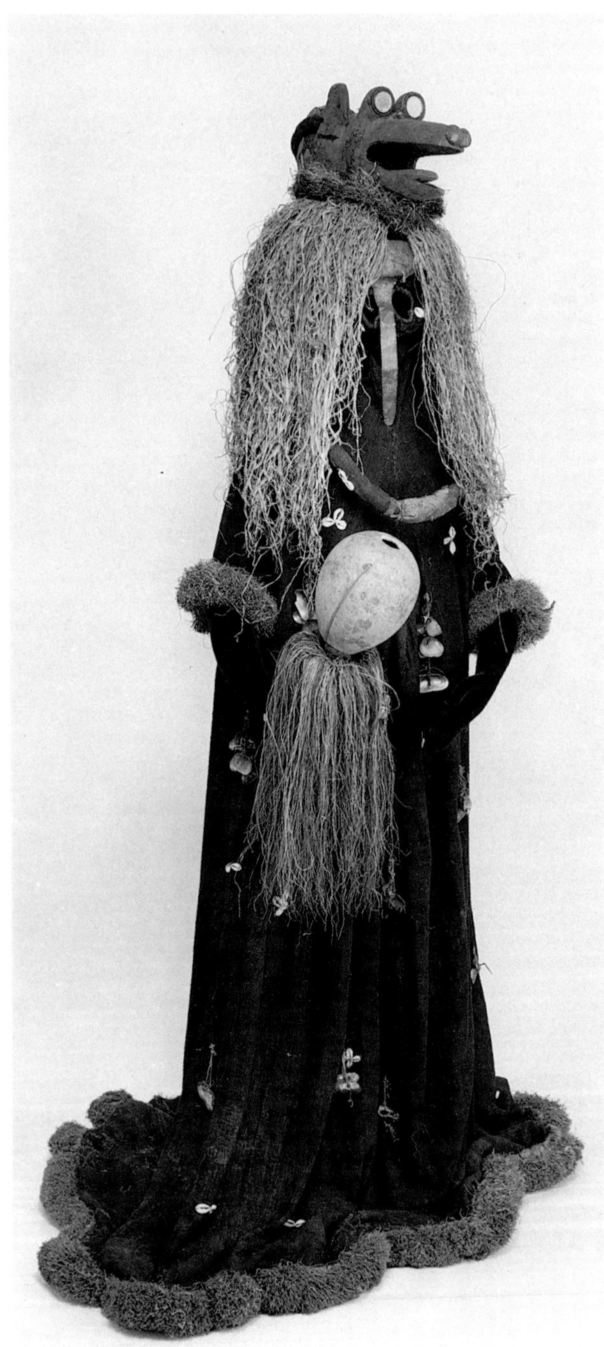

197

of sacrificial gifts (egg with yellow camwood powder) remain on the mask surface.

The costume is of indigo-dyed cotton with raffia fiber fringe. The decoration of the robe, preserved only in part, consists of pairs of fresh-water-mussel shells, and cowries applied in groups of four. This latter arrangement recalls the four-leaf ornament of the Benin plaques (see Nos. 168–70) and of the body decoration of the female figure on the Ejagham headdress mask (No. 189). Two small wooden boards resembling Koran tablets are attached to the back of the robe at waist level. A piece of diamond-shape lizard skin is attached to each. A calabash rattle (seen here) as well as a machete (missing here) are part of this mask costume.

Mask and costume are feared instruments of the *basinjom* association. Among their powers is the ability to provide enlightenment in connection with events ascribed to sorcery. The mirror eyes, said to insure the identification and conviction of witches, substitute for the water divination, which exposed sorcerers in pre-colonial days. The water oracle's suppression by the colonial authorities contributed to the quick rise of the *basinjom* association, active today in most large villages from southern Nigeria to western Cameroon. Its crocodile mask is even more respected than the leather-covered headdress mask of the *ekpo* society (see Nos. 188–90). According to Koloss, the crocodile head with feather ornament symbolizes the power to pursue sorcerers on both land and water—that is, in the realm of the crocodile but also in that of the bird. This earth and water symbolism, together with the crocodile-and-bird, also exists in *ekpo* traditions.

Length of mask 43 cm., height 20 cm. 26-46-½

Length of costume 195 cm.
Acquired from J. F. G. Umlauff 1926

Lit.: H. Ganslmayr 1969, pp. 9-37; H. J. Koloss, in F. Küssmaul 1981, pp.108-9, and personal communication; M. Ruel 1960, pp. 210-13; P. A. Talbot 1912, pp. 52, 198, 1923, pl. p. 258; R. F. Thompson 1974, pp. 209-14.

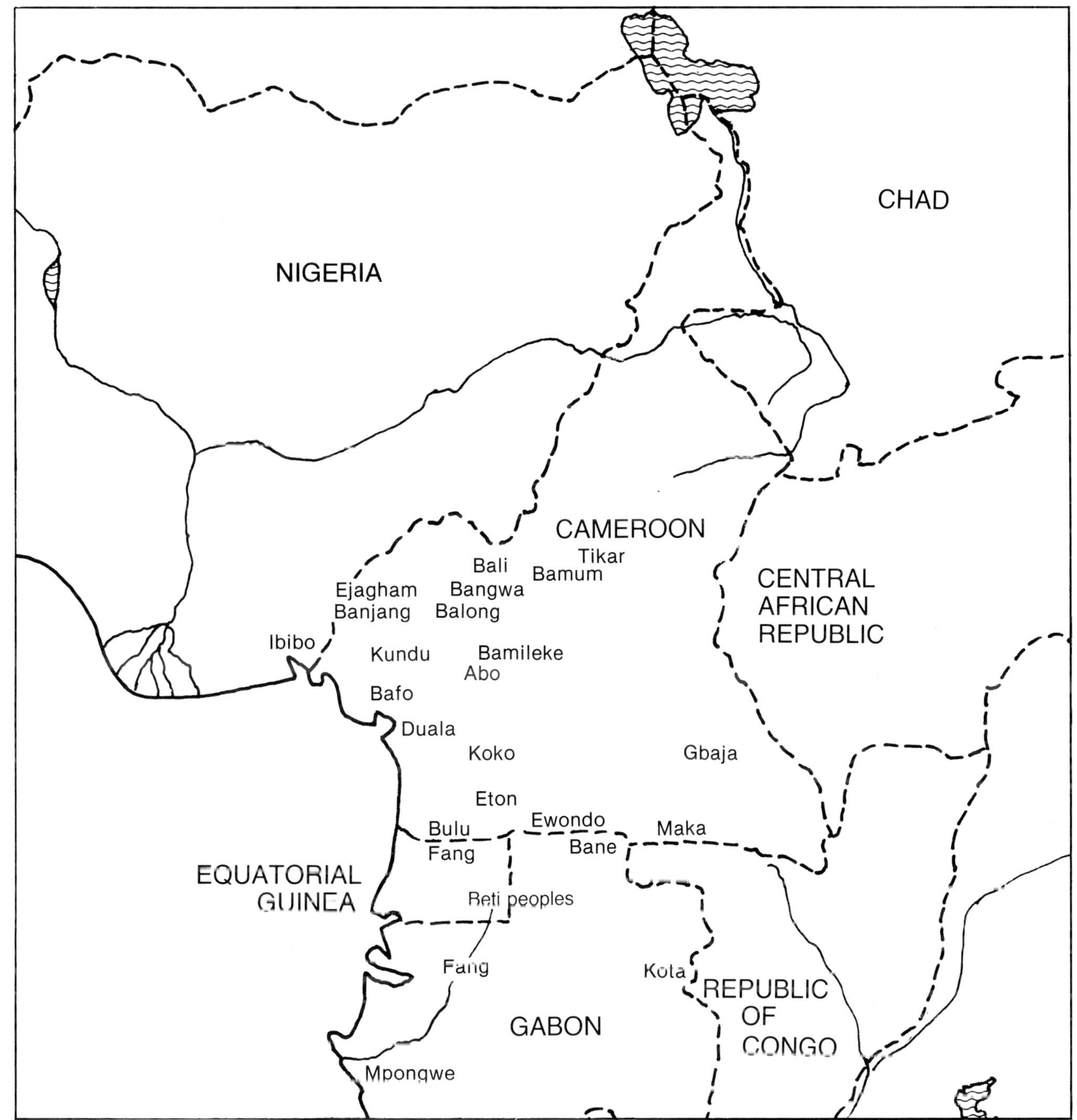
CHAD
NIGERIA
CAMEROON
Tikar
Bali
Bamum
CENTRAL
AFRICAN
REPUBLIC
Ejagham
Bangwa
Banjang
Balong
Ibibo
Kundu
Bamileke
Abo
Bafo
Duala
Koko
Gbaja
Eton
Ewondo
Bulu
Maka
Fang
Bane
EQUATORIAL
GUINEA
Beti peoples
Fang
Kota
REPUBLIC
OF
CONGO
GABON
Mpongwe

Cameroon Grasslands

A multitude of ethnic groups without linguistic, cultural, or political unity inhabit the open savannas of the south-central Cameroon highlands. No empires arose in the grasslands, but numerous small, occasionally even minute, kingdoms did grow up there two to three hundred years ago under the influence of comparatively late waves of immigration from the southern Chad region. Their rulers frequently had little military power, but the pattern of grasslands social strata, bureaucracies, and court ceremonials resembles that of the empires—of ancient Mali and Ghana and the kingdoms of the Guinea coast.

Although the kings' power was limited by secret societies and councils of clan elders, the institution of kingship and the king's person were considered sacred, though not divine. Considerable authority rested with kings, who were responsible for executing certain rites that assured the country's fertility and the inhabitants' wealth. Among the kings were outstanding personalities who ruled their small realms in exemplary fashion and who, like the Bamum king Njoya (1889-1933), introduced important reforms. Modern Cameroon respects these kings—now practically powerless—as guardians of tradition who fill ceremonial and priestly roles. Their residences were, and in part still are, centers of traditional artistic activities where craftsmen mainly carried out commissions for the king and court but also produced wood sculptures, pottery, and other objects for associations and clans. In the case of certain object types such as wood sculpture and pipe bowls, an independent grasslands tradition arose. In comparison with other West African areas its art is intensely expressive and bold, occasionally crude or coarse. Human images are lively and dynamic, sometimes humorous and even caricatural, but there is no uniformity of style. In the multiplicity of local workshop traditions there are at least three regional stylistic groups: the Bamileke-Bangwa groups in the southwest, the Tikar groups in the north and east, and the Bamum group in the center. Pinpointing the origin of an object is often difficult, for trade among these regions frequently led to wandering art works. Then, too, rulers traditionally exchanged gifts as a means of strengthening mutual political ties. Therefore, embellished utilitarian objects such as tobacco pipes, bead-covered calabashes, clay and wood vessels, garments, fabrics, and metal ornaments, as well as sculpture such as masks and figures, migrated from one place to another.

Lit.: R. Brain & A. Pollock 1971, p. 13; W. S. Ellis 1974, pp. 141ff.; P. Gebauer 1979, pp. 32-36; H. J. Koloss 1977, p. 6.

198 Figure of a king *(lefem)*, wood.
Cameroon, Bangwa.
(see color plate p. 269)

Although the face of this king shows figures typical of Bangwa-Bamileke art—rimmed eyes, mouth open to reveal rows of teeth, small projecting ears—and a tendency to stylization, the artist has created an individual, realistic impression. The slight turning of the upper body heightens this effect and lends vitality to the entire figure. The king is shown nude though wearing the royal insignia: knobbed cap, glass bead necklaces, a leopard-skin belt, ivory bracelets, and plaited strings around his ankles and knees. The gourd bottle in his right hand indicates that the king is about to pour a libation.

A portrait figure of each Bangwa king, carved immediately upon his accession to the throne, was kept with statues of his predecessors. This ancestral

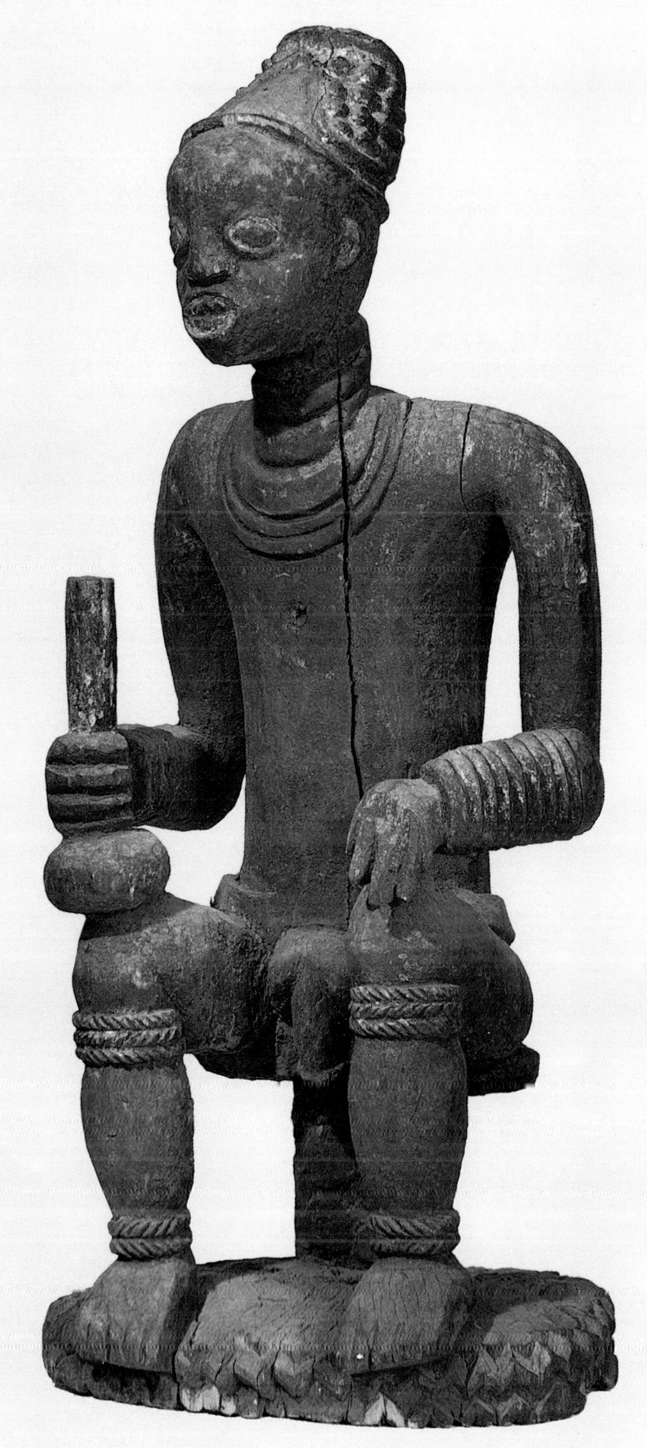

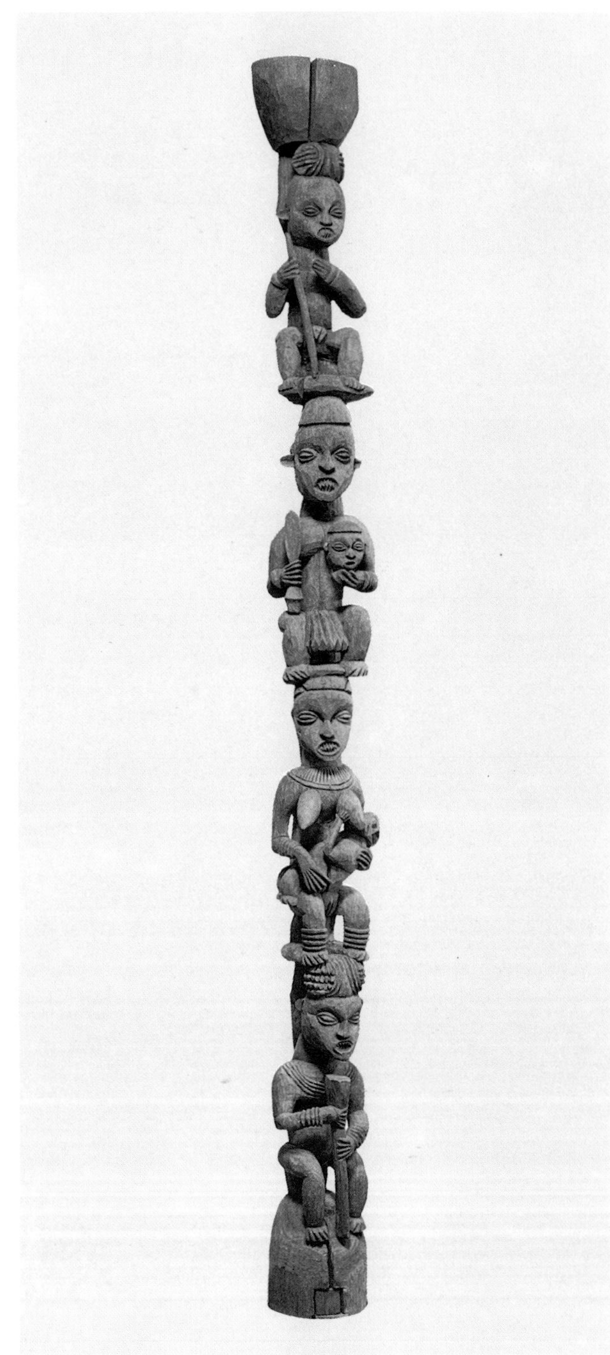
199

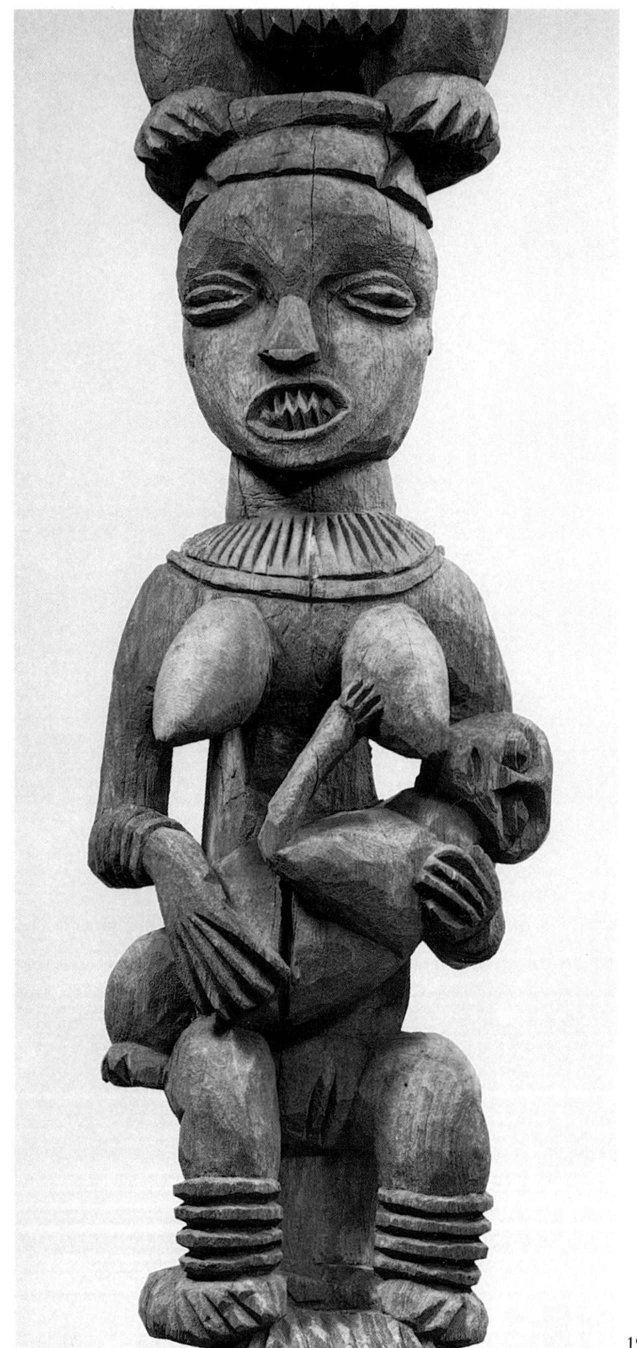
199

group usually comprised up to nine generations, which made vivid the history of the dynasty, expressing the continuity that furthered the preservation of the realm. These figures were seen publicly only during the *lefem* society's performances at their annual ceremonies, at the burial of a king, or at the accession of a new king.

As they were not considered cult objects, these figures received no offerings. If statues of royal forebears were destroyed by termites or fire, the ruler borrowed from distinguished families the number of figures required to legitimize his dynasty. Besides rulers, dignitaries such as the queen mother, favorite royal wives, and priests and priestesses of the earth cult were portrayed.

Height 91 cm. 05.230
Acquired from Berke 1905

Lit.: R. Brain & A. Pollock 1971, pp. 118-20.

199 Pillar, wood.
Cameroon, Bangwa.

Tall pillars such as this support the heavy straw roofs and eaves that project far beyond the square buildings, forming a covered veranda. Pillars at the king's palace, the houses of dignitaries, and the men's meetinghouse are richly ornamented with carved figures whose motifs symbolize social stratification: just as the pillars support the roof, so the king and court support society. Depicted here are the ruler, one of his wives holding a child, a victorious army leader, and a dignitary whose cap and staff indicate his notability.

Height 3 m. 05.242
Acquired from Berke 1905

Lit.: P. Gebauer 1971, p. 41.

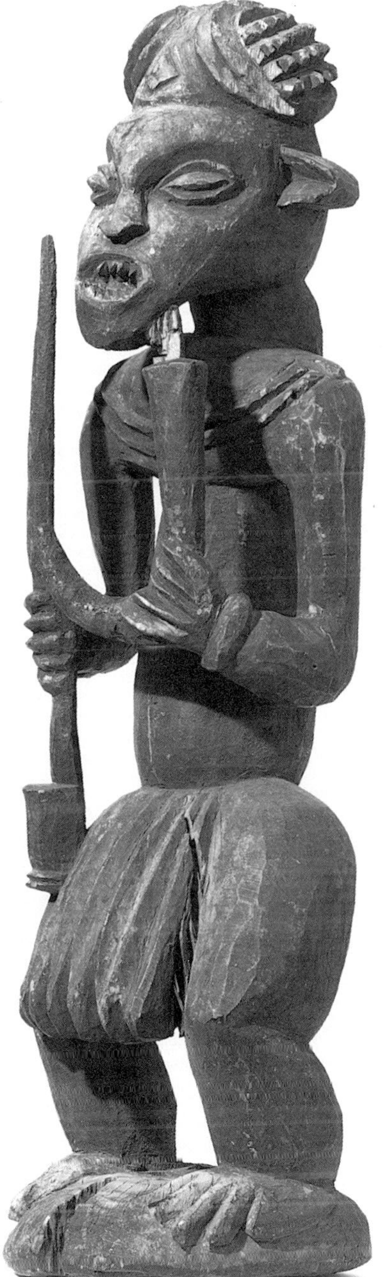

200

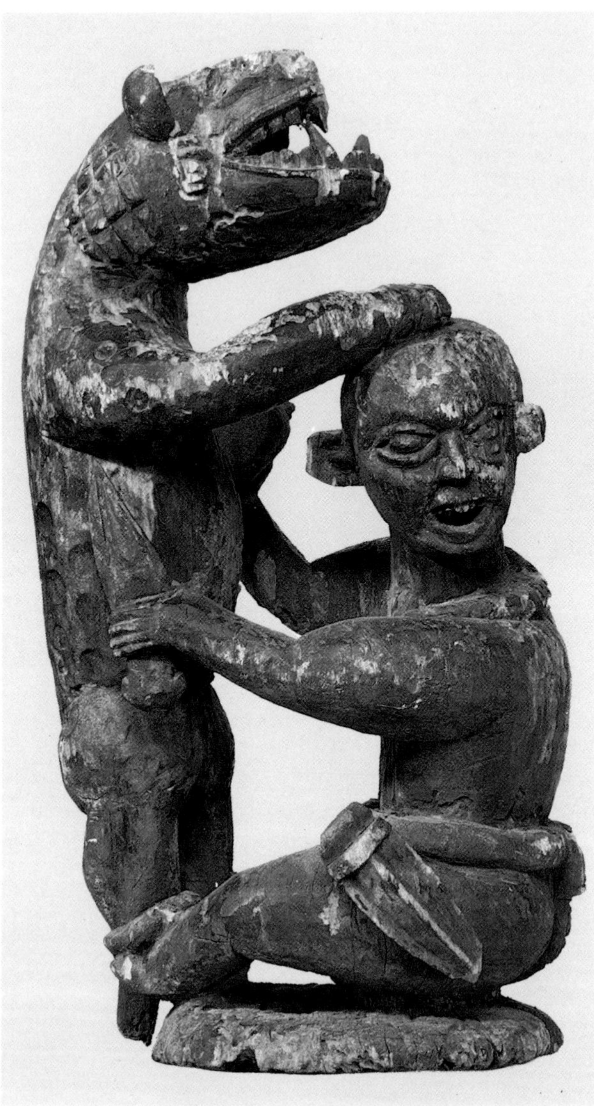

201

200 Figure of a king *(lefem),* wood.
Cameroon, Bangwa.

This figure displays elements typical of Bangwa carving: the slightly turned torso with massive shoulders and a grooved backbone, the bent legs, and the inclined, blackened head. Among frequently occurring Bangwa insignia are the knobby cap and multiple necklaces seen above, the loincloth of bark cloth (with five to seven folds, according to rank), the tobacco pipe, and the ceremonial drinking horn for palm wine.

Such figures were kept in the sanctuary of the royal ancestors along with elephant tusks and the skulls of deceased rulers, and were venerated with offerings. They were temporary abodes for the royal ancestors, whose cult was an important part of the religion. Members of each clan revered their own ancestors ritually. In most cases the ancestors were more significant than deities, not just in Cameroon but in other parts of sub-Saharan Africa as well. Since the births of children, health, and rich harvests depended mainly upon the benevolence of ancestral spirits, the ancestor cult's widespread importance is easy to understand. A large part of this region's creative art is thus rooted not in aestheticism but in the effort to represent ancestors appropriately.

Height 92 cm. 05.229
Acquired from Berke 1905

Lit.: R. Brain & A. Pollock 1971, pp. 60, 85; T. Northern 1985, pp. 86–87.

201 Hunter and leopard, wood.
Cameroon, Bamileke.

This sculpture melds the artist's personal style with typical Bangwa traditional features: movement is indicated, the upper body is turned, the shoulders are massive, there is a deep backbone groove, the shaved head has projecting ears, the open mouth reveals rows of teeth, and the eyes are noticeably rimmed. The subject and type of narrative representation, however, are foreign to the artistic traditions of the Bangwa and their neighbors. In correspondence, Harter has drawn our attention to the fact that even before World War I colonial officials were already commissioning secular, narrative carvings from Bangwa and Bamileke artists; our example would seem to be one of these.

Two more details that support this assumption are the pose of the rearing predator standing at the hunter's feet and its being killed with a hunting knife at the moment of attack—both very old motifs in European art.

Height 76 cm. 80-301-294
Acquired from W. Bareiss 1980

202 Part of a doorframe, wood.
Cameroon, Bamileke.

The grasslands peoples, especially the groups called Bamileke, produced significant works in both sculpture and architecture—meetinghouses, royal palaces, and dwellings of the nobility, made of raffia-palm wood and clay. They are technical and aesthetic masterpieces, where the most ornate elements are the entrance and roof pillars, which are often richly carved with human and animal figures. This piece, part of a doorframe, is a good example: its rhythmically distributed high-relief figures, presumably representing a ritual act, are arranged as nude couples one above the other. In the middle, one plays a flute; at the top is a leopard, an important royal symbol.

Such doorframes are conceived entirely for frontal effect. The carvings on the jambs resemble one another, as if they were mirror images, whereas those on the threshold and lintel differ. Characteristic of these doorways is the high threshold.

Height 191 cm. 15-17-63
Acquired from the Museum für Völkerkunde Berlin 1915

Lit.: P. Gebauer 1979, pp. 69-70; R. Lecoq 1953, p. 65, pls. 33-49.

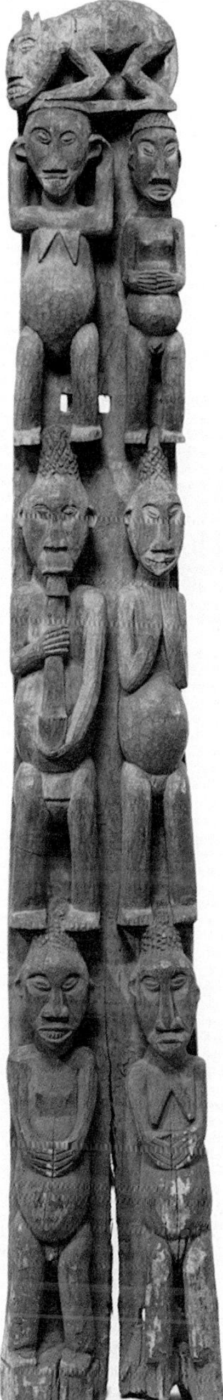

202

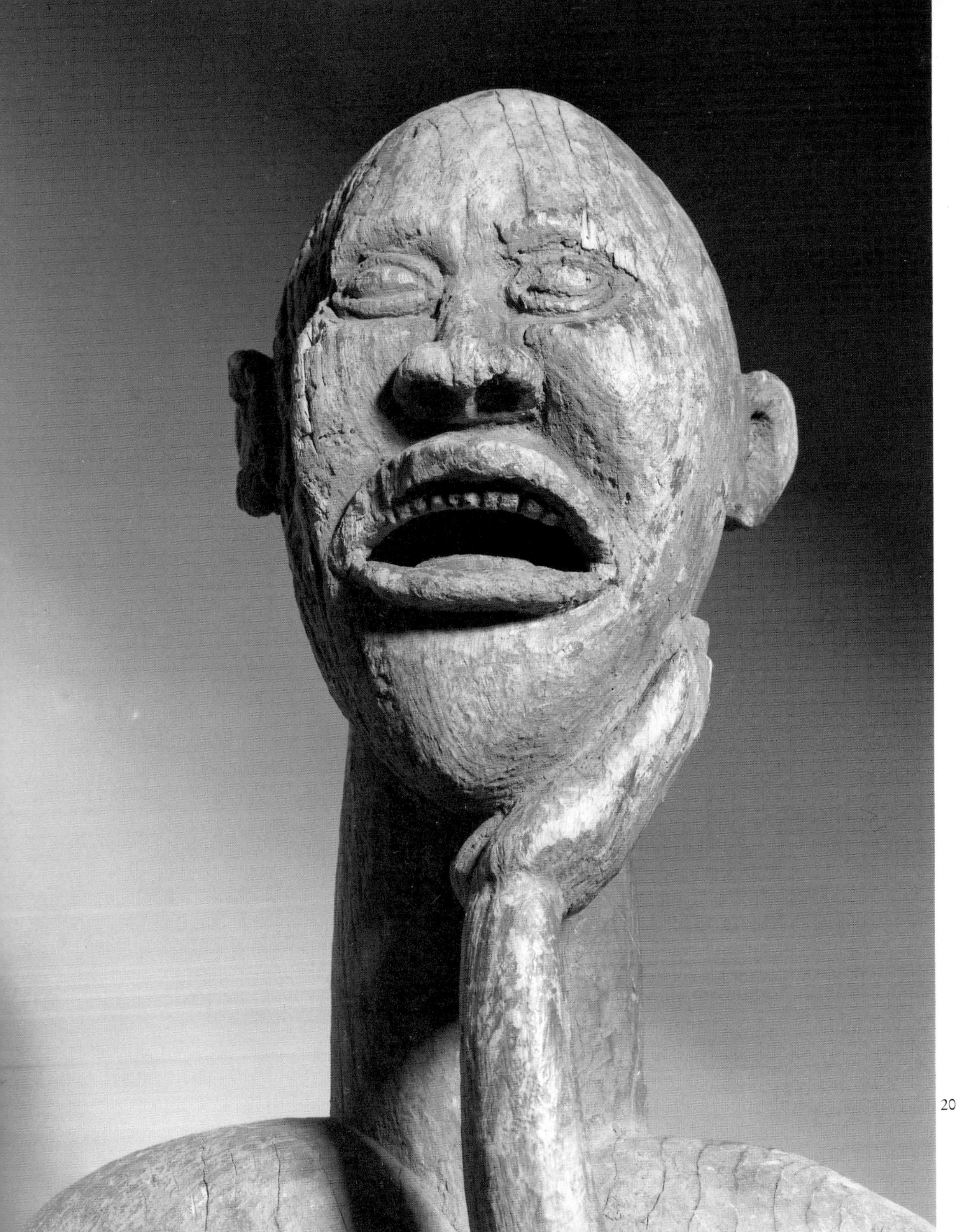

203 Figure of a pregnant woman, wood. Cameroon, Bamileke, Papit village, east of Bangante.

Throughout Africa, court art tends to conform to a canon that prescribes symmetrical, static figures with finely polished surfaces and idealized faces. In contrast, this sculpture, the work of a creative personality who enriched traditional style, is asymmetrical, expressive, shown as if in movement, and its rough surface left its natural color. The pain-distorted face, announcing the commencement of labor, deserves special attention. The sunken abdomen and the legs with inwardly turned feet bent beneath their burden testify to the imminent delivery. The breasts, elongated through frequent nursing, indicate that this is a fertile woman who has borne several children. The figure is carefully worked on all sides, and the shoulder blades, backbone groove, and buttocks are precisely rendered.

Bamileke chiefs had several such figures set up under the protection of their projecting eaves. Three subjects were usually represented—chiefs, pregnant women, and nursing mothers—all attributed with the power of promoting fertility. These figures were also considered temporary abodes for souls of the dead. They were expressively and naturalistically rendered, though in no way equal in quality. Many of them—and our piece is among these—are the most worthy Bamileke art works, while others are rudely carved imitations of older models.

Height 161 cm. 79-300-913
Acquired from H. H. Rayfield 1979

Lit.: R. Lecoq 1953, pp. 117-27.

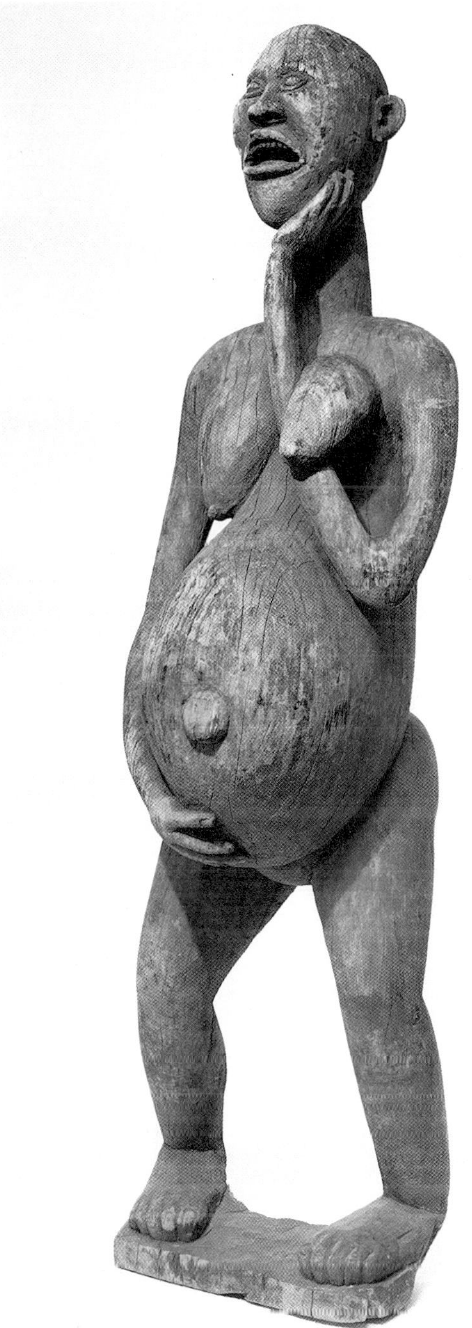

203

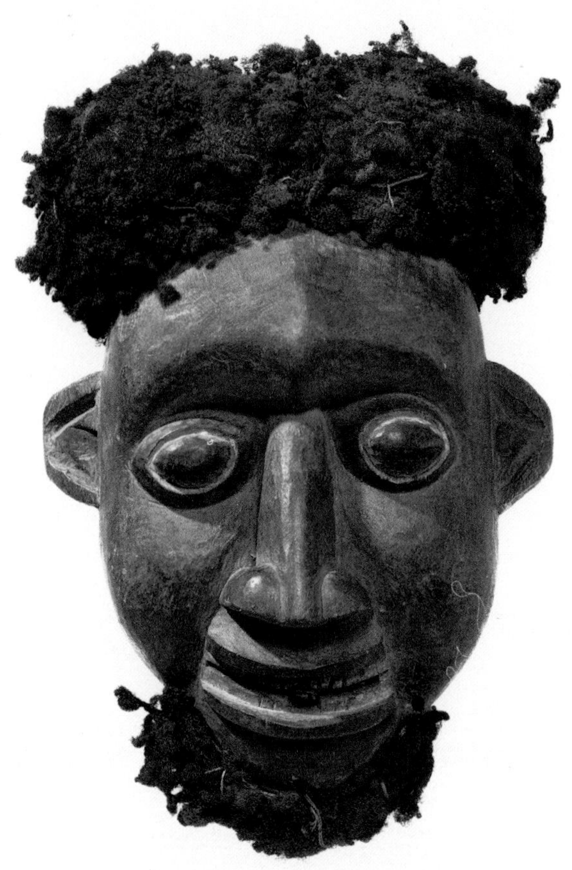

204

Masks of the Cameroon Grasslands (204–209)

Most masks of this region are oversize with stylized faces, both human and animal. The masks are of two types: the head with neck (see Nos. 206 and 207) and the face alone with broad rim (see Nos. 204 and 205). Both are worn on the crown of the head as headdress masks; dancers wearing the second type must bend forward so that the mask can see the spectators. The dancer's face is covered with cloth or netting, and he wears the garment prescribed for his particular mask: raffia with feathers or human hair and, in recent times, cotton or other similar cloth printed or dyed indigo.

For the most part, the pieces shown here are from the northern grasslands—specifically Aghem and neighboring Kom. Characteristic are the large rimmed eyes, the strong noses with prominent nostrils, the protruding mouth open to reveal pointed teeth, the simplified projecting ears, and a variety of head coverings. The surface colors range from dark brown to black and show traces of red and white paint.

Owners of the masks were, and still are, the numerous men's associations. In some areas there are also women's associations, but they do not use masks. The most important occasion on which these masks appear is the commemorative ritual at the death of a society member. Without such a ceremony, the deceased's soul cannot enter the realm of the dead. Some masks also serve as instruments of authority—they provide surveillance of communal work, control fires in domestic hearths during the dry season, pursue criminals, and deliver royal messages. Before it appears, each mask is charged with magically potent plant matter to imbue it with power. In contemporary pidgin English, this is called *juju,* or medicine. There is a hierarchy among the masks according to shape and type of magical treatment. Some are considered especially dangerous, others less so.

Lit.: H. Baumann & L. Vajda 1959, pp. 246-54; E. M. Chilver & P. M. Kaberry 1967, pp. 123-29; C. Geary 1979, p. 64; P. Gebauer 1968, n.p.; H. J. Koloss 1977, pp. 35-47, 62; T. Northern 1973, pp. 29, 54; P. Valentin 1977, p. 176.

204 Mask, wood, human hair.
Cameroon, Bamenda-Tikar, Kom?

This headdress mask represents the type called *kam* or *akam* and is from the western kingdoms of Bamenda province—that is, Oku. A unique feature of this mask and its costume is that they are partially covered with human hair. The mask probably represents a dead king or family head and is one of the most feared and respected mask types. It may appear either alone or with other masks. In Oku the mask group consists of seven to fifteen mask personae led by this one. Each group of masks led by a *kam* represents one of the societies that exist in every large village.

Height 41 cm. 05.251
Acquired from Berke 1905

Lit.: H. J. Koloss 1977, p. 49; T. Northern 1973, pp. 30-31.

205 Mask with knobbed cap, wood.
Cameroon, Bamenda-Tikar, Kom?

This type of headdress mask is worn by members of the dancing groups of various associations. The grinning mouth indicates that the wearer has assumed the role of a monkey—the messenger of the leader (*kam;* see No. 204). In Oku the monkey character supervised certain communal work and may represent the leader at burials. Both animal and human features appear on this headdress mask. The stylized knobs on the head represent the cap worn by notables, the exaggerated grinning simian mouth shows pointed teeth, and the ears are decorated with an abstract frog motif.

Height 43 cm. 05.250
Acquired from Berke 1905

Lit.: H. J. Koloss 1977, pp. 50-51; T. Northern 1973, pp. 29, 39.

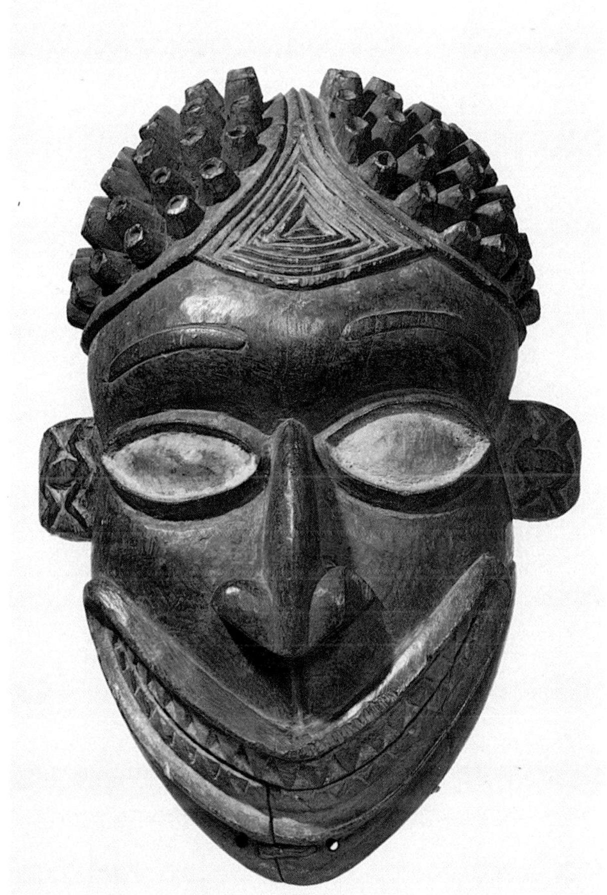

205

206 Mask with openwork cap, wood.
Cameroon, Bamenda-Tikar, Aghem (Wum).

This headdress mask with openwork superstructure on a powerful forward-leaning neck belongs to the category of masks that appear in groups (see also Nos. 204-207). The full-cheeked face—a symbol of prosperity—is characteristic of Bamum style. The turbanlike spider-patterned head covering indicates

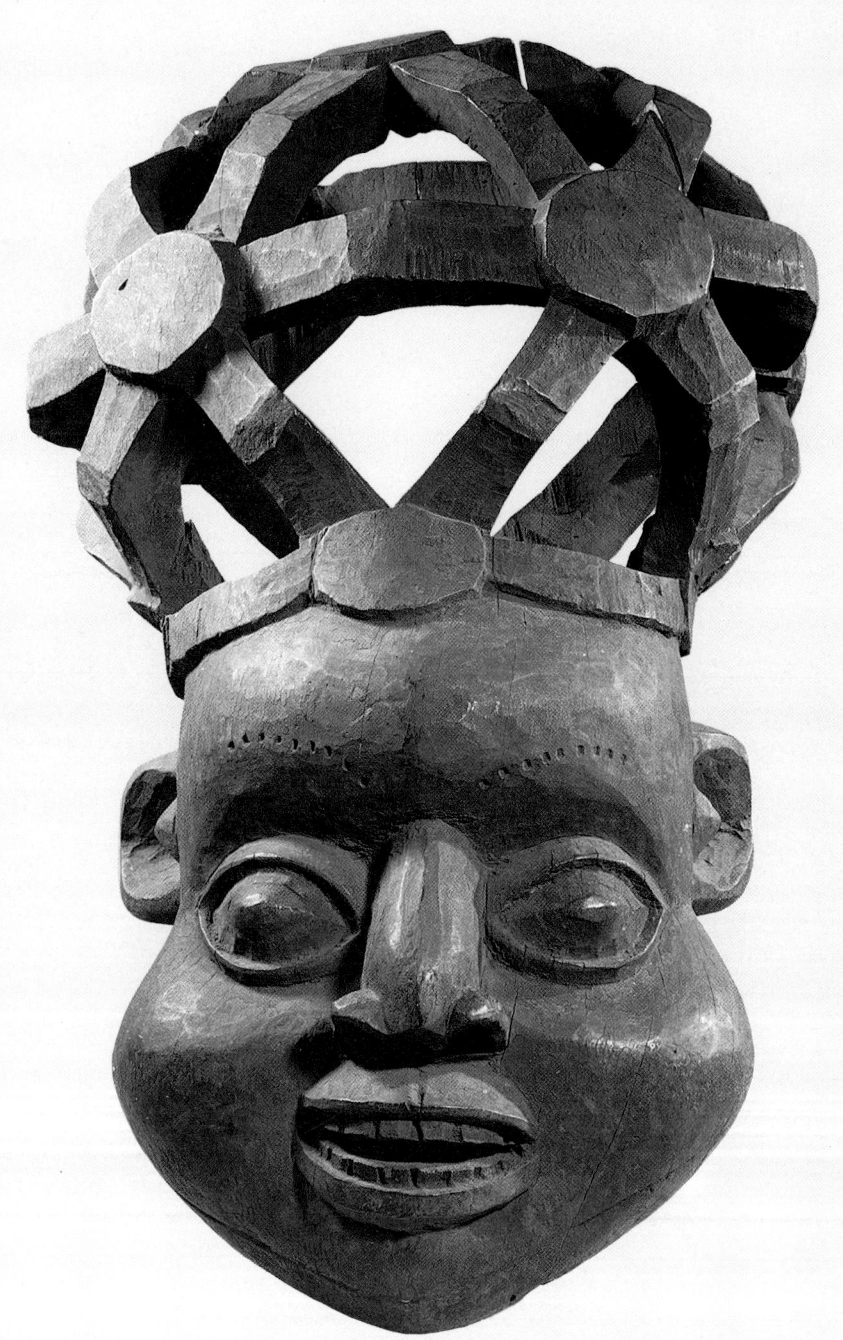

the masked dancer's importance and originally was probably a sign of the social position of a high dignitary or clan elder. In the Tikar kingdom, the field spider was not only used for divination and as a symbol of the sun or death but was also a royal emblem. The mask's original significance is lost, and the explanation given in 1976-77 by a Tikar informant in Oku, east of Aghem—that the head ornament represents a basket for crops or other goods—scarcely explains the significance of this important attribute.

Height 62 cm. 14-71-110
Acquired from E. Mack 1914

Lit.: P. Gebauer 1964, p. 42, 1979, p. 153; H. J. Koloss 1977, p. 50; T. Northern 1973, p. 33.

207 Mask with female face, wood.
Cameroon, Bamenda-Tikar, Aghem (Wum).

Characteristics of the Kom style apparent in this headdress mask include the marked nape and white-rimmed mouth and eyes. Whereas Nos. 204–205 represent only the face, this mask consists of the whole head. The dancer who wears such a mask need not bend to let the mask look forward, for the strong nape supports it upright on top of his head (his face is not covered). The raised, almond-shape hair on the top of the head, retaining remnants of redwood paint, represents a female coiffure. Since grasslands carvers rarely distinguish female faces from male, only the coiffure indicates when a mask is a female—*ngoin* or *ngon,* wife of the *kam* (see No. 204). All masks, including the females, are worn by men. This piece shows traces of use. A similar mask symbolizes both the royal wives and womanhood in general.

Height 30 cm. 14-71-107
Acquired from E. Mack 1914

Lit.: H. J. Koloss 1977, pp. 40, 49-50; T. Northern 1973, pp. 36-37, 1984, p. 146.

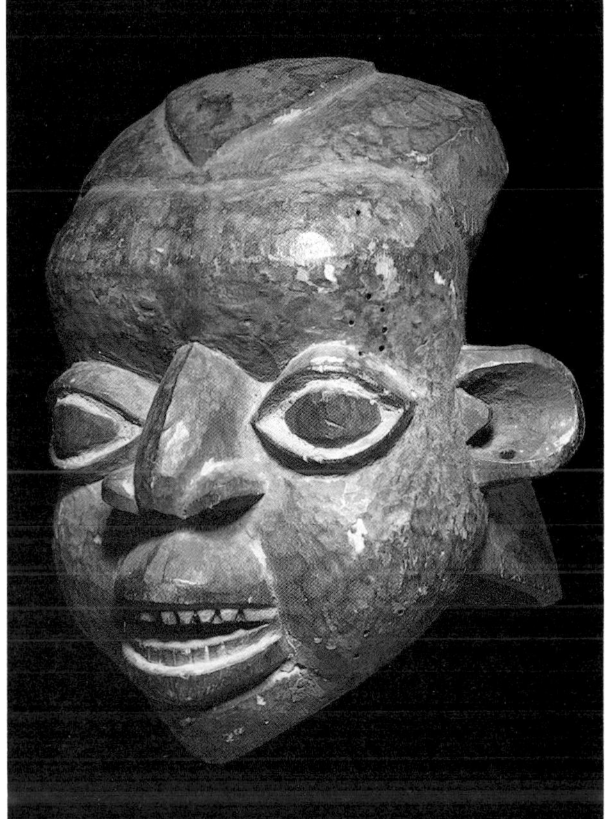

207

208 Buffalo (?) mask, wood.
Cameroon, Bamenda-Tikar, Aghem (Wum).

This headdress mask has an open mouth that reveals rows of teeth, and horns, ears, eyes, and teeth colored with bright white clay. The horns are not natural but stylized. This mask's function is the same as that of No. 209.

Height 51 cm. 50-11-89
Acquired from the Deutschen Museum 1950 (E. Mack Collection 1914)

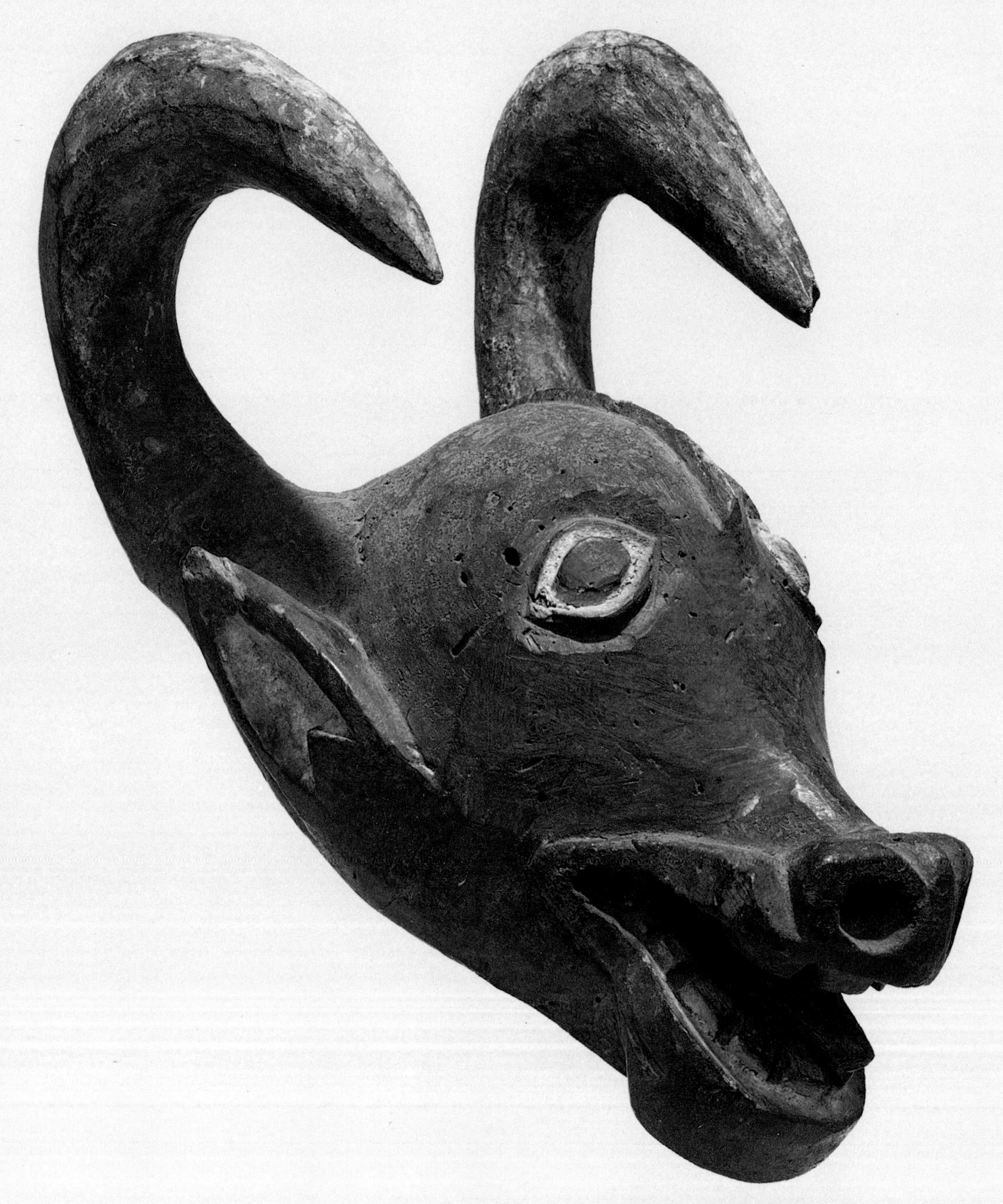

209 Buffalo mask, wood.
Cameroon, purchased at Ebolome, southern Cameroon.

Bold outlines enliven this headdress mask. Although it is said to have been bought from the Bulu in southern Cameroon, it is a typical work of grasslands sculpture and, unless the alleged provenance is incorrect, must have been carried south. Similar masks are known from the grasslands, from both the Bamum and Bamenda-Tikar regions. The sharply contoured nostrils link it to the grasslands buffalo masks. Among the grasslands peoples, animal masks, most frequently buffalo masks, perform in dancing groups (see Nos. 204 and 205). The buffalo-mask dancer is feared, for he carries a spear to keep enemies away from the masked group.

Length 82 cm. 14-67-3
Acquired from K. Ritter 1914

Lit.: P. Gebauer 1979, p. 155; H. J. Koloss 1977, p. 51.

210 Elephant mask, cotton, glass beads.
Cameroon, Bamum, from Fontemena.

A cotton-cloth cap covers the wearer's whole head, while the long flaps fall across his chest and back like a cape. Animal and human features are combined: eyes, nose, mouth, teeth, and the notables' knobbed cap represent human features, while the long strip hanging down the front depicts an elephant's trunk. The prominent beaded circles on either side of the face represent elephant ears.

This was an important ritual object of the elephant society, whose membership was reserved exclusively for rich noblemen. Only they could afford to pay the society's admission fees and to buy the elephant masks, which were extremely expensive because of the costly glass beads. Closely linked to the royal court, the society's members served the king as warriors or administrators. Their relationship

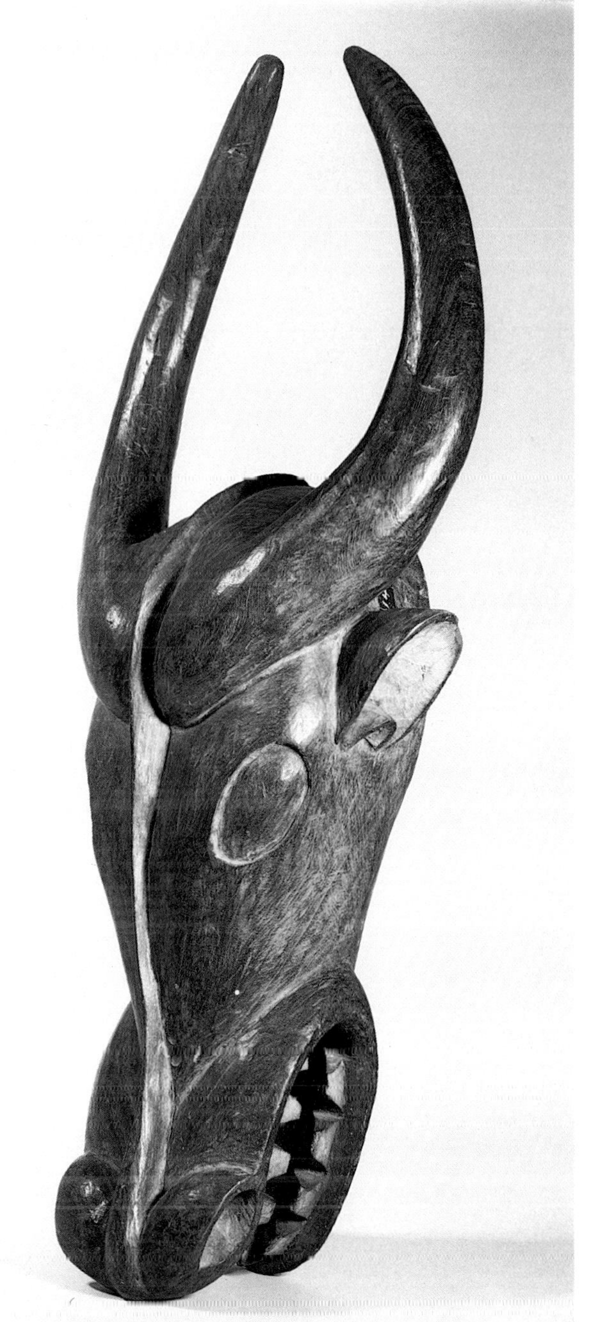

209

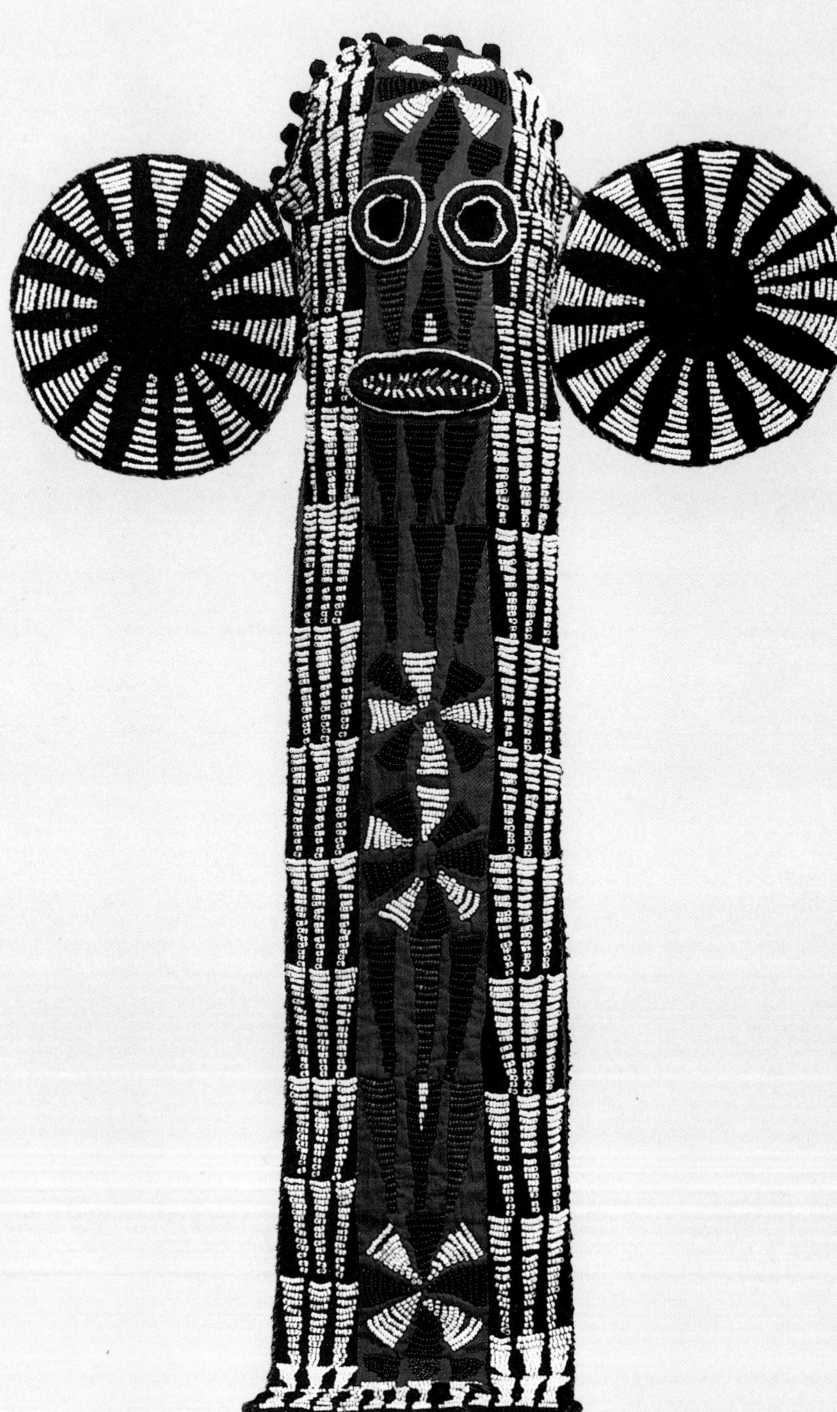

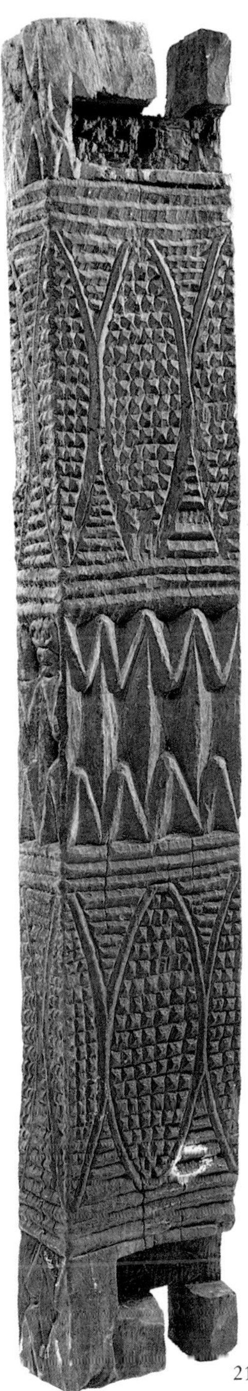
213

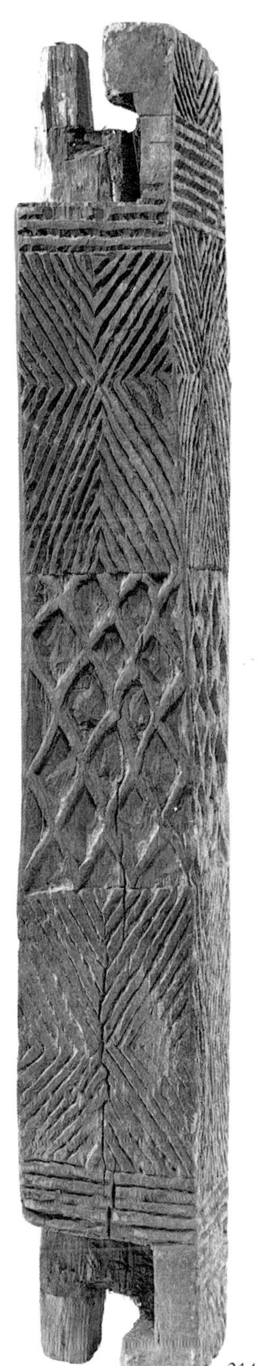
214

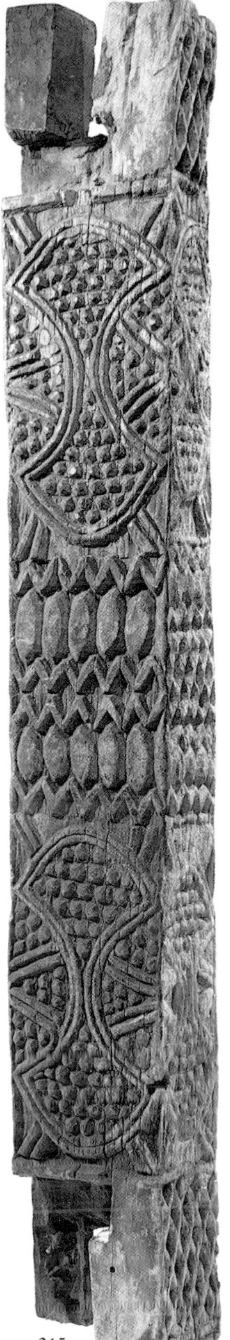
215

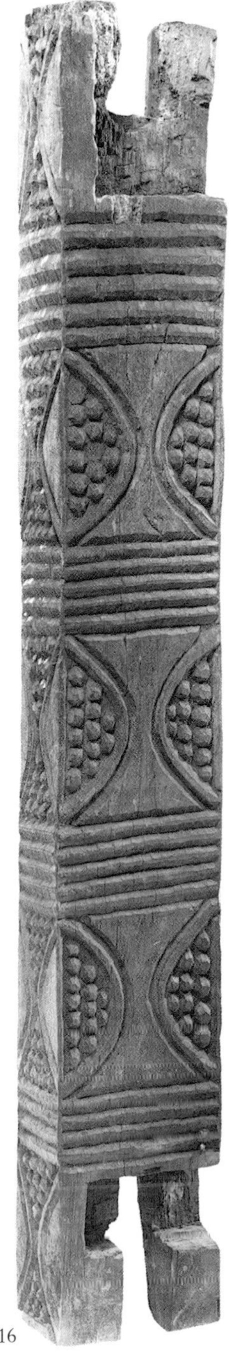
216

Pipe bowls are usually of clay, as only members of the royal court could use cast-bronze bowls. Decorative motifs were taken largely from traditional art, but around the turn of the century, after the weakening of this tradition, European motifs and grotesque new creations appeared.

The owner's social position may be ascertained from his pipe. Simple pipes, with or without geometric decoration, may be smoked by anyone. Pipes with special animal motifs are reserved for members of cult associations. Anthropomorphic bowls or metal pipes with ivory stems may be used only by members of the royal court, including the royal wives and the ruler himself. The ceremonial pipe of the kings of Bamum, used at state festivals and receptions, has a gigantic clay bowl and a wooden stem adorned with filigree carving covered with metal foil. Its unusual size and excessive decoration developed under King Njoya (1889-1931). This pipe is kept by a specially appointed royal wife, lighted at ceremonies by a second wife, and filled with tobacco that is stored by a third.

Clay pipe bowls are formed by hand with a stick or modeling iron and are then slowly dried and fired. Decoration is completed during firing when red camwood powder is brushed into the hollows so that the color is burned in. Tobacco juice is let out through a small hole in the base of the pipe, which is usually plugged with cotton cloth. Metal pipes are modeled individually and cast in lost-wax molds. Most are made by Fumban (Bamum) and Bagam craftsmen.

The pipe industry received a new stimulus in colonial times when pipe bowls became popular souvenirs. Grasslands pottery settlements became production centers: while the women modeled pottery for domestic use, the men made pipe bowls.

Lit.: H. Baumann & L. Vajda 1959, pp. 286ff.; P. Gebauer 1979, pp. 249-50; P. Harter 1973, pp. 18ff.; F. Hutter 1902, p. 405.

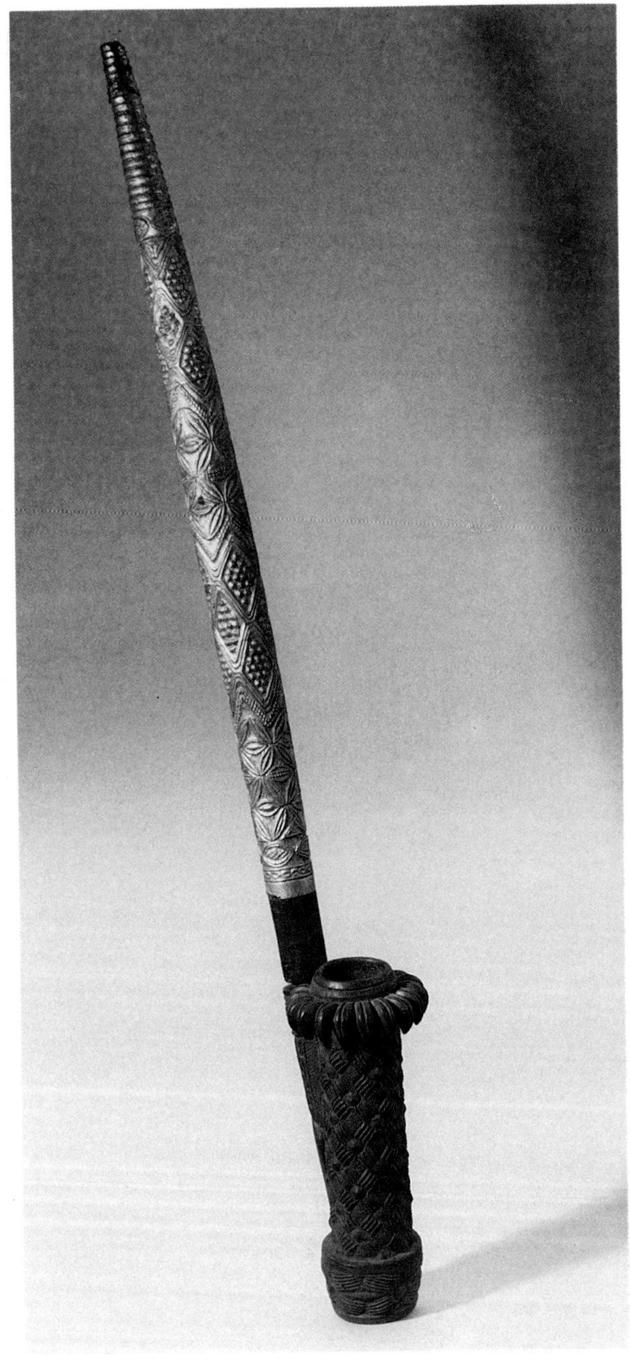

217

217 Royal tobacco pipe, clay, wood, metal.
Cameroon, Bamileke or Tikar, Bafut.

Spider-pattern ornament decorates this pipe bowl. At the upper rim of the bowl a wreath of arches with median grooves curves outward and downward—a decoration that is frequently found on Oriental pipe bowls. Although some Bamileke and Tikar interpret this pattern as leopard claws and others as the hornbill's beak or the fruit of the *mbure* tree, these may well be secondary interpretations of a motif originally introduced from the Orient. Geary is of the opinion that such pipes are typical of Bamum work.

The pipestem is carved with abstract decoration, including lozenges and rosettes, characteristic of the grasslands (see also Nos. 213-16). Possessing a pipestem covered with metal foil like this one was a royal privilege.

Height (pipe bowl) 33 cm. 15-17-3

Length of stem 118 cm. 31-54-30
Acquired from the Museum für Völkerkunde Berlin 1915 (bowl), J. Frick 1931 (stem)

Lit.: H. Baumann & L. Vajda 1959, p. 287; C. Geary 1983, p. 89, illus. 43,44; P. Harter 1973, pp. 27, 1.

218 Pipe bowl, clay, paint.
Cameroon, Bali.
(see color plate p. 268)

This old pipe bowl, made at the end of the nineteenth century, bears traces of use. The head, greatly enlarged in relation to the body, is characteristic of human representations from the Guinea coast, but is also frequenty found in the art of Cameroon. The seated figure of the king, rendered in a unique style, is particularly fine: the representation as a whole is graceful, the curves are gentle, there are half-closed almond-shape eyes without pupils, and minute stylized ears, fine incisions, and painted ornament.

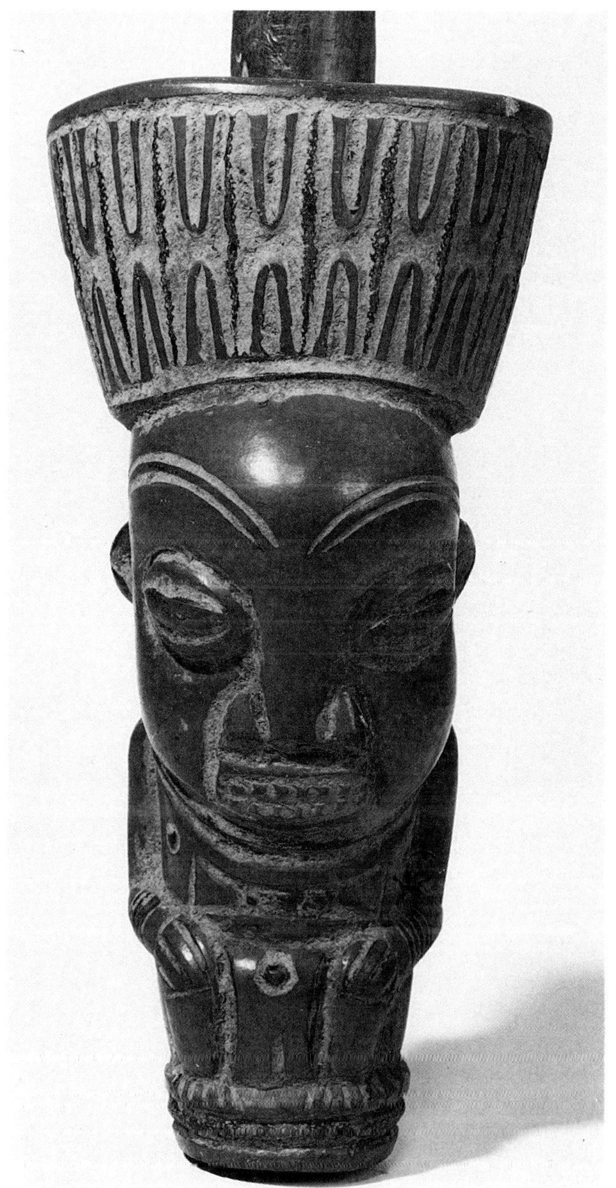

218

Height 24 cm. 93.316
Acquired from F. Hutter 1893

Lit.: P. Harter 1973, p. 23.

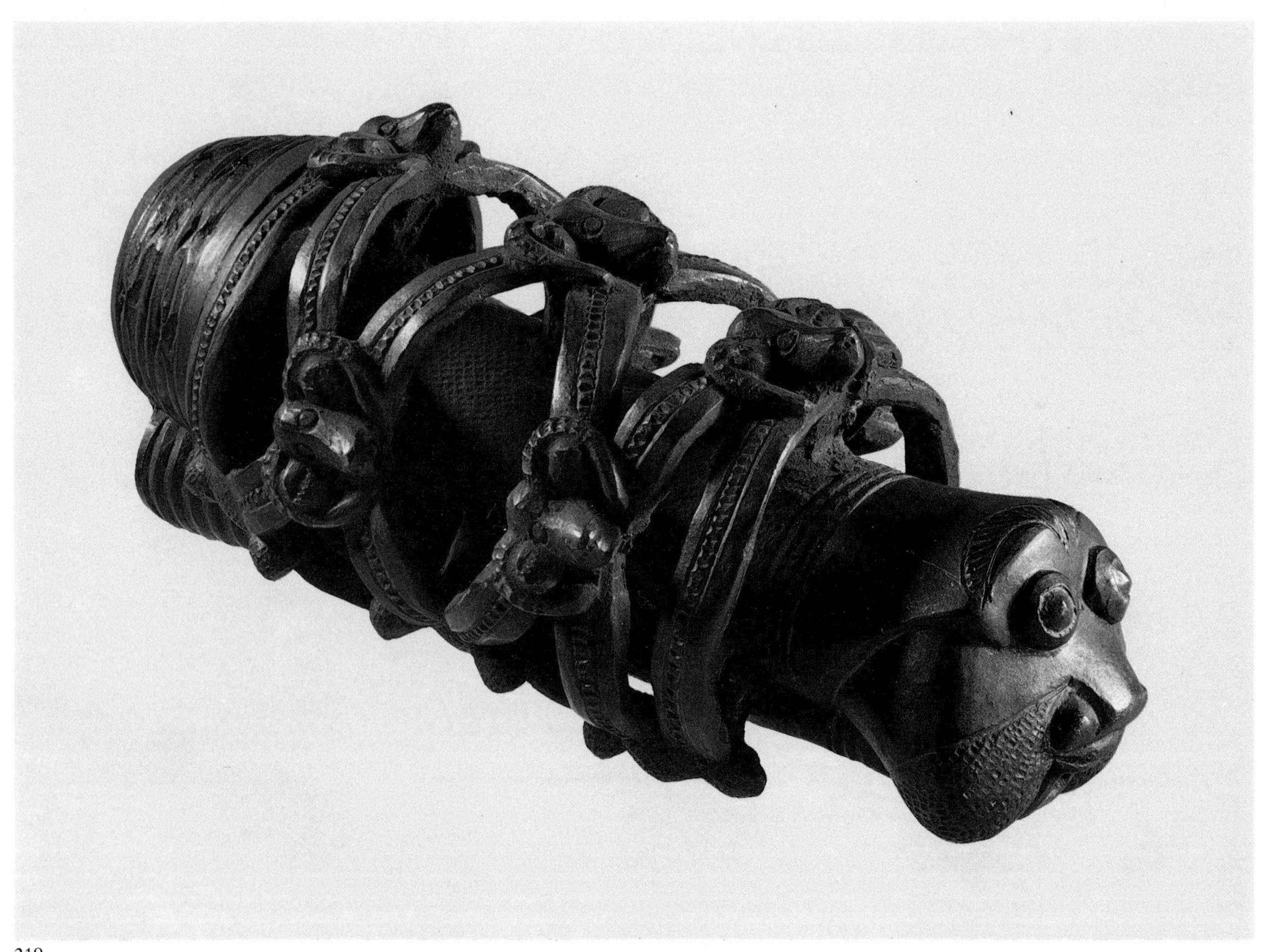

219

219 Pipe bowl, clay, graphite, paint.
Cameroon, Bamum (?), collected in Bali.

The full-cheeked face of this pipe bowl, with distended nostrils and circular eyes with pupils, is typical of Bamum art. The latticework around the pipe bowl forms a stylized spider pattern. The ram's heads at the points of intersection were shaped of clay pellets, stuck on, and finished. Pipe hearth and lower half of face are covered with the same cross-hatching.

Height 27 cm. 21-8-10
Acquired from F. Hutter 1921

Lit.: H. Baumann & L. Vajda 1959, pp. 287-89; C. Geary 1983, p. 89; P. Harter 1973, pp. 26-28.

220 Double-bowl pipe, graphite, red pigment. Cameroon, Bamum (?), collected in Bali.

All the details of this old, finely worked piece are treated with equal intensity. The right to use double pipes, which could be smoked without pause (while the tobacco in one bowl was still burning, the other could be refilled), was granted only to fathers of twins. This fact is affirmed by the depiction of a male/female twin pair. In the grasslands, where twins were considered an exceptional blessing, their parents were held in high regard.

This example shares a number of characteristics with No. 219: the almost circular face has round eyes, the nose has distended nostrils, the face is divided into two sections, there are neck rings, and the pipe bowl is crosshatched.

Height 14 cm. 93.318
Acquired from F. Hutter 1893

Lit.: P. Harter 1973, p. 21; F. Hutter 1902, p. 406.

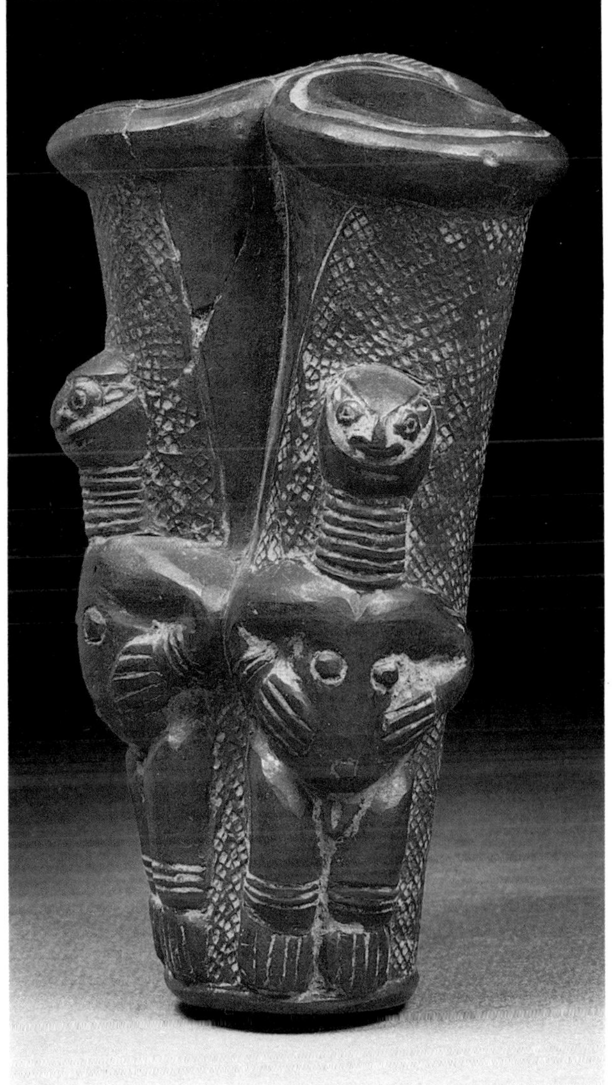

220

221 Pipe bowl, clay, red pigment. Cameroon, Bali.

This pipe bowl decorated with stylized, grotesque animal heads is of a type found mainly in the central area of the Bamileke. This unwieldly example was probably made as a souvenir.

Height 21 cm. 21-8-9
Acquired from F. Hutter 1921

Lit.: P. Harter 1973, p. 8.

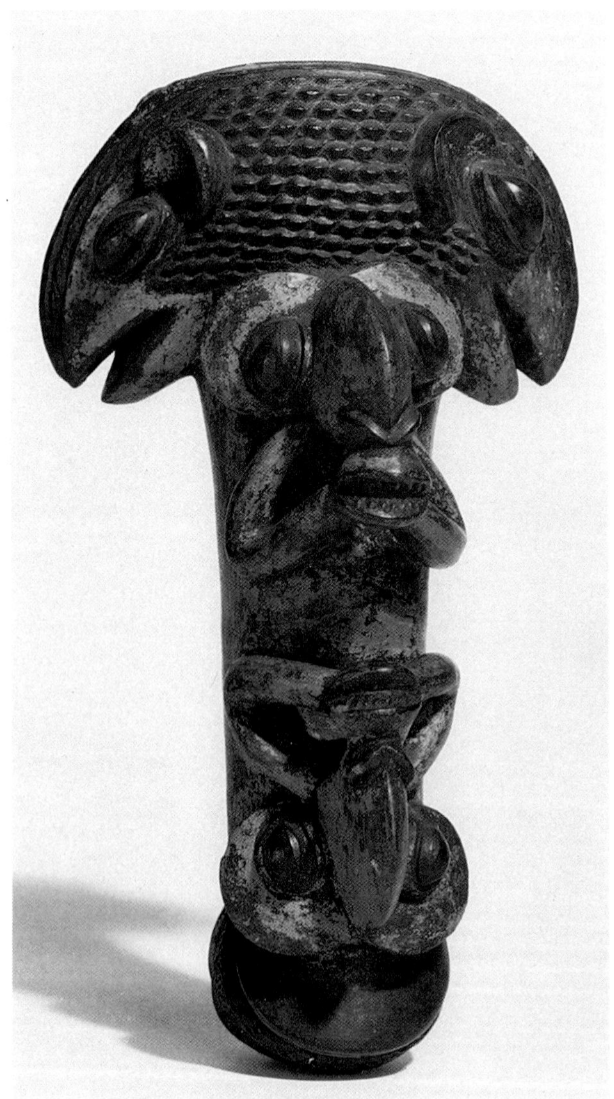

221

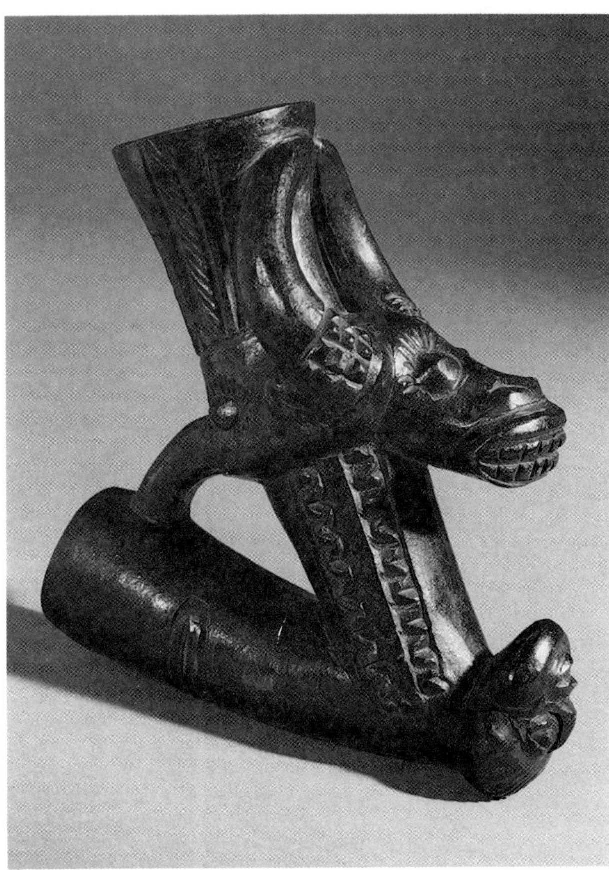

222

222 Pipe bowl, clay, graphite.
Cameroon, Babungo.

Depictions of masks were often found on pipe bowls. Here the head of a buffalo confronts a human-faced mask. The pipe's owner was presumably a member of a cult society that used such a mask.

Height 18 cm. 15-17-10
Acquired from the Museum für Völkerkunde Berlin 1915

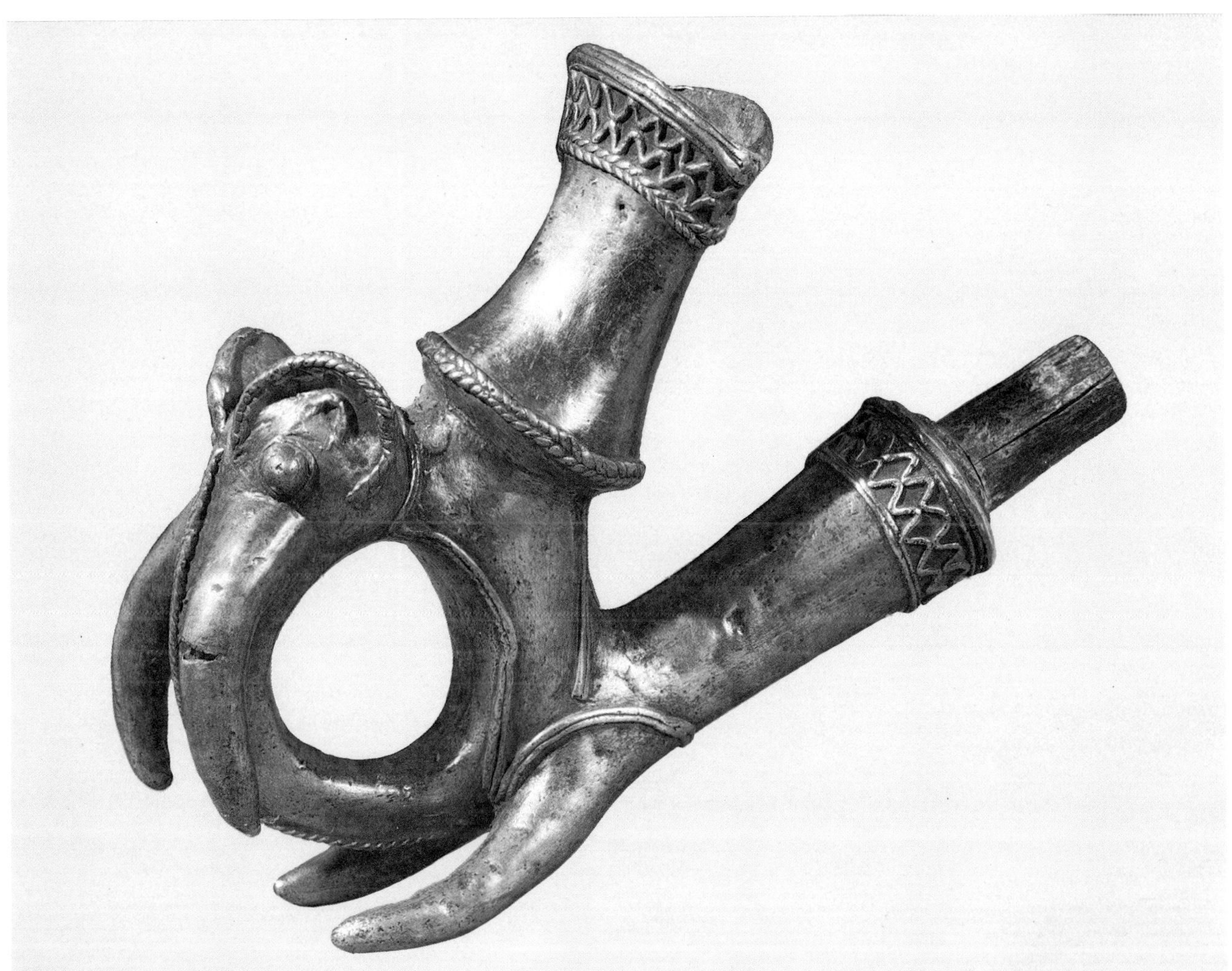

223

223 Pipe bowl, brass, reed.
Cameroon, Bamenda Tikar.

The use of the elephant motif highly stylized here—was a royal privilege, as was the possession of brass pipe bowls. We can be certain that this piece originally belonged to a ruler.

Height 21 cm. 20-3-87
Acquired from A. Grubauer 1920

Lit.: P. Gebauer 1979, pp. 249, 251; T. Northern 1973, p. 28.

224 Pipe bowl and stem, brass, reed.
Cameroon, Tikar, collected in the Dschang area.

Like brass pipes in general, this typical pipe bowl with bird figure in the round was made for a chief. A short piece of reed that originally held the bowl and stem together is inserted.

Length 31 cm. 31-54-31
Acquired from J. Frick 1931

Lit.: F. Thorbecke 1919, III, p. 52.

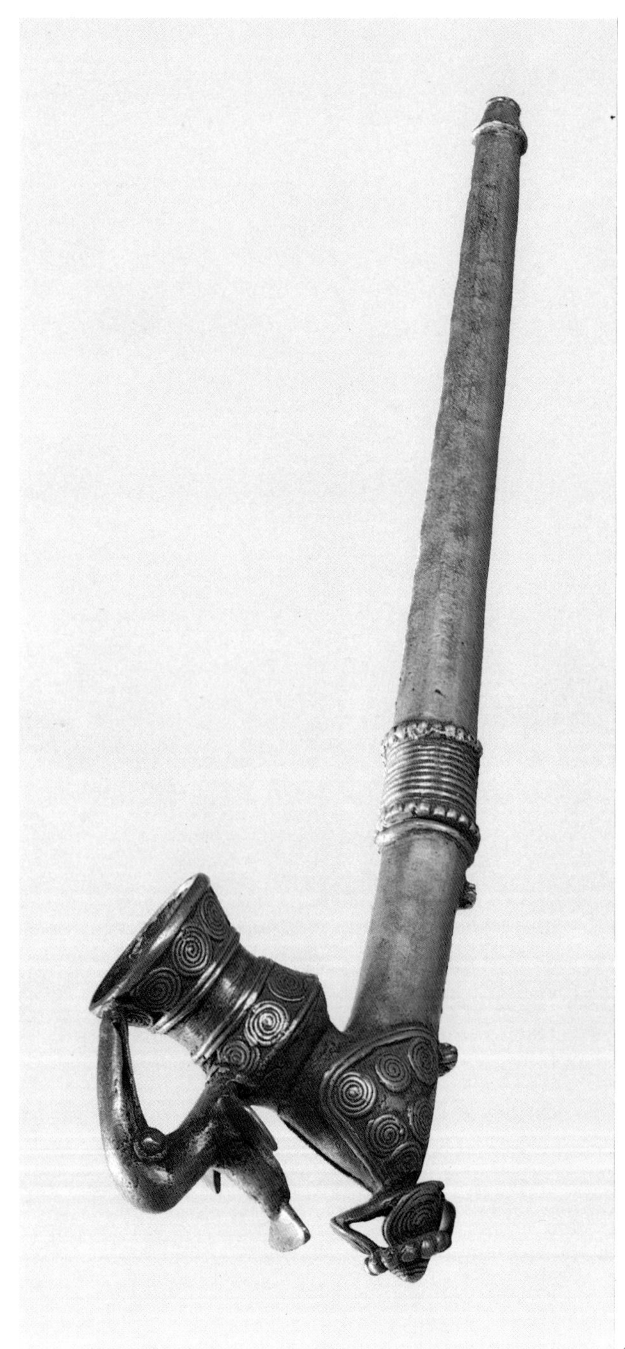

224

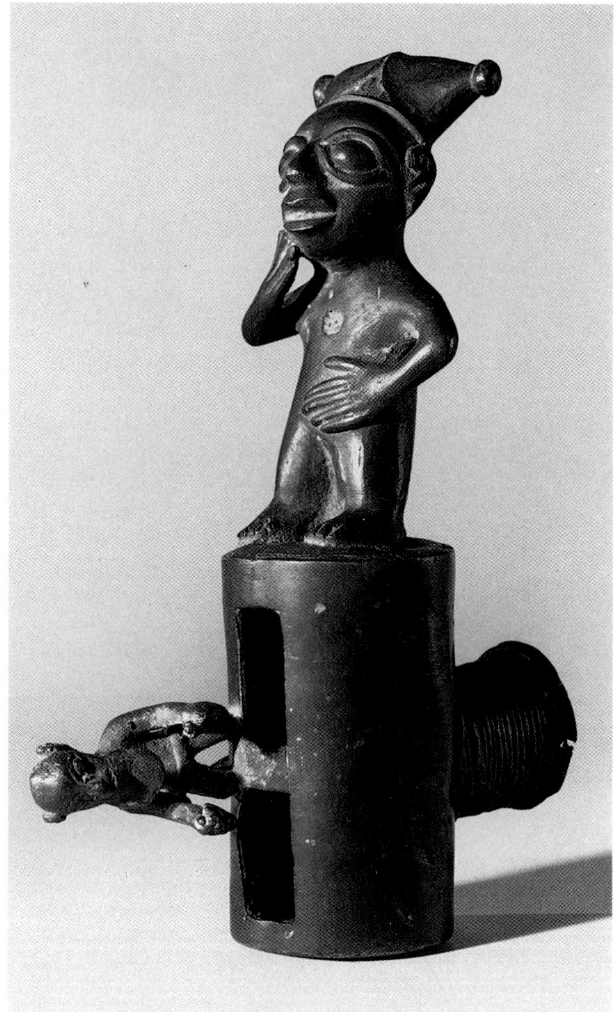

225

225 Hammer or staff top, brass.
Cameroon, Bamileke.

This unusual cast-brass composition, arranged on vertical and horizontal axes, represents a bearded drummer with large slit drum (state drum?) and a second male figure wearing a dignitary's cap. The wooden staff on which this was mounted is missing. A European court mallet may possibly have served as the model for this piece.

Length 22 cm., width 14 cm. 81-301-495
Acquired from R. L. Stolper 1981

226,227 Two pendants, brass.
Cameroon, Bamum.

Like the elephant, the buffalo was respected for its physical strength and cunning—attributes also ascribed to the king, chiefs, and clan elders. In the council at Fumbam, the capital of Bamum, the highest dignitaries sat upon buffalo skulls. They wore iron neck rings (see drawing) strung with dozens of small buffalo-head pendants, which were placed in their graves after death. These insignia lost their importance when the traditional political structure gave way, and by the turn of the century such pendants were being worn by only a few women as neck or girdle ornaments.

Height 3 cm., 4.5 cm. 18-7-18,19
Acquired from L. Frobenius 1918

Lit.: P. Gebauer 1979, pp. 234, 246; T. Northern 1985, p. 126.

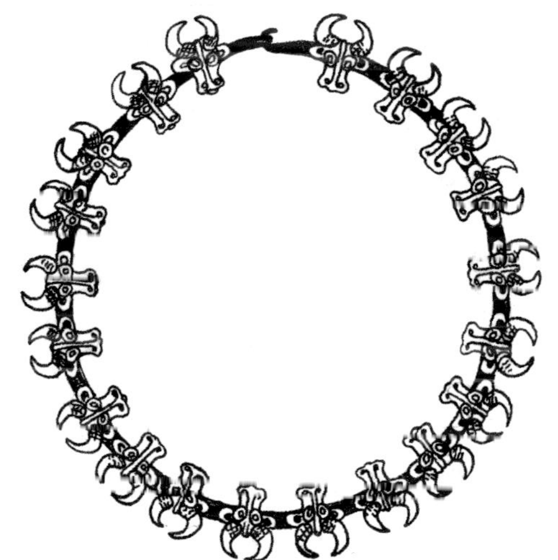

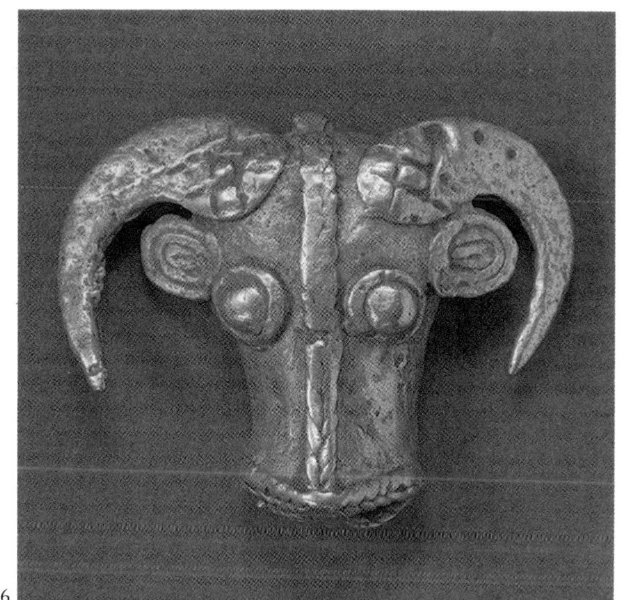

226

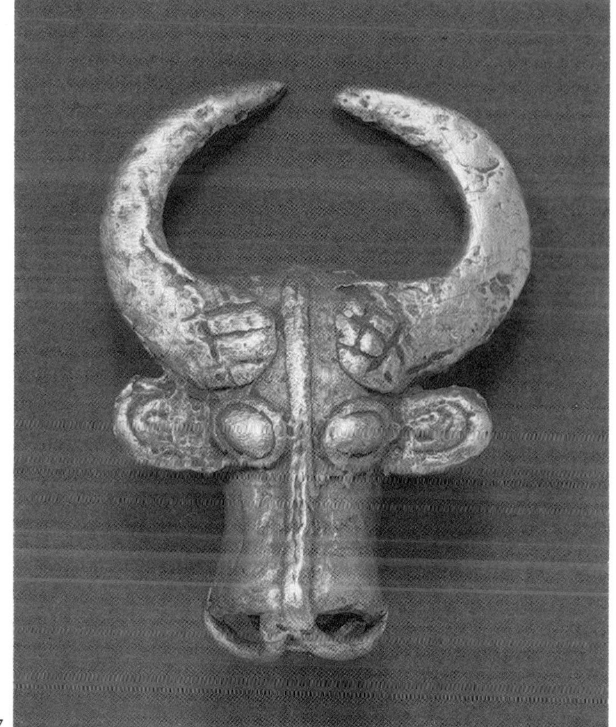

227

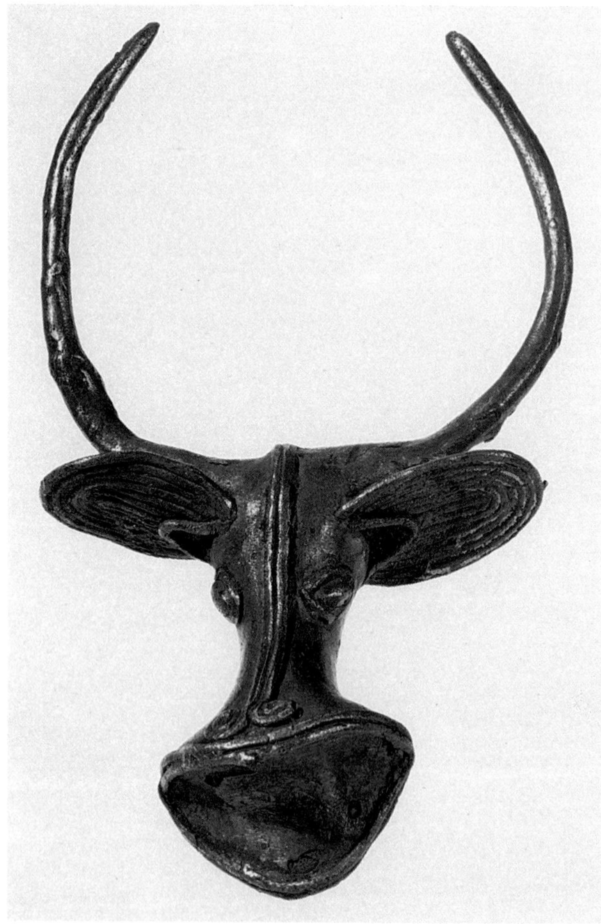

228

228 Bovine head, cast brass.
Cameroon, Bamum (?), collected among the Balong.

Probably an example of souvenir art, this massively cast piece was carried from the grasslands to the Balong, in the forest area.

Height 14.5 cm. 12-42-11
Acquired from G. Witthoft 1912

Lit.: K. Krieger 1967, III, illus. 103.

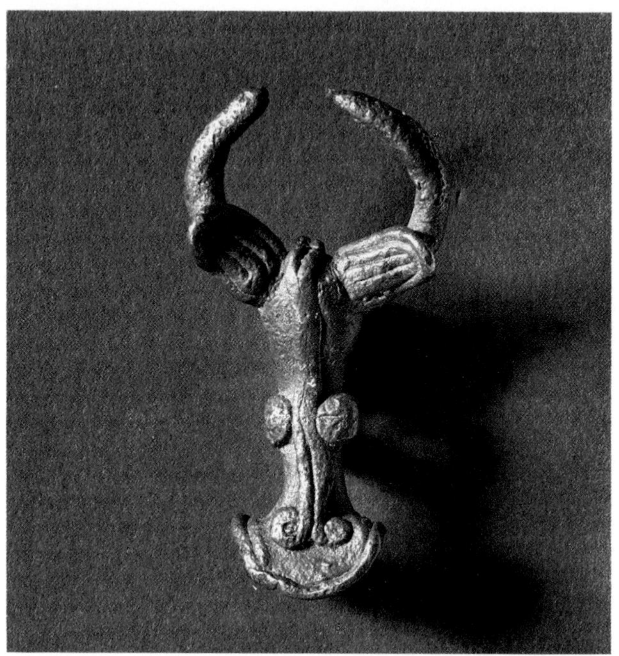

229

229 Bovine head, cast brass.
Cameroon, Bamum.

Similar to No. 228 but corresponding in size to Nos. 226 and 227, this piece is distinguished by a very small loop on the back. It may have been attached to a finger ring.

Height 4.5 cm. 18-7-34
Acquired from L. Frobenius 1918

Lit.: K. Krieger 1967, III, illus. 100.

230 Resist-dyed fabric, cotton.
Cameroon, Bamum.

This textile has been made of twenty long, narrow bands of plain-weave unbleached cotton. It has been dyed in a sew-resist technique by covering all the white areas in lightly sewn raffia fiber, which the indigo dye does not penetrate. After dyeing, the raffia fiber is removed.

230

This method of cloth making and style of decoration comes from the Jukun of northern Nigeria. Their textiles were imported by Hausa traders until the grasslands developed its own cloth industry as a royal monopoly. At the turn of the century at the court of King Njoya, work was carried out on 310 looms under the supervision of the royal treasurer. The king presented the cloths, status symbols, to his subjects, who made them into garments, wore them at the festivals, or used them as wall hangings at the festival site. Inequilateral triangles dominate the decoration—a pattern, according to Northern, that symbolizes leopard skin.

Length 304 cm., width 112 cm 74-1-1
Acquired from L. Bretschneider 1974

Lit.: R. Boser-Sarivaxévanis 1972, pp. 8, 52; R. Bravmann 1973, p. 76; T. Northern 1975, p. 58; A. Rhein-Wuhrmann 1925, pp. 89-90

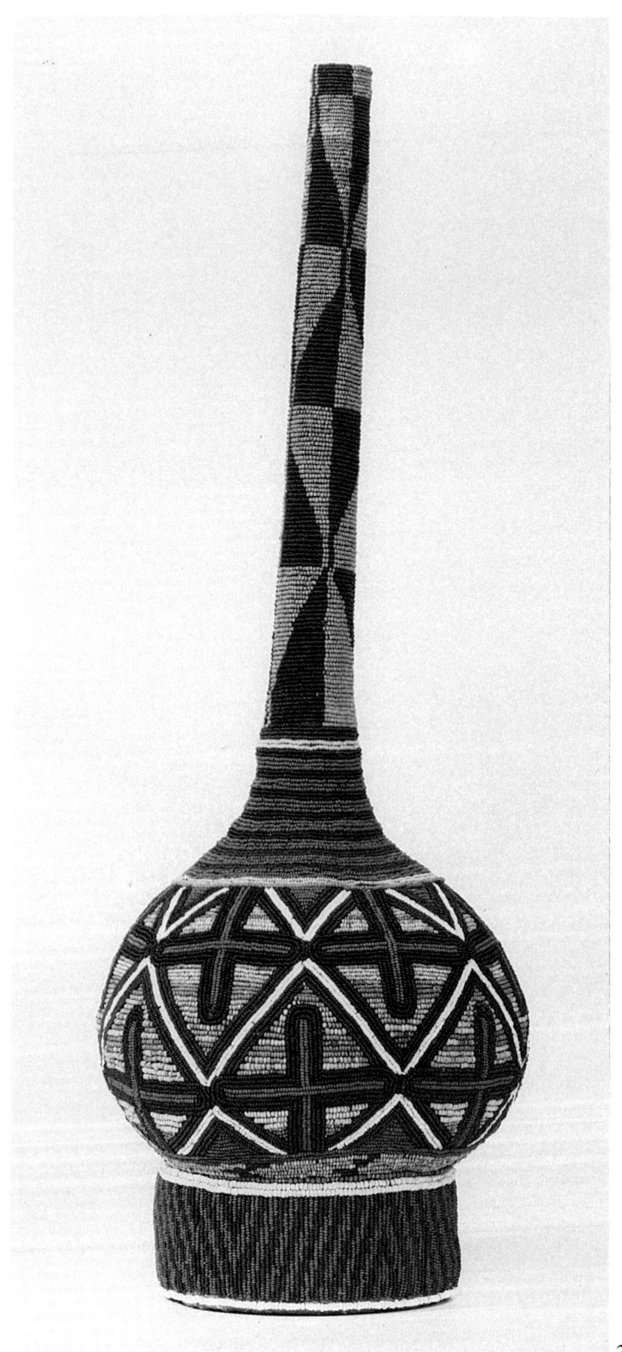

231

231 Calabash vessel, cotton, glass beads.
Cameroon, Bamum.

Calabashes, sometimes entirely bead covered like this one, or with a stopper ending in a sculptured animal, serve as containers of the palm wine that is indispensable at festivals or sacrificial observances. Even at ordinary drinking rounds a libation for the ancestors is first poured on the ground. In earlier periods, glass beads decorated only the calabashes used at court ceremonies. Today at such receptions, each of the king's wives, standing behind the throne, holds a richly adorned calabash, though now it is empty. Ornament on the recently manufactured pieces still indicates their courtly origin: the crossed and zigzag lines on our piece are presumably abstract spider and frog motifs (see also No. 212), whereas the design on the neck of the vessel suggests leopard-skin markings (see also No. 230).

Height 51.5 cm. 05.282
Acquired from Berke 1905

Lit.: P. Gebauer 1968, n.p., 1979, p. 201; T. Northern 1975, pp. 55-58; C. Savary & P. Harter 1980, pp. 15-16

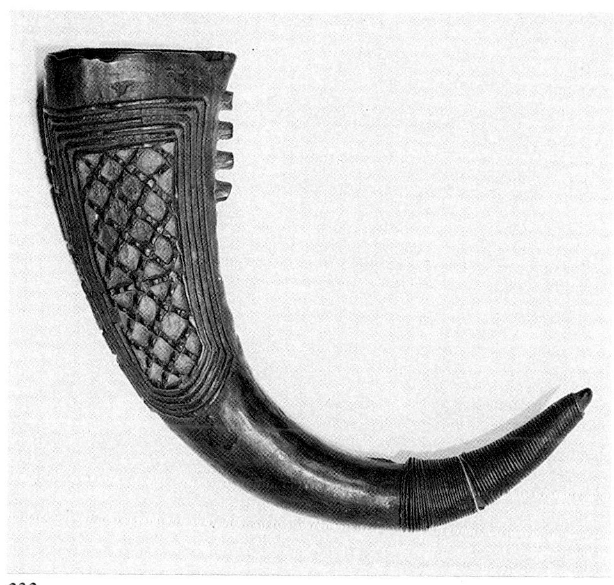

232

232 Drinking horn, cow horn, copper wire.
Cameroon, Bamenda-Tikar (?), Babanki-Tungo (?)

Drinking vessels of polished and more or less richly carved horn, formerly buffalo but now cow horn, were symbols of nobility. The simple folk used mainly calabashes. Presenting a drinking horn as a gift was a ritual gesture of friendship, and examples of these horns circulated among members of chiefly families. This horn is carved with a spider design framed by parallel ridges.

Length 18 cm. 74-10-3
Acquired from K. F. Schädler 1974

Lit.: P. Gebauer 1979, p. 215; T. Northern 1975, pp. 126-27

233,234 Two male figures, wood, barkcloth, cowries, fiber, beads.
Cameroon, eastern Gbaja, from Bogoto.

The same carver made both of these rough pole-style figures. Each has a broad, round upper body, angular shoulders, and bulbous neck. The thin arms stand out in relief, while the short legs with blocky knees and small feet are sculptured in the round. Genitals are merely suggested. The carver included some anatomical and ornamental details such as the pierced nostrils, upper lips, and ear lobes and adorned them with wooden sticks. He achieved the effect of an iris by inserting cowries into the eye sockets of No. 233.

A comparison of these pieces with the drawings of the Gbaja sculpture published by Tessman (p. 220) the original was destroyed by fire in Berlin—suggests that the Munich figures are mediocre copies of the piece that reached Berlin. The noses are too high, the eyes too low, and the ornate Gbaja coiffure, with its many horizontally and vertically arranged braids, is here placed so low that the forehead virtually disappears.

Tessman's assertion that these figures depict ancestors does not entirely accord with the facts. They are, rather, objects used to instruct youths during initiation—an interpretation supported by the

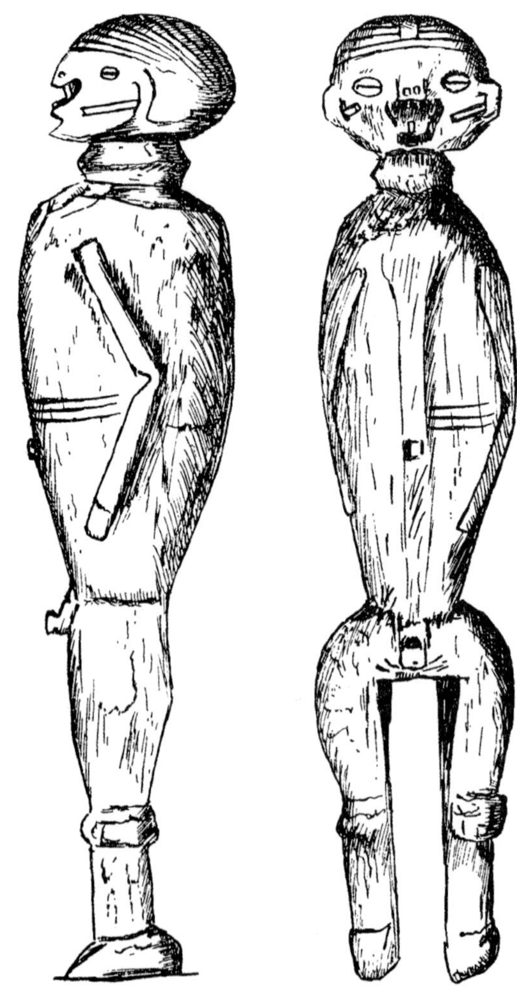

presence of so-called *labi* (initiation) cuts near the navel area (see drawing). The reddish brown loincloth with a belt of twisted plant-fiber string was part of the initiates' costume. On the youths themselves, the grass stalks that were first used in newly pierced nostrils, ears, and lip were replaced by pegs of other materials during the course of the initiation ceremonies. It was for purposes of instruction that the carver placed such emphasis on the face, stressing the characteristic perforations and filling them with

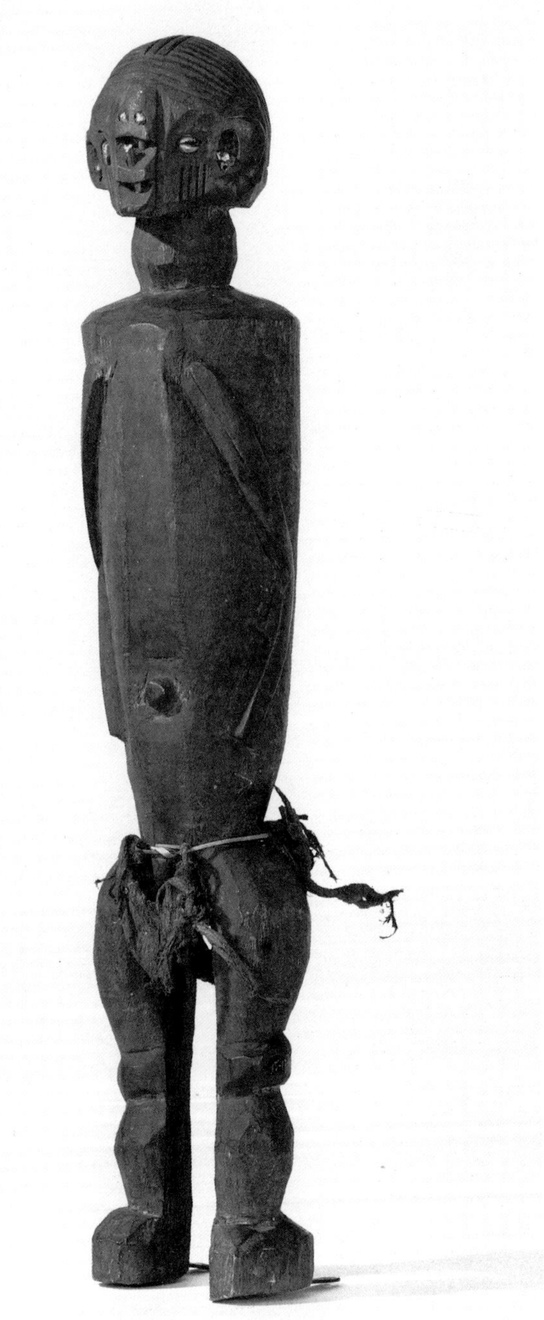

233

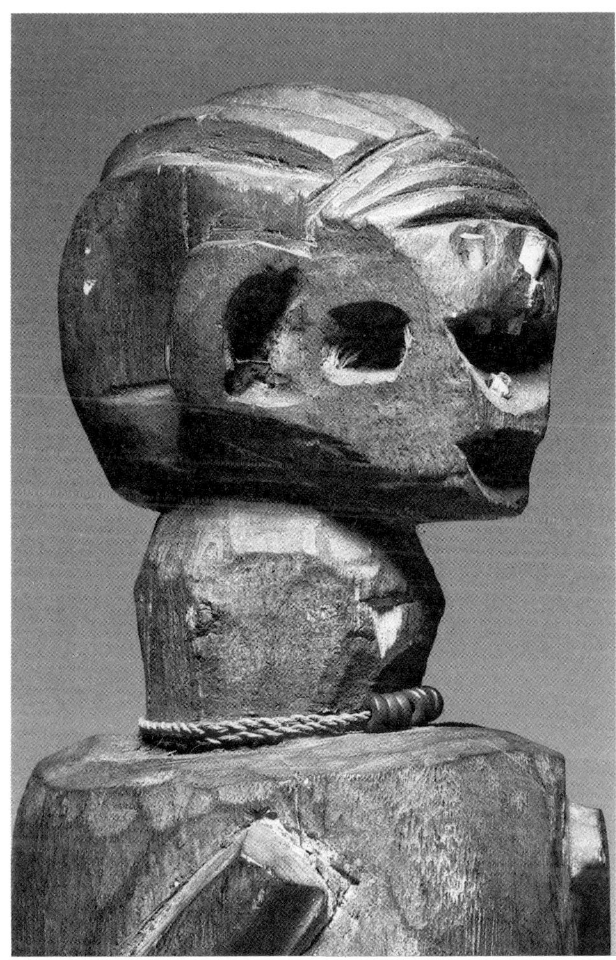
234

wooden sticks. Although these wooden figures thus presumably represent male initiates, this would not necessarily exclude an eventual secondary use in the ancestral cult.

Length 50 cm., 52 cm. 15-17-17,18
Acquired from the Museum für Völkerkunde Berlin 1915 (Collection Bartsch)

Lit.: Lieutenant Bachmann 1923-24, p. 55; E. Bartsch 1914, p. 123 and Table XIII; G. Tessman 1934, I, pp. 117-18, 127, 195, II, pp. 62, 81.

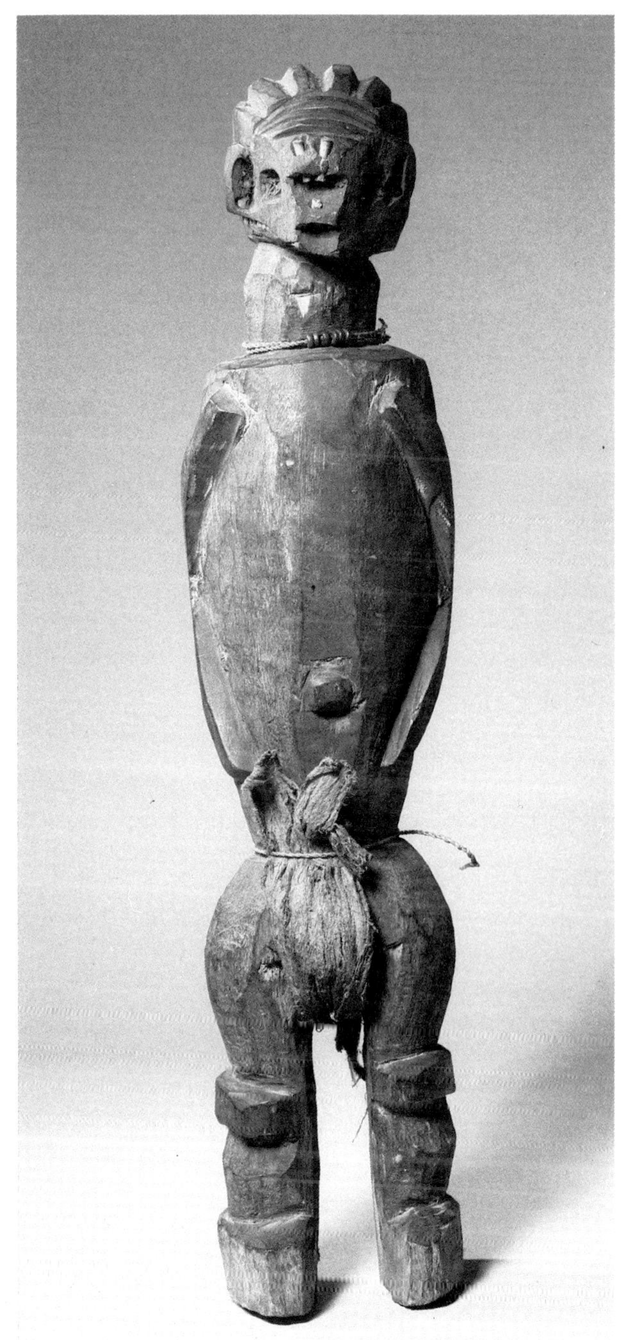
235

The Duala and Their Boats (235-244)

The history of the Duala has been extremely eventful in the last two and a half centuries. Under pressure from Beti (Fang) peoples invading from the north, the Duala migrated from the interior to the Cameroon coast, reaching their present location north of the mouth of the Sanaga River about 1750. There they were influenced first by Islamic and later by British and German traders and colonial settlers. The former forest farmers thus began to specialize in trade during colonial times. In their long dugout canoes they transported goods such as palm kernels and oil, ivory, rubber, and, until 1841, slaves to the trading stations on the coast.

The resulting European influence produced quite a remarkable hybrid style in Duala carving. European carpentry techniques and bright paint were adopted, and foreign and traditional elements were fused into a formal repertoire. Ancestral figures disappeared completely and mask art deteriorated. In their place, ornamentation of the now all-important canoes and paddles flourished. Both the paddles and the long, narrow boats, seating fifty and more, were painted with polychrome floral and geometric patterns on both sides along the gunwales.

On festive occasions there were processions of boats and regattas. Canoes that took part in these were adorned with long artistically carved and brightly painted prows in complicated openwork designs abundant in figures and curves—pieces that closely resembled objects made before Duala artistic traditions were lost. At the same time, these sculptures revealed the strength of foreign influence in their incorporation of numerous undeniably European elements.

Only a few examples of this unique Duala coast art have been preserved, and the two pieces here are among the best of their kind. Their history mirrors that of the Duala in the 1880s, as competition between the British and Germans led to the rise of mutually antagonistic partisans among the Duala. When this rivalry ended in 1884, in the defeat of the group led by pro-British chief Lock Priso, Max Buchner, then chief curator of the Munich Museum für Völkerkunde, succeeded in securing the most important booty—the carved prow of Lock Priso's boat (No. 235). A few years later the museum was able to buy the prow ornament of King Bell, Lock Priso's Germanophile opponent (No. 236). Besides being ornamental, the purpose of the boat prows was apparently similar to that of European heraldic devices.

Lit.: K. Born in H. Baumann 1975, p. 697; M. Buchner 1914, p. 194; H. Dominik 1902, p. 31; F. Hutter 1902, p. 7; T. Northern 1984, p. 179.

235 Boat prow *(ndenge),* wood, paint.
Cameroon, Duala.

The only detail here that indicates European influence is the clothing worn by the three human figures, two men and a woman, presumably to display their social status. However, painting their faces white, the ritual color, corresponds to local tradition. Further motifs have parallels mainly in the Orient. The man holding a wriggling snake in each hand, for instance, was said to symbolize the course of the sun and moon, or the "beneficent cosmic potencies" in the ancient Orient—a motif with astral significance. The depiction of the struggle between bird and snake was first used in Babylon three thousand years ago and spread from there to both Asia and Egypt; it is found in Greco-Roman, Renaissance, and pre-Columbian art. In these cultures, the motif was interpreted in its astral context but was given numerous new meanings: the struggle between light and dark, between heavenly and (under)worldly powers, between good and evil, between one's own king (or his dynasty) and the hereditary foe, and so on.

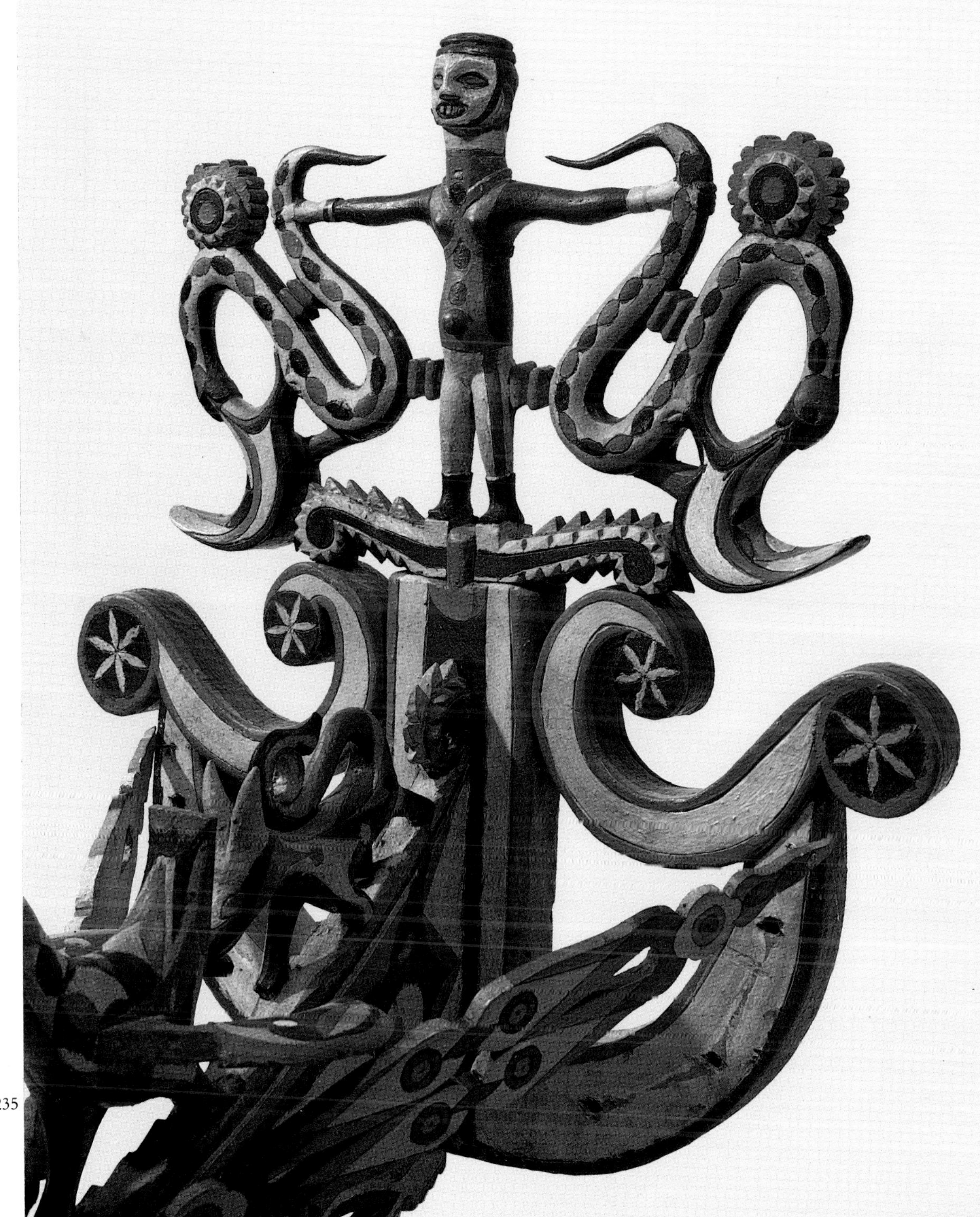

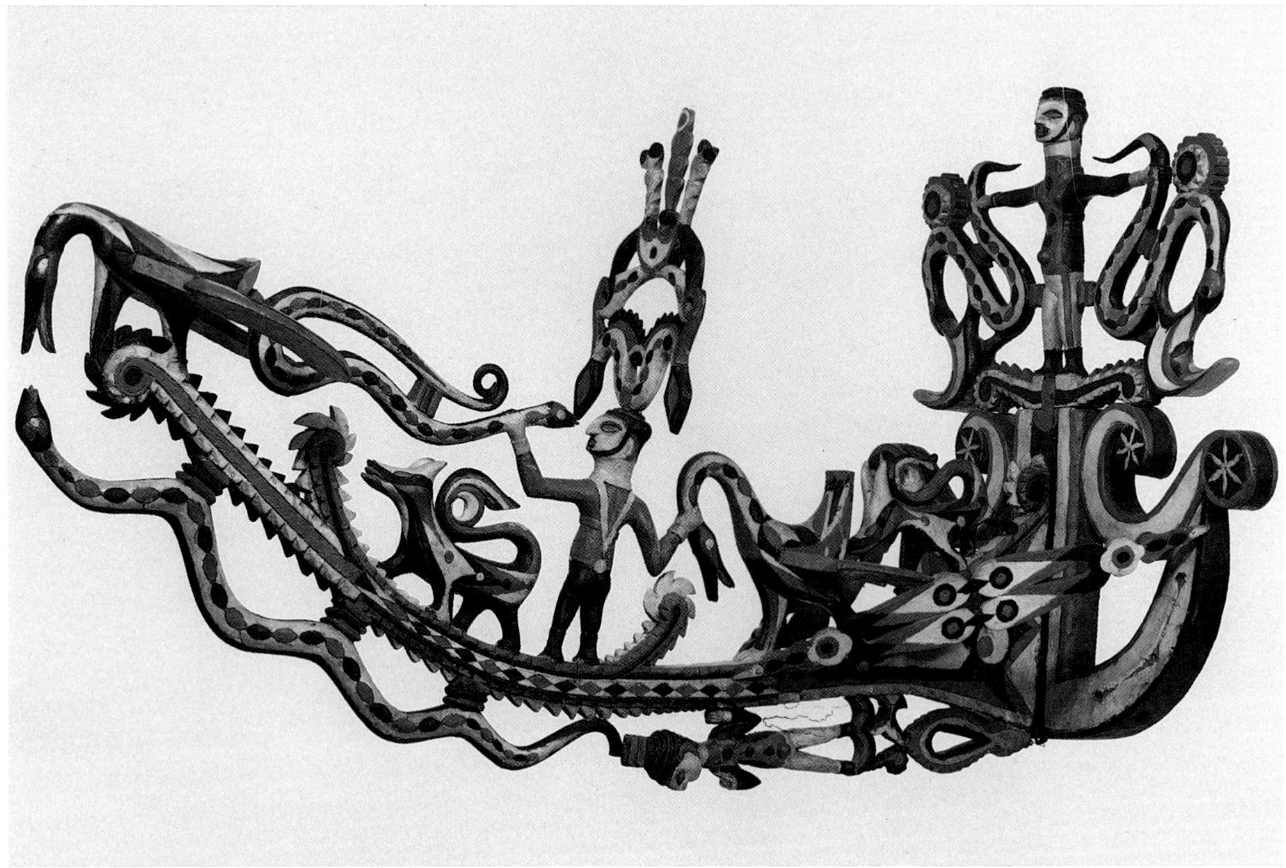

235

Besides the Duala, other West Africans, especially peoples of the Guinea coast—among them the Baule, Asante, Yoruba, and Bini—adopted the motif, apparently using it as a symbol of royalty, or possibly as an amulet. By which route, through whose mediation, and in what period these motifs reached West Africa from the pre-Islamic Orient—and, once arrived, what significance they acquired—are questions still largely unanswered. Frobenius's theory that the bird figure in the Duala carvings represents the bird that leads the souls of the dead into the beyond may not be altogether wrong but remains unproved. The frequently recurring circle and rosette decorations on our boat prow are also possibly of Oriental derivation. Used in connection with boats, these motifs might be a variant of the eyes that ward off evil on so many boats in the Mediterranean Sea and Indian Ocean.

According to the inventory, this piece was among "King Bell's possessions, more exactly those of his son-in-law, Ekwe, who was also the craftsman."

Length 150 cm., height 75 cm. 89.584
Acquired from F. A. Schran 1889

Lit.: R. LeB. Bowen 1955, pp. 5-48; L. Frobenius 1897, p. 38; A. Gottlicher 1972, pp. 59, 61-62; F. Hutter 1902, p. 7; R. Wittkower 1938, 39, pp. 312ff.

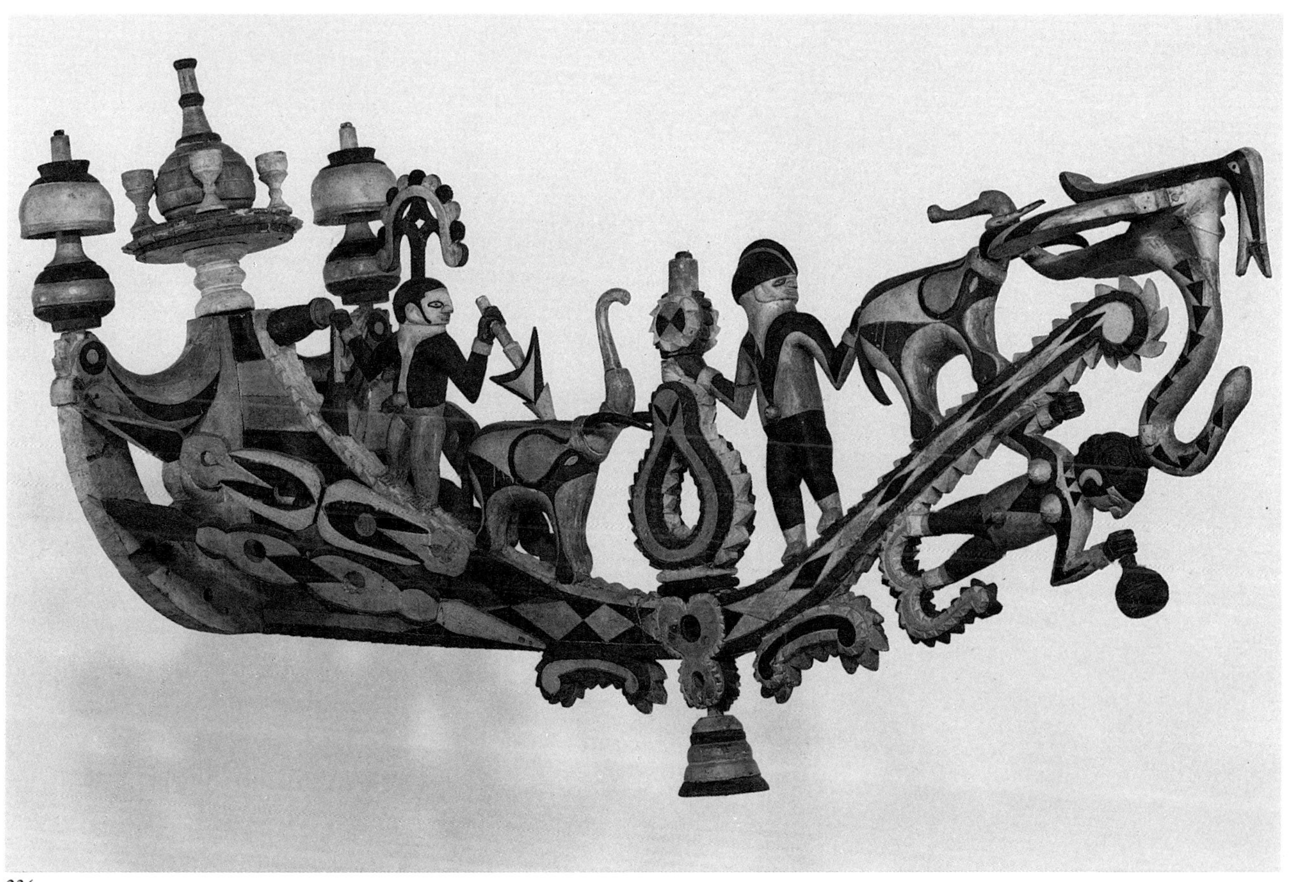

236

236 Boat prow (*ndenge*), wood, paint.
Cameroon, Duala.
(see color plate, p. 266)

Like No. 235, this sculpture, once part of Chief Lock Priso's boat, displays both indigenous and, in the widest sense, Oriental and modern European motifs: the chief as tamer and killer of elephants, the struggle between bird and snake, and European dress combined with white ritual body paint. Also noteworthy is the graphic representation of the alternating peace-and-war strategy of the colonial powers. Under the group (on the left) that includes a table with liquor flask and glasses set between two paraffin lamps is a cannon pointed directly at the elephant killer (is it protecting or threatening?) The artist seems to have considered the European clothing (worn by Africans as a status symbol) and ship's bell embodiments of wealth and technical superiority.

Length 145 cm., height 70 cm. 7087
Acquired from M. Buchner 1884

Lit.: M. Buchner 1914, p. 194.

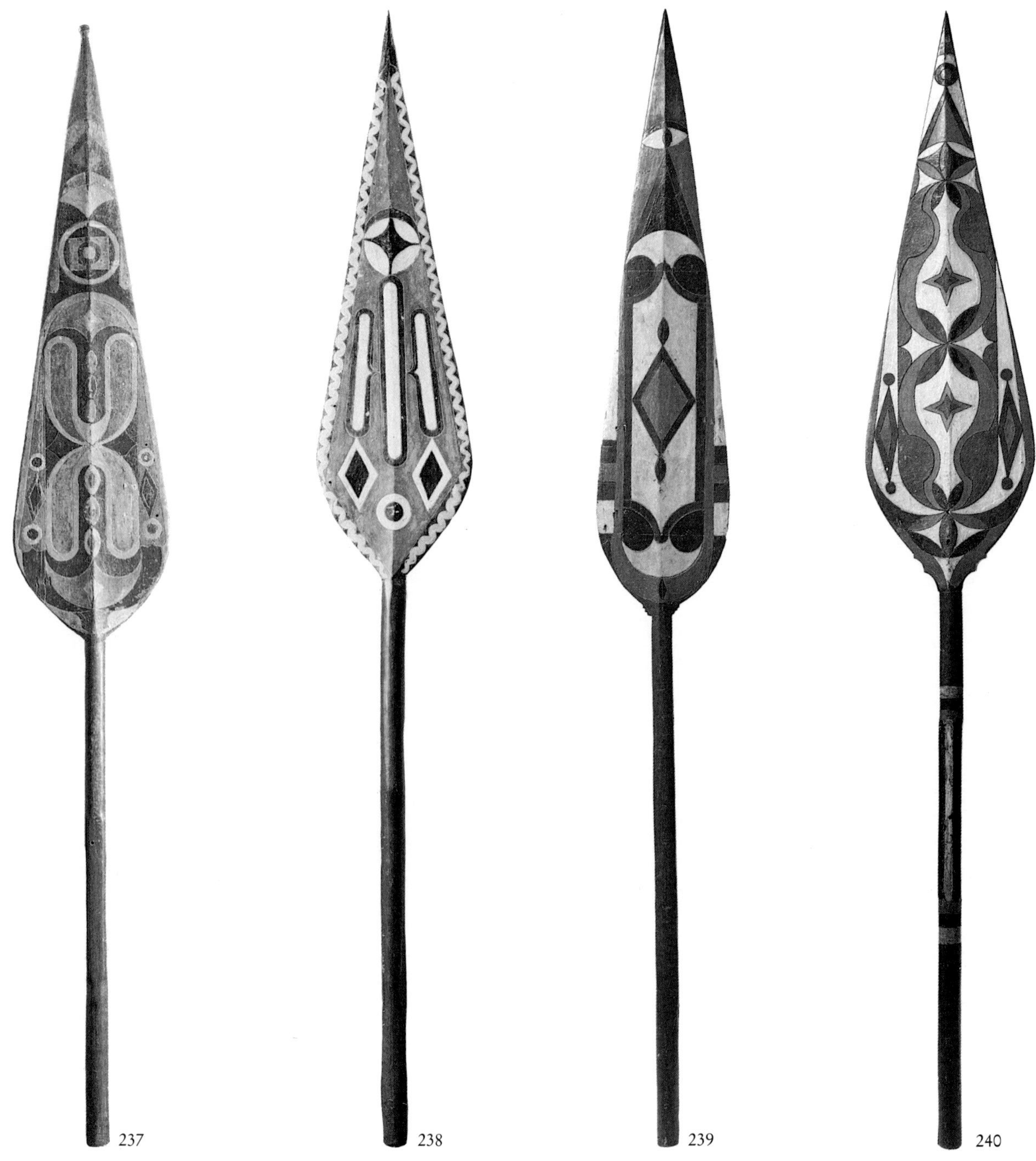
237
238
239
240

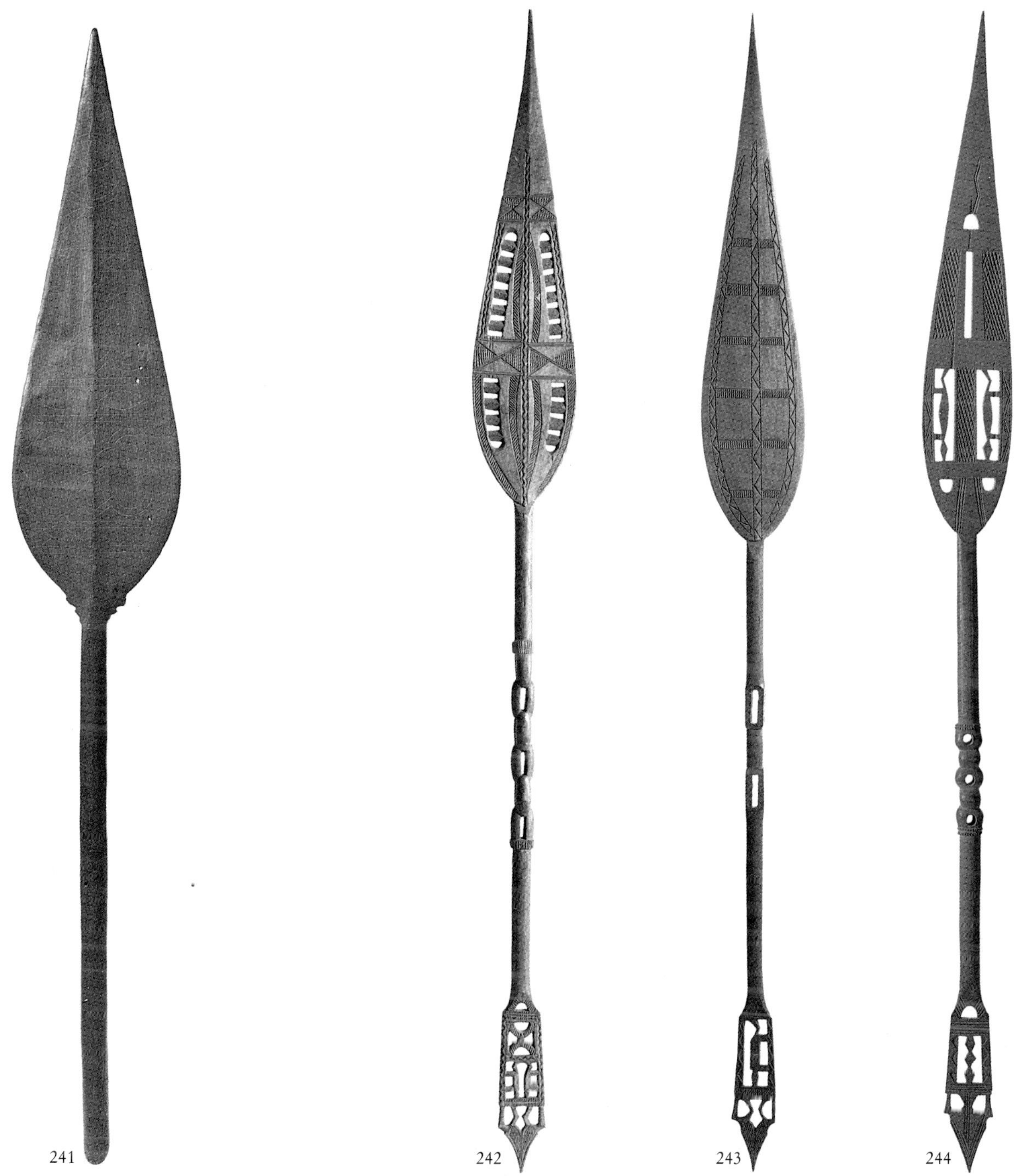

241 242 243 244

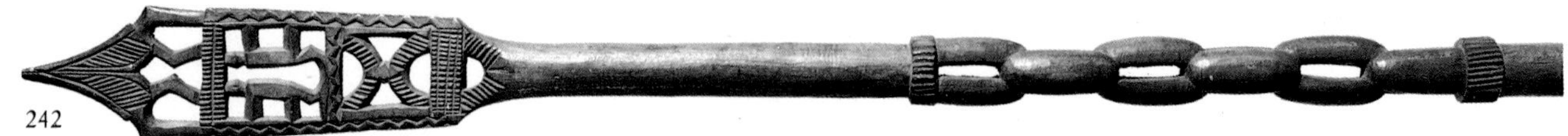
242

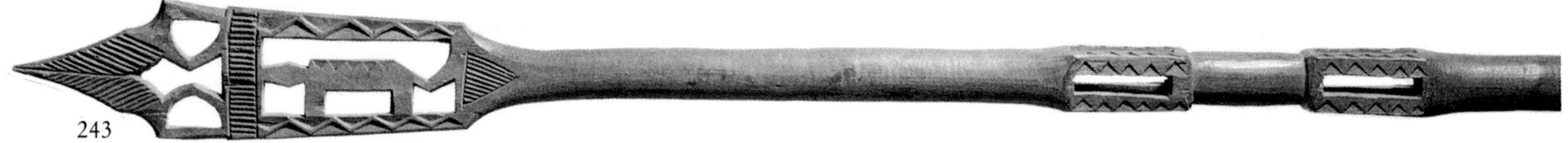
243

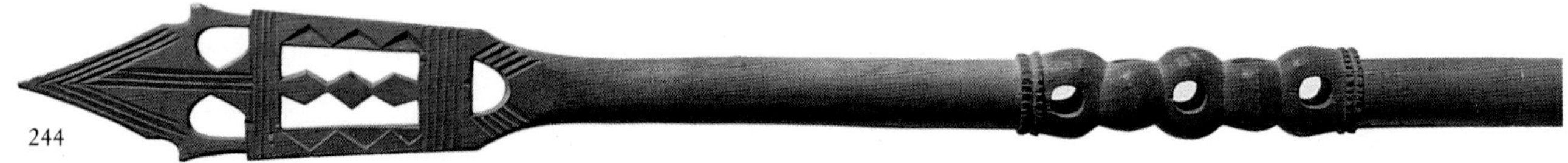
244

237-244 Eight paddles, wood.
Cameroon, Duala, and Nigeria, Niger Delta peoples.
(see color plate p. 267)

The Duala used richly ornamented paddles at festive boat processions and regattas (see p. 222), but it is questionable whether all surviving painted and carved paddles were actually used. It would seem that by the turn of the century such pieces were being produced for sale to Europeans. Four paddles with broad blades (Nos. 237-40) have been painted with enamel whose predominating colors, red, yellow, and black, were popular in local art long before chemical paints were introduced. Along with geometric forms, the ornament consists of floral motifs like those of Cross River tribal art. Another broad-bladed paddle (No. 241) is an actual working paddle, stained dark brown and ornamented with finely incised designs.

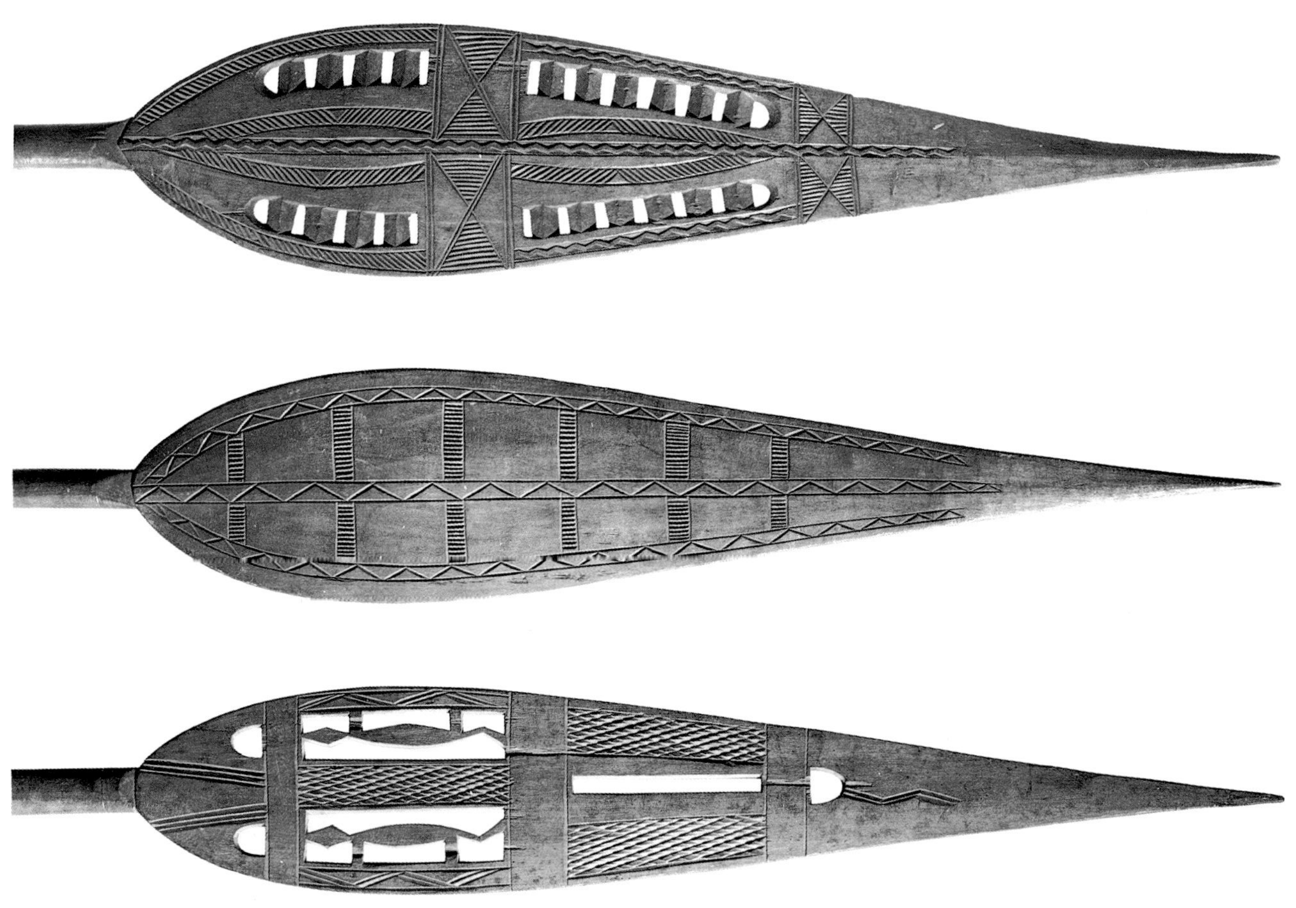

Three paddles (Nos. 242–44) are unpainted but incised, and openwork patterns are carved on both their narrow blades and their handles. The incised ornaments are purely geometric, but among the openwork patterns there is the stylized figure of a chameleon. These three paddles, collected in the Duala country, are typical ceremonial examples from the Itsekiri, Urhobo, and Ijo of the Niger Delta. A large number of paddles are placed blade downward in the back of water-spirit shrines, "to show how many paddles the water spirit concerned has to paddle his canoes" (Fagg, citing Horton, verbal communication)

Length 150–165 cm.
Acquired from M. Buchner 1884 — 7064–7067
F. A. Schran 1888 — 88.128
Schubert 1889 — 89.155,156
Transferred from Bayreuth 1973 (old collection) — 73-1-44

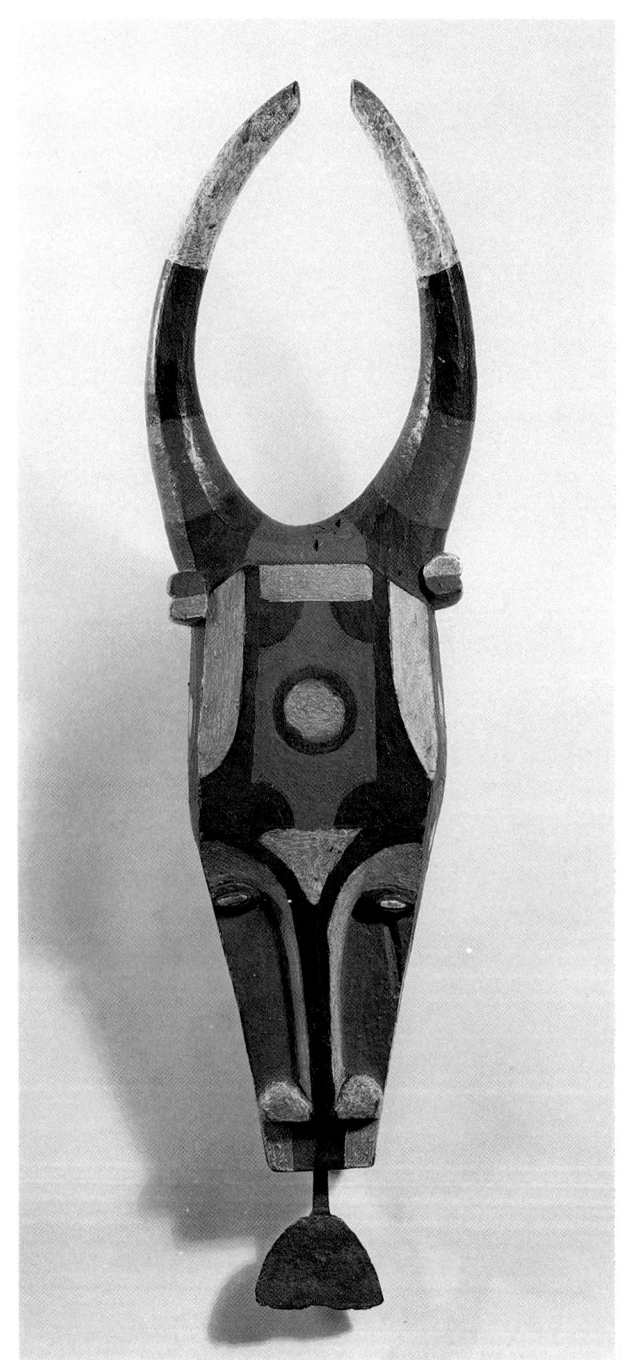

245

Horned Masks of the Cameroon Coast (245–247)

The influence of grasslands art (see p. 190) extended to the Duala, Abo, Kossi, and neighboring coastal peoples, but the models underwent considerable change at their hands. Animal masks in the round became flat; outlines and decoration were geometrized (see Nos. 245 and 247). Ears, eyes, and horns were formed in a great variety of ways. In addition, the grasslands monochrome treatment was more or less replaced by polychrome in either the indigenous light-dark or imported red, yellow, and black palette.

The horned masks belonged to the cult association (*isango;* plural, *losango*). Among the Duala, the *ekongolo* and *elong* associations seem to have been the important institutions of social control. Masked members severely punished and, on occasion, killed anyone who threatened the social order. In addition, association members appeared masked at other members' funerals (see Nos. 204 and 205).

Lit.: M. Buchner 1887, p. 26; I. Ittmann 1936, pp. 305-6; R. Karutz 1901, p. 25; P. Valentin 1979, pp. 143ff.

245 Horned mask (*niati*), wood, paint, iron. Cameroon, Duala.

The angular form and polychrome painting of this *ekongolo* association mask are typical of Duala work in the early colonial period. Other works of the turn of the century (see also No. 247) also have tongues made of old iron hoe blades. The black-rimmed circular forehead ornament may well be a sun symbol.

Length 87 cm., width 26.5 cm. 73-1-40
Transferred from Bayreuth 1973 (old collection)

Lit.: L. Franz 1967, pp. 104-107; L. Frobenius 1954, pp. 134-139; R. Karutz 1901, pp. 8-13.

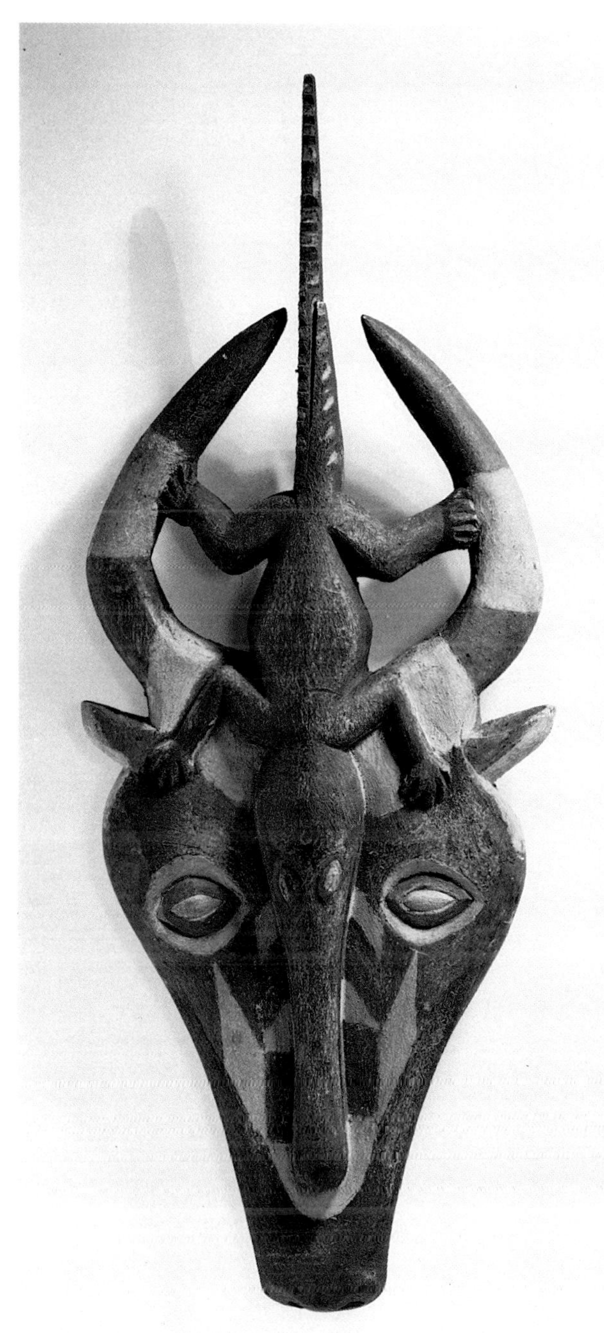
246

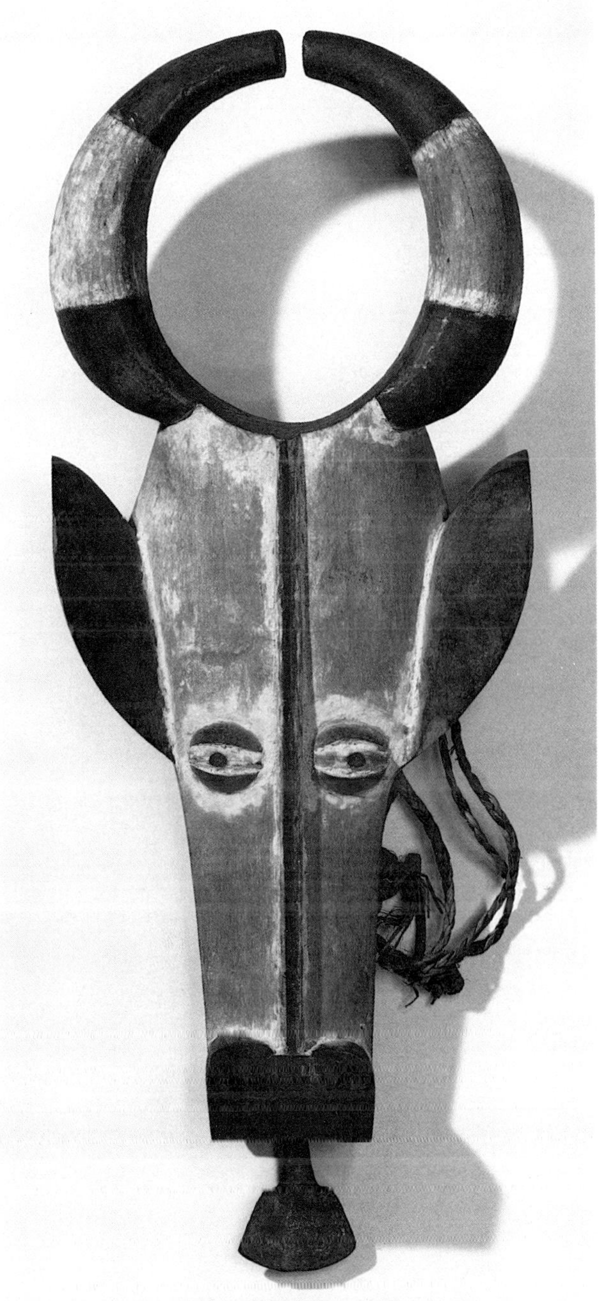
247

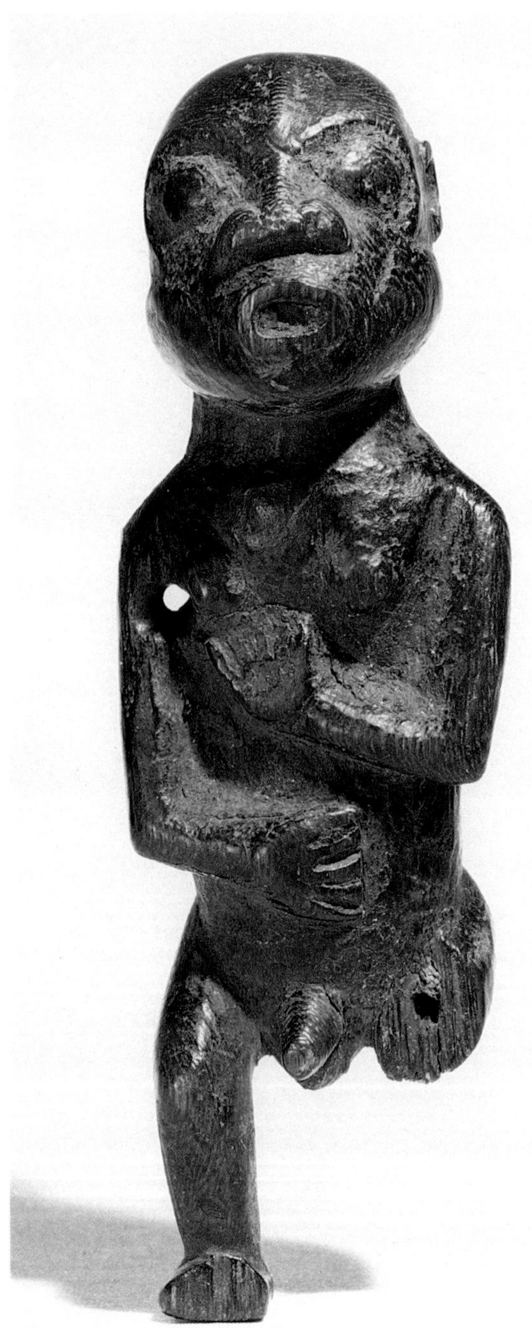

246 Horned mask (*niati*), wood.
Cameroon, Duala or Abo.

This *ekongolo* association "buffalo" or cow mask is sturdier than Nos. 245 and 247 but has softer contours and is painted various hues of brown and white. A crocodile crawls down the center. It is not known what ideas were associated with this combination of crocodile and buffalo or cow.

Length 91 cm., width 35 cm. 88.83
Acquired from F. A. Schran 1888

247 Horned mask (*niati*), wood, iron, paint.
Cameroon, Abo.

This flat *ekongolo* association mask with midrib and angular outlines is an example of the coastal masks painted white and black whose dark parts are produced by scorching the wood with a poker. An iron hoe blade is used as a tongue (see also No. 245).

Length 83 cm., width 31 cm. 88.2
Acquired from F. A. Schran 1888

Art of the Western Cameroon Forest

The ethnic groups that settled in the forest (Abo, Balong, Kundu, and Bafo) live in small communities governed by clans led by councils of elders, without any larger political organization. Although their work lacks the richness of form and variety of types of carved objects that we find in the grasslands courts, the quality is just as high in forest work as in grasslands. In the dense forest with its difficulties for communication, the traditional style survived for a longer period than in the open savanna. Thus perfunctory execution and other phenomena of deterioration are rarely observed in forest carvings.

Characteristic of the western Cameroon forest in both sculpture and high-relief carving is a certain configuration of the human figure: soft, flowing
248 lines; slightly bent legs; and stiff, angular arms with

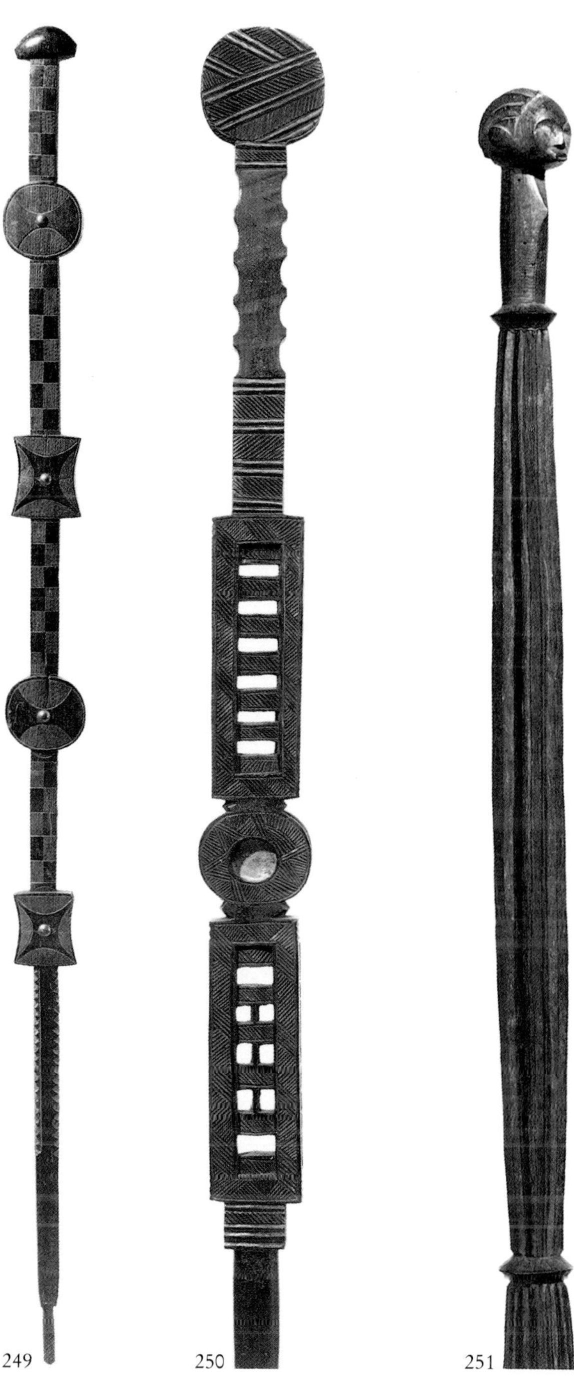

249 250 251

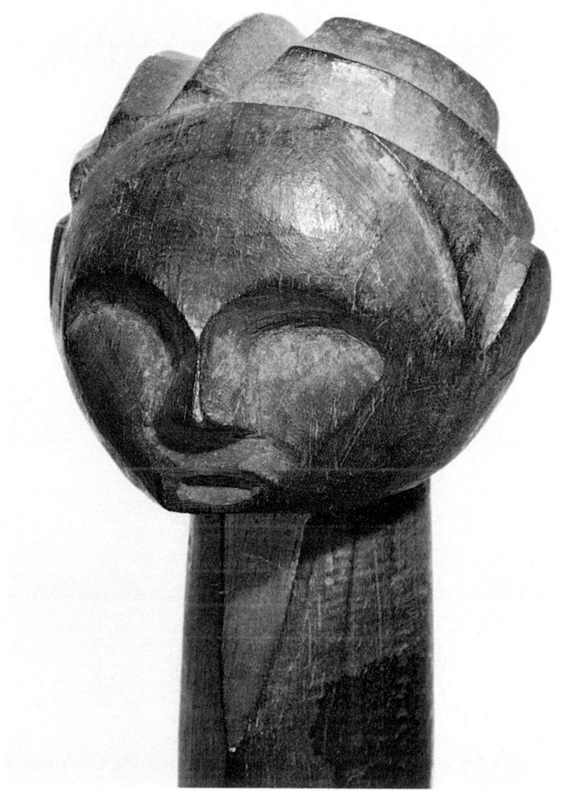

251

hands together below chin or pointed beard. The long, narrow head is usually without coiffure; the concave heart-shape face is reduced to essentials; the button- or almond-shape eyes are sculptural. Flat nose and open mouth with protruding lips are also characteristic. A circular ornament appears on many carvings, often in a central position, but its significance is unknown. The same ornament is found in the art of the Cross River peoples. According to Mansfeld it represents the moon, while Thompson believes it to be the quartered *nsibidi* sign, symbolizing the meeting of heaven and earth, of man and woman.

Lit.: E. Bufe 1913, p. 224; A. Mansfeld 1908, pl. V/29; R. F. Thompson 1974, p. 181.

248 Male figure, wood.
Cameroon, Abo (?).

This carefully carved figure with typical heart-shape face is representative of the miniature art of the forest area. Its function is unknown, though possibly it was worn on a string to protect its owner from danger.

Height 12 cm. 05.301
Acquired from Berke 1905

249-251 Three staffs, ebony, tacks, glass.
Cameroon, Abo or Wuri.

Widespread symbols of honor and prestige, staffs exhibit workmanship that often reflects the owner's social standing. Presumably, these painstakingly worked pieces belonged to members of the highest social stratum.

The carvers of Nos. 249 and 250 divided their staffs rhythmically by alternating circles with squares and lighter with darker surfaces, the latter achieved by crosshatching. Both works reveal the influence of carvings from the Cross River area—No. 249 in the fine incised decoration and No. 250 in the circular mirror insertion. A carved human head enriches the top of No. 251. Shaped by a carver with a delight in detail (note the Adam's apple and the neck ring), this head, especially in its asymmetrical coiffure above a heart-shape face, recalls the sculpture of the Beti, who live farther south. The Peabody Museum in Cambridge, Massachusetts, possesses a fully sculptured wooden figure with a similar coiffure, ascribed to the Beti (Fang) group of the Bane.

Length 106 cm., 118 cm., and 126 cm. 02.43-45
Acquired from A. Diehl 1902

Lit.: W. Fagg 1970, p. 73; W. Schilde 1930, pp. 83-91.

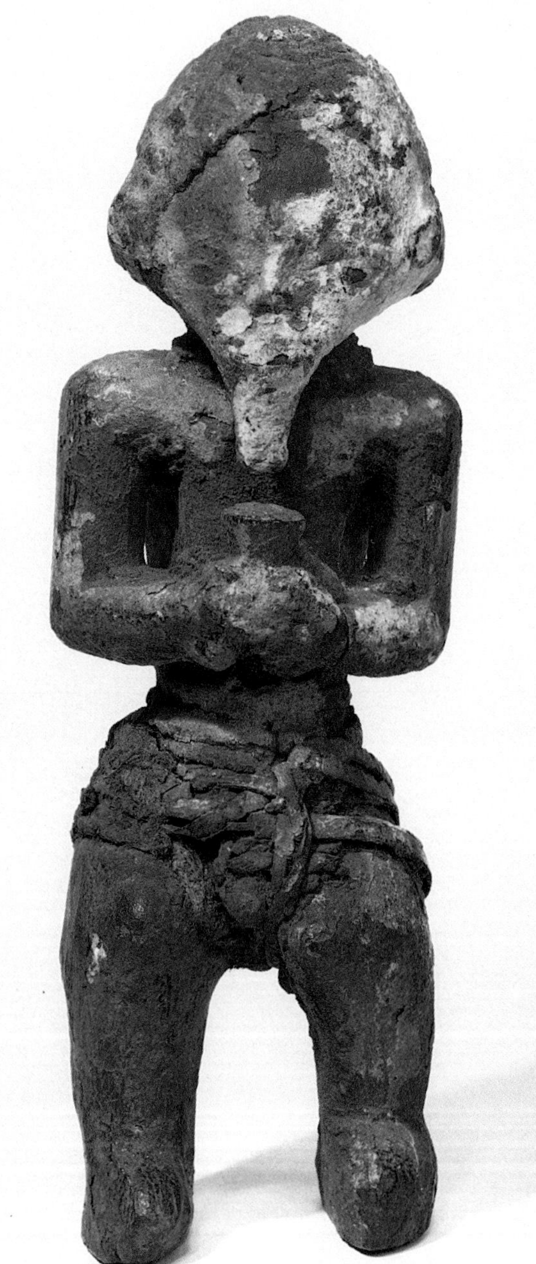

252

252 Small male figure, wood, leather, string.
Cameroon, Balong.

The composition of this figure's upper body and head reveals the influence of the Beti and the peoples of the lower Congo. The plaited beard as insignia is particularly common in the Congo basin. The figure, covered with sacrificial patina and holding in its hands a horn—a container of magical matter—is reminiscent of the *musongo* figures of the neighboring Kundu, before which persons accused of a crime had to affirm their innocence. *Musongo* punished perjury by inflicting disease.

Height 22 cm. 16-13-7
Acquired from H. Rolle 1916

Lit.: E. Bufe 1913, p. 234; W. Schilde 1930, p. 54.

253 Ornamental ax, wood, iron.
Cameroon, Balong.

This ornamental ax is a woodcarver's trademark, or the insignia of a chief. Such axes are especially common in the Congo basin, and presumably found their way from the basin to southern Cameroon.

Length 31 cm. 16-13-8
Acquired from H. Rolle 1916

Lit.: C. G. Widstrand 1958, pp. 143-44.

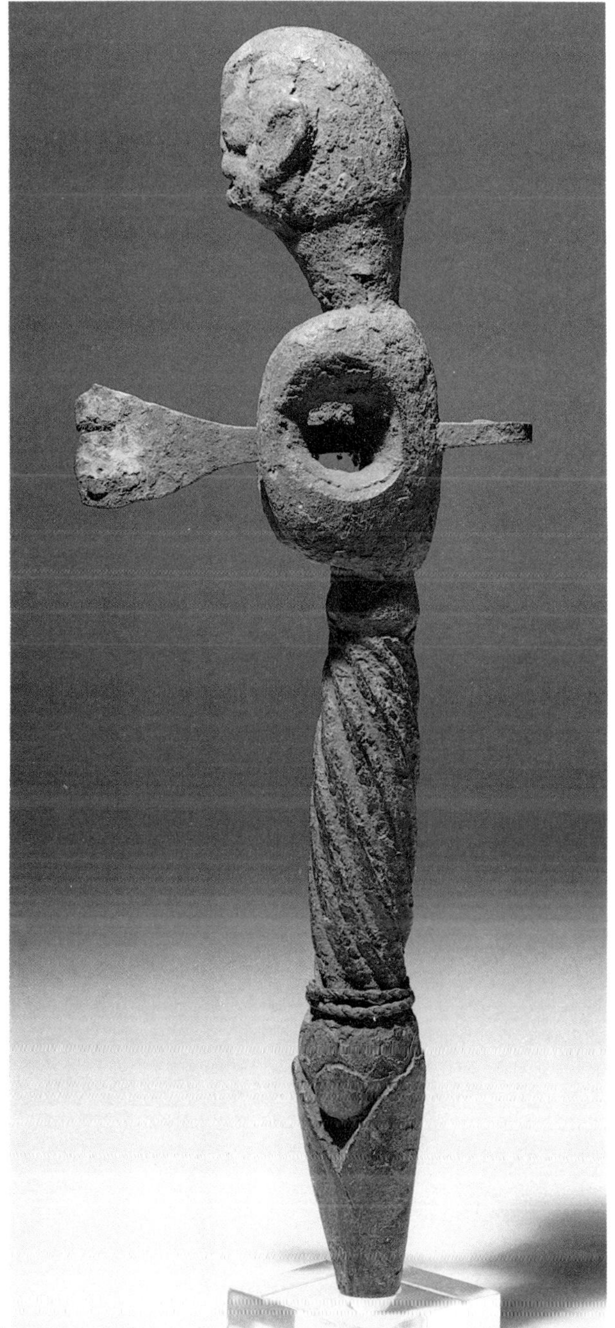

253

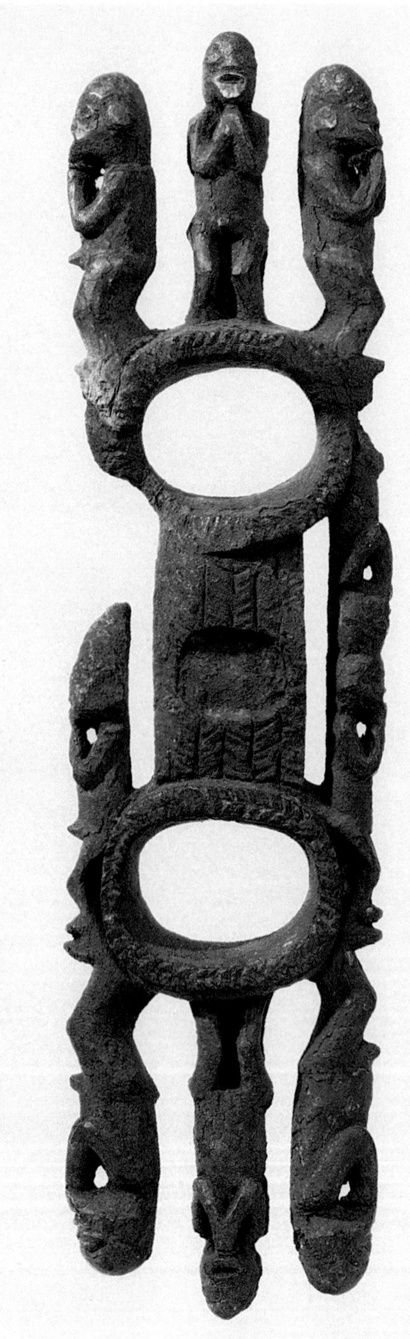

254

254 Carving with several small human figures, wood.
Cameroon, Kundu (?), Balong (?).

As early as the beginning of the twentieth century, a unique style of miniature sculpture flourished in the hinterlands of the Cameroon coast. The products of this school—predominately sculptures of high quality—have become known as *Kundu* figures. If they came from the Kundu, they were probably also from the Balong, and eventually also from the Bafo and other ethnic groups of the rain forest of western Cameroon. Especially characteristic of this tradition are compositions in which two or more fully sculptured human figures, very often in eccentric positions, stand back to back or one on the head of the other.

In nearly all cases the hands are folded under the chin. Nothing is known of the function of these figures, although Bohner has stated that "box after box of them was shipped to Europe" as early as the end of the nineteenth century.

Stylistically this object belongs with the Kundu figures, though it occupies an exceptional position because of its mirror-image composition and two elliptical openings (circle ornaments?). Referring to its counterpart in their collection, the Basler Mission Museum offers nothing more than the noncommittal "ceremonial utensil, use unknown."

Height 44 cm. 94.417
Acquired from E. Zimmerer 1894

Lit.: H. Bohner 1898, pp. 376, 382; E. Bufe 1913, p. 238; P. Valentin 1972, p. 44 & Illus. 23, unpublished manuscript.

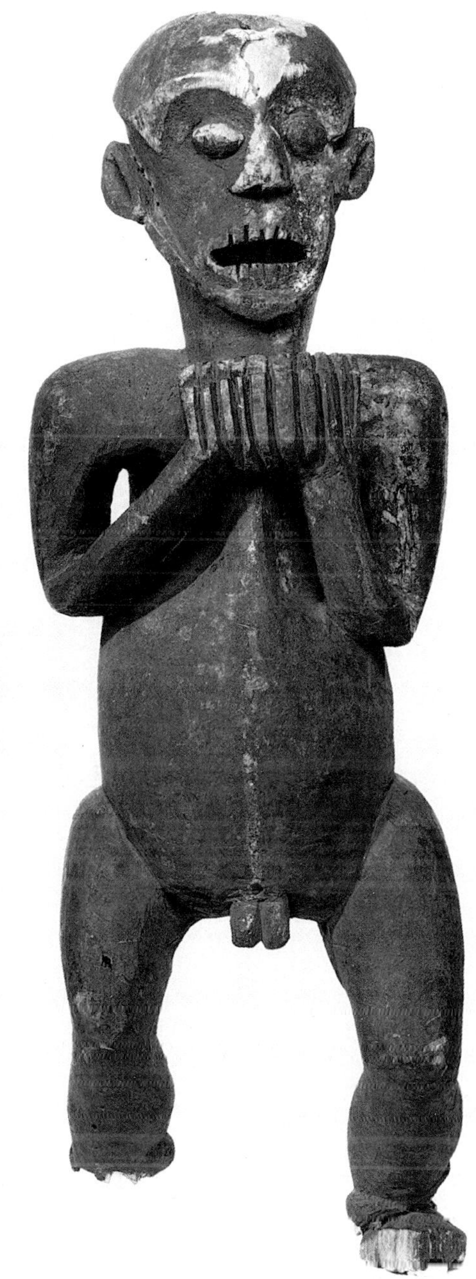

255

255 Male figure, wood.
Cameroon, Bafo (?), Bangwa (?).

Possibly this object, whose provenance is given simply as Cameroon, comes from the Bangwa (Mbanwe), the western neighbors of the Bamileke. It is probably a *lekat* figure, used by the Kungang society in its battle against witchcraft. Anyone suspected of practicing sorcery can escape death only by affirming his or her innocence under oath before the *lekat* statue. In case of perjury the accused will contract dropsy and die, as the swollen belly of the figure threateningly indicates. The *lekat* figures were carved by the same artists who produced the ancestral and royal portrait figures. But whereas the latter are mostly influenced by the art of the Grasslands peoples, the *lekat* figures are related to woodlands styles—hands raised to chin, flowing body lines, and smooth round head—and are counterparts of the plastic figures of the Kundu (Nos. 252, 254, and 255).

Height 70 cm. 93.15
Acquired from von Stetten 1893

Lit.: K. Born 1981, pp. 9, 24 & Illus.29; R. Brain & A. Pollock 1971, pp. 2, 3, 117, 127-129.

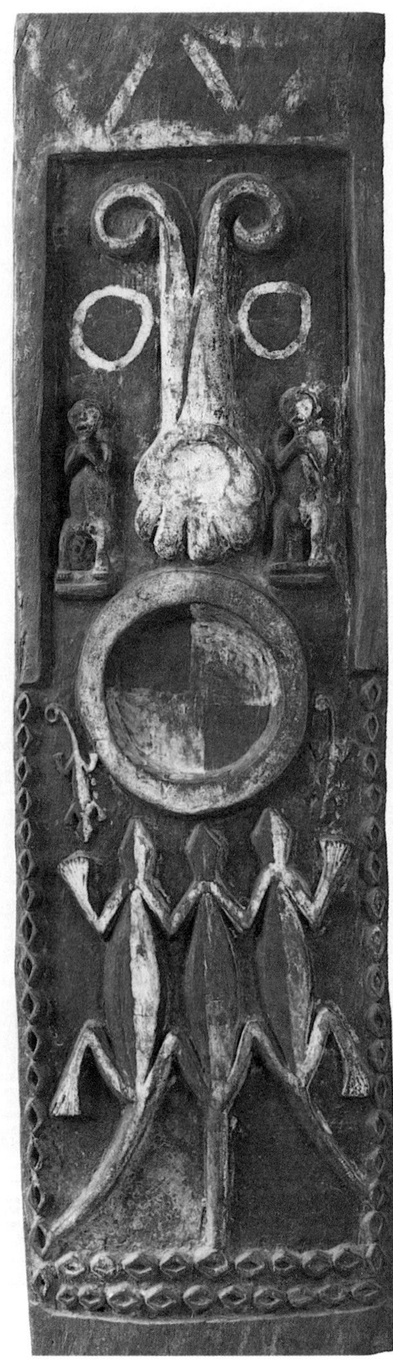

256

256,257 Two carved wooden blocks.
Cameroon, Bafo (?), Beti (?).
(see color plate p.72)

No details whatsoever are available concerning the provenance, function, or meaning of the ornament of these rectangular wooden blocks. No. 256 is carved on one side, No. 257 on both. It may be assumed that both objects belonged to the cult houses. Possibly the block with carving on only one side stood against the wall or formed part of it; the other may have served as pillar. In each case, the middle of the carved front surface is occupied by a double-rimmed circle, the back of No. 257 by a square. Predominantly figurative carvings are arranged in horizontal zones above and below the center. It is conceivable that these refer to the mythical primordial age, depicting the original relationship between the large lizards and the ancestral pair. If this is so, we have a kind of genealogical tree before us. Painted lines divide the central double-rimmed circle of No. 256 into four parts. The horizontal diameter corresponds to the gap where the sections of the rim, with and without decoration, meet. Animal representations predominate. Above the central circle is an enigmatic image consisting of two pipelike formations, each curving upward and outward (plants? horns?), and what seems like a stylized hand. To the right and left are circles above male or female figures with hands folded at the chin, painted half white, half black; in most cases these colors signify life and death.

Human figures predominate on No. 257, painted red, white, and black. Besides the ancestral pair, there is a bearded male figure. In the middle of the reverse side is the above-mentioned "pair of horns" with hand. W. Kandinsky admired this wood sculpture so greatly that he often went to see it.

Height 130 cm., 182 cm., 93.14/13
width 36 cm., 32 cm.
Acquired from von Stetten 1893

Lit.: Peg Weiss 1982, Illus.305.

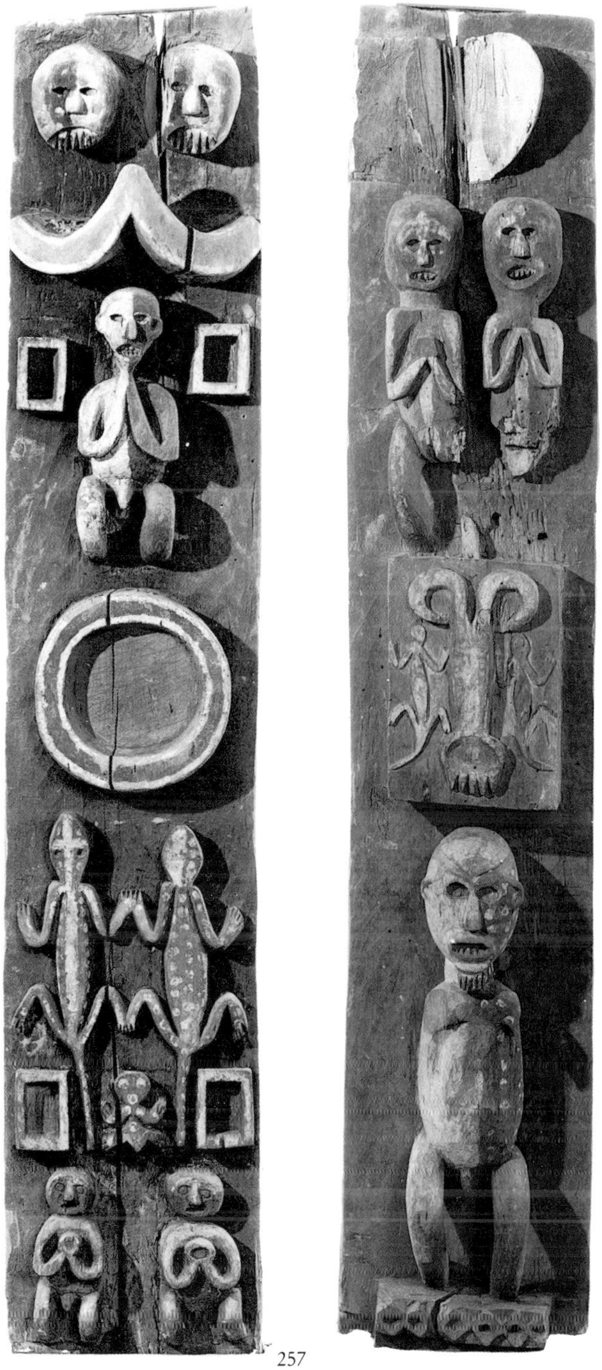

257

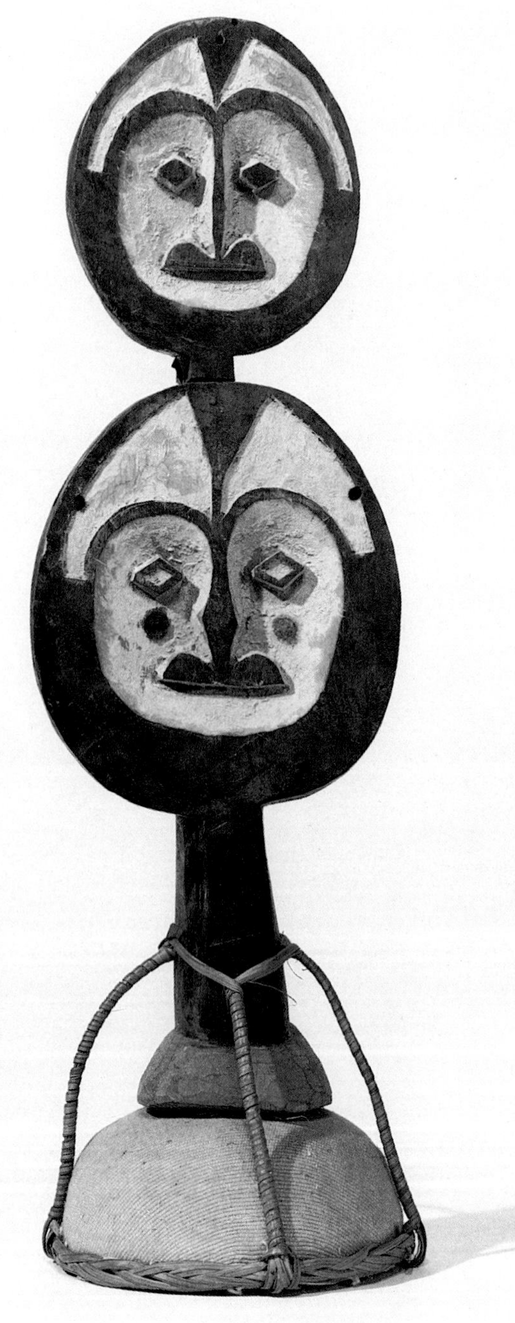

258a

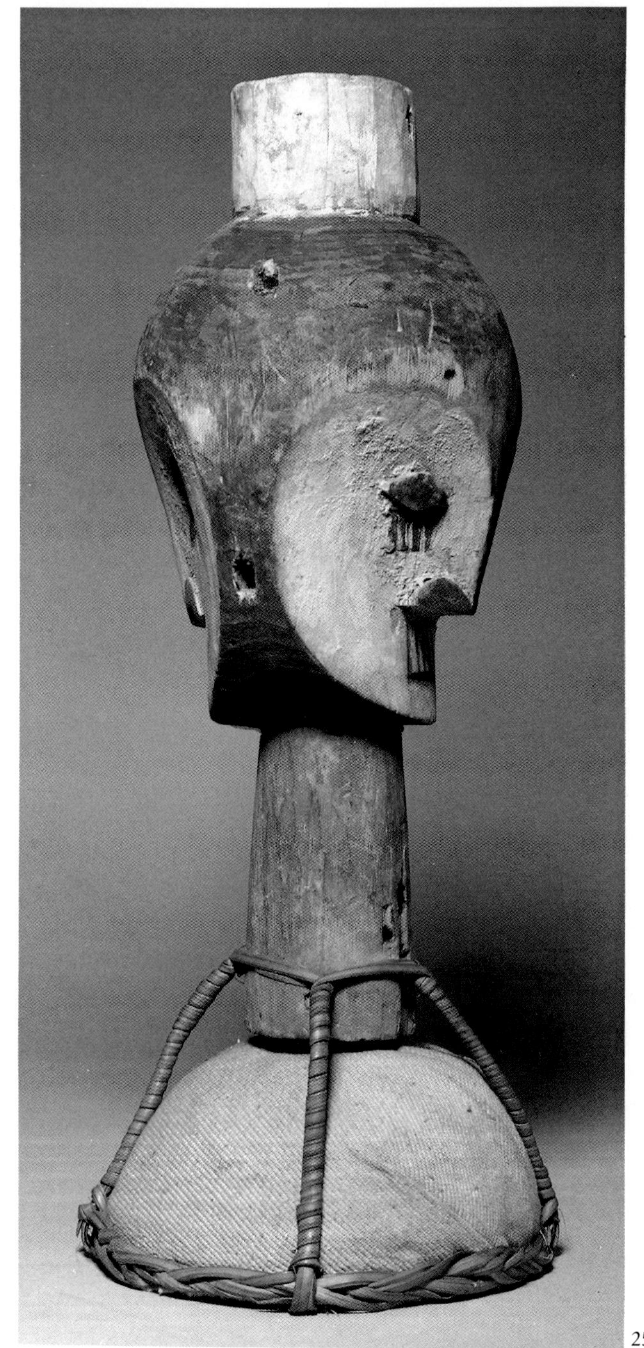

258b

258a,b Two headdress masks, wood, rattan plait. Cameroon, Bafo.

The idea of the headdress mask traveled from the north, in the Cross River area on the border between Nigeria and Cameroon, to the south as far as the Bafo region. Though also influenced by the art of the Kwele (Republic of Congo), the Bafo masks took a radically different form: northern examples, naturalistic in shape and color, became flat abstract disks in contrasting black and white. The double-faced compositions of the models were transformed into two faces, one above the other. Eyes, nose and mouth stand out in relief against the ornamental heart-shaped, slightly concave faces. Originally, stylized horns rose from these masks, of whose function little is known.

Height 65 cm., 48 cm. 94.53 2/3
Acquired from E. Zimmerer 1894

Lit.: E. G. Bay 1975, p. 243; I. Bolz 1966, pp. 202, 3.

Art of the Southern Cameroon Forest

The southern woodlands were the setting of many migrations, and the area's turbulent history is mirrored in the multiplicity of stylistic trends found there. The last great movement, the slow migration of Beti peoples from the Sudan, began sometime in the eighteenth century. These warlike groups, strong in numbers, had no central organization but were divided into clans led by councils of elders. As they moved into the woodlands, they partly dislodged the resident population and partly superimposed their own culture on remaining residents, uniting the indigenous culture with their own. In their former home in the Sudan, the Beti probably were skillful craftsmen, but they produced no sculpture. In the woodlands, they developed sculpture of high quality by adopting already existing styles and perfecting them through their strength in craftmanship (Nos. 286-90). Strongly stylized masks (Nos. 284 and 285), helmets, and metal products such as weapons and ornaments were made as a result of this fusion of style and technique.

Lit.: H. Baumann 1940, p.,169; K. Born, in H. Baumann 1975, I., p. 687; I. Bolz 1966, pp. 85-89; C. P. Ngumu 1977, p. 16-17.

Koko Wood Sculpture (259-263)

In precolonial times, the Beti (Fang) displaced the Koko from the interior of Cameroon, causing them to retreat to their present home on the lower Sanaga River. During the first years of German colonial rule, the Koko engaged in several armed conflicts with German troops because the foreigners' trade route was to run through Koko territory into the interior of Cameroon. Hans Dominik, the leader of a German military expedition, observed that there were "in most villages fetishes carved in wood in the shadow of a tree or in a thicket surrounded by a fence or hedge." Little of what must have been a rich stock of cult figures has survived.

The five Koko sculptures in the Munich collection can be divided into two groups that differ considerably in wood, size, shape, color, and ornament. Despite these differences, all five figures are more or less typical of the so-called pole style, whose chief characteristic is that the tree trunk or natural "pole" from which the figure was cut can still be recognized. In contrast to most round style human figures, pole figures generally follow the natural proportions of the body. Recent research refutes the previously prevalent opinion that this kind of sculpture represents a "primary style." Rather, the pole style was the result of a long, consciously abstract stylistic development.

Lit.: H. Baumann 1969, pp. 8ff.; T. Bodrogi 1968, Illus. 125, 126; H. Dominik 1902, pp. 83-85, 118-19, 131; E. Leuzinger 1970, p. 15.

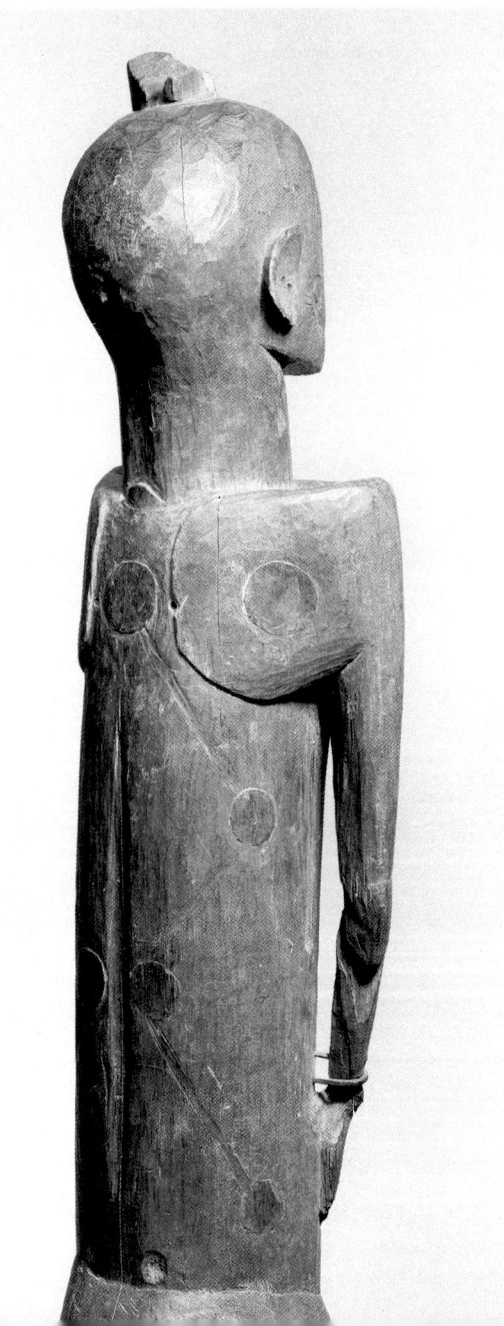

259

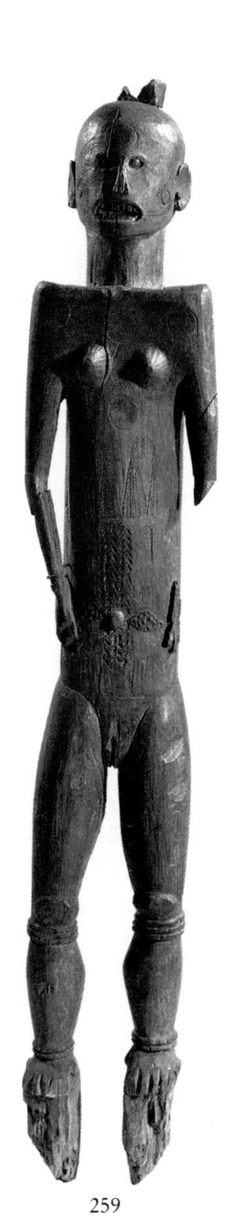

259

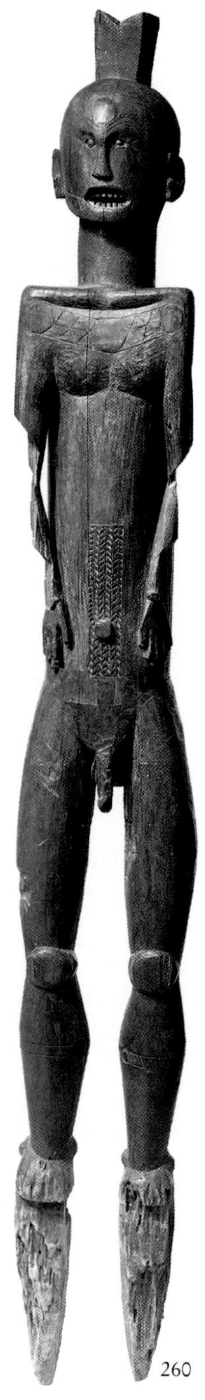

260

259,260 Pair of figures, wood, glass beads.
Cameroon, Koko, Edea.

Of all the human figures shown, these two most clearly represent the pole style. Various stylistic groups influenced the details of pole-style figures. Their faces, for instance, recall those of Cross River figures, with open mouth revealing rows of teeth, and alien material inserted as eyes. But the circular ornament between the eyes is believed to have been the tribal mark of the Koko; the circle is combined with a whirl pattern in the female figure's forehead and also on her cheeks. Chip-carved decoration in a herringbone pattern surrounds the navel of each figure. The modeling of the back, with its tapering groove representing the spinal column and its suggestion of shoulder blades, is remarkable: the flat, angular shoulders, hunched forward and broadened, seem to imitate those of the famous Beti watchmen figures (see Nos. 286-90). The human representations from the second group of Koko sculptures (Nos. 261 and 262) have counterparts in the cult figures of the Beti of Eton (No. 283). Nos. 259 and 260 probably served as supports for a sanctuary's roof or rafter. We may assume they are depictions of a significant ancestral pair, perhaps the clan founder and his wife, and thus objects of cult worship. Possibly the Koko themselves damaged the figures' arms to annul their magic power.

Height 161 cm., 130.5 cm. 95.6/7
Acquired from E. Zimmerer 1895

Lit.: H. A. Bernatzik 1947, pp. 673ff.; H. Dominik 1902, p. 85.

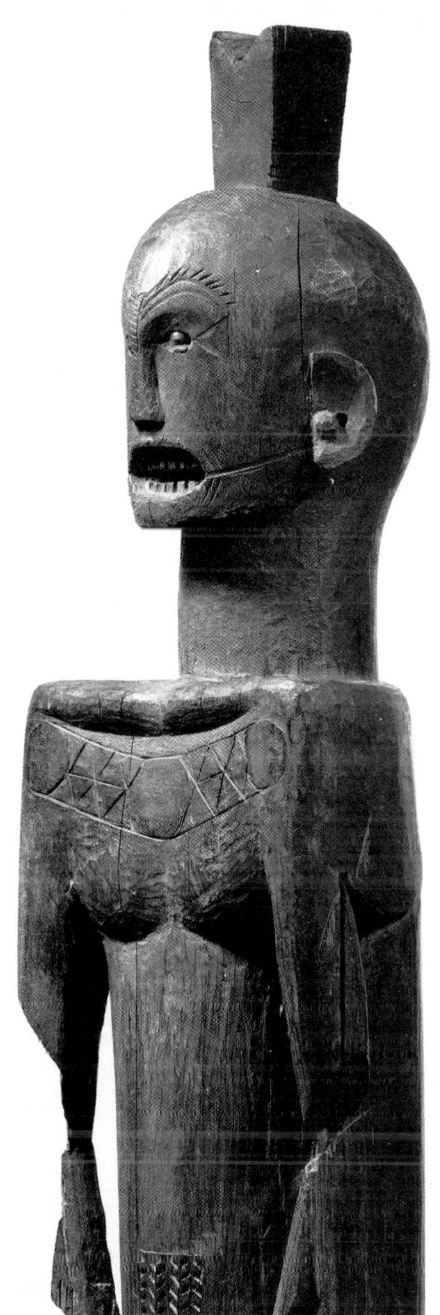

260

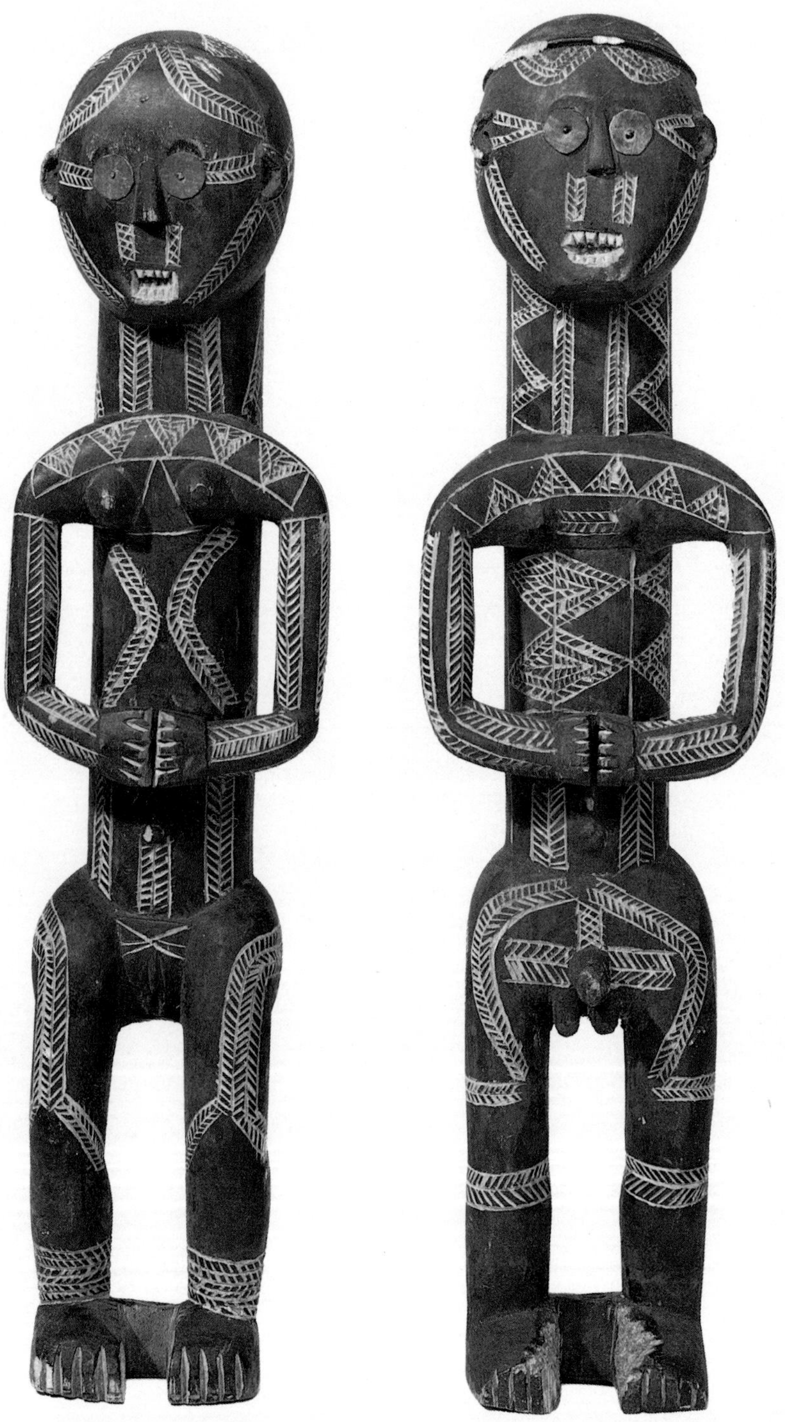

261-263 Human pair and leopard figure, wood, brass.
Cameroon, Koko.

All three of these figures display characteristics of the pole style: torso, neck, and head form a single pillar, and arms and legs are arranged in parallel lines. Again the modeling of the shoulder area is striking and the arms are set forward (see also Nos. 259, 260, and 283). The Beti (Fang) influence is visible in other aspects as well: the structure, size, and proportions of the figures, the position of the arms, and the use of metal. The artistic quality of these pieces, however, is far below that of their models (see Nos. 286-90).

Enlivening the dark brown stained surface with incised drawings is a unique contribution of the Koko. These designs correspond to the tattoo marks of persons who have passed through initiation. We are not sure of the function of these human figures, nor do we know the meaning of the tattoos, though the Koko very likely considered them magical. The desire to repel evil by inserting foreign matter under the skin probably played a greater role in their use of tattoos than the desire to provide an erotic stimulus or to increase beauty. The skin decoration of the leopard, however, consists of circles burned into the light backgound with a red-hot poker. See No. 170 for an explanation of leopard symbolism.

Height 45 cm., 46 cm. (human figures)
Length 56 cm. (leopard) 27-24-16/18
Acquired from A. Gopfert 1927

Lit.: G. Tessman 1913, I., pp. 199ff.

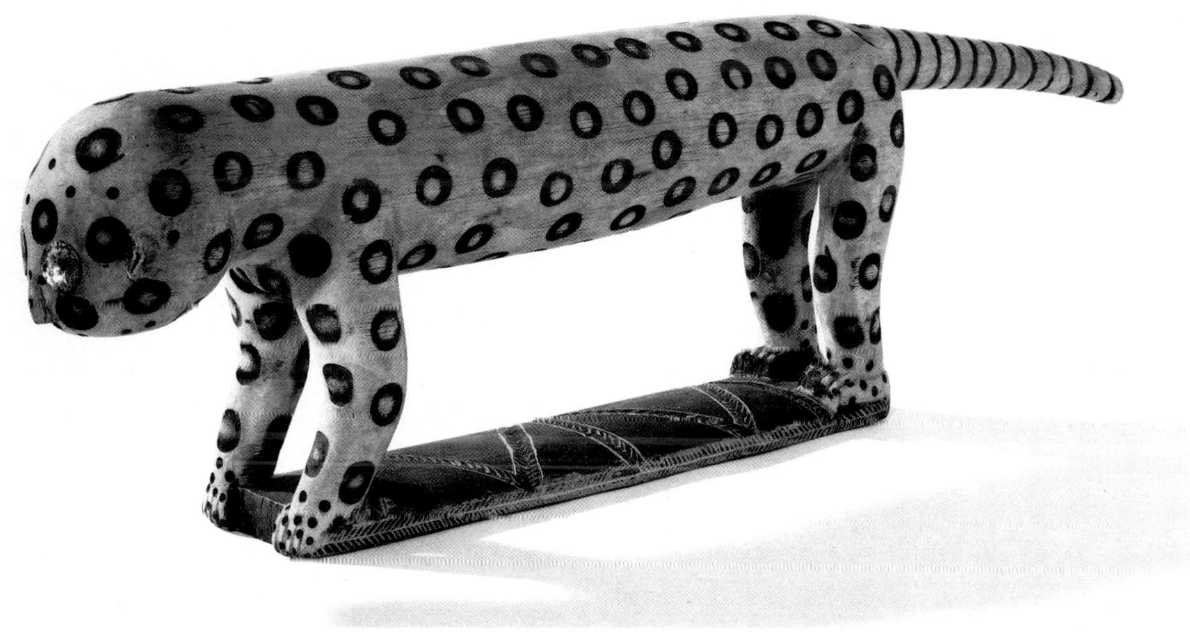

262 263

Gambling Chips (264-266)

The game of chance called *abia* is widespread among Cameroon woodland peoples. Despite official prohibition of the game, the Beti in particular are known to be passionate players. Four or more persons may participate. Seven pumpkin disks and a chip from each player are thrown into the air from a wicker plate. The number combination of disks and chips that fall with the smooth (carved) side or the rough (uncarved) side up indicates the winner. The stake consists of goods, such as iron rods and money. It is said that in the past desperate players even offered to stake their relatives or themselves, and if they lost they became slaves of the winner.

Each participant brings his own counters to the game. The counters' incised patterns and figures are not part of the game itself, but all players believe in their counters' lucky qualities. The counters are manufactured from the fruitstone of the *Mimusops congolensis* tree. Whereas the Maka, from whom the Beti adopted the game, adorn their counters with abstract motifs (see Nos. 264-66), the Beti often prefer animals, humans, utensils, and sometimes even small narrative scenic compositions. The frequency of certain motifs is perhaps explained by the fact that the Beti believe they produce magical effects. Birds, antelopes, and beings that play an important role in woodland myths and festivals predominate.

The incised patterns of the counters embody a tradition of relief sculpture which, in comparison with three-dimensional sculpture, plays a minor role in sub-Saharan Africa. The contrast between dark background and light incised lines lends a special charm to these small carvings, which are often worked with great care. Stylistic unity is a notable feature of Beti game counters.

Lit.: C. Beart 1955, p. 428; M. Perves 1948, pp. 26-41; F. Quinn 1970, pp. 30-32; O. Reche 1924, p. 3; G. Tessman 1913, II, pp. 315-17.

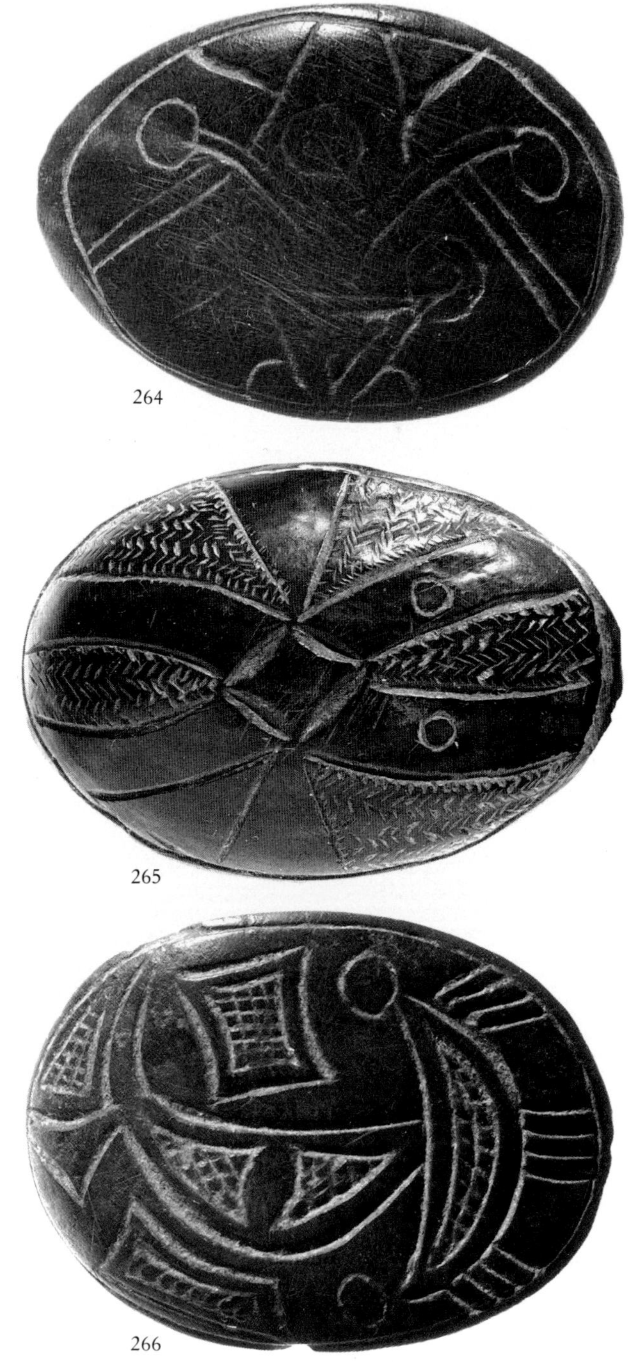

264

265

266

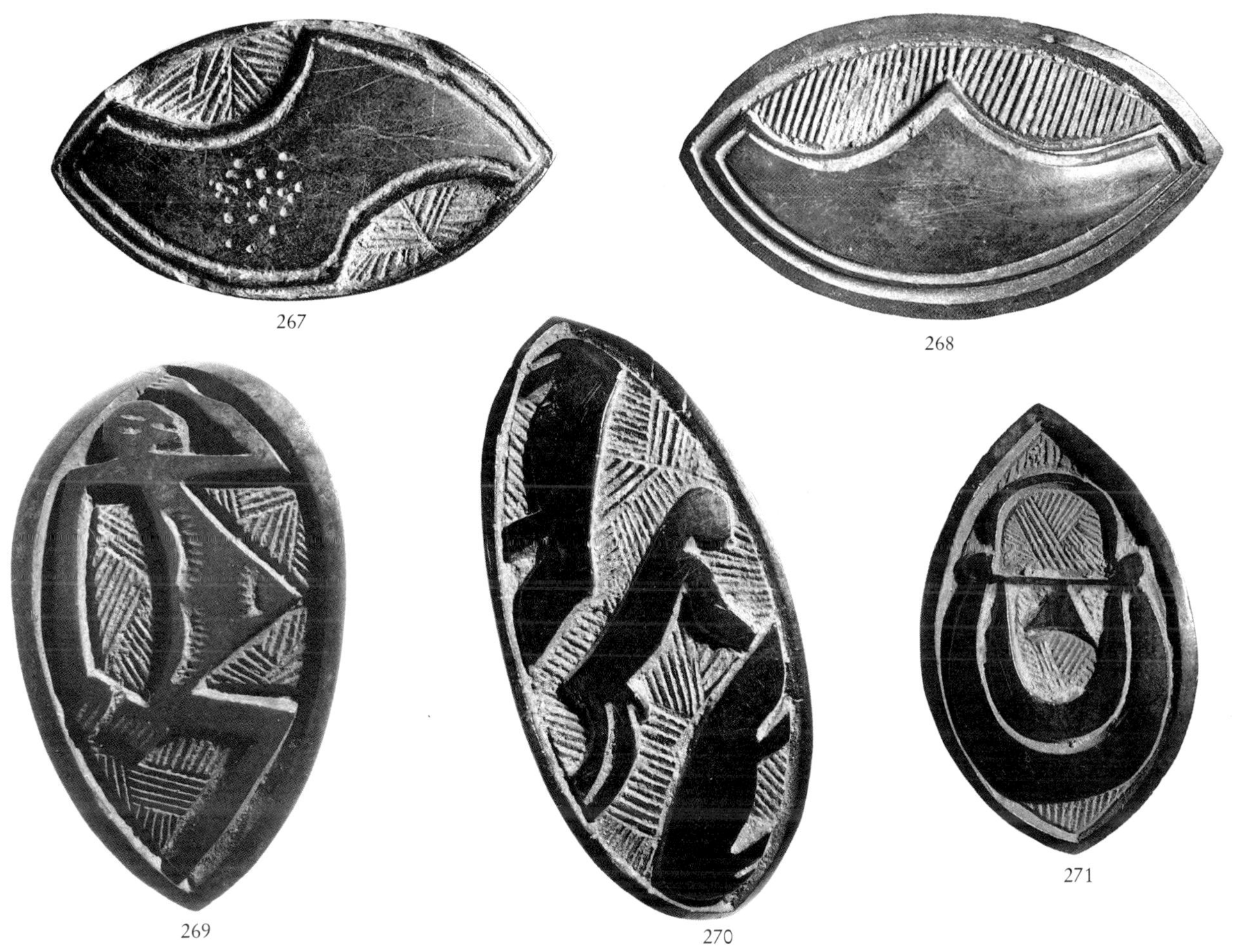

267 268 269 270 271

264-266 Three game chips *(abia)*, fruit stone. Cameroon, Maka.

These Maka *abia* ornamented with abstract motifs show signs of wear. Maka *abia* are usually larger than those of the Beti.

Length 3.7-4.6 cm. J 180-182
Acquired from R. Flegel (collected before 1888)

267-282 Sixteen game chips *(abia)*, fruit stone. Cameroon, Ewondo.

Nos. 267 and 268 are decorated with abstract motifs, No. 269 with a woman wearing a breechcloth, No. 270 with a man and two hippopotamuses, No. 271 with a carrying bag, Nos. 272 and 273 with birds, No. 274 with an armadillo, No. 275 with a crocodile, No. 276 with a tortoise, No. 277 with two fish, and Nos. 278-82 with various species of antelope, including one dead animal (No. 281).

Length 3-4.2 cm. 42 9 1
Acquired from A. Priester 1942

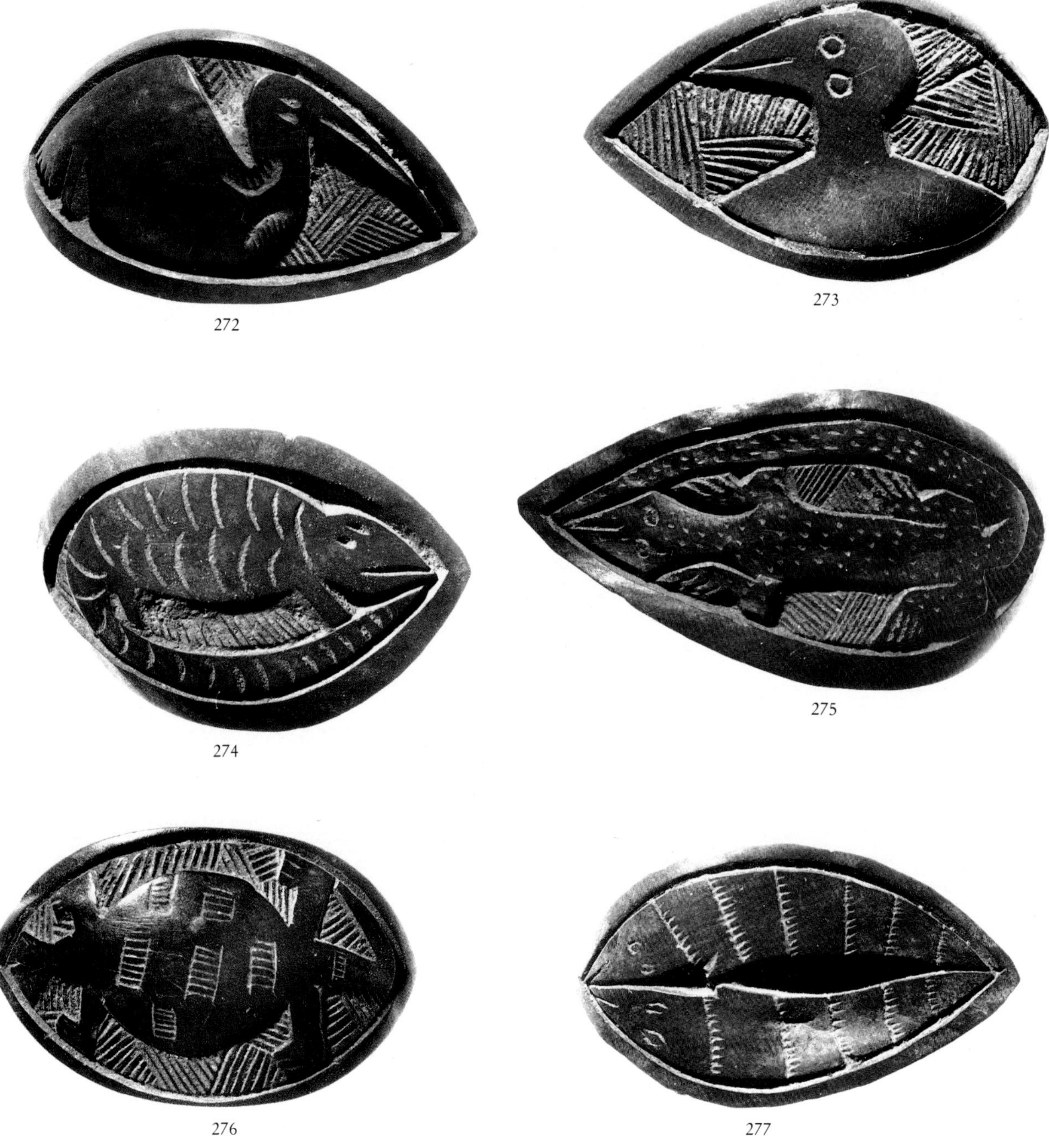

272

273

274

275

276

277

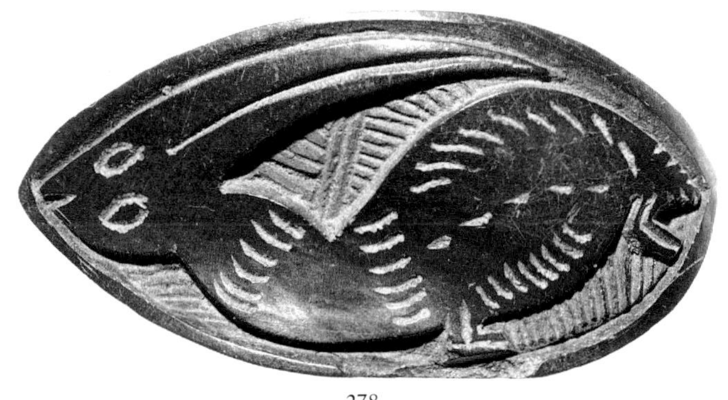

278

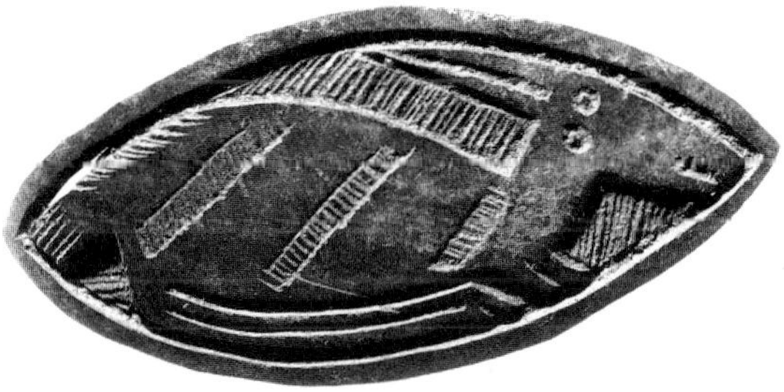

279

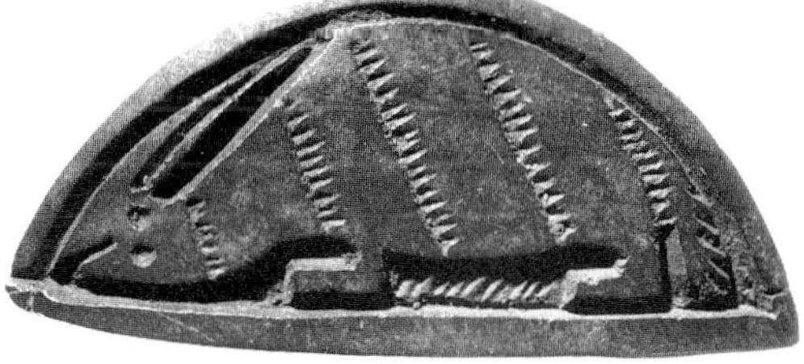

280

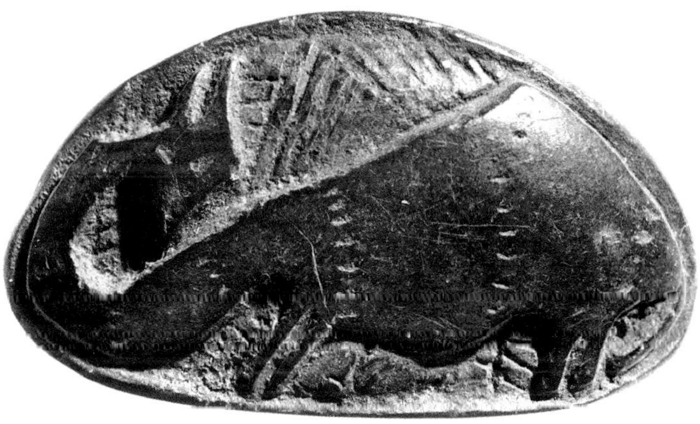

281

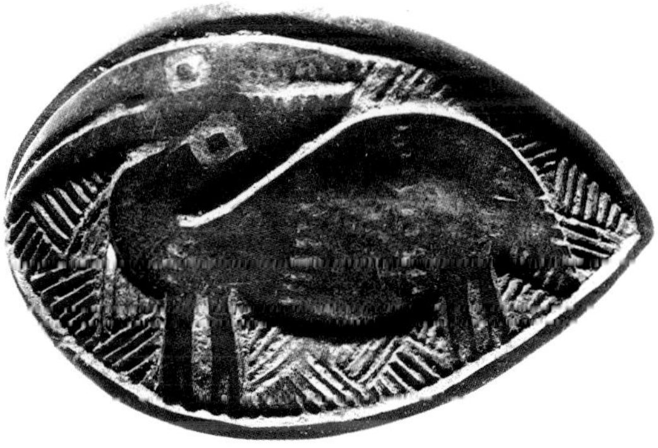

282

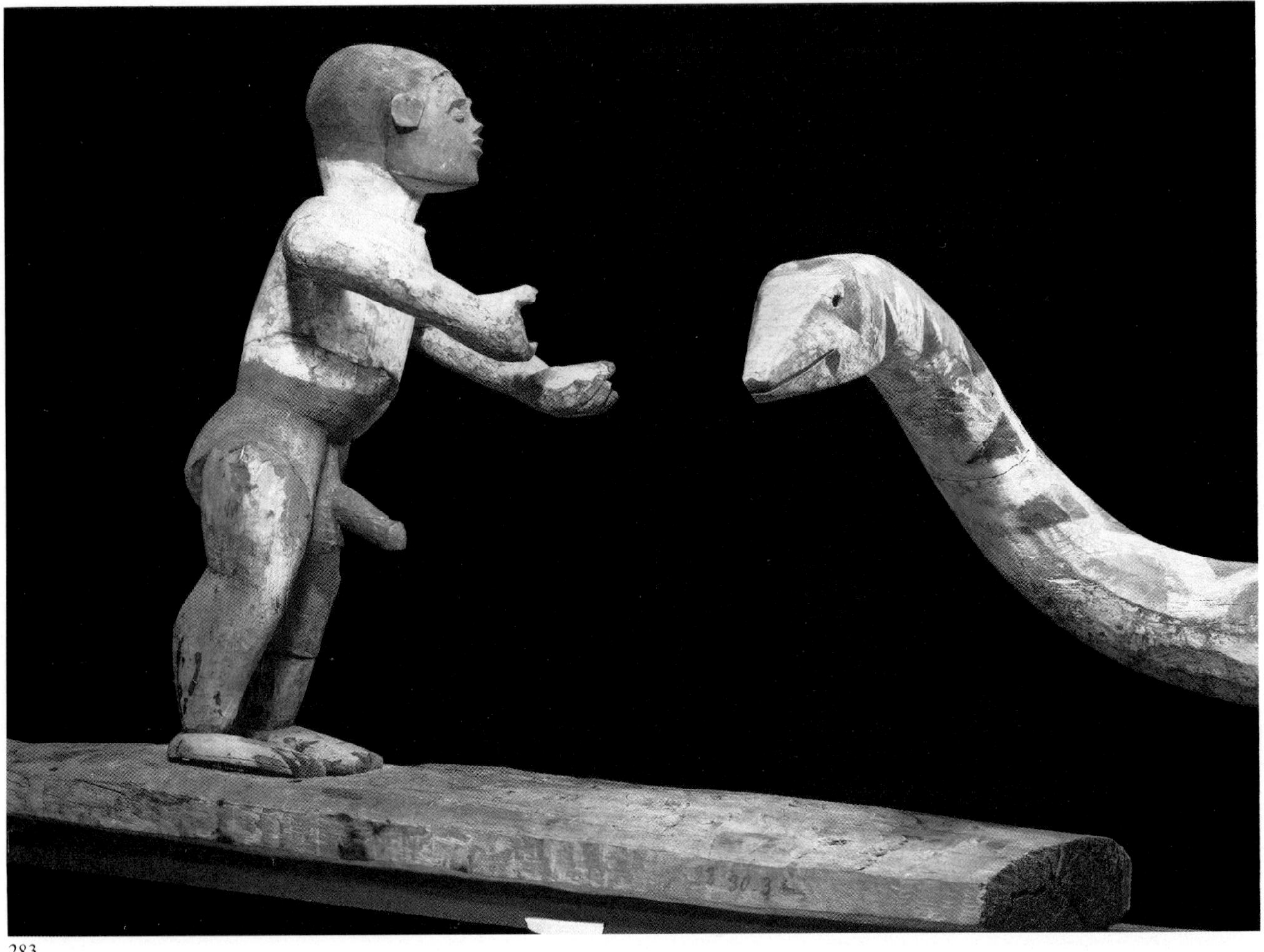

283

283 Ritual sculpture (*njom*), wood, paint. Cameroon, Beti, Eton, Yaounde district.

This massive board and the figures mounted on it were originally carved from a single tree trunk. Because of its state of disrepair, the enormous object was cut into several pieces while still in Africa and the middle section of the board replaced. The human figures were severed from the base at ankle level and repaired with new wooden parts, especially the lower bodies.

The restorer undertook alterations. For instance, the abdomens became slimmer and the male genitals more pronounced. The arm of the figure facing the snake is set onto the body incorrectly, while the weapon the figure originally held was lost (see the drawing made from Nekes's field photo). The distribution of black and white paint was also changed. The restorer disregarded the horizontal grain of the wood and carved his additions against the grain. There are some indications that our *njom* sculpture was originally identical with that collected by Dominik and published by Nekes, which still appears to be intact in the 1913 photograph. But whether the striking differences between the piece in the photograph and ours are due to later restoration is uncertain.

Among the few known pieces of this type, our example is artistically and iconographically one of the most significant. Such sculptures were made to be used one time only during puberty rites (at the end of the preparatory period and before actual instruction). They were set up on two forked posts or between tree branches at a height of about two meters in the bush camp of the initiates. When the ceremonies were concluded everything in the camp was left to decay. Our piece, in a neglected state, was standing abandoned in the woods,, when Hans Dominik discovered it sometime between 1894 and 1900. Such beams usually had an elongation at each end that served as a platform for dancing; this, presumably, was originally the case with our piece.

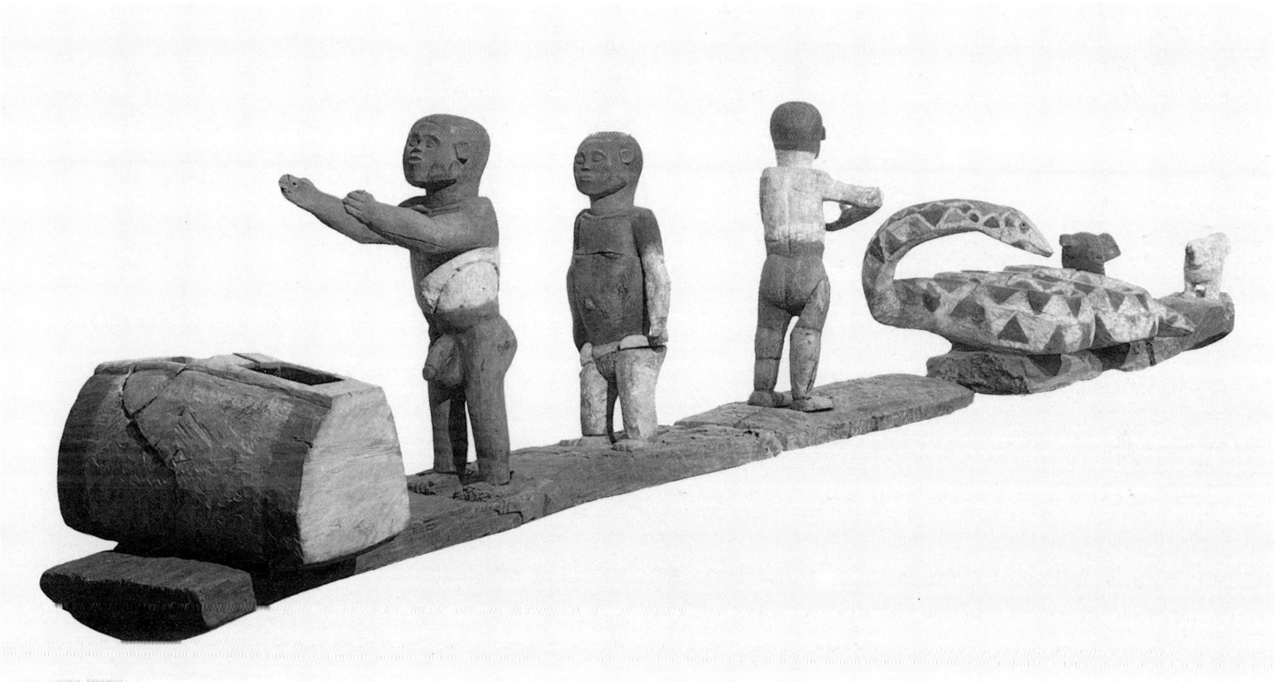

283

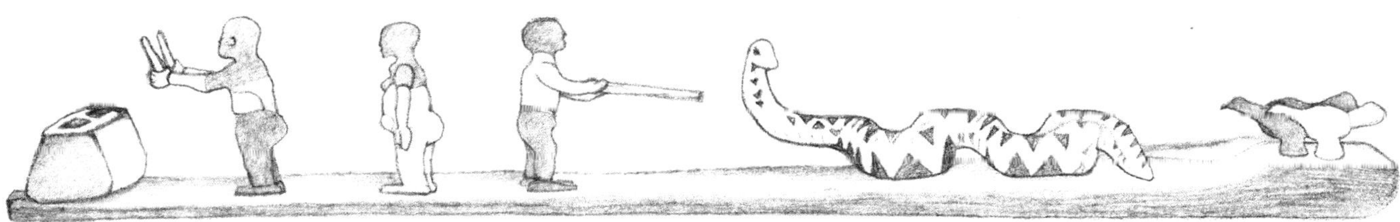

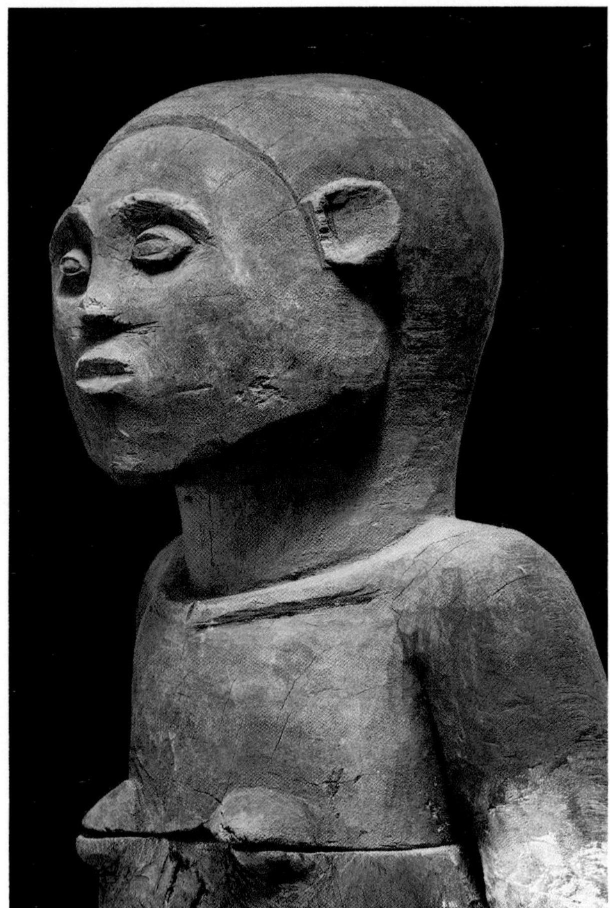

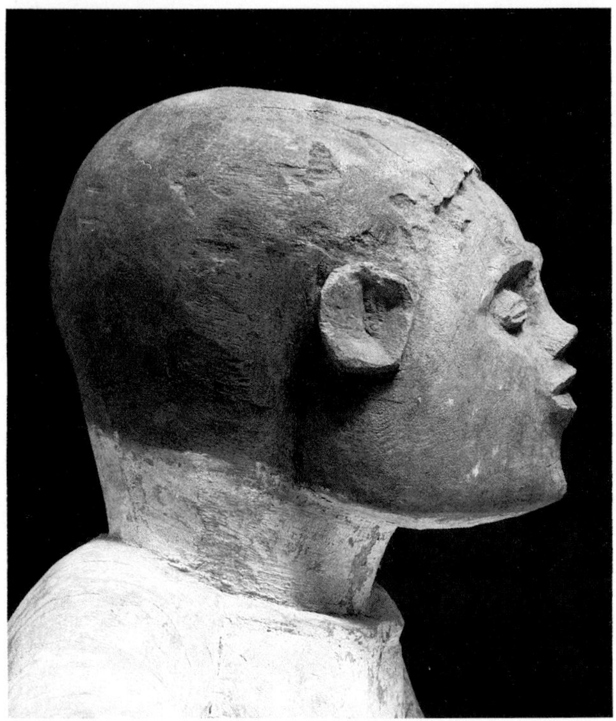

283

The board is a symbolic bridge between the here and the hereafter, which the candidate had to cross before reentering the social world as an adult. Freed of certain prohibitions after the ceremony, he could marry and participate in the great communal hunts. According to Siroto, each of the figures exhibits a wealth of symbolic details. The massive snake, shown as if in movement, also represents a kind of bridge. It recalls the mythical snake of primordial times that placed itself across the border river, enabling the ancestors to immigrate to the present community's area. Juxtaposing the snake and the young man in the center suggests other possible interpretations, such as the snake as symbol of masculinity, rebirth, or immortality. The gun the youth originally held probably represents the Beti ideal of a successful hunter. The two woodfowl may also have been associated with differing symbolic values, for such birds are considered symbols of femininity, peace, stability, and passivity (in contrast to the

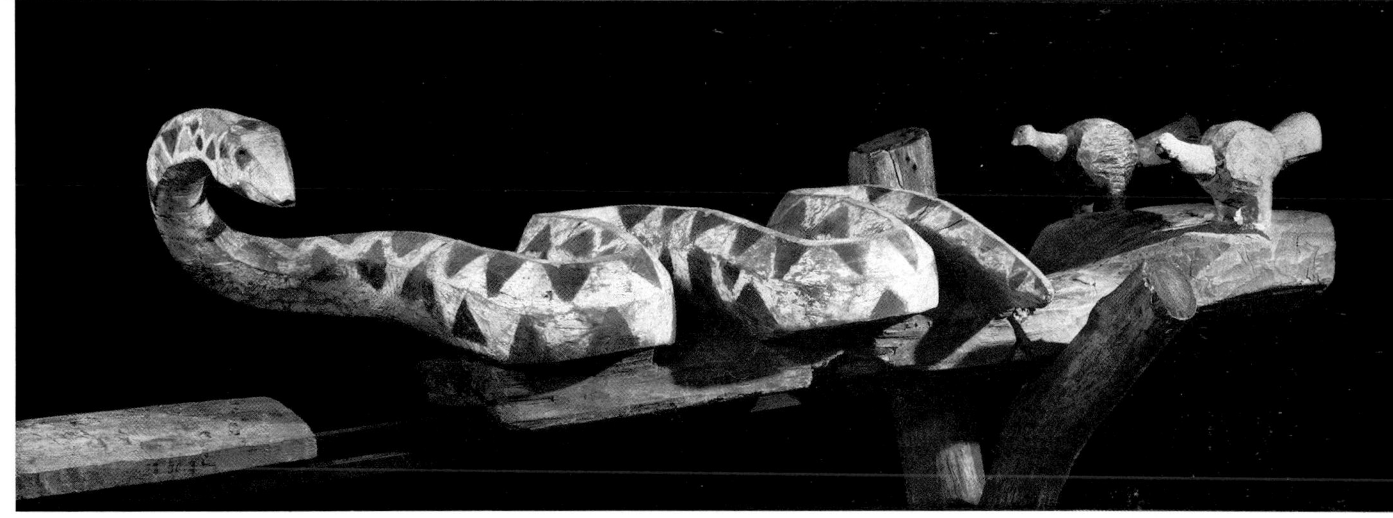

aggression and vigor of the snake). However, woodfowl were also feared as bad omens. The figure of the drummer on the opposite end—his sticks have been lost—may refer to the conclusion of the puberty rites and the beginning of the festival. The female figure perhaps reminded the youths that, after their return from bush camp, they would be permitted to choose a partner.

The human figures are sturdy and thickset, with features natural to youth. The accentuated neck, clavicle and shoulder area are notable (see also Nos. 259-62 and 286-89). The black and white paint (with red used sparingly) may well hint at the idea of death and resurrection that underlies initiation: the child must die to rise again as an adult.

Length 460 cm.
(portions of the beam are missing) 22-30-3
Height 63 cm., 65 cm., 64 cm. (human figures)
Acquired from H. Rolle 1922
(Collection H. Dominik)

Lit.: H. Dominik 1901, pp. 164-66; P. C. Ngumu 1977, pp. 155-57, H. Nekes 1913, pp. 209, 10; L. Siroto 1977, pp. 38 51, 90, 91, 1978, pp. 86, 87; G. Tessman 1913, II, pp. 45, 50-51; G. Zenker 1895, pp. 55-57.

Fang and Mpongwe White Masks (284,285)

The Fang and Mpongwe, who belong to the Beti tribe, exercise social control in their community through masks. They have developed a mask style that gives strong evidence of the influence of their eastern neighbors, the Kwele. The heart-shape face occurs in Kwele masks "with the greatest clarity," according to Fraser. Characteristically, the masks are carved of wood, light in both color and weight, and are linear and planar rather than supple. The slightly concave large-planed form of the heart-shape face, frequently mouthless, is given a narrow, often disproportionately long nose and almond-shape slit eyes. The face is always painted white, heightening the contrast of the heat- darkened symbols (groups of lines, angular decorations, rows of dots), which reproduce the tattooing characteristic of the individual groups. The hair style reproduces the ornate coiffure of the Beti. The white masks of the Fang and Mpongwe gave impetus to European modern art of the early twentieth century.

Lit.: E. G. Bay 1975, pp. 252-54; I. Bolz 1966, p. 181; L. Perrois 1973a, pp. 41, 42, 465ff.; W. Rubin 1984, pp. 20ff.

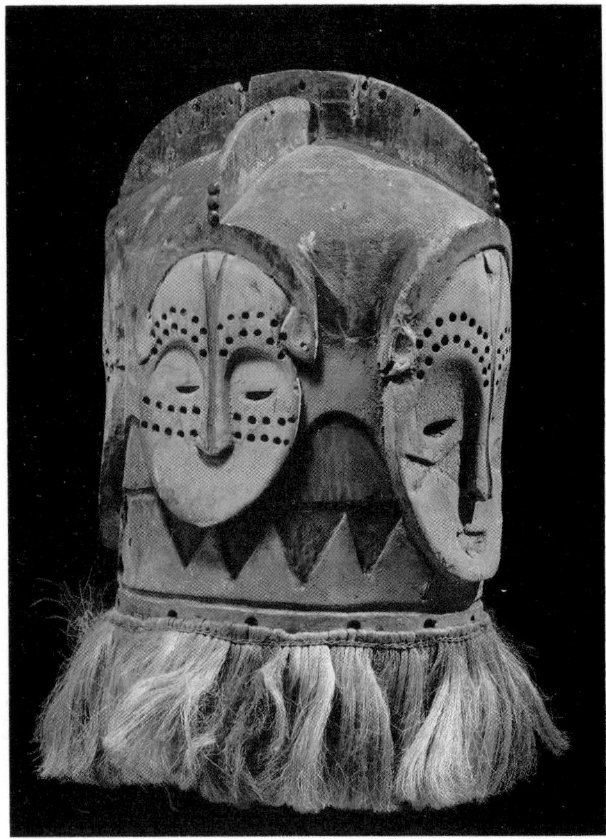

284

284 Four-faced headdress mask (*ngontang*), wood, raffia, tacks.
Gabon, Mpongwe.

From the eyebrows down, the heart-shape faces of this mask are composed of concave planes broken by rows of dots and finely incised lines, the latter reproducing tattoos characteristic of their makers. The high crested-helmet coiffure connecting the four faces represents a traditional hair style. Such many-faced masks probably first appeared only a few decades ago, and our piece, acquired in 1928, is one of the earliest examples. Quadrupling the face was more likely a means of creating rhythmic accentuation than of meeting a functional requirement. With the help of such masks, sorcerers were detected and punished by magical means.

Height 34 cm. 28-22-12
Acquired from P. Guillaume 1928

Lit.: I. Bolz 1966, p. 194, 95; L. Perrois 1973a, p. 42; S. Vogel & F. N'Diaye 1985, p.144.

285 Mask (*ngel*), wood, paint.
Gabon, Fang (acquired among the Bulu in Eboloma).

From an aesthetic viewpoint, this is one of the most significant masks in our African collection. The *ngel* is the best known of the three Fang mask types. It represents the spirit of a deceased person. The spiritualized, slightly concave, heart-shape face is mouthless, with eyes reduced to slits. The delicate forehead tattoos are of the southern Fang type. Parallel lines running the length of the face not only divide it symmetrically in half but also increase the effect of elongation.

Height 35 cm. 14-67-1
Acquired from K. Ritter 1914

Lit.: I. Bolz 1966, p. 189; L. Perrois 1973a, p. 39.

Guardians of the Ancestral Skulls (286-293)

The Fang and their Kota neighbors preserved clan founders' skulls and certain bones in cylindrical bark boxes or in baskets. The carved wooden head that was originally fixed to the rim of this container was

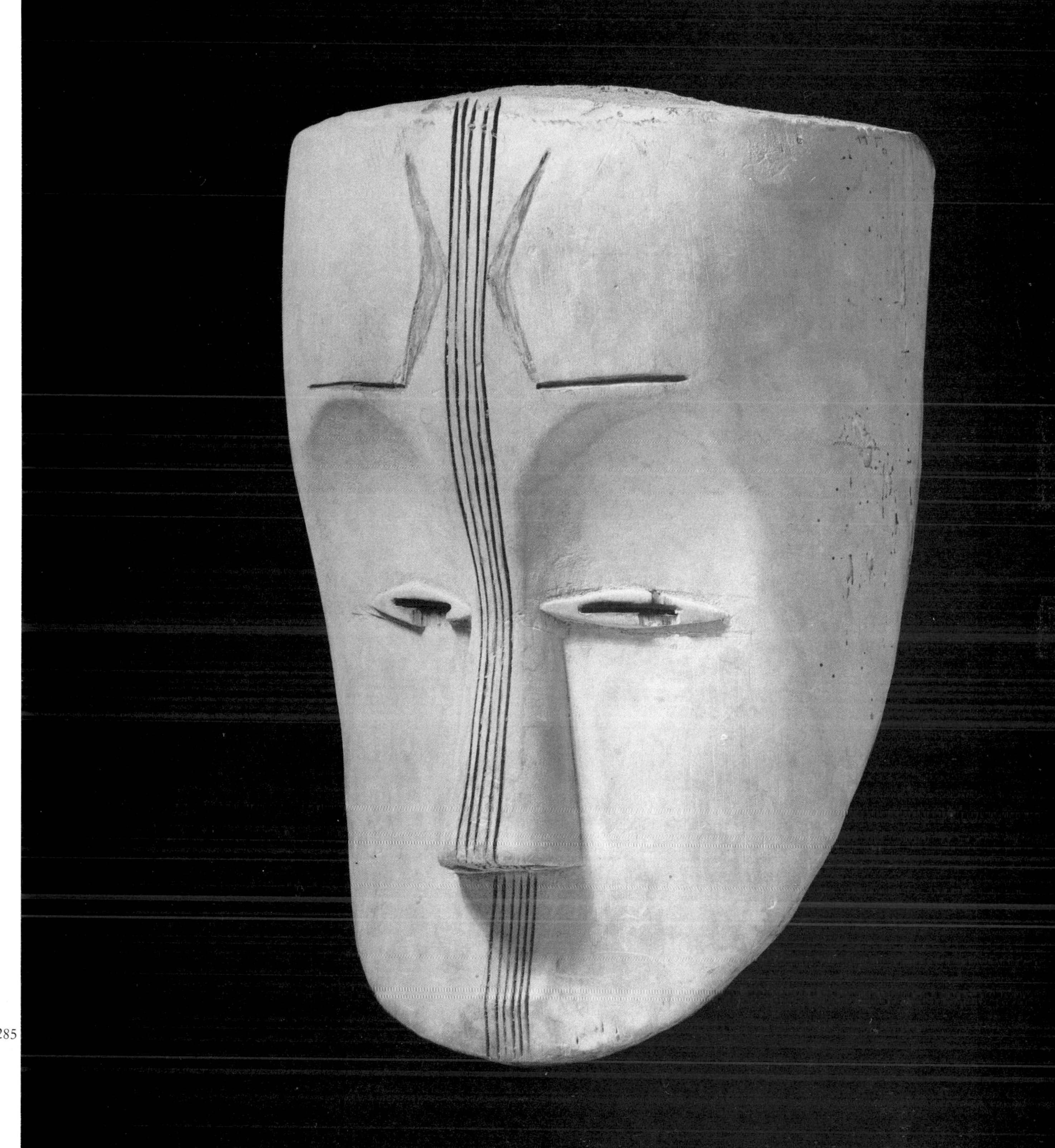

285

later replaced by one or more figures. The Fang and the Kota created widely differing versions of this guardian figure: those of the Fang were three-dimensional sculptures, while those of the Kota were strongly stylized two-dimensional heads. They share the feature of sheet-metal overlays that are more (Kota) or less (Fang) rich. Besides the relics of clan founders, skulls and bones of other distinguished persons, such as famous healers, judges, and the mothers of many children, were also preserved. That this honor was sometimes accorded exceptionally skilled craftsmen indicates the esteem in which these peoples held their artists.

Reliquaries, kept in the clan elder's dwelling, were taken outside only on those occasions when the clan elder assumed the role of priest and offered sacrifices to the relics. Young men who had not yet undergone initiation were excluded from such rites, as were most women and children.

The spiritual significance of the guardian figures is still under discussion. One opinion is that they represent the clan founder, another the totality of the ancestors. Fernandez recognizes in the proportions of the human bodies and in some stereotyped details what he considers to be intended similarities with the bodies of newborn babies; he explains this as an artistic expression of the reincarnation of ancestors in their descendants. Other scholars do not exclude this possibility, but neither do they accept it as the most likely consideration. Tessman's reports suggest that these guardian figures were of little significance in themselves, for, while the skull and bone relics were revered and never under any circumstances sold, there seemed to be no such scruples about selling the wooden guardians. The irreverent handling of these figures is apparent in the drawing made from a field photo by Tessman (p. 257).

Lit.: K. Born, in H. Baumann 1975, p. 713; A. Chaffin 1973, p. 14; J. W. Fernandez 1974, p. 76, 77; P. C. Ngumu 1977, pp. 169-72; L. Perrois 1973b, p. 21; L. Siroto 1968, p. 22; G. Tessman 1913, II, pp. 113, 117.

a) *Byeri* or *malan* Figures of the Fang (286-289)

The guardian figures of the Fang of southern Cameroon, Equatorial Guinea, and Gabon make up one of the most important types of African art south of the Sahara. Form, expression, proportion, and surface treatment testify to a feeling for high quality and symmetry. Metal overlays emphasize all important parts of the body and fuse harmoniously with the wood. Hair styles represent the various padded coiffures of the Beti (Fang) peoples. Many male figures hold an antelope horn filled with charms. Such "medicine horns," regarded as amulets and occasionally as cult instruments, play an important role among both hunters and peasants.

The *byeri* figures, also called *bian, malan,* or *ngun melan,* can be divided into two main groups on the basis of characteristic proportions—length of torso and neck in comparison with total height—but cannot be sharply separated from one another. The eighteenth-century Ntumu area is considered to be the place where the *byeri* heads originated. There, probably one century later, the full-figure sculptures evolved from the heads. The wood, in most cases light hued, was treated with pulverized charcoal, palm oil, and resin, and sometimes also with red camwood powder. The metal sheeting came from European brass bowls.

Apart from their function as guardians of relics, the *byeri* were the community's watchmen, warding off prowling sorcerers. The metal-framed glass eyes warned that neither hidden nor future events could escape their clairvoyance. All guardian figures seen here date from the nineteenth century, and the majority represent the Ngumba style of the northern Fang.

Lit.: K. Born, in H. Baumann 1973, I, p. 713; A. Chaffin 1973, p. 26; J. W. Fernandez 1974, p. 76, 77; P. C. Ngumu 1977, pp. 168, 69, 224-25; L. Perrois 1972, pp. 11-20; A. Raponda-Walker & R. Sillans 1962, pp. 62ff., 67.

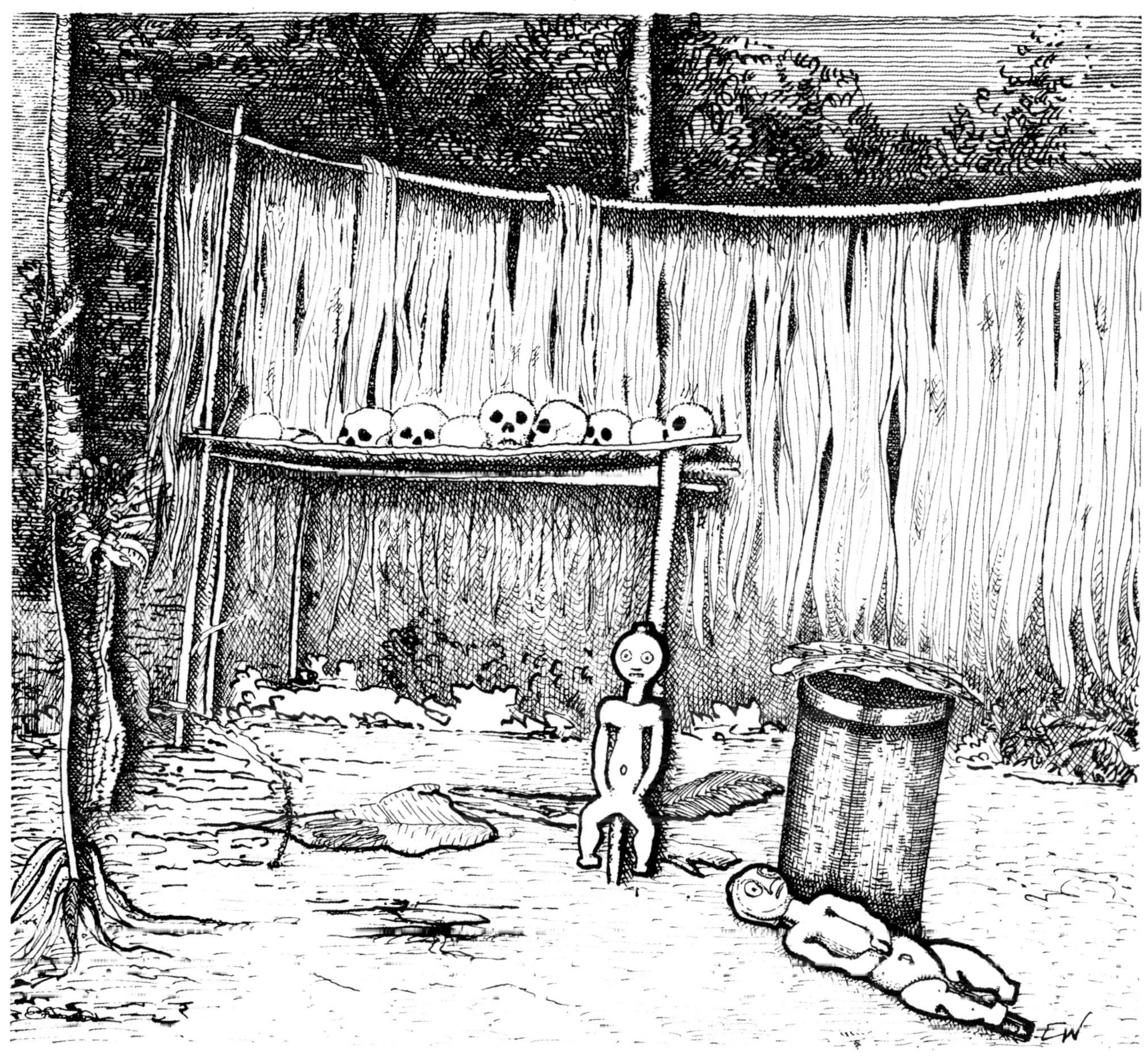

286 Reliquary guardian: seated female, wood, brass, glass, teeth, shells.
Gabon, Fang.

The only female among the guardian figures exhibited here is distinguished by a slight turning of the body, a three-part coiffure, and ornamental chains—

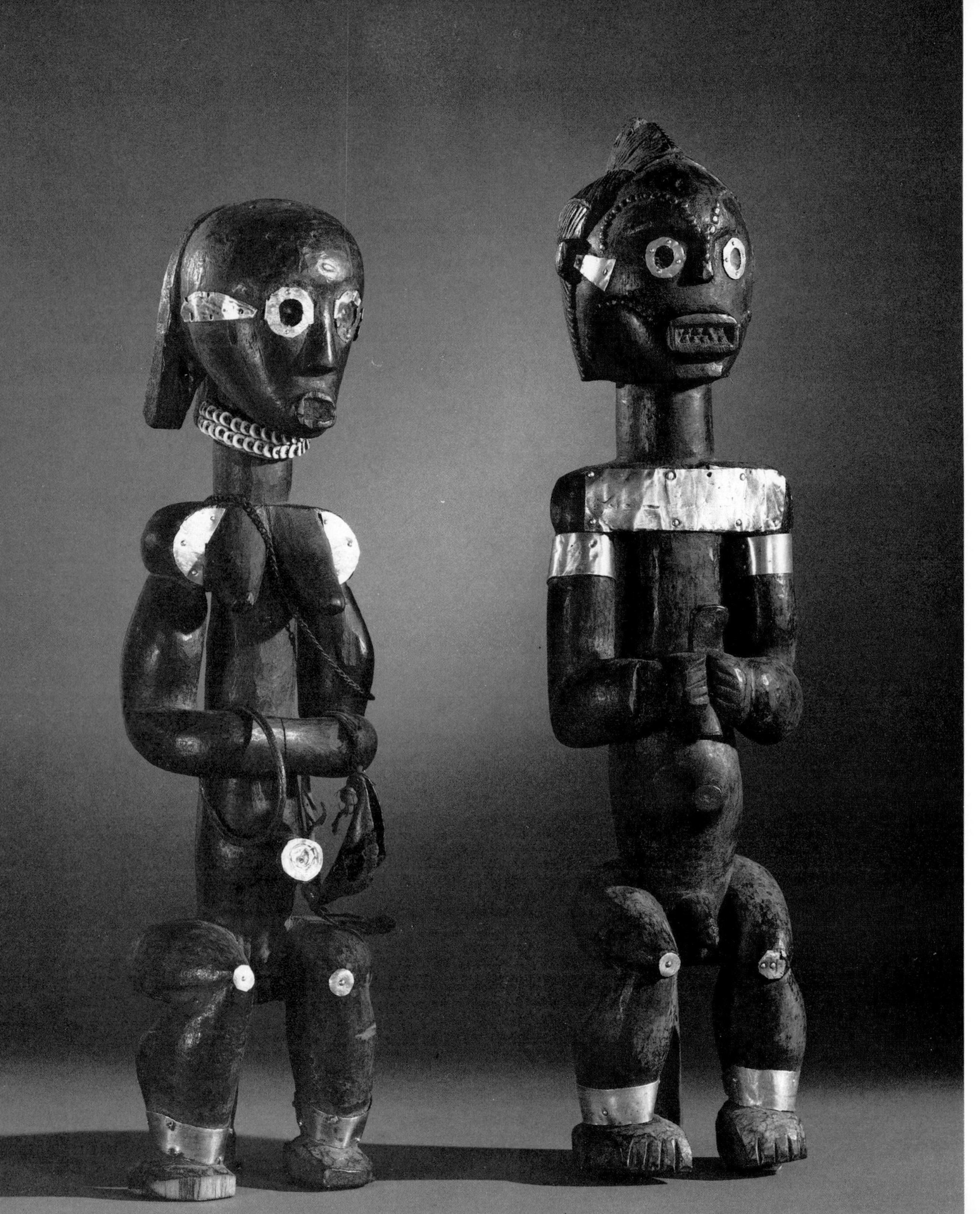

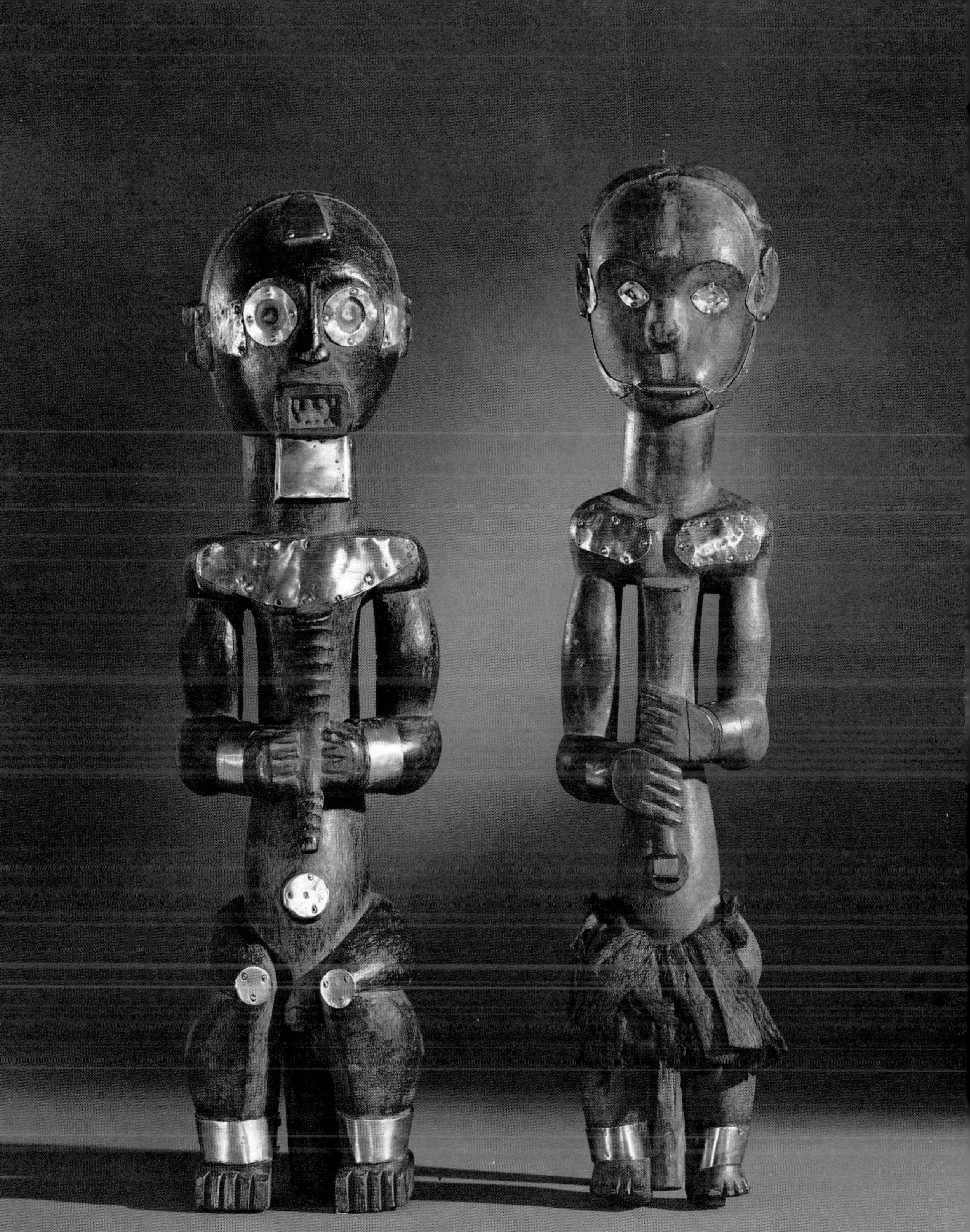

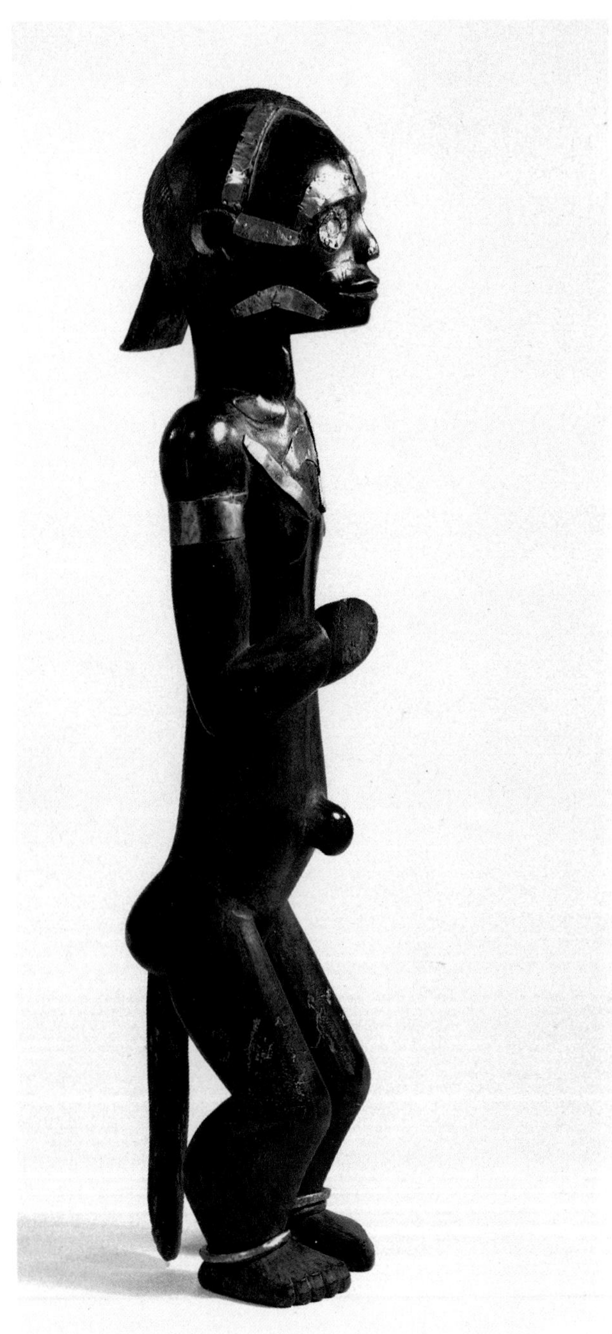

290

among them a shell necklace from Oceania probably added in Europe. This figure does not hold an antelope horn—this magical or ritual implement is used exclusively by men. The artist was unsuccessful here in finding a satisfactory solution for the hands. Characteristic of this sculpture, in the *Ngumba* style of the southern Fang, are the shoulders and hips of equal width and the long, straight, slender back.

Height 46.5 cm. 29-34-11
Acquired from E. Fischer 1929

Lit.: L. Perrois 1972, pp. 65, 66.

287 Reliquary guardian: seated male, wood, brass, glass.
Southern Cameroon, Fang.

This figure has a facial tattoo indicated by iron pins, a padded coiffure with incised detail, and teeth filed to points. Our inventory includes the information that this sculpture was acquired "probably by First Lieutenant Bartsch during his war at Aktona on the Niong (Nyong) River in Yaounde," and that the figure is "certainly Nsumba, Highland of South Cameroon" (Dorbritz VIII, 1921).

Height 57.5 cm. 96.245
Acquired from Captain of the Horse Guards von Stetten 1896 (Collection Bartsch?)

288 Reliquary guardian: seated male, wood, brass, glass, teeth.
South Cameroon, Fang.
(see color plate p.265)

This figure is distinguished by its cubistic structuring. The head is spherical; the caplike coiffure ends in a well-sculptured horizontal roll at the back of the neck; beard and mouth are nearly squares; and the open mouth reveals rows of filed teeth. The circular, metal-enframed eyes are of glass disks, with pupils of human or animal teeth. The hands and magic horn

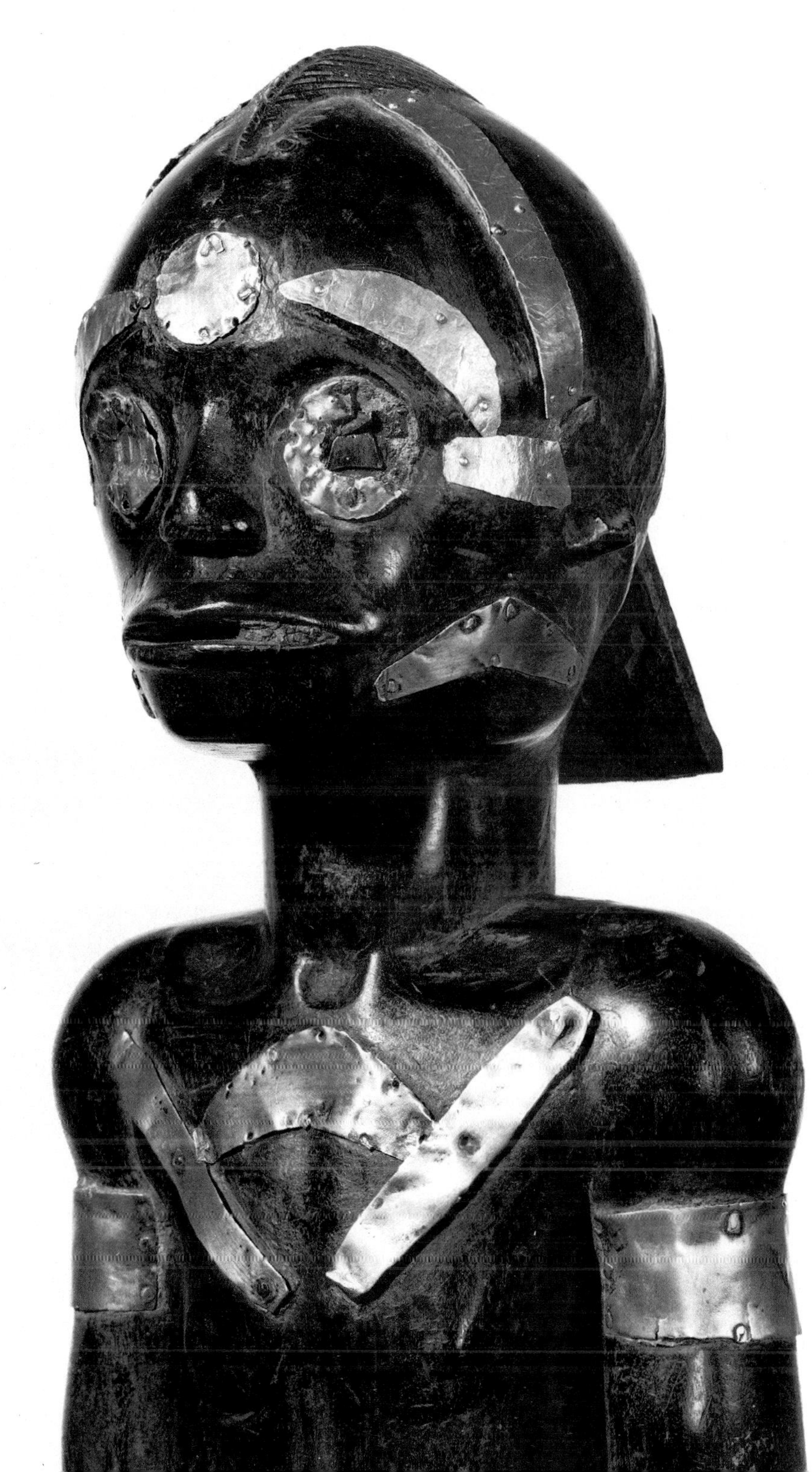

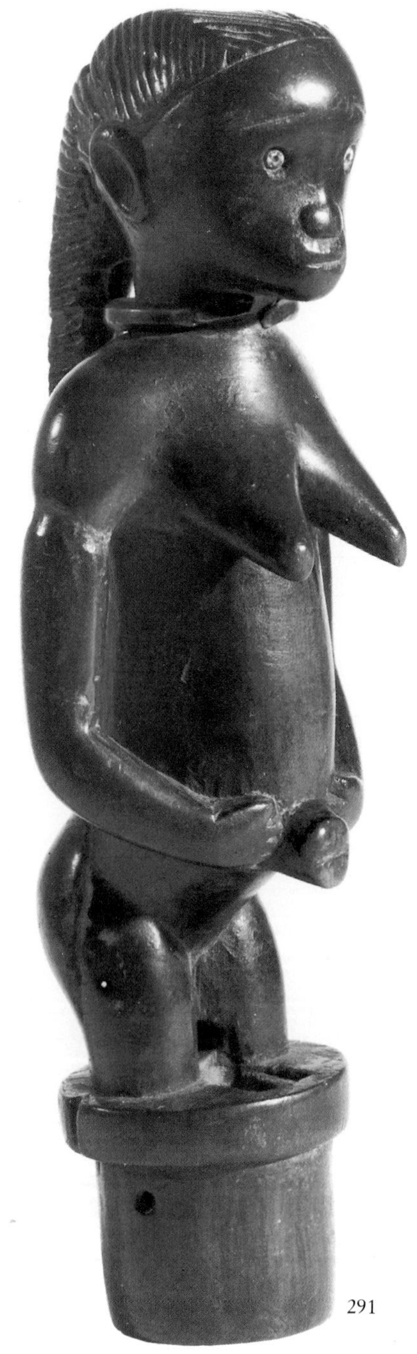
291

form a symmetrical composition. The inventory contains the note "Certainly Ngumba, South Cameroon."

Height 68 cm. 00.109
Acquired from B. Rippel 1900

289 Reliquary guardian: 'seated male, wood, brass, iron, glass, bark cloth.
Southern Cameroon, Fang.

Despite its striving for symmetry and stylization, this piece displays a tendency toward naturalism. The collar bone and neck hollows are depicted, the buttocks are divided and rounded, the backbone is grooved, and the hands are placed in an asymmetrical position. According to the inventory, this is of the Ngumba type.

Height 59 cm. 00.108
Acquired from B. Rippel 1900

290. Reliquary guardian: male, wood, brass, iron, glass.
Gabon, Fang.

This figure, representative of the southern style, was made by the Nzaman-Betsi or Okak (see also No. 291). A high-quality work, it differs from other such figures in style and size. The carefully executed head and torso tend toward idealized naturalism. the well-proportioned, harmoniously composed face has small closed lips; the coiffure ends in a kind of nape protector. Shoulders, clavicle, base of throat, breast, nipples, navel, genitals, and backbone groove are all finely worked. The buttocks are naturalistically formed, in contrast to those of the other four figures. The legs are strong and slightly bent. Exceptionally, the head is one fifth the height of the body.

Height 76 cm. 49-1-1
Acquired from E. Mayer 1949

Lit.: L. Perrois 1972, pp. 62, 247, 254.

291 Whisk handle, wood, brass, iron.
Cameroon or Gabon, Bane.

This female figure recalls the guardian figures of the southern Fang, especially those of the Okak style. The body has been shaped with great sensitivity. The composition is reminiscent of a certain type of Fang female figure holding a medicine box. The neck ring corresponds to the typical high brass collars of the Beti (Fang). An armlet (now missing) presumably rested in the groove on the upper arm. The surface is dark and polished.

Breasts and navel form a counterweight to the precisely rendered long, braidlike coiffure. Small iron rings have been inserted as eyes. The long arms pressed against the body end in tiny hands that rest on either side of the protruding navel.

Height 22.5 cm. 40-14-1
Acquired from D. J. Fuchs 1940

Lit.: T. Celenko 1981, p. 38; L. Perrois 1972, pp. 191, 290; M. Plass & W. Fagg 1964, p. 145.

292 Staff, wood.
Gabon, Bane.

This staff, in the Mvai style of the southern Fang, served the head of a clan as an official insignia. Its top has been carved into a seated male figure in the style of the guardian figures, with a reserved facial expression and a high coiffure divided into thirds in back. The navel protrudes and the legs are strikingly long with short thighs and strong calves. The magic horn the figure originally held has been broken off.

Length 105 cm. 13-7-4
Acquired from J. Kometzko 1913

Lit.: L. Perrois 1972, pp. 62, 87; G. Tessman 1913, I., p. 275.

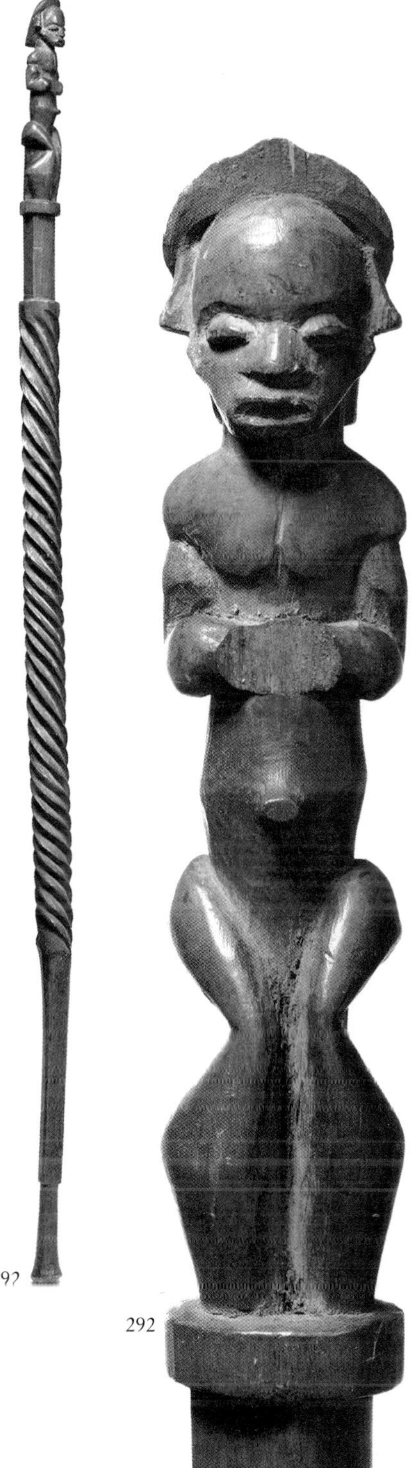

292

292

b) Kota reliquary guardians (*mbulu* or *mwete*)

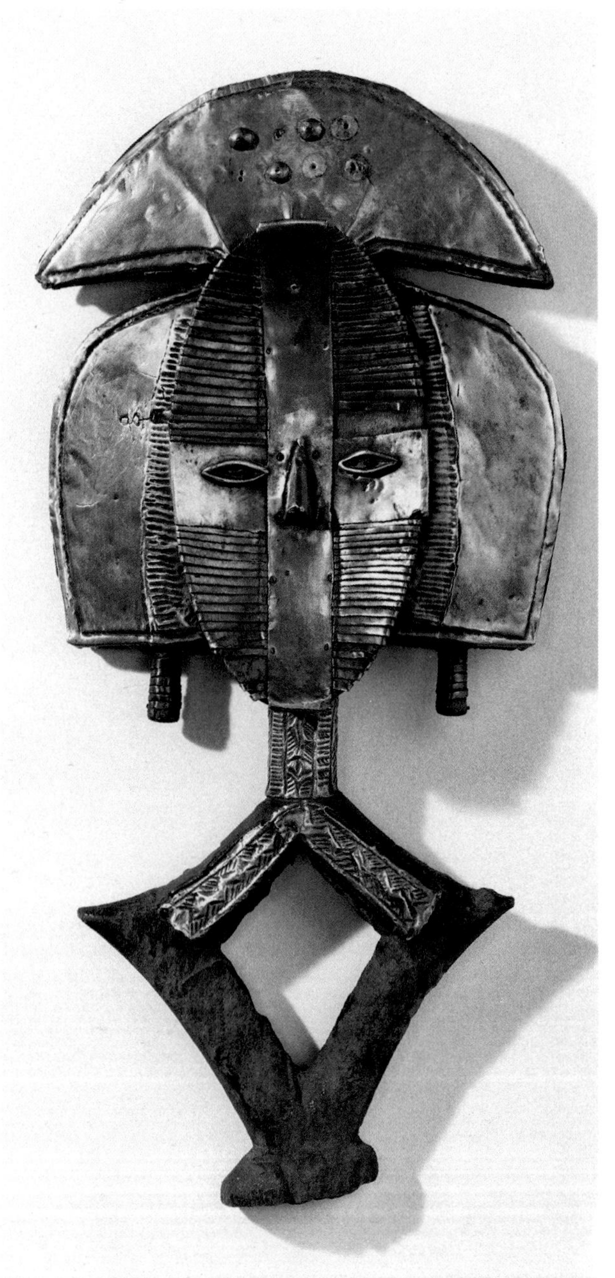

293

293 Reliquary guardian: wood, brass, copper. Gabon, Kota, Ogowe River area.

In the past these guardian figures were called *mbulu-ngulu;* today *mwete* or *mboy* is usually used. They are representative of the southern style of the Obamba and Mindasa groups and are characterized by faces that are oval, concave, and mouthless with almond eyes. The coiffure, in crescent form above the face, has lateral lobes framing the cheeks and ending in an appendage. A long thin neck rests on a diamond-shape handle that was plaited into the lid of the skull basket and thus shows signs of decay. Low-relief carvings on the back apparently represent the two forms of "blade" currency.

Smiths often made such heads, which perhaps explains the simple reduced molding that edges the coiffure and the frequent choice of metal as the medium. Presumably an earlier, pre-European style of such head sculptures existed. Besides the tutelary function of the *mwete,* they were regarded as oracles that were questioned before important decisions, and were considered protection against sorcerers. The latter, particularly dangerous during the night, were driven away by the gleam of the *mwete,* which reminded them of the coming daylight.

Height 54 cm. 31-60-1
Acquired from Cranmore Ethnological Museum 1931

Lit.: A. & F. Chaffin 1973, pp. 14, 16ff., 26; L. Perrois 1973b, p. 25, 26; L. Siroto 1968, pp. 22, 23, 86, 87.

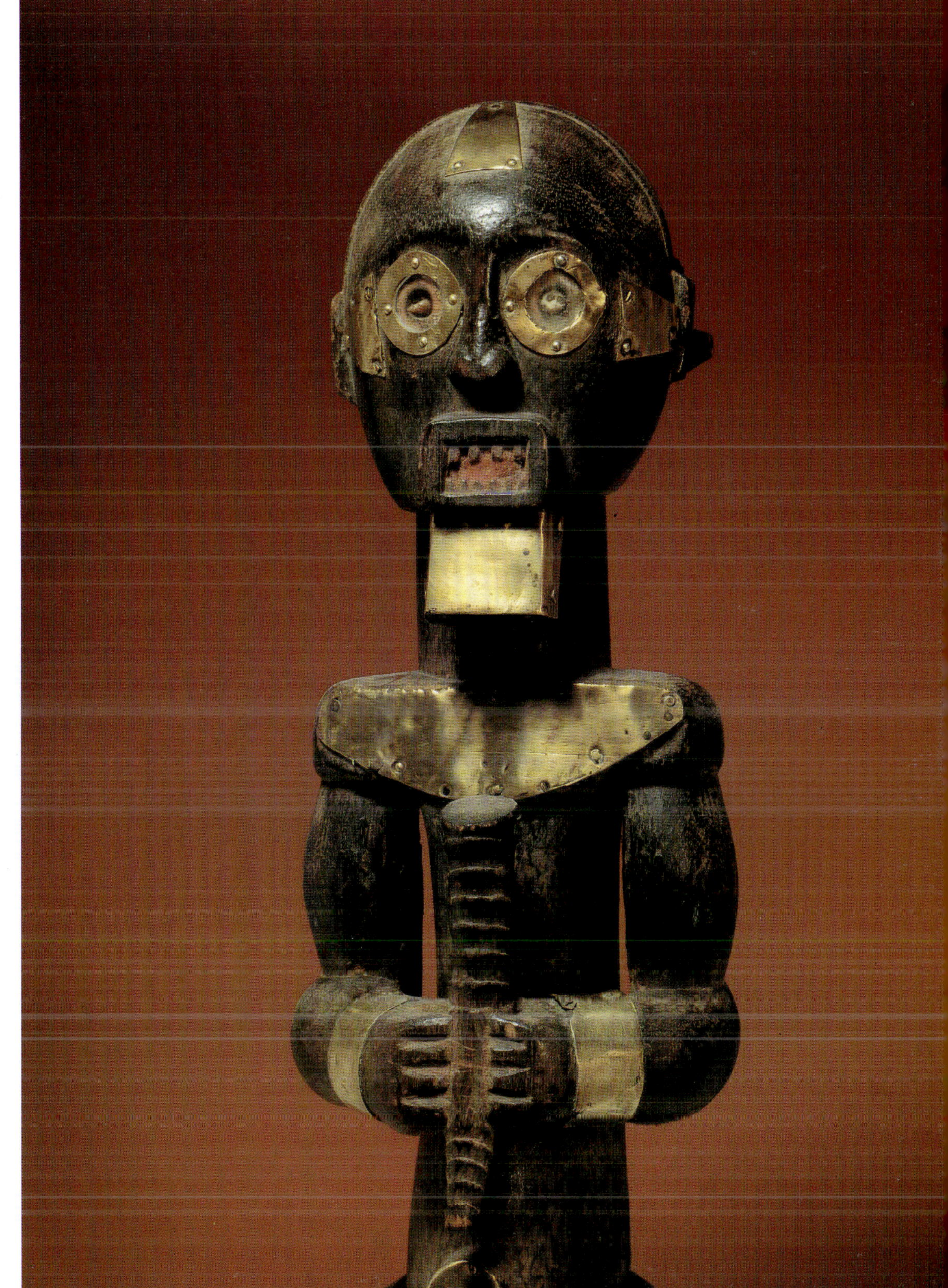

See page 260
Cat. No. 288

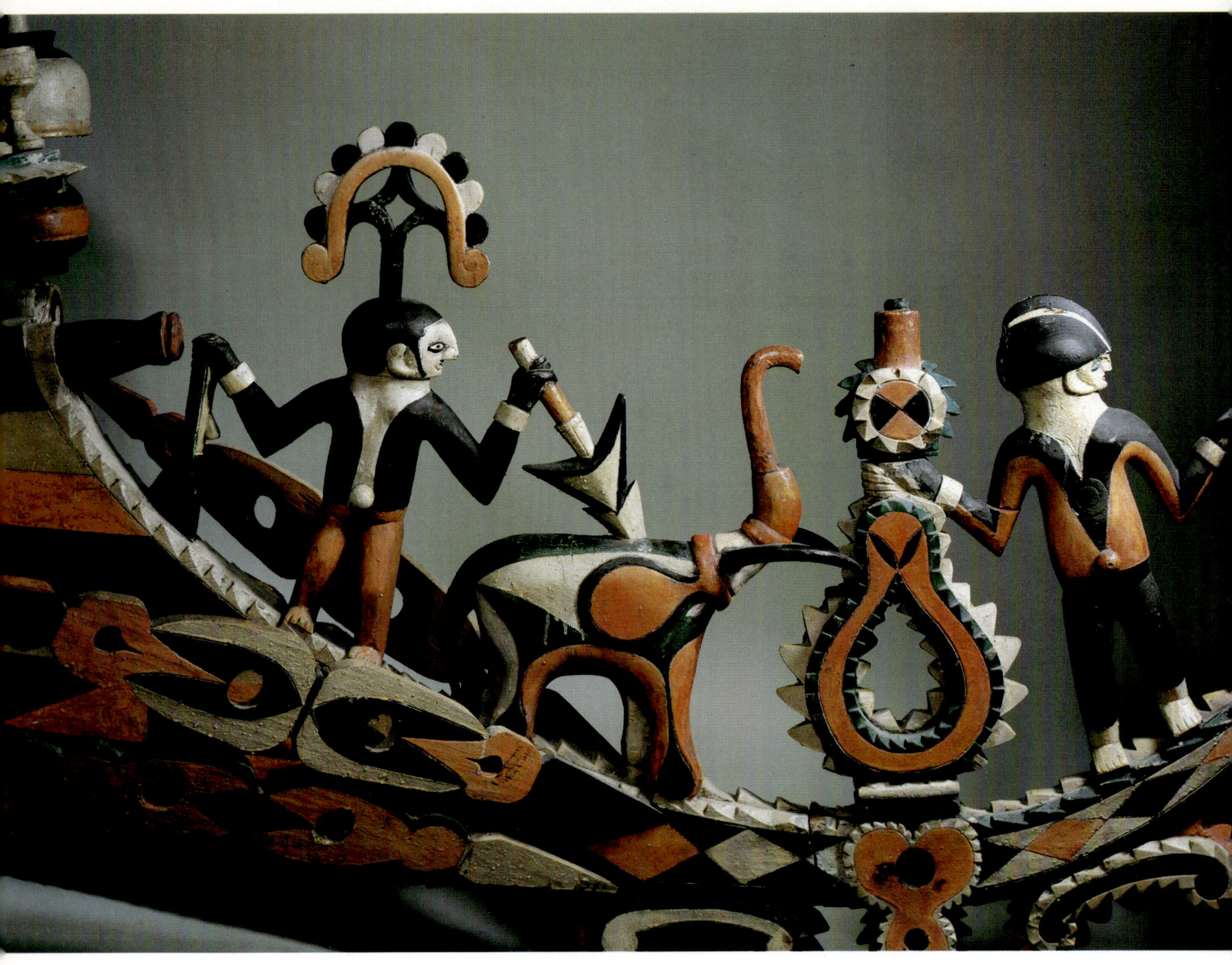

See page 225
Cat. No. 236

Page 267
See pages 228-229
Cat. Nos. 235-242

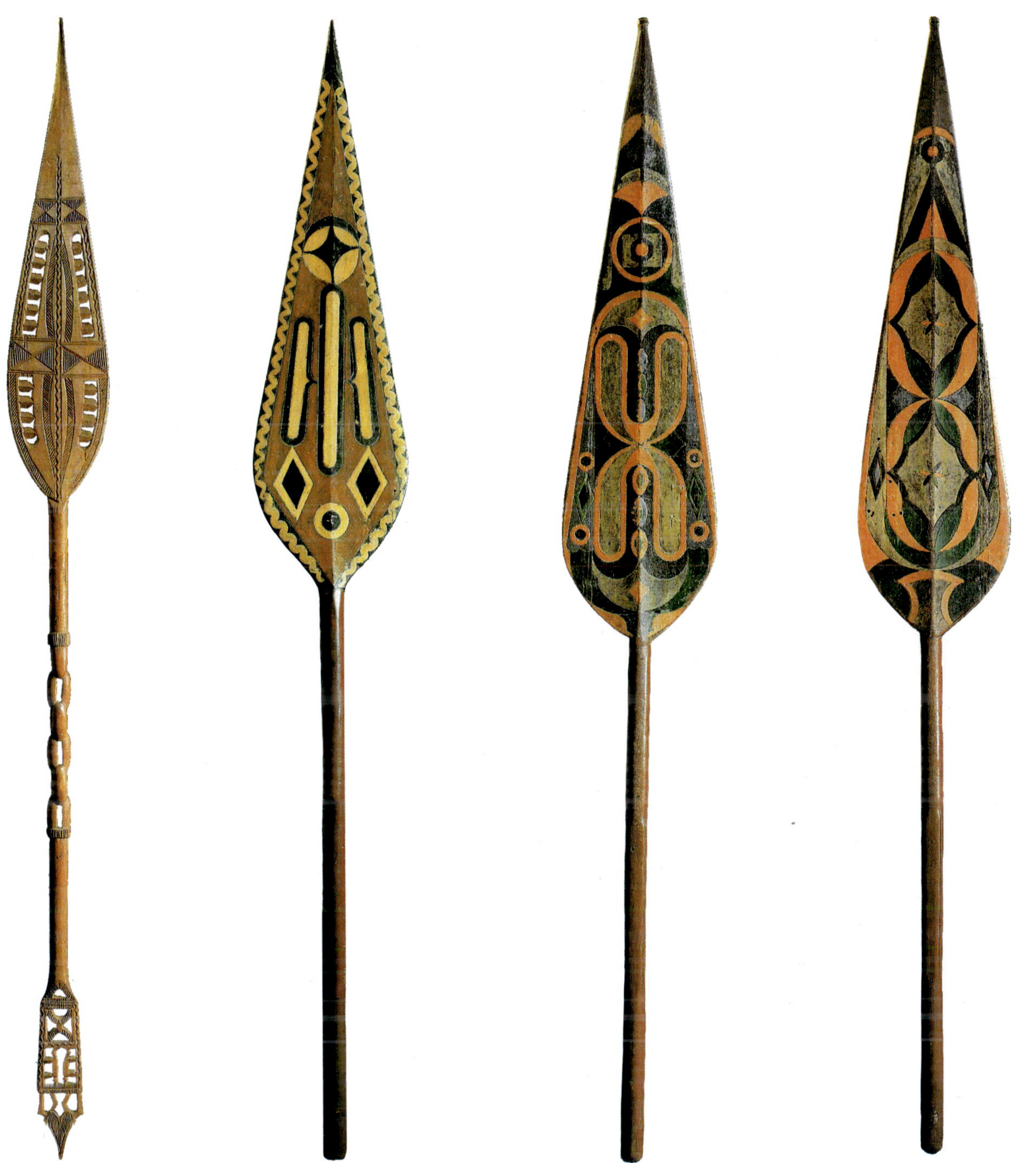

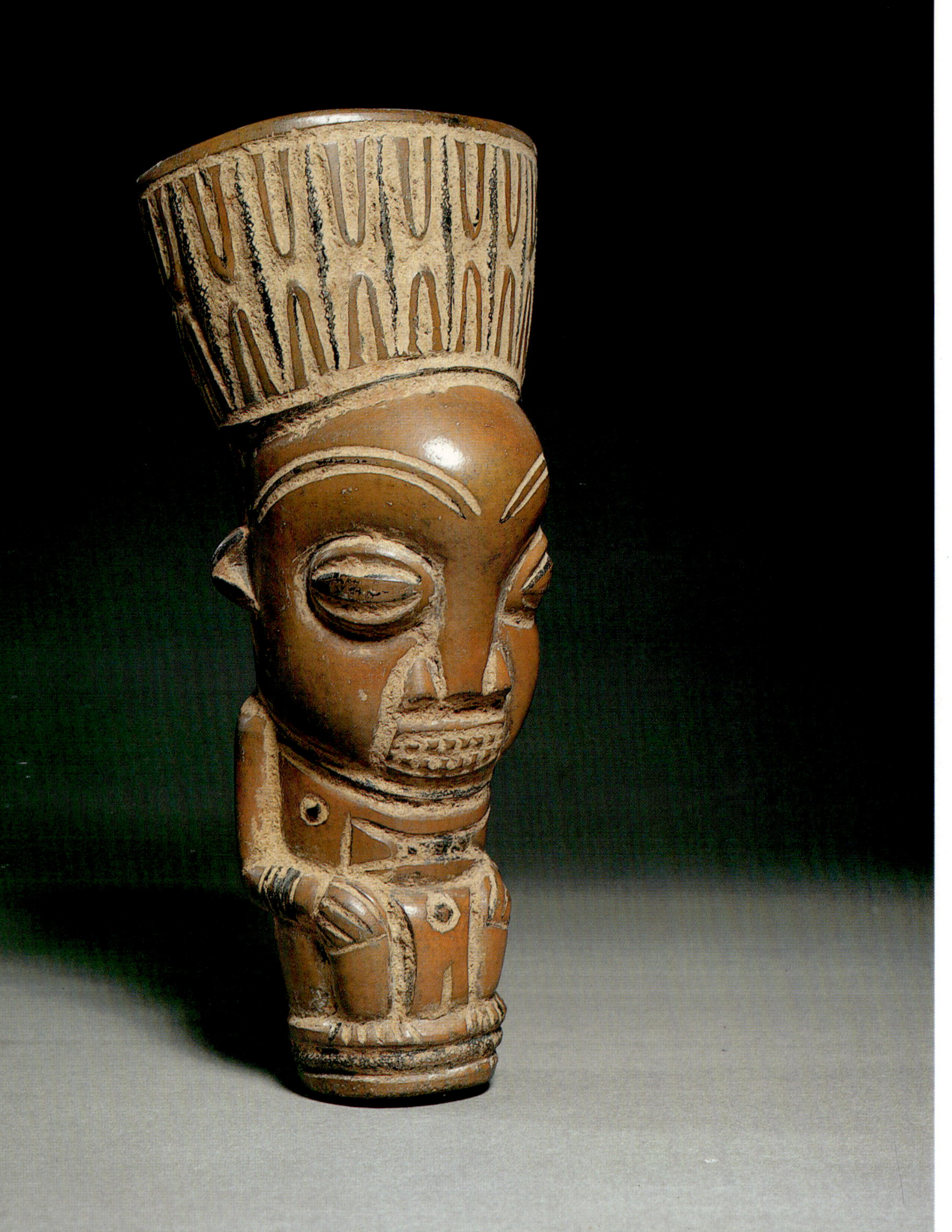

See page 209
Cat. No. 218

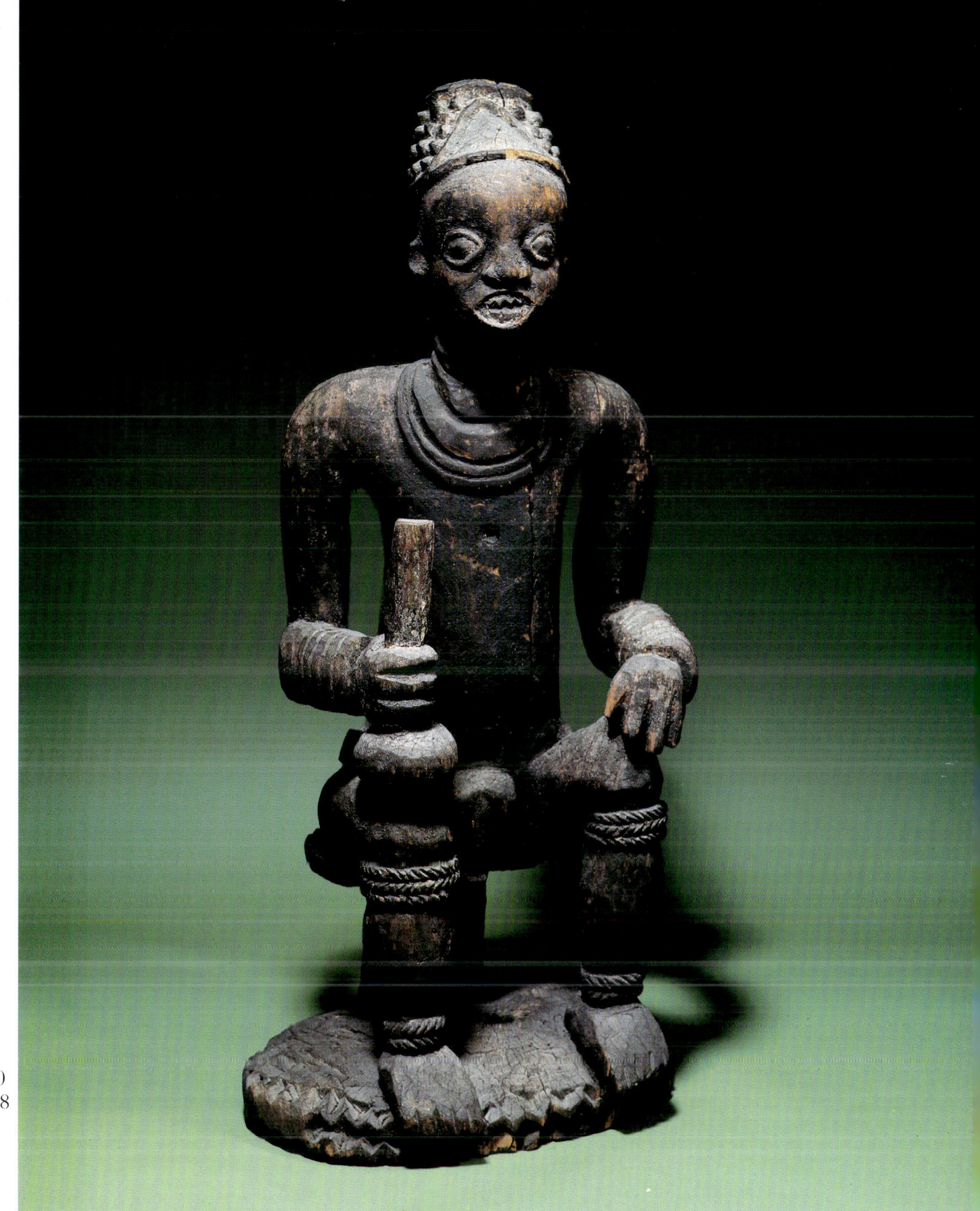

See page 190
Cat. No. 198

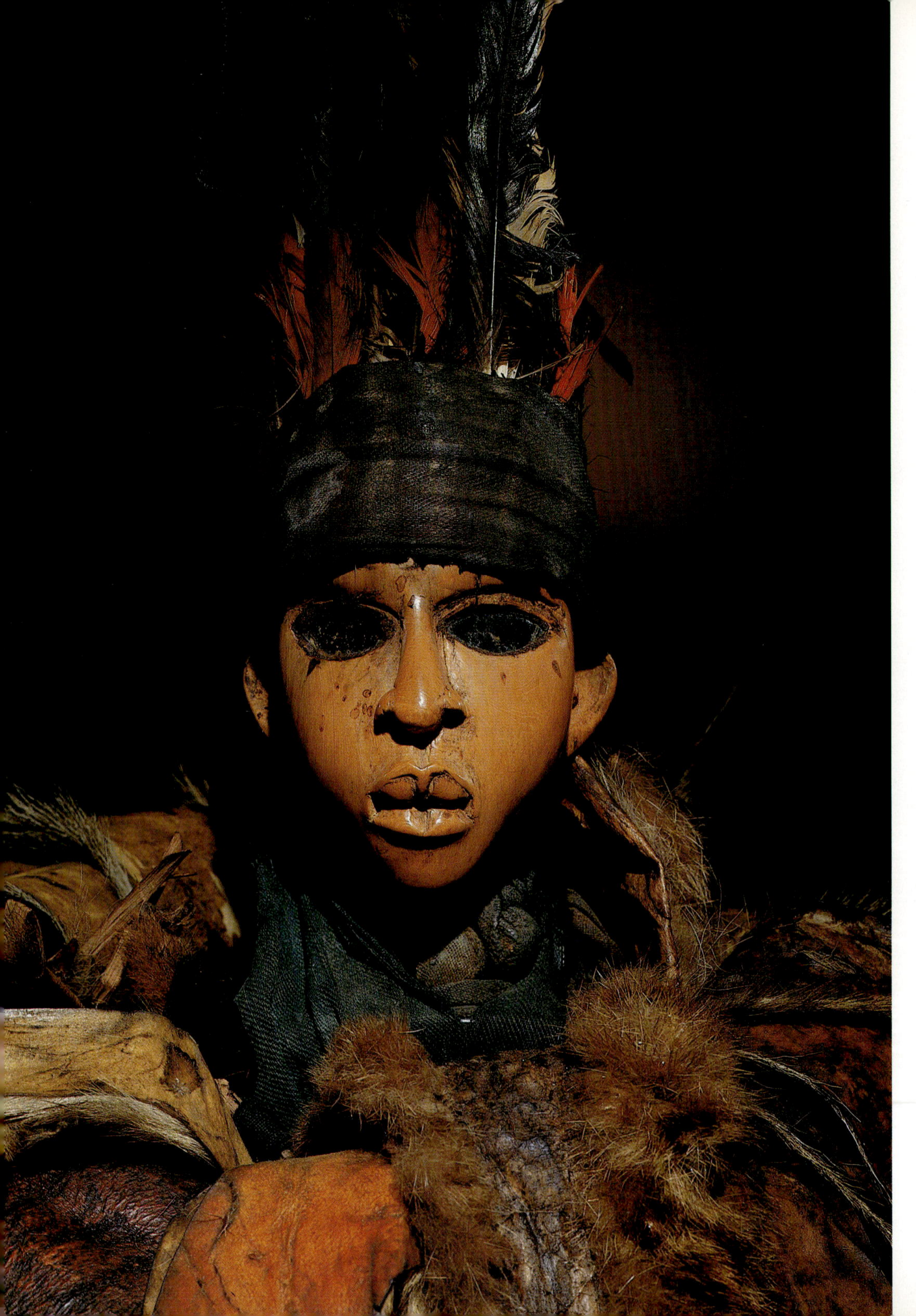

See page 294
Cat. No. 299

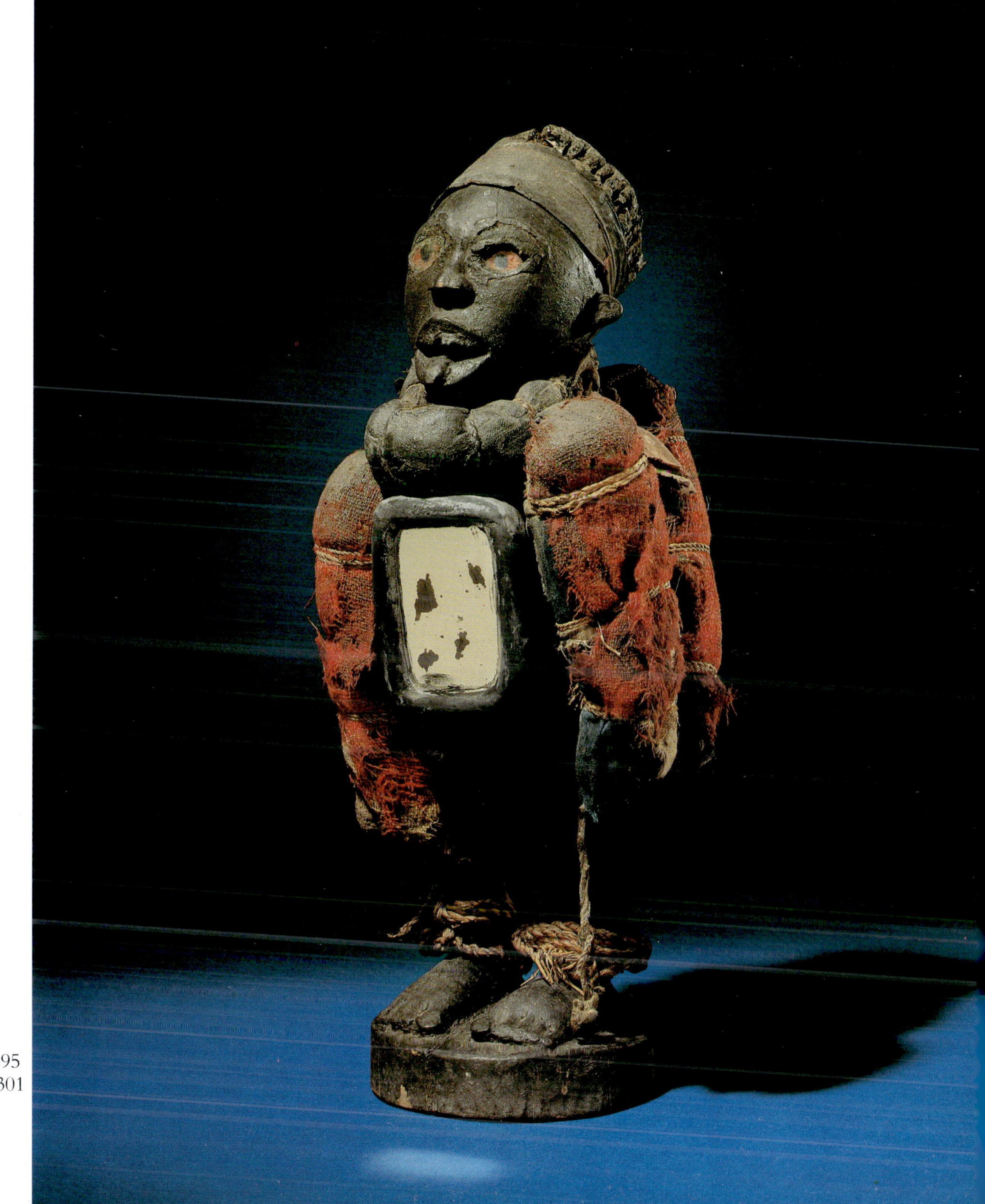

See page 295
Cat. No. 301

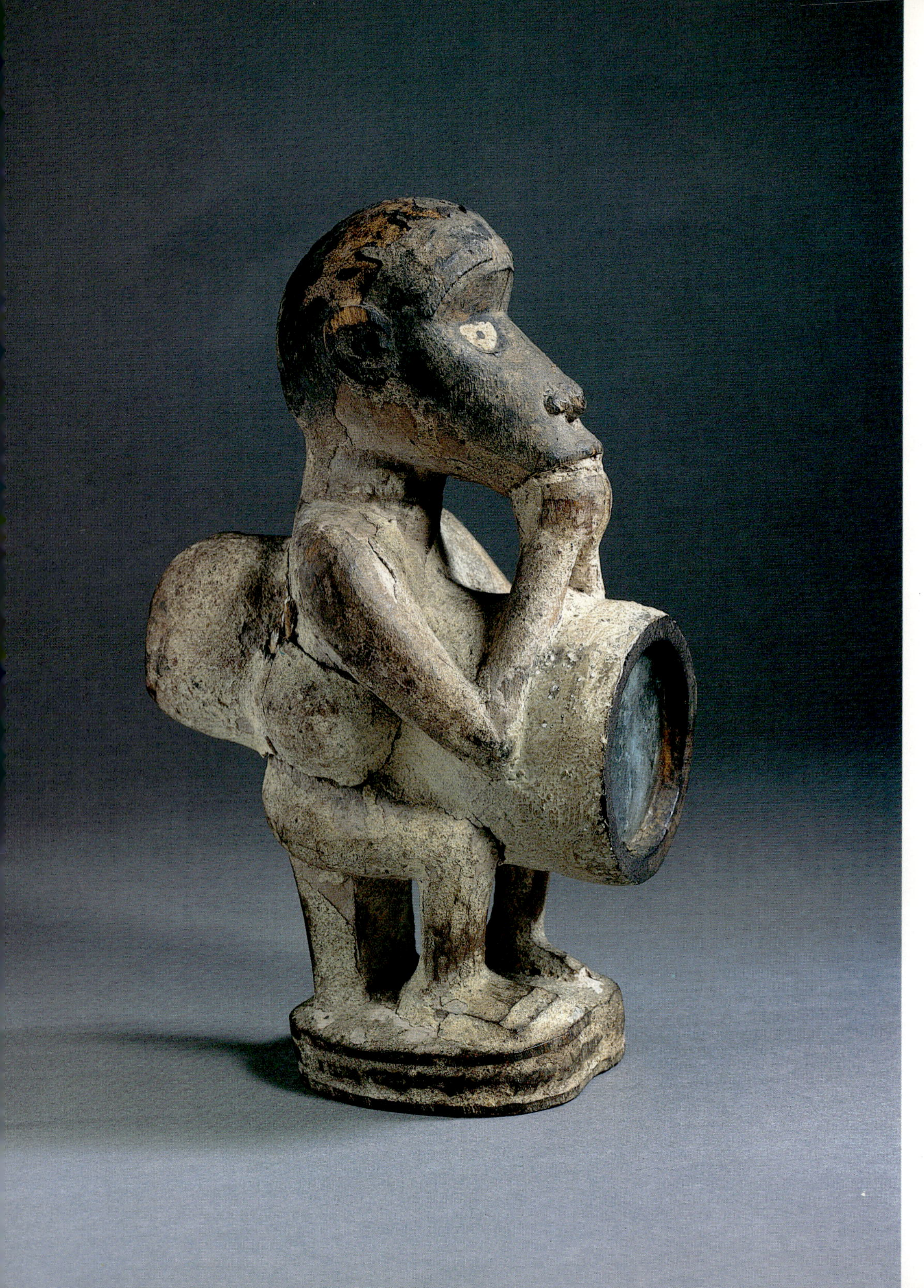

See page 299
Cat. No. 307

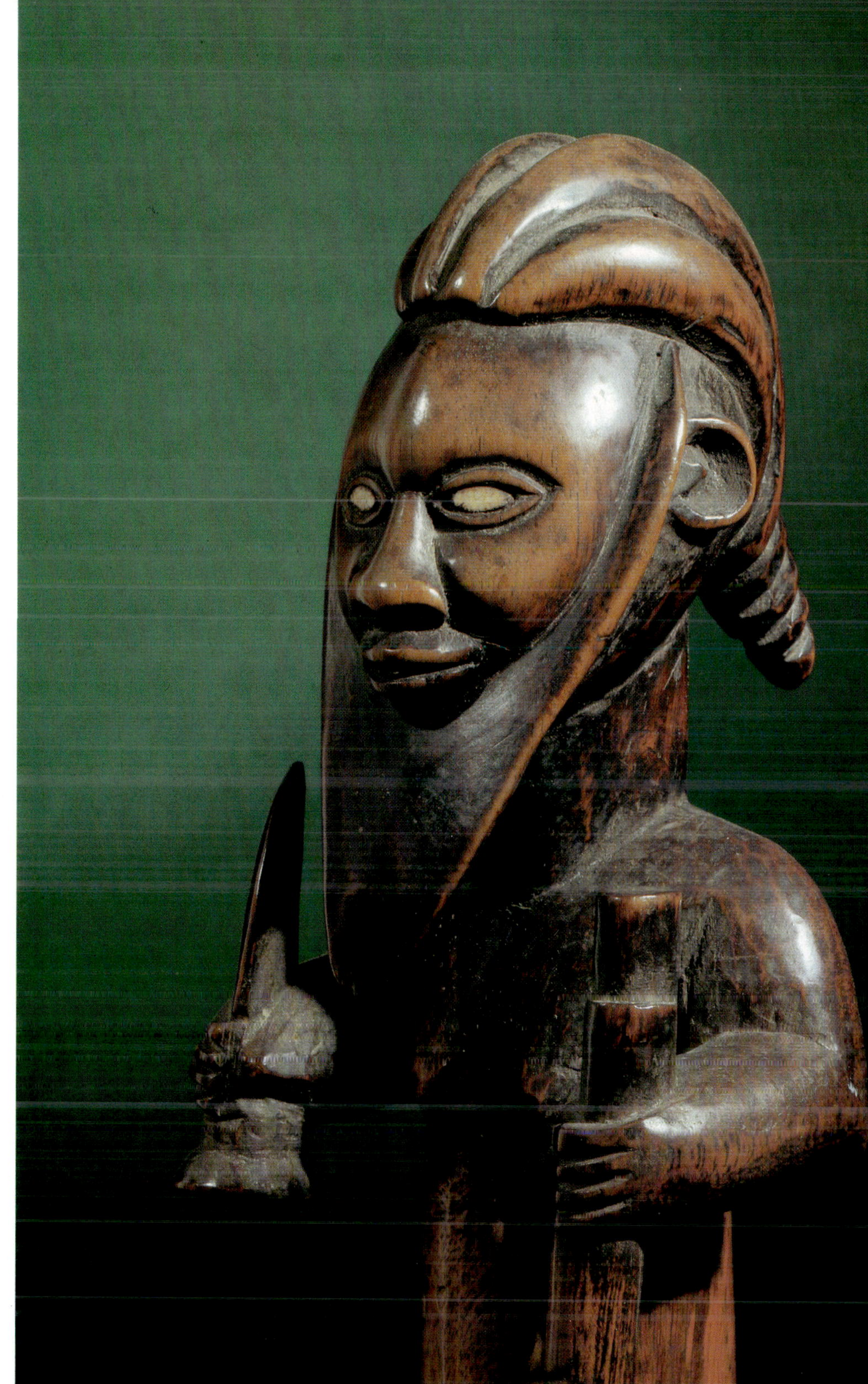

See page 306
Cat. No. 314

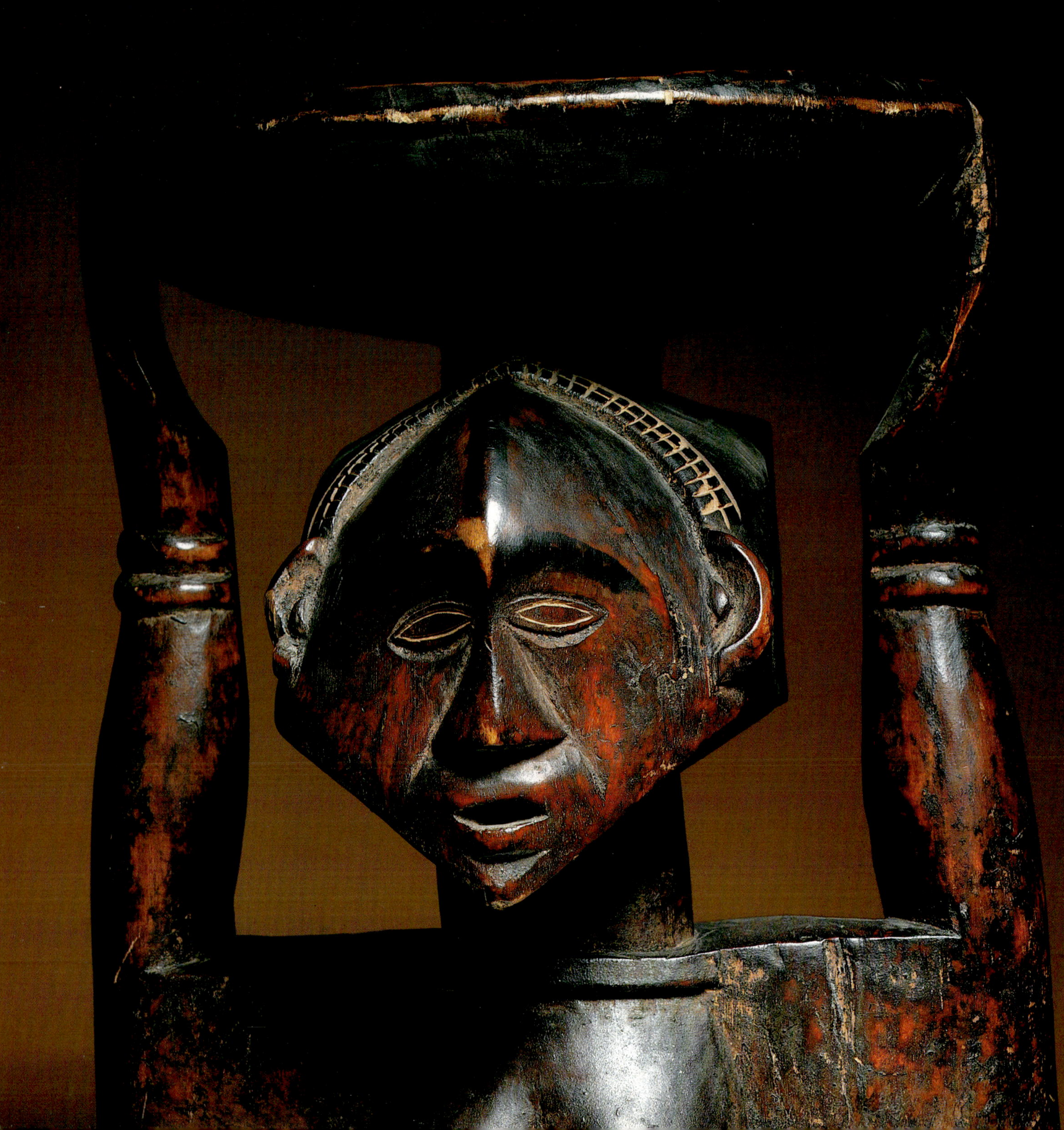

Page 274
See page 366
Cat. No. 384

Page 275
See page 317
Cat. No. 325

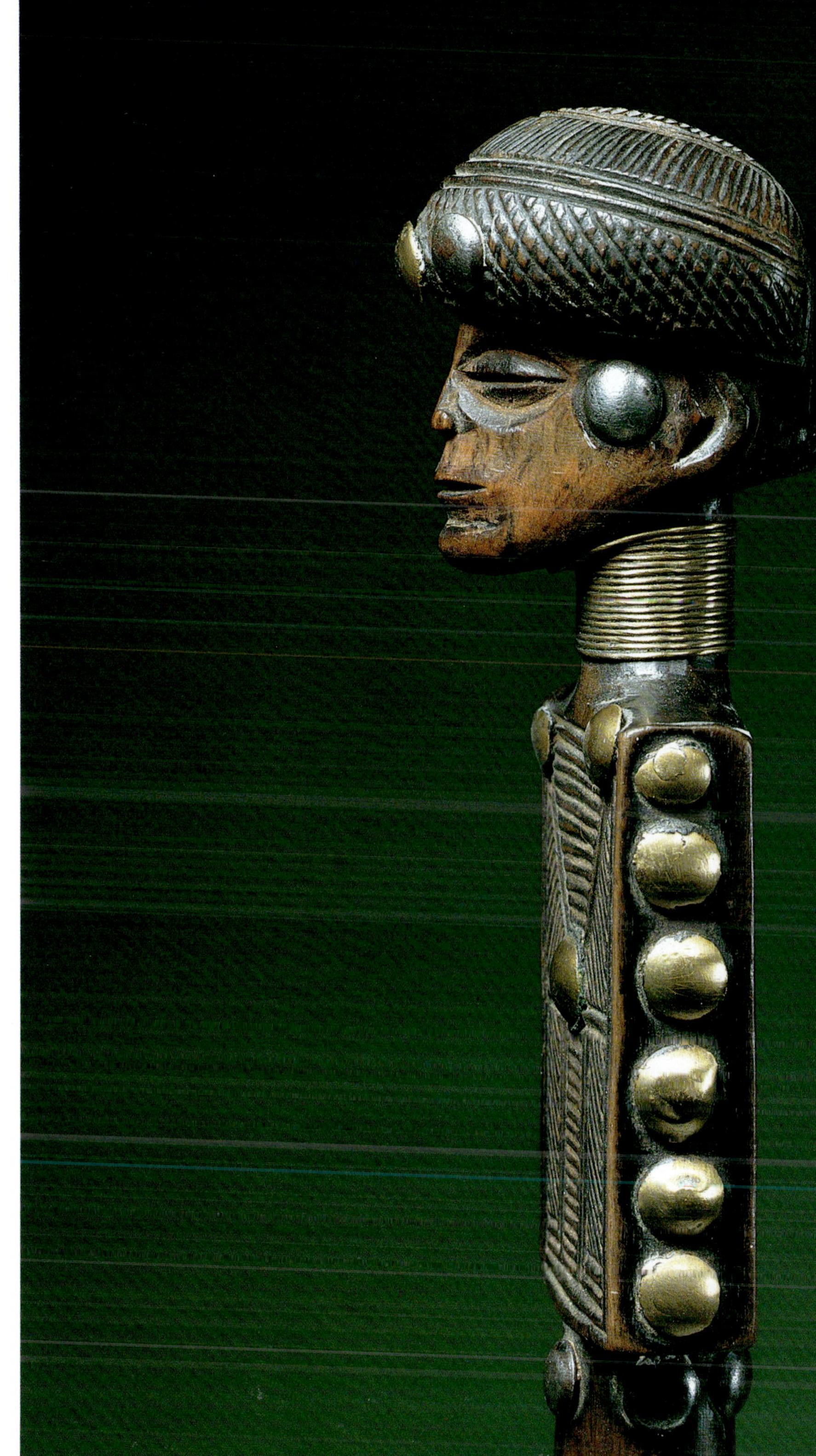

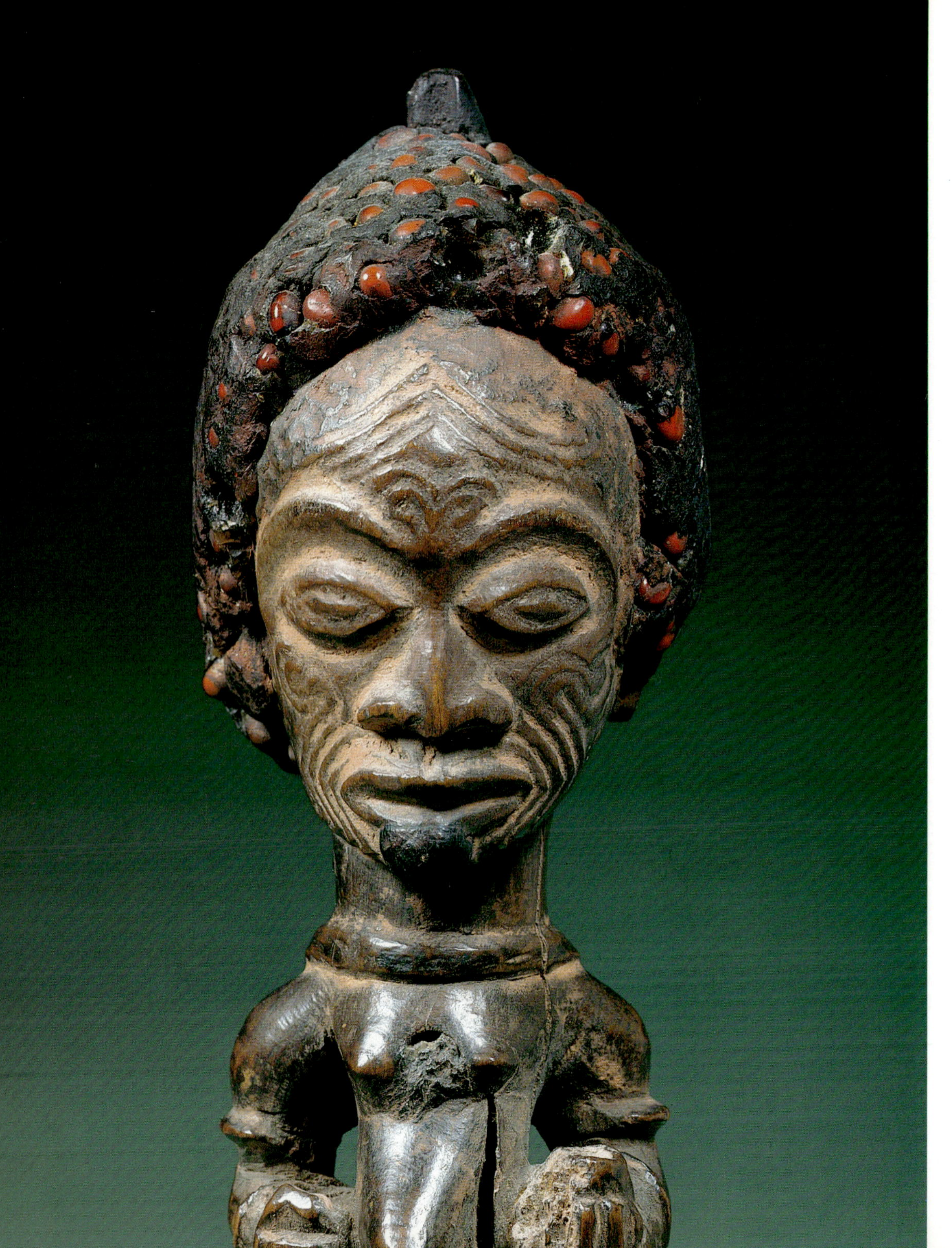

See page 343
Cat. No. 364

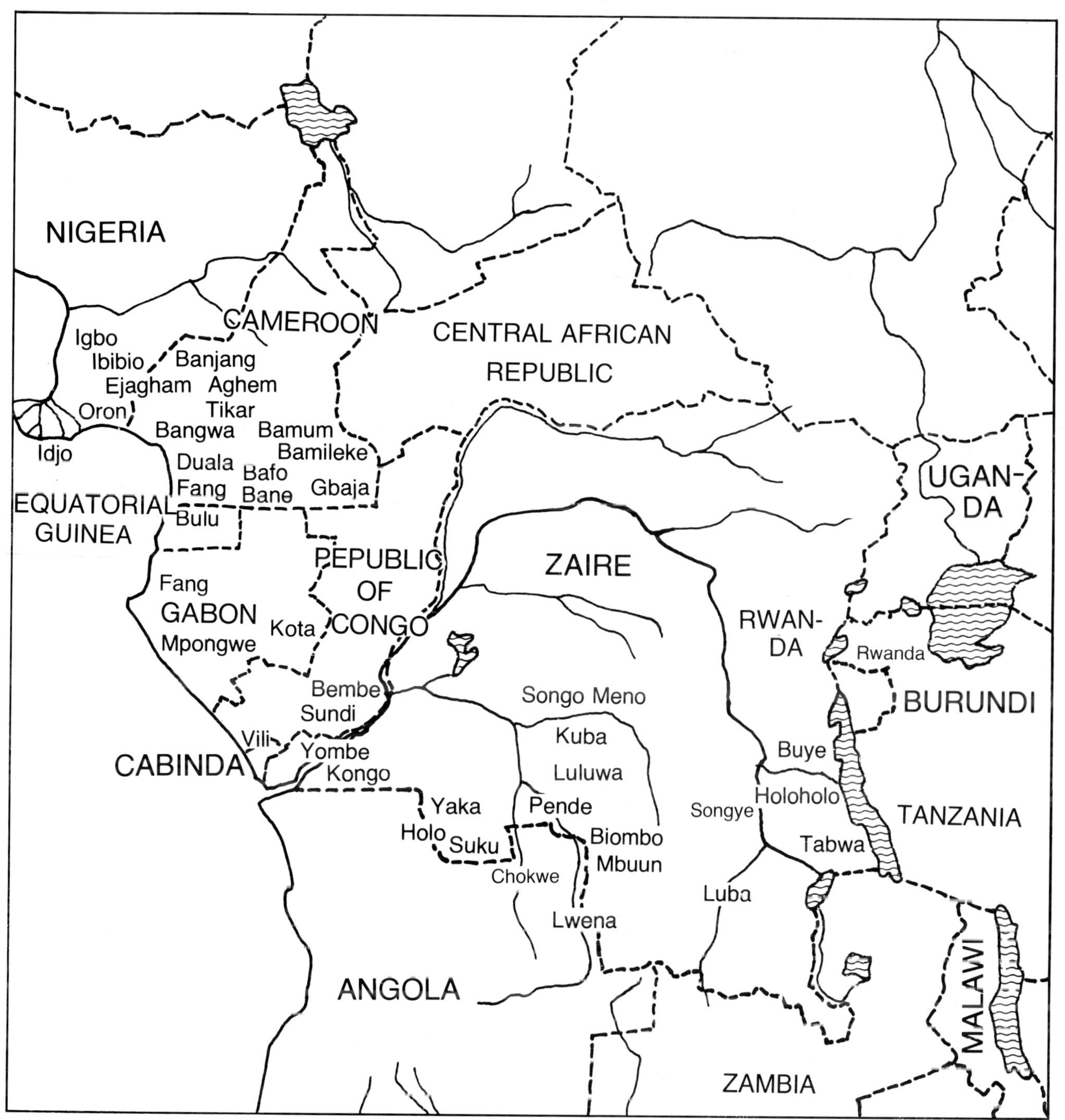
NIGERIA
CAMEROON
CENTRAL AFRICAN
REPUBLIC
Igbo
Ibibio
Banjang
Ejagham
Aghem
Oron
Tikar
Bangwa
Bamum
Bamileke
Idjo
Duala
Bafo
Fang
Bane
Gbaja
EQUATORIAL
GUINEA
Bulu
UGAN-
DA
REPUBLIC
OF
CONGO
ZAIRE
Fang
GABON
Mpongwe
Kota
RWAN-
DA
Rwanda
Bembe
Sundi
Songo Meno
BURUNDI
Kuba
Vili
Yombe
Kongo
CABINDA
Luluwa
Buye
Yaka
Pende
Songye
Holoholo
TANZANIA
Holo
Suku
Biombo
Mbuun
Chokwe
Tabwa
Luba
Lwena
MALAWI
ANGOLA
ZAMBIA

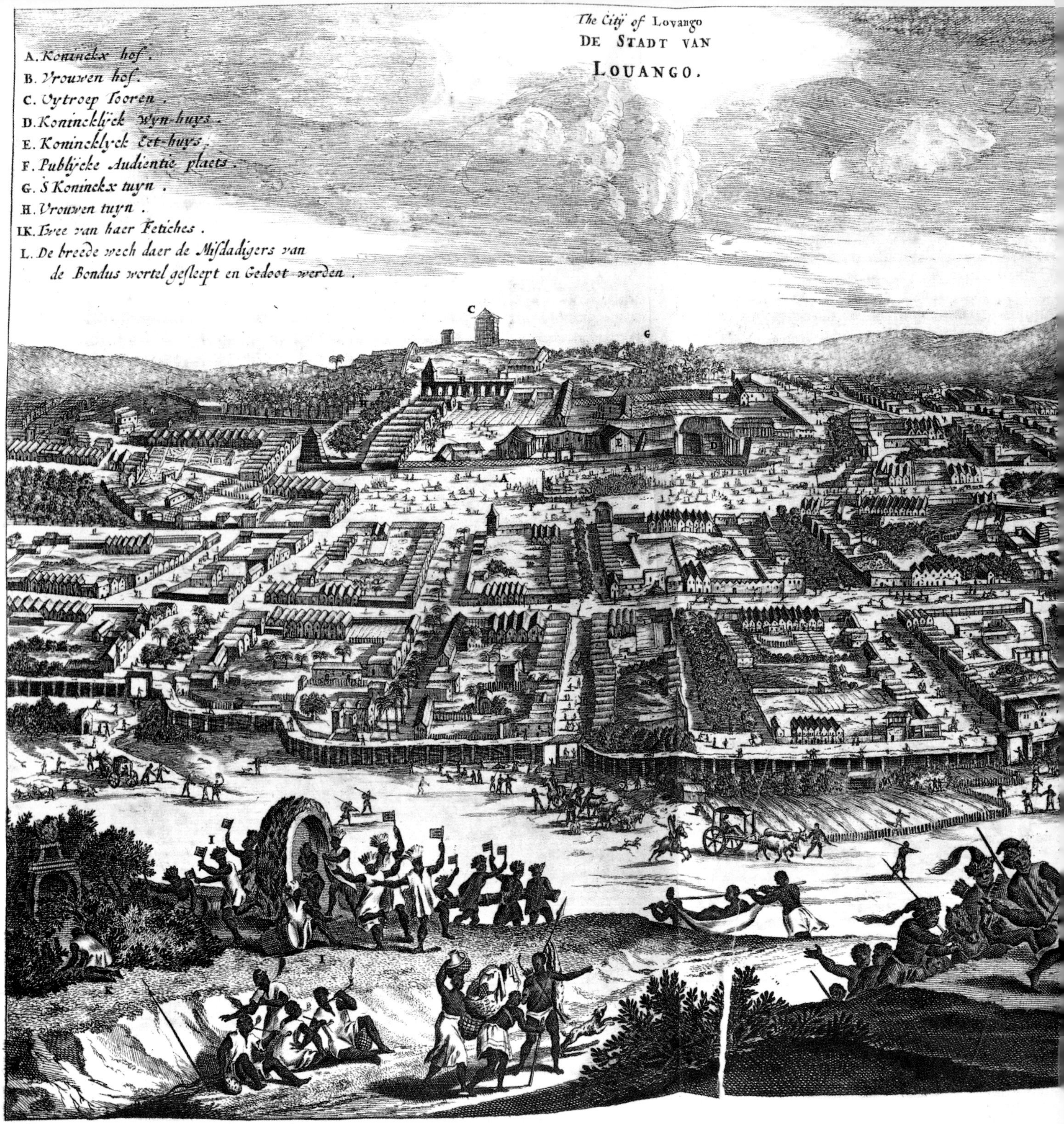

The City of Lovango

DE STADT VAN LOUANGO.

A. Koninckx hof.
B. Vrouwen hof.
C. Uytroep Tooren.
D. Konincklijck Wyn-huys.
E. Konincklyck Eet-huys.
F. Publijcke Audientie plaets.
G. 'S Koninckx tuyn.
H. Vrouwen tuyn.
IK. Twee van haer Fetiches.
L. De breede wech daer de Misdadigers van de Bondus wortel gesleept en Gedoot werden.

Kingdoms of Lower Zaire

When the first European seafarer, the Portuguese Diego Cao, reached the mouth of the Zaire River in 1483, he found a flourishing kingdom. Trade was established between this Congo realm and Portugal and soon developed into a complex system with economic, political, and cultural aspects. Thus began an experiment unique in the history of Afro-European relations which proved successful for two hundred years. The Congo kings sent their sons to be educated in Portugal, adopted Christianity, and supported the missionaries in building churches and schools. Ambassadors traveled between Portugal and the Congo. Numerous Europeans, among them many craftsmen—settled in the capital city Mbanzakongo (San Salvador) and at other important points in the kingdom, especially on the coast. An Afro-Portuguese culture with a patina of Christianity arose and enriched indigenous traditions with new ideas and new forms of expression.

The effects of this cultural exchange extended far beyond the borders of the Congo. From the sixteenth century on, a number of kingdoms—among them Loango, north of the mouth of the Zaire River—have been repeatedly mentioned as trading partners or allies of the Portuguese and, occasionally, of the Dutch as well. Dapper, who in 1670 compiled a history of what was then known of Africa, described the capital of Loango as a flourishing town equal in size to Amsterdam, with wide streets and an extensive palace compound. Ivory and slaves were by far the most important exports, but redwood, raffia plushes, and other products were also in demand.

This promising early attempt to establish regular contact between Europeans and Africans eventually foundered because the Portuguese government did little to curtail the activities of slave traders. The development of a Christian, or Christian-tinged, Kongo culture was thus interrupted, and even the missionary work had to be started afresh in the nineteenth century.

Lit.: O. Dapper 1670, pp. 506, 508ff.; D. Westermann 1952, pp. 390-406.

294 Square cloth with fringe, raffia pile cloth. Zaire, Zaire estuary.

In no other part of old Africa did textile arts attain such a degree of perfection as in the coastal zones north and south of the Zaire estuary. As far back as the sixteenth century, Portuguese, Dutch, and Italian reports spoke admiringly of the beauty and technical perfection of the various types of patterned fabrics woven from raffia fibers. Their suppleness was achieved by soaking the fabric in water, then kneading and beating it. Embroidered pile cloths were especially treasured (for an explanation of the technique, see p. 340). These were made in pillow-size pieces and sewn together to make such articles as blankets, clothing—in the sixteenth and seventeenth centuries, several Catholic missionaries possessed vestments of Kongo pile cloths—and shrouds. They also served as currency. The coastal population of Loango and the Congo carried on a lively trade in these fabrics. In Loango, weaving was for a time one of the most lucrative trade items: according to a report of 1611, twelve thousand to fifteen thousand pieces of first quality and forty thousand to fifty thousand pieces of medium quality were produced there annually. The Portuguese purchased these in exchange for salt, shells, and ornaments. Further

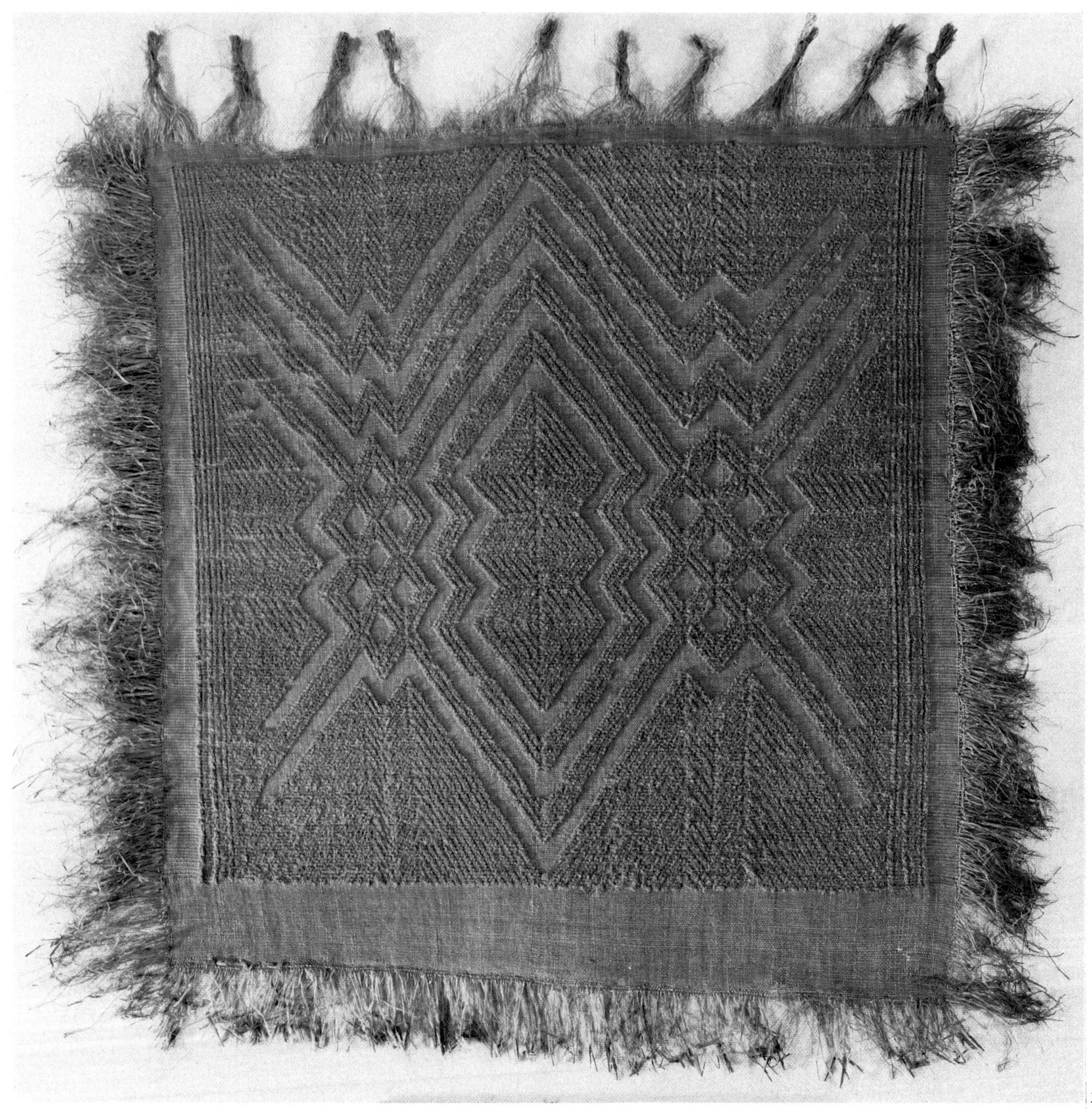
294

south, in Angola, they bartered such textiles for slaves, who were then sold at a considerable profit in Portugal or South America.

Few specimens of these once so famous west-coast pile cloths have survived. In the nineteenth century they were manufactured only in the Kuba area, deep in the interior of the continent. Thus the antique piece shown has a special documentary significance: it comes from the Zaire estuary region and reached Europe sometime before 1857, probably as early as the eighteenth century.

Measurements: 42 x 41 cm. No.895
Acquired from the Royal Bavarian Ethnographic Collection (Collection Prince Leuchtenberg 1858)

Lit.: E. Bassani 1977b, p. 176; O. Dapper 1670, pp. 506, 512; A. Stritzl 1971, pp. 37-48; J. Vansina 1978, pp. 220, 21.

Ivory Carvings for Europeans (295-297)

In the nineteenth century a professional ivory-carving industry developed on the lower Zaire. Its products—richly carved blowing horns, staff handles, and similar objects of elephant tusk or rhinoceros horn—were made for sale to Europeans. This tourist-souvenir industry was, however, rooted in traditional themes and forms. Human beings and animals, frequently arranged in rows that wind spirally or wrap around the longitudinal axis of the tusk, were the most important motifs of the figurative carvings. The representations reflect the artist's efforts to come to terms with the cultural changes of his time. Africans, for instance, recognizable by their precisely depicted hair, do not appear in traditional garb but often in grotesque combinations of wraparound skirt and raffia cap with European jacket and similar articles. Their faces usually appear in profile. They are

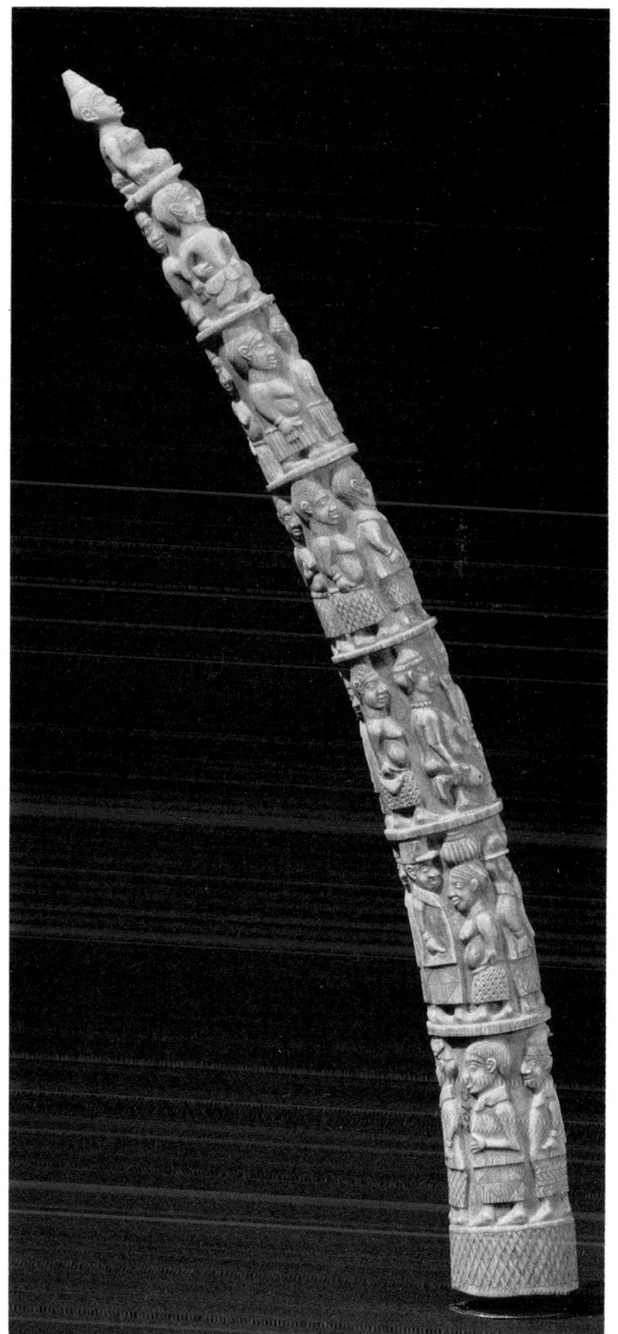

295

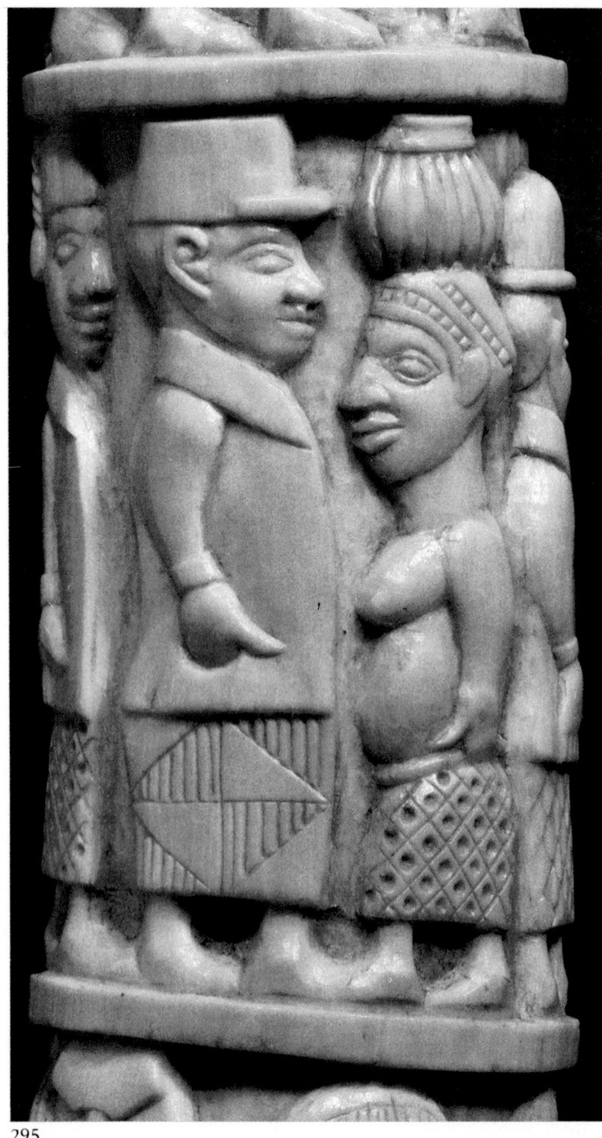
295

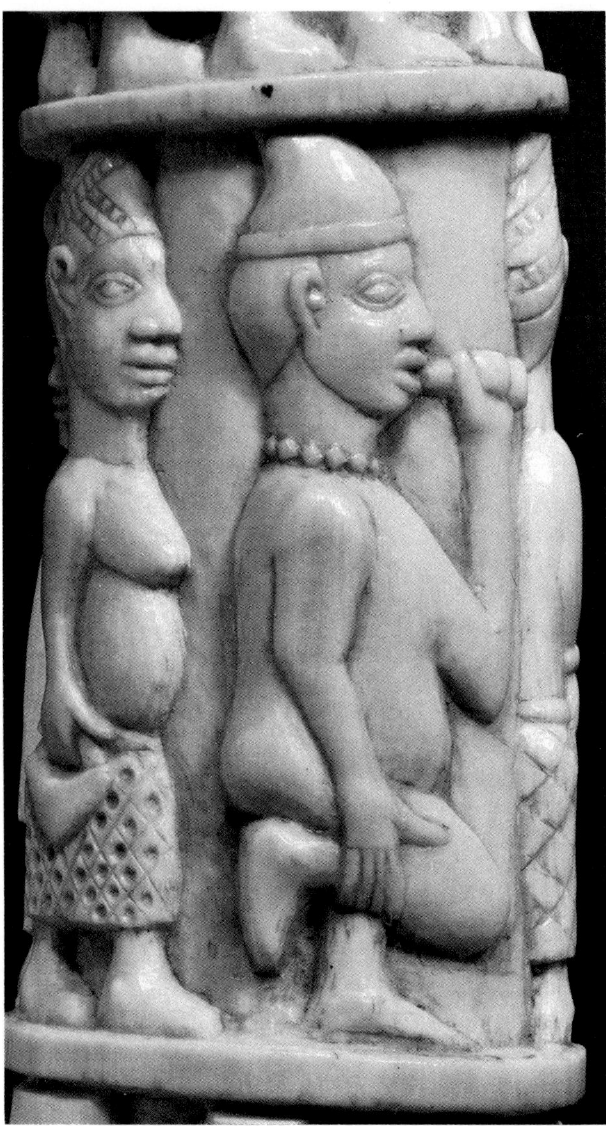
295

schematized and expressionless, but occasionally characterized by a naive striving for exactness. As a consequence, artists adopted the curious habit of occasionally suggesting the second eye or the hidden half of the face at the edge of the profile. Artists' tools were very simple. According to Bastian, who mentions the ivory craft center Chiluango (in Cabinda), sharpened nails served as carving tools.

Lit.: A. Bastian 1874, p. 156; P. Gussfeldt 1875a, pp. 195ff., 1875b, pp. 142ff.

295 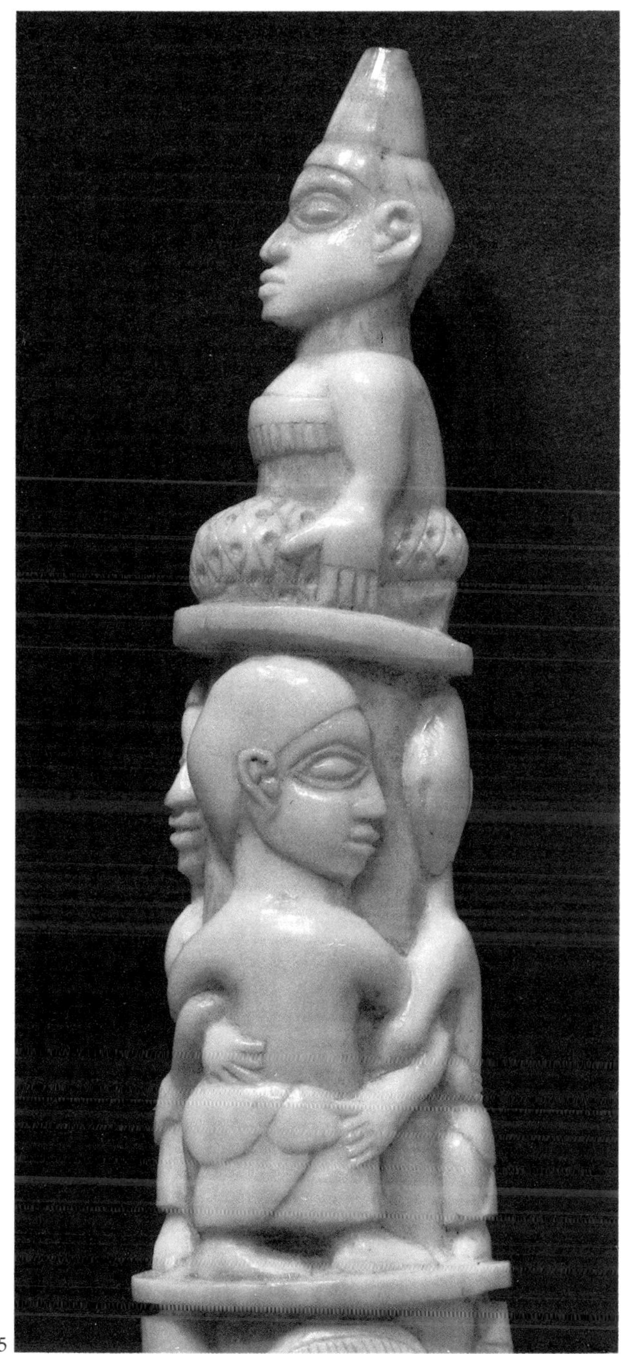

295 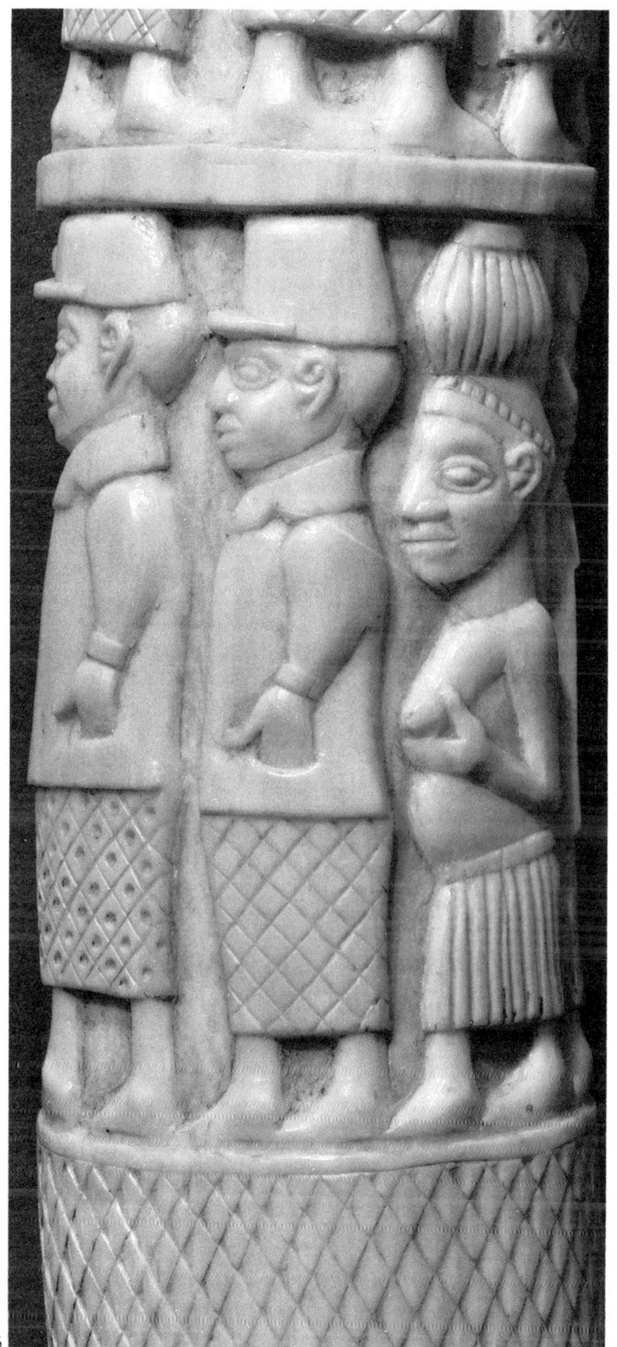

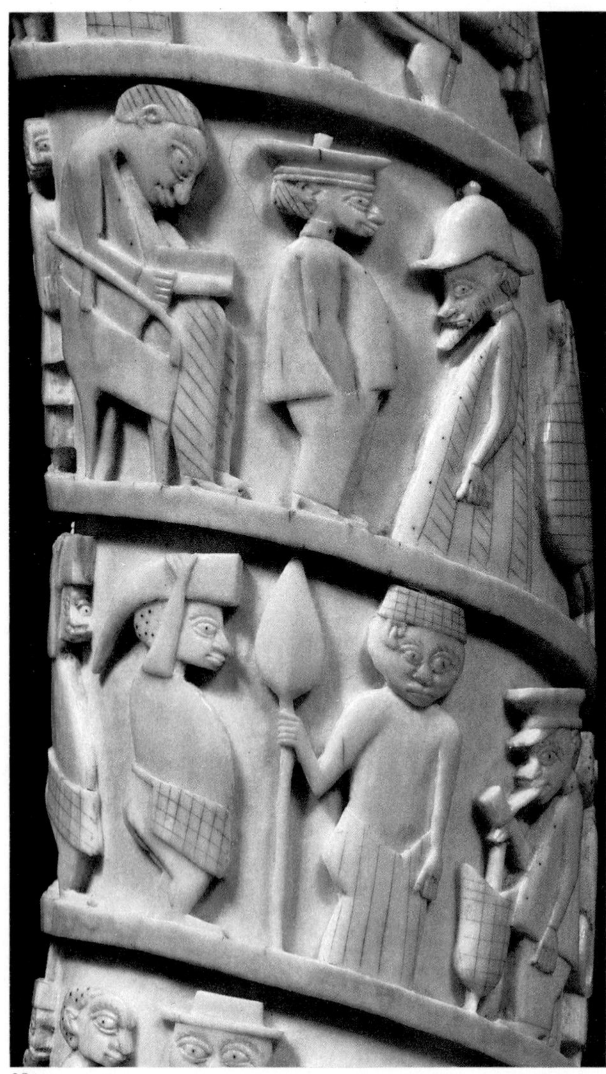
296

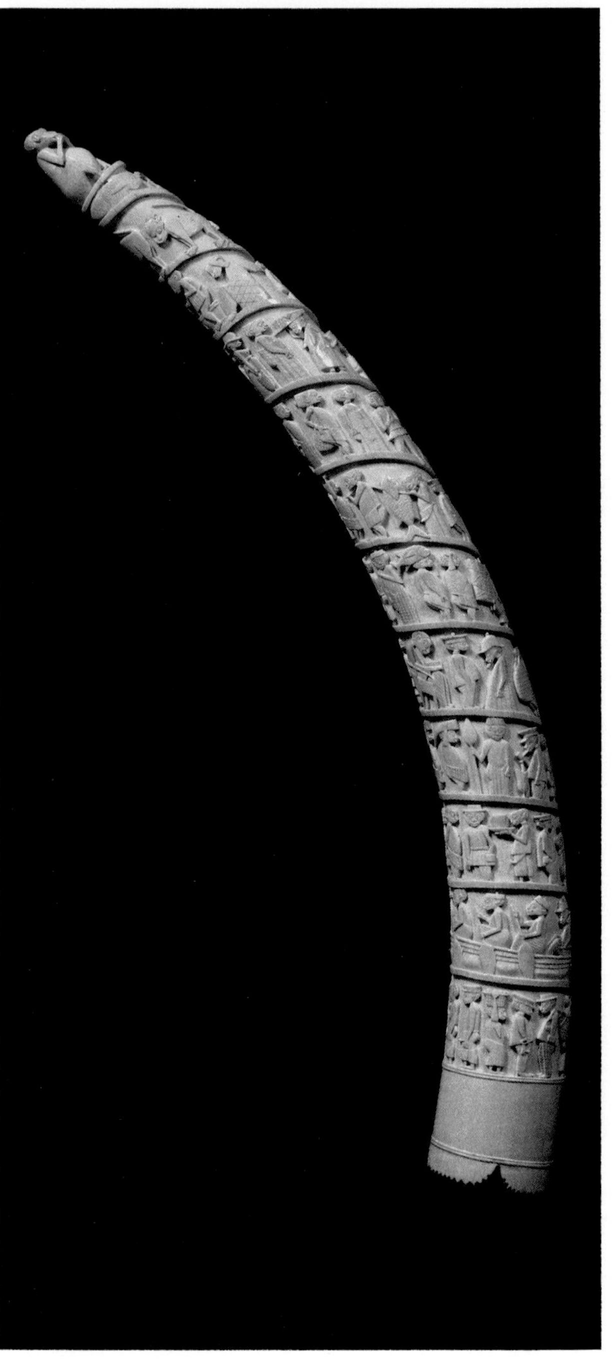
296

295 Elephant tusk carved in relief.
Cabinda (?), Loango (?).

The entire surface of this tusk is divided into six panels, seven if the figure on the tip is included, arranged one on top of the other. The edges of the figures are carefully rounded. Prominent Africans are represented in dress corresponding to fashions

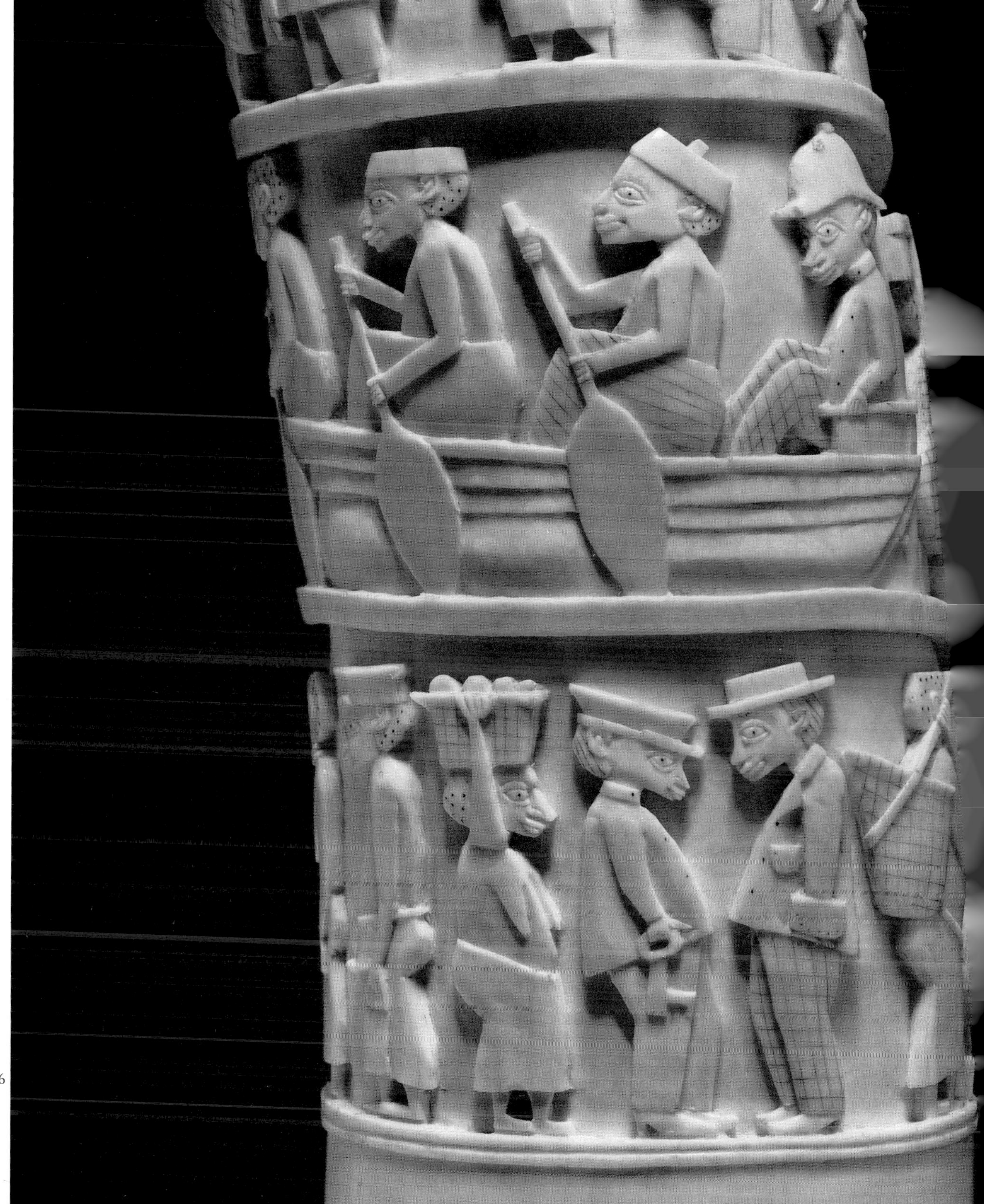

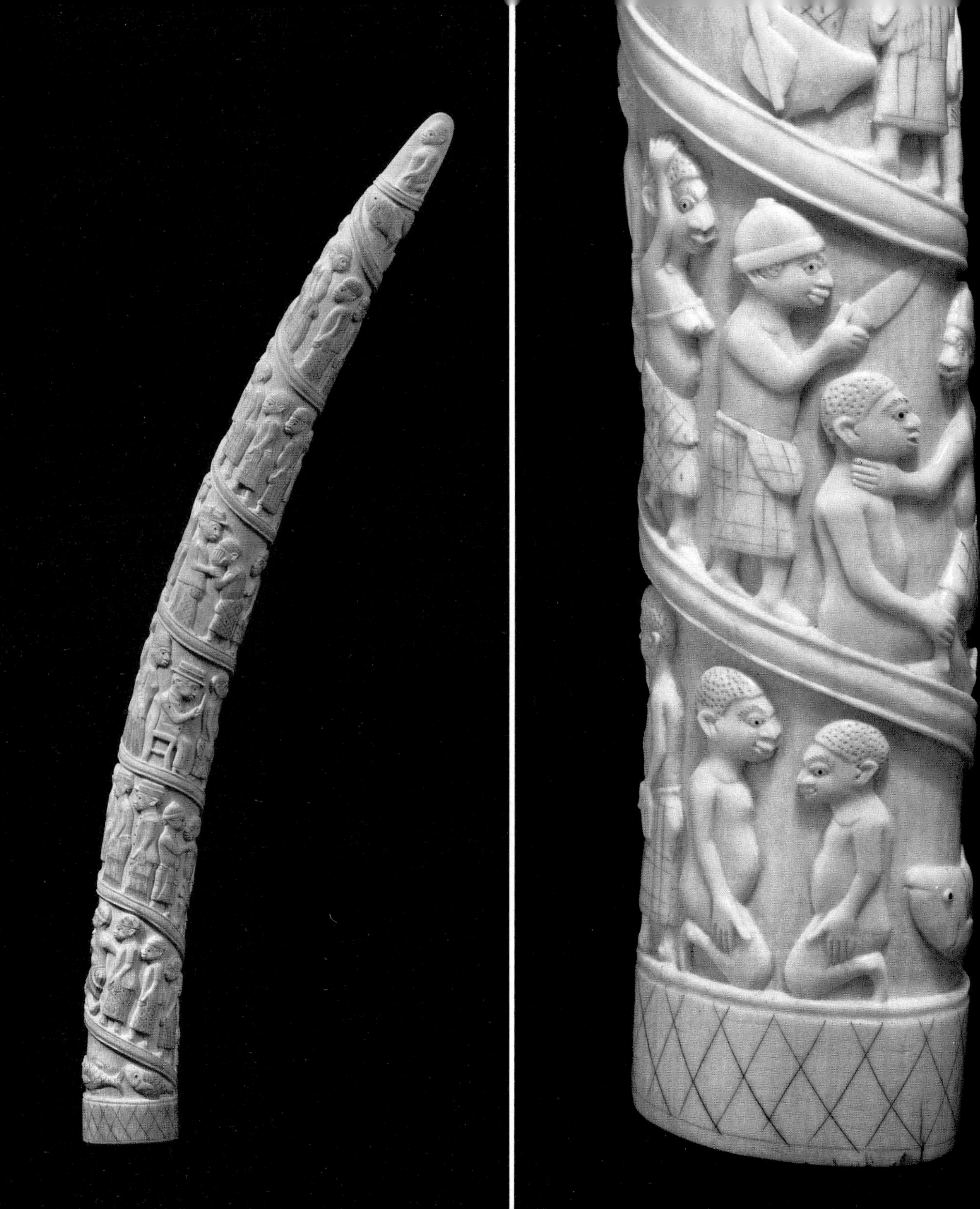

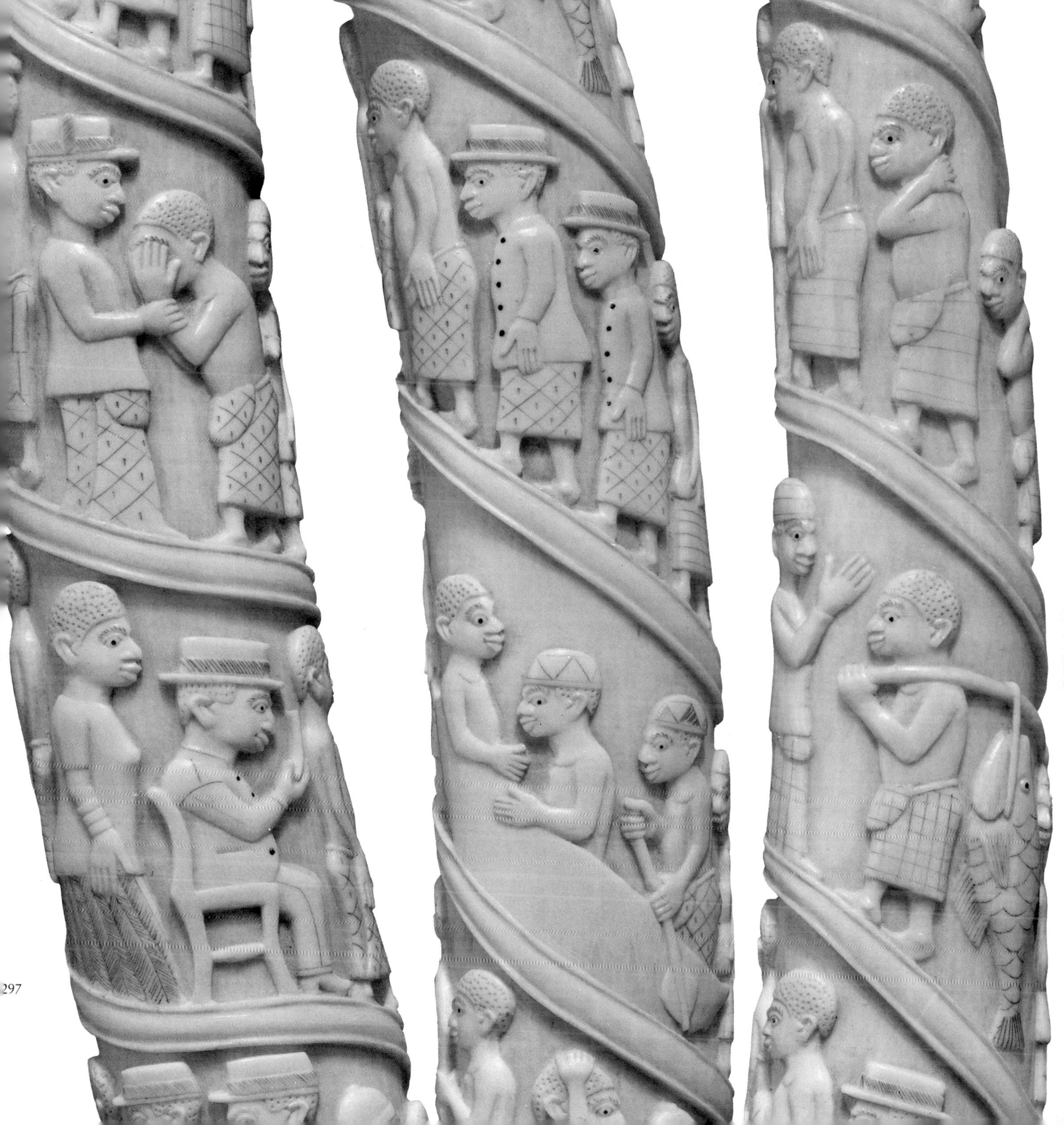

297

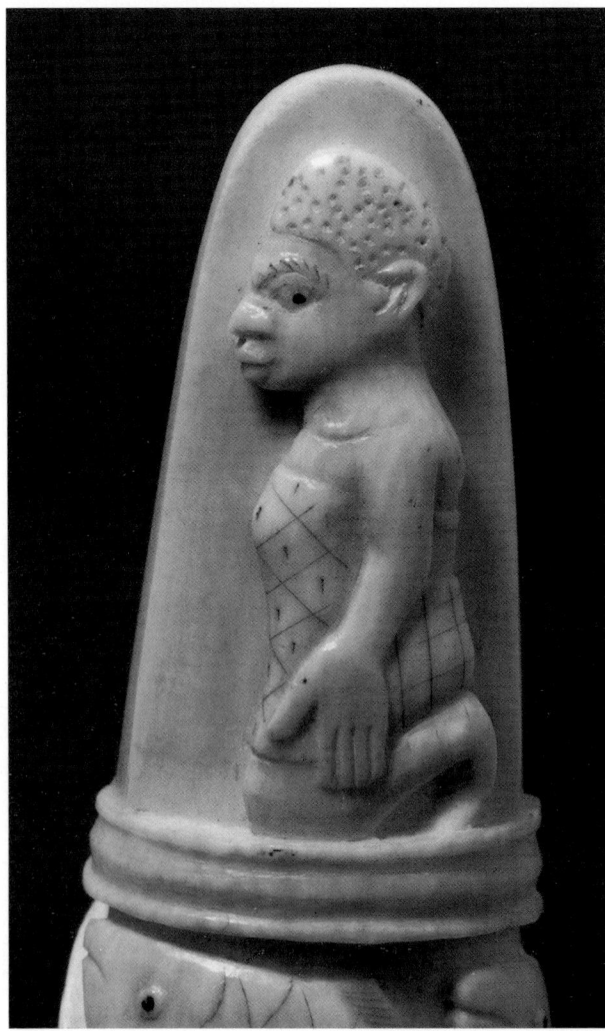
297

popular on the coast, according to travel books, at the end of the nineteenth century: brightly colored wraparound cloths, men's jackets (mostly English), and a multitude of foreign headcoverings (the fez, bowler, and peaked cap among them). The three-dimensional kneeling figure of the king at the top of the tusk, however, wears traditional regalia: raffia-fiber cap (*ngola type*) and pectoral band. The king depicted in the third row can also be recognized by his *ngola* cap.

The king's necklace of unusually large beads is a sign of his wealth, as is the liquor flask, undoubtedly acquired from European merchants, from which he is taking a hearty swig. Some of the female figures wear traditional raffia-fiber skirts, artistic upswept coiffures, and patterned head coverings (see also No. 310). This piece was made sometime before 1859 and is, we believe, the oldest among the ivory carvings from the lower Zaire shown here.

Length 40.3 cm. (end to end) 3702
Acquired from Schilling (before 1859)

296 Elephant tusk with relief, ivory.
Cabinda (?), Loango (?).

The surface of this piece is divided into twelve spiral registers, thirteen including the figure at the tip. All the figures except five are in profile, with sharply edged contours. Africans are easily distinguished from Europeans, for the formers' hair, like the eyes and the clothing buttons, are traced with graphite. Colonial officials, travelers, traders, missionaries, and a few elegant ladies, all dressed in turn-of-the-century fashion, are recognizable. The image of a European seated in his chair reading a book also appears in No. 297. The many small scenic depictions include a trip in a boat, various ways of carrying loads (elephant tusks among them), and a European lady with her hand extended to be kissed. At the tip is the three-dimensional figure of a monkey (holding a maize cob?).

Length 68.5 cm. (end to end) 14-32-3
Acquired from Oriola 1914

297 Carved elephant tusk, ivory.
Cabinda (?), Loango (?).
(illustrated on pages 286-88)

Outstanding craftsmanship distinguishes these nine spiral registers. All details are carefully executed, the edges of the relief are rounded, the faces are full of expression. Eyes and dress buttons are indicated by tacks, fabric patterns and eyebrows are traced with graphite. All the scenes seem to be associated with the royal court: slaves kneel at the bottom; in an execution scene above them the executioner wears a cap with brim (?), and behind him stands the queen, a pectoral band indicating her status, her hands raised in a plaintive gesture. The single European sitting on a chair reading (see also No. 296) is the only figure wearing shoes. (Africans, on the whole, were adverse to imitating Europeans in the wearing of shoes.) The scenes with boat and carriers, including that of the men with the large fish, recall those of No. 296.

Length 42 cm. 93.449
Acquired from F. Martin 1893

298 Female figure, ivory.
Zaire, Woyo.

This kneeling female figure, naked except for broad bracelets, wears the embroidered raffia cap of the *mpu mpembe* type that is the traditional sign of high social rank. She holds a ceremonial knife that shows her to be a queen, for the queen was guardian of this status symbol which was considered her special insignia. Among the Woyo, as among many other peoples of the Zaire region, the power of the queen was considerable: she had the right, for example, to settle all affairs of government in the absence of the king.

Height 8 cm. 14-57-6
Acquired from Brummer 1914

Lit.: F. Neyt 1981, p. 86; Z. Volavkova 1982, pp. 52-59.

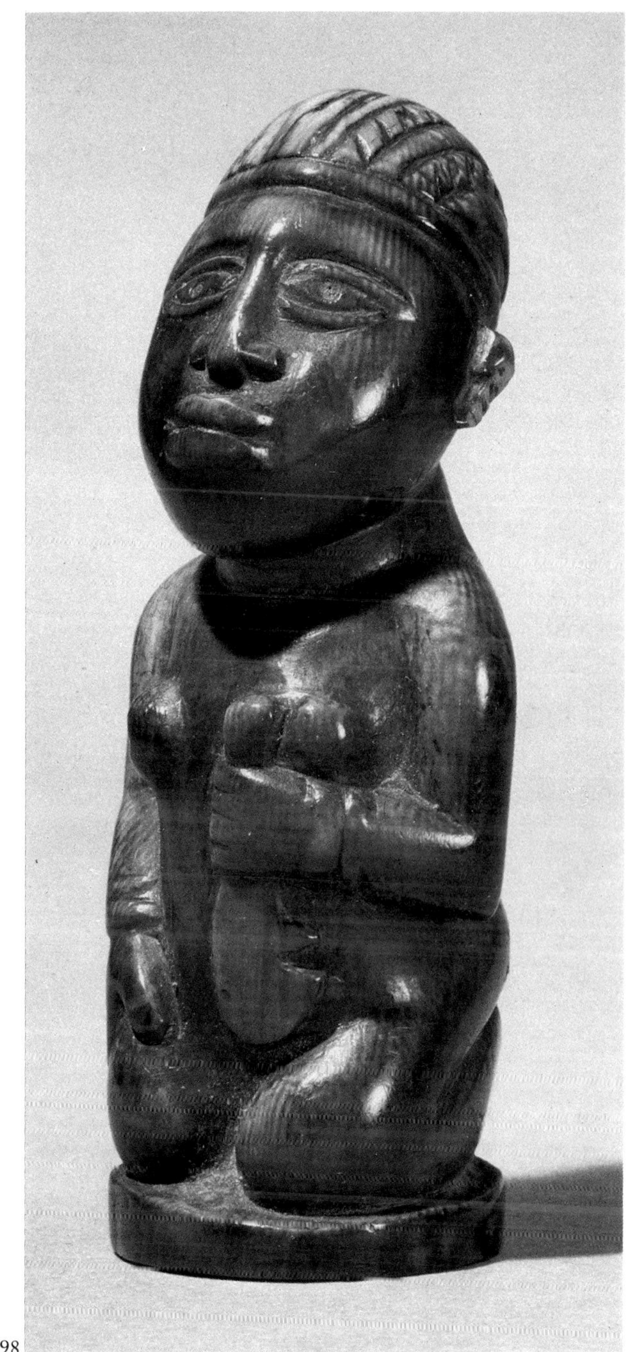

298

Lower Zaire Power Figures with Mirrors and Nails

One of the most important groups in the Munich collection is that of magical figures, often equipped with bits of mirror *(nduda)* or spiked with nails *(nkondi),* from the region of present-day Zaire. The pieces shown, all acquired in Mayombe in 1893 by the Bavarian agronomist Martin, are of excellent quality and are typical of figurative sculpture produced exclusively in the lower Zaire region. This sculpture is characterized by the foreign matter, partly organic, partly inorganic, added to the wood, the basic material.

The works' creation was undertaken in two stages. The artist first carved the figure, which the ritual specialist *(nganga)* then furnished with certain substances considered magically effective. The most potent magical substances were placed in a boxlike hollow or a lump in or on the figure's abdomen, chest, back, or head and sealed in with a mirror. The object was then considered to be "charged," and its stored magical power *(nkisi)* could be activated by means of spells or certain other manipulations. One of these activating techniques was "waking" the *nkisi* by driving strong nails into the wooden figure.

Information about the function of these figures is fragmentary. The smaller ones presumably were owned by chiefs or village priests, and perhaps also by private individuals, while the larger pieces, which reach a height of some 100 centimeters, were described in early reports as "village fetishes." (The term "fetish," from the Portuguese *feitico,* "product," is no longer current in ethnology.) The figures themselves were not revered. Upon proving ineffective a figure was either thrown away or returned to the ritual specialist. The latter, after renewing its magic, might sell the figure to another client.

Apparently each figure had its own special functions: warding off sorcerers and thieves, neutralizing misfortune, healing illness, and confirming oaths were among the most important. There was, perhaps, a link between their defensive functions and the mirrors found on most figures. Some researchers are of the opinion that the evil spirit or malevolent human could be driven away by the sight of his own face; others believe that the mirror could retain the image of the evildoer so that he could later be destroyed by the figure's potent magical substances.

The figures are mostly male, but there are a few female ones, and some animals. The carver devoted the greatest care to human facial features, and in some cases created masterpieces of realism. This was especially true when a threatening attitude—wide-open, staring eyes, and bared teeth in an open mouth—was employed as an additional means of averting evil. The body, often covered with skin, fabric, and feathers, was frequently less carefully depicted.

Some scholars feel that this type of art was based on Christian models. Images such as that of St. Sebastian pierced by arrows may have inspired the "nail fetishes." Reliquaries in human form may have influenced the boxlike hollow for magical substances in the figure's chest. There is no proof for this hypothesis, however, and in contradiction to it is the fact that magical "nailing" was most probably practiced with wooden pegs long before European iron nails were imported. Nevertheless, the area of distribution of these figures is almost identical to that most influenced by the very successful Christian missions of the sixteenth and seventeenth centuries.

Lit.: H. v. Geluwe, in J. Fry 1978, pp. 153-62; W. Hirschberg 1972, pp. 107-15; D. G. Jongmans 1962, pp. 50-62; R. Lehuard 1980, pp. 10, 12, 139-81; J. M. Janzen & W. McGaffey 1974, pp. 87-89; J. Maes 1930, pp. 347-59, 1935, Pl. X; F. Martin 1893, pp. 26-32; H. Palme 1976, pp. 154-82; E. Pechuel-Loesche 1907, pp. 347ff.; R. F. Thompson 1978, pp. 212, 13; Z. Volavkova 1972, pp. 52-59; J. Zwernemann 1961, pp. 15-32.

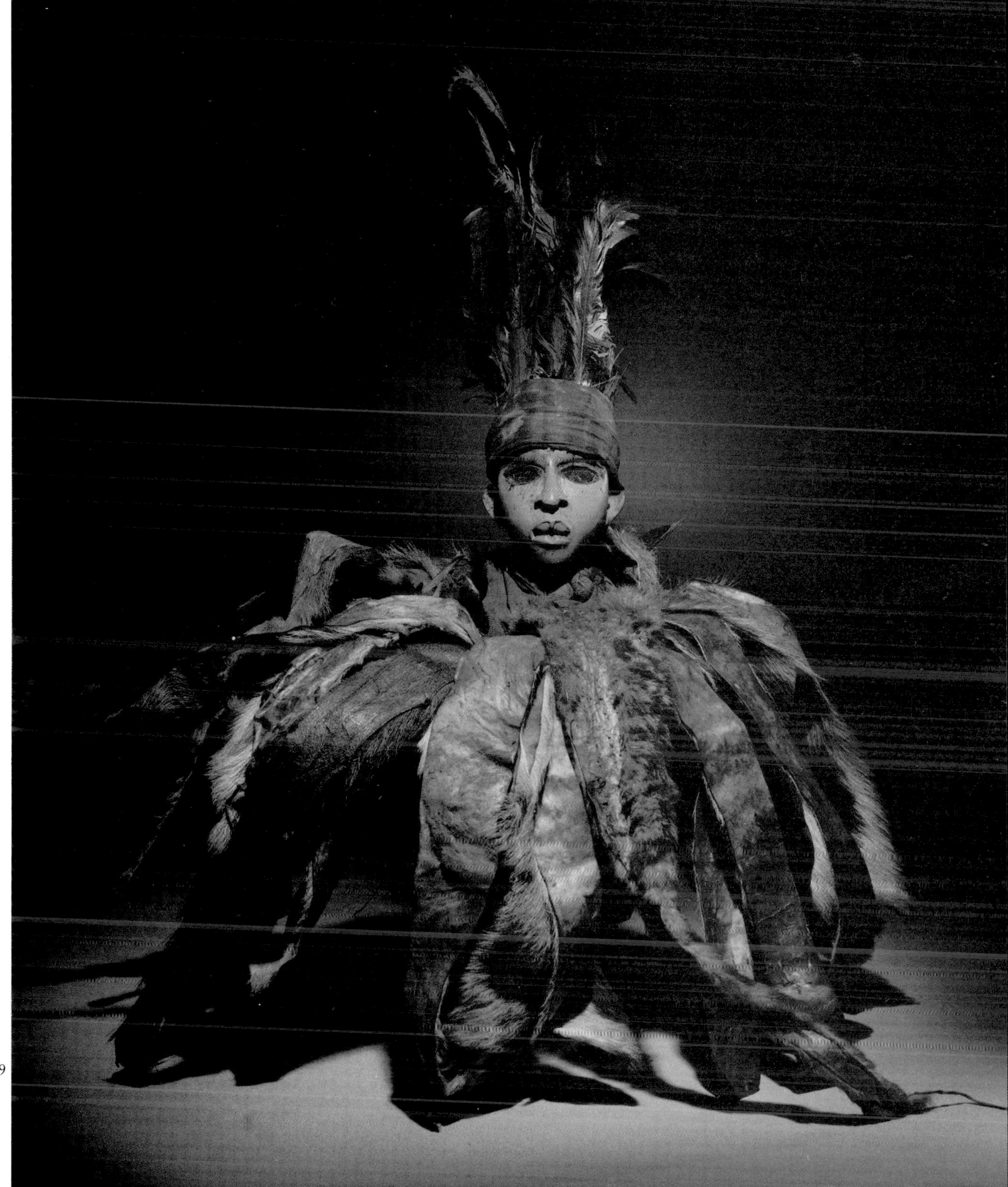

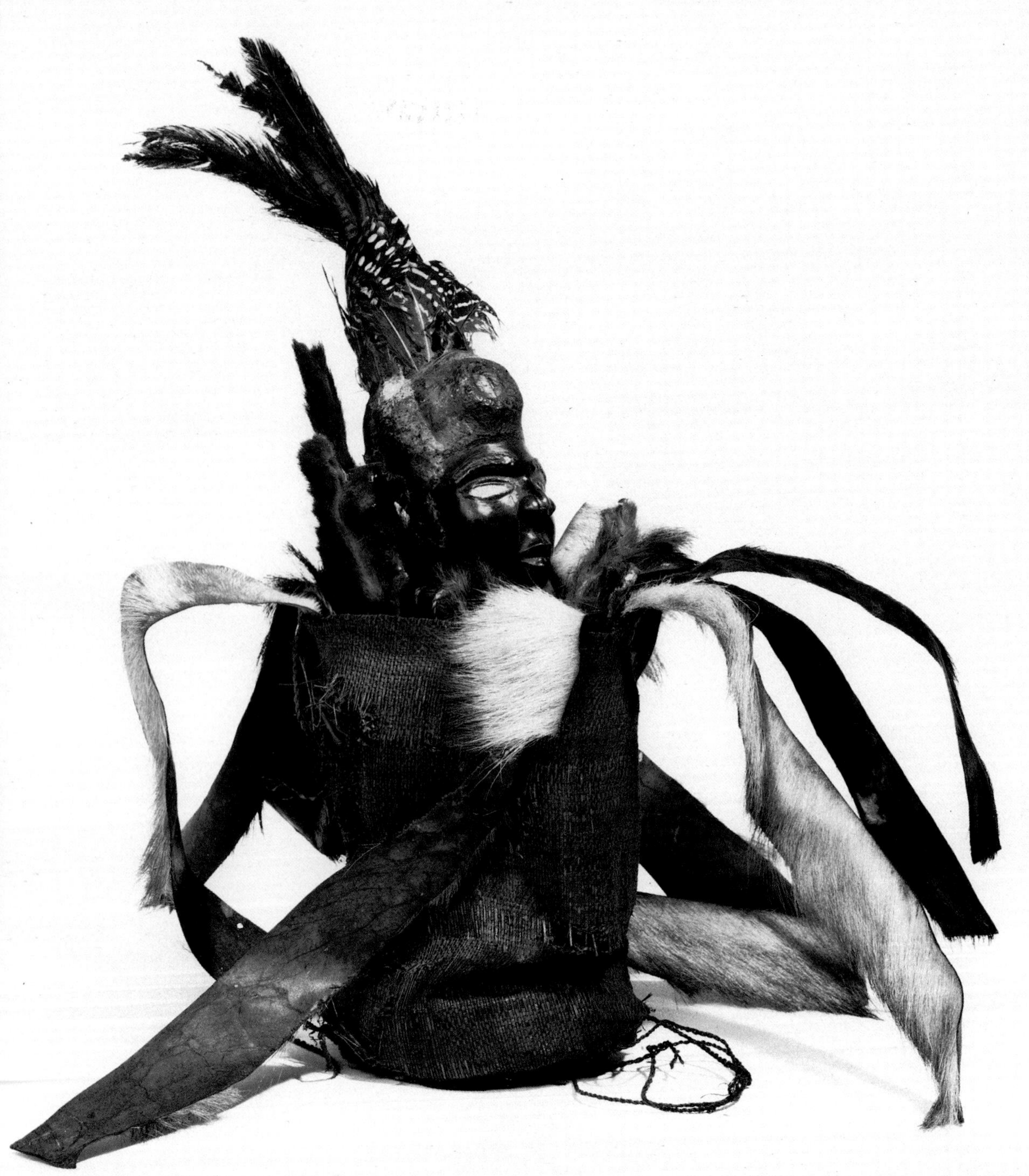

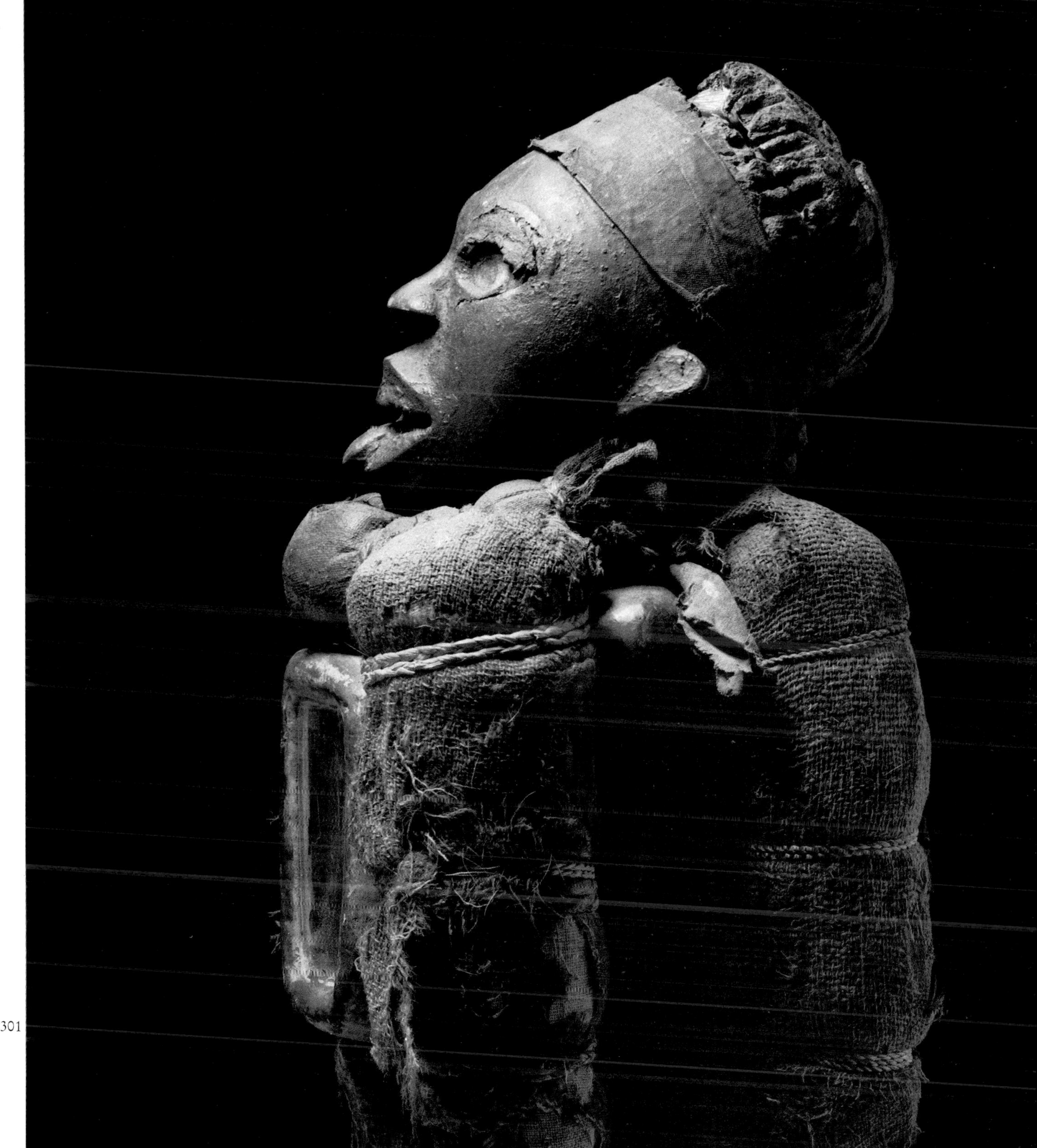

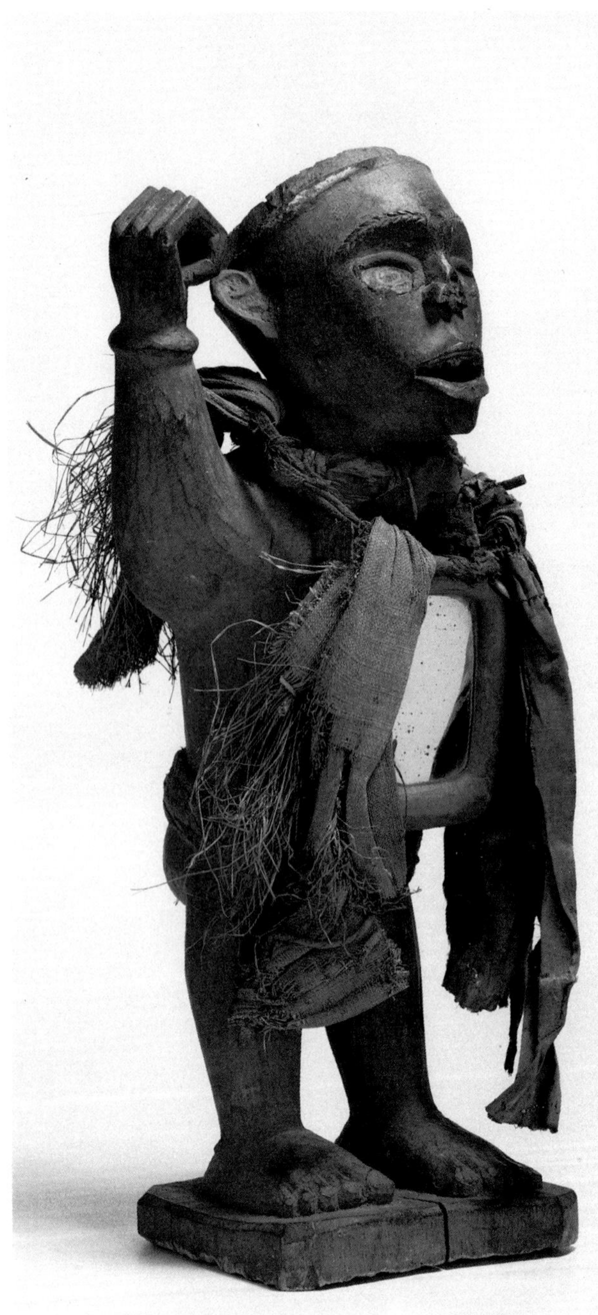

302

299 Magical figure (*nduda*), wood, glass, leather, feathers, cloth.
Zaire, Yombe.
(see color plate p. 270)

This magical figure, an outstanding piece of realistic art, is in excellent condition. The head and face—the mouth in particular, with protruding closed lips cut off at the corners in a straight line—were rendered with a degree of realism that is completely unimpaired by the bits of mirror glass inserted as eyes. The realism is actually heightened by the light brown face color. (In lower Zaire, among the Vili of the Loango realm, nineteenth-century travelers observed the relatively high incidence of individuals with light or bronze skin.

This richly outfitted figure, with its feather ornament, recalls depictions of royalty (see No. 300). The artist expressed the figure's inherent power through the imagery of royal insignia.

Height (without feathers) 34 cm. 93.630
Acquired from F. Martin 1893

Lit.: P. Gussfeldt 1876, p. 204.

300 Magical figure (*nduda*), wood, glass, leather, feathers, resin.
Zaire, Yombe.

In quality and state of preservation, this figure is comparable to No. 299. Except for the mirror-glass eyes and the geometrically stylized eyebrows, the face is again realistic. In this case the skin is dark and the nose broad. The armlets and cap with feathers are royal insignia that convey the power of the figure—or, more precisely, of the magical substances it contains.

Height (without feathers) 24 cm. 93.631
Acquired from F. Martin 1893

301 Magical figure (*nduda*), wood, glass, resin, cloth, reed, fiber strings.
Zaire, Yombe.
(see color plate p. 271)

This figure, including its long, tightly fitting trousers and its head fillet, is entirely covered with a dark resinous substance. The mouth is half open, showing the chiseled gap in the upper row of teeth characteristic of the Yombe-Woyo. The protruding tongue probably served as a magical defensive. The eye sockets are lined with red cloth and covered with glass. The eyebrows gain relief from the resinous matter but do not have the geometric patterns seen in Nos. 300 and 305. Fingers and toes have distinctly worked nails. The carved plaited raffia bands that adorn the upper arms are emblems of royalty.

The figure's original attachments are almost completely preserved. Magical substances are in mirrored boxes on its chest and back, as well as in a hollow in back of its head, and are sealed in with resinous matter. At the back of the head, palm nuts and small bamboo splinters (see also No. 308) can be discerned at the edge of the seal. Each of the cloth pads suspended from the shoulders contains a piece of slender hollow reed wrapped in several layers of different fabrics. In the reed itself, as well as between the cloth layers and inside the mirrored boxes, are numerous small crystals, detected by X-ray. These are probably saltpeter, used in the production of gunpowder and therefore valuable.

Height 41.5 cm. 93.628
Acquired from F. Martin 1893

Lit.: H. Dechamps, 1981, pp. 68, 69.

302 Magical figure (*nduda*), wood, glass, plant and cotton fiber, iron.
Zaire, Yombe.

This figure, which has a few nails and blades driven

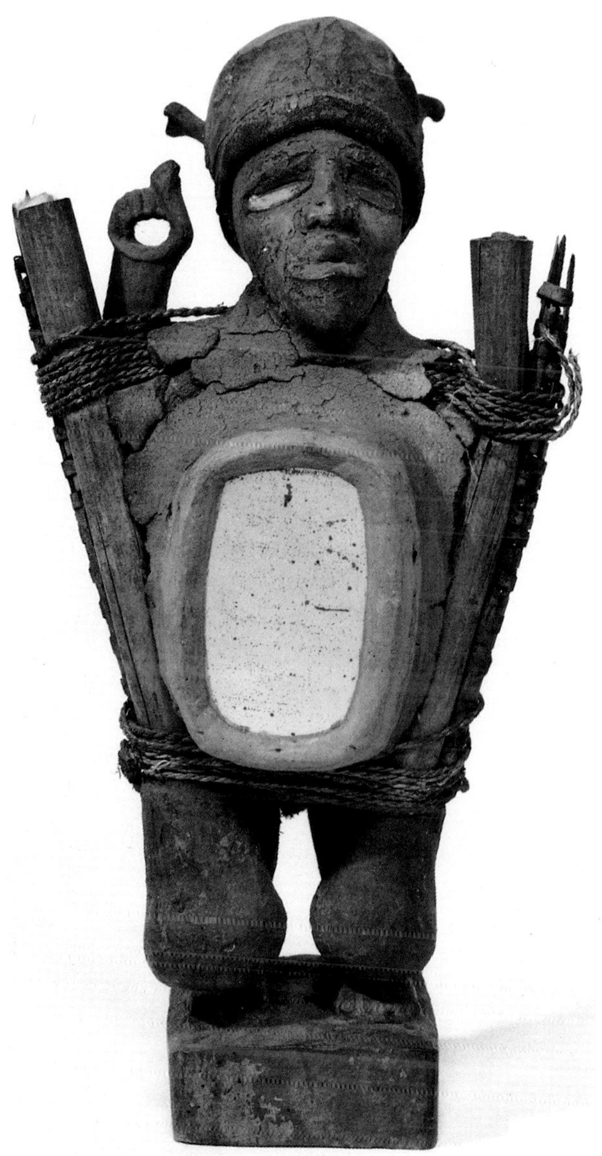

303

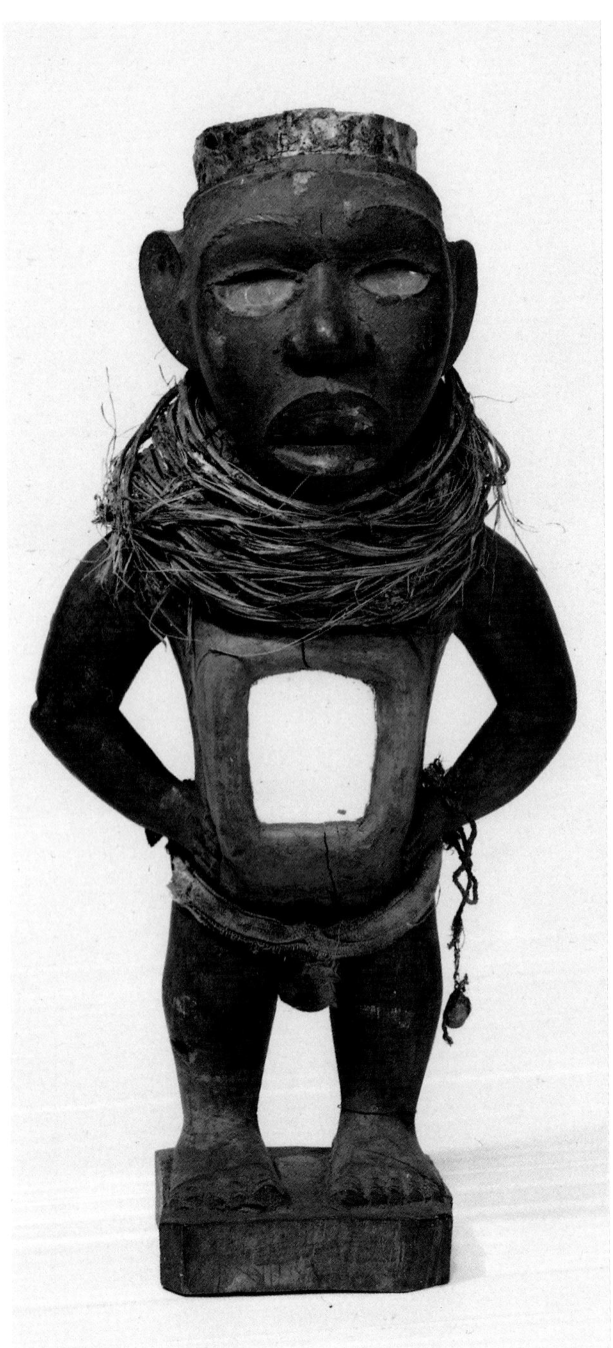

304

into it, has a mirrored box on its chest only. The face is finely worked, and the sculptured eyebrows are emphasized by a herringbone pattern. The lips of the slightly open mouth are carefully formed, and the upper teeth have the chiseled gap characteristic of the Yombe. The figure wears a loincloth (*dhoti*) and carved bracelets. Since it is painted red, the body was presumably not meant to be covered. A spear, originally held in the raised right hand, and magical accretion once on the head are missing. The twisted roll around the neck is covered with depilated skin.

Height 42 cm. 93.627
Acquired from F. Martin 1893

303 Magical figure (*nduda*), wood, glass, resin, bones, bamboo, plant fiber, cords.
Zaire, Yombe.

The idea of magical defense finds powerful expression in this figure. Its almost completely preserved attachments include two reeds, filled with gunpowder and sealed with resinous paste, from which symbolic shots were fired at the enemy. The raised right hand is meant as a warding-off gesture. The front of the figure is painted in gray, and the back is red under a dark brown surface. In the cap, a symbol of high social position (see also Nos. 299-302), are small bones—bearers of magical potency.

Height 32 cm. 93.626
Acquired from F. Martin 1893

304 Magical figure (*nduda*), wood, glass, fabric, plant fibers.
Zaire, Yombe.

The forward-tilted body with hands on hips conveys concentrated power. Red glass-covered eye sockets with large black pupils are set in a somewhat insensitive face. The mouth is realistically shaped, with

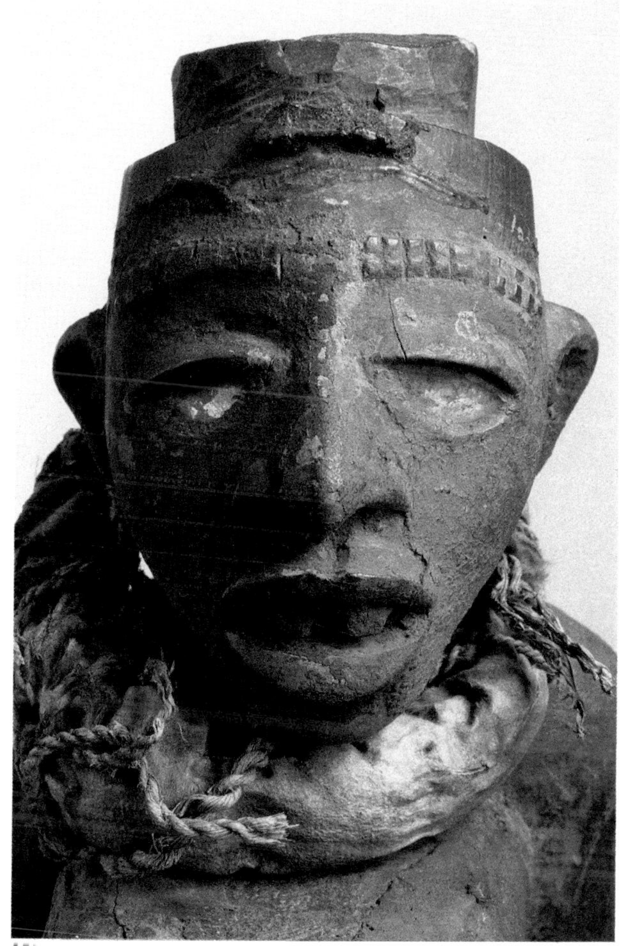

305

open lips that reveal not only the chiseled teeth but gums as well. Feet and toes are carefully depicted. Loincloth, neck ornament, and black-painted body indicate that the figure was not meant to be dressed. Head covering and a second container for magical substances on the back of the figure are missing, possibly retained by the owner when he sold the piece.

Height 40 cm. 93.629
Acquired from F. Martin 1893

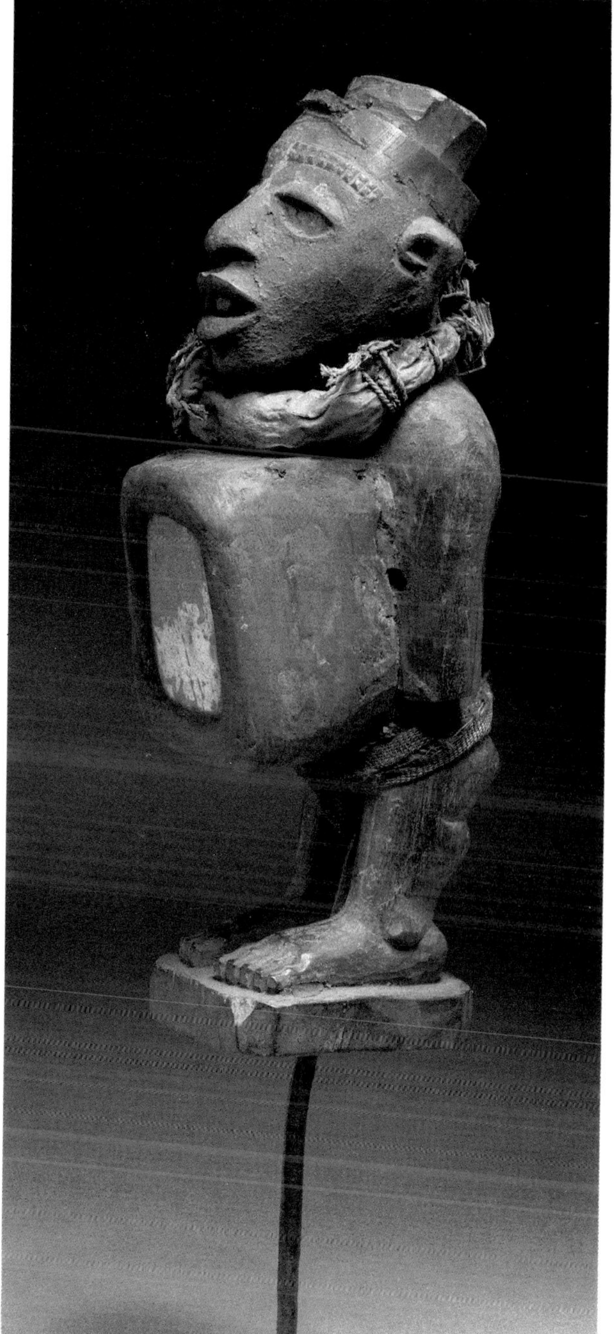

305

305 Magical figure (*nduda*), wood, glass, iron, leather.
Zaire, Yombe.

This artistically significant piece has only one container of magical substances, in its chest. The expressive face, painted red on one side and black on the other, displays eyebrows adorned with a geometric pattern in relief. The thick, finely shaped protruding lips reveal filed upper teeth; the ears and feet are carefully shaped; the dress is relatively scanty. A roll of depilated skin is twisted around the neck, and the figure stands on an iron rod.

A small figure in the museum at Louvain-la-Neuve is strikingly similar to our piece, except for the absence of the chest receptacle for magic that was apparently once attached with iron pins. Both pieces were probably made by the same master.

Height 35.5 cm. 93.625
Acquired from F. Martin 1893

Lit.: F. Neyt 1981, p. 97.

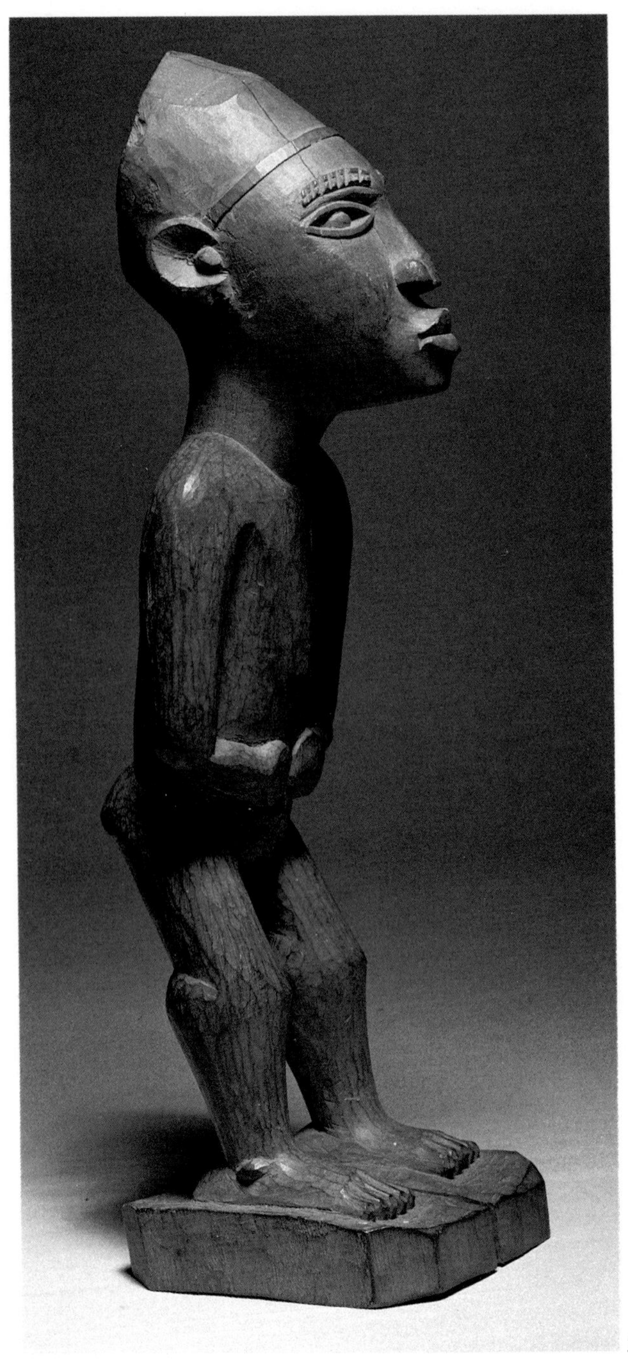
306

306 Human figure (*nduda* or *ndoki*), wood.
Zaire, Yombe.

The carver completed this figure, but the ritual specialist did not add the magical substances, so it is impossible to determine whether it was meant as a mirror figure (*nduda*) or a nail sculpture (*ndoki*). The body bends forward slightly, the face is worked in detail, and the eyebrows are sculptured with a geometric pattern. The difference between the finely structured feet and the rather negligently treated hands is striking; presumably the latter were to be hidden by the magical attachments.

Height 32 cm. 93.621
Acquired from F. Martin 1893

307 Animal figure (*nduda*), wood, glass, quill.
Zaire, Yombe.
(see color plate p.272)

While the facial features of this figure are those of a realistically depicted monkey, the china eyes with eyebrows in patterned relief remind us of anthropomorphic magical figures. The body and seated posture on the stool, which is a sign of high office, also appear human. The figure's equipment, if this has been wholly preserved, is meager in comparison with that of other power figures. It consists only of mirror containers on chest and back and black-and-white coloring.

Height 19.5 cm. 93.623
Acquired from F. Martin 1893

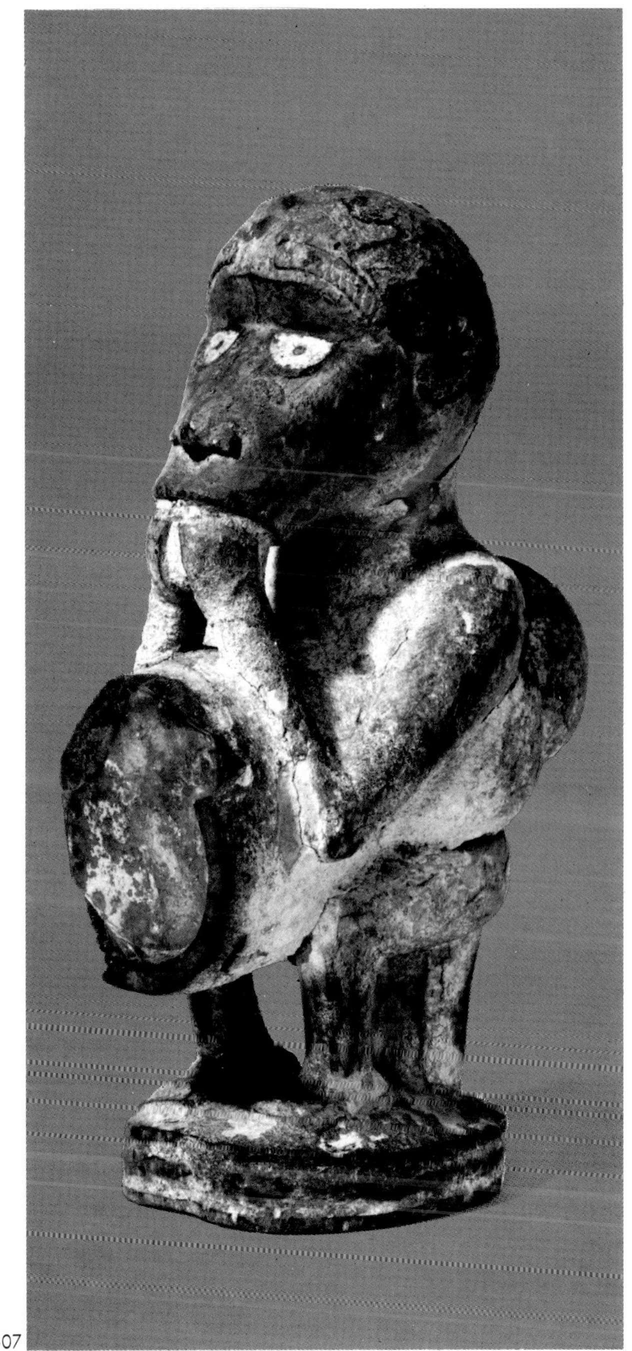
307

308 Animal figure (*nkondi*), wood, resin, reed, iron.
Zaire, Kongo.

The animal figure in itself has no independent ritual significance, but the representation of a powerful beast of prey was thought to strengthen and intensify the magical potency with which it was imbued. The large canine teeth on this piece suggest that it was conceived as a leopard. Bits of reed and small wooden pegs were inserted into a lump of resinous matter on the figure's back. In lower Zaire, long before the importation of European iron nails, this ancient "nailing" by means of *binko* (wooden pegs, wedges, and so on) was the customary form of waking dormant powers of defense in such figures.

Length 30 cm. 57-13-5
Acquired from L. Bretschneider 1957

Lit.: R. F. Thompson 1978, p. 212.

309 Two-headed animal (*nkondi*), wood, resinous mass, iron.
Zaire, Vili

This figure, acquired by missionaries sometime be-

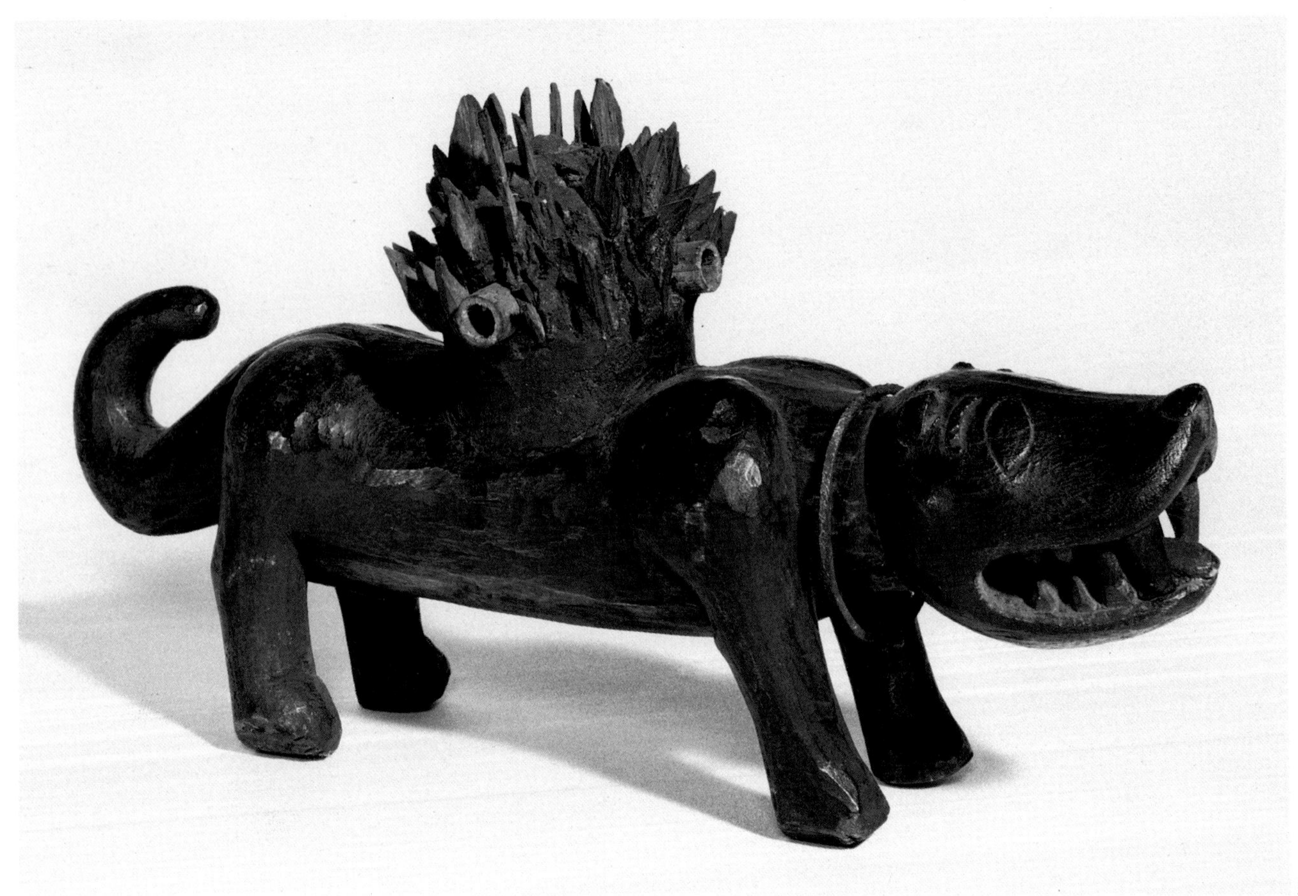

308

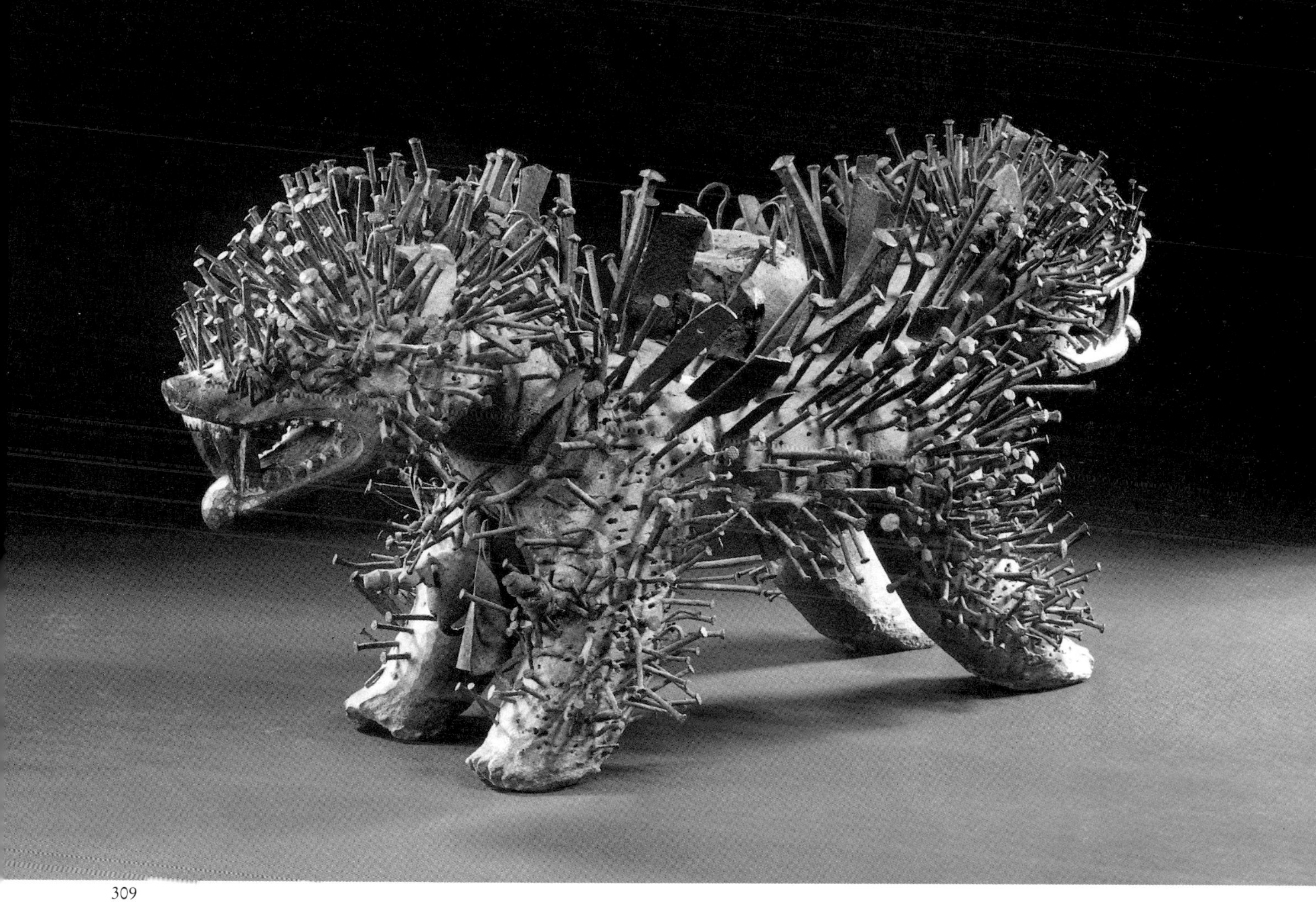

309

fore 1912, is said to have been used mainly to repel evil. To assist in this function, both ends of the body have heads—a composition not infrequent among magical animal figures with open mouths, bared teeth with large canines, and outstretched tongues. Around one of the necks hang small animal figures, perhaps leopards or dogs, which, like the double heads, probably intensify the beast's power. The most important magical substances are to be found in the resin lump on the animal's back.

The nails driven into the wooden figure are mostly European. From an artistic point of view the figure is of little importance, but it is remarkable that both the pointed and the drooping ears are precisely shaped, in contrast to the summary presentation of all other details.

Length 74 cm., height 35 cm. 57-13-5
Acquired from L. Bretschneider 1957

Lit.: R. Lehuard 1980, pp. 140, 168-81.

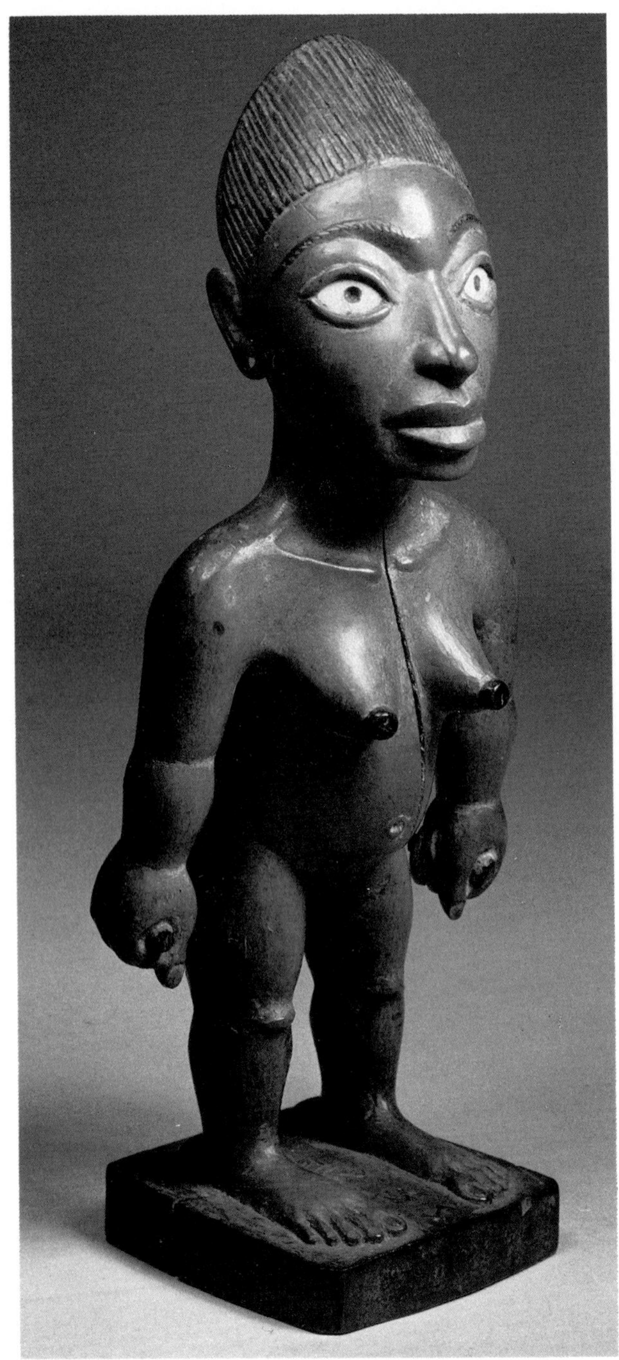

310

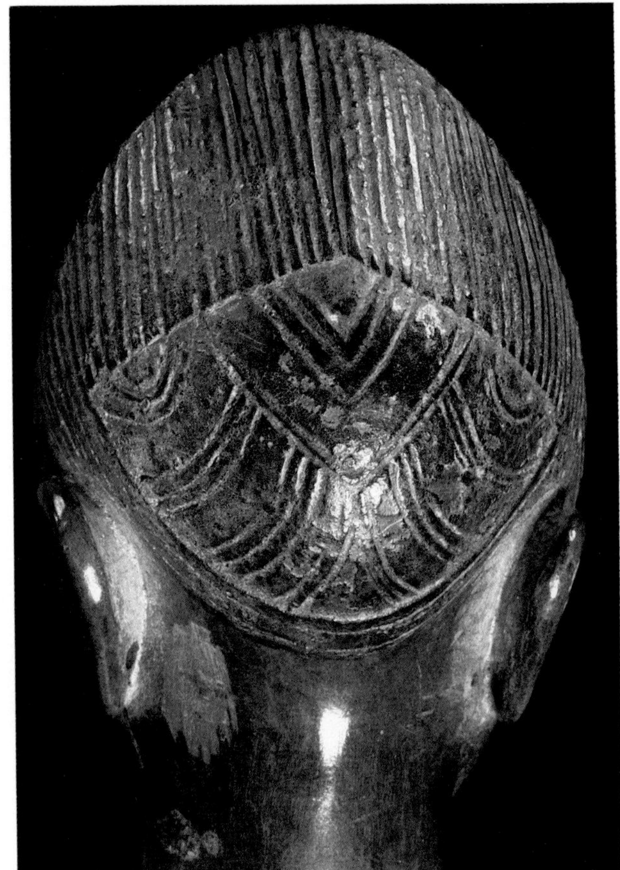

310

Female Figures of Lower Zaire (310-312)

The sculpture of the peoples of lower Zaire is by no means limited to magical mirror and nail figures. Female figures in a variety of attitudes form a further group. Their functions are similarly varied—among them divination and fighting disease—but hardly anything is known of the ideas associated with them. It must be assumed that the artistic tradition that so faithfully retained the various iconographic types outlived the ideas associated with them.

Father Laman, who spent almost thirty years among the (Ba)Kongo people as a missionary, places most of these statues in the category of "*nkisi* figures." He also enumerates many "*nkisi spirits*" that in one way or another torment or aid the living. However, even his ample information offers no explanation why certain *nkisi* are always presented the same way, as kneeling girls or as women holding their breasts.

Lit.: K. Laman 1962, particularly Chapters IX-XIV; F. Maes 1935, p. VIII, Illus. 5; A. Maesen 1981, p. 47.

310 Female figure, wood, porcelain.
Zaire, Yombe.

The texture of the wood as well as the oil polishing give this figure a silky, shining middle-brown tone that corresponds to the skin color of many inhabitants of the lower Zaire region. Further naturalistic details of this carefully worked sculpture may be seen in the sensitively depicted face, the shoulder area with suggested shoulder blades, the breasts, and the feet. In contrast are the staring porcelain eyes. Incised lines form an elaborate miter-shape coiffure combed high on the head, re-creating the lower Zaire fashion of adorning the crown or back of the head with shaved-out patterns. The earlobes are pierced. The hands enclose what may be small medicine containers.

Height 27 cm. 93.622
Acquired from F. Martin 1893

311 Female figure, wood, iron rings.
Zaire, Yombe.

This standing figure, holding her breasts, wears a high pointed cap with delicate linear decoration, and metal rings on her ankles. Disk-shape depressions on the abdomen and the back of the head still contain

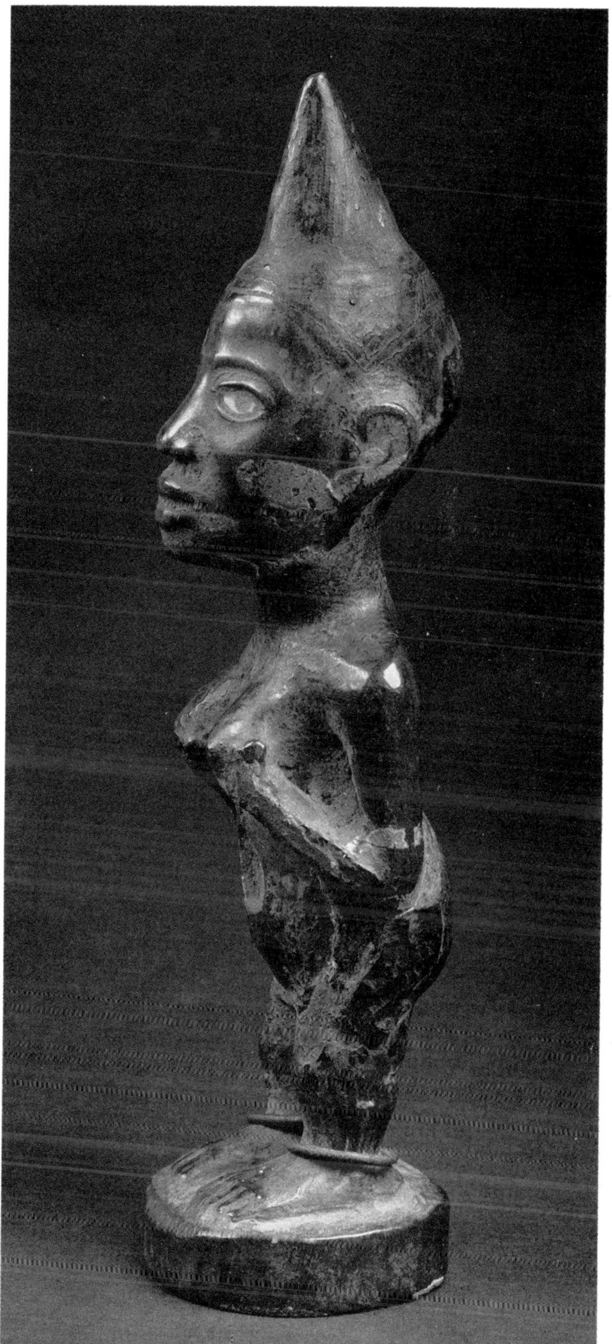
311

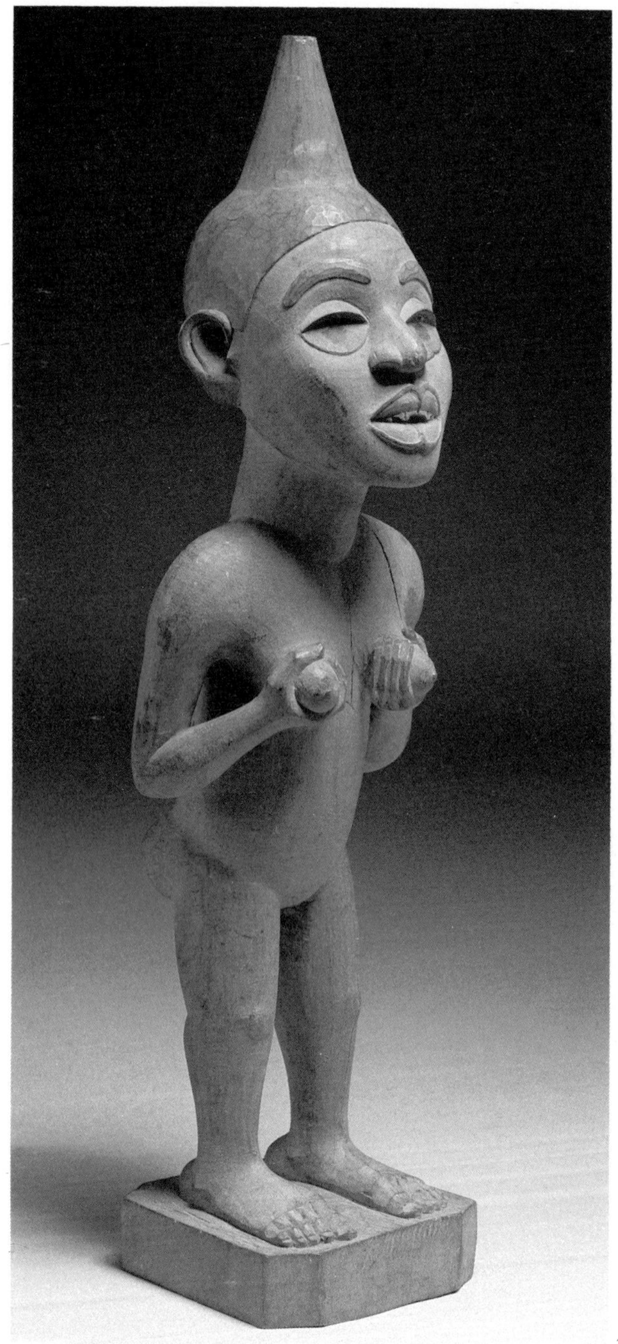

312

remains of red *tukula* powder (see p. 332). Traces of wear suggest frequent use.

Height 16.5 cm. 34-32-3
Acquired from L. Bretschneider 1934

312 Female figure, wood, porcelain.
Zaire, Yombe.

This figure's porcelain eyes are half hidden by eyelids, and the slightly open mouth with protruding lips reveals the typical gap between the chiseled teeth. The coiffure and eyebrows are somewhat darker than the body. Since the figure shows neither patina nor traces of wear, it was probably completed by the carver but never dedicated. Though without hollows or metal ornaments, it is similar to No. 311.

Height 28.5 cm. 93.616
Acquired from F. Martin 1893

313 Bellows wood.
Republic of Congo, Sundi, west of Luozi.

This is a two-drum wooden blacksmith's bellows; the lower part of the clay air tube has been broken off, and the membrane, probably moved by sticks, are also missing. The handle, formed as a human head wearing the cap of notables, and the suggestion of pubic hair, give the impression of a female figure—if the two drums are interpreted as breasts. Such a shape for an important smith's implement is no arbitrary frivolity. Rather, it suggests an analogy between metallurgy and copulation. Frequent reports of smelting furnaces in the south of Zaire furnished with sculptured breasts and tattoo marks symbolizing fertility support this sexual interpretation.

Height 62 cm. 79-300-823
Acquired from L. Bretschneider 1979

Lit.: H. Baumann 1935, p. 93; W. Foy 1909, p. 199; M. Leiris & J. Delange 1968, p. 196.

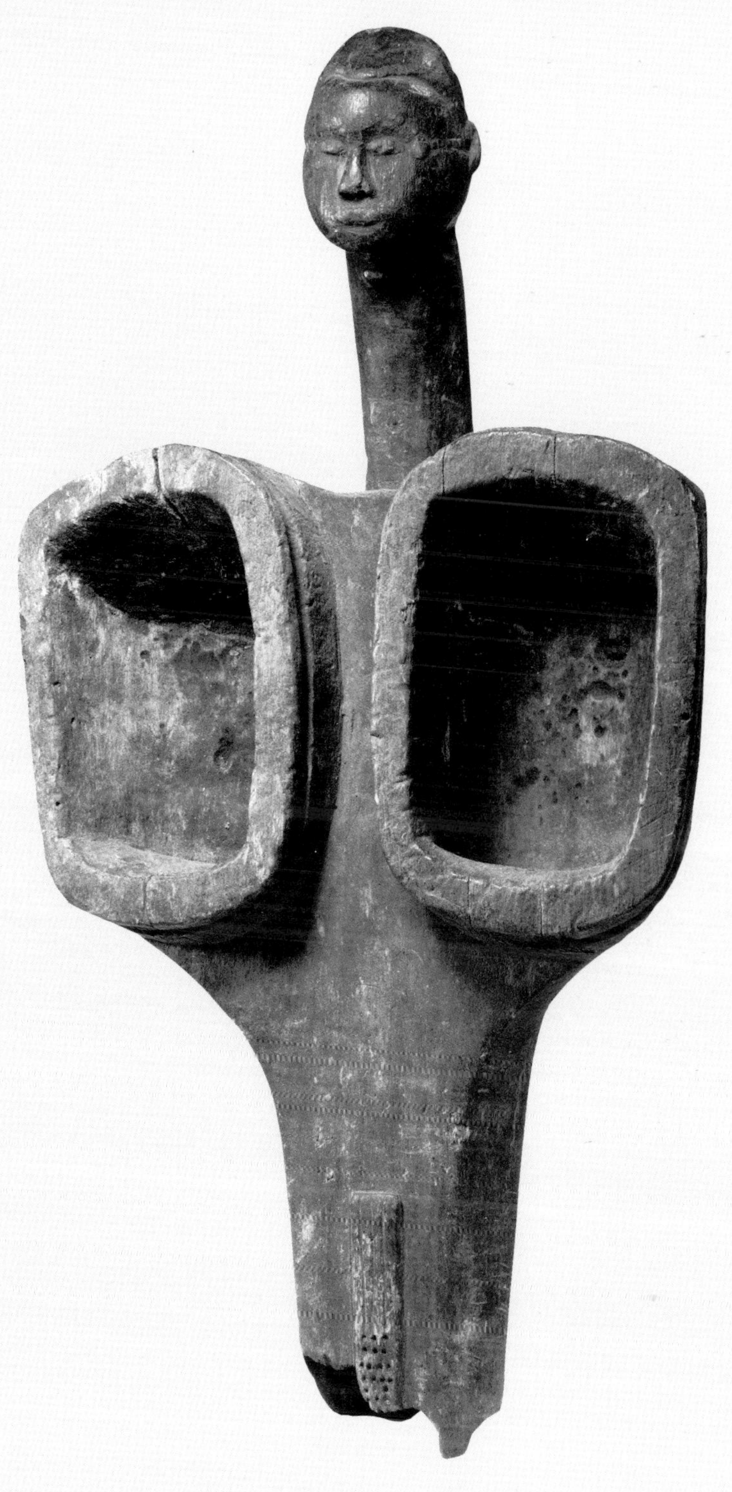

313

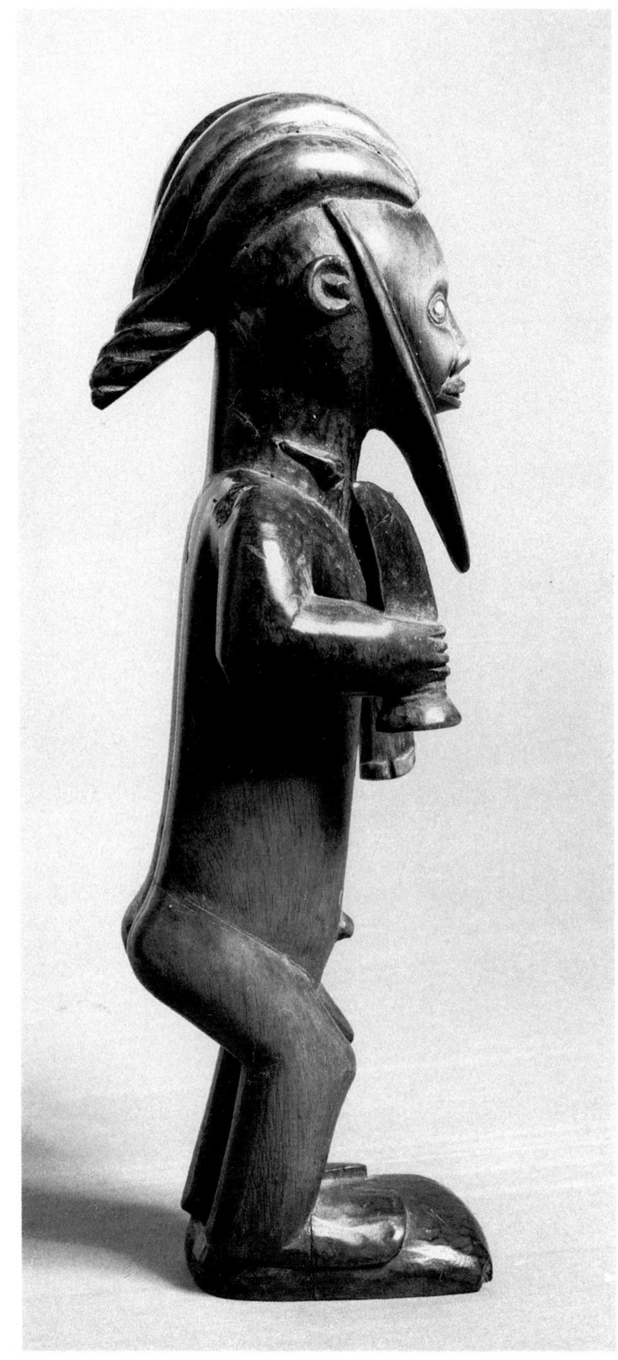

314

314 Male figure, wood, porcelain.
Republic of Congo, Bembe, from Sibiti.
(see color plate p. 273)

This carefully carved, stained, and polished figure is typical of Bembe art. The realistic treatment of the face, with eyes composed of porcelain fragments, is remarkable. Except for a long ornamental scar on the right side of the neck, characteristic Bembe torso cicatrices are missing. In contrast to the power figures of the lower Zaire, those of the Bembe have no receptacles for magical matter, but a magically potent substance has been fitted into a small hollow between the legs in this figure. Equipping the figure, as bearer of magical power, with the insignia of a chief does, however, recall the lower Zaire figures. These insignia include a superbly rolled coiffure ending in a braid, an artificial beard, and, a chopping knife and its sheath. The Bembe, believe that these figures have the capacity to repel misfortune, and they also use them for divination and as temporary abodes for ancestral spirits.

Height 26.5 cm. 28-22-4
Acquired from P. Guillaume 1926

Lit.: B. Soderberg 1975, pp. 15-37.

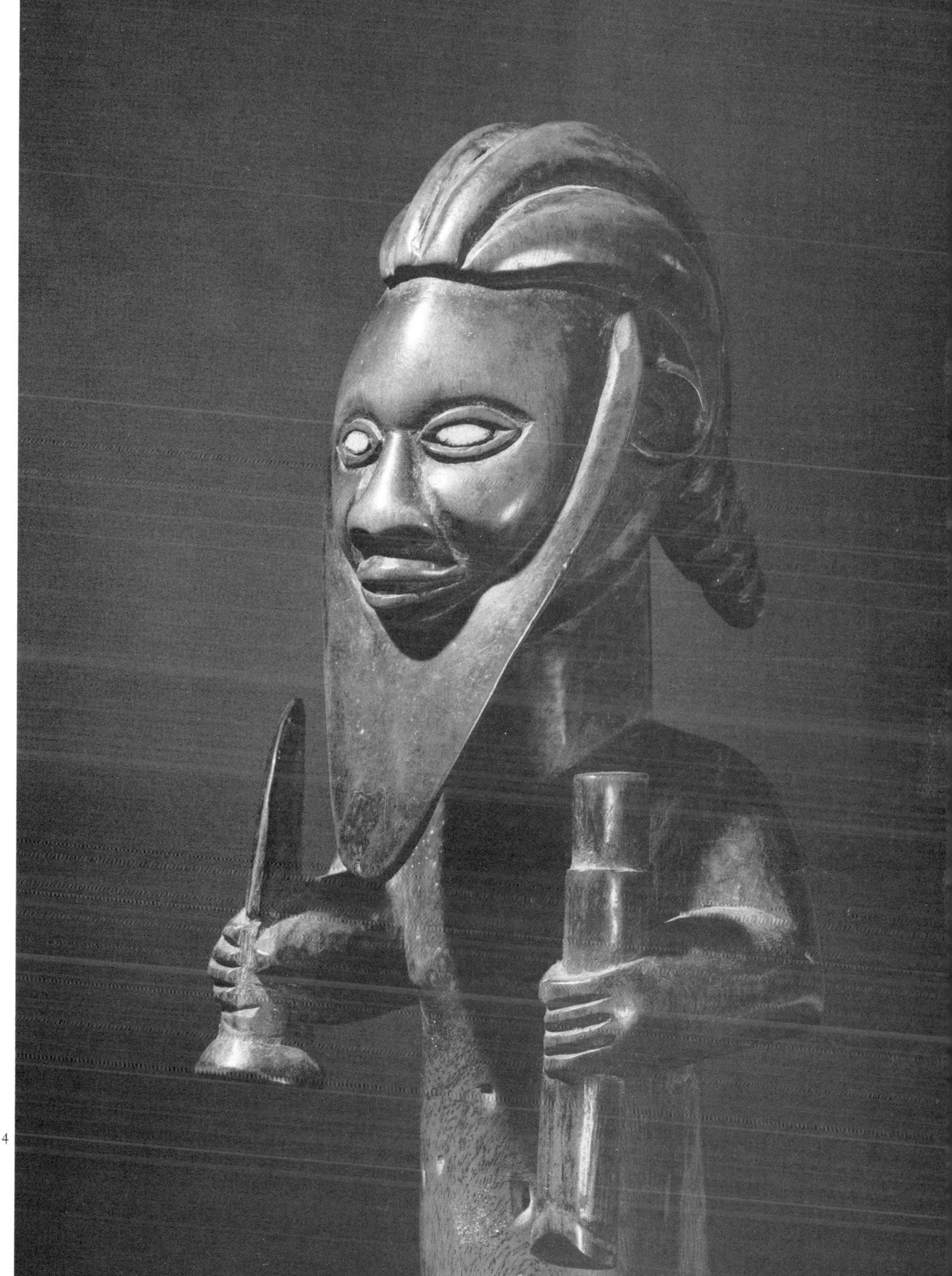

315,316 Two helmet masks (*hemba*), wood, paint, raffia.
Zaire, Suku (East Yaka).

Hemba masks are used in boys' initiation ceremonies, in the magical treatment of disease (particularly gynecological disorders), and to insure luck in hunting, as well as in other endeavors. There are both male and female faces; in the past the masks always presented themselves in pairs.

The longitudinal axes of these more or less lozenge-shaped faces may be clearly traced from the angular centers of the bulbous foreheads through the pointed turned-up noses and the beards. The large coffee-bean-shape eyes with slits and the large for-

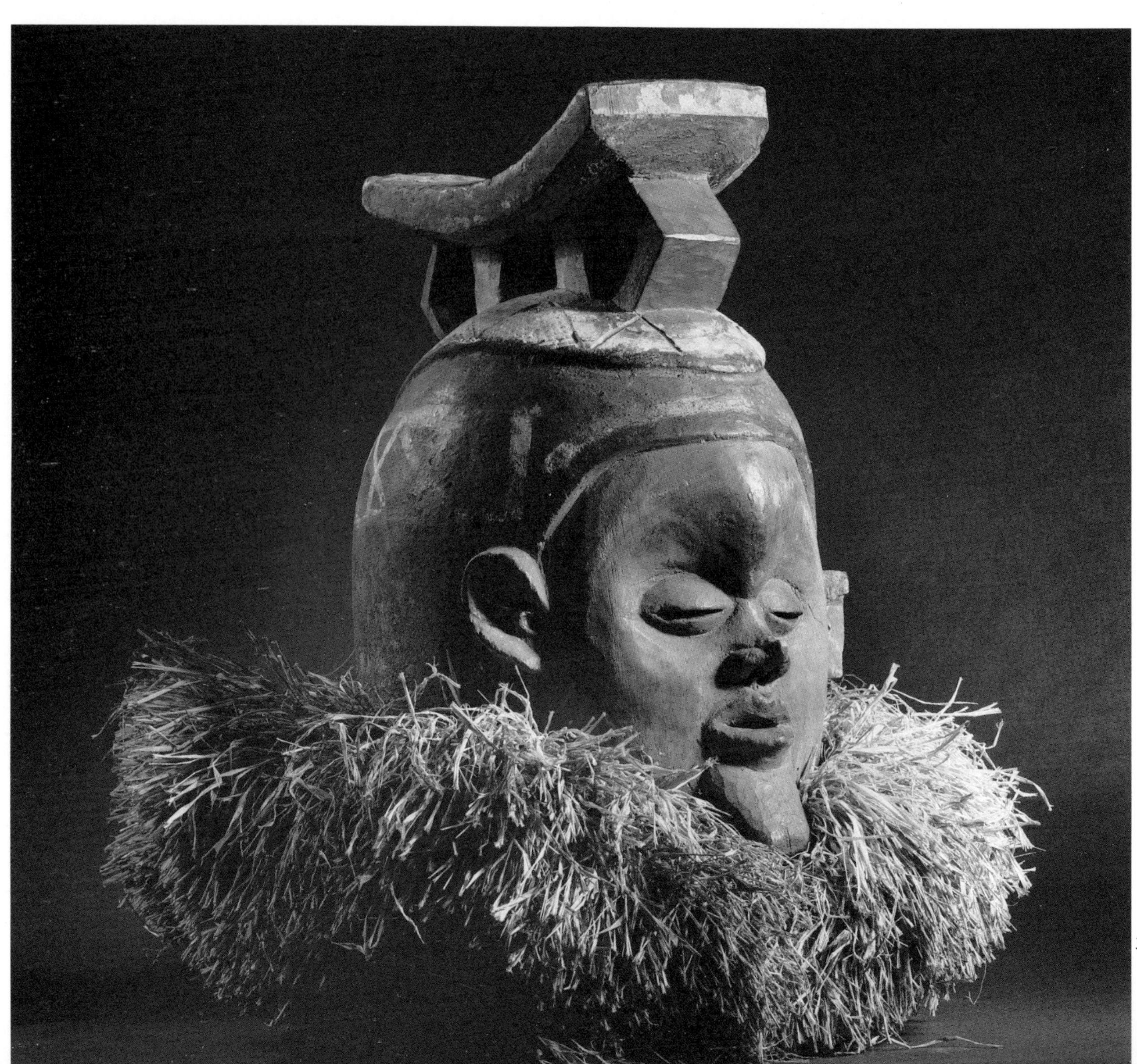

315

wardly placed ears form the transverse axis. Eyebrows and cheek tattoos are indicated by finely incised lines. A white band composed of geometric ornaments encircles the sharply delineated hair. Above this and on No. 316 is the model of a bench or headrest, and on No. 316 is the high, padded coiffure typical of this region.

Height 37 cm., 39 cm. 39-11-6/7
Acquired from L. Bretschneider 1939

Lit.: A. P. Bourgeois 1981, pp. 26-28, 30, 32, 37, 38.

317 Comb, wood.
Zaire, Yaka.

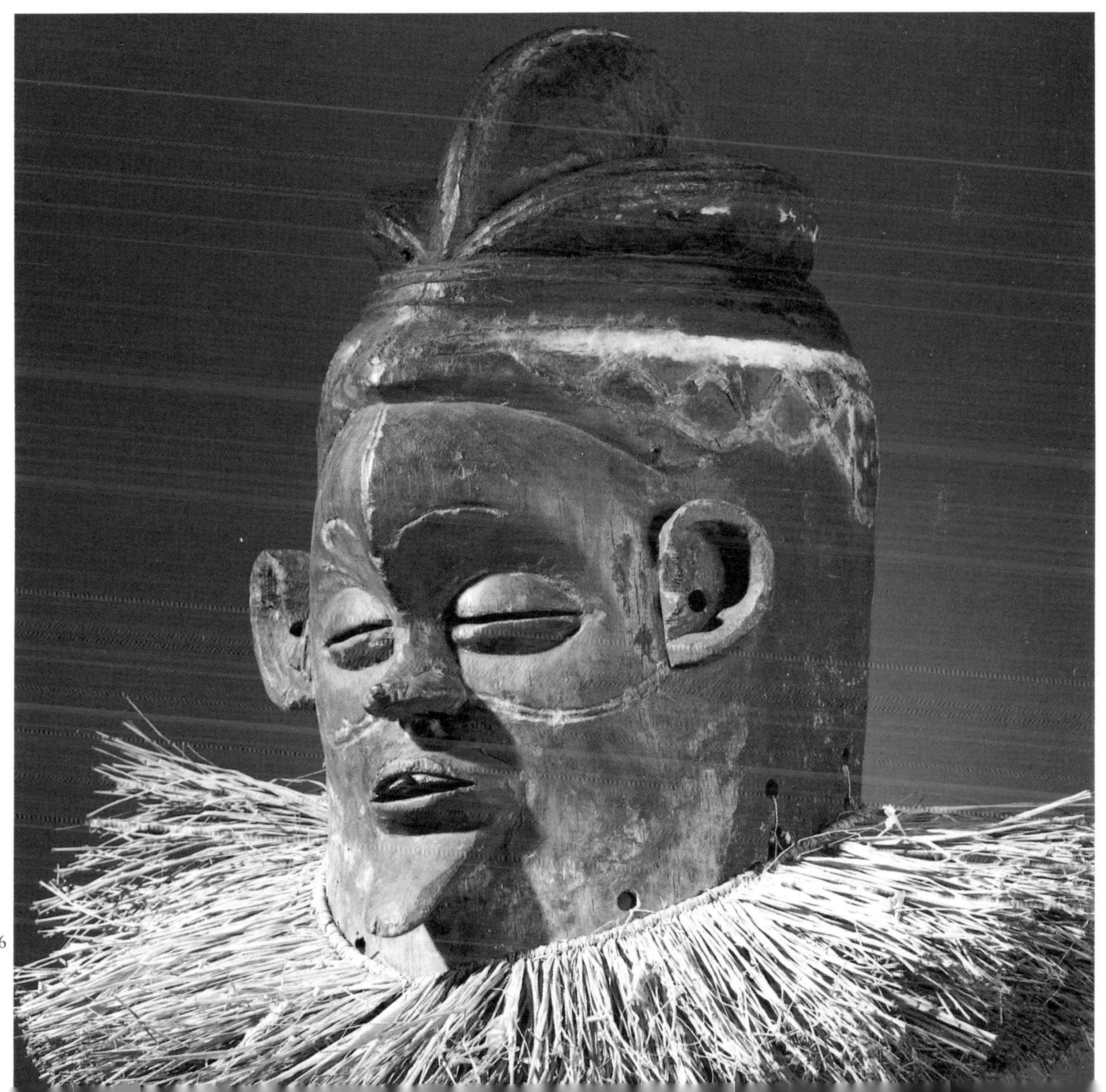

316

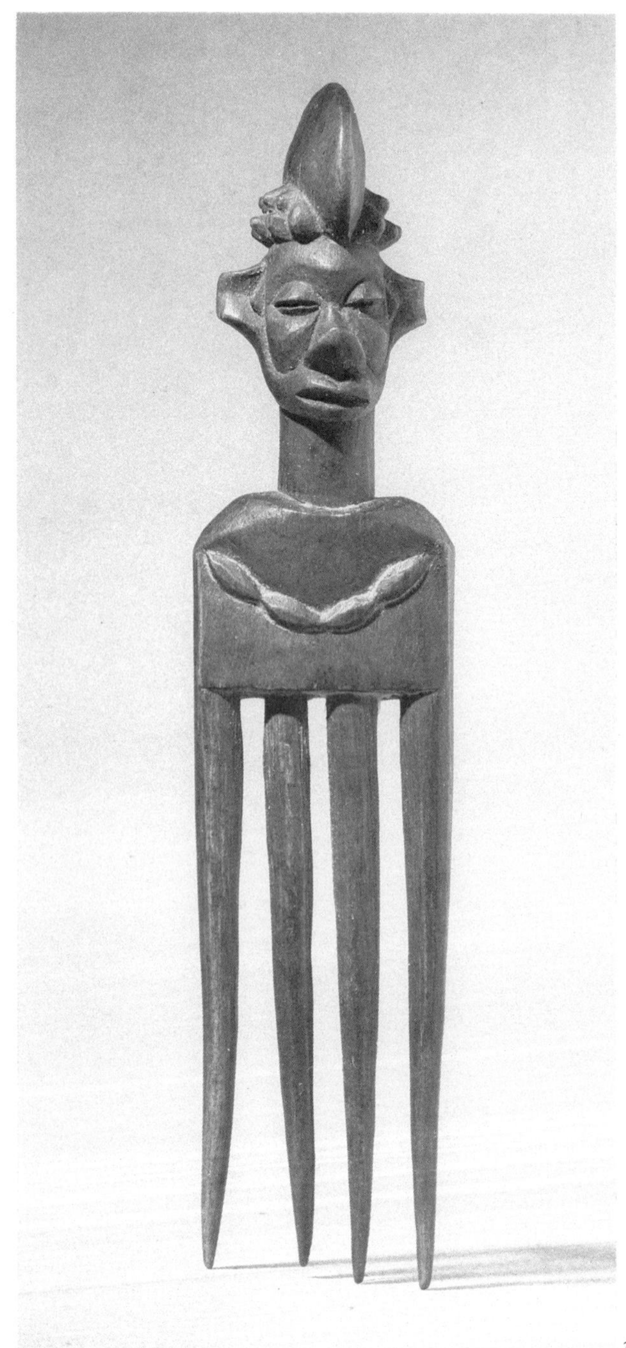

317

The artistically carved miniature head exhibits many characteristics of Yaka sculpture. Its prominent facial features include a large upturned nose, large coffee-bean eyes, cheek tattoos, and a protruding mouth. The angular ears, to the head, extend at right angles to the high, padded coiffure.

Length 15 cm. 28-22-15
Acquired from P. Guillaume

318 Male figure, wood.
Zaire-Angola, Holo (?), Kwango area.

This nude male figure, with almost horizontally extended arms ending in oversize hands, stands in a frame carved in geometric patterns. Carvings of this kind are common among the various peoples of the Kwilu area, but the pose with outstretched arms, and the placement of the figure in a frame are unusual. Most scholars are of the opinion that European influence is at work here: the position of the arms may derive from crucifixion scenes; the frame probably imitates the framed religious pictures of the Catholics. This theory is supported by the fact that in the Kwango area there are many other examples of syncretism, with ideas, rites, and symbols that have evolved from the combination of indigenous and Christian elements. Among these syncretic phenomena, which in some cases go back to the seventeenth century, are the framed figures of the *nzambi* cult. Although their ideological significance has become detached from the probable Christian model, in many parts of western Africa the name *nzambi* designates a high god of obvious Christian influence. The *nzambi* cult, however, is directed to the ancestors, and the male figure is sometimes replaced by a female or even by a pair of figures.

Height 26 cm., width 17.5 cm. 82-301 777
Acquired from L. Bretschneider 1982

Lit.: J. Cornet 1973, p. 97ff.; W. Hirschberg 1963, pp. 163-79, 1972, pp. 98-113; A. Maesen 1960, Pl. 14; J. F. Thiel & H. Helf 1984, p. 101, Illus. 116-23.

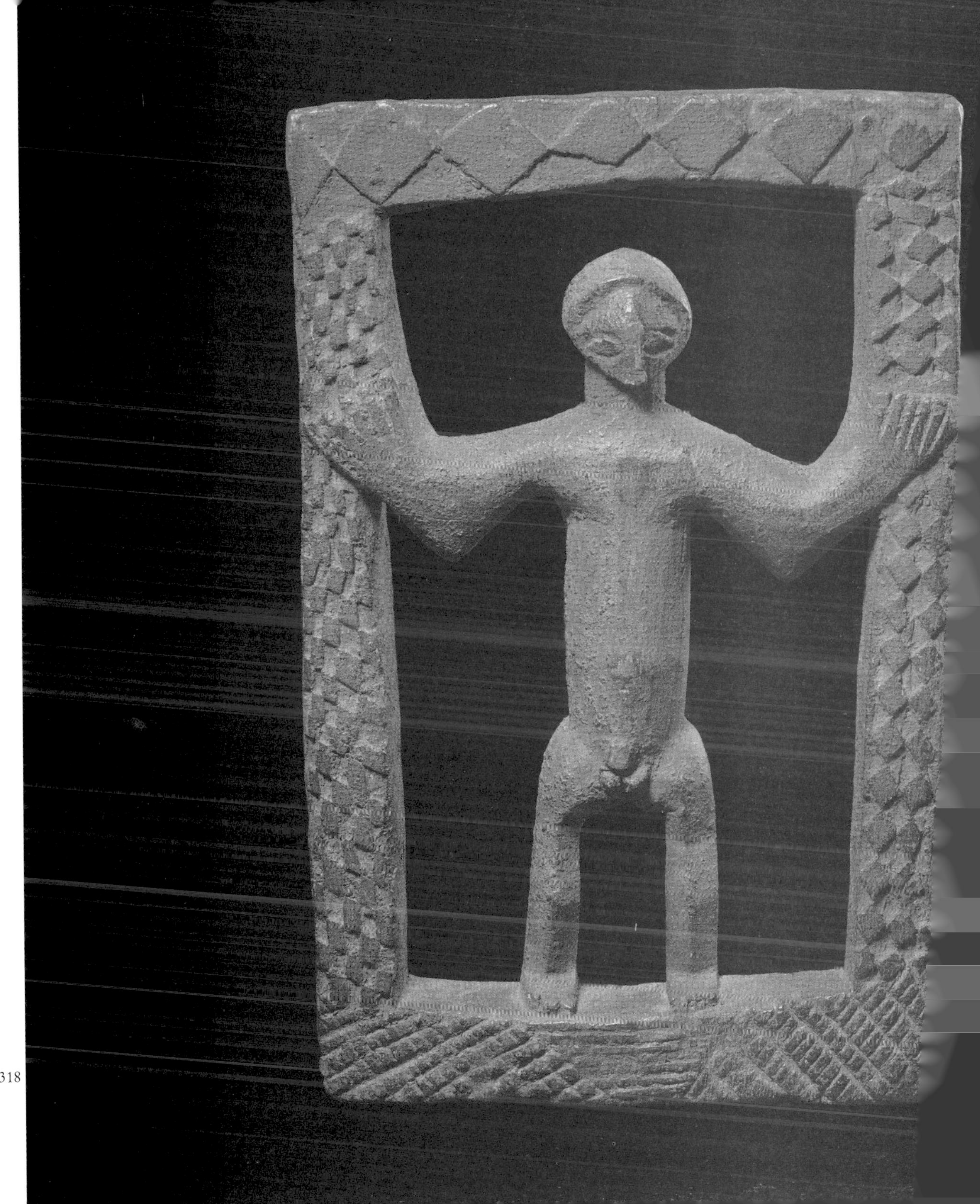

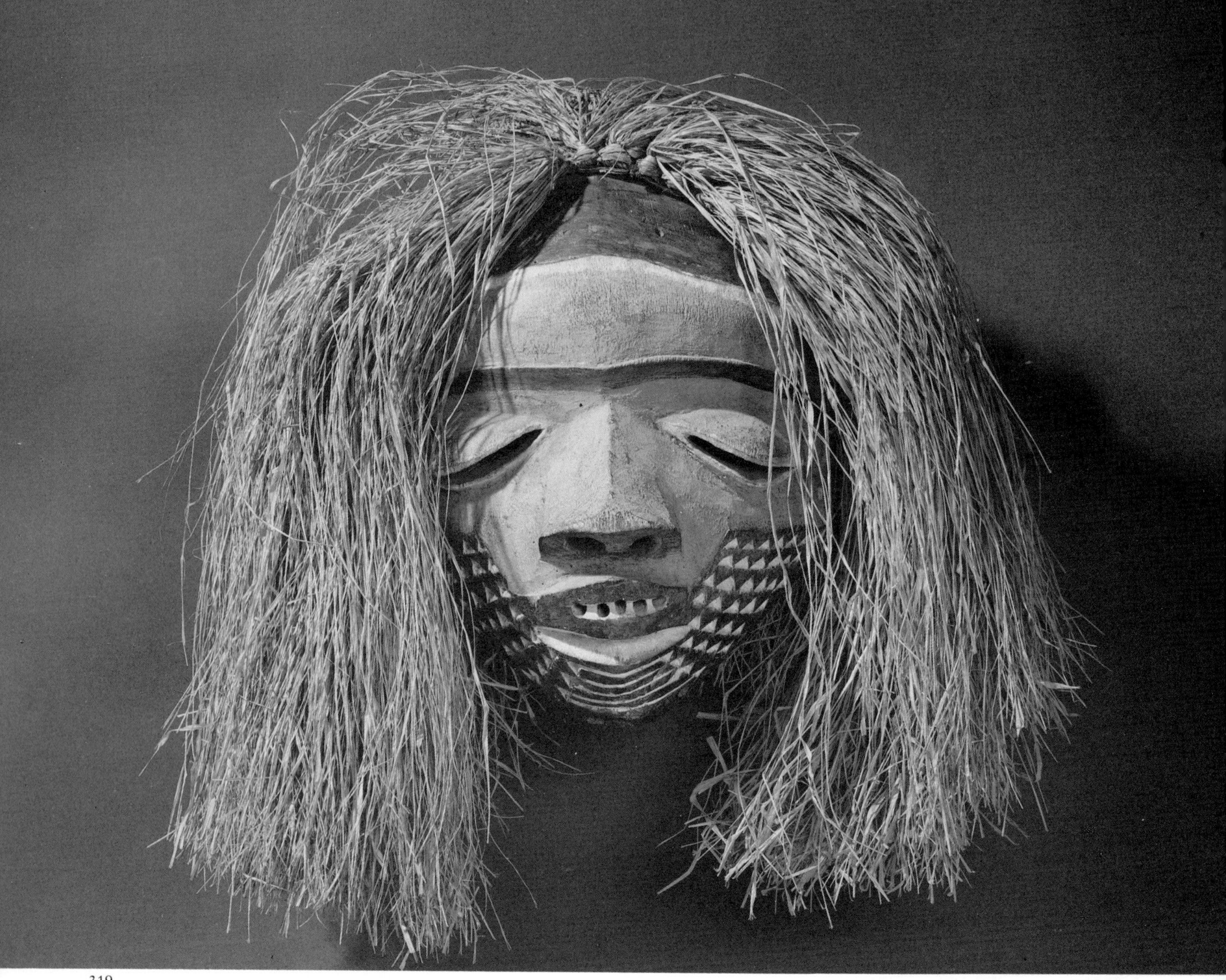

319

319-321 Three masks (*mbuya*), wood, raffia. Zaire, Western Pende.

All three of these masks have a characteristic profile created by a salient forehead, pointed upturned nose, and narrow jutting lips, the latter either pressed together (as in Nos. 320 and 321) or slightly open (as in No. 319). Further characteristics include eyes narrowed to slits and a raised unbroken eyebrow ridge that extends the full width of the face. The faces are nearly lozenge-shape with cheekbones more or less strongly emphasized.

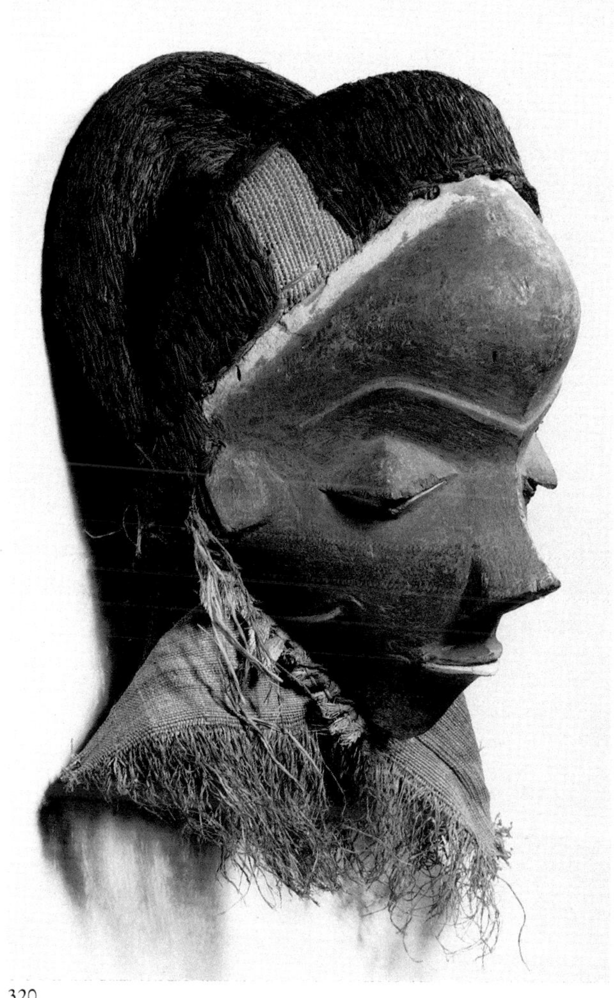

320

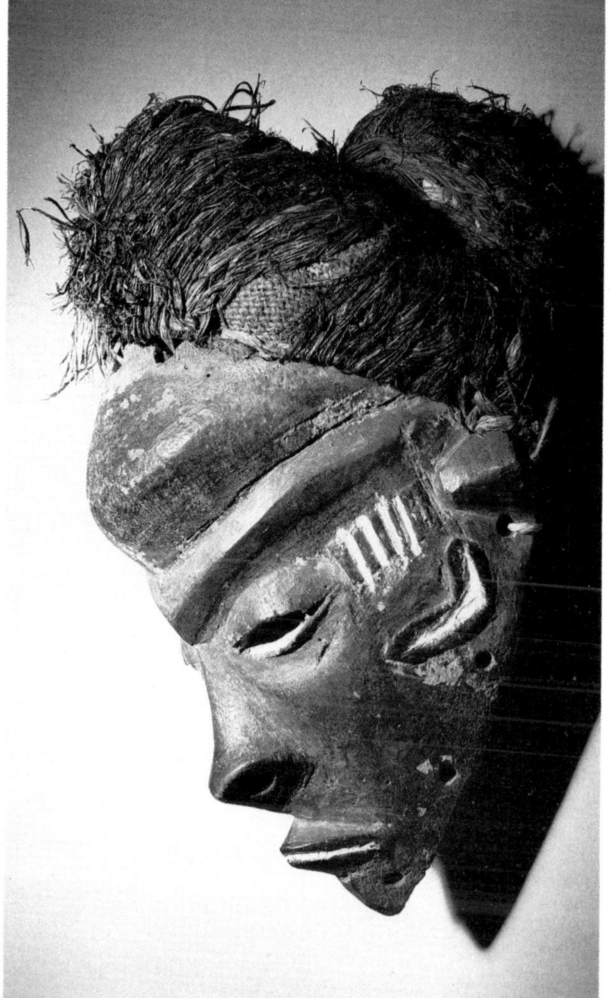

321

Mbuya were formerly considered manifestations of ancestral figures. Their most important performance took place during the boys' initiation: after the preparatory tests and the candidates' public confession, the adult men's secret was revealed– that the masks were not the ancestors themselves but disguised humans. To demonstrate this truth, the masks were then removed. In recent times *mbuya* have served simply to entertain spectators with small sketches on such occasions as the accession of a new village or district chief. The carvers' scrupulousness waned as the masks' significance diminished. Newer masks are all more or less alike, with no individual features; some cannot even be worn as masks but only rest on the forehead.

Height 33 cm., width 30 cm. 61-7 1
Acquired from E. Beer 1961
Height 29 cm., width 21 cm. 26-3-24
Acquired from O. W. Oldman 1926
Height 28 cm., width 20 cm. 63-2-1
Acquired from I. Esberg 1963

Lit.: J. Cornet 1973, pp. 104-09; L. de Sousberghe 1959, pp. 29-32, 39-42.

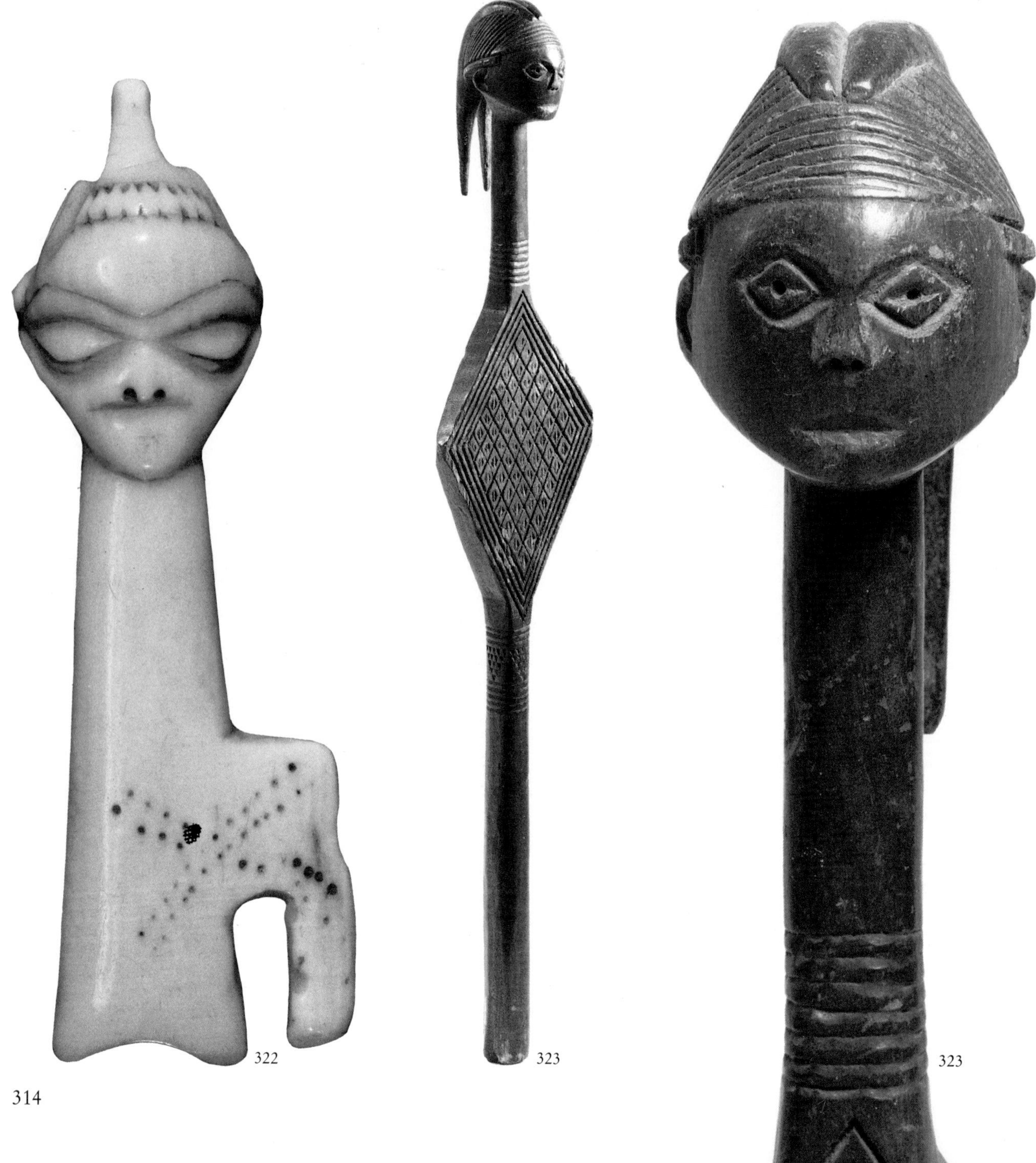

322

323

323

322 Whistle, ivory.
Zaire, Pende.

The shape of this rare type of whistle, known only among the Pende, imitates that of old European keys. Even the X symbol, formed by rows of dots on that portion corresponding to the key bit, can be traced to keys common in Europe decades ago. Apparently the Pende had observed that some Europeans, among them perhaps a few particularly respected persons, could produce whistling sounds with their keys. In contrast to this precise adoption of a foreign model is the exquisitely worked human head at the closed end of the whistle. It represents in altogether exemplary fashion the traditional art of the Pende, with its characteristic diagonal surface arrangement and continuous eyebrow line (see also Nos. 319-21).

Height 9.5 cm. 51-29-4
Acquired from L. Bretschneider 1951

Lit.: L. de Sousberghe 1959, pp. 83-85.

323 Speaker's staff (*muhango*), wood.
Zaire, Mbuun (lower Kwilu River).

In the chiefdoms of the lower and middle Kwilu, each clan owns a special speaker's staff that is kept by the clan speaker (*ngambi*), who is elected by the elders. In legal quarrels between two clans the speaker represents his clan's case, holding the staff in his hand to secure the ancestors' support. Our piece represents the type of speaker's staff characterized by a human head on a broad lozenge-shape abstract body with chip-carved decorations. The head-hugging coiffure with sculptured braids, rare in wood carving, and the neck rings indicated by incised lines (see also No. 341) are external signs of the high social rank of a figure representing the

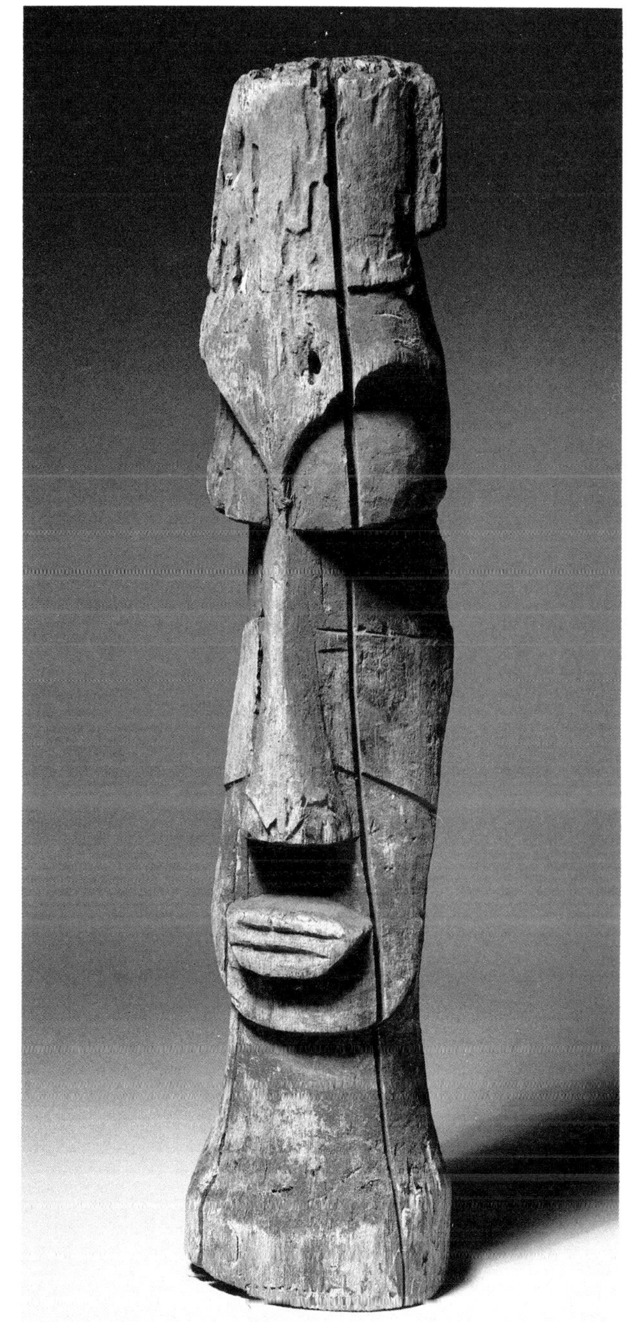

324

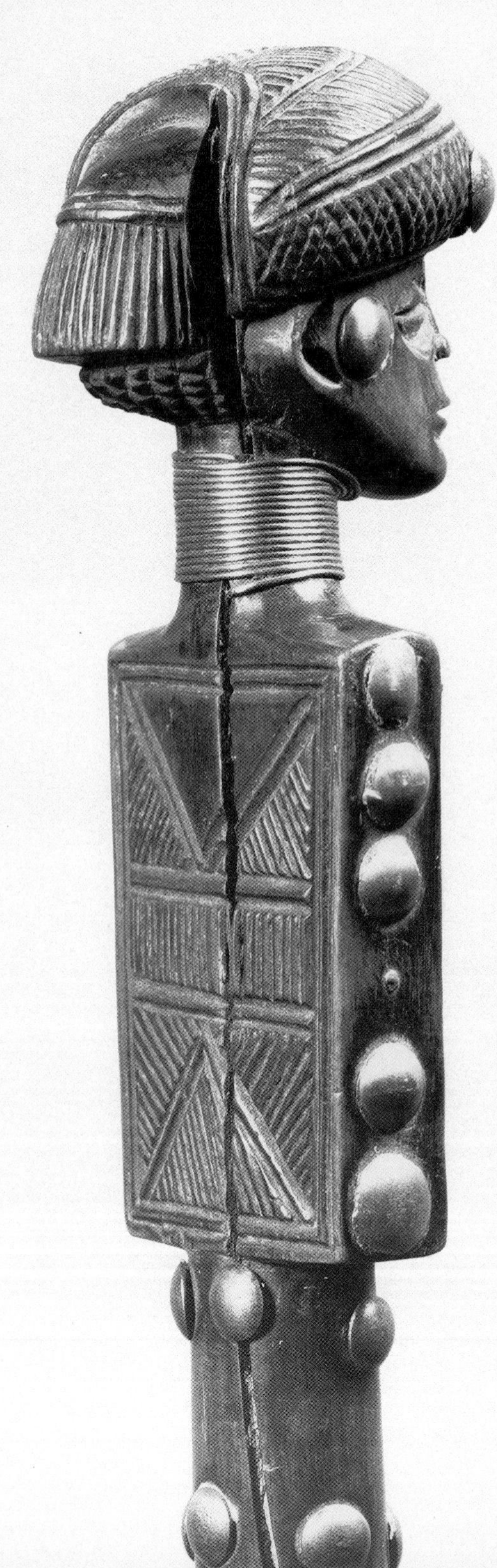

325

ancestors. The unadorned lower portion of this staff must originally have been about eighty centimeters longer.

Height 41 cm. 28-22-9
Acquired from P. Guillaume 1928

Lit.: L. de Sousberghe 1959, pp. 97-104, 159-60, Illus. 149-83.

324 Head from a pole, wood, paint.
Zaire, Biombo.

The Biombo have become known chiefly through their mask art, which bears a formal resemblance to their less well-known pole figures, as this head illustrates. In the characteristic decoration of the face, for instance, there are rows of small diamonds or triangles between two lines, a feature that is almost completely effaced here.

Height 52 cm., width 14 cm. 51-3-4
Acquired from H. Himmelheber 1951

Lit.: H. Himmelheber 1960, p. 353, 54; K. Volprecht 1967, Illus. 132.

Chokwe Art

The region of northeastern Angola and southern Zaire where the Chokwe live is considered one of the most flourishing art provinces in Africa. The Chokwe achieved a high level of craftsmanship and aesthetics in wood carving of figurative sculpture and in the applied arts particularly staffs, stools, combs, musical instruments, and tobacco pipes. Among the rich vocabulary of geometric ornaments, combinations of rectilinear elements dominate. Bastin states that their designations in the Chokwe language suggest that they are, at least in part, simplified representations of animals, plants, celestial bodies, and the like. So far, the use of such imported European commodities as wire (see No. 336), has enriched Chokwe art without affecting its substance.

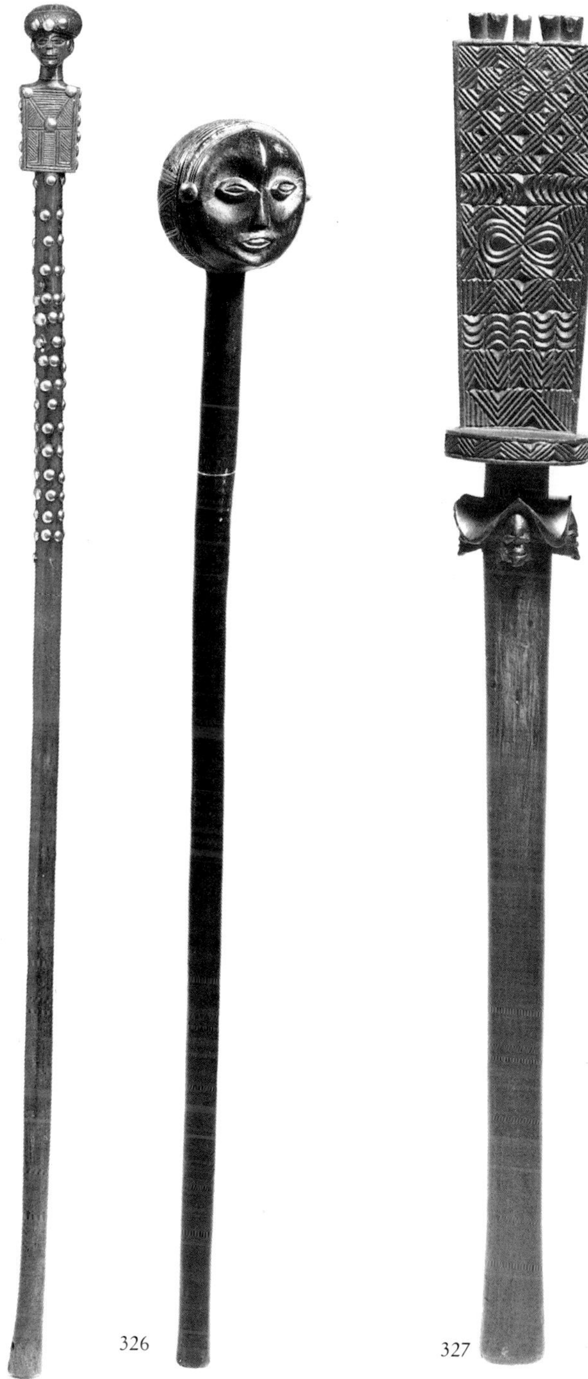
325 326 327

In the past, artistic activities were closely associated with chiefs' courts. Promoted by their rulers, Chokwe artists also worked in the Lunda empire, whose art was thus strongly influenced by them, as was the art of linguistically related neighboring peoples such as the Lwena and Mbunda. Like the Chokwe, the Kuba were masters of allover surface ornament (see Nos. 339-59), and apparently a mutually fruitful relationship existed between the two provinces. In the Munich collection the important Chokwe style is represented by only a few divination figures and ceremonial staffs.

Lit.: M. L. Bastin 1961, pp. 21-32, 57-64; 1968, pp. 41-47, 63, 64; J. Cornet 1973, pp. 171-79.

325-327 Three ceremonial staffs (*mbweci*), wood, brass tacks, wire.
Angola, Lwena, Chokwe.
(see color plate p. 275)

These short examples served women as dancing staffs at ritual performances. Men carried other staffs—some furnished with female heads—on their visits to other villages. Two of the pieces shown end in a female head, possibly representing a mask. The staff with the brass-wire collar (No. 325) shows the coiffure Lwena women wore at the *ciwila* festival, a kind of second intiation. The head of No. 327 is decorated with purely geometric motifs. Just below, under a wavy royal hood, a small head, perhaps a mask, is repeated four times. The repeated head is reminiscent of depictions of the legendary hunter Tshibinda Ilunga Katele, the ancestor of the Lunda kings, from whom the Chokwe rulers are also descended.

Height 94.5 cm., 59 cm., 60 cm. 29-22-2,26-3-26,26-3-29

Acquired from Kammel 1929 and O. W. Oldman 1926

Lit.: M. L. Bastin 1961, p. 287, Illus. 40, 1968, pp. 41ff.

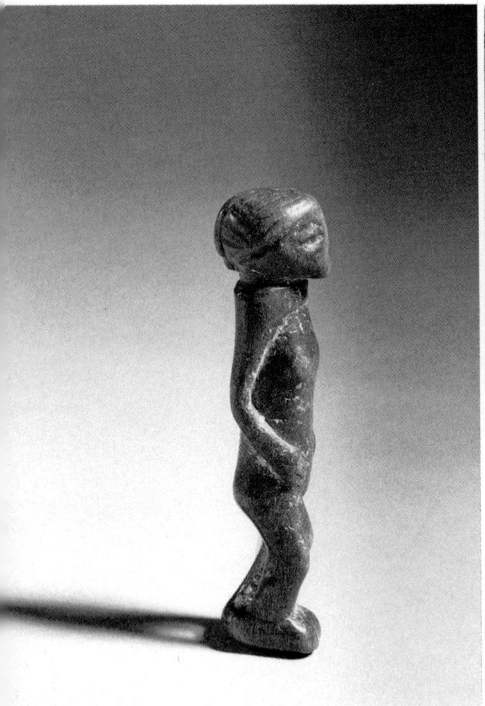

328 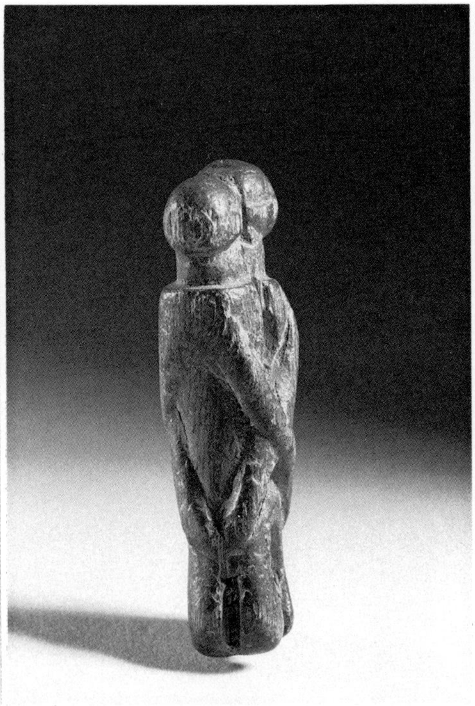 329 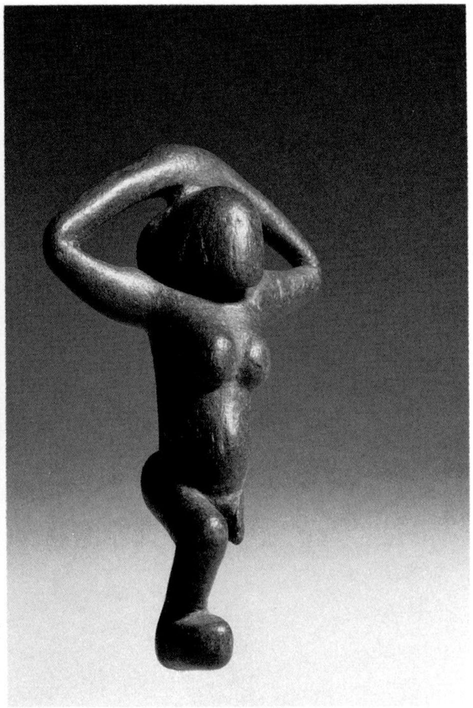 330

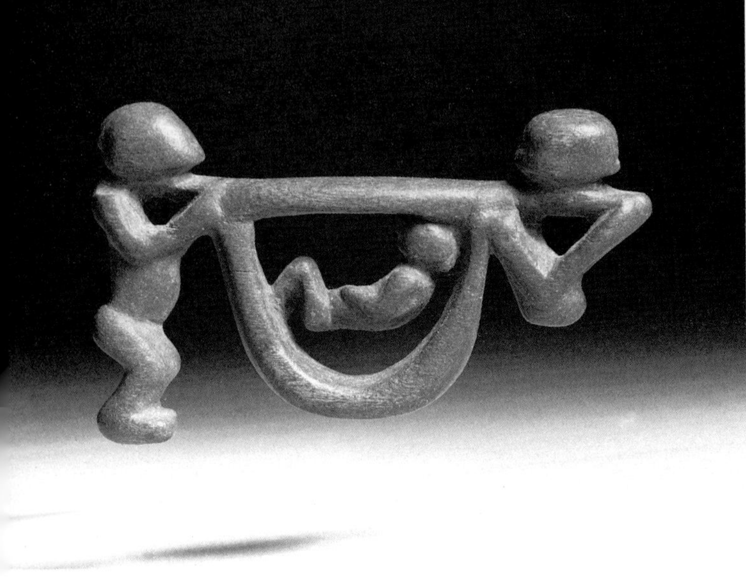

Chokwe Divination Figures (328-334)

The figurative wood carving of the Chokwe of northeast Angola is represented in the Munich collection by a number of stylistically diverse divination figures. Patina and traces of wear attest to the figures' great age and frequent use. They were kept in a basket reserved for divination purposes (*ngombo ya cisuka*) together with various objects considered magically effective: bones, snail shells, animal claws, and so on. The diviner, possessed by the ancestral spirit (*hanba Ngombo*), shakes the basket and, from the position of the figures on top or at the front edge of the basket, attempts to find answers to the questions put to him. The number and kind of figures and other objects used fluctuate; there are, however, typical figures considered basic divination equip-

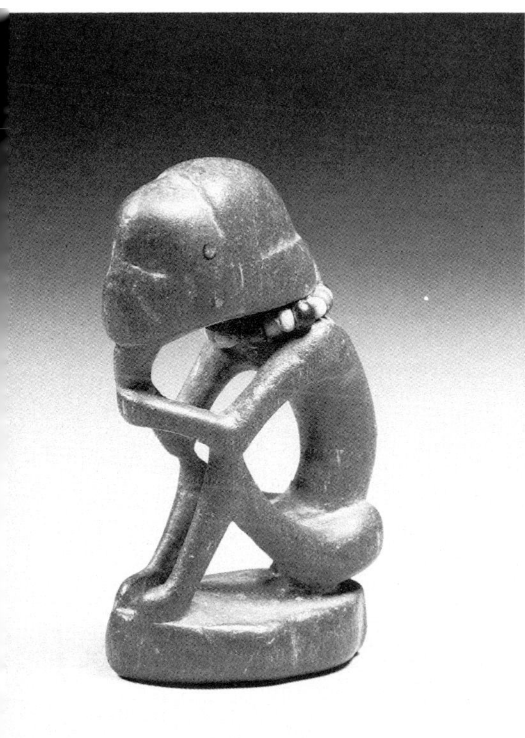

2

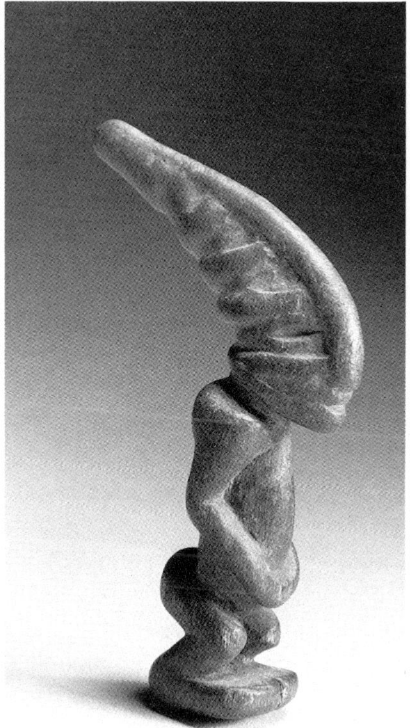

333

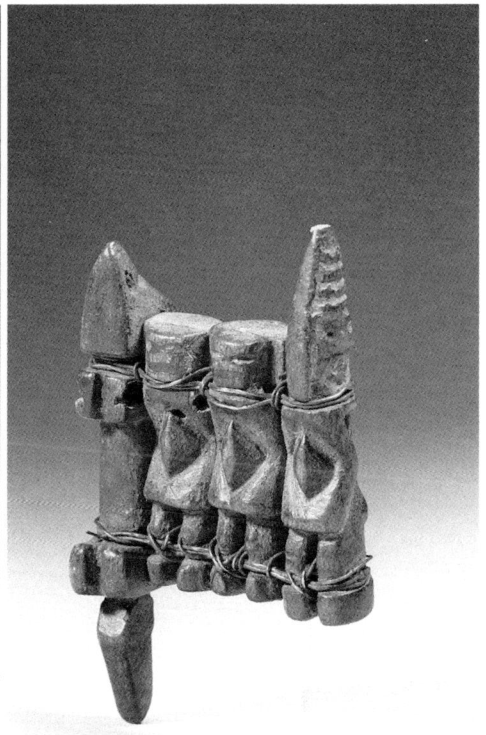

334

ment, which are present in almost all cases. These were designated "father," "mother," and "child" by Baumann and "ancestor," "ancestress," and "wearer of the mask" by Rodrigues de Areia.

Height 4,5-8 cm. 33-30-1/8
Acquired from C. Schomburgk 1933

Lit.: H. Baumann 1935 pp. 165-70; T. Delachaux 1946, pp. 48-72, 138ff.; A. Hauenstein 1961, pp. 132-43; A. Monard 1930, pp. 107ff., 118ff.; M. L. Rodrigues de Areia 1978, p. 34; 1985, pp. 175-92, 206ff., 246ff., 270ff.

328 Female figure (*kalamba kuku wa puo*), wood. Angola, Chokwe.

This figure represents the mother or ancestress of the basic divination group. Its significance in divination varies according to the position it occupies: feet upward, death; body horizontal, illness; head upward, life—that is, possible recovery.

329 Copulating couple (*mbate* or *yikoyi*), wood. Angola, Chokwe.

Figures of this kind are associated with marital problems or the prospective blessing of children.

330 Female figure (*katwambimbi*), wood. Angola, Chokwe.

With arms folded above the head and one leg broken off, this figure is interpreted as "mourner"—that is, a messenger of impending death, in certain cases through sorcery.

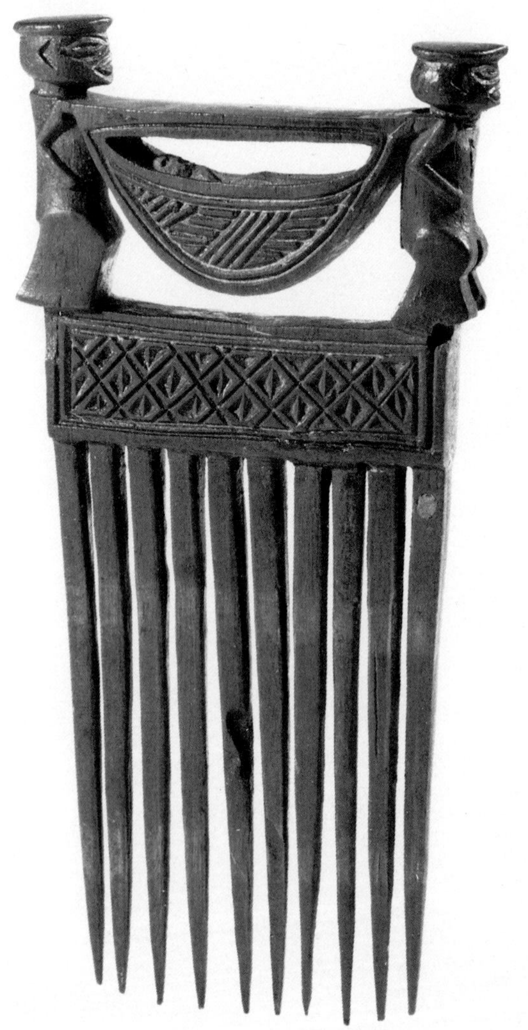

335

331 Group of persons on the way to a funeral, wood.
Angola, Chokwe.

The bier (see also No. 335) does not seem to appear among other types of divination figures. This could represent a burial scene that the artist has misunderstood. The corpse (*mufu*) is carried to its grave in a sling attached to a carrying pole. In the divining process this funeral scene signifies which one of the ancestral spirits, determined by the preceding throw, the client is to appease through sacrifice.

332 Male figure (*kalamba kuku wa lunga*), wood, beads.
Angola, Chokwe.

The father or ancestor, recognizable by his sitting posture with elbows propped on knees, is part of the basic divination ensemble. Whereas most of the other published pieces are rather simply carved, this one is of conspicuously high quality. The supple body, asymmetrical attitude of the limbs, and complicated coiffure suggest that the artist created the figure in response to exacting individual demands.

333 Masked dancer (*cikunza*), wood.
Angola, Chokwe.

Baumann states that this figure, easily recognizable by its head covering, represents the hunting spirit found in almost every divinatory basket. If this figure moves to the top when the basket is shaken the diviner interprets it as luck in hunting or the blessing of children. To assure such success, either in hunting or for his wife in childbearing, the client must order a small *cikunza* figure and carry it as an amulet either on his belt or bound to his hunting weapon.

334 Four figures bound together, wood, brass wire.
Angola, Chokwe.

This group consists of cubistically shaped figures of three humans and a dog. For its interpretation the position of the *cikunza*—the figure wearing the mask—is decisive (see No. 333). Since the figure of the dog may refer to either hunting or pregnancy, the combination of the mask wearer with the dog allows various interpretations.

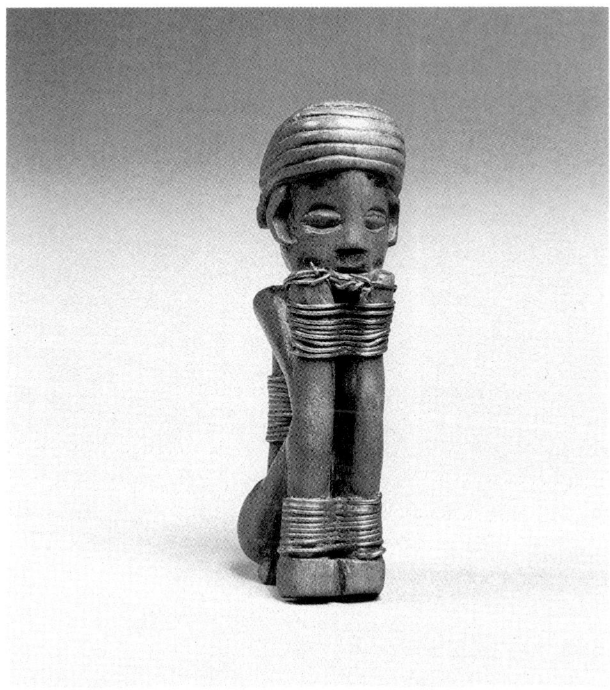

336

335 Comb with figures, wood.
Angola, Chokwe.

The openwork scene on top of this comb consists of two male figures carrying a third in a hammock (*tipoya*). The Portuguese had become acquainted with the hammock in Brazil and introduced it to West Africa in the sixteenth century. It became a royal insignia in many places.

Height 13.8 cm. 33-30-10
Acquired from Schomburgk 1933

Lit.: M. L. Bastin 1961, p. 328; K. G. Lindblom 1928, pp. 5-11.

336 Female figure, wood, brass wire.
Angola, Lwena.

The collector obtained this piece from the Chokwe, who used it as a divination figure, as the female

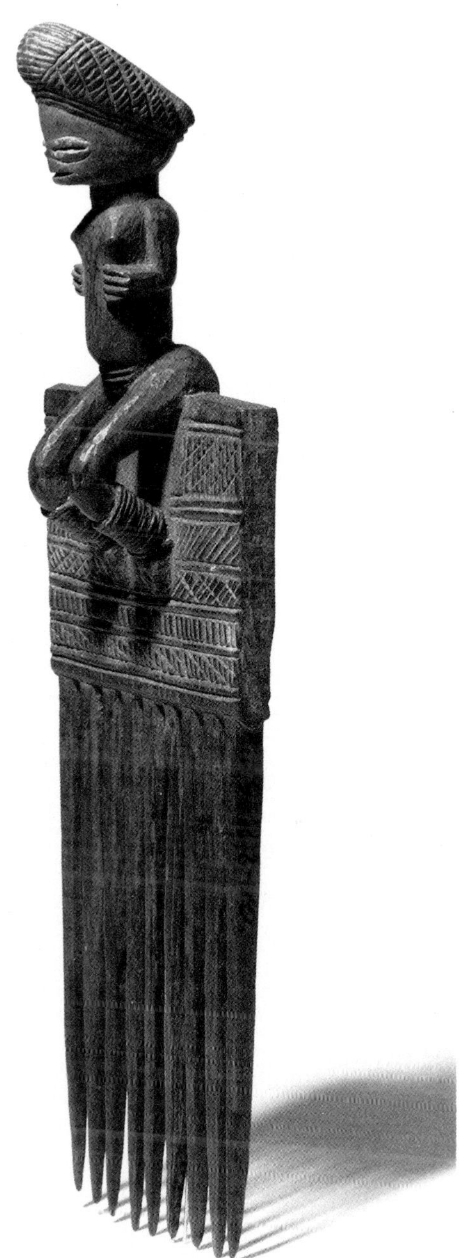

337

companion to the father or ancestor (No. 328). But here function and place of discovery are secondary, for the figure originally formed the handle of a comb (see No. 337), and characteristics of style suggest that it is the work of the Lwena rather than the Chokwe. The human body presented as compact block is notable. Coiffure and metal ornament—wire coiled around both legs as in No. 337—reveal that the figure represents a noble lady.

Height 6.5 cm. 33-30-5
Acquired from C. Schomburgk 1933

Lit.: M. L. Bastin 1961, Illus. 134, 135.

337 Comb (*tsisakulu*) with female figure, wood, brass wire.
Angola, Mbunda.

The carefully carved combs of the Mbunda, Chokwe, and their neighbors, used only by men, are for the most part adorned with chip-carved patterns and three-dimensional figurative sculpture. This is a frequently recurring figure—a female with artistic coiffure and anklets, represented by brass wire coiled around both legs.

Height 16.5 cm. 29-22-10
Acquired from Kammel 1929

Lit.: H. Baumann 1935, p. 35.

338 Chair, wood, leather, tacks.
Angola, Chokwe, Lwena.

The late-Baroque chairs that Portuguese officials imported from Europe were imitated by the Chokwe and Lwena and used by village chiefs as status symbols. Whereas their structure and shape correspond exactly to the European model, the ornament is entirely in a traditional African style. The lozenge decoration and the pair of sculptured figures of a chief and his wife with cap and coiffure designating no-

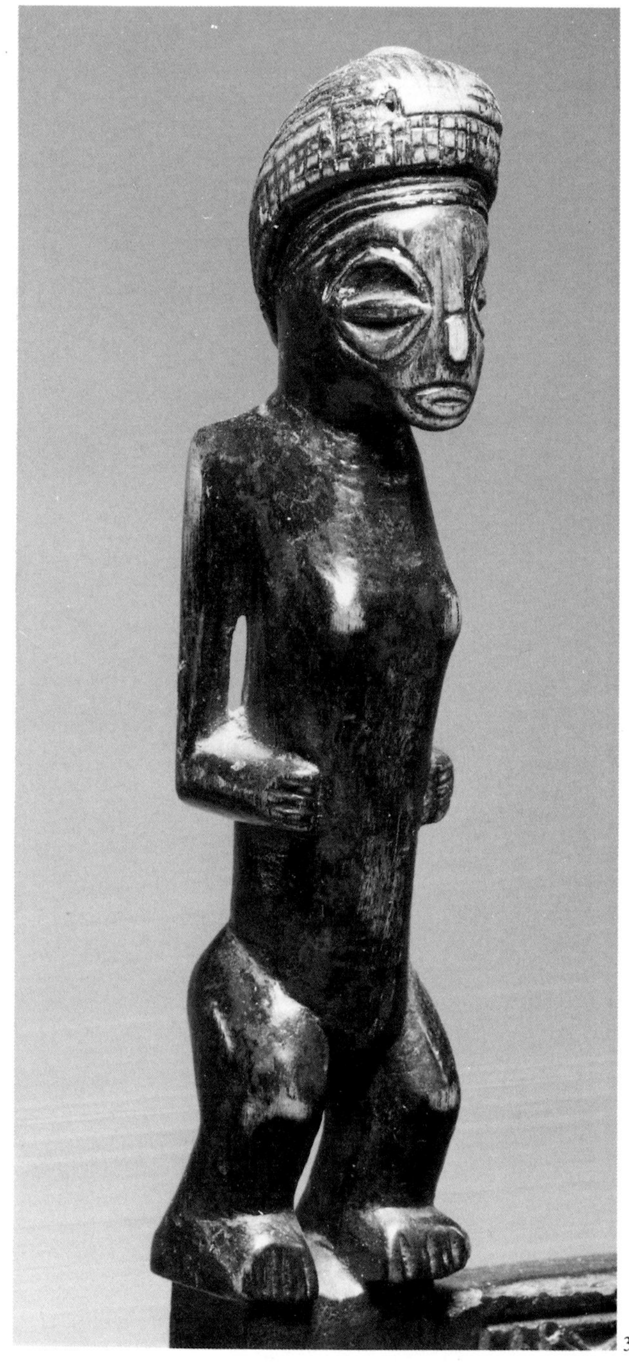
338

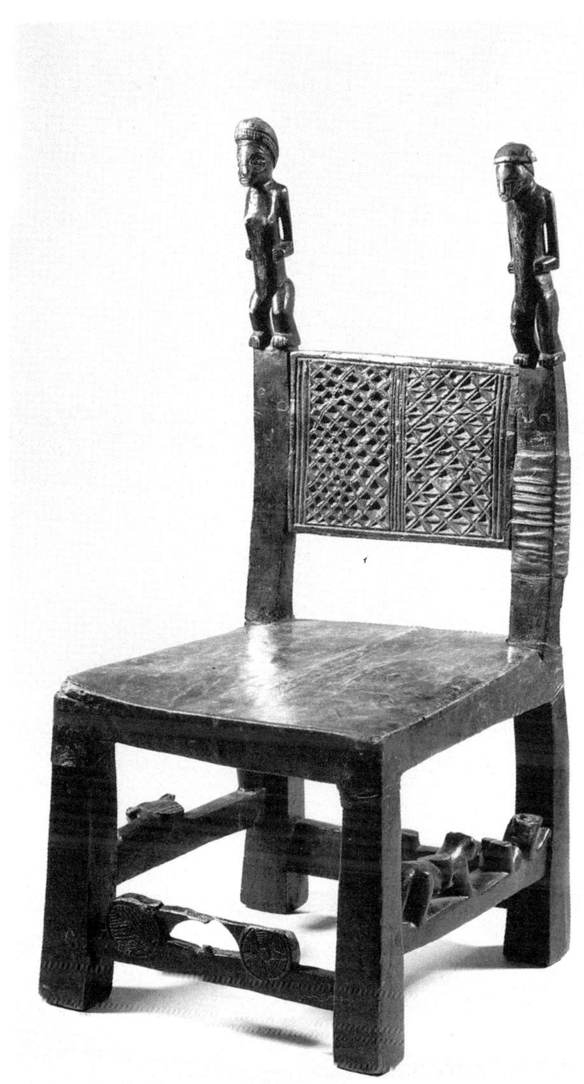

338

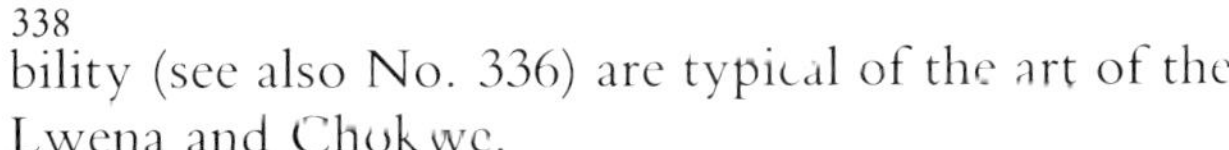

bility (see also No. 336) are typical of the art of the Lwena and Chokwe.

Height 56.5 cm., width 23 cm. 80-301-290
Collected by S. Fohn 1933, in the Museum since 1980

Lit.: M. L. Bastin 1961, pl. 182-89; L. de Sousberghe 1959, p. 114.

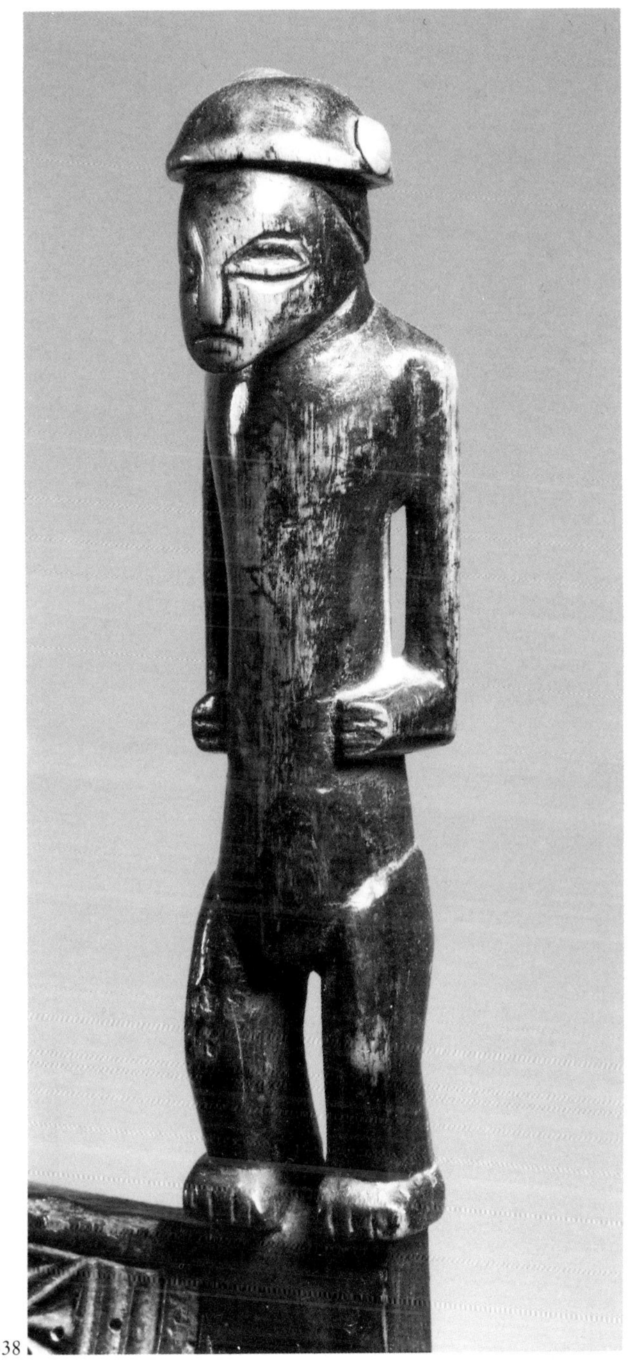

338

The Kuba Empire and its Neighbors

Toward the end of the Middle Ages between the Kasai and Sankuru rivers the great Kuba or Bushongo empire arose out of an alliance of many small states. The Kuba kings promoted the arts, and groups of well-trained craftsmen (among whom the woodcarvers enjoyed especially high esteem) worked constantly for the court. Much of the extraordinarily rich art of the Kuba probably originated in that splendid court, becoming common property only in the course of time. In any event, highly developed geometric ornament, for instance, was already widespread throughout the Kuba empire by the nineteenth century and was applied not only to almost all ritual objects but also to most everyday utensils. this ornament, comprising triangles, diamonds, zigzags, and plaited and looped bands, is always diagonally arranged—possibly a sign that it originated in basketry. A few decades ago these patterns were to be seen everywhere: woven of palm-leaf ribs on house walls, in plush fabrics for blankets and clothing, and on jars, beakers, spoons, and other utensils carved of wood.

The Kuba empire has a very detailed oral tradition that describes past kings as political reformers and cultural heroes. One of the most important rulers, who reigned from 1600 to 1620, is said to have introduced the art of royal sculpture, the splendid raffia fabrics, and the use of certain types of ornament in wood carving and basketry. According to legend, he received his most important inspirations while on a study tour in Pende country situated west of the Kuba empire on the upper Kwango River. The Pende, an artistic people have become especially famous for their carving of masks and ivory miniatures.

Lit.: E. Torday & T. A. Joyce 1910, p. 9ff.; J. Vansina 1954, p. 3, 4.

339 Mask (*ngady a mwaash*), wood, paint, brass. Zaire, Southeastern Kuba.

This mask appeared at initiation and funeral ceremonies and acted as guardian of the initiates' bush camp. It probably represented Shene Malula, also called Mweel, sister and wife of the mythical first ancestor.

This is a characteristic example of one of the three main types of Kuba masks. Distinctive features are the expansive, bulbous forehead, domed at the center and tapering back and up to a pointed hairline (see also No. 342), and protruding eyes surrounded by holes through which the wearer may see. The eyes, of the so-called chameleon type, have pupils of brass nails. The nose is strong and pointed with curved nostrils; the rimmed, crescent-shape mouth is connected to the nose by a straight line. The face is divided by white, black, and yellow lines, straight and zigzag, with interstices precisely filled with rows of triangles. A cap of raffia fibers adorned with cowries and glass beads was originally attached to this light-wood mask.

Mask representations have become popular in the applied art of the Kuba, appearing on lidded wooden boxes, on beakers and drums, and on the handles of vessels and spoons (see Nos. 340-42, 344, and 358).

Height 26 cm., width 21 cm. 15-26-39
Acquired from L. Frobenius 1915 (Weber collection)

Lit.: F. Neyt 1981, pp. 159-61; E. Torday & T. A. Joyce 1910, pp. 87, 250; E. Torday 1925, p. 100; J. Vansina 1978, p. 216.

340 Wooden bowl with handle. Zaire, Songo Meno, Dibele.

This bowl displays geometric decoration altogether typical of Kuba art, although it comes from their northern neighbors. A variant of interlace ornaments it; on the handle is a mask face ending in a human hand.

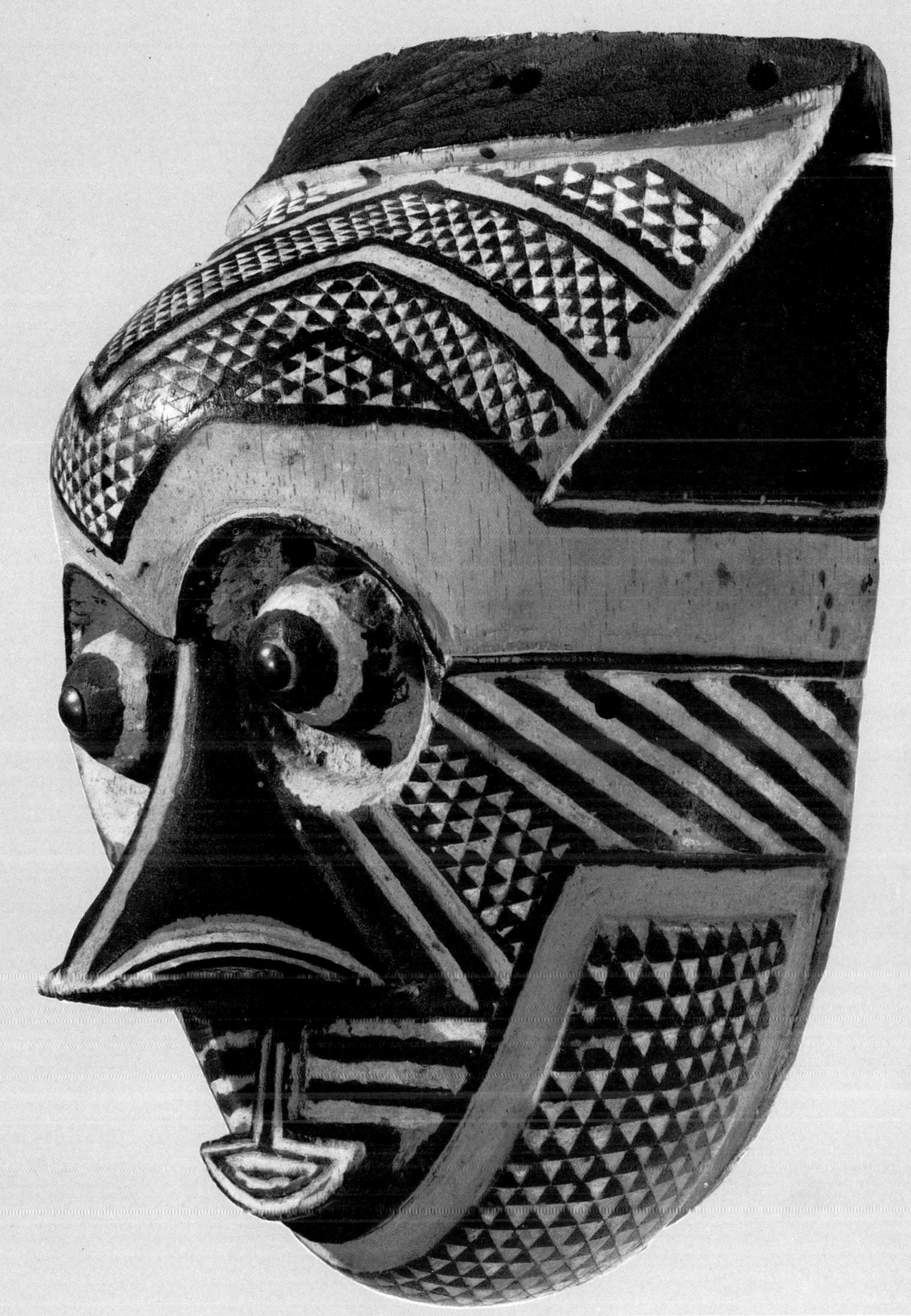

Height 7.5 cm. 15-12-11
Acquired from L. Frobenius 1915 (Weber collection)

Lit.: E. Torday & T. A. Joyce 1910, pp. 204, 210, 11, 264.

341 Fragment of a spoon handle, wood.
Zaire, Shoowa, Butala.

The triangular head of this abstract female figure, increasing upward in width, is presumably modeled on a mask (see No. 339). The diagonal lines under the eyes represent tears; the several lines incised into the neck supposedly suggest necklaces (see also No. 323). Breasts and genitals appear on the boardlike torso as raised forms in a shape that recalls cowrie shells, which served as both adornment and currency and were also considered symbols of fertility.

Length 23 cm. 18-22-13
Acquired from L. Frobenius 1918 (Mignon collection)

Wooden Beakers

Anthropomorphic wooden beakers and wooden cups of geometric shapes (cylinders, cones, or goblets), are famous for their rich decoration. The guilloche and its variants—entwined rectangles, Solomon's knots, heart or kidney-shape patterns, and figure eights—predominate. Like most other Kuba carvings, the wooden beakers were imitated by neighboring peoples. Such beakers were used mainly for secular purposes (to serve palm wine, for example), but finely adorned beakers were also used to administer the poison to test accused persons in the poison ordeal.

Lit.: H. Baumann 1964, pp. 29-57; W. Deonna 1952, pp. 163-70; H. U. Hall 1924, pp. 7, 9; H. Himmelheber 1960, pp. 370-73; L. Segy 1951, 52, pp. 39-41; H. Straube 1965, pp. 242-44.

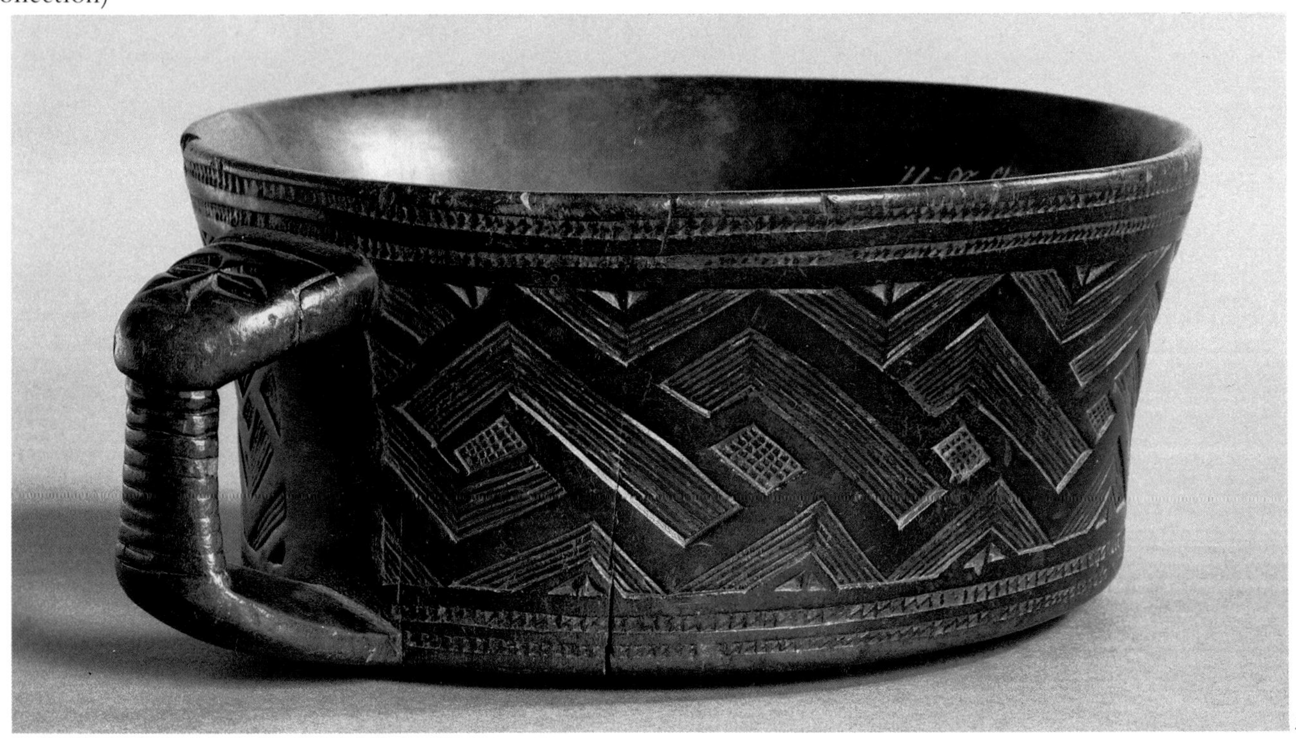

340

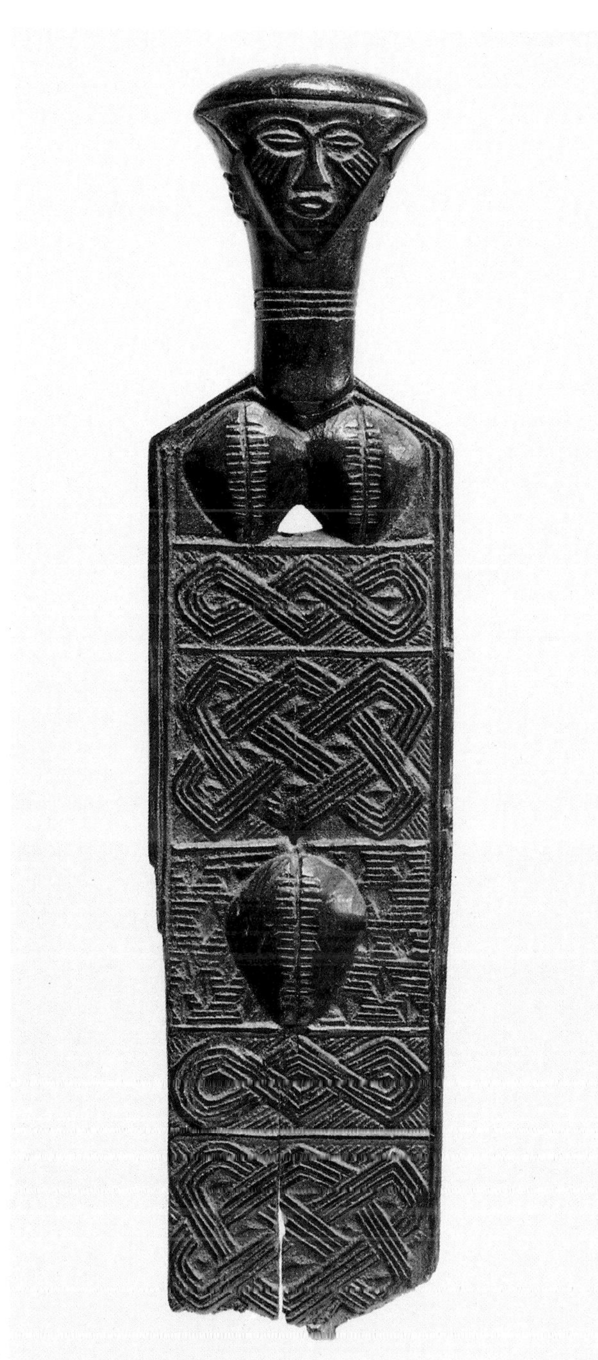

341

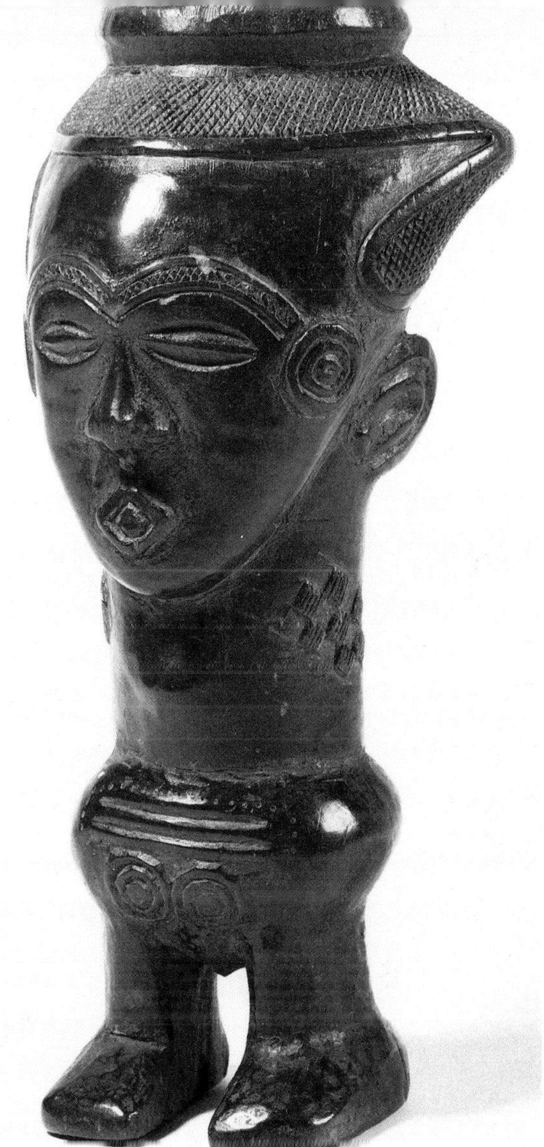

342

342 Anthropomorphic beaker, wood.
Zaire, Songo-Meno, Futu.

The human figure in this beaker is reduced to head, abdomen, and legs. The head, widened at the tem ples and the shaved-out corners of the forehead, simulate the horned coiffure that was the right of chieftains and of women after the birth of the first

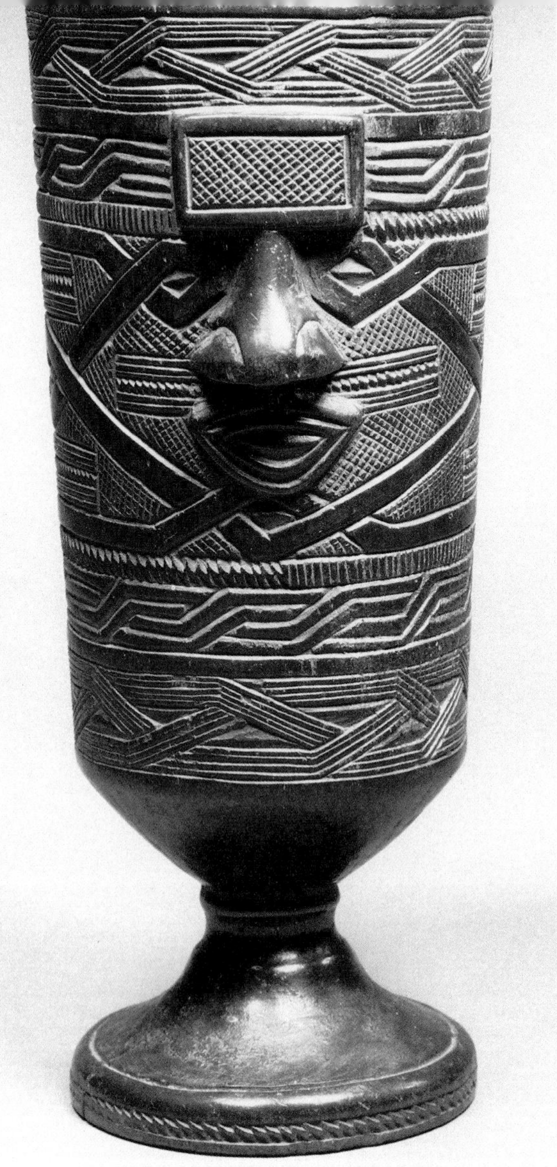

343

child. Also typical are the almond-shape eyes, ornamental cicatrices formed of concentric circles, and mouth in diamond form.

Height 23.5 cm. 18-22-1
Acquired from L. Frobenius 1918 (Mignon collection)

Lit.: E. Torday 1925, p. 100.

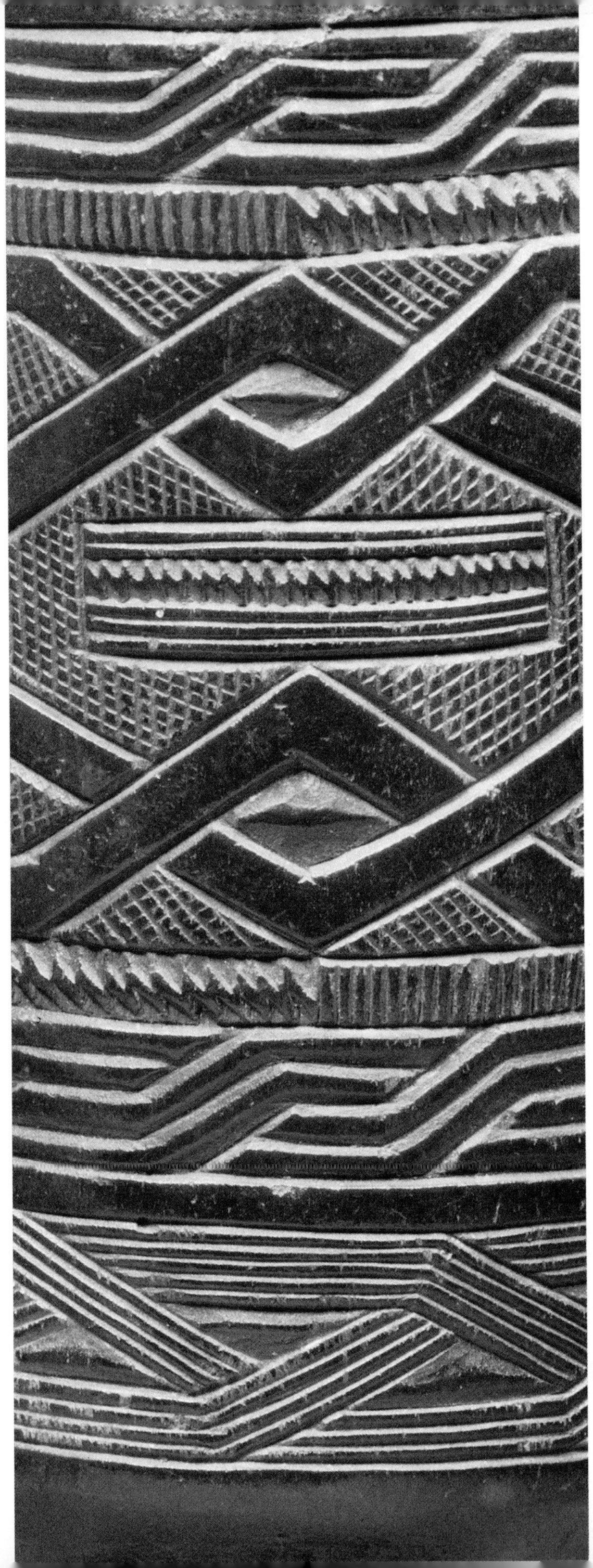

343

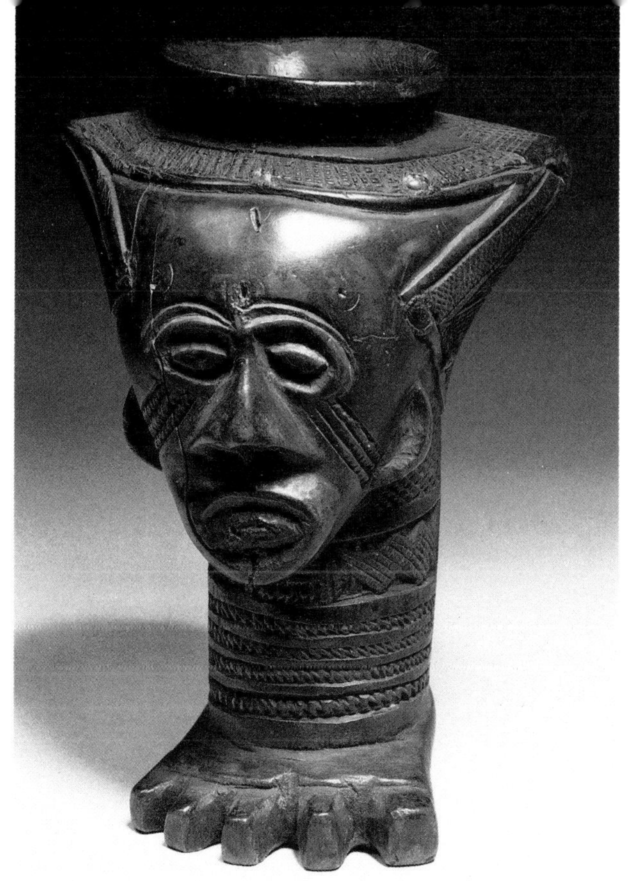

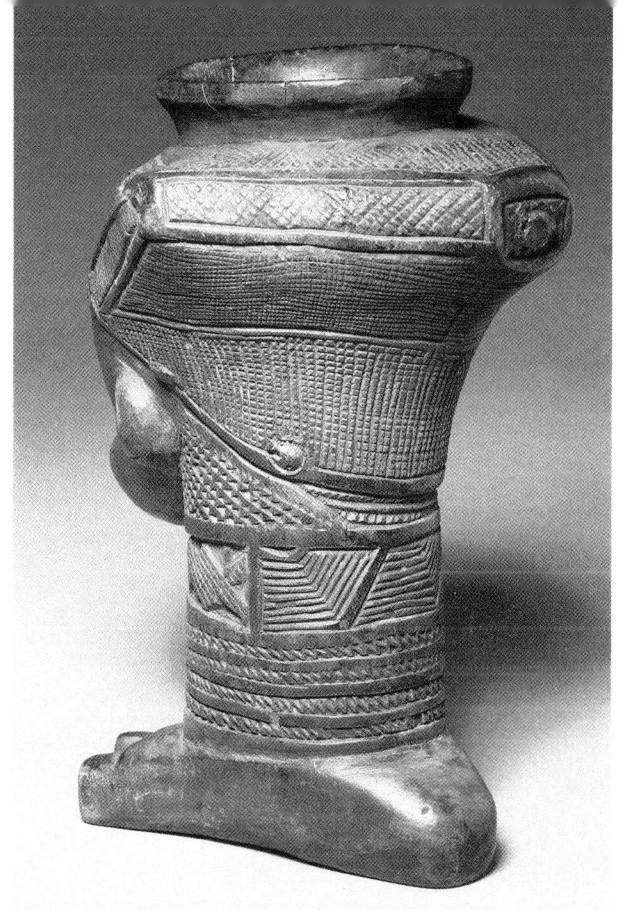

344

343 Goblet-shape beaker, wood.
Zaire, Kuba.

High quality craftsmanship and a playful but judiciously devised composition make this an impressive piece. The contours and eyes of the human face arise out of the flat relief bands that ornament the vessel. Only the strong, beautifully shaped nose, stylized mouth, and the rectangle above them form sculptured elevations.

Height 22 cm. 18-22-6
Acquired from L. Frobenius 1918

344 Footed head beaker, wood.

Although otherwise similar to No. 342, this face is especially expressive of sadness. The richly varied decoration on the back of the elongated head and neck probably represents an artistic coiffure or a cap of some kind.

Height 18 cm. 18-22-4
Acquired from L. Frobenius 1918

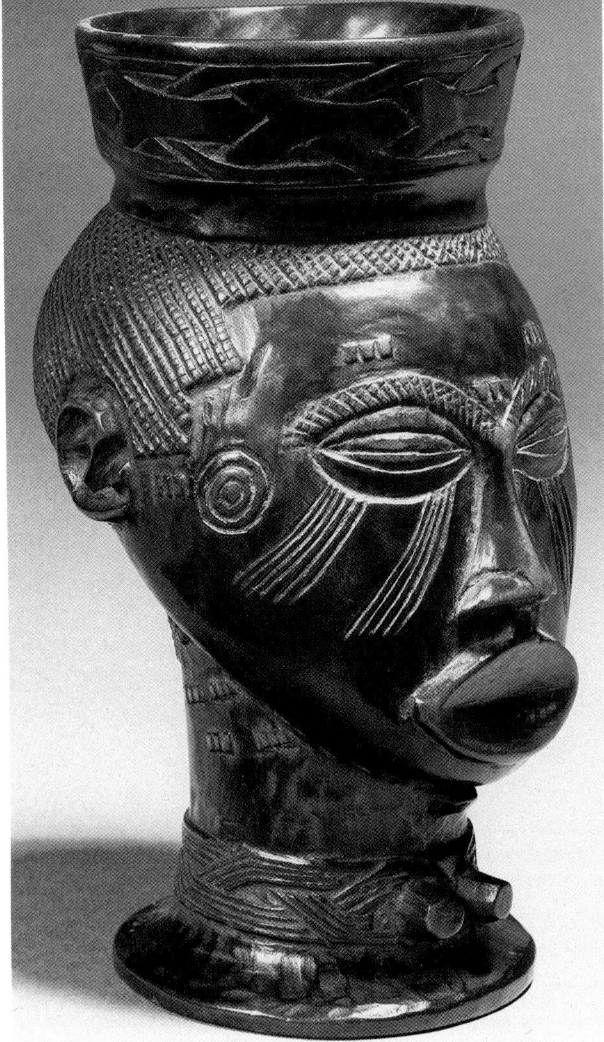

345

345 Head beaker on pedestal, wood.
Zaire, Wongo (?).

The roundness and naturalistic nose, mouth, and ears of this head make this more realistic than others. The groups of lines below the almond-shape eyes and the concentric circles at the temples depict ornamental scars.

Height 18 cm. 14-49-2
Acquired from Kropp 1914

346 Cylindrical beaker with human figures, wood, tacks.
Zaire, Pyaang.

Carved in high relief with bodies suggested by flat-carved geometric bands, the three human figures in this unusual composition have only faces, hands, and legs. The broad lozenge-shaped faces recall the *pwevo* mask of the Chokwe. Chokwe divination figures (see Nos. 33 and 336) may have inspired the hunched pose with elbows resting on the knees.

Height 19 cm. 18-22-7
Acquired from L. Frobenius 1918

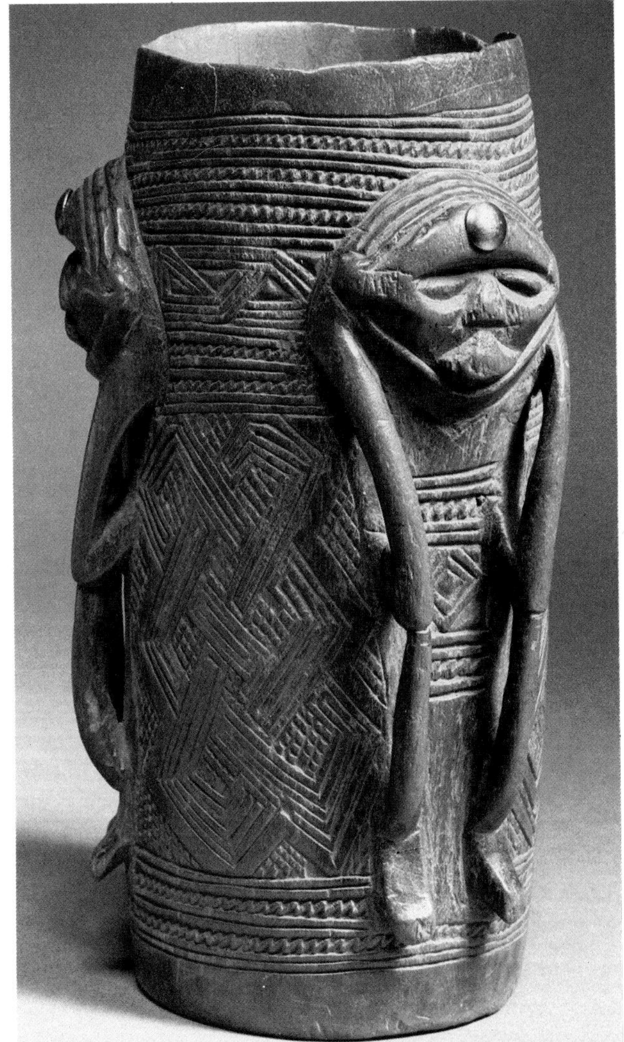

346

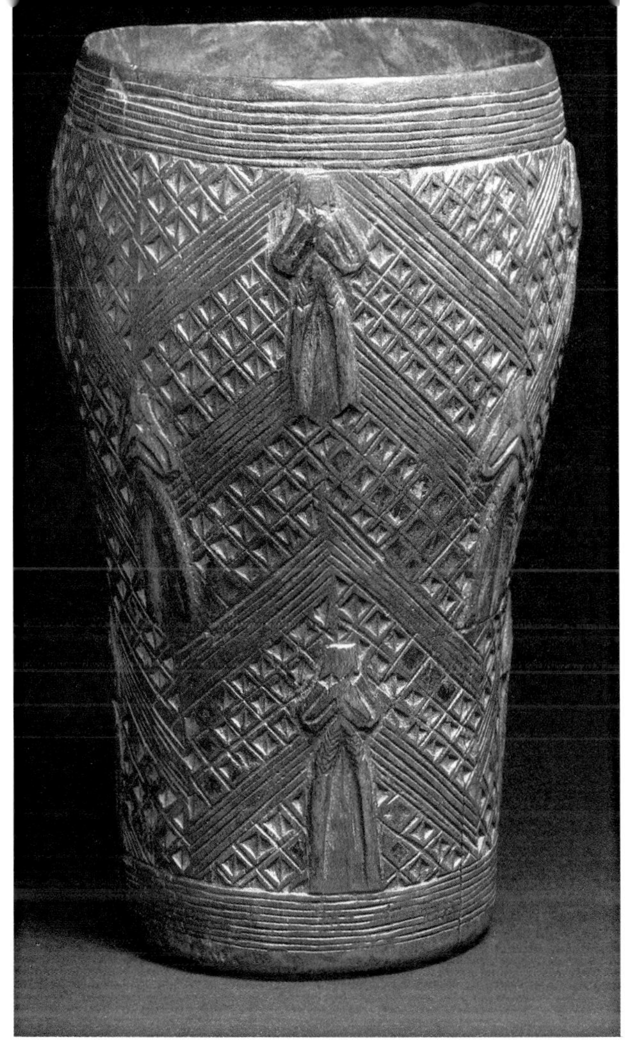

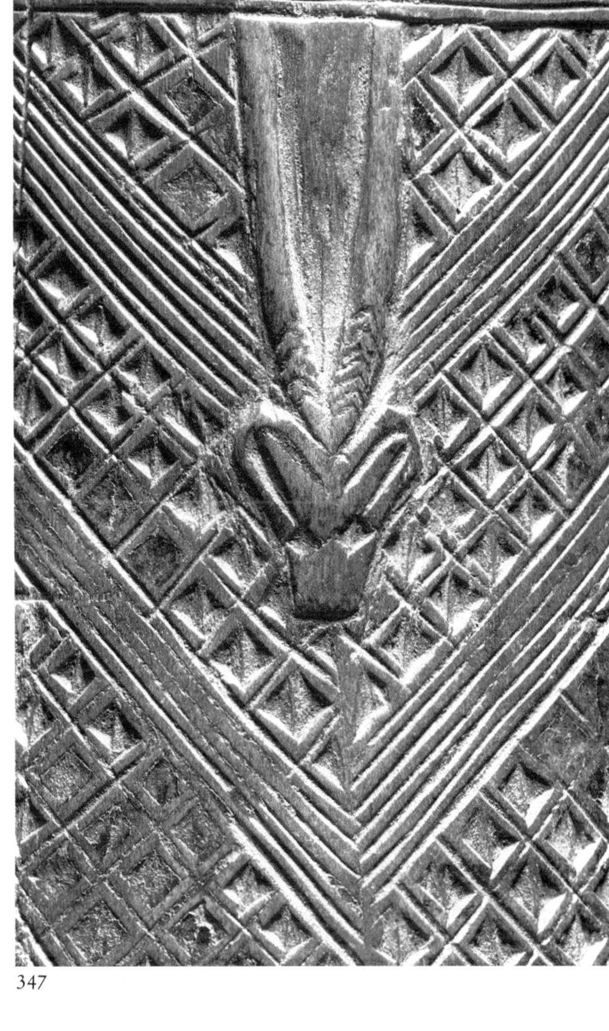

347

347 Vaselike beaker, wood
Zaire, Kuba.

Bold zigzag bands stand out against a ground covered by small diamonds. Upside down long horned antelope skulls carved in higher relief appear at intervals.

Height 19 cm. 18-19-8
Acquired from L. Frobenius 1918

Lit.: E. Torday & T. A. Joyce 1910, p. 211.

348 Beaker with circular pedestal, wood.
Zaire, Kuba.

The carver of this vessel worked with a particularly light touch in dividing the openwork base into four feet. Among the Kuba there are drums with similar structure and ornament.

Height 17 cm. 15-26-8
Acquired from L. Frobenius 1915
(Weber collection)

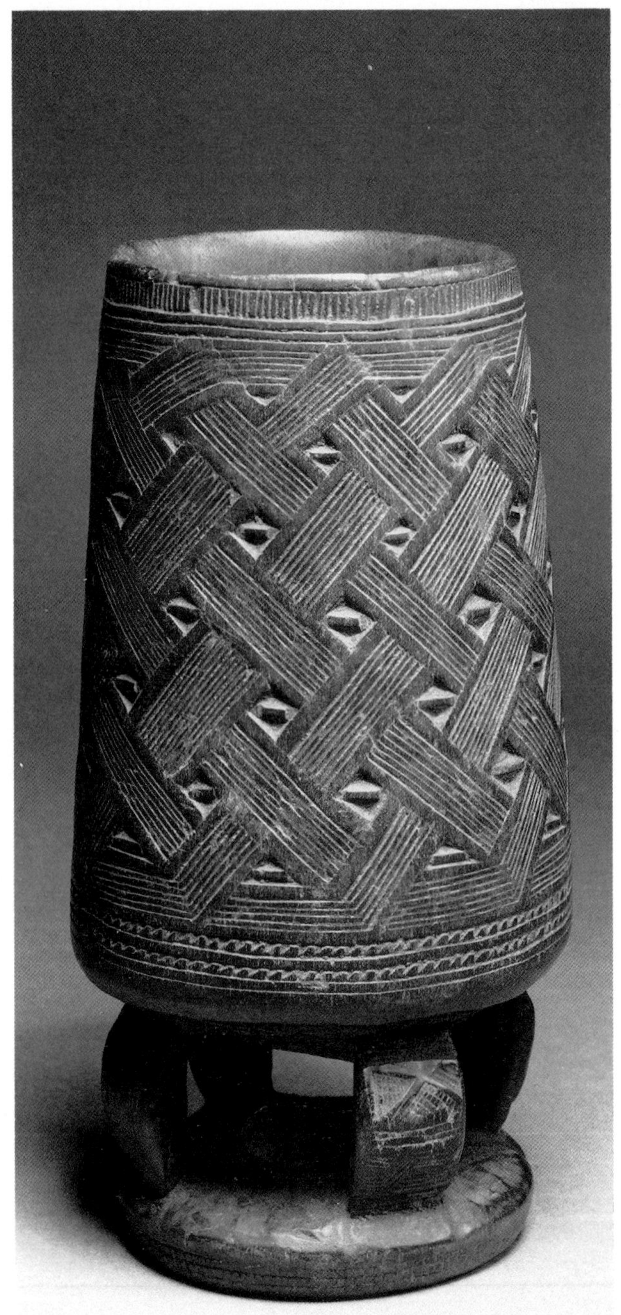

348

Boxes and Jars for Redwood Paste (349-359)

The fragrant red paste called *tukula* is made of powdered camwood, or amboyna wood (from the *Pterocarpus indicus* tree) and is uşed chiefly as body paint and fabric dye. Great amounts of it are used for festivals in general, but particularly at dances. In Kuba color symbolism, red is connected with funeral rites and *tukula* is applied to corpses. Splendidly adorned boxes and jars are employed to prepare, though not to store, the paste. The most recent and most frequent containers are crescent-shape. Older and rarer forms include cylindrical jars whose shapes are reminiscent of lidded baskets and square, oval, and semioval pieces with mask faces. The sides and lid are ornamented with many varieties of interlace pattern (see also No. 340).

Lit.: H. Straube 1960, pp. 401-04; E. Torday & T. A. Joyce 1910, pp. 112, 127, 165, 206.

349-351 Three cylindrical jars, wood.
Zaire, Kuba.

Almost the entire surfaces of Nos. 349 and 350 are decorated with variants of the interlace ornament. The large sculptured insect on the lid of No. 350 serves as a handle. Circular ornaments considered to represent the sun and zigzags with star motif decorate No. 351. The tall jar reminiscent of Kuba woven lidded baskets, No. 349, is a notable example of this type of vessel.

Height 18 cm. 15-26-28
17 cm. 18-19-10
11 cm. 15-26-16
Acquired from L. Frobenius 1915 (Weber collection) 1918

Lit.: E. Torday & T. A. Joyce 1910, pp. 210-14, 223.

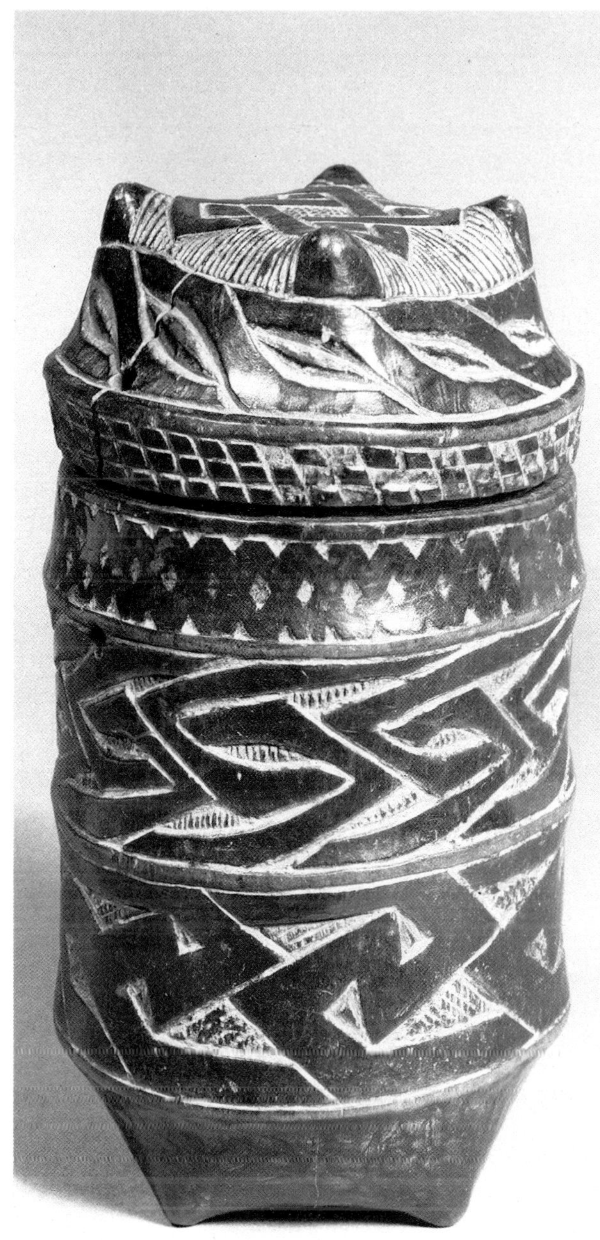

349

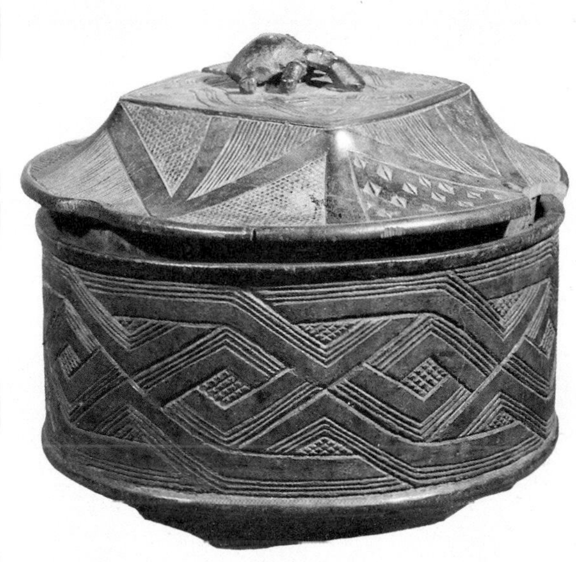

350

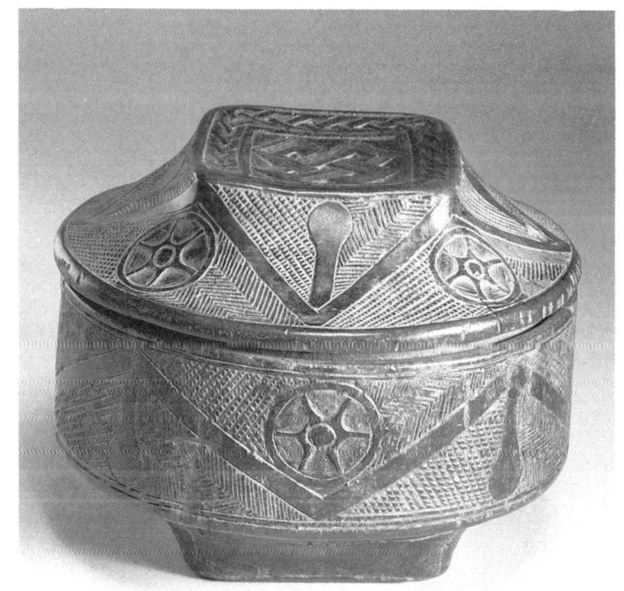

351

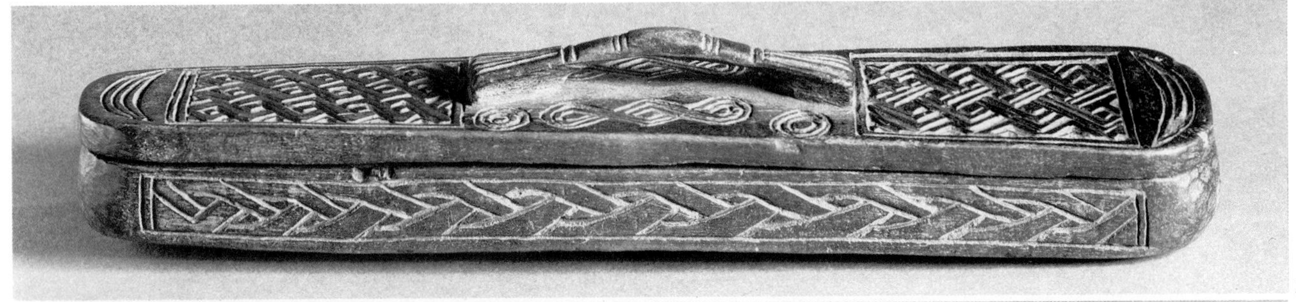

352

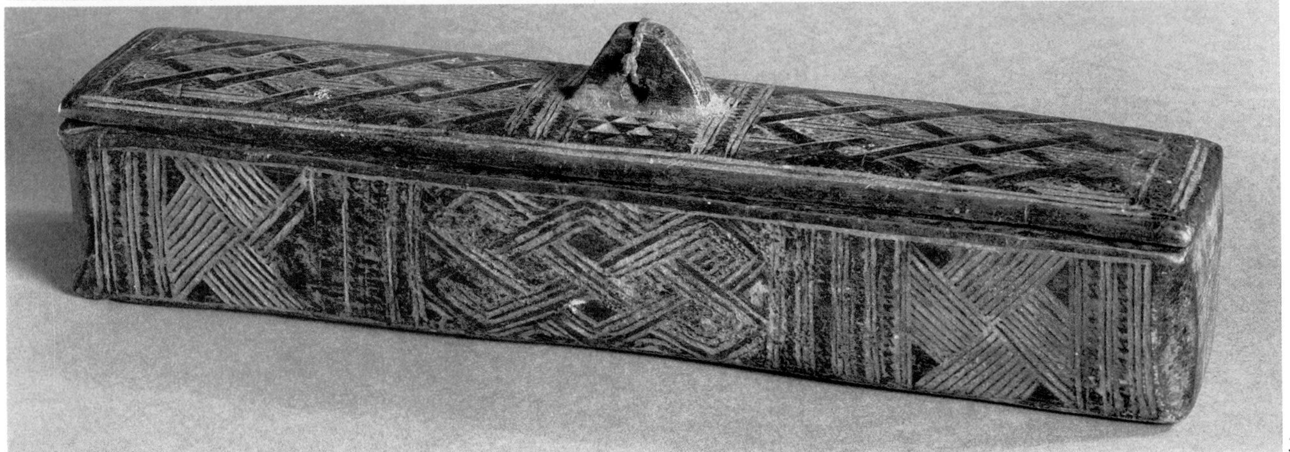

353

352,353 Two rectangular lidded boxes, wood.
Zaire, Kuba.

Redwood paste (*tukula*) remains in the recesses of these boxes, the larger of which (No. 353) is more finely ornamented than No. 352. They may perhaps have been used as containers for shaving knives.

Length 25 cm., 28 cm.
Acquired from L. Frobenius 1918 — 18-19-1
L. Kegel 1951 — 51-3-11

354,355 Two half-moon-shape lidded boxes, wood.
Zaire, Kuba.

Sculptured carvings ornament the lids of these boxes. The face of No. 354 is reduced to eyes and mouth. Sun symbols, finely carved antelope horns, and a bow-shaped handle ending in hands decorate No. 355.

Height 4.8 cm., length 18.3 cm. — 18-19-4
5.5 cm., length 30.5 cm. — 15-26-24
Acquired from L. Frobenius 1915 (Weber collection) 1918

356,357 Two square, lidded boxes, wood.
Zaire, Kuba.

Lids, walls, and bottoms of these boxes are decorated, one with a "Solomon's knot," the other with an incised chameleon. It is worth noting that the drawings on both bottoms have double contours. Casket and lid are tied together loosely.

Height 7 cm., length 18 cm. — 15-26-21
7 cm., length 17 cm. — 18-19-2
Acquired from L. Frobenius 1915 (Weber collection) 1918

Lit.: E. Torday & T. A. Joyce 1910, pp. 208, 09, 212.

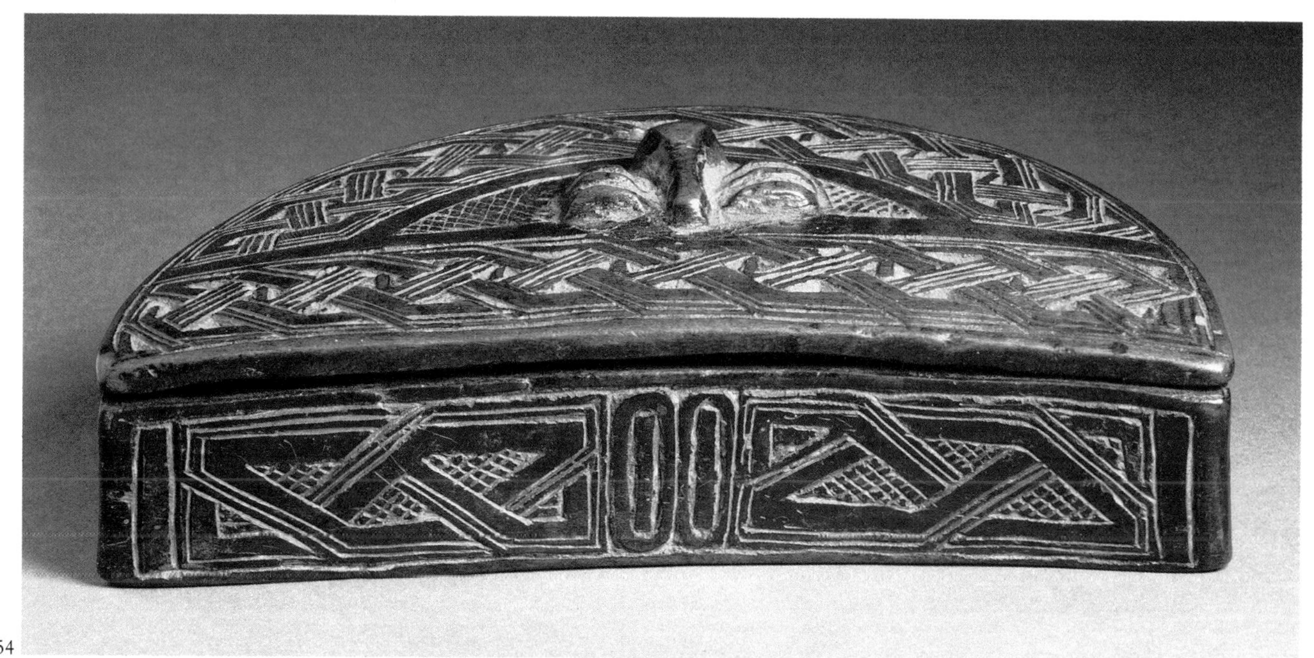

354

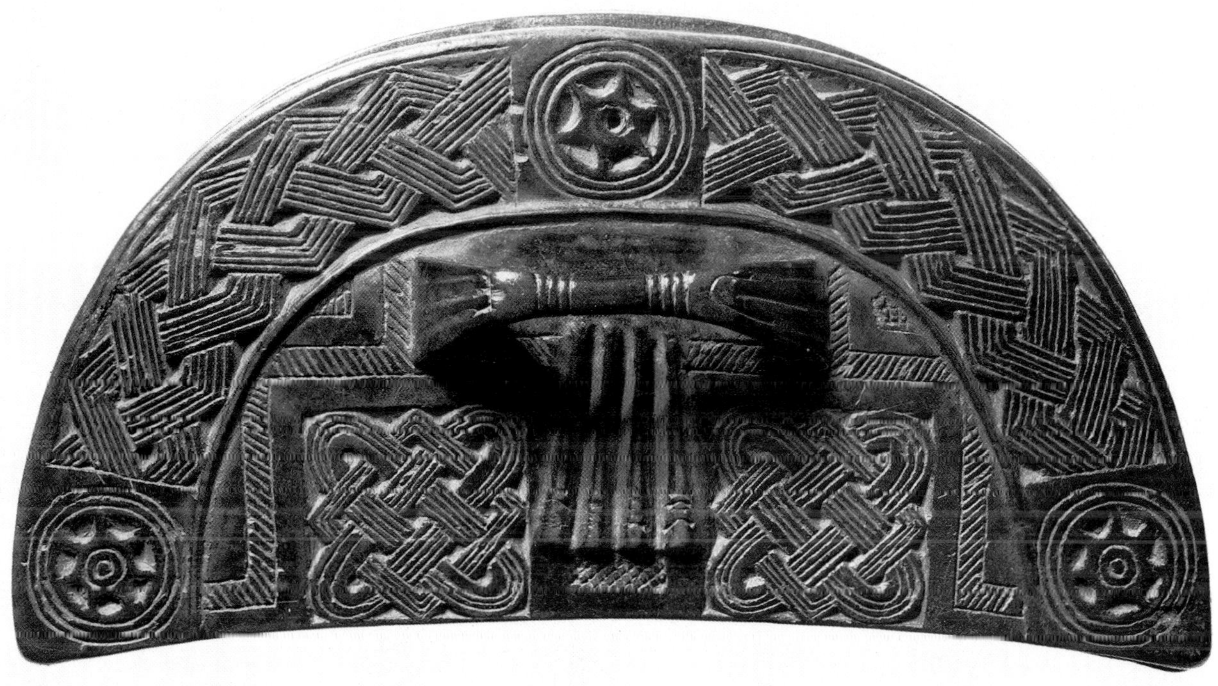

355

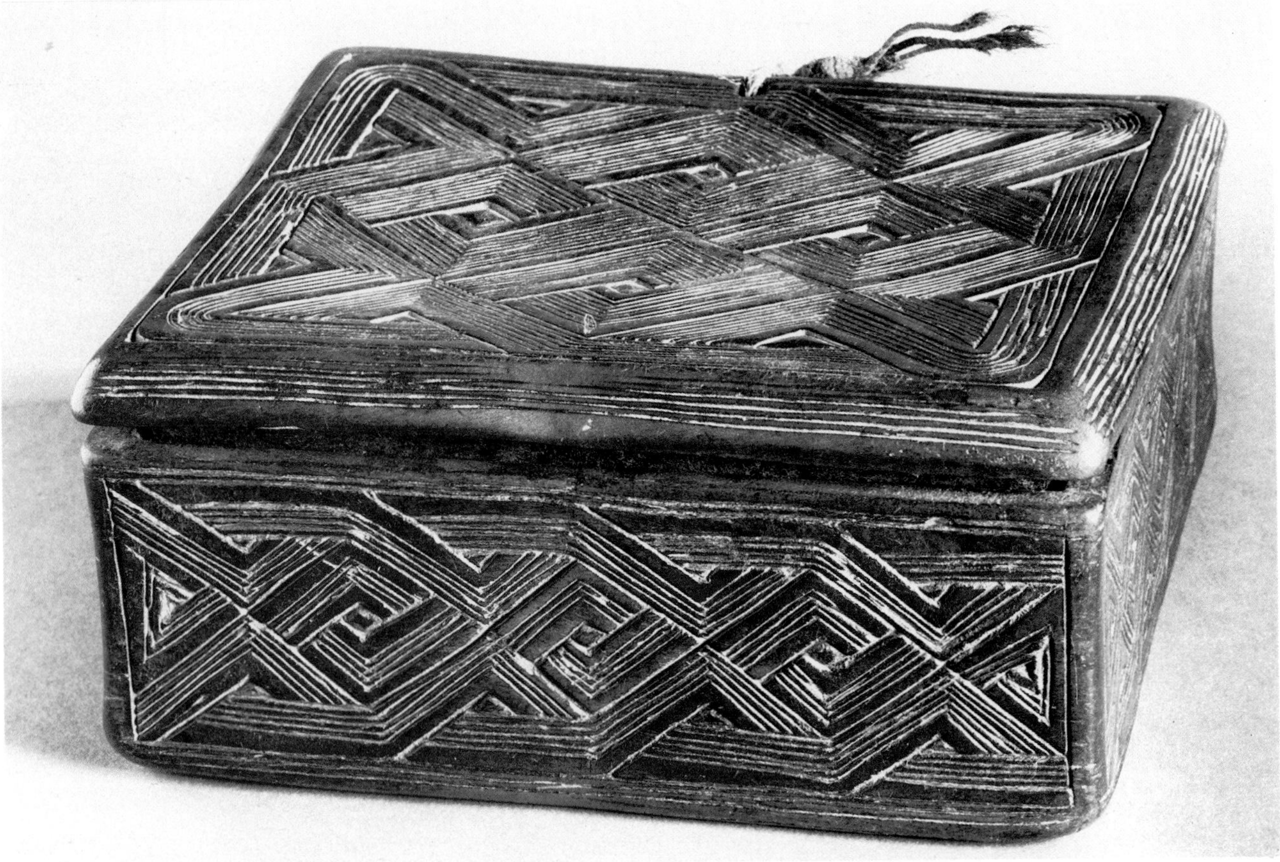

356

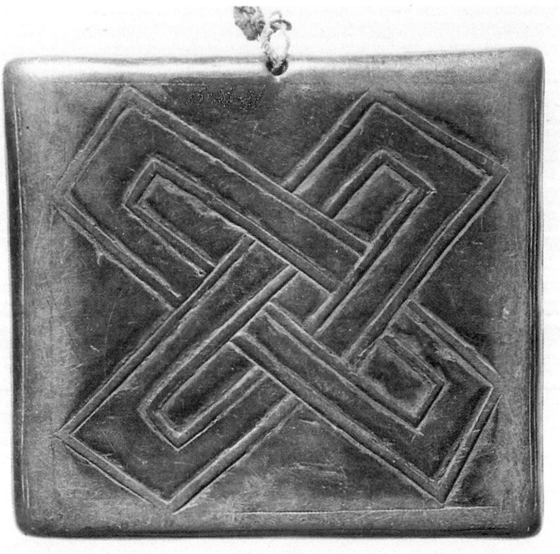

356

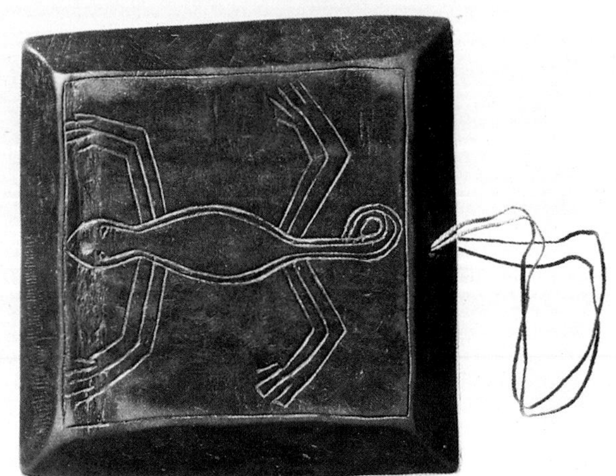

357

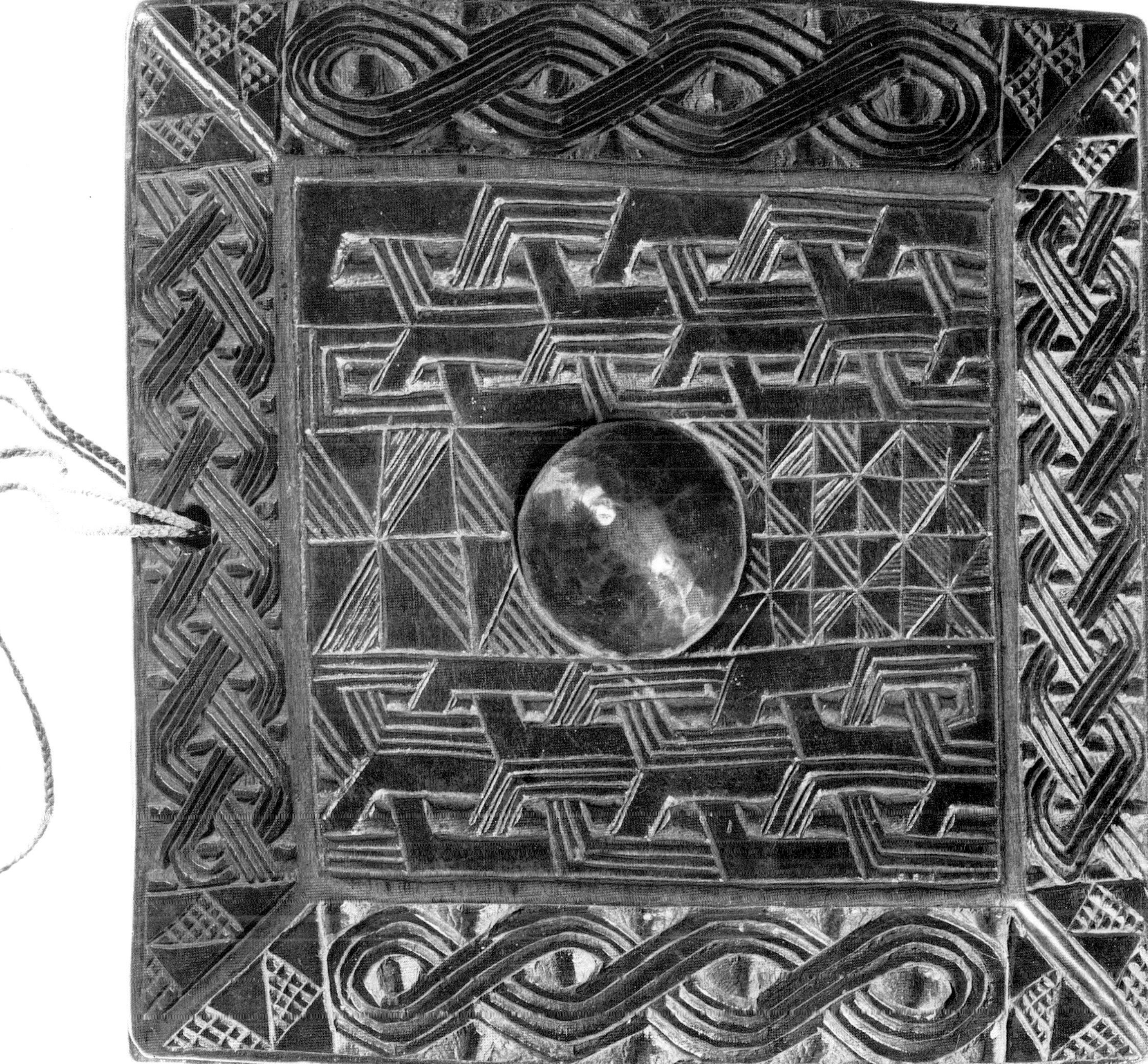

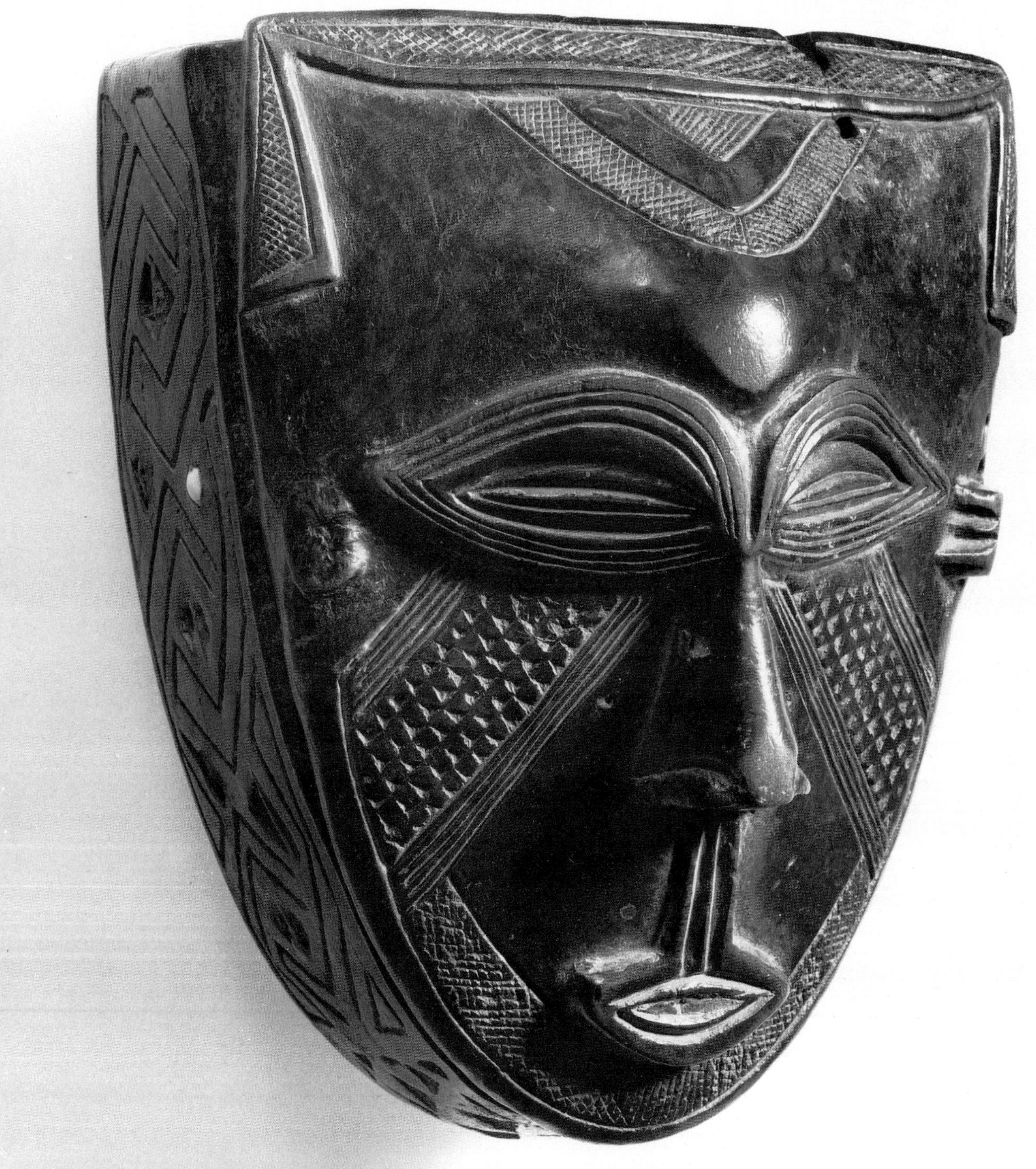

358 Lidded box, wood.
Zaire, Kuba, Ifuta.

The distinctively drawn face on the lid of this box has narrowed, rimmed eyes, a forehead that bulges in the middle and has shaved-out corners, a slender, pointed nose, an almond-shape mouth connected to the nose by straight lines, and oblique lines under the eyes (see also No. 339).

Height 21 cm., width 16 cm. 15-26-26
Acquired from L. Frobenius 1915 (Weber collection)

359 Lidded box, wood.
Zaire, Central Kuba area, Lubundi River.

This rare type of *tukula* casket is in the form of a gabled house with detachable roof—a faithful imitation of a chief's house, whose walls consist of richly ornamented matting. Casket and lid are tied together.

Length 13 cm., height 11 cm. 15-26-12
Acquired from L. Frobenius 1915

Lit.: F. Neyt 1981, p. 150.

359

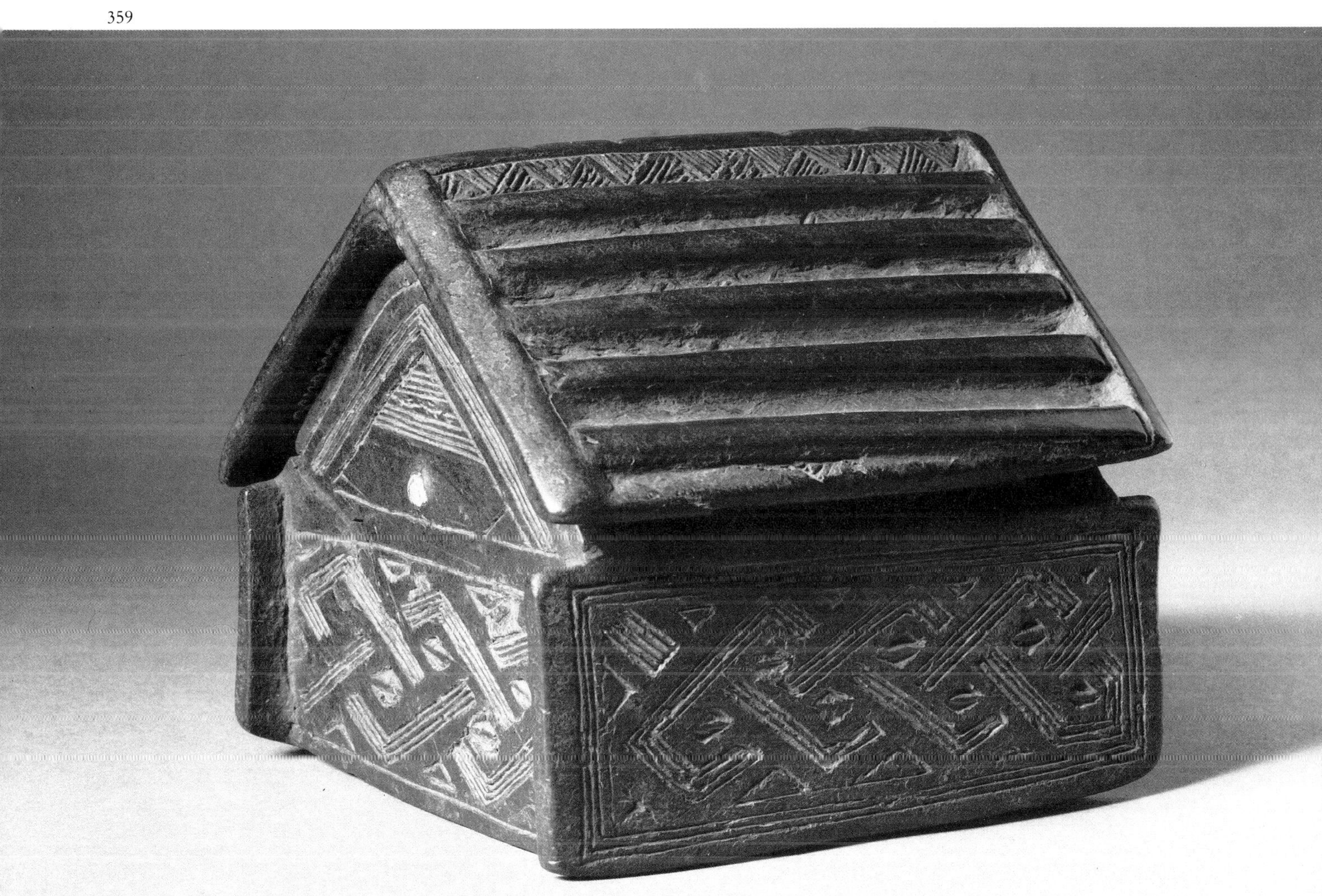

Embroidered Raffia Pile Cloth (360-62)

Embroidered raffia pile cloth (fabric made of raffia that has a soft plushlike pile) is among the famous applied arts of the Kuba region. It surpasses all comparable products in Africa south of the Sahara in the harmonious colors of its compositions and the balanced rhythm of its patterns despite the surprising breaks (or "leaps") in the ornamental rows. On the average, individual pieces are no larger than thirty by sixty centimeters, so several are usually sewn together. Closely embroidered cloth with especially splendid patterns was so valuable that only the rich and privileged had many, for only they had enough wives to engage in the time-consuming decoration.

The pile-making technique is simple, but requires much time and patience. After men weave a broad band of fabric from raffia fibers—left in their natural colors or dyed yellow, brown, or red to serve as background—the women embroider in one or more colors. They work the bamboo, bone-splinter, or iron needle (later, a European embroidery needle) between weft and warp so that no stitch is visible on the underside. Immediately after taking each stitch, the craftswoman cuts off the thread over her left thumbnail and fringes it out with a trapeze-shape knife.

Blankets sewn together from pile cloth were worn as ceremonial dress, used as wrappers for newborn babies, and as shrouds for dead kings. They also covered royal stools. Such garments were not for sale and changed hands only as heirlooms, presents, or as a means of settling damage claims. Today pile cloth is produced for sale and is of far poorer quality than earlier examples. In order to save time, today's craftspeople use coarse basic textiles and embroidery threads and garish chemical colors. The patterns are monotonous, and lack the animation created by the traditional pattern "leaps."

No one has yet satisfactorily explained why and how the Kuba came to produce pile cloth embroideries. According to oral tradition, the Pende wives of the Kuba kings introduced them, but since it can be proved that the art was indigenous to the west coast, most scholars think that the Kuba took up pile cloth embroidery after the coastal peoples gained access to imported European fabrics and ceased the tradition.

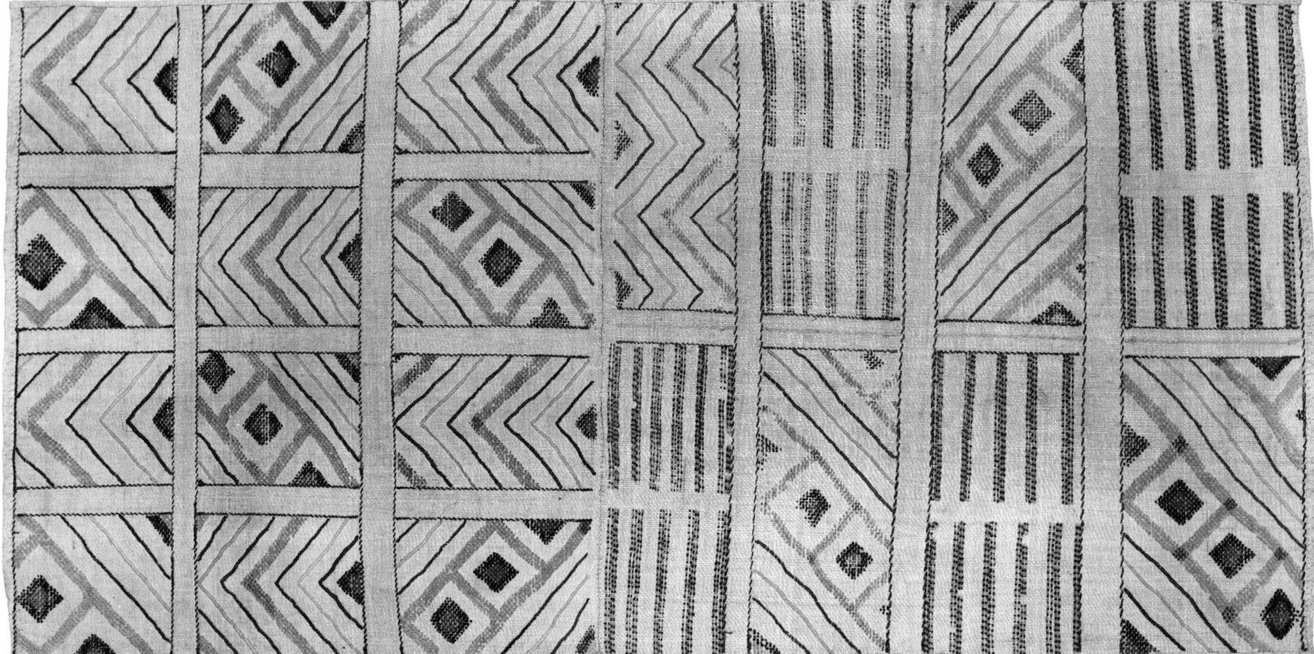

360

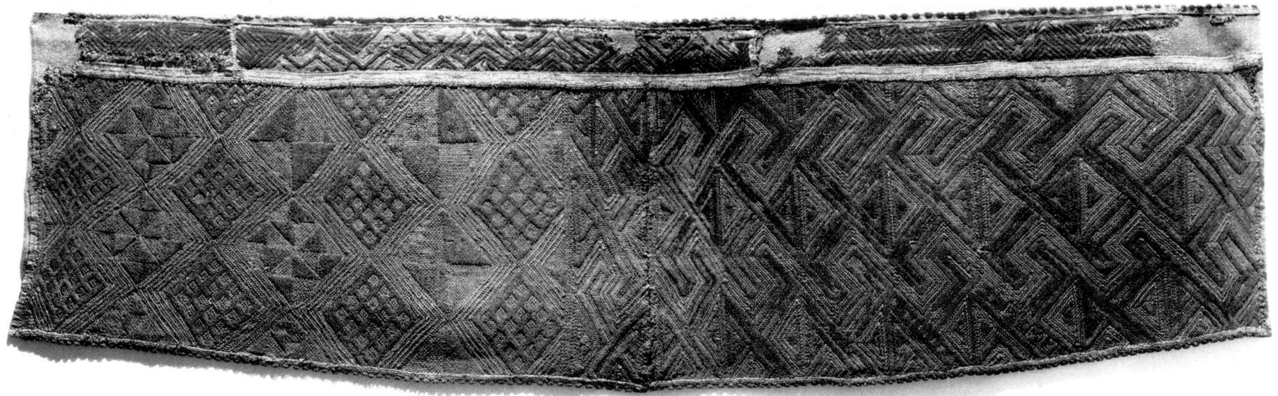

361

Lit.: M. Adams 1978, pp. 24-30; J. Picton & J. Mack 1979, pp. 198-203; A. Stritzl 1971, 10, 11; E. Torday & T. A. Joyce 1910, pp. 184-91; J. Vasina 1978, pp. 219-22.

360-62 Three raffia pile cloths.
Zaire, Kuba.

Length 136 cm., width 68 cm. 15-26-44
Length 150 cm., width 30 cm. 18-22-17
Length 156 cm., width 34 cm. 52-2-2
Acquired from L. Frobenius 1915, 1918, L. Kegel 1952

362

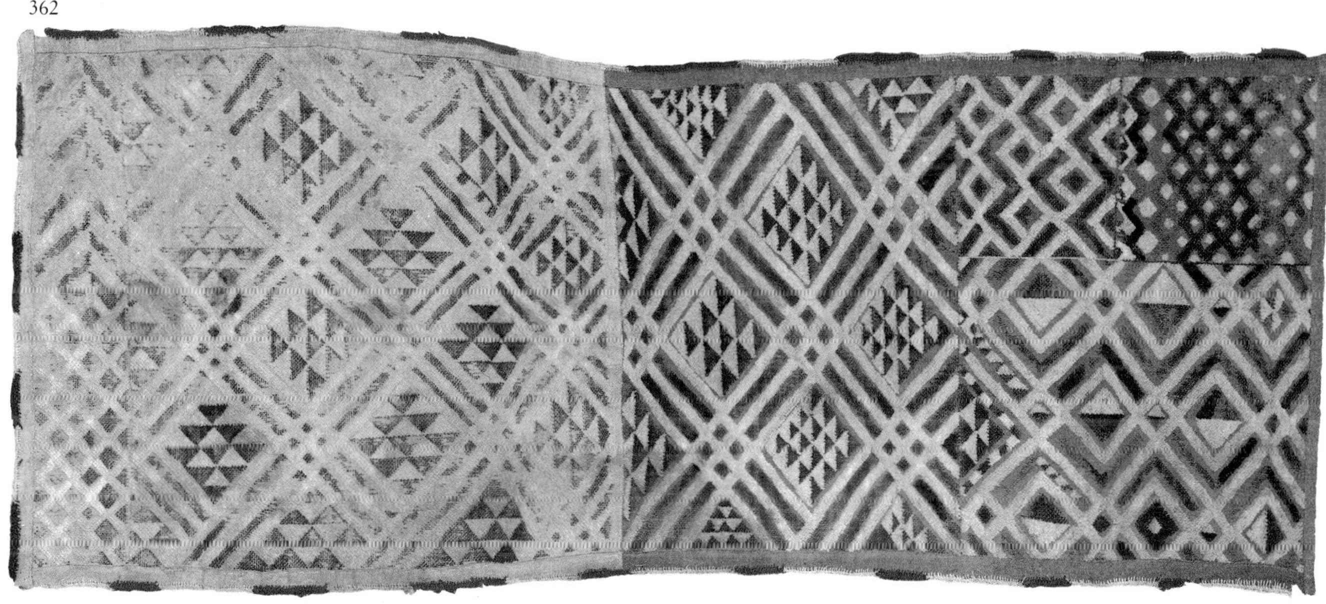

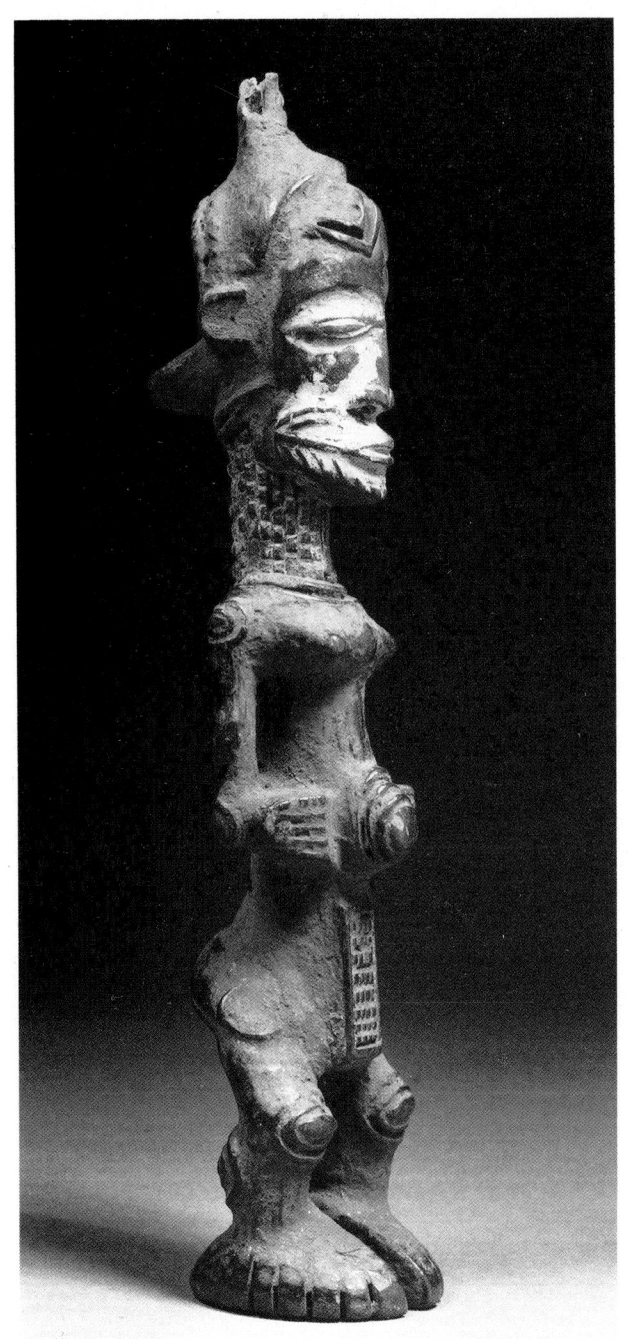
363

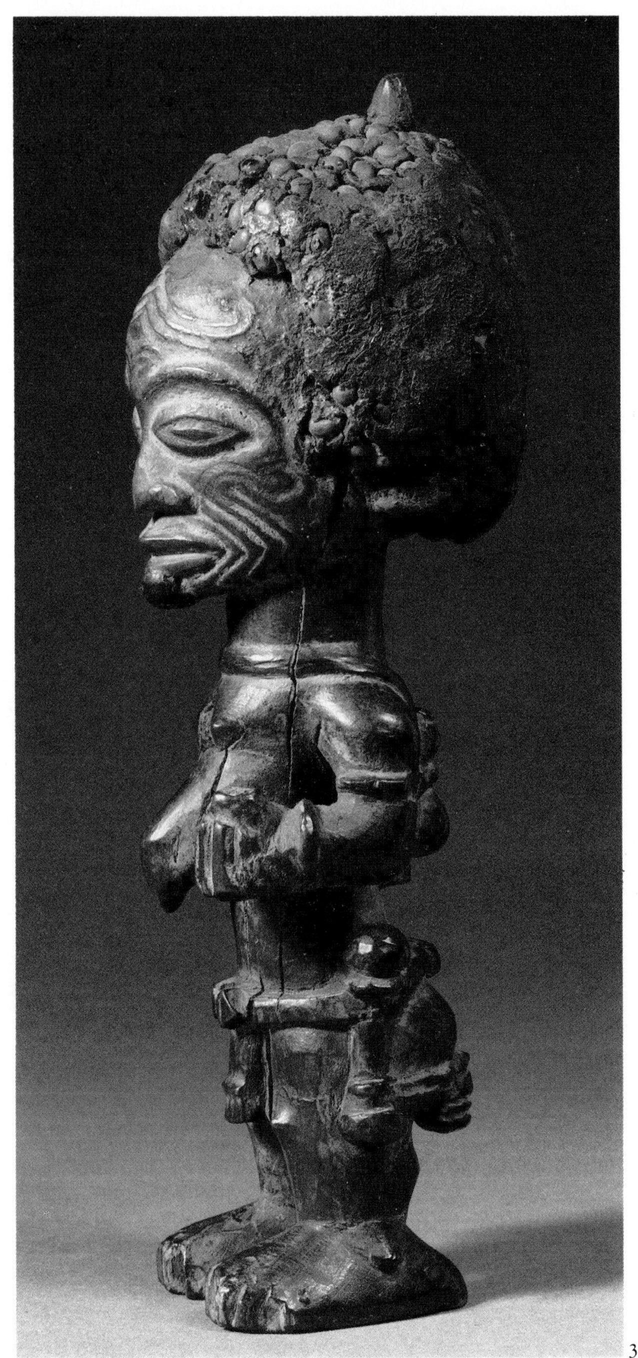
364

363,364 Two male figures (*mbulenga*), wood, resin, seeds.
Zaire, Luluwa.

Ethnic and political differences account for the variety in Luluwa styles. Both pieces shown here represent a single type, however—the *mbulenga* figures from the districts around Demba, Luebo, and Kazumba. They are believed to be responsible for beauty, health, and luck, which they secure by establishing links with guardian spirits. The numerous ritual and magic societies frequently use these carved figures.

Although on the whole they display a tendency toward abstraction, the figures have abundant, exactly depicted facial and neck cicatrizations, for these are felt to be particularly significant. Like many *mbulenga,* both figures hold a minute bowl containing magical substances. Marks representing cicatrices or body painting form concentric circles on shoulder joints, elbows, thighs, buttocks, calves, and knees. The red camwood paint, still visible, was renewed from time to time to "animate" the *mbulenga* power or to serve as a sacrifice to the tutelary spirit being summoned.

The decoration of the leopard-skin apron of No. 363 is like that of its neck ornament. No. 364, whose protruding navel looks like a bird's beak, is richly outfitted, wearing a necklace with a medicine calabash suspended from the back, upper-arm rings, and ivory beads hanging from the belt. All these are royal emblems.

Height (in both cases) 21 cm. 51-3-7; 15-26-33
Acquired from L. Kegel 1951, L. Frobenius 1915

Lit.: J. Cornet 1973, pp. 153, 157; P. Timmermans 1966, pp. 17, 18, 22, 23.

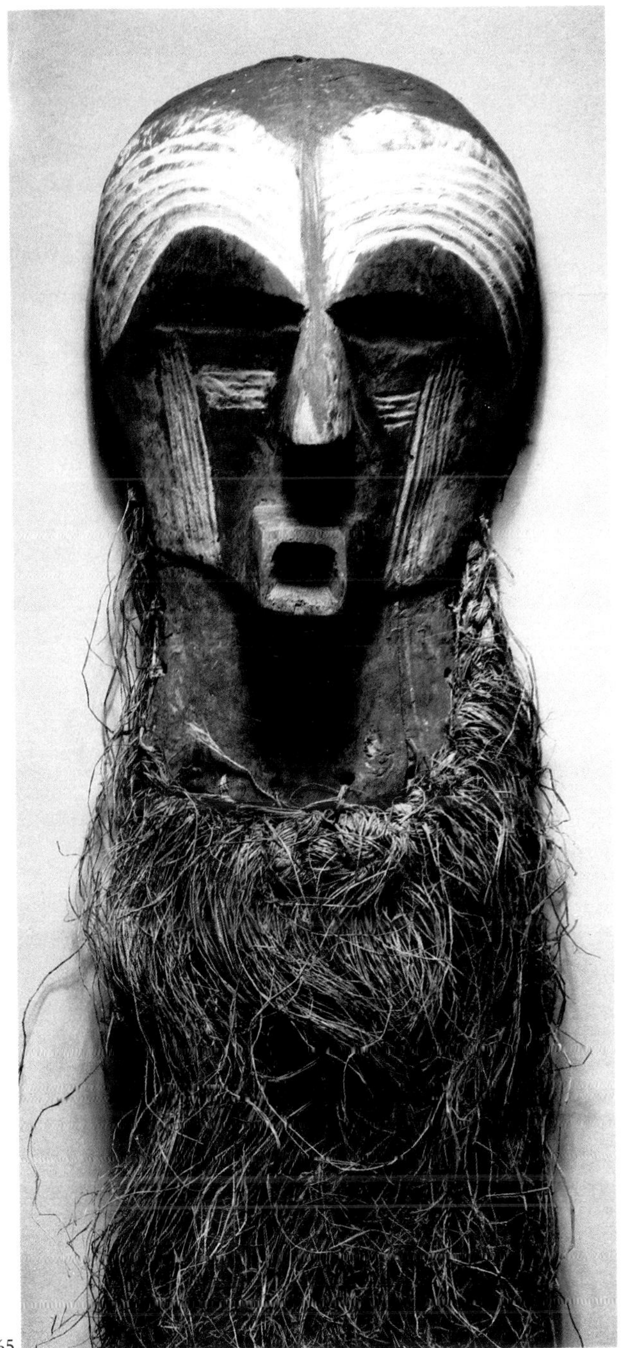

365

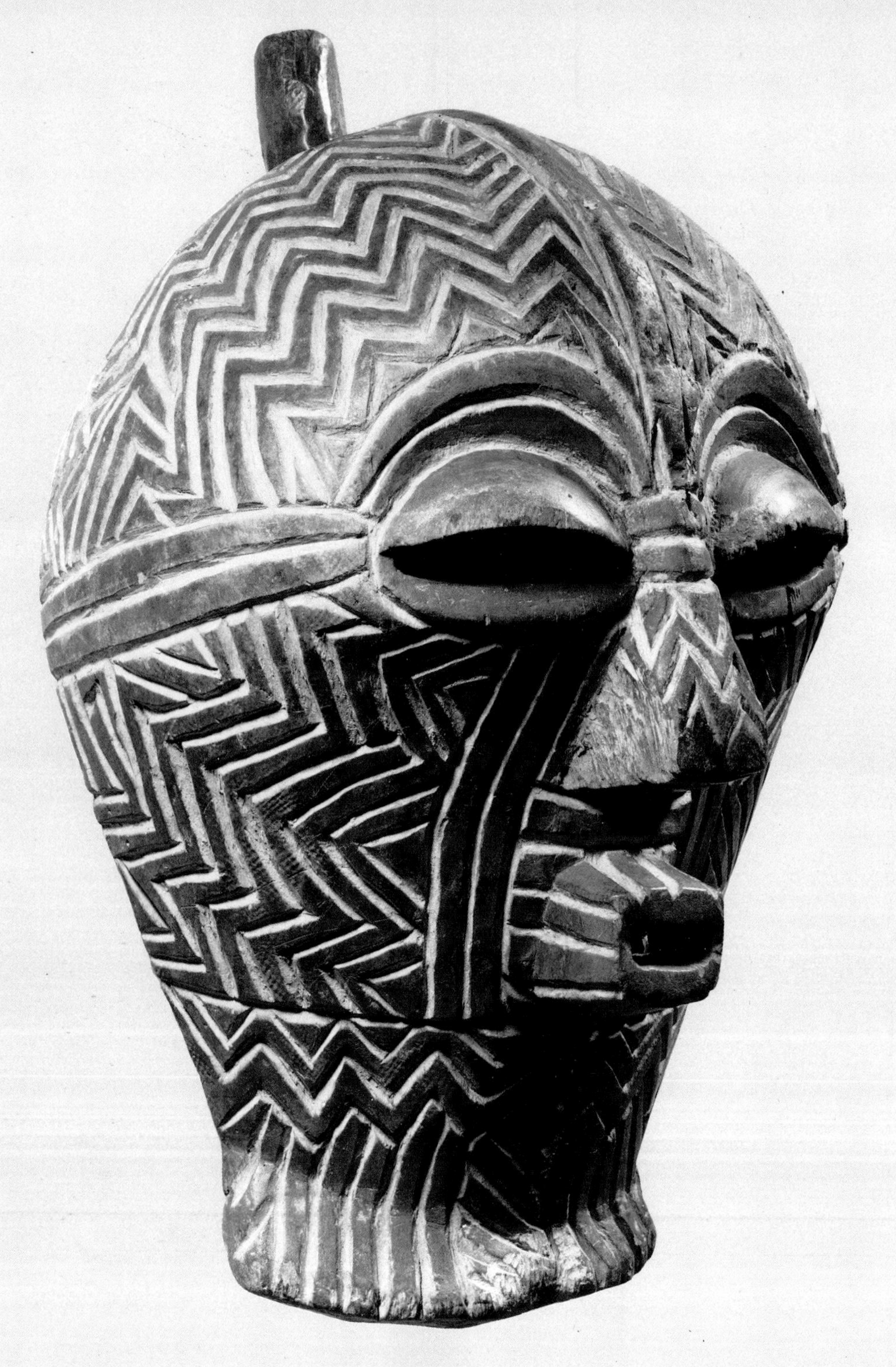

365,366 Two masks, wood.
Zaire, Songye-Luba, west of Kituri (Lomami).

No clear boundary separates the Songye (Songe, Yembe) from the linguistically related Luba on the Kasai River and in Katanga, and our objects are similarly transitional. This type of cubistic mask is designated *kifwebe* or *tshifwebe,* which simply means "mask." The entire surface is divided into geometric fields of white lines, straight or curved (No. 365), or of incised white lines in zigzag patterns (No. 366). The large rimmed eyes, projecting nose, and the distinctive four-cornered mouth are further features of this style. No. 365 has a beard of raffia fiber.

Little is known of the function of such masks. They often appear in male-female couples and seem to represent ancestors. They are brought out especially under the threat of a natural catastrophe such as the outbreak of disease, war, or death of a chief. According to the collector's report, the healer occasionally wore such a mask when treating the sick.

Height 45 cm., width 27 cm. 11.1464/65
Acquired from F. Mitchell 1911

Lit.: J. Cornet 1973, pp. 247, 249; J. Maes 1924, pp. 36-43.

367 Amulet mask, wood, raffia, feathers, mixed media.
Zaire, Songye-Luba, Kituri.

Such miniature masks were often worn as amulets to repel malevolent powers, and were probably also employed in ways unknown to us. Various articles including seven small horns, two small whistles, and several little wooden plugs with a suggestion of facial features, are suspended from the edge of the mask. This was probably part of a healer's paraphernalia.

Height 16 cm., with feathers 40 cm. 11.1466
Acquired from F. Mitchell 1911

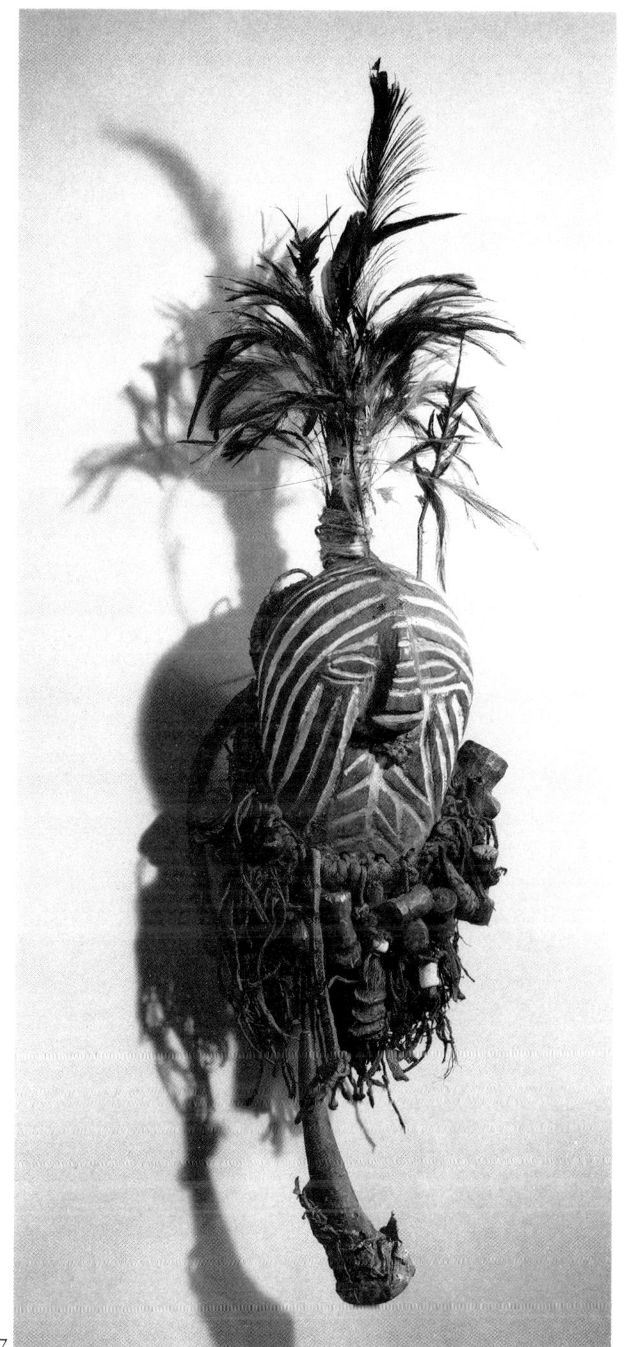

367

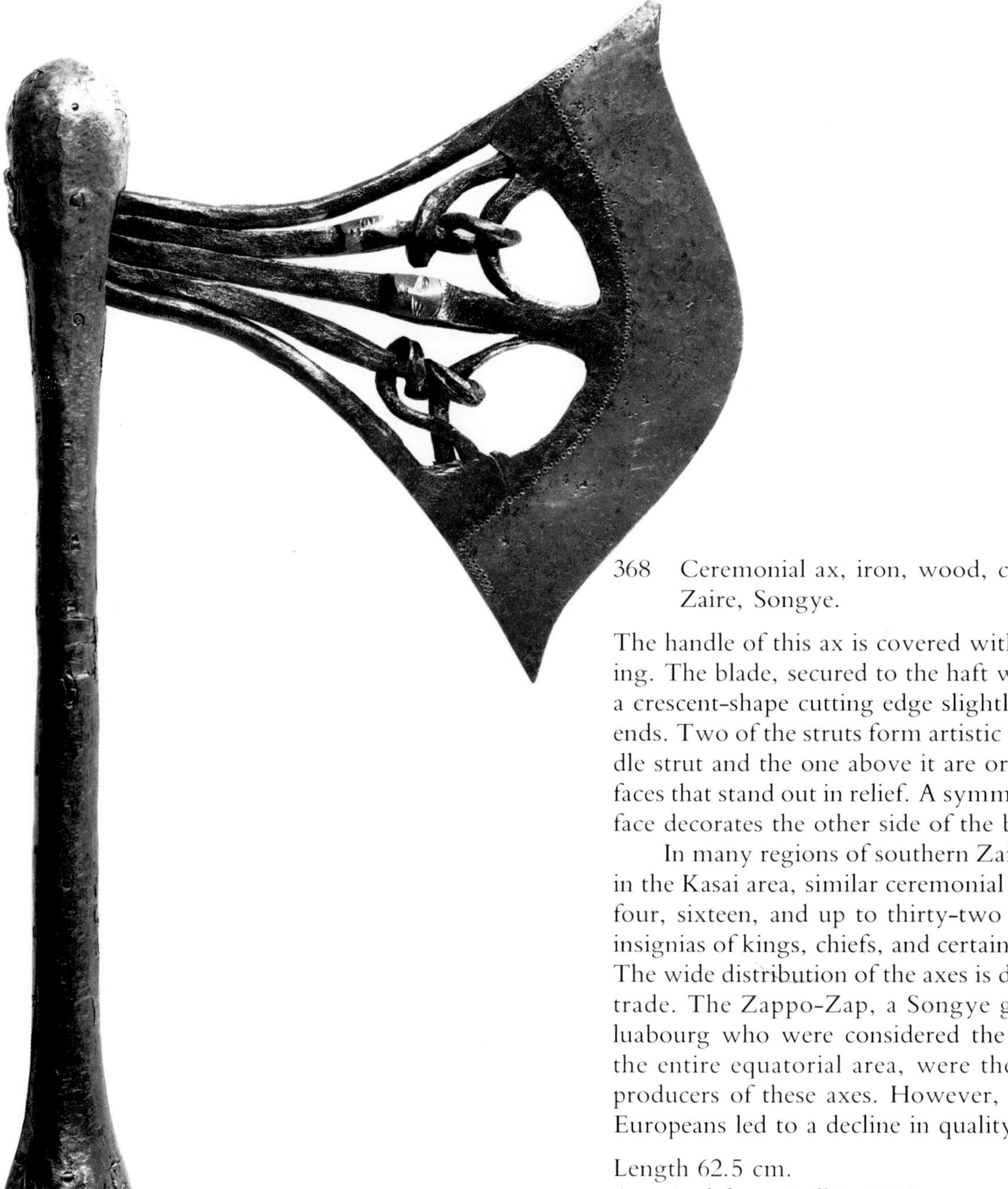

368

368 Ceremonial ax, iron, wood, copper. Zaire, Songye.

The handle of this ax is covered with copper sheeting. The blade, secured to the haft with a rivet, has a crescent-shape cutting edge slightly waved at the ends. Two of the struts form artistic knots; the middle strut and the one above it are ornamented with faces that stand out in relief. A symmetrically placed face decorates the other side of the blade.

In many regions of southern Zaire, particularly in the Kasai area, similar ceremonial axes with two, four, sixteen, and up to thirty-two faces served as insignias of kings, chiefs, and certain court officials. The wide distribution of the axes is due to extensive trade. The Zappo-Zap, a Songye group near Luluabourg who were considered the best smiths in the entire equatorial area, were the most prolific producers of these axes. However, production for Europeans led to a decline in quality.

Length 62.5 cm. 03.22
Acquired from Helbig 1903

Lit.: C. D. Widstrand 1958, pp. 50, 52, 53, 143, and Map 5.

The Luba Empire and Borderland

The Luba empire (situated between the Kasai River and Lake Tanganyika, with southern Katanga as the core area) was the most powerful and culturally important of the states that previously occupied the eastern part of present-day Zaire. This empire was possibly founded before the thirteenth century, though researchers disagree about the various waves of immigration that contributed to its founding and about subsequent Luba history as well. What is certain is that from the very beginning, the population of the empire was ethnically heterogenous, for although common political ties promoted assimilation, ethnic identities remained strong. The Luba empire flourished through the end of the nineteenth century: it was not rigidly organized but rather a centralized confederation which new groups joined as others dropped out.

An extraordinary wealth of art styles coexisted in the Luba area. Artistic motifs were equally diverse, though the female figure was common in all Luba art. (The respected status of women was anchored in mythology and strongly influential in Luba social life as well.)

The classic art center in the Luba realm was probably Katanga. From its workshops come the most accomplished sculptures and the finest crafts. Human representation is characterized less by abstraction than by idealization: symmetrical construction, motionlessness, carefully rendered face and coiffure. Variety in facial expression, from deepest gravity to dreamy melancholy, from bitterness to irony, stands in strange opposition to the solemn stasis of the figures.

Our objects, made predominantly in the nineteenth century, come from the eastern Luba part of the empire and from neighboring areas formerly in the administrative districts of Manyema and Urua. These regions were, and are, inhabited not only by the Luba themselves but also by Luba-influenced groups, among them the Hemba, who live in many small scattered chiefdoms. An exact differentiation of these ethnic groups—Katanga-Luba, Hemba, Niembo, Mambwe, Buye, Bembe, Boyo, Kusu, Bangubangu, and Tabwa—and the objects they made, which used to be called simply "Luba," has now been made possible by the detailed studies undertaken in recent years by Biebuyck, Neyt, Maurer, and Roberts.

Lit.: D. Biebuyck 1981, pp. 45-52; O. Boone 1961, pp. 112, 13, 130, 31, 145; E. M. Maurer & A. F. Roberts 1985; F. Neyt 1977, pp. 233-57; F. M. Olbrechts 1959, pp. 64-75.

369 Mask, wood, paint.
Zaire, Luba.

The main feature of this mask type, usually called *kifwebe (tshifwebe),* is its division into stripes of contrasting color. The Luba adopted it from the Songye, but Luba masks rarely attained the quality of the models: the composition of Songye masks is more refined (see Nos. 365 and 366), the tendency toward geometrization stronger, and the execution more exact.

Height 44 cm. 05.76
Acquired from H. Deininger 1905

Lit.: R. P. Colle 1913, Vol. II, p. 440; J. Cornet 1973, p. 208, 09; J. Maes 1924, pp. 36-43.

370 Mask, wood.
Zaire, Luba, Manyema.

This rare mask as yet has no known counterpart. In size and breadth of face this example is reminiscent of No. 369, but it is flatter and more sparingly decorated.

Height 40 cm., width 31 cm. 91.1075
Acquired from von Gravenreuth 1891

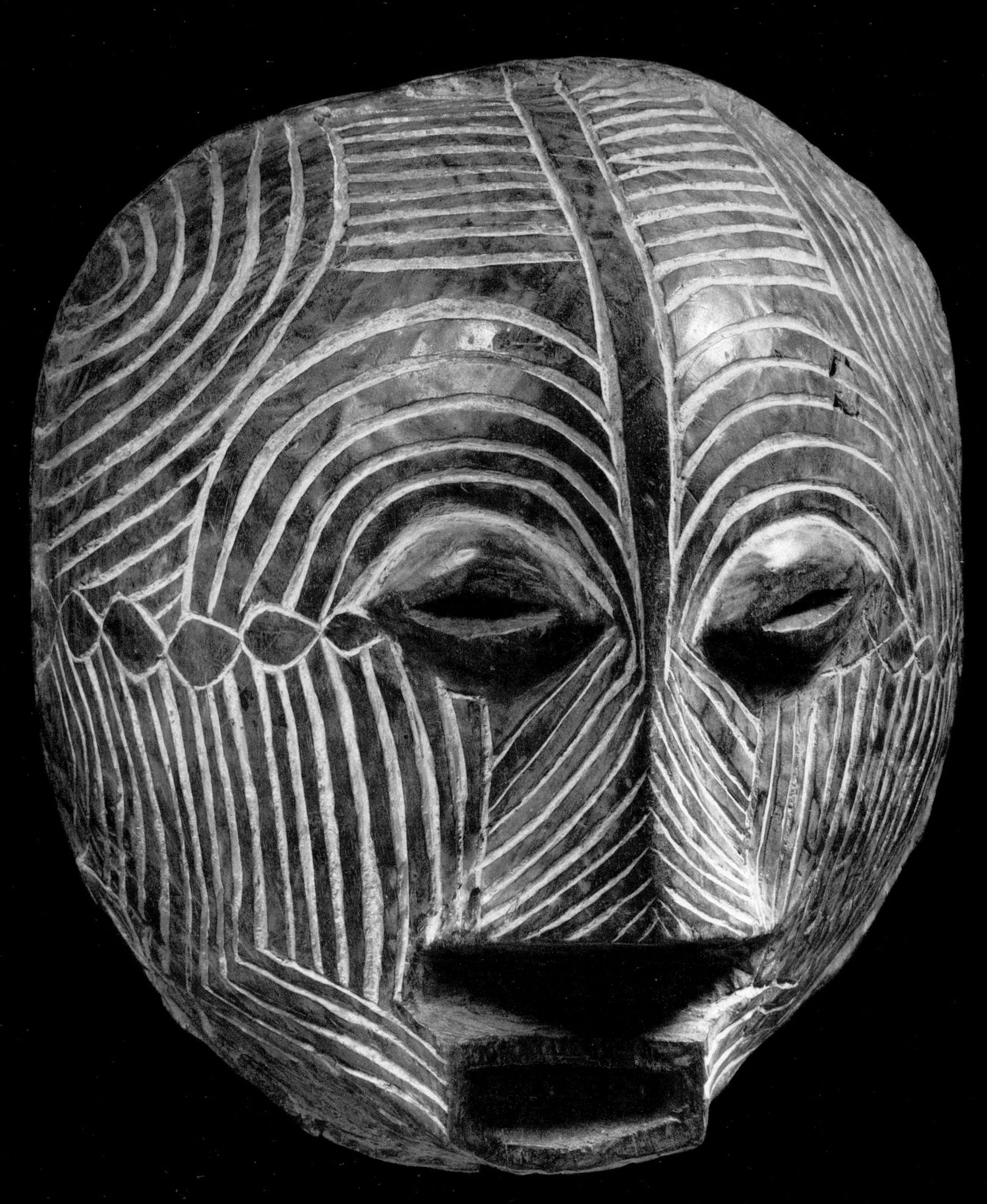

3

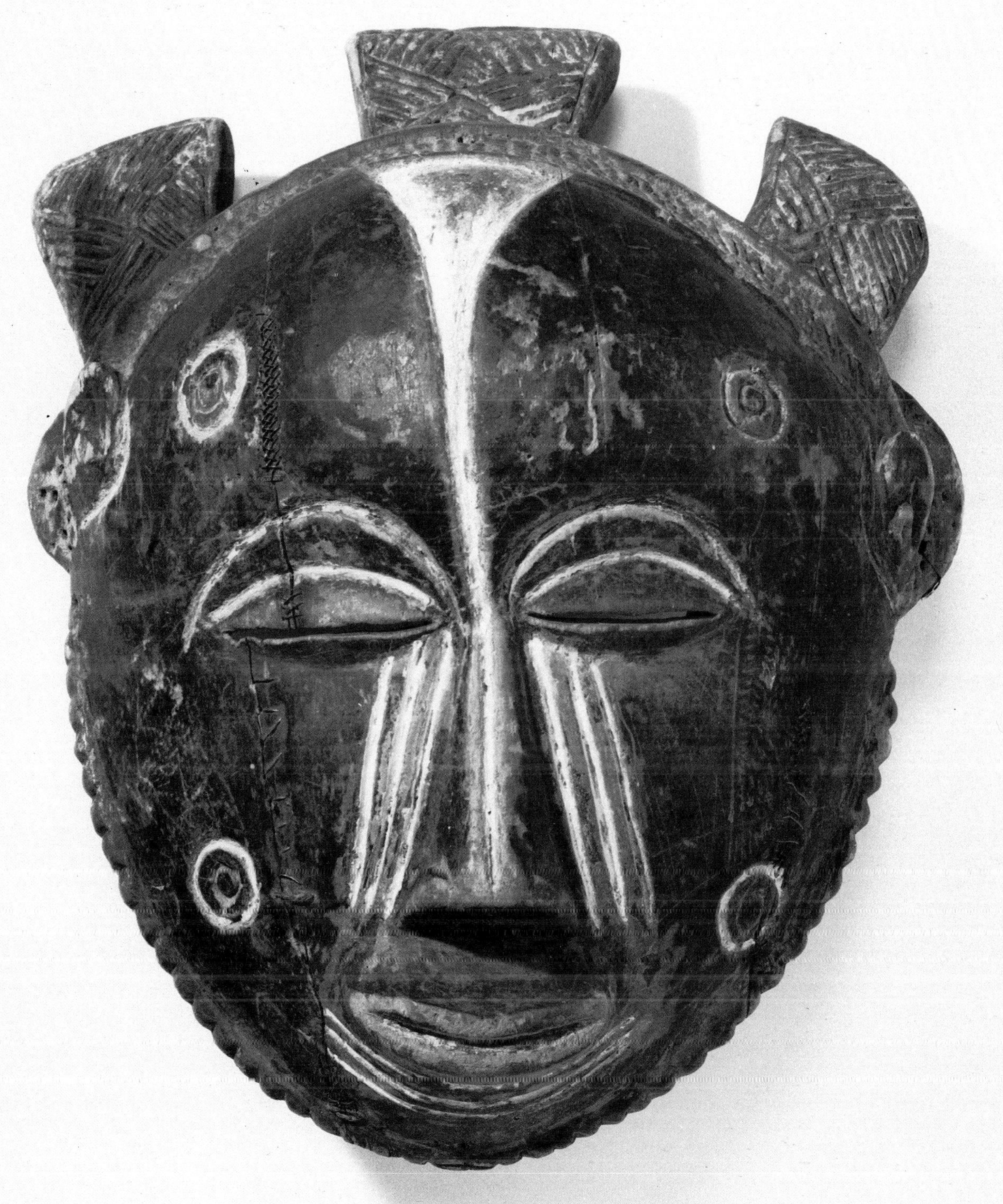

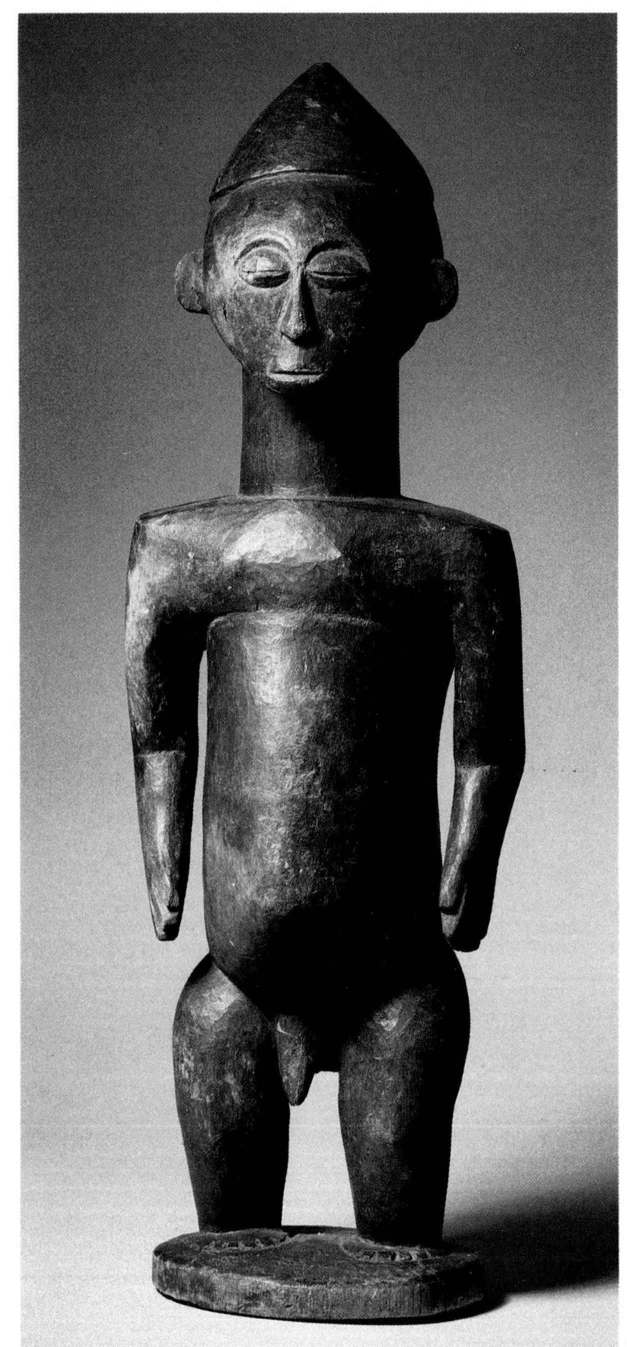
371

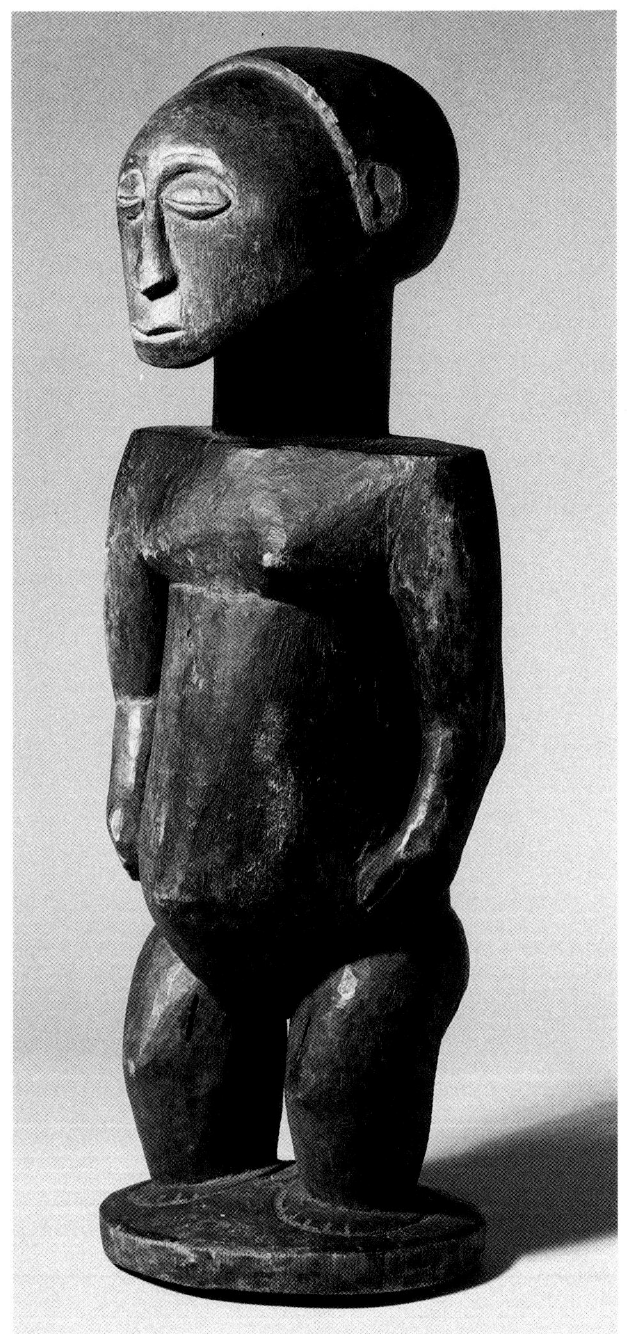
372

Luba-Hemba Ancestral Figures (371-378)

Some Luba ancestral representations are freestanding figures and some are bases of chieftains' stools or bearers of ritual bowls. Most are complete figures, fifty to one hundred centimeters high, though occasionally only head and torso appear. Face, coiffure, and cicatrices are always precisely executed. While the curves of the torso are anatomically correct, arms and legs are often negligently formed.

Only outstanding personalities who had enjoyed high prestige during their lifetimes were commemorated with such figures. The figures kept the memory of these important forebears alive and also served as temporary abodes for ancestor spirits, who helped in all circumstances of life. The close link between these sculptures and religious veneration of ancestors is revealed in a curious iconoclasm at the end of the nineteenth century: an ecstatic mass movement in the western Luba area, the *riamba* cult (so named for the important role of hemp, *riamba*), was hostile to tradition and intolerant toward ancestral veneration. Cult members destroyed most of the ancient ancestral figures and in doing so confirmed their religious significance.

Lit.: W. F. P. Burton 1961, p. 50; R. P. Colle 1913, II, pp. 427-36; H. v. Wissmann 1891, pp. 156, 159.

371,372 Two human figures, wood.
Zaire, Luba-Hemba, Manyema.

Squat and broad-shouldered, these figures are geometrically structured. Their basically cylindrical bodies curve only slightly. Their faces jut forward, and the tips of their noses point down. Eyebrows and nose form one unit, lips are narrow and pressed together, and the small ears are simplified. Short, almost unstructured legs end in feet simply carved on the base in very low relief. The man is wearing

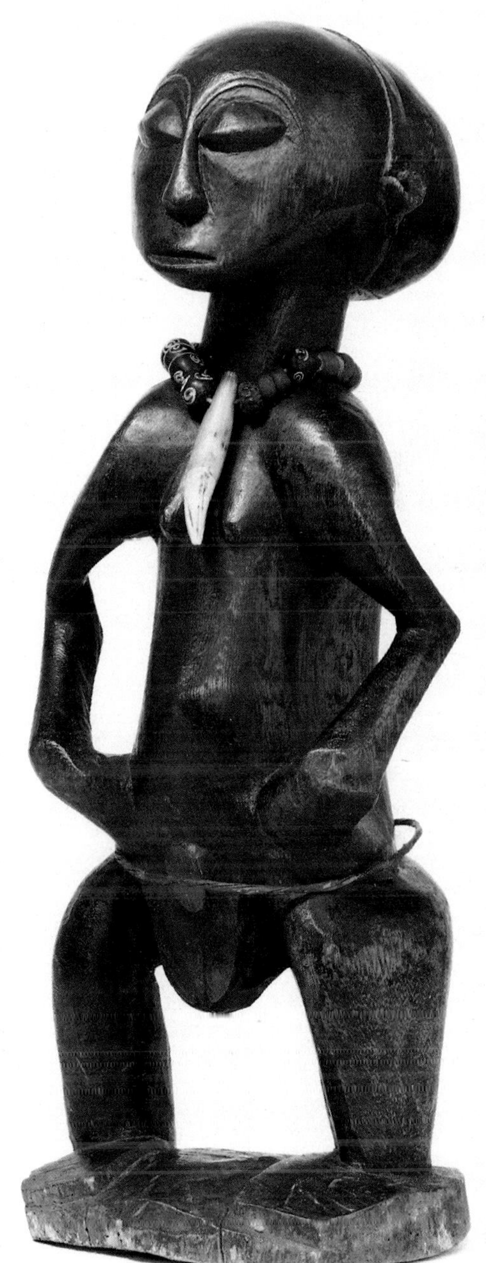
373

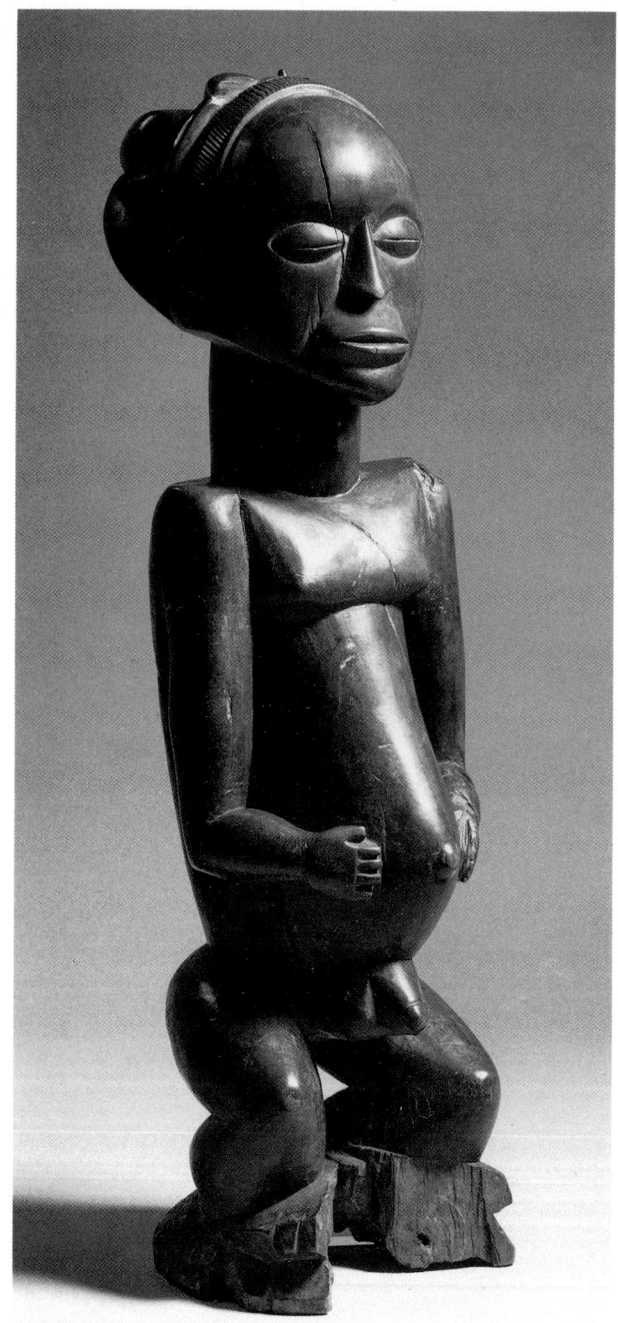

a conical cap, the woman a smooth coiffure. The two figures were conceived as a pair.

Height 60 cm., 56 cm. 05.66, 05.67
Acquired from Deininger 1905

373 Male figure, wood, bead necklace with animal tooth.
Zaire, Luba-Hemba, Manyema.

This piece, in many respects similar to the pair of figures in Nos. 371 and 372, is more sophisticated artistically. The markedly prognathous face with half-closed eyes expresses reserve, perhaps even aloofness. The shaping of the narrow shoulders, drawn forward, and of the thin handlelike arms with angular elbows is notable. Legs straddle the base and end in flat feet that turn inward. The penis has been broken off. The bead necklace with an animal tooth pendant was probably worn as an amulet.

Height 47 cm. 05.68
Acquired from H. Deininger 1905

374 Male figure, wood, copper.
Zaire, Luba-Hemba, Urua.

Although most Luba sculptures are carved of lighter woods, this polished figure is of a heavy brown wood. The lines of its face are sharply defined, the lids of its large coffee-bean eyes are half closed, and its mouth and nose protrude. Both the cruciform coiffure and the fillet are most carefully worked, and a copper pin with conical upper end is stuck into the crown (see also No. 413). Face, pointed abdomen, blocky chest with broad, angular shoulders, and upper arms parallel to the body all display a tendency toward geometrization (see also No. 372). The legs, with bulging thighs and calves, are bent. Tiny hands rest on the abdomen.

374 Height 48 cm. 13-57-146
Acquired from H. Deininger 1913

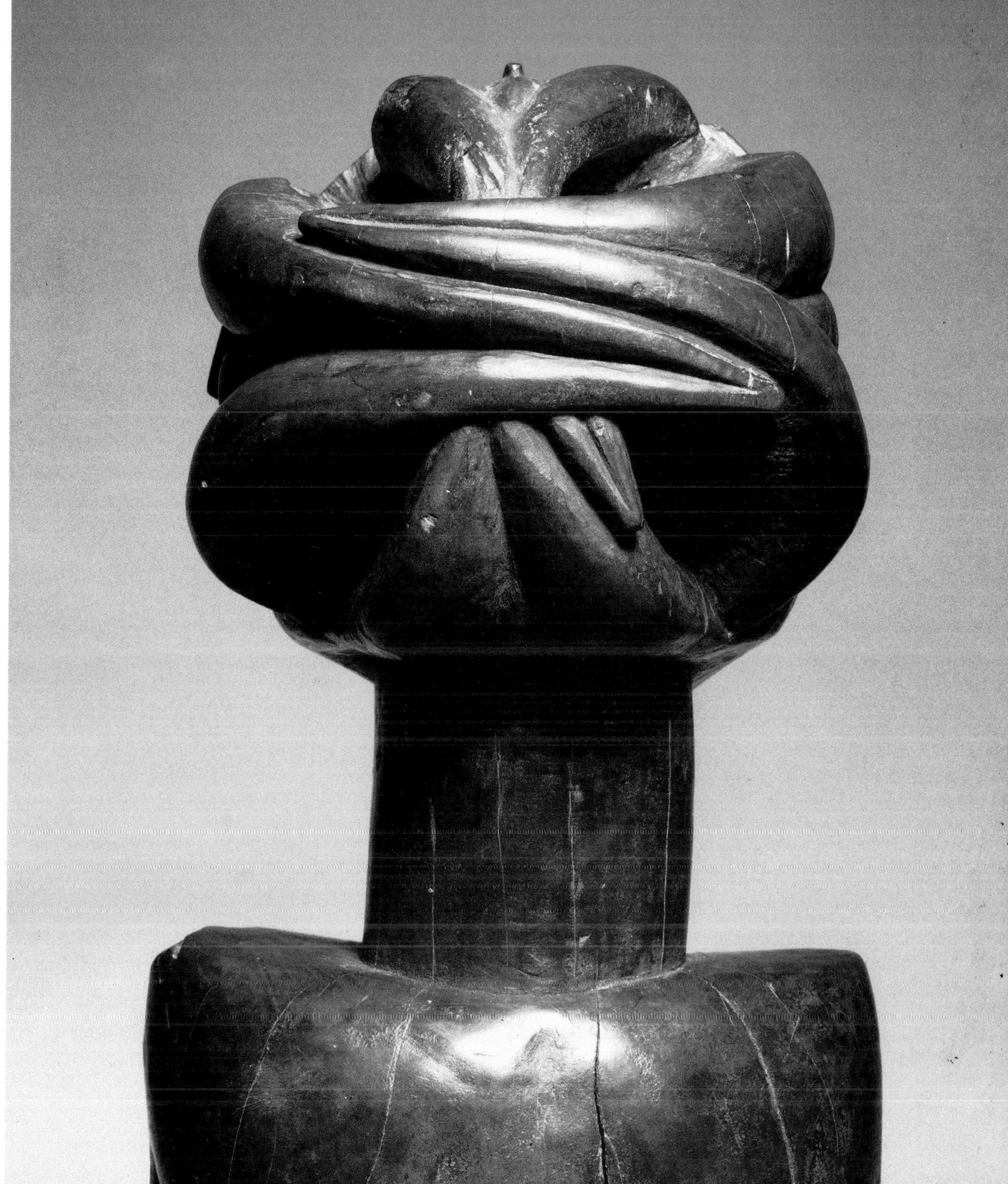

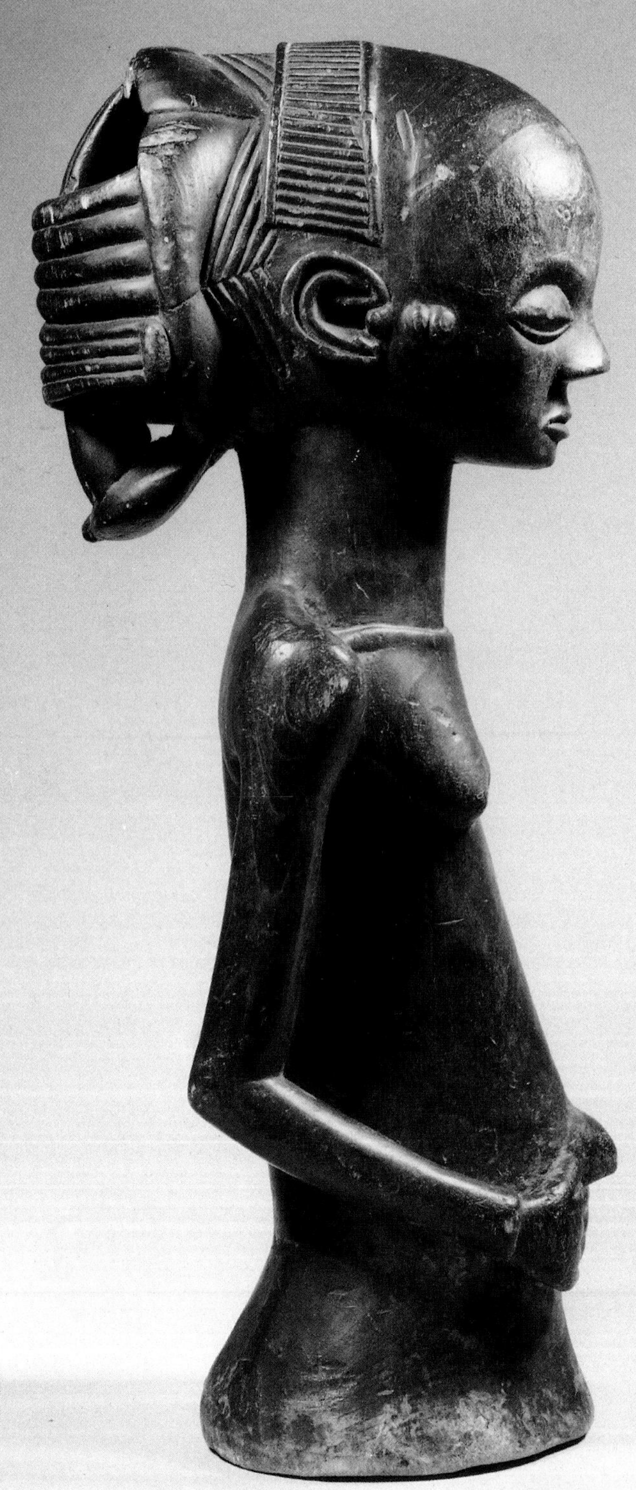

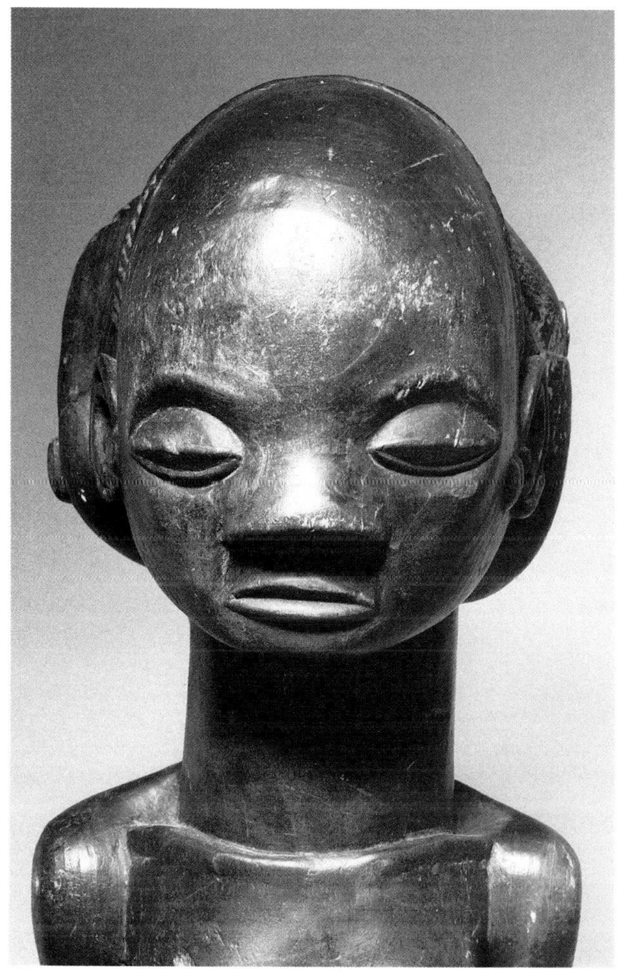
375

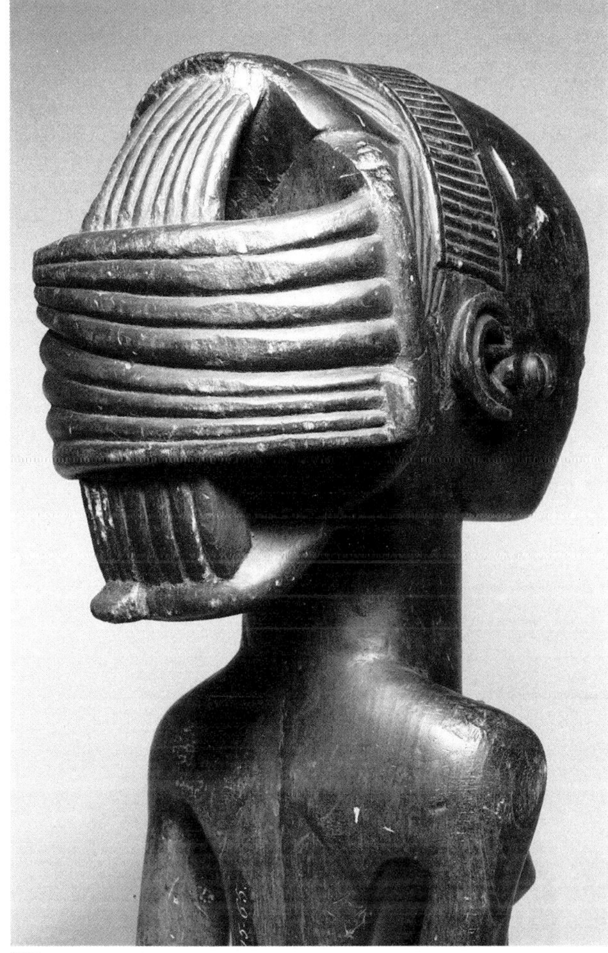
375

375 Female figure, wood.
Zaire, Luba-Hemba, Manyema.

In Luba sculpture nearly all half-figures are made for divination purposes (see No. 378); this secular piece is an exception. Of very high quality, the figure is also exemplary for its idealized naturalistic style. Its face is finely worked, with large coffee-bean eyes, short broad nose, narrow lips, and scant cicatrization. The ears, too, are artistically formed, with double raised outlines. The artist devoted greatest care of all to the elaborate coiffure, composed of braids arranged at right angles to each other, and the fillet with narrow raised parallel lines. The plastically rendered clavicle, shoulder blades, and navel are remarkable. The torso is long, the arms thin and angular; the large hands rest on the abdomen.

Height 62 cm. 05.65
Acquired from H. Deininger 1905

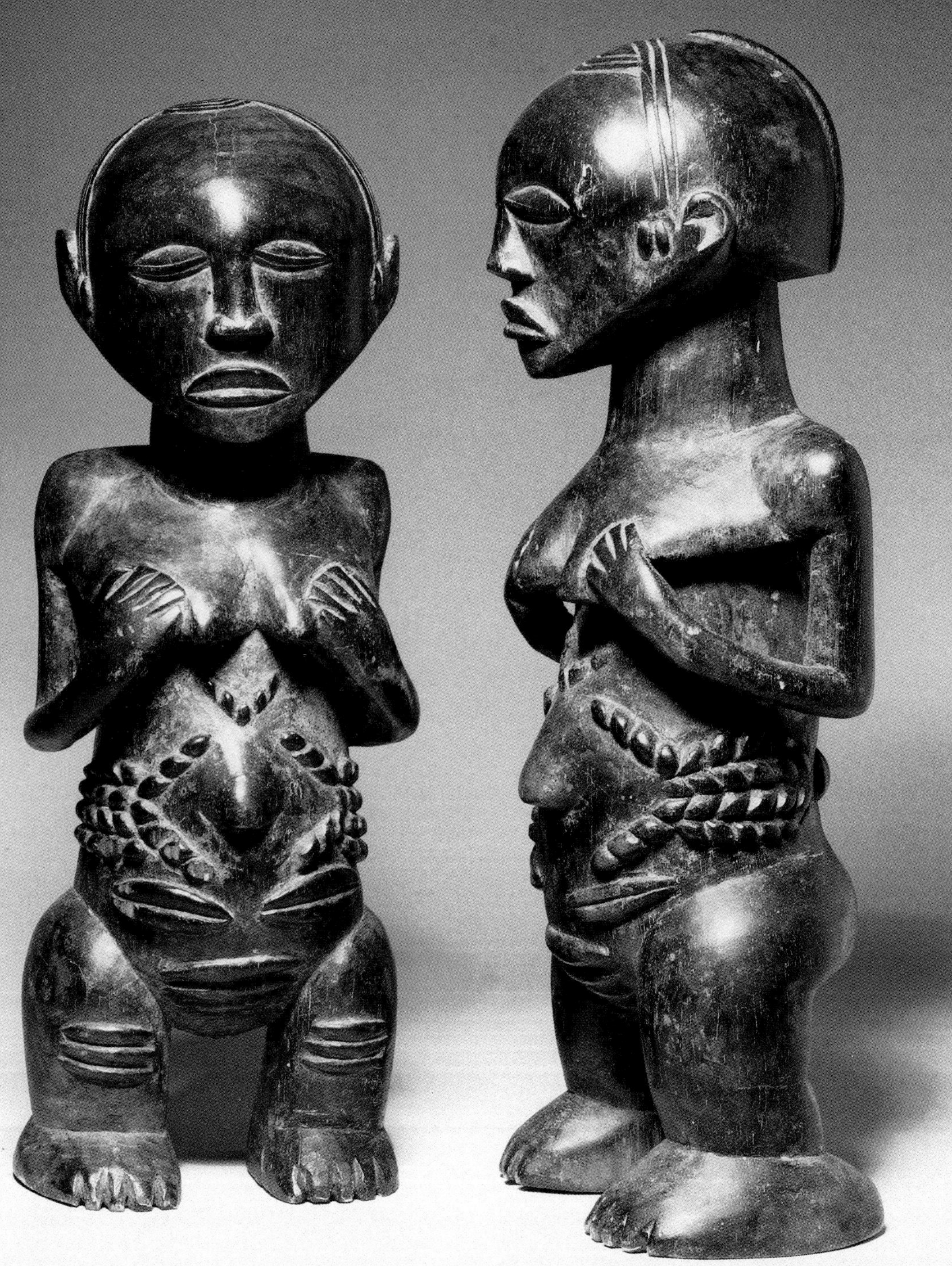

376/37

376,377 Two female figures, wood.
Zaire, Luba.

These standing female figures hold their breasts; downturned mouths give their faces serious, even bitter expressions. Coiffures are simple and head hugging. Bodies are squat, and the abdomens are covered with vigorous cicatrization. The arms are thin, but the legs are short and sturdy, with notched toes. The feet serve as the base; there is no pedestal. According to the inventory, such figures stood in the storage section of the dwelling.

Height 33 cm., 35 cm. 11.1450, 11.1451
Acquired from F. Mitchell 1911

378 Female figure, wood.
Zaire, Luba, Manyema.

This half-figure (see also No. 375) typifies the local style of long-faced figure with slim torso and precisely carved cicatrices. The backround was often light yellow, with details emphasized in dark brown, as here. A hole in back from the base to the crown of the figure contains a rag, visible from outside, that is a magical insertion.

The base of this figure was probably a calabash stopper. In many places calabashes with figural stoppers were important divination implements. Such vessels in the possession of the Buhabo (Bahabo, Bugabo, Bwabo) society widespread throughout the Luba region, were famous. This society, which struck fear into outsiders, extorted payments by means of threats and, allegedly, poisonings. On the other hand, the society was considered a reliable source of medical knowledge. Calabashes with figural stoppers were employed in the society's healing activities.

Height 27 cm. 13-57-142
Acquired from H. Deininger 1913

Lit.: R. P. Colle 1913, II, pp. 601-17; H. v. Geluwe, in S. Vogel 1981, pp. 223-25; F. Neyt, in J. Fry 1978, pp. 169-72.

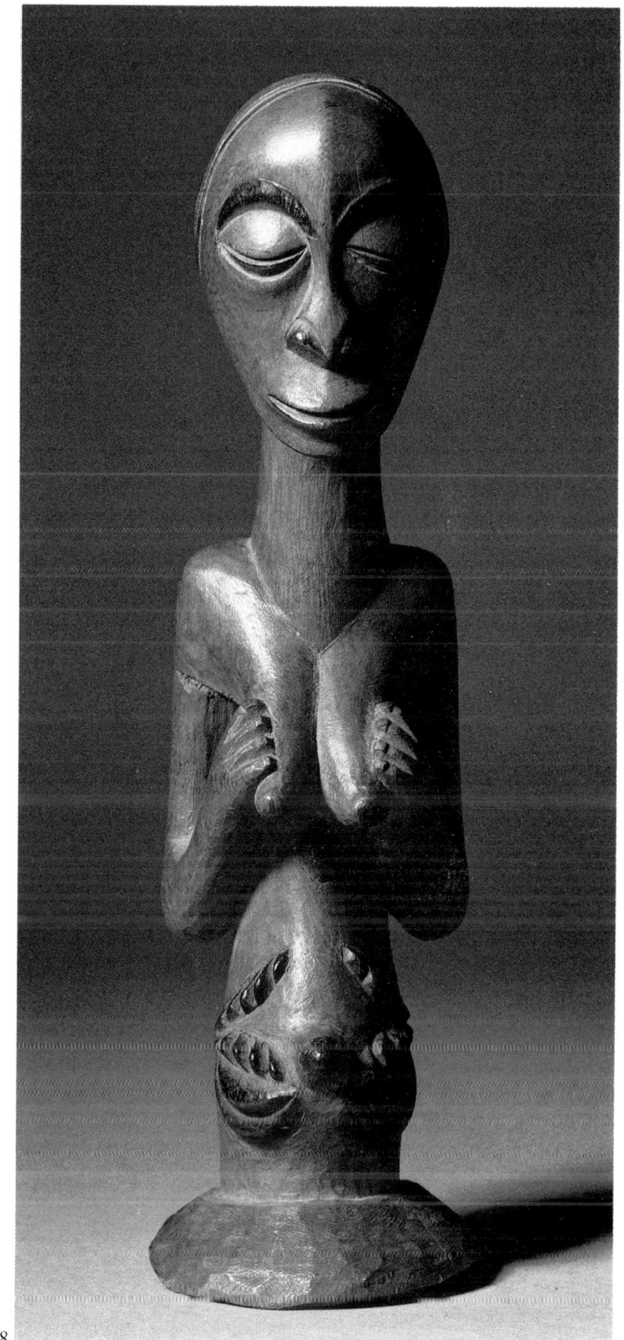

378

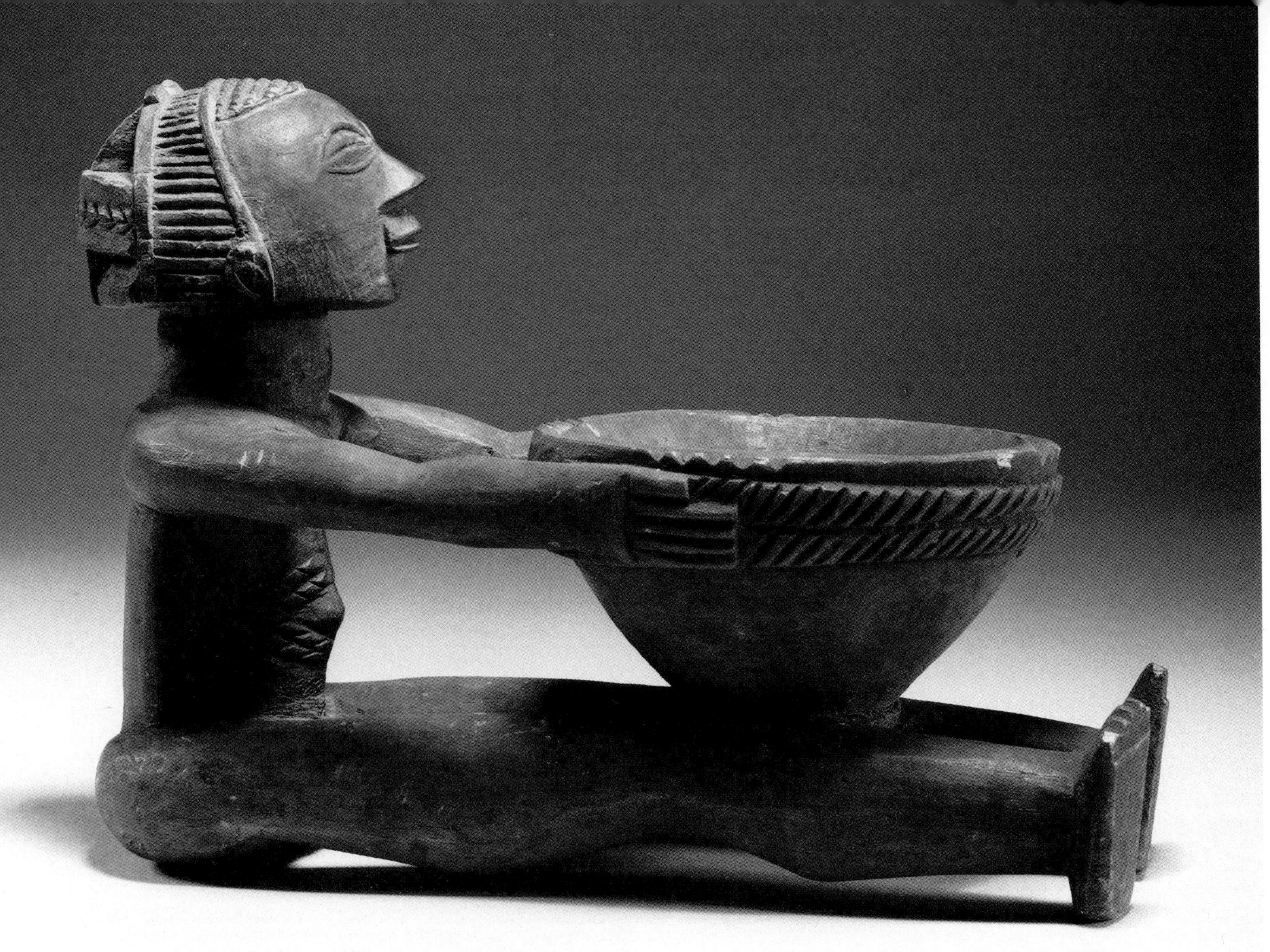

379

Bowl Figures (379-382)

Female—and, very rarely, male—figures, sitting or kneeling with a bowl in their hands, are among the most impressive subjects in Luba sculpture. Little is known of their function other than that such a figure is placed before the house of a woman after childbirth so that passersby can put gifts of cowries into the bowl.

In the past such a figure was referred to as a *kabila* ("beggar woman"), but according to some recent authors the correct name is *mboko* ("calabash"). Others feel that the latter designation is only a cover because the Luba consider uttering the real but secret name, *kitompa kya muchi* ("divination bowl of wood"), dangerous. According to recent research, there are several types of bowl-holding figures, whose functions differ throughout the Luba region, and this may explain the confusion in terminology.

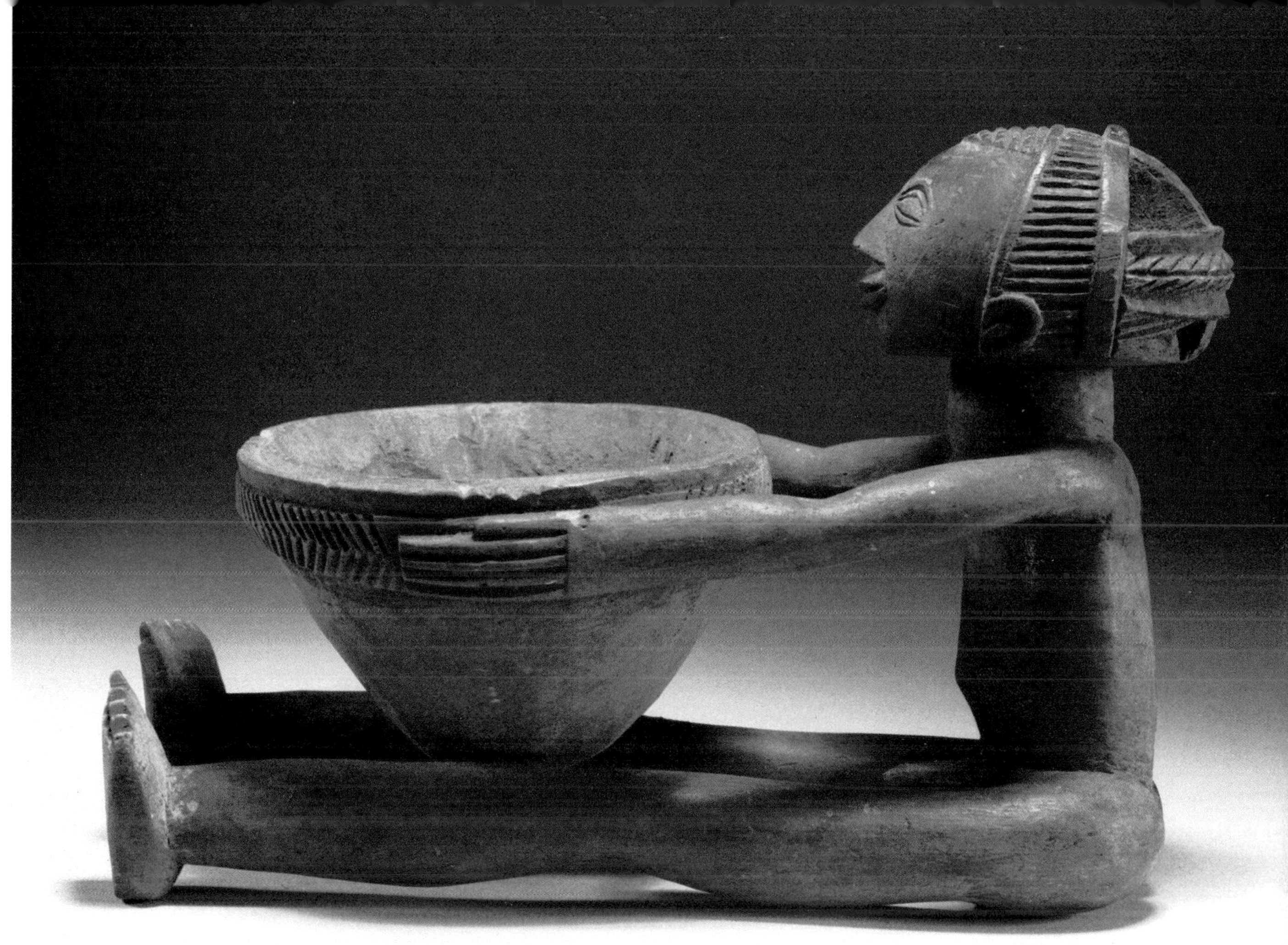

380

A close link with divination and healing seems to be common to all the bowls. For such purposes at least some of the bowls serve as receptacles for the white kaolin used in rituals. The color white is prescribed for all contacts with spirits, and the diviner therefore paints a client with white earth; he also paints himself white after all important ritual acts. When a chief takes office the first wife hands him a sacred calabash with white earth, the symbol of power. Other bowl holding figures are considered the abode of the spirit with whose help the diviner heals the patient. Often the patient simply takes the bowl in his hands, is painted white, and immediately feels himself cured. Some patients must then spend their lives as slaves of the spirit, that is of the diviner.

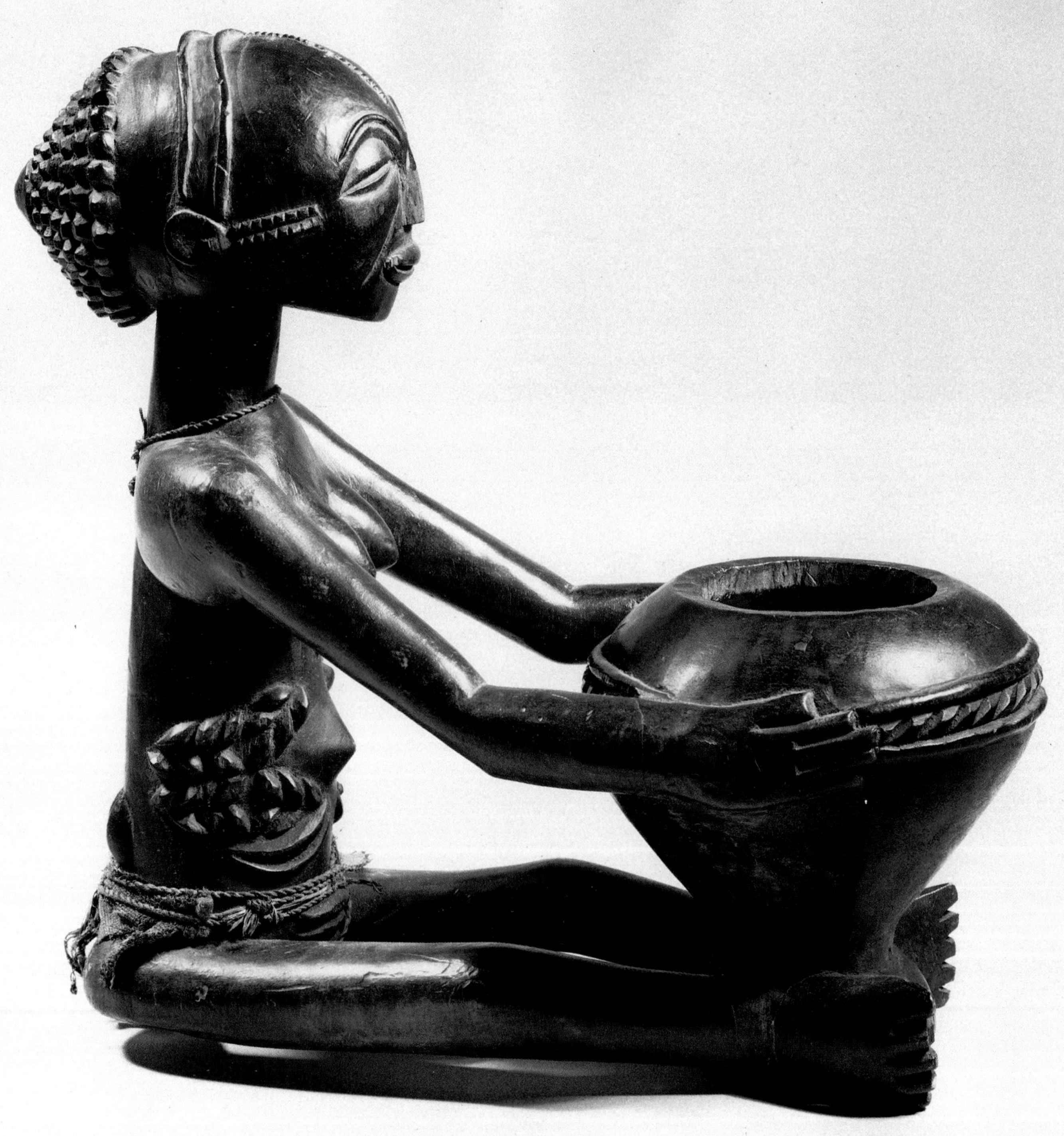

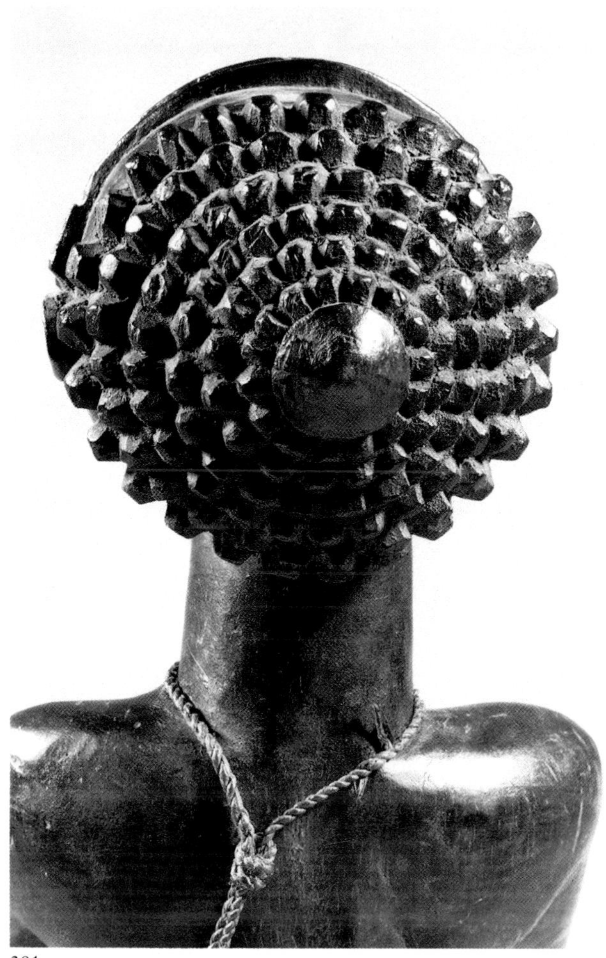

381

Very probably the four bowl-holding figures shown differed in their significance. The two smaller ones (Nos. 379 and 380), a pair, are simple pieces, while the two larger ones (Nos. 381 and 382) are of high artistic quality. Since such pieces were mentioned among chiefs' insignias, carvers would certainly have received court commissions from patrons who were exacting in their demands.

Lit.: J. Agthe 1983, pp. 11, 17; M. F. P. Burton 1961, p. 59; R. P. Colle 1942, Vol. II, p. 436 & Illus. 47, 8; J. Maes 1942, pp. 249, 252, 258; R. Wassing 1968, Illus. 112.

379,380 Two bowl-holding figures (*mboko*), wood.
Zaire, Luba, Kasingi.

These relatively small figures of a man and a woman are obviously a pair, but their significance—the overwhelming majority of such figures is female—is not known. (In Colle's illustration of such a pair from the northern Luba region the man and woman are sitting opposite each other with a bowl between them.) The differences between these two figures are negligible. The female has ornamental scars on her abdomen, while her partner is unadorned. The long-limbed, somewhat rigid figures are of a very light wood (probably rhicinodendron) simply stained a dark color; there is no dark polish as there is on Nos. 381 and 382.

Height 16.5 cm., 16 cm. 11.1467, 11.1468
Acquired from F. Mitchell 1911

Lit.: R. P. Colle 1913, Vol. II, Table II.

381 Bowl holder (*mboko*), wood, raffia-fiber fabric.
Zaire, Luba-Hemba, Urua.

This figure's round, broad-planed face, from which eyes, nose, and mouth scarcely protrude, is similar to those of the masks in Nos. 369 and 370). The scarification patterns are a remarkable combination: the narrow geometric bands at the temples and in the middle of the forehead recall those of Tabwa figures (see Nos. 420 and 421), but the striking group around the navel is typically Luba. The nubbed coiffure is rare, and the fillet is without decoration. The proportions of the long-limbed figure correspond approximately to nature. The hands and feet are negligently treated; by contrast the small breasts are finely shaped.

Height 37 cm. 13-15-147
Acquired from H. Deininger 1913

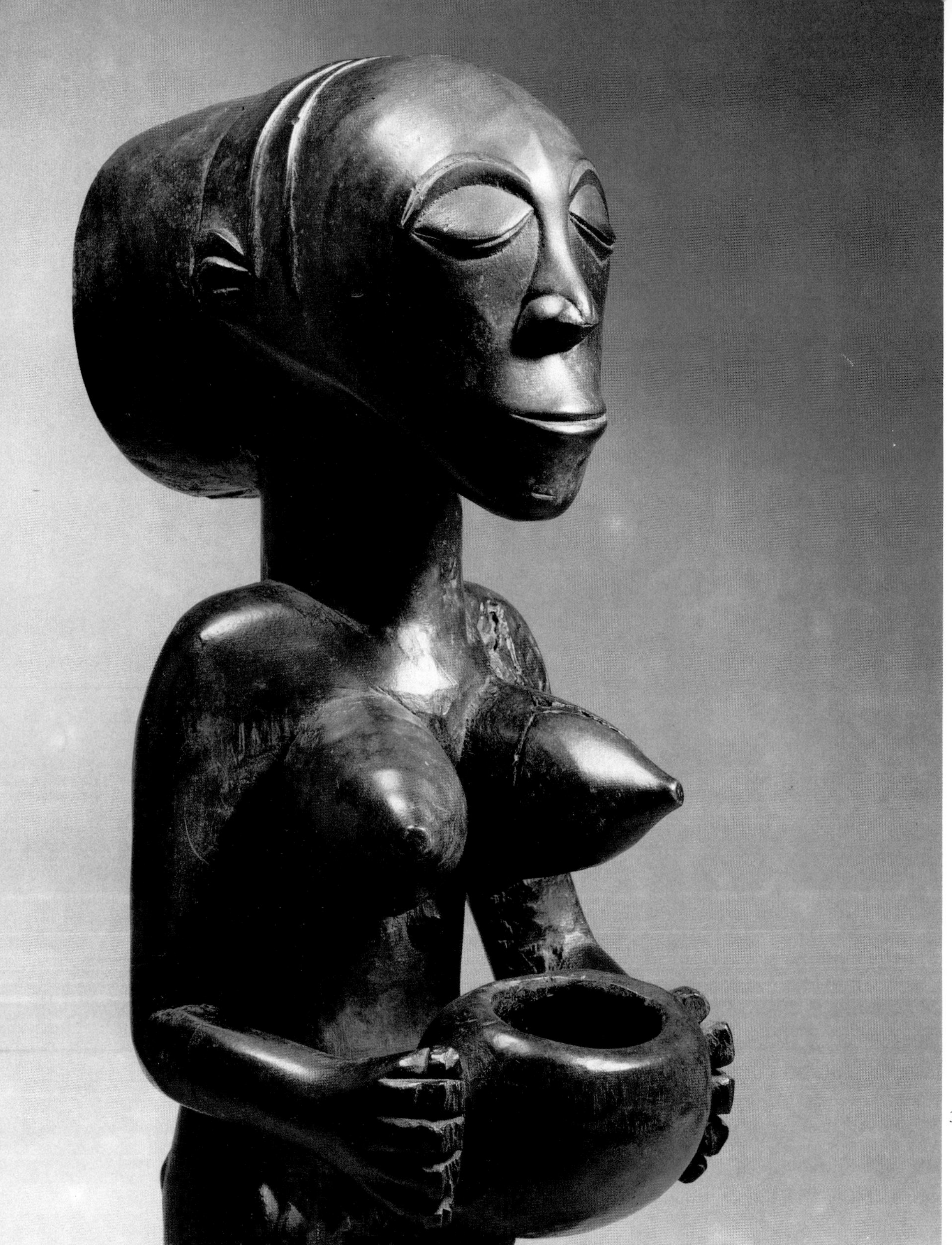

382

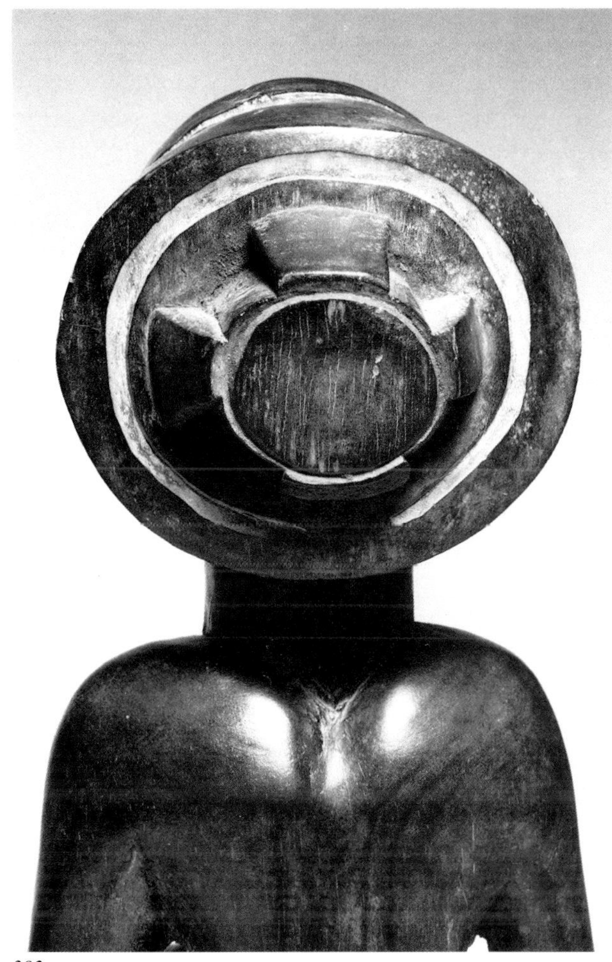
382

382 Bowl holder, wood.
Zaire, Luba-Hemba, Urua.

The artist concentrated on the face and plump jutting breasts of this important Luba piece. The long, expressive face is reserved; the line of the upper eye continues into that of the nose; and the narrow lips are pressed together. The ponderous coiffure accentuates the dominant head, which appears even larger in comparison with the short legs.

The careful execution of shoulders and chest and the exact depiction of scarification are characteristic of the idealizing realism of many bowl-holding figures.

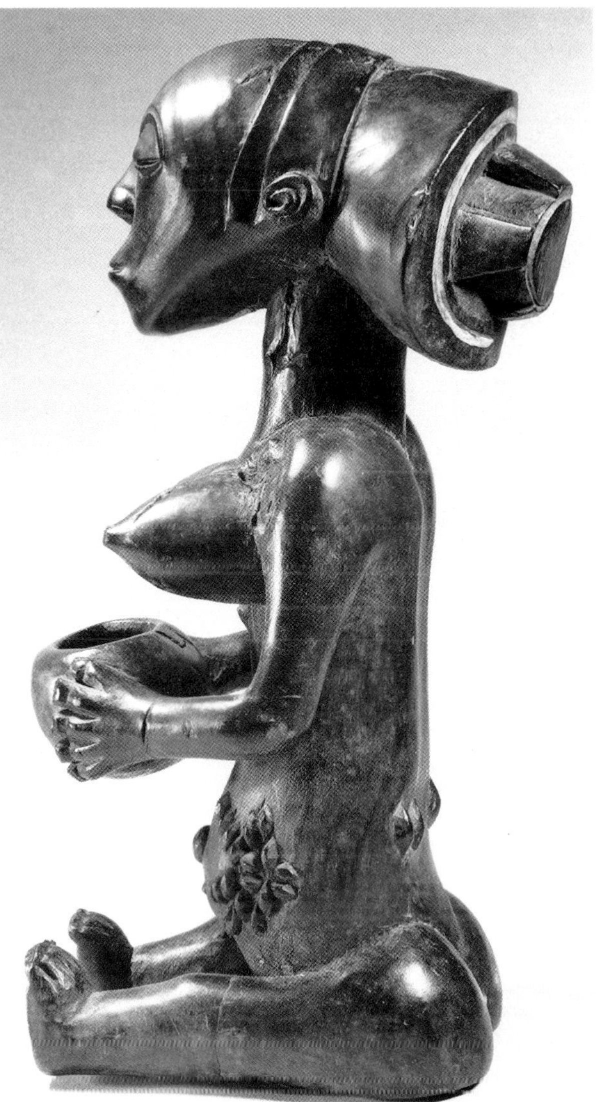

Height 48 cm. 05.57
Acquired from H. Deininger 1905

Royal Stools (383-389)

These stools are symbols of royal authority and of the highest office. Each is carved from a single block of wood. The circular seating surface is supported by one or more fully sculptural figures. These mostly female standing or kneeling figures are distinguished by abundant scarification and splendid coiffures, which indicate the highest social position. They are presumably royal ancesors, of decisive importance in a royal succession determined by matrilineal descent. They were also considered mediators between the reigning chief and his matrilineal ancestors. The artistic quality of these figures equals that of free-standing ancestral figures, though there are certain differences. In the majority of cases, for example, the carrying position of these figures led to distorted proportions. The legs are shortened, often appearing crippled, and the carefully carved hands are usually enlarged. Royal stools were kept in a house exclusively reserved for them and were cared for by one of the chief's wives.

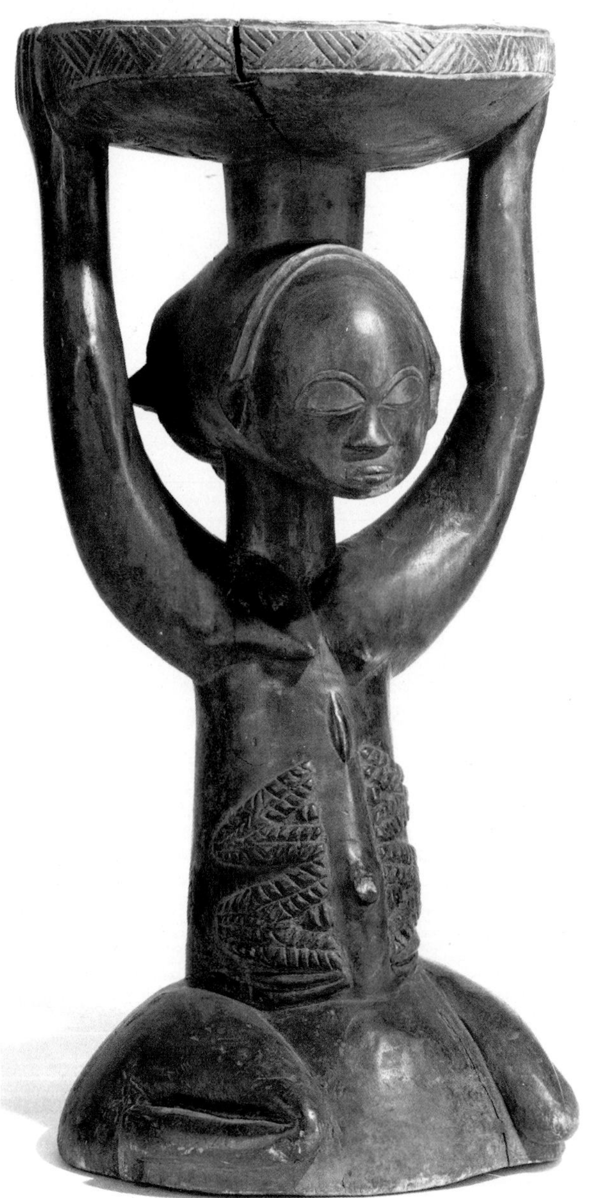

383

383 Stool with female caryatid figure, wood. Zaire, Luba.

This squatting female figure (see also No. 386) is thoughtfully stylized: body and neck taper gradually, giving them a conical form. Lowered lids and narrow pressed lips lend the face a melancholy expression. Body scarification is geometrized, and the doubled-up legs are much shortened.

Height 57.5 cm. 13-57-149
Acquired from H. Deininger 1913

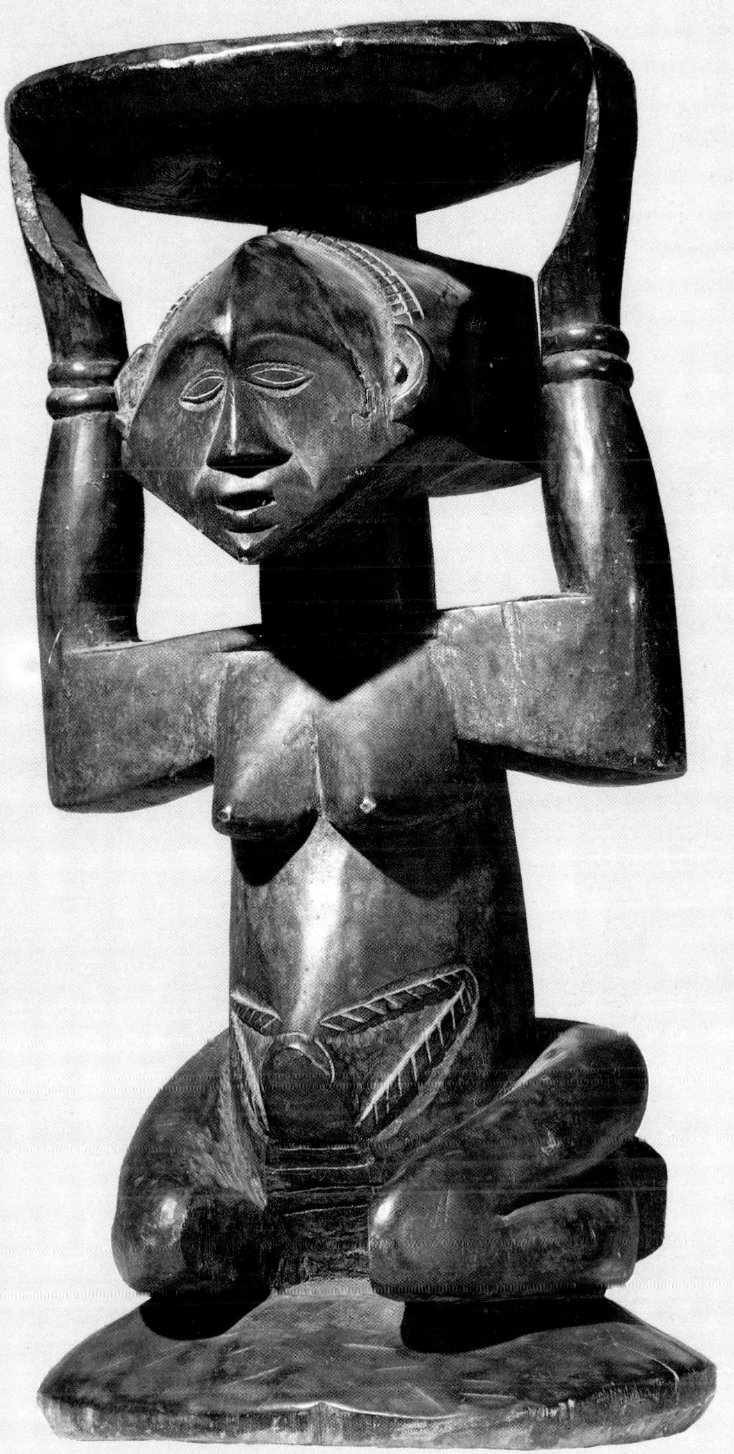

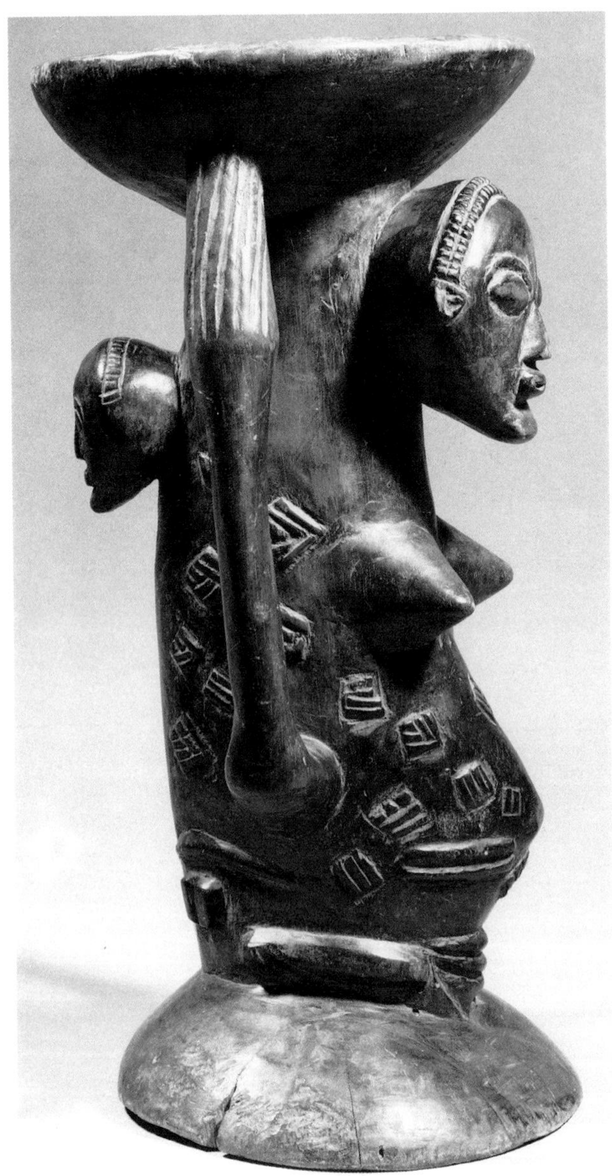

385

384 Stool with female caryatid figure, wood.
Zaire, Luba.
(see color plate p. 274)

This female figure, crouching on doubled-back legs,

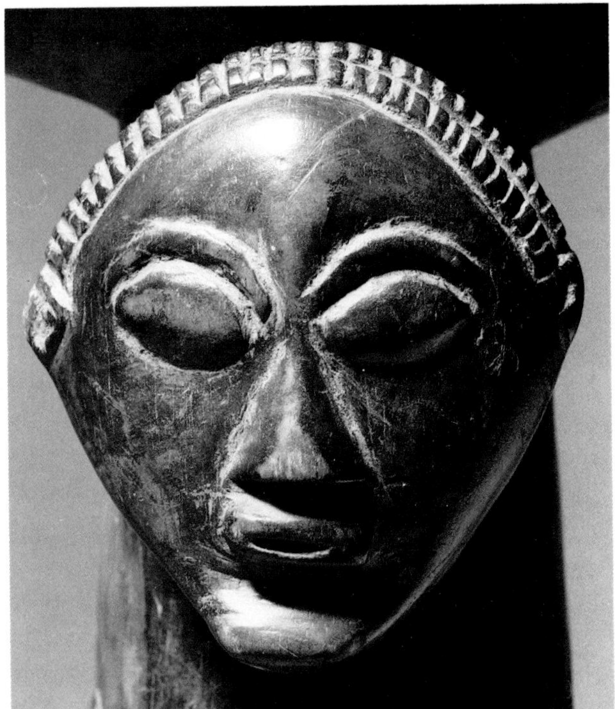

385

has a diamond-shape face and angular coiffure, shoulders, and upper arms that are cubistic in style—a rare phenomenon among these predominantly idealized female sculptures. Despite this geometrization, the face is expressive. The head fillet and the scarifications are indicated in low relief with simple incised lines.

Height 48 cm. 25-18-15
Acquired from F. W. Goring 1925

385 Stool with mother-and-child caryatid figure, wood.
Zaire, Luba.

This piece is the most abstract of the royal stools shown here. Heads of mother and child jut from opposite sides of the central pillar. Their faces are diamond-shape, their coiffures largely geometrized.

The mother's arms, with their large hands, have been placed low on the body and are therefore too long, as if the artist intended to stress their carrying function. Legs and scarifications are cursorily indicated. This sculpture bears some resemblance to the headrest in No. 409 and to the staff in No. 410.

Height 48.5 11.1456
Acquired from F. Mitchell 1911

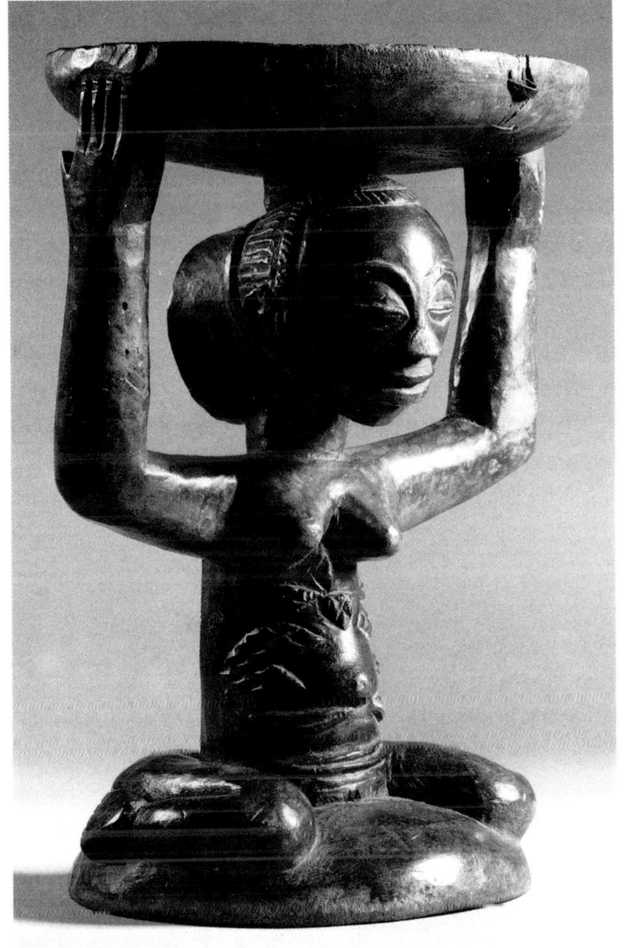

386

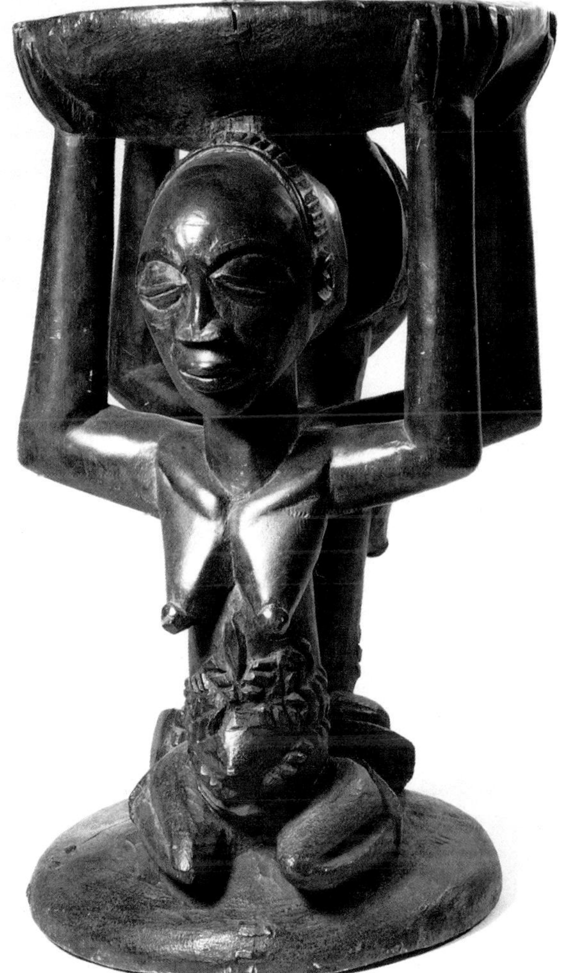

387

386 Stool with female caryatid figure, wood. Zaire, Luba.

This figure is similar to No. 383, but smaller. There is less geometrizing here, but the facial expression is livelier.

Height 31 cm. 11.1459
Acquired from H. Deininger

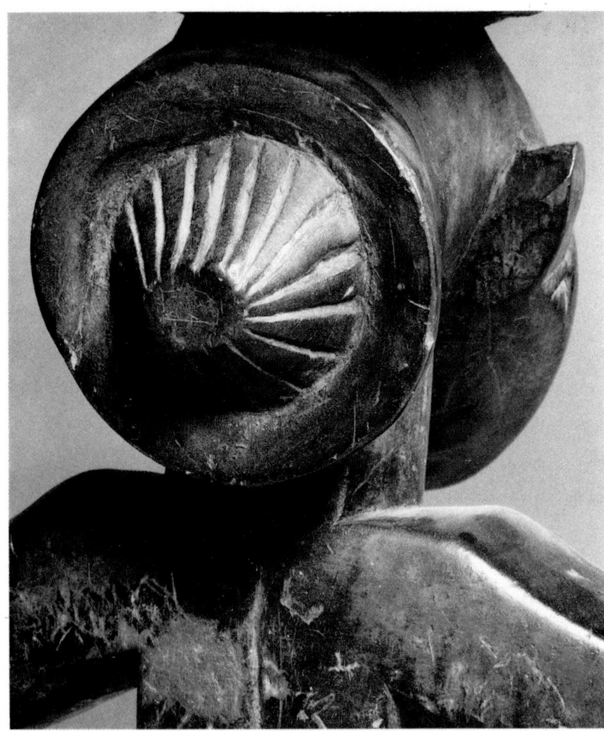

388

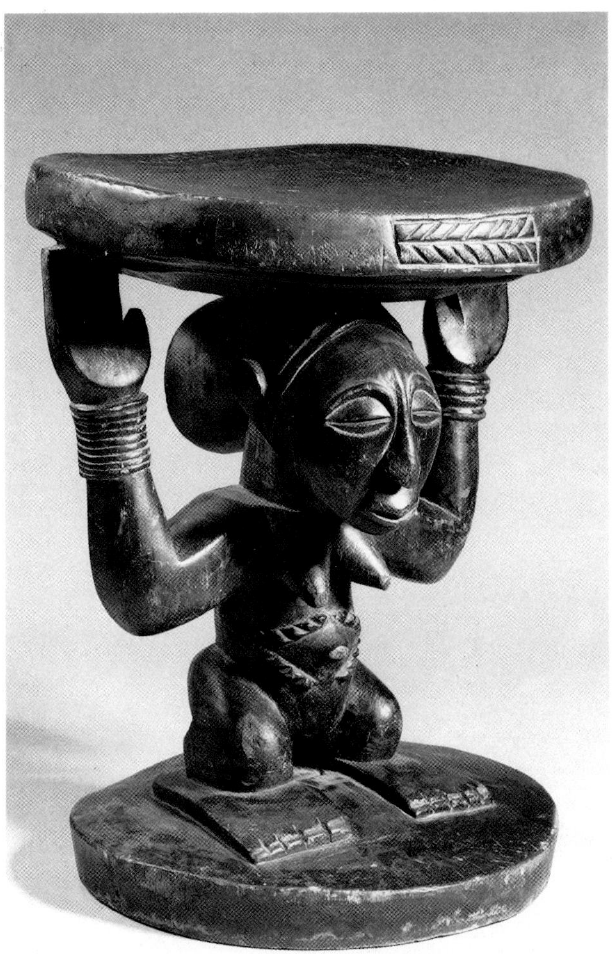

387 Stool with two female caryatid figures, wood.
Zaire, Luba.

The realistic figures of the two women squatting back to back to form the base of this stool exemplify the classical Luba style. The high-relief body scarifications and the pendulous breasts with large nipples are notable.

Height 50 cm. 25-18-16
Acquired from F. W. Goring 1925

388 Stool with female caryatid figure, wood.
Zaire, Luba.

All details of this standing female figure—the rich scarification, the chignon, and the bracelets—are executed with the greatest care. Sadness emanates from the expressive face. The strong, squat bodybuild and the very short legs with large flat feet stress the figure's carrying function.

Height 40 cm. 11.1449
Acquired from F. Mitchell 1911

389 Stool with female caryatid figure, wood.
Zaire, Luba.

This standing female figure with comparatively long

legs (in contrast to those of No. 388) probably comes from the eastern Luba area. The triangular face, the heavy sharp-edged coiffure, and the angular shoulders express a geometric tendency that is further apparent in the hair patterns and the scarifications. In contrast, the back, especially the shoulder blade area, is executed in a manner that shows the beginnings of a realistic approach to the body.

Height 59.5 cm. 13-57-148
Acquired from H. Deininger 1913

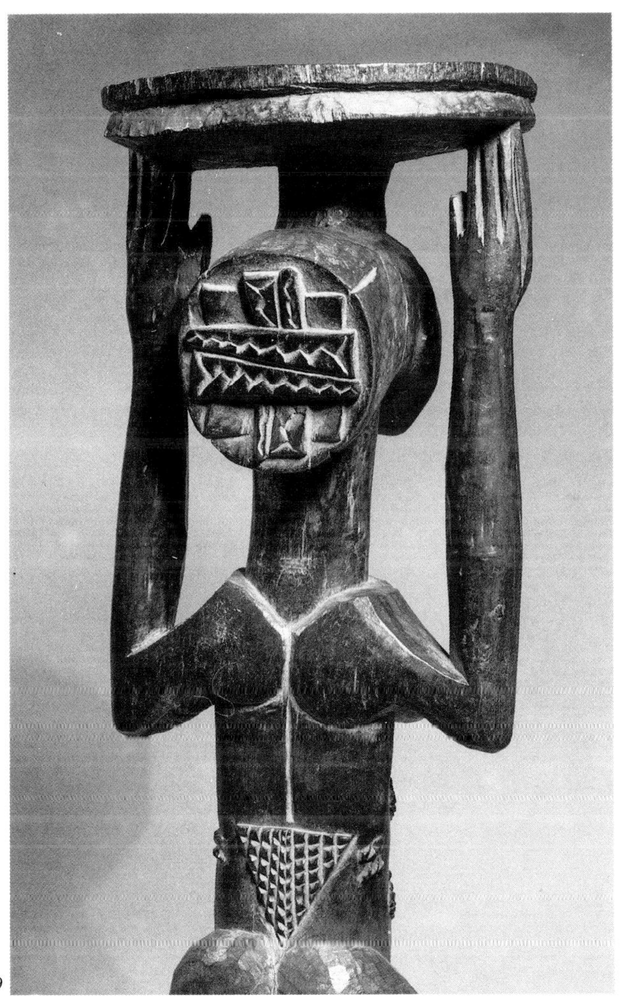

389

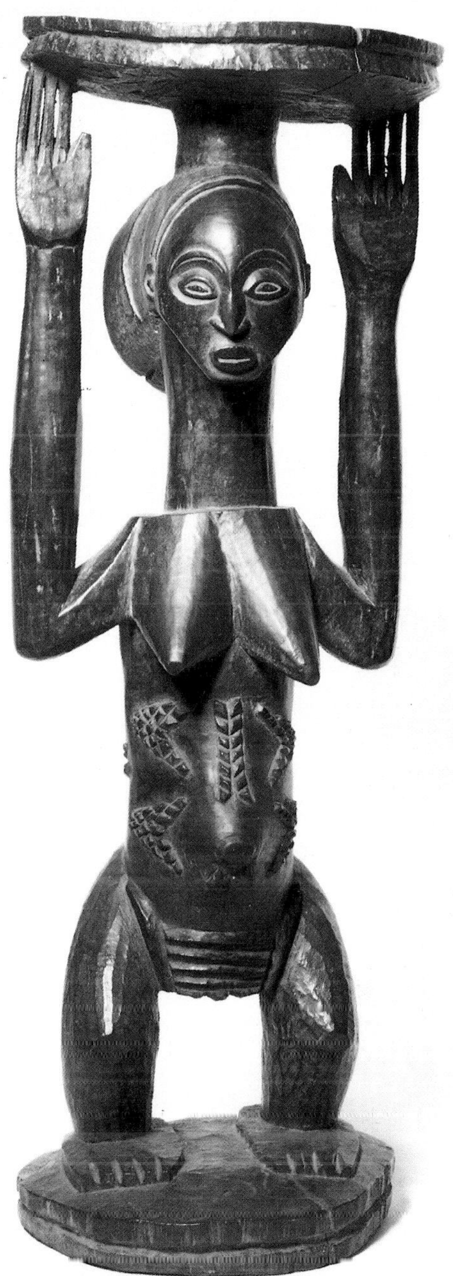

389

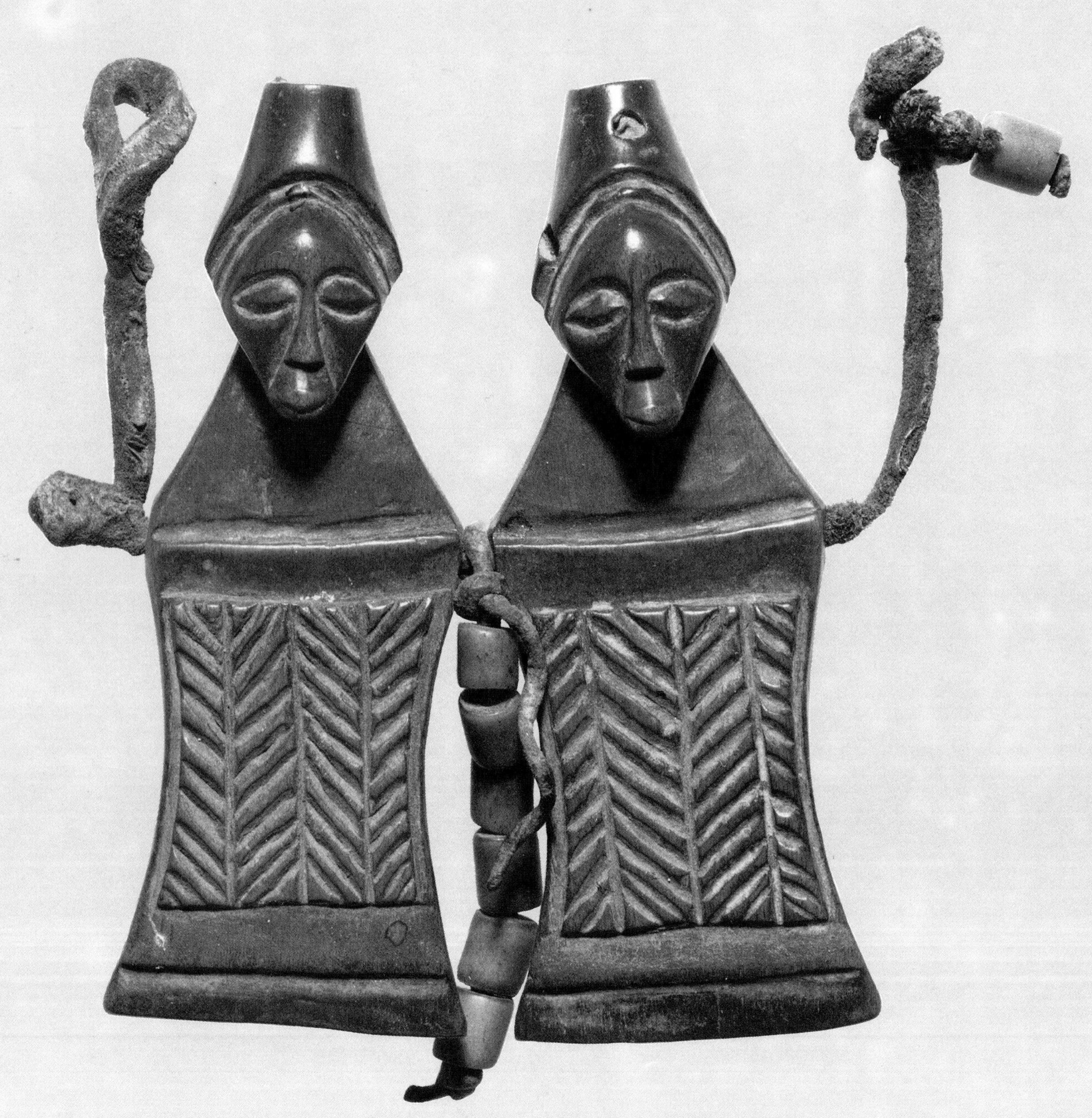

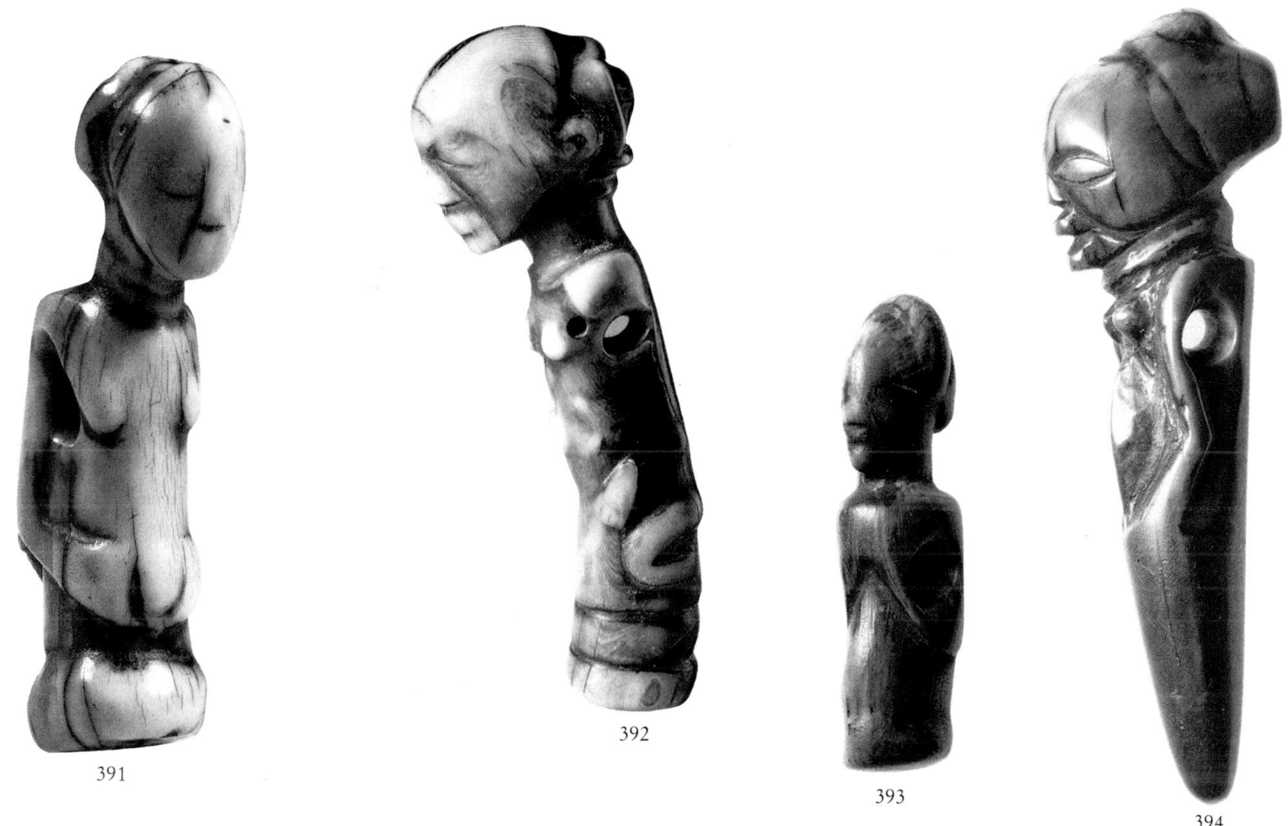

391

392

393

394

390-402 Amulet figures.
Zaire, Luba.

Among the miniature sculptures of the Luba, amulet figures carved in bone, ivory, hippopotamus tooth, boar tusk, and occasionally wood (No. 390) are particularly charming. In most cases they represent women, frequently holding their breasts. Complete figures were made, as well as busts on pedestals. The face is sometimes large and round, sometimes long and oval, sometimes triangular; they are no more uniform than the large wood sculptures. Most necks are ringed to represent high collars, and one of the figures even has a metal neck ring. Circle and point ornaments or imitation scarifications decorate some bodies, though just as often there is no body adornment.

In accordance with definite precepts, these amulets were threaded, singly or in groups, and worn on belt, neck, or upper arm, or even under the arm. A certain effect was ascribed to each amulet: some protected their wearers from sorcery, including disease and other misfortune, others secured luck in hunting, repelled thieves, and so on. The powers they were believed to have are described in various ways. According to some reports, an impersonal, extraordinarily effective power (*bwanga*) is active in them. Other reports claim that the Luba link them with spirits, ancestors, and even the high god. There

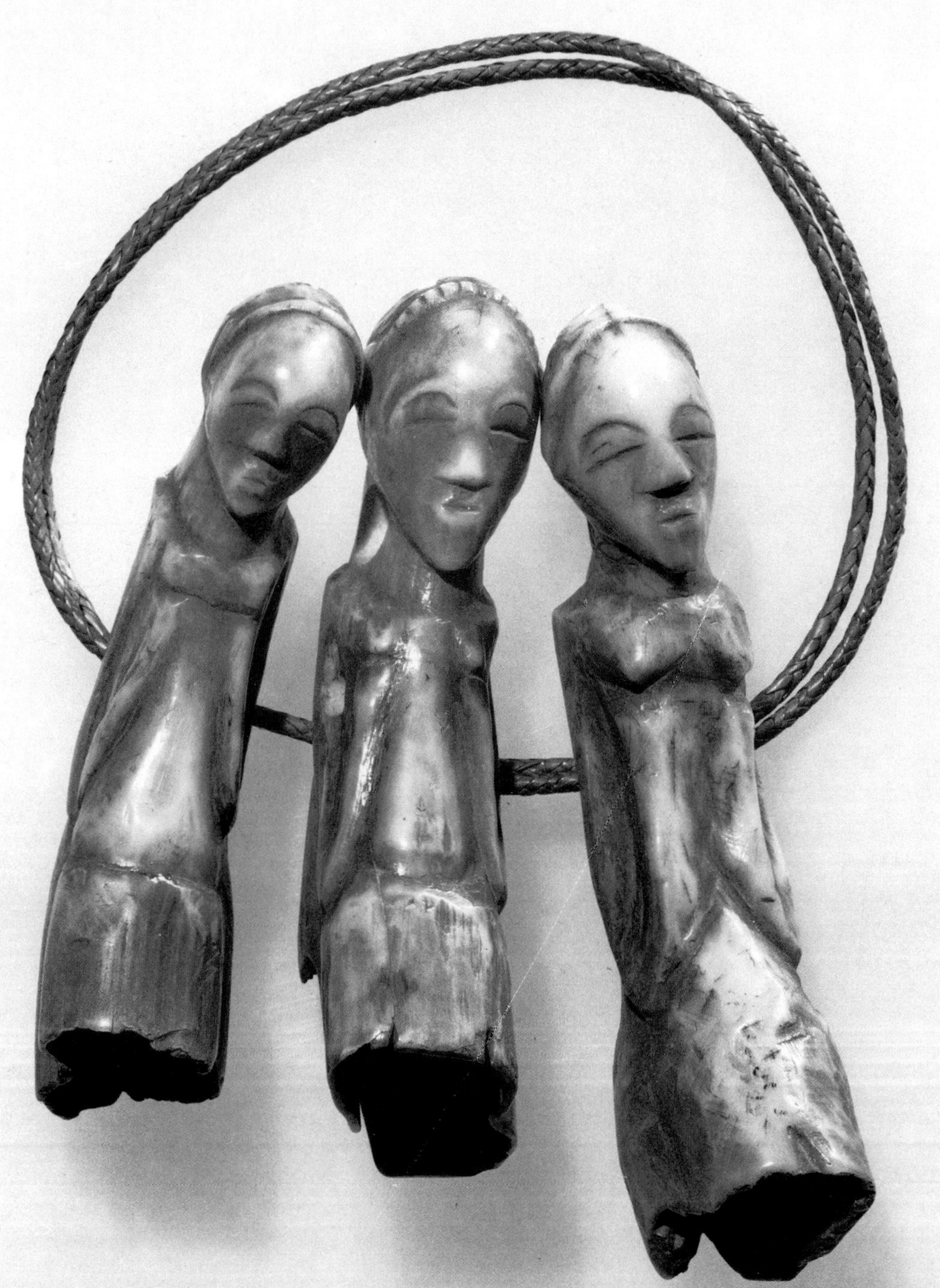

395
396
397

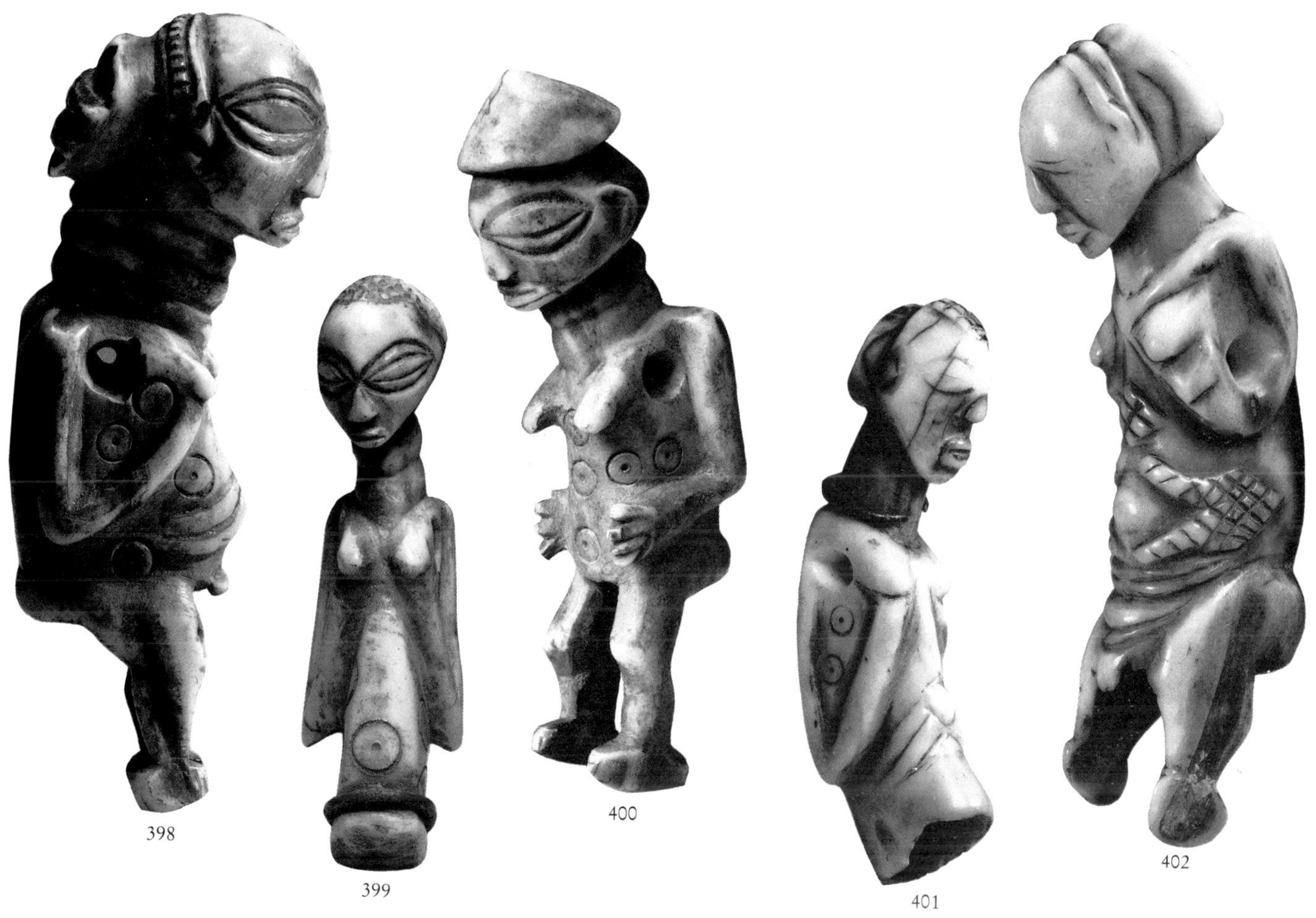
398 399 400 401 402

is probably no general explanation, for these ideas vary from region to region and from individual to individual. It is also possible that special types of amulet are associated with certain ideas. According to Colle, the figures are named for the deceased person from whom they obtain their power, though it is doubtful whether this would hold true for the whole Luba region. It is known that from time to time the figures are rubbed with palm oil—hence the silky reddish surface; the dark patina is simply the result of long use. It is often impossible to decide whether the custom of rubbing with oil is observed in order to activate an impersonal power or to sacrifice to the spirits of the amulet.

Height 8-11 cm. 11.1555a-d, 13-57-150-4, 13-57-188, 51-29-2-3

Acquired from F. Mitchell 1911, H. Deininger 1913, Bretschneider 1951

Lit.: W. F. P. Burton 1961, pp. 44, 91, 92; R. P. Colle 1913, Vol. II, p. 435; J. Cornet 1913, p. 212.

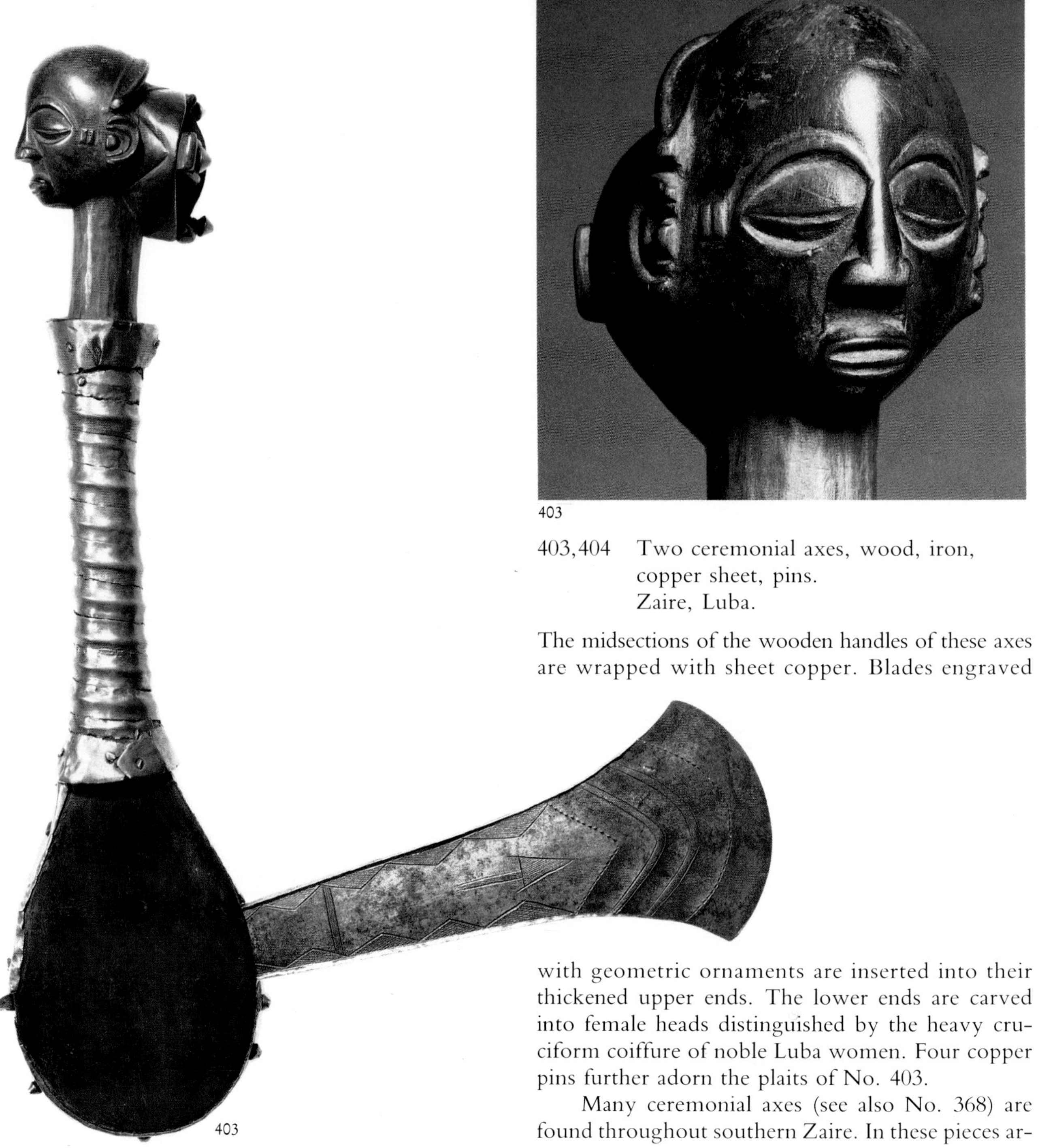

403

403

403,404 Two ceremonial axes, wood, iron, copper sheet, pins.
Zaire, Luba.

The midsections of the wooden handles of these axes are wrapped with sheet copper. Blades engraved with geometric ornaments are inserted into their thickened upper ends. The lower ends are carved into female heads distinguished by the heavy cruciform coiffure of noble Luba women. Four copper pins further adorn the plaits of No. 403.

Many ceremonial axes (see also No. 368) are found throughout southern Zaire. In these pieces artistic quality is determined by the skill of the carver rather than by that of the smith. They were neither weapons nor tools but were used in various symbolic and ritual ways—as symbols of office or profession, as implements for ordeals or cult ceremonies, as amulets, and so on. It is not known for what purpose our pieces were used.

Length 66.5 cm., 56.5 cm. 13-57-127, 11.1521
Acquired from H. Deininger 1913, F. Mitchell 1911

Lit.: C. G. Widstrand 1958, pp. 56, 124, 131, 143.

405 Staff with female figure, wood, iron pin.
Zaire, Luba from Maniema.

This figure's full form, light body color, richly ornamental scarifications, melancholy facial expression, and artistic coiffure with massive chignon ally it with the Buli (long-face) style associated with famous Luba masterpieces.

Length 122 cm. 05.72
Acquired from H. Deininger 1905

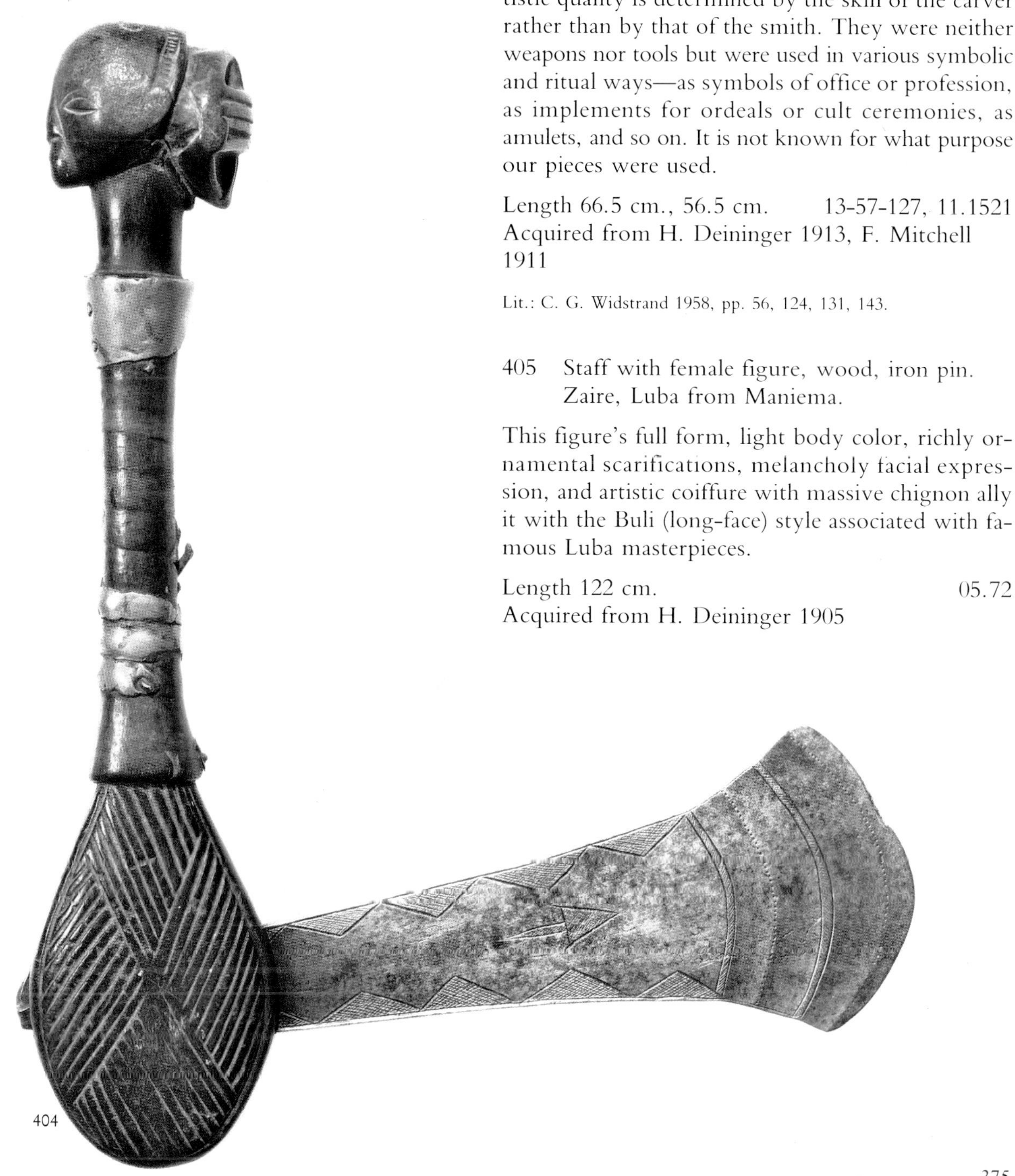

404

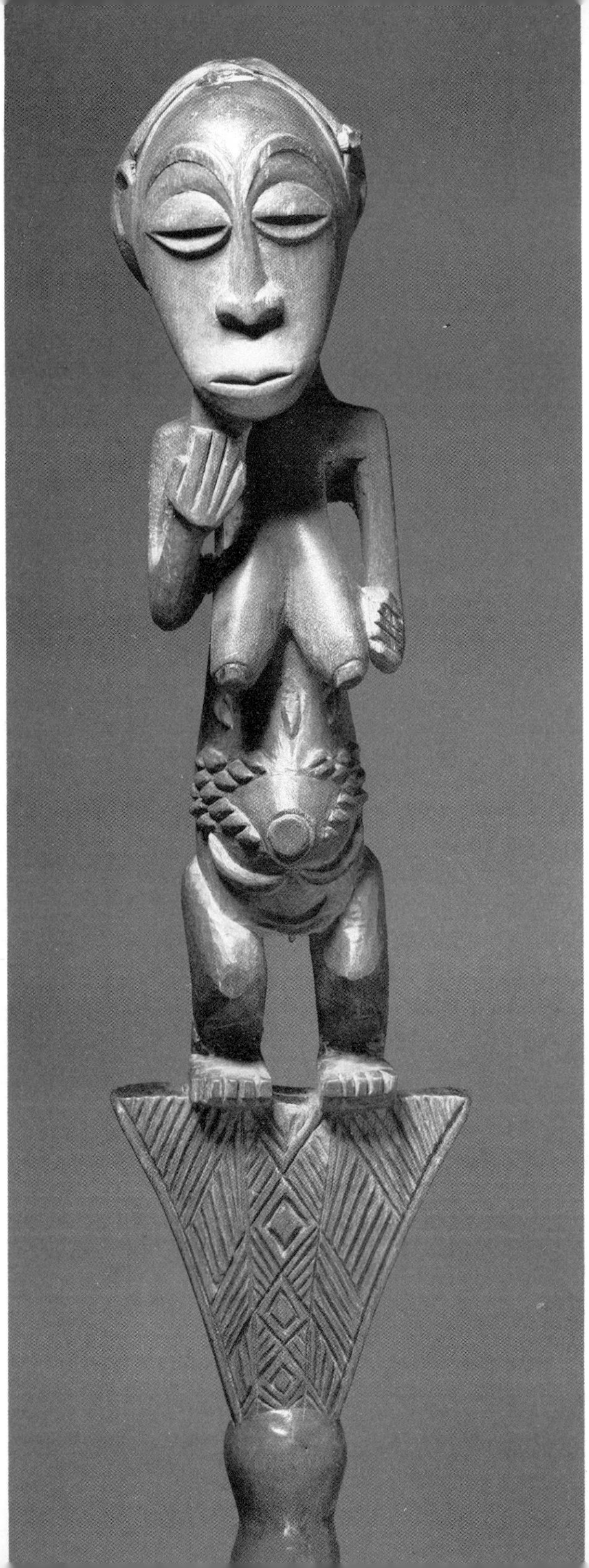

405

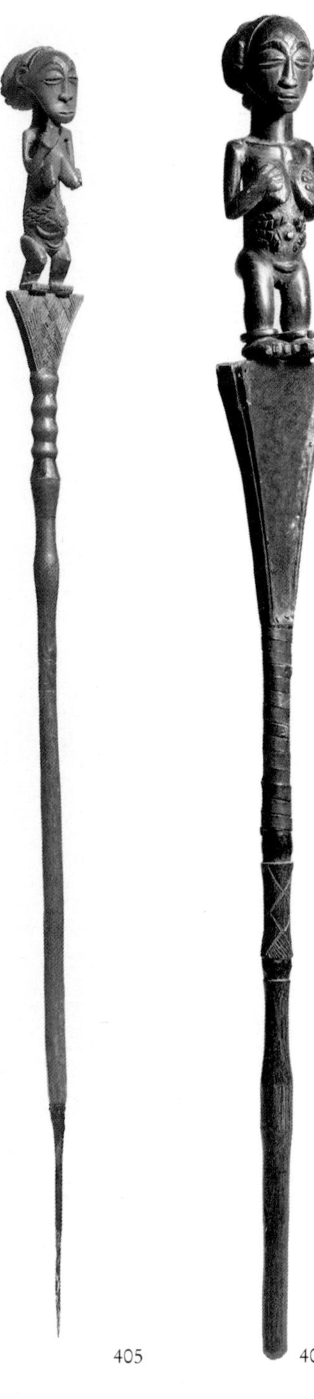

405

406

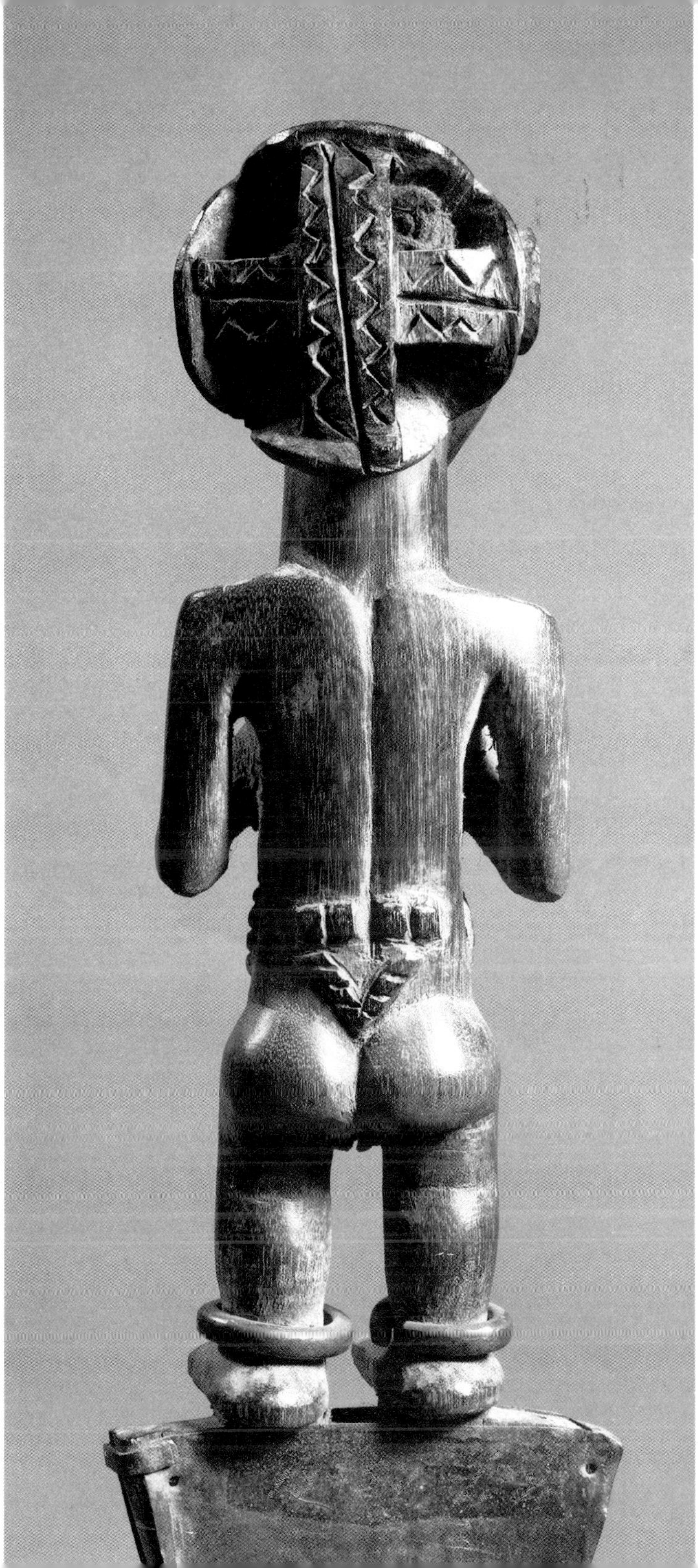

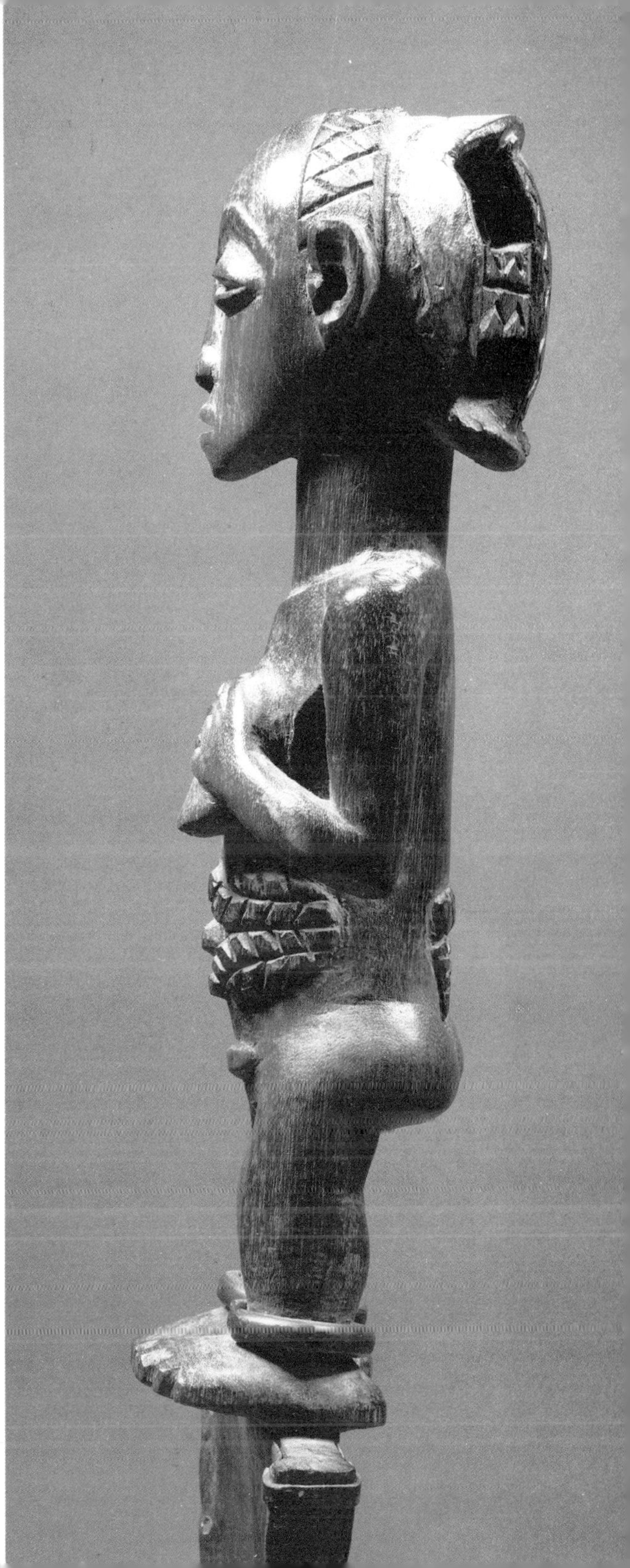

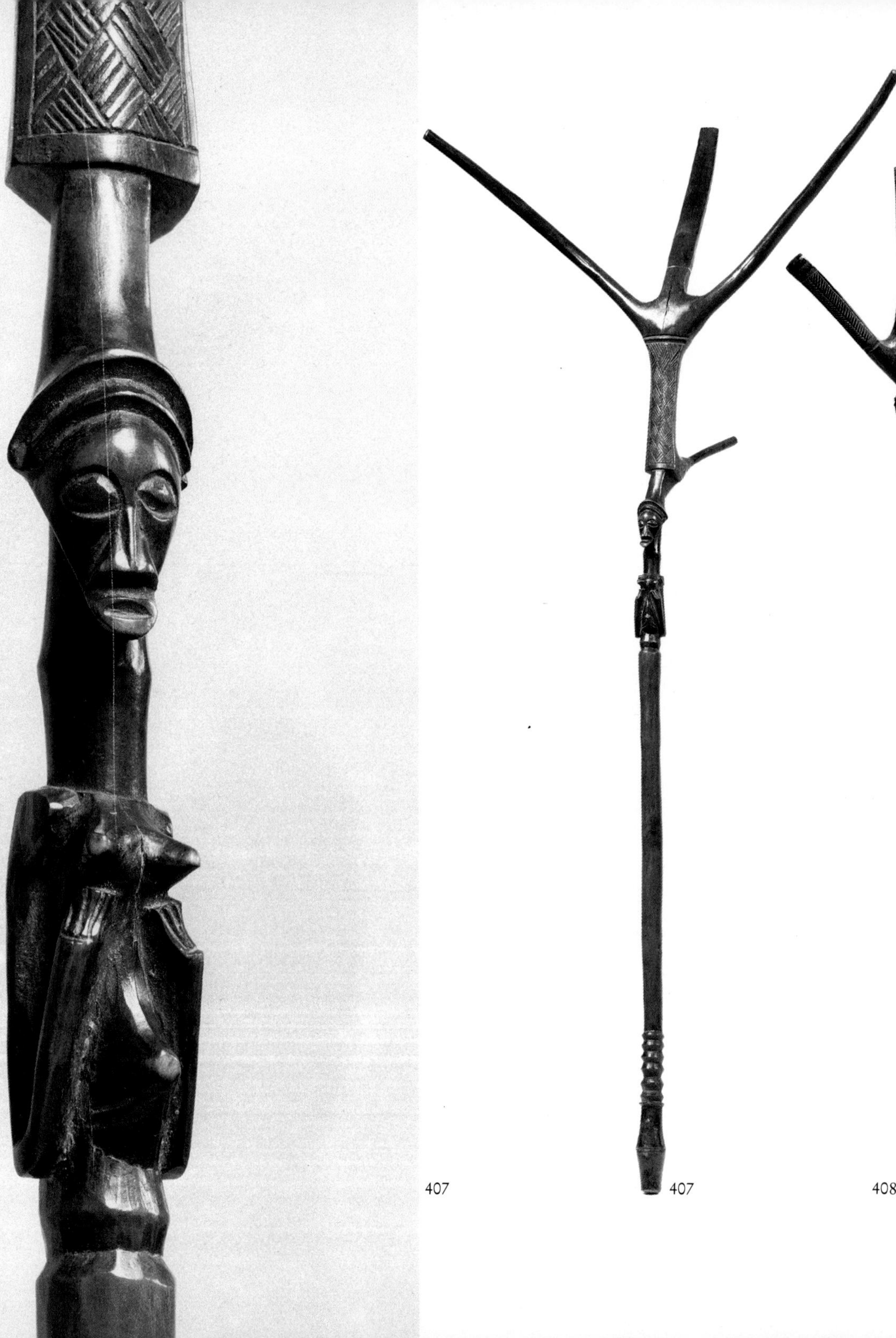

407 407 408

406 Staff with female figure, wood, iron sheet and rings.
Zaire, Luba-Hemba, Uroa.

This figure's hands rest on her breasts. Her cruciform coiffure and dark abdominal and back scarifications are carefully worked. There is a piece of red cloth in the hollow of the coiffure behind the plaits.

Length 82 cm. 13-57-137
Acquired from H. Deininger 1913

407,408 Two bow and arrow holders, wood.
Zaire, Luba-Hemba, Urua.

Bow and arrow holders, terminating in three arms and often adorned with high-quality sculptured female figures, were originally a special attribute of Luba royalty. The holder was usually stuck into the ground in front of the royal palace and, together with the royal bow and arrows placed in it, was an insignia of the ruler. Guarding these power symbols and the royal stools was an important office entrusted only to a woman of the highest social rank. In the course of time the exclusivity of bow and arrow holders diminished. High court officials and then district chiefs employed this insignia until at last, around the turn of the century, it was to be found in the houses of ordinary Luba, usually standing between the marriage bed and the wall.

Although their provenance is said to be the same, the two exhibited pieces are very different in style. The face of No. 407 reminds us of Songo art, that of No. 408 of Luba.

Length 75 cm., 122 cm. 13-57-122, 13- 57-123
Acquired from H. Deininger 1913

Lit.: R. P. Colle 1913, Vol. I, pp. 167, 68; J. Cornet 1973, p. 210; S. Lagercrantz 1950, pp. 368, 69.

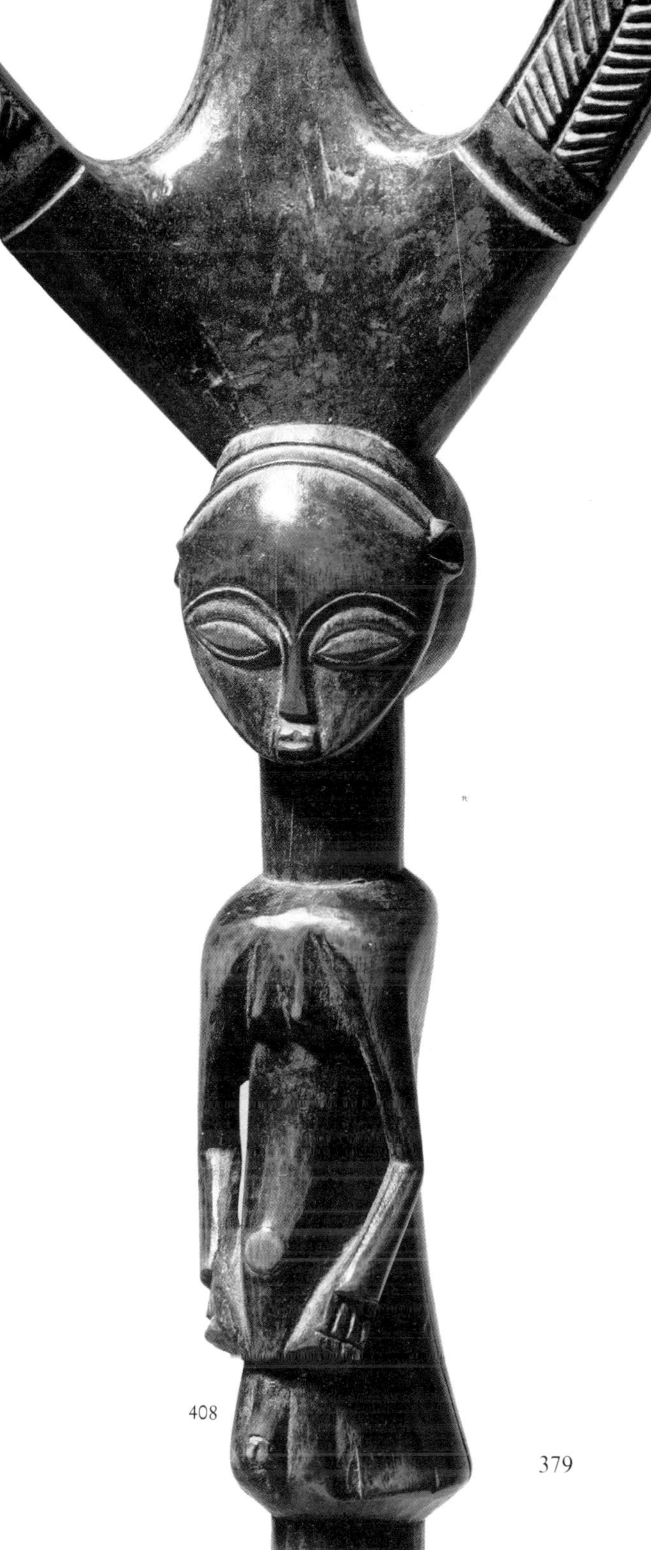

408

409 Headrest, wood.
Zaire, Luba-Hemba (Kunda?).

A headrest served as a pillow during sleep and helped protect the artistic coiffure. This supporting function suggests why the base of the headrest was sculptured anthropomorphically, like the royal stools (Nos. 383-89).

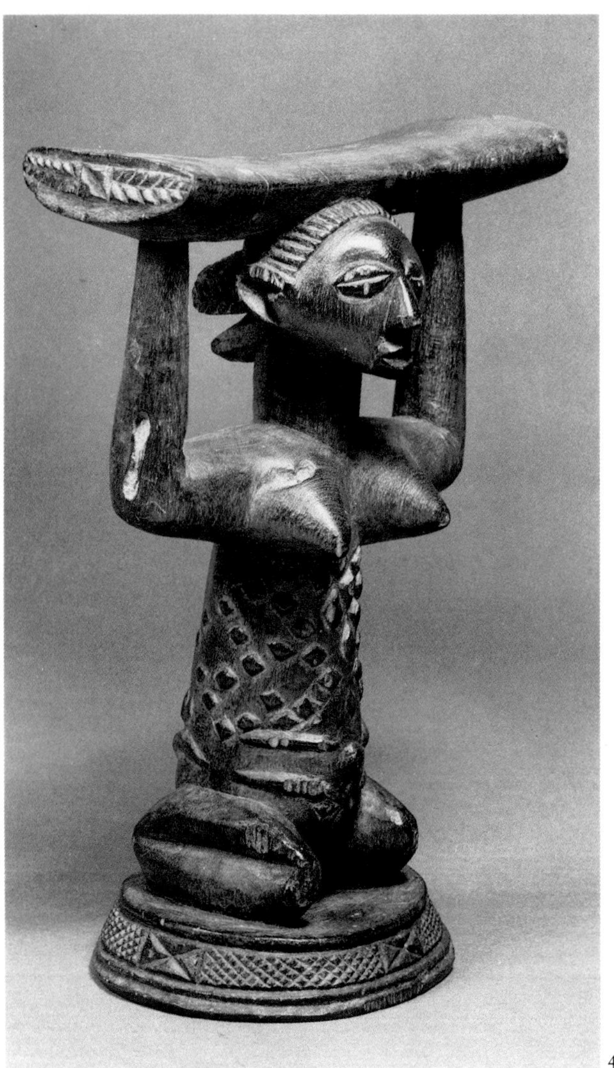

409

According to Neyt, this seated figure has characteristics of Luba-influenced Kunda figures: a diamond-shape face, a graduated coiffure, and an extended torso with elaborate scarification. The legs folded under the sitter have been simplified to a creased oval.

Height 20 cm. 11.1501
Acquired from F. Mitchell 1911

Lit.: F. Graebner 1927, pp. 1-13; F. Neyt, personal communication.

Royal Staffs (410-413)

The staffs of the Luba area, symbols of office that are embellished with sculptured figures, have a unique form different from that of royal staffs made in other regions of southern Zaire. Whether the broad flat ends of the staffs actually indicate their evolution from earlier emblematic oars or paddles (and thus allude to their fisher forebears or to their immigration by boat) as is sometimes claimed, is debatable. In any case, the paddlelike broadening offers carvers a surface to fill with fine ornament suggestive of wickerwork. The sculptured human figures on the staffs shown represent various styles, ranging from naturalistic to abstract.

Lit.: A. Massion 1964, pp. 157ff.

410 Royal staff with female figures, wood, iron.
Zaire, Luba, Lake Kisale.

The figures in this composition are similar to that of No. 409, but more abstract. The top figure's hands rest on its chest; the lower (double) figure stands on bent legs, rather than kneeling as the top figure does.

Length 170 cm. 11.1442
Acquired from F. Mitchell 1911

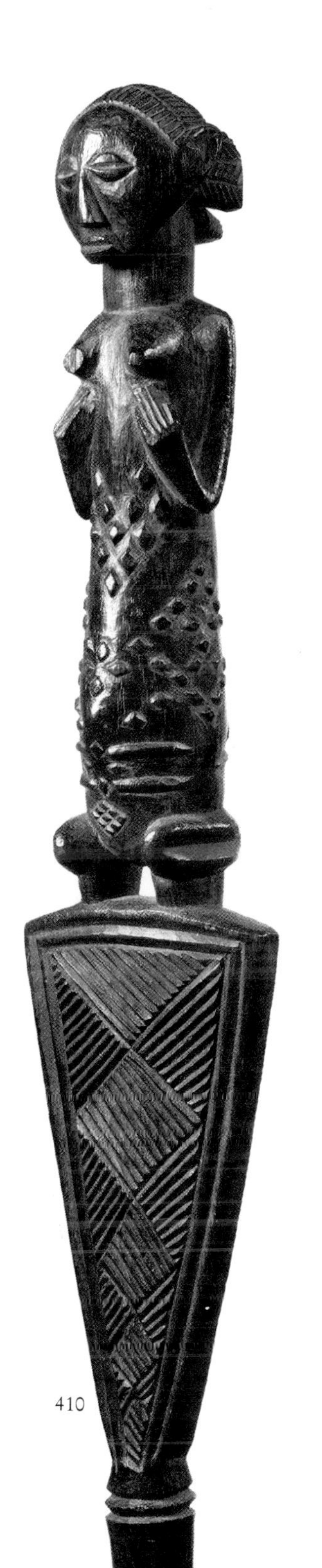

410

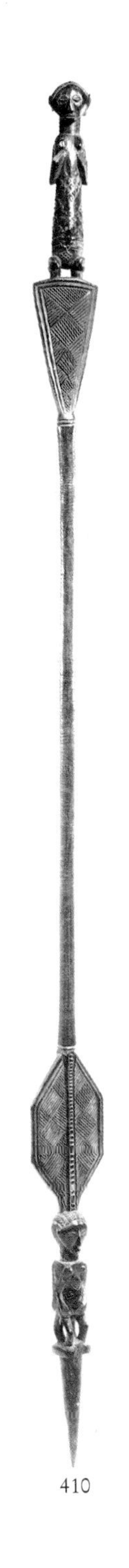

410

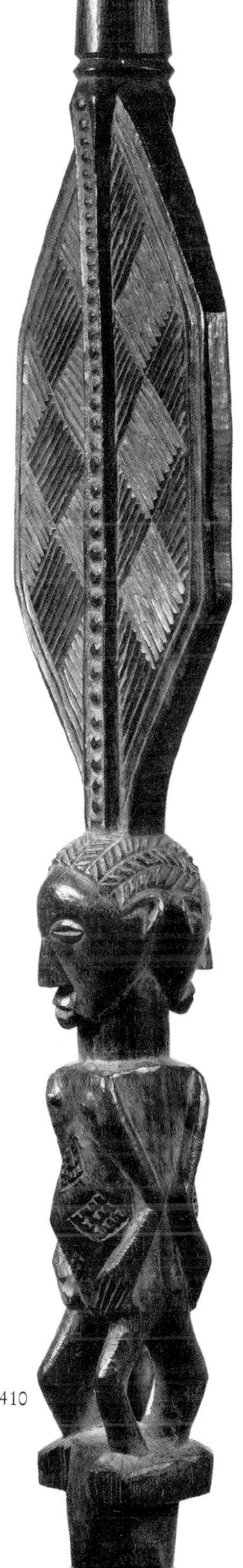

410

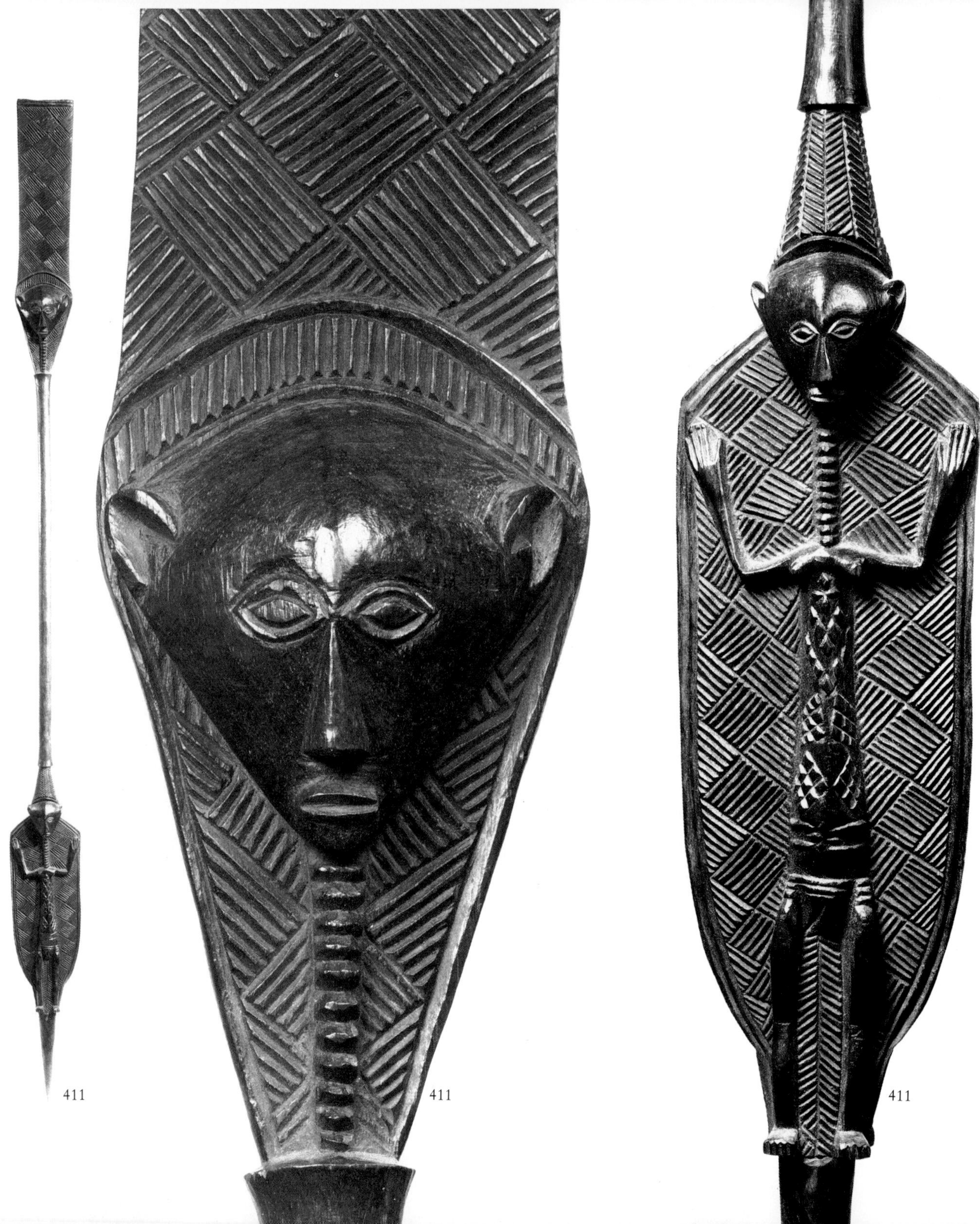

411

411

411

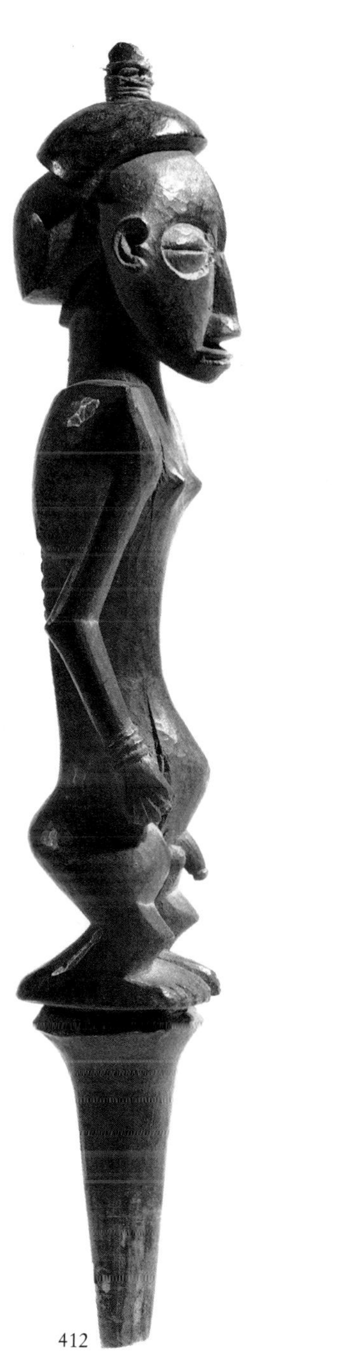
412

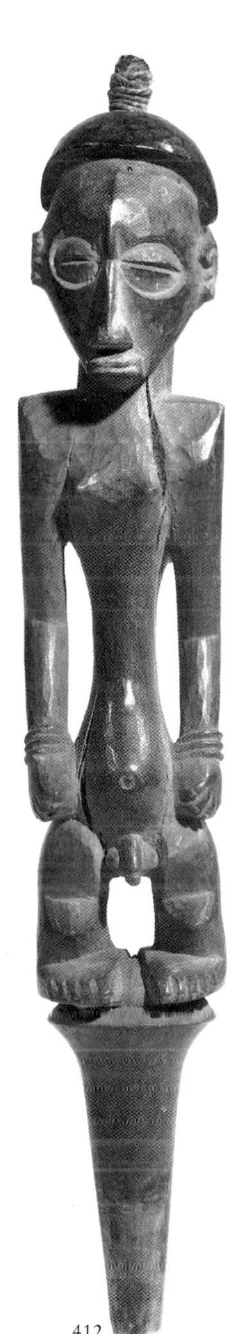
412

413

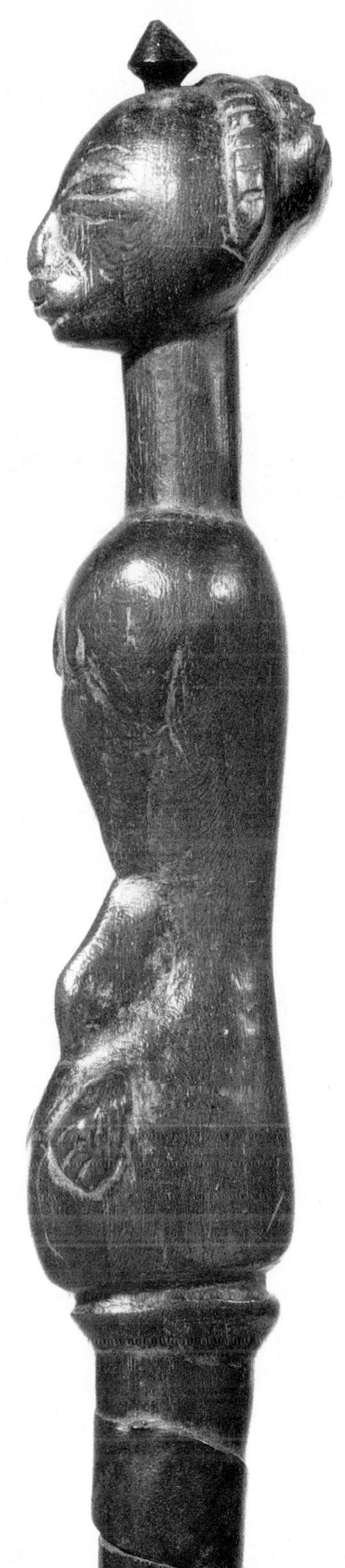

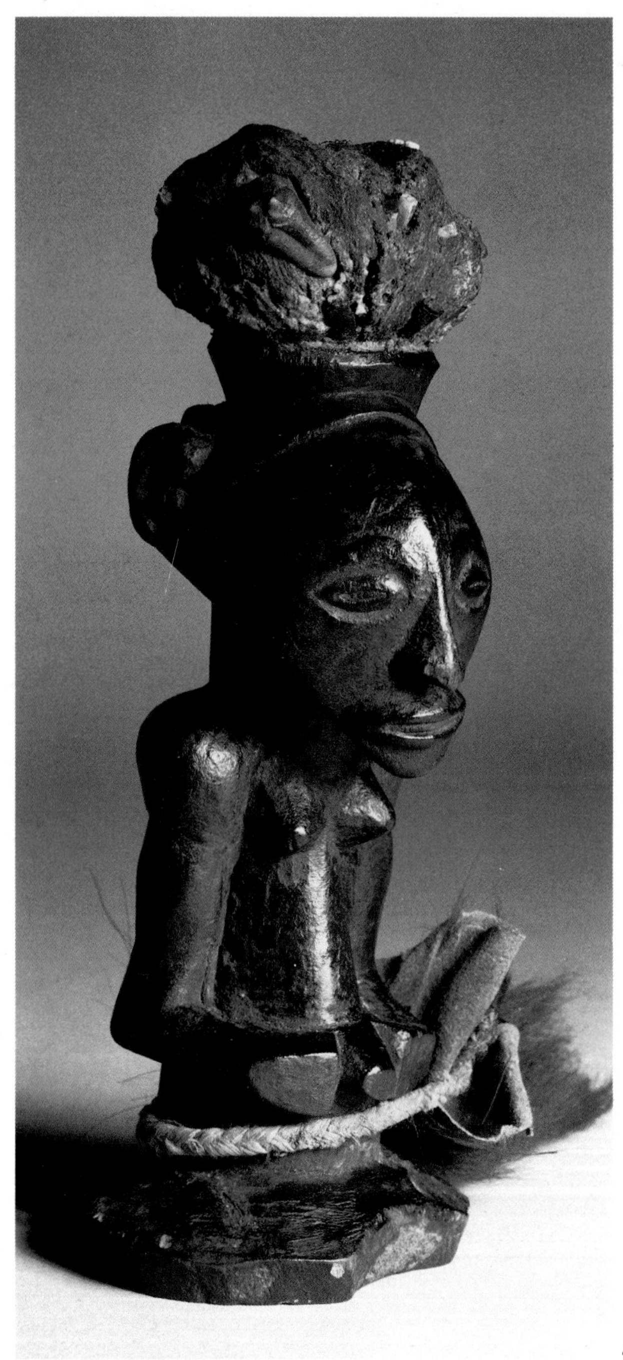

414

411 Royal staff with figurative relief, wood.
Zaire, Luba-Hemba, from Lake Kisale.

The paddle-shape section of this exquisitely carved staff displays a relief of an upright human figure with raised hands, its body adorned with scarifications. On the broad upper end is a relief of a head and neck only. These carvings are in a mature abstract style that employs the human figure purely as ornament. The triangular faces and long, ringed necks are essentially identical. Back and front are identical as well.

Length 169 cm. 11.1441
Acquired from F. Mitchell 1911

412 Handle of a fly whisk, wood, iron.
Collected in Urua, Zaire.

The small male figure at the tip of this fly whisk handle is remarkable because of its overly long torso with narrow constricted waist (see also No. 416). As usual, the head dominates the composition. Both the face, divided by conspicuous transverse and longitudinal lines, and the angular shoulders express a tendency toward geometrization that is repeated in the zigzag rhythm of the body profile. A dark-colored graduated coiffure crowns the head and is topped by an iron pin. The arms, adorned with bracelets, are comparatively thin and angular; the very short legs are bent. This type of figure is classified as belonging to the pre-Bembe style.

Length 25 cm. 13-57-139
Acquired from H. Deininger 1913

Lit.: D. Biebuyck 1981, Illus. 35,36.

413 Staff with male half-figure, wood, copper.
Zaire, Luba.

In basic concept this piece resembles No. 412, but it represents a distinct stylistic variant characterized

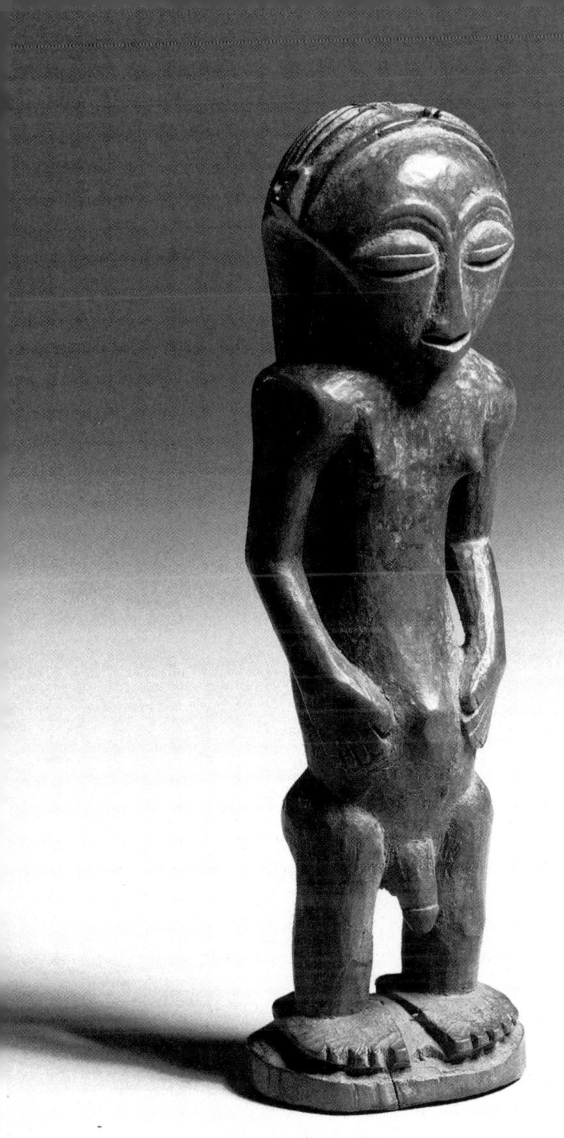

415

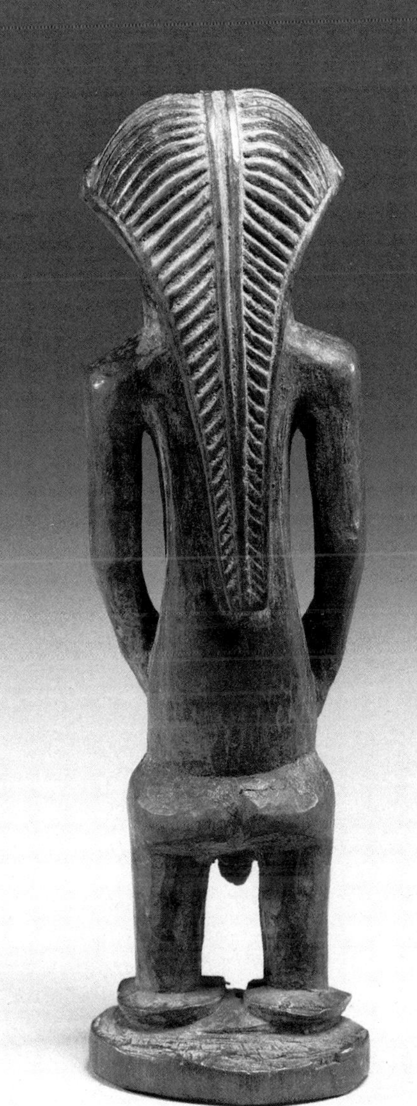

415

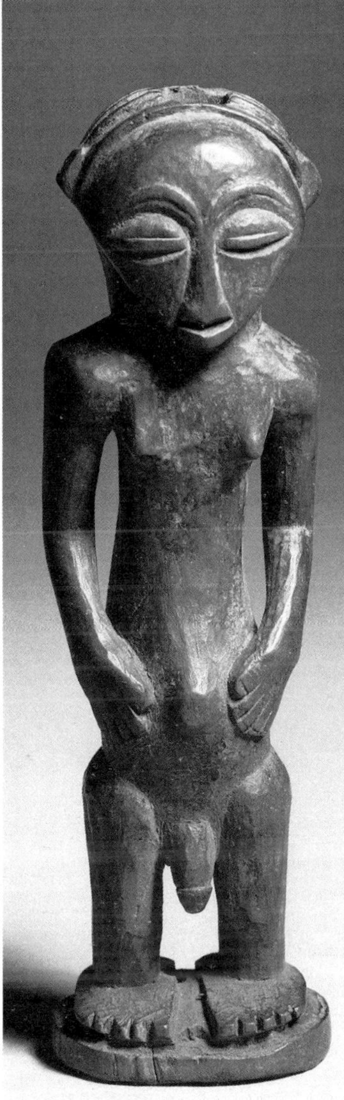

415

by prognathous face, long neck, vaulted chest, and narrow waist. Arms are faintly suggested, but only the hands are represented. The copper pin in the crown of the head is very like that in No. 412.

Length 98 cm. 13-57-136
Acquired from H. Deininger 1913

414 Half-figure with bundle of medicines, wood, skin, resin, plant fibers.
Zaire, Luba, Buli (Kunda?).

The face of this half figure is diamond-shape; the almond eyes are open—a detail comparatively rare in Luba art. The line of the eyebrows continues to

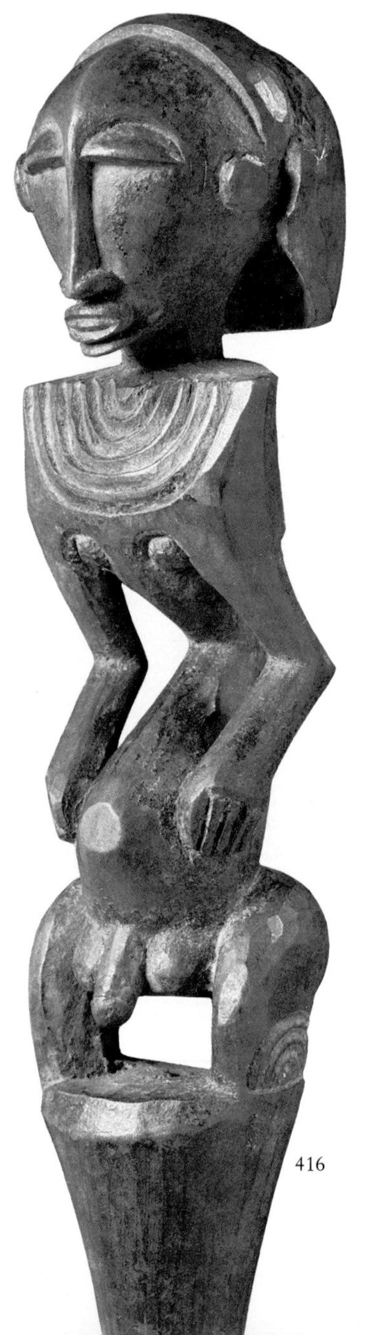

416

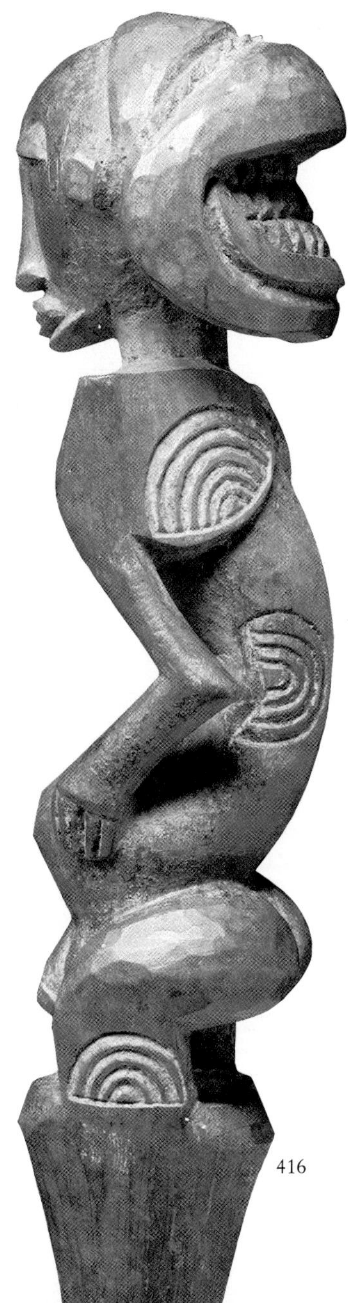

416

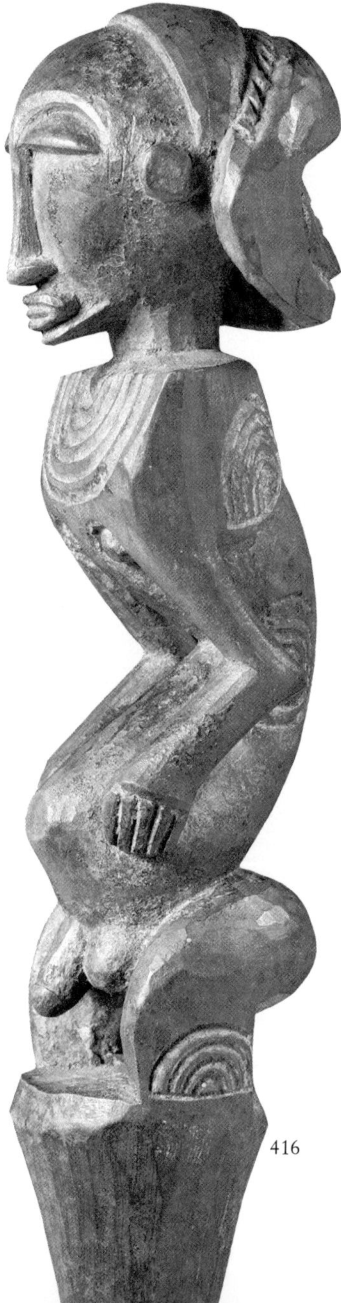

416

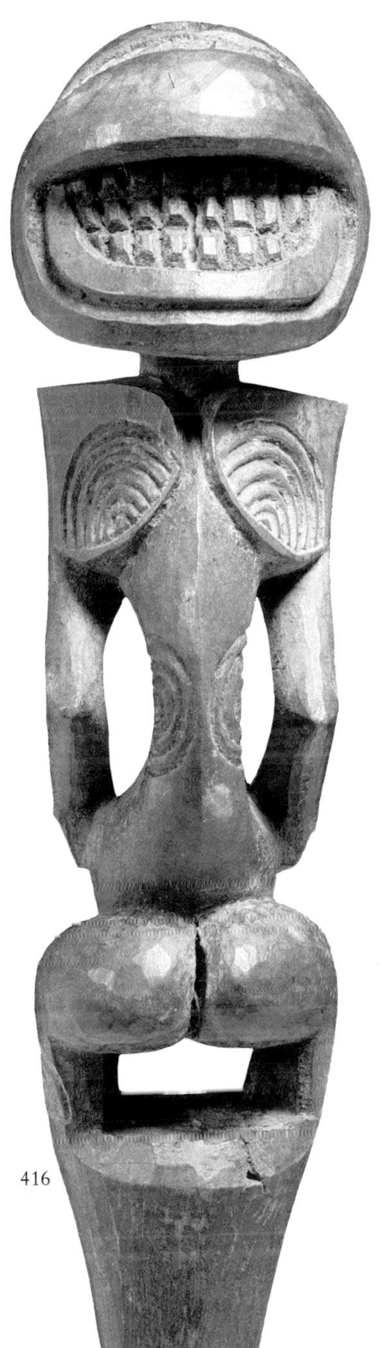
416

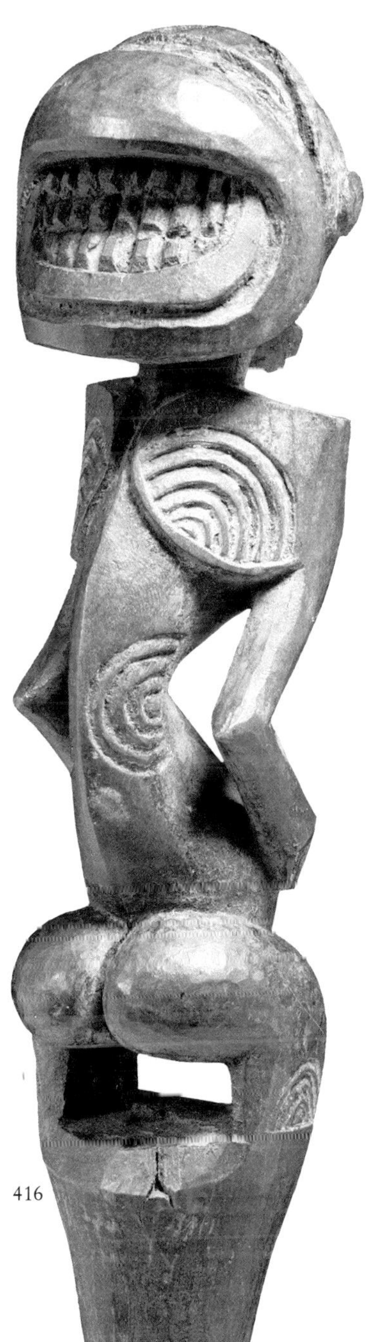
416

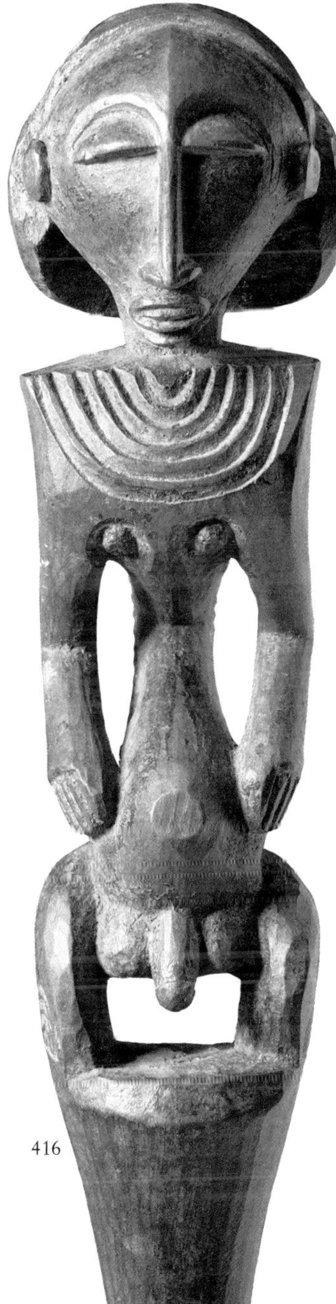
416

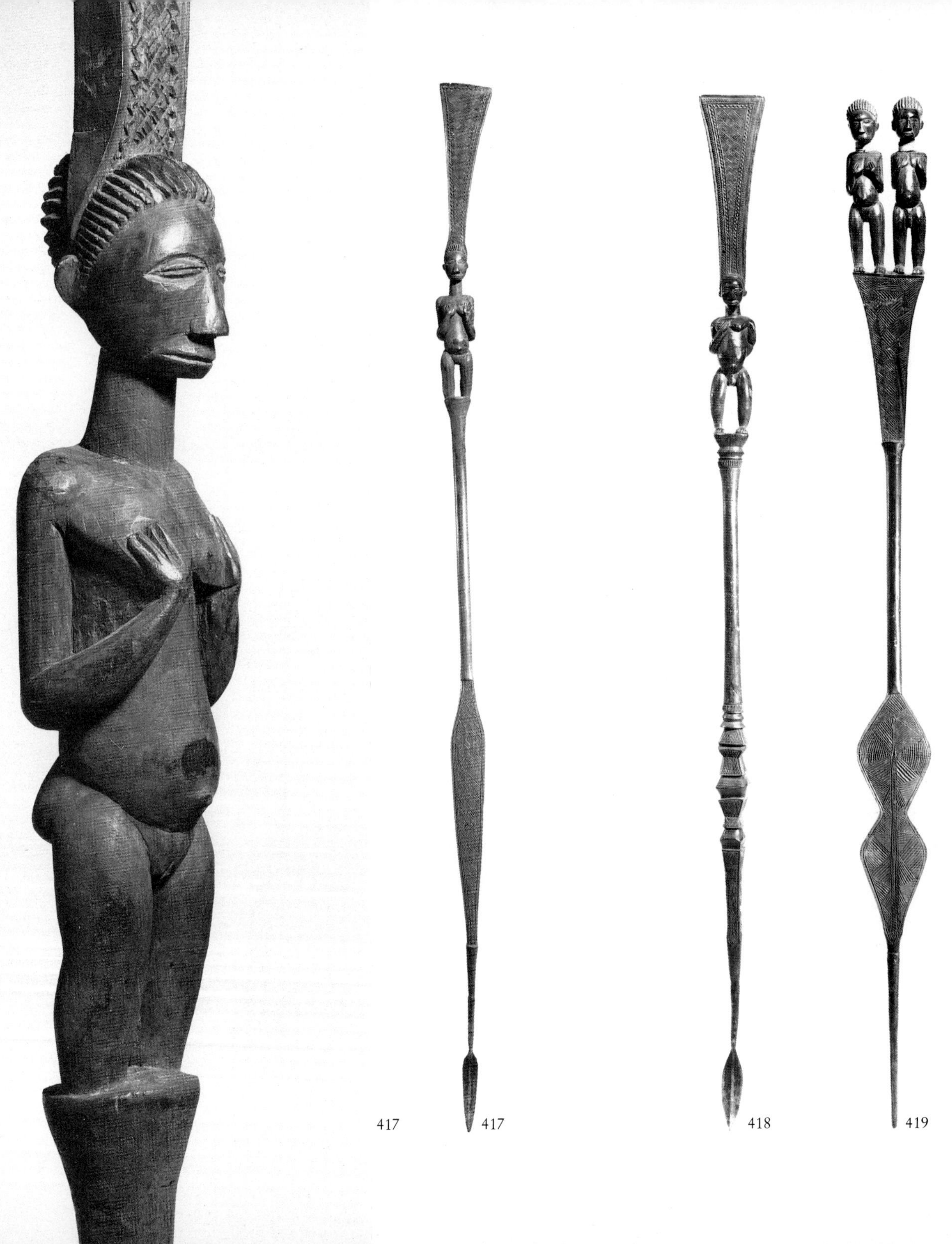

417 417 418 419

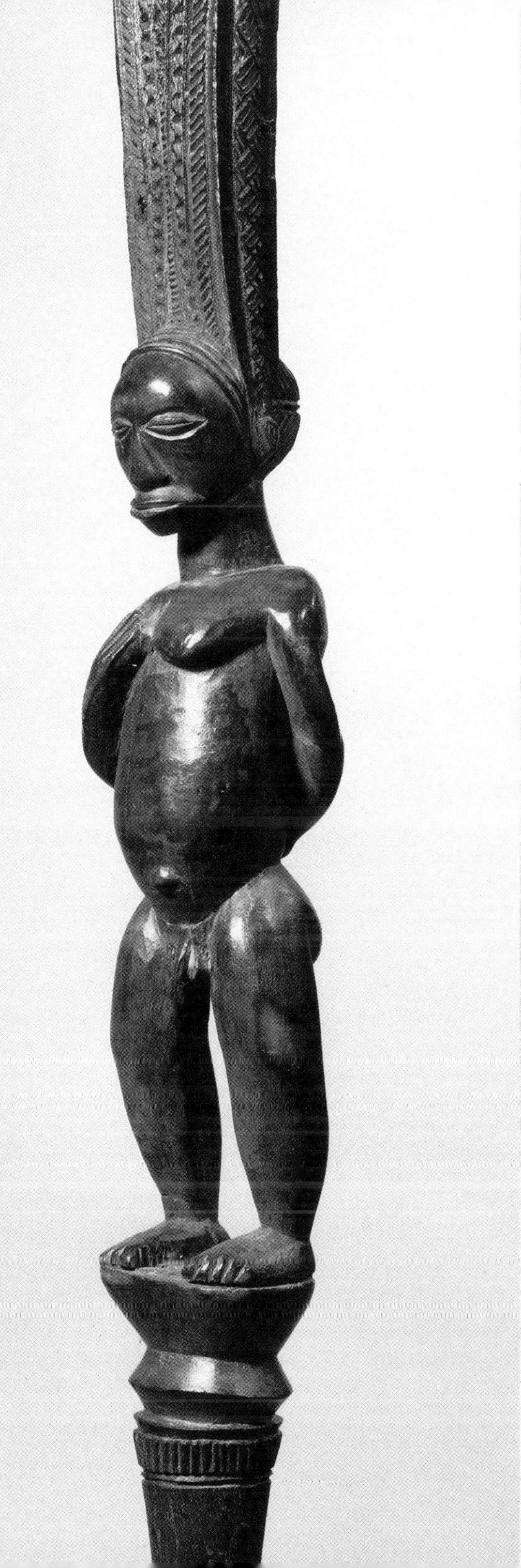

418/419

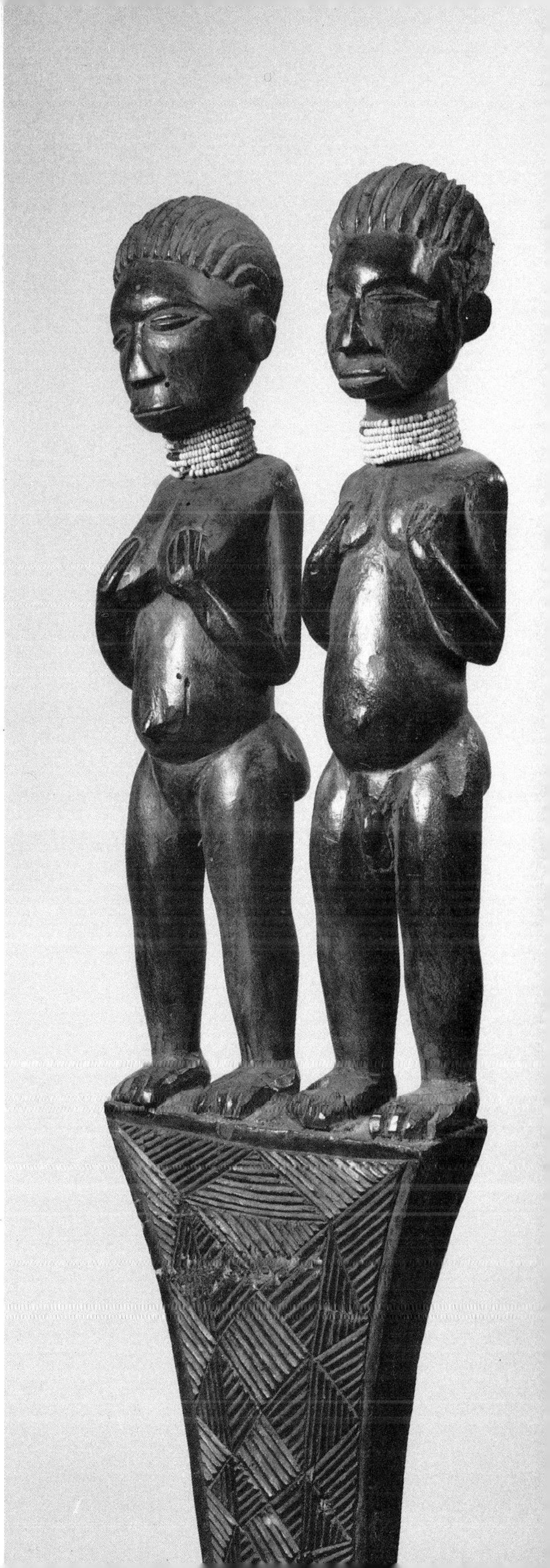

form the bridge of the nose; the mouth thrusts forward. Small hands rest on the slightly protruding abdomen.

The base of this figure serves as a calabash stopper (see also No. 378). The vessel is said to have been used in divination, which accounts for the medicine bundle on the small figure's head. The horn filled with magical substances, once part of the figure, is missing. Possibly the stopper's original owner withheld the horn when he sold the object.

Height 20 cm. 11.1483
Acquired from H. Deininger 1911

415 Male figure, wood.
Zaire, collected in the Luba area, Mambwe (?).

This fine small sculpture with diamond-shape face has large rimmed eyes, raised eyebrows, and protruding mouth. The long ribbed coiffure is characteristic of the Mambwe style. The torso is elongated; the large hands have clearly recognizable fingers and nails; the feet are flat. There is a hole for the magic horn (now missing) in the crown of the head. These small figures modeled on larger ones represent deceased chiefs.

Height 14.5 cm. 13-57-138
Acquired from H. Deininger 1913

Lit.: F. Neyt 1977, pp. 291-95, 412, 13; F. Neyt, in A. F. Roberts & E. M. Maurer 1985, pp. 70-73.

416 Handle of a fly whisk, wood.
Zaire, Buye (Boyo).

A male figure forms the tip of this fly whisk handle. The figure is a small masterpiece with the characteristic features of the considerably larger Buye ancestral figures. The artfully designed body creates a singular rhythm that is further accentuated by segments of low-relief concentric circles. The exaggerated, stylized face balances the heavy intricate coiffure.

From the quality of the piece, we may assume that it was part of the ceremonial paraphernalia of a prominent man. In many parts of Africa, the fly-whisk is a sign of office of the ruler and also occasionally of certain courtiers, priests, diviners, and so on. (See also No. 412.)

Length 27.5 cm. 13-57-140
Acquired from H. Deininger 1913

Lit.: N. de Kun 1979, pp. 29-44.

417 Chief's staff with female figure, wood.
Zaire, Holoholo (?).

This sculpture resembles those of No. 419 but has no string of beads. It is a breast-holding figure with deepened navel.

Length 183 cm. 09.493
Acquired from Arneth 1909

418 Chief's staff with male figure, wood, iron.
Zaire, Holoholo (?).

The artist who created this realistic figure quite consciously defied the tradition of symmetrical representation by placing one of the figure's hands in front and the other in back. The lower half of the staff, adorned with singularly carved geometric patterns, ends in an iron spear blade hafted in a socket.

Length 154 cm. 09.494
Acquired from Arneth 1909

419 Chief's staff with pair of figures, wood, glass beads.
Zaire, Holoholo (?).

Except for overly long legs, the proportions of these bodies are almost natural. Strings of beads clasp the figures' necks; the coiffures are simple.

Length 155 cm. 09.495
Acquired by Arneth 1909

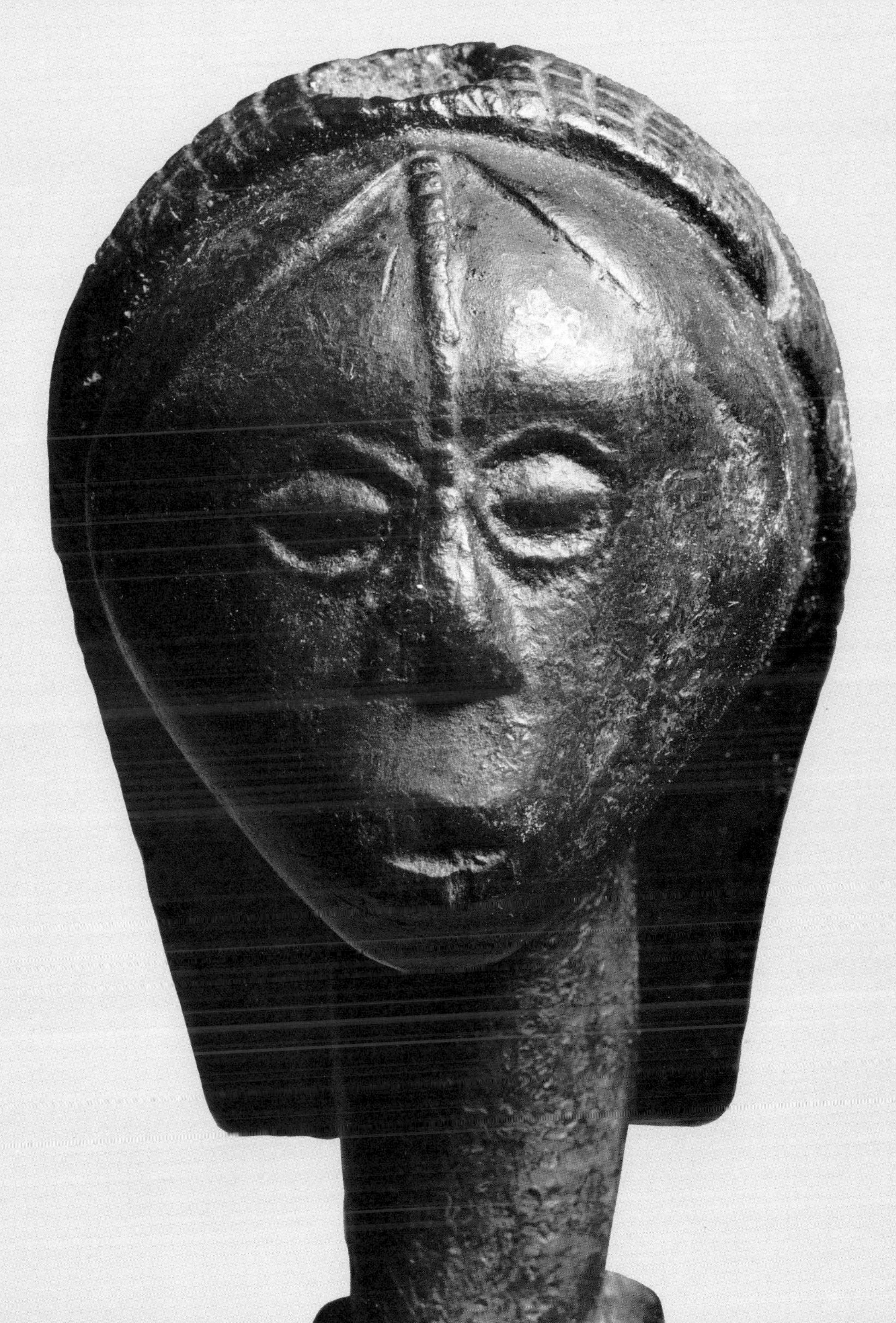

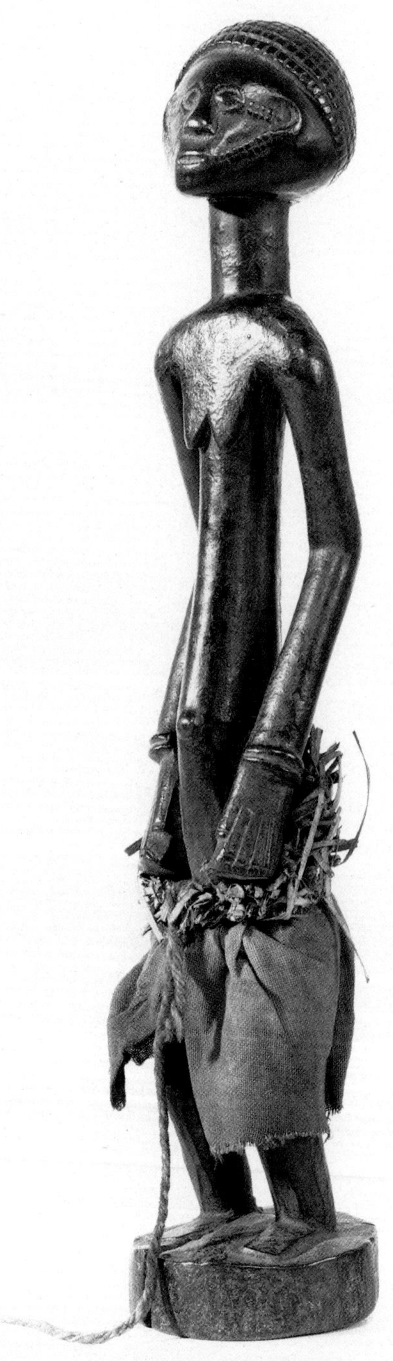

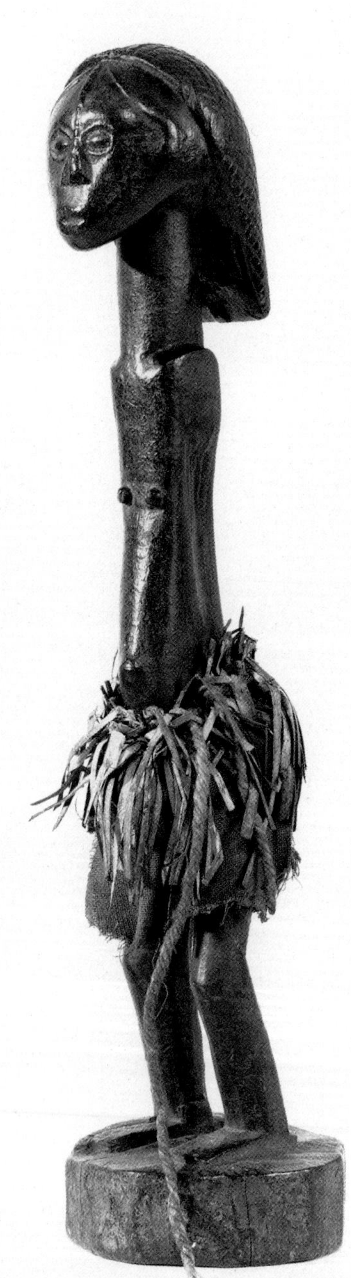

420/421

420,421 Female and male figures, wood, plant-fiber fabric, cotton.
Zaire, Tabwa.

The figure with short hair represents a woman, the other a man. Cicatrizations adorn these broad stylized faces, which also have large rimmed open eyes, broad noses, and narrow protruding lips. The ornamentally sculptured spinal columns are striking. The man's arms were presumably broken off and the break later retouched. Also noteworthy is the detailed sculpturing of hands and feet, with fingers and toes cut in deeply, steplike. The rich patina testifies to a long period of ritual usage.

Height 33.5 cm., 36.5 cm. 05.52/3
Acquired from H. Deininger 1905

Lit.: A. F. Roberts & E. M. Maurer 1985, pp. 118, 19.

422-424 Two single female figures and a couple, wood.
Zaire, Tabwa.

These pieces are further variants of the Tabwa style, one with broad face (No. 422), two with longish protruding faces (Nos. 423 and 424). The upper bodies are tattooed. No. 424 has no base but stands on thick blocky feet. No. 423 shows a man carrying a woman on his shoulders, a rarity because there are few figures in action in traditional African sculpture. The ritual piggyback ride, however, is recorded in many parts of the continent. Usually the ruler was prohibited to touch the ground and was therefore carried on a slave's shoulders—a custom also in the ancient kingdoms of southern Zaire. Among the Luba, Hemba and other peoples, novices and young girls were also carried piggyback at initiation cere-

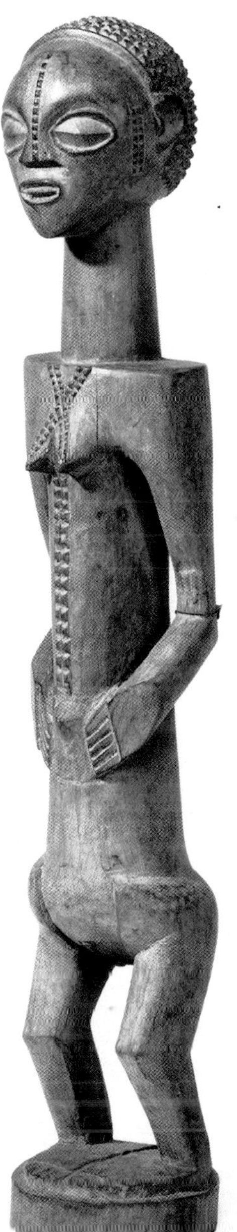

422

monies. The Tabwa, in Urua and elsewhere, also carried a bride at her wedding.

Height 35.39 cm., 70 cm. 05.54/58
Acquired from H. Deininger 1905

Lit.: V. L. Cameron 1877, Vol. II, p. 75; R. P. Colle 1913, Vol. II, pp. 592, 594; S. Lagercrantz 1950, pp. 331ff.

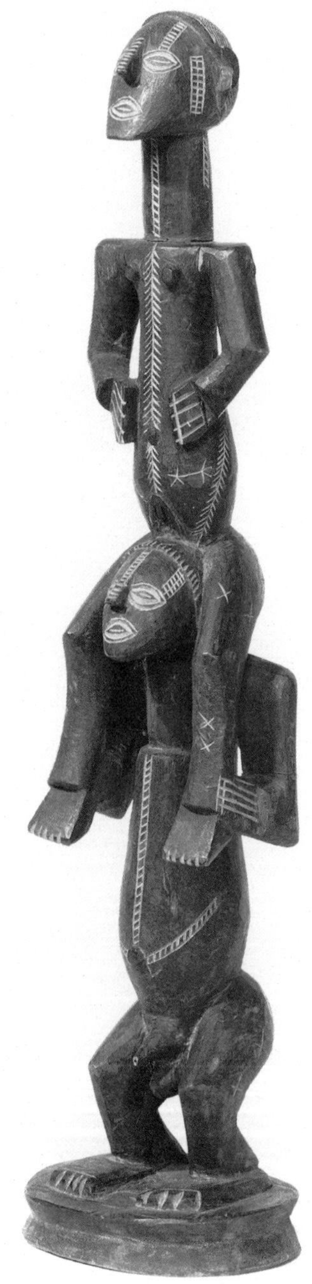

423

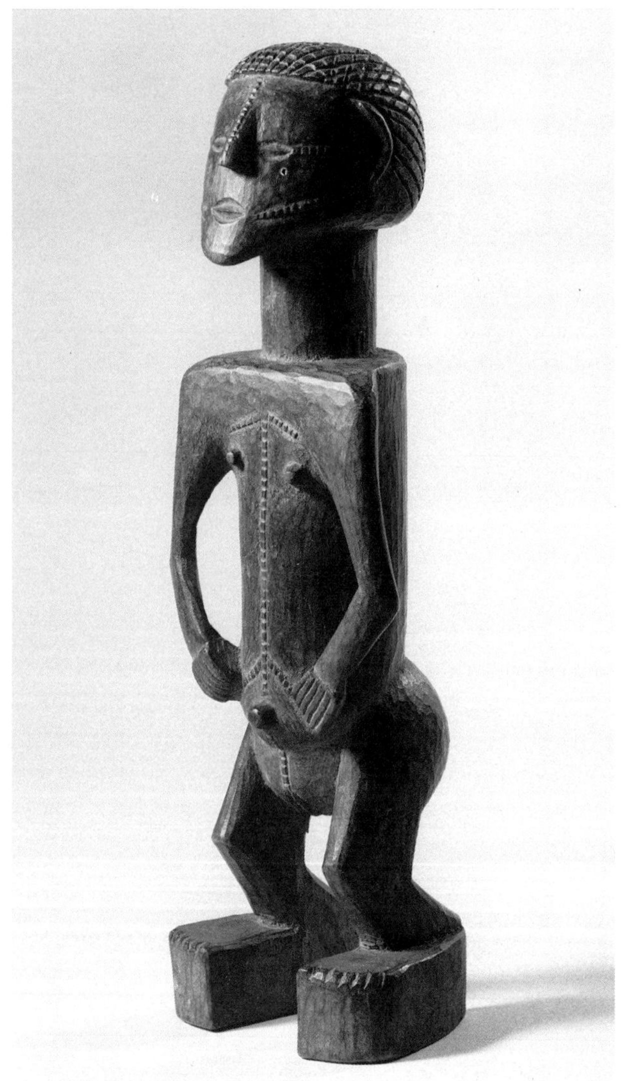

424

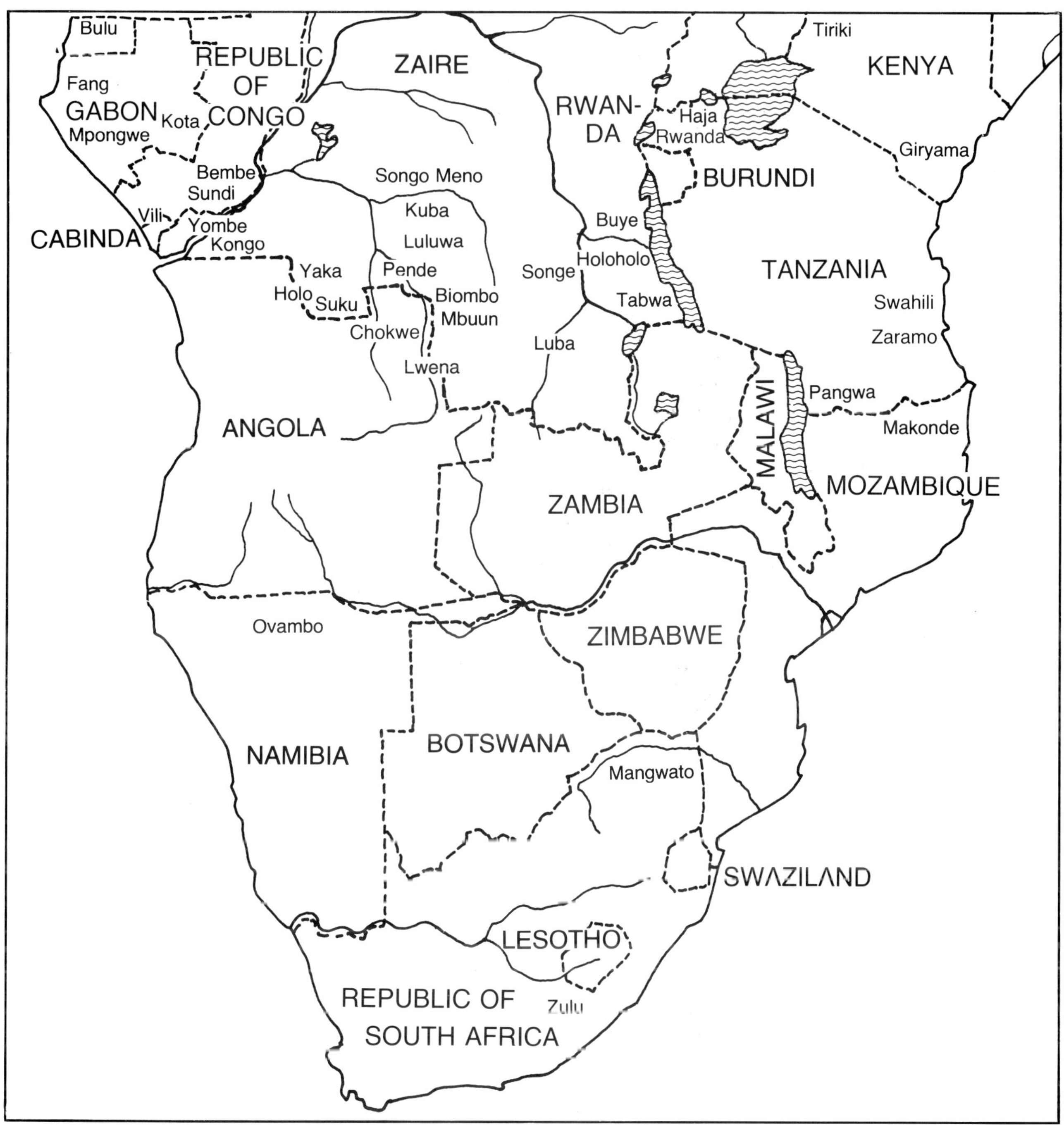
Bulu
REPUBLIC OF CONGO
ZAIRE
Tiriki
KENYA
Fang
GABON
Kota
Mpongwe
RWAN-DA
Haja
Rwanda
Giryama
Bembe
Sundi
Songo Meno
BURUNDI
Vili
Yombe
CABINDA
Kongo
Kuba
Luluwa
Buye
Holoholo
Yaka
Pende
Songe
TANZANIA
Holo
Suku
Biombo
Mbuun
Tabwa
Swahili
Chokwe
Zaramo
Luba
Lwena
Pangwa
MALAWI
ANGOLA
Makonde
MOZAMBIQUE
ZAMBIA
Ovambo
ZIMBABWE
NAMIBIA
BOTSWANA
Mangwato
SWAZILAND
LESOTHO
REPUBLIC OF SOUTH AFRICA
Zulu

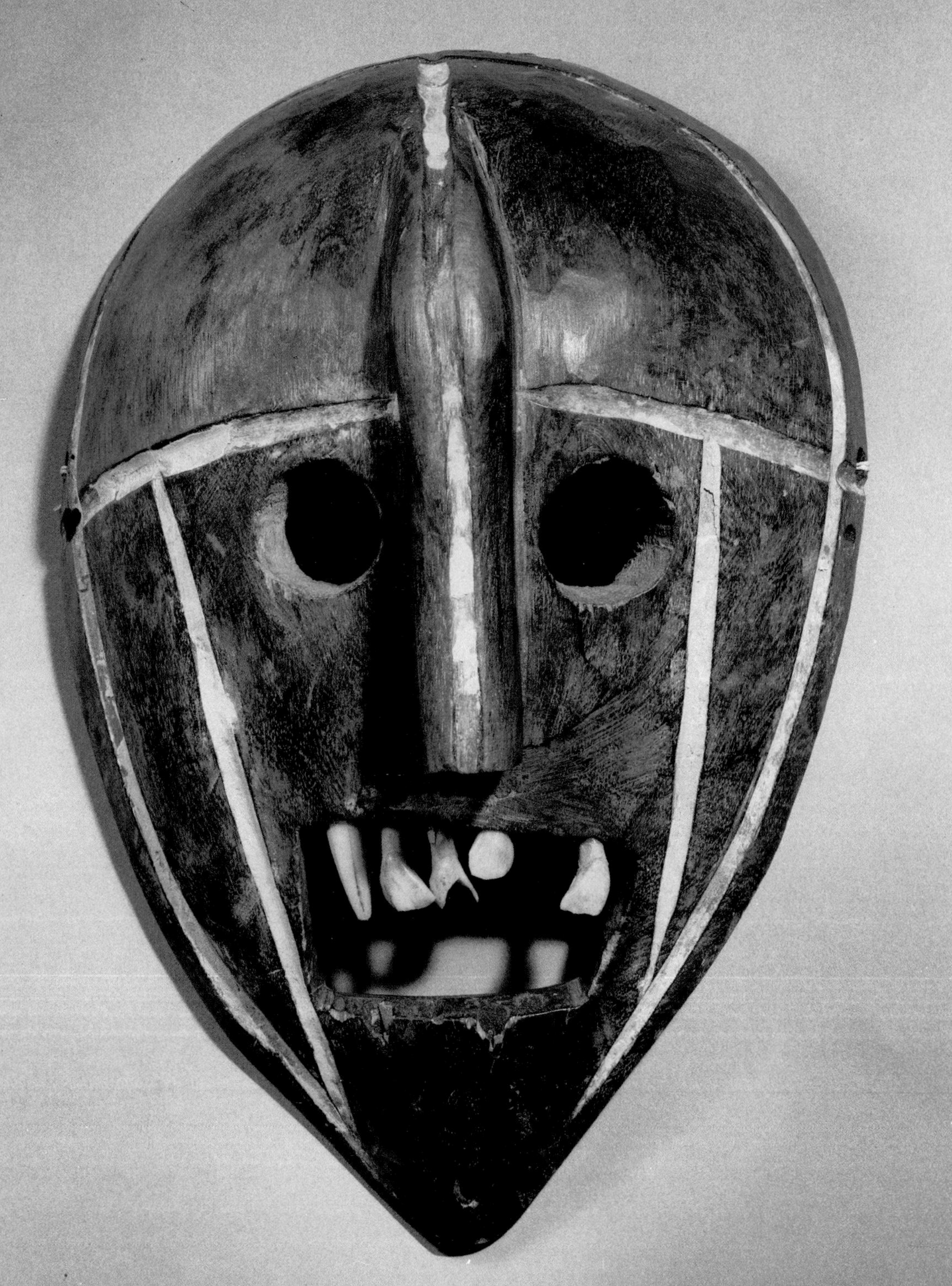

Eastern and Southern Africa

The fine arts seem to occupy a strikingly modest place in the traditional cultures of eastern and southern Africa. In some areas migrations of pastoral peoples may have made it difficult to preserve figurative traditions. In other instances belief in a high god may have displaced the ancestral cult, which had always stimulated the arts. Presumably, the literal iconoclasm of Islamic orthodoxy impaired art life in large parts of eastern Africa, either directly or indirectly. But the "artistic poverty" of eastern and southern Africa frequently mentioned in research studies was not always characteristic of that area. Besides thousands of rock paintings and engravings, scattered traces of ancient clay sculpture give evidence of former epochs of figurative art. The historical causes of the eclipse of art were not the same everywhere.

In the nineteenth century and the first part of the twentieth, most figurative sculpture was restricted to fertility and toy dolls and to the decoration of carved staffs, stools, musical instruments, and so on. Only a few peoples produced, for instance, anthropomorphic grave posts (the Mijikenda of the east coast) or masks (the Makonde in southern Tanzania and northern Mozambique). Nonetheless, though the stock of figurative art is on the whole modest, there can be no talk of a comprehensive poverty in art, for a richly developed applied art exists everywhere: there are outstanding works of pottery, plaiting, smithwork, and bead embroidery. Even wood carving, so poor in the figurative area, flourished in that of beautifully formed combs, spoons, pipes, and other utensils, often ornamented.

Also significant are the traditions of body adornment. These include ornaments to be worn as well as shaped coiffures, body painting, and scarification. Craftsmen of the region have also skillfully adopted alien models. Figural wood carving, for instance, has developed rapidly among the Kamba of Kenya; in recent times and in the past, southern African leather dolls were similarly borrowed and produced successfully.

Lit.: L. Holy 1967, pp. 16-40; G. W. Hartwig 1969, pp. 25-51; A. v. Gagern, H. J. Koloss & W. Lohse 1974, pp. 38-42, 45, 46.

425 Mask, wood, human teeth.
Tanzania, Haya (Ziba).

This dark pokerwork mask is divided into panels by white lines. The nose of the oval face continues well into the forehead. Both jaws originally contained human and animal teeth, but only the upper jaw has retained them. No doubt the holes at the edge of the mouth were intended to hold long tufts of animal hair, though they were never inserted. The mask, in fact, seems never to have been used. Rehse is the only scholar to have observed such masks in use. Early in this century he was present when king Karagwe's court jester (*nshegu*) performed antics in such a mask. It seems questionable, though, whether these masks were originally intended to be worn by court jesters. Several Haya masks of this kind are in European collections.

Height 26 cm. 25-18-8
Acquired from F. W. Goring 1925

Lit.: E. Cesard 1936, pp. 493, 94; L. Holy 1967, p. 17 & Fig. 18-20, H. Rehse 1910, pp. 64, 65

426 Lidded vessel plaited banana leaf and grass.
Tanzania, Haya, Bukoba.

This form suggests foreign influence, and the model may well have been a European perfume flagon with stopper. However, the materials—extremely narrow dark brown strips of the sheath of the banana leaf

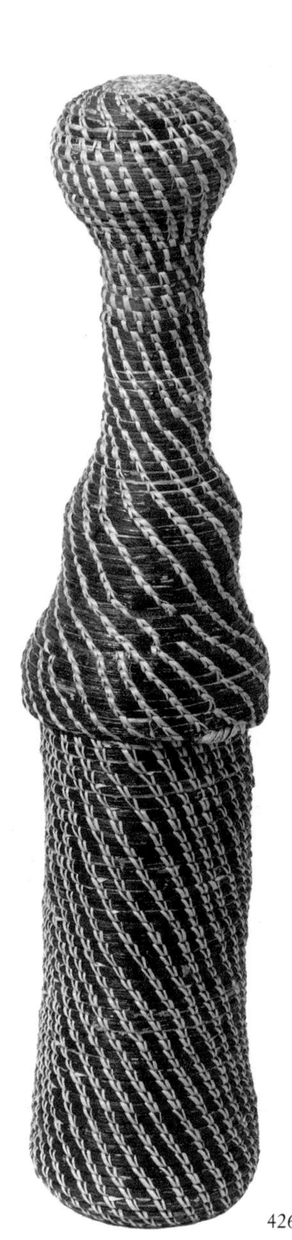
426

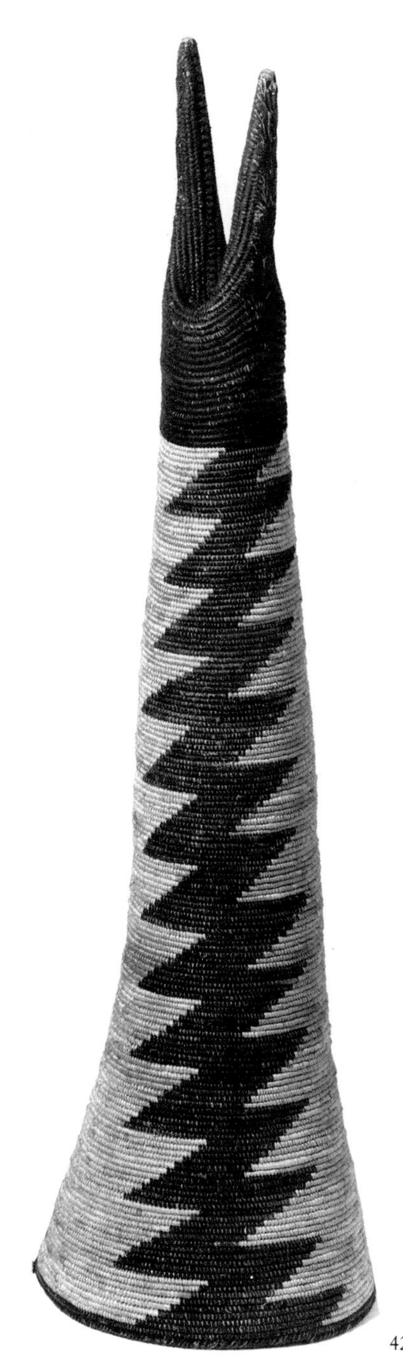
427

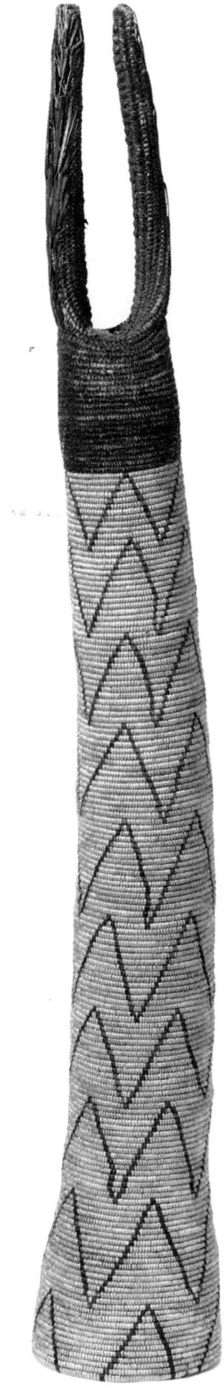
428

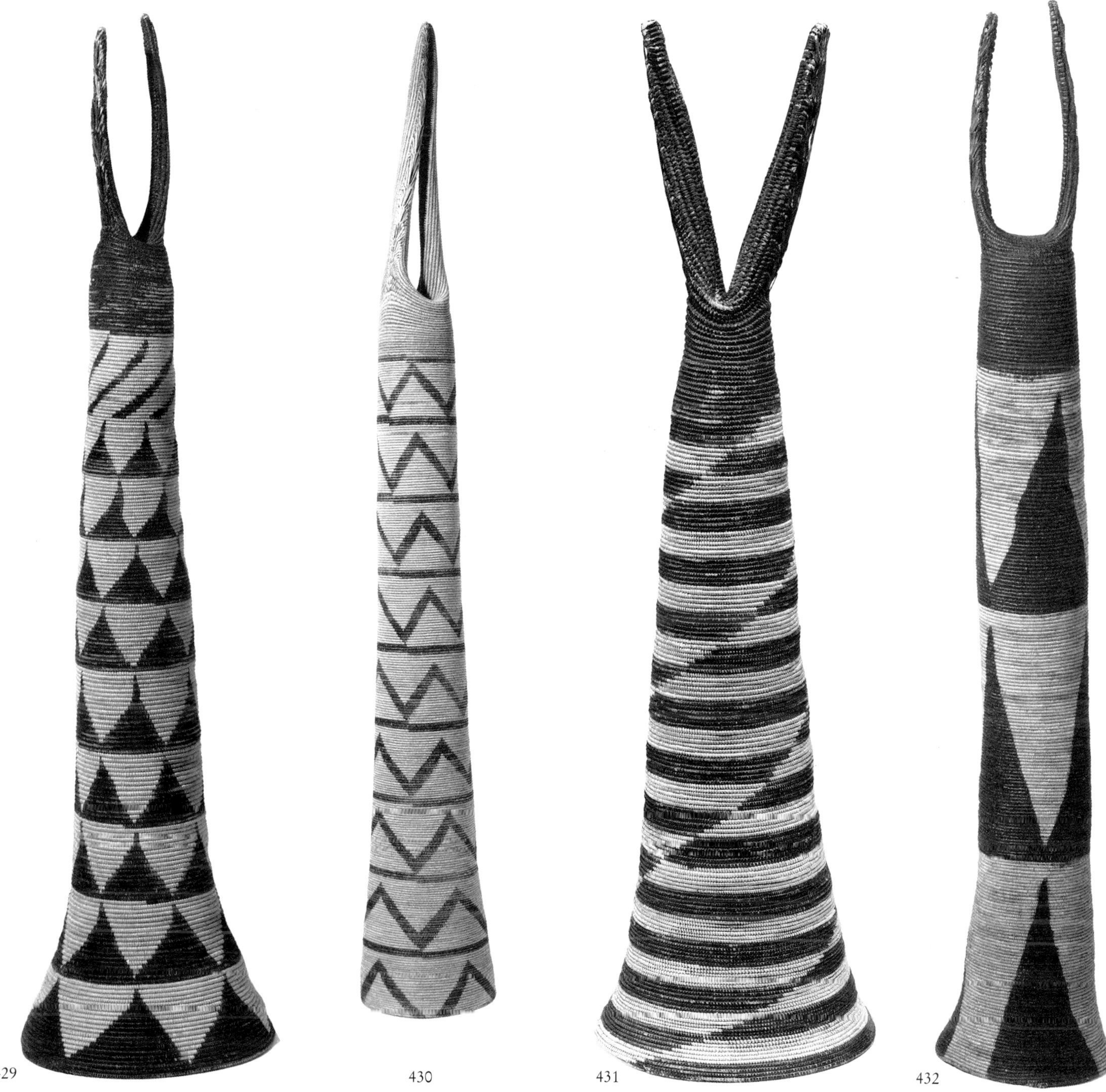

429

430

431

432

woven with split grass blades in natural hues—and the coiling technique are indigenous.

Height 25 cm. 08.562
Acquired from M. Schleifer 1908 (Collection H. v. Gotsch)

427-432 Lids for gourd vessels, plaited banana leaf, and grass.
Tanzania, Ruanda, and Uganda, Haya from Bukoba.

These plaited funnel-shape forms were placed over the necks of gourds to protect the banana wine from insects. The long-neck wine gourds are specially cultivated for men, who drink from them with a straw.

Banana wine plays an important role in social life. At all meetings strict conventions govern the offering and drinking of the wine, and significance is therefore attached to particularly decorative lids. They are coiled of split grass in natural hues and plaited with dark fibers of the banana-leaf sheath. Each pattern has its own name, and each black element and the light shape it produces in the grass section are classified as a unit. The peaks at the top, also characteristic of calabash lids of the interlacustrine region, presumably represent horns. These symbolized the livestock that was esteemed above all else by the cattle breeders of this region.

Length 47-57 cm.
08.571/3/5, 09.515, 13-57-113, 17-7-10
Acquired from M. Schleifer (Collection H. v. Gotsch)

Lit.: R. Kandt 1904, pp. 339, 353, 54, 356, 57; P. Kollmann 1898, p. 64; H. Rehse, pp. 5556.

Giryama Grave and Commemorative Posts (433, 434)

Only influential old people, healers or members of a cult society—usually male-receive a carved grave or commemorative post after their death. These may be set up months, years, or even decades later, when a restless spirit appears to relatives in a dream. After the family consults the diviner, the wood carver is commissioned to make a post and given exact instructions as to details. The post is then set up either at the head of the grave or in the former dwelling of the deceased, within or without the sacred area (*kaya*). Food and libations are then brought to this simple monument.

The custom of erecting grave or commemorative posts is known among all the Nyika or Mijikenda groups and the Giryama of the coastal region. Some posts are pillarlike objects with heads sculptured in the round and are often compared with the grave poles of the Konso of southern Ethiopia. Planklike examples with rich chip-carved ornaments resemble carved objects made by the Swahili, coastal peoples whose culture is strongly influenced by Islam (their doorposts with geometric and floral decor are an example).

The grave-post tradition is as likely to have originated in the first homeland of the Mijikenda, who migrated from the hinterland of Somalia southward in the seventeenth century, as in their present home near the coast. Although it has never been substantiated that such posts were customary among the Mijikenda before the end of the nineteenth century, it is believed that in other parts of the east coast pillar-form grave monuments of stone, wood, or clay were probably erected even earlier. This older period of grave art seems ultimately to have occurred as a result of Arabic-Persian influences, however.

Lit.: J. Adamson 1975, pp. 287-97; J. L. Brown 1980, pp. 36-39; W. G. Hartwig 1961, pp. 10-15; J. Kanderl 1984, Illus. L; H. Straube, personal communication.

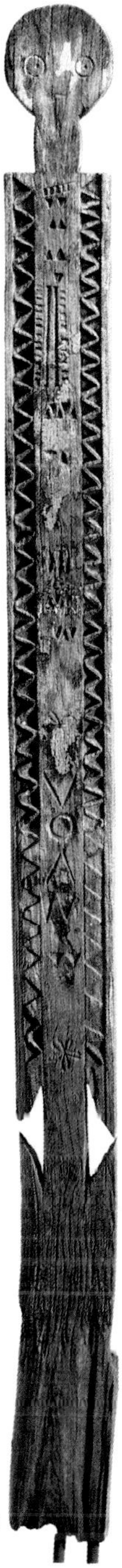

433

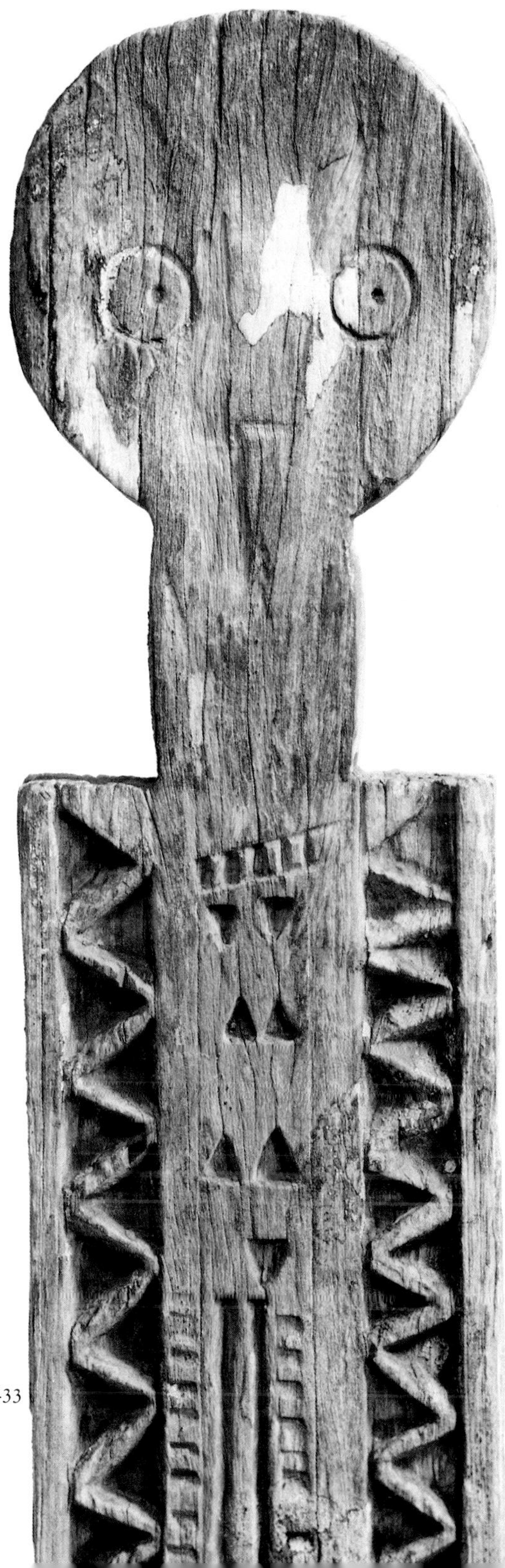

433

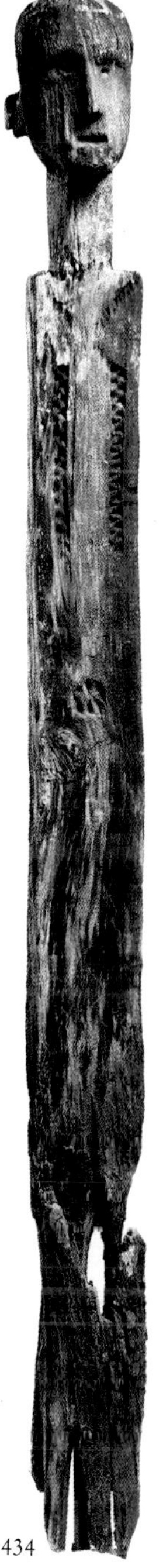

434

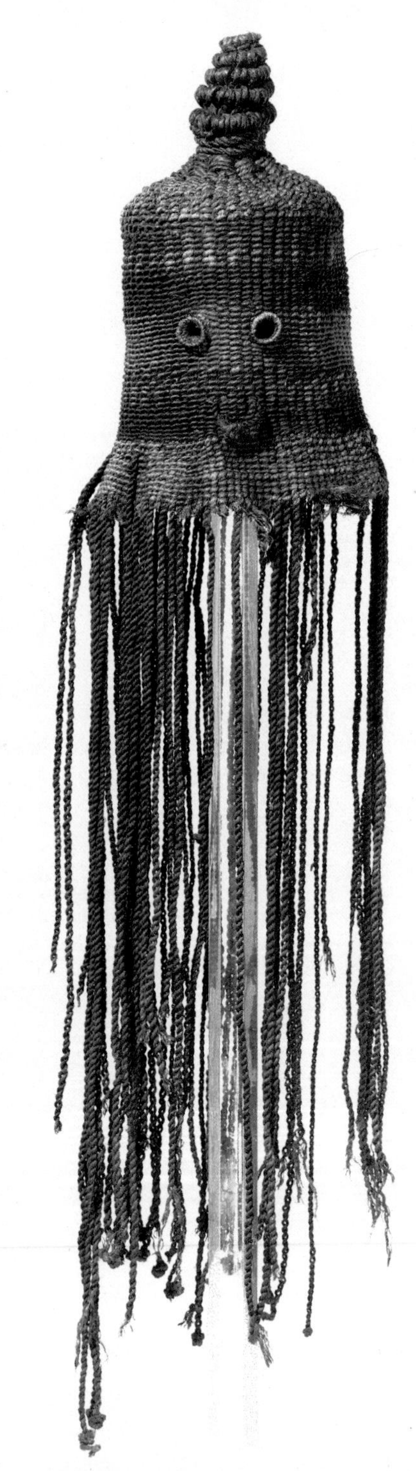

435

433 Grave and commemorative post (*kigango*), wood, paint.
Kenya, Giryama.

This planklike post with chip-carved front edges is a decidedly abstracted human representation in the so-called pole style. The deep regular zigzag decoration of the edge contrasts sharply with the faintly worked irregular decor of the central panel. This consists of triangles, squares, rosettes, and a circle, which supposedly indicate parts of the human body (the chest, navel, and genitals). Deep triangular notches are cut out of the lower end.

Length 199 cm. 82-301 780
Acquired from W. Ketterer 1982 (Collection K. F. Schadler)

434 Grave and commemorative post, wood.
Kenya, Giryama.

This man is much more naturalistically represented than the figure in No. 433. Although the body is also planklike, with shoulders at right angles to the plank, the neck is rounded. The fully sculptured head is without coiffure. Facial features are gentle, with concave cheeks and a strikingly long narrow nose. Uniform chip-carved zigzag lines and rosettes sparingly adorn the front of the post.

Length 168 cm. 81-301-522
Acquired from W. Ketterer 1981

435 Helmet mask, plant fiber.
Kenya, Tiriki.

This mask is plaited with alternate light and dark strands that perhaps had a symbolic significance. The face is reduced to tubular eyes and a linear mouth.

The helmet mask is part of the initiation costume in which youths appeared in public when they temporarily left the bush camp. It is a disguise, primarily a kind of protection for the initiate during the transition from childhood to manhood; at this time he finds himself in an extraordinary psychic state that is generally considered sacred in Africa. We do not know whether dances were performed in the mask costume.

The mask with a fiber costume is made by the initiate's mentor and is stored for the next group after the festival. The few published Tiriki masks were apparently adorned during use with a kind of palm-leaf crest on the peak.

Length 110 cm. 72-4-2
Acquired from L. Bretschneider 1972

Lit.: J. Adamson 1975, pp. 130, 31; W. Bohning & J. Kalter 1972, Illus. 32, p.58.

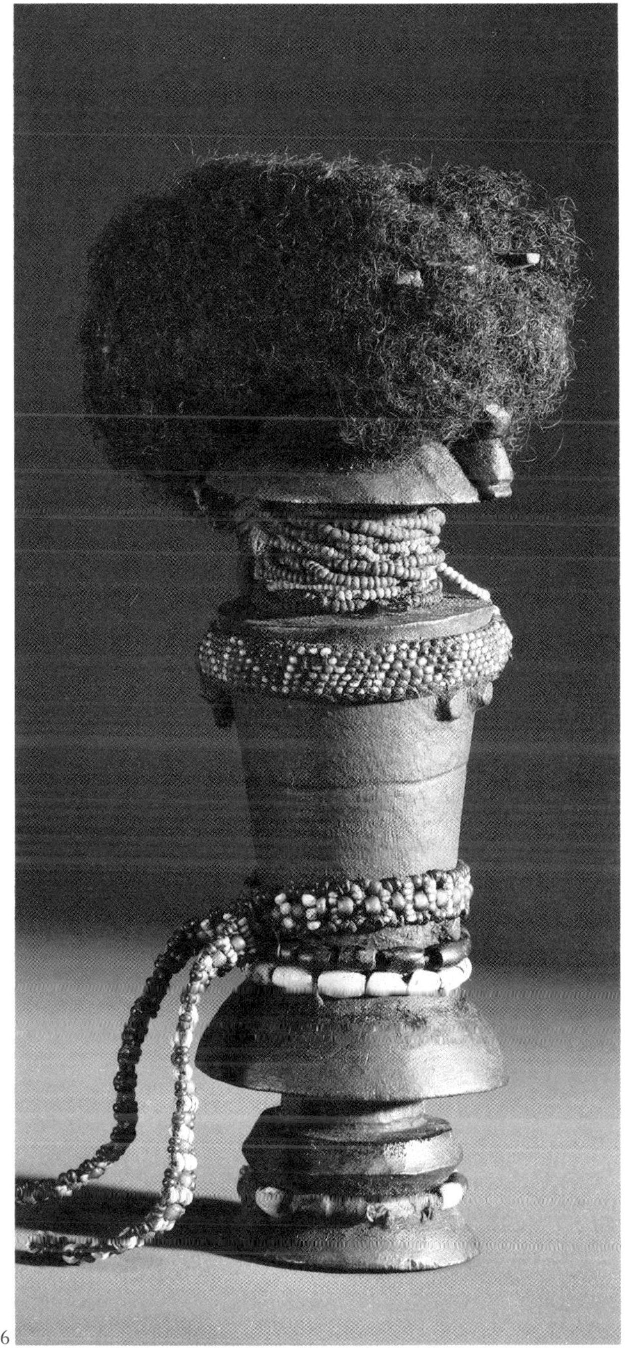
436

436 Fertility doll (*mwananyanhiti*), wood, human hair.
Tanzania, Zaramo.

This cunningly abstracted type of small human figure without arms or legs is found mainly among the Swahili and those eastern African groups strongly influenced by the coastal culture—the Zaramo, Doe, Kami, and Kerewe. This piece is very richly outfitted, and its various strings of glass beads were apparently selected and arranged according to definite precepts. Two long arrowlike hairpins are stuck into the human hair, which largely hides the face, leaving only the nose and mouth showing. A minute notch marks the mouth, and the eyes are suggested through the downwardly drawn hair. Breasts and navel are indicated by small disks on the cylindrical torso.

Such small figures, some carved in wood, others constructed of calabashes (see Nos. 445 and 446), were the constant companions of girls separated from their families during initiation. The girls cared lovingly for these dolls, even feeding them. After the initiation ceremonies were concluded, the girls, now considered nubile, continued to carry the dolls, usually hung on a cord around their necks. Childless married women also carried such dolls. Some scholars' view that the doll magically insures the capacity

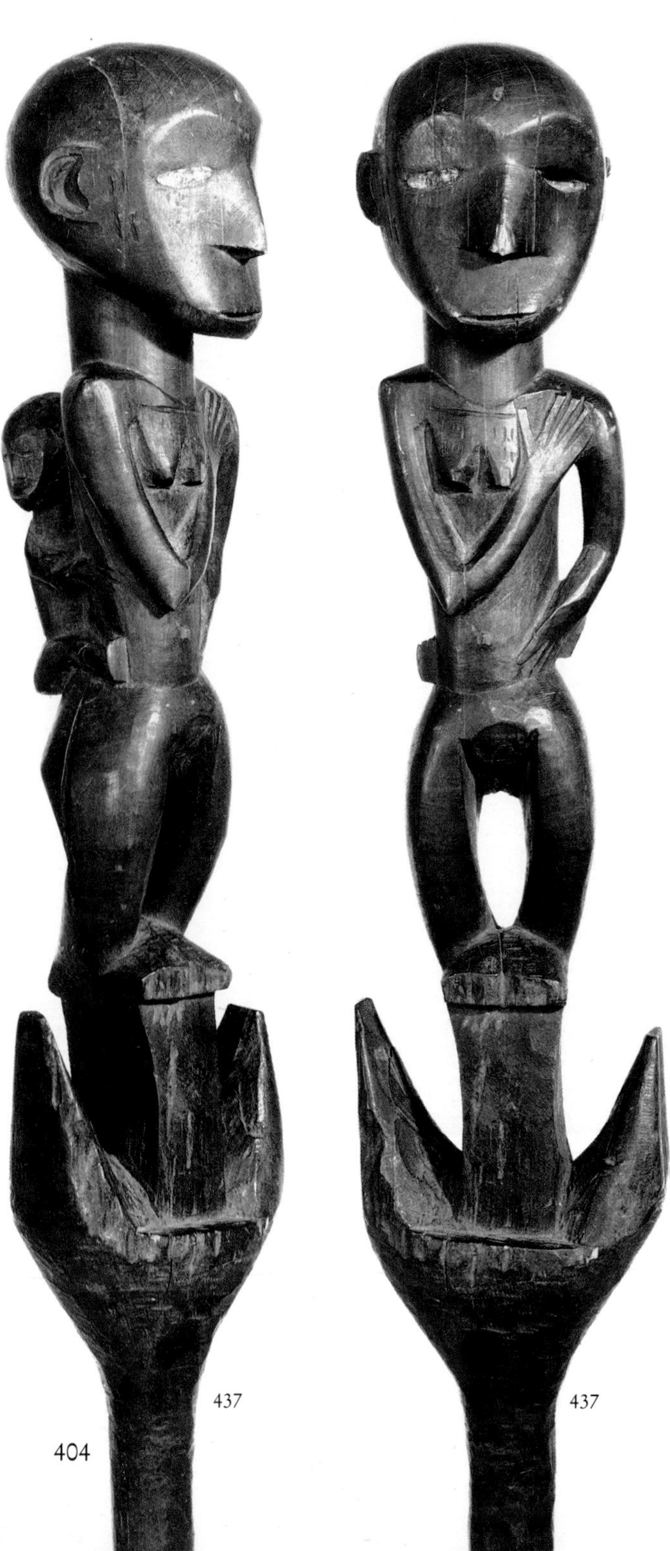

to bear children is contended by other scholars. Actually, such figures were also often stuck onto the ends of musical instruments or walking sticks (our piece has a small hole in the bottom). Despite such secular uses, the dolls have, or at least in the past had, a magical significance.

Height 19 cm. I.1360
Collector unknown

Lit.: G. W. Hartwig 1969, p. 37; J. R. Harding 1961, p. 72; H. Kraus 1907, pp. 358, 59; F. Stuhlmann 1910, p. 32; J. A. R. Wembach-Rashid 1970, pp. 358, 59.

437 Staff with carved human figure, wood, mussel-shell eyes.
Tanzania, Zaramo.

The asymmetrical position of the arms and the inlaid eyes of this three-dimensional figure recall those of the figure with bowl zither (No. 438), though the execution is less skillful. Since the artist obviously wanted to depict both the characteristic gesture and the scarified breasts, he placed the latter in an unnatural position. According to the inventory note, probably from the collector himself, this piece is a magical staff with mother and child. But the small figure carried piggyback does not appear to be that of a nursling. It is more probable that the composition refers to the part of initiation when boys and girls are carried piggyback by their tutors to prevent their walking "a dangerous path" on their own. If this is the correct interpretation, the conductor of the initiation ceremonies used the staff in a ritual.

Length 130 cm. 17-14-98
Acquired from H. Kraus 1917

Lit.: M. Kecskesi 1982, pp. 52-55.

438 Soundboard of a bowl zither with carved handle (strings and resonance box are missing), wood, glass beads.
Tanzania, Makonde.

This type of instrument usually has six to ten strings, which are actually a single cord wound back and forth on the board. A calabash beneath the dished soundboard serves as a resonance box. The three-quarter human figure on the handle is of unusually fine quality in comparison with most eastern African figurative carvings. The remarkable movement created by the asymmetrically positioned arms is rare. The tiny white beads with boreholes indicate both eyes and pupils. The small torso displays no sexual characteristics but is richly adorned with scarifications. According to inventory entries, this piece was obtained from the Makonde, though its style seems to be that of the Kewere.

Length 64 cm. 17-7-8
Acquired from E. Hintz 1917

Lit.: B. Ankermann 1901, p. 27; G. W. Hartwig 1969, p. 43.

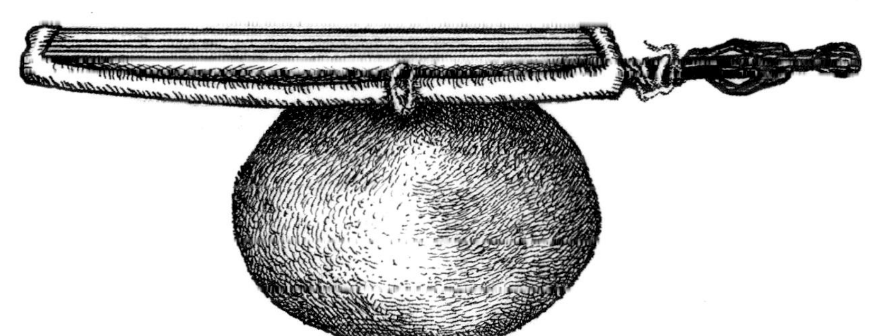

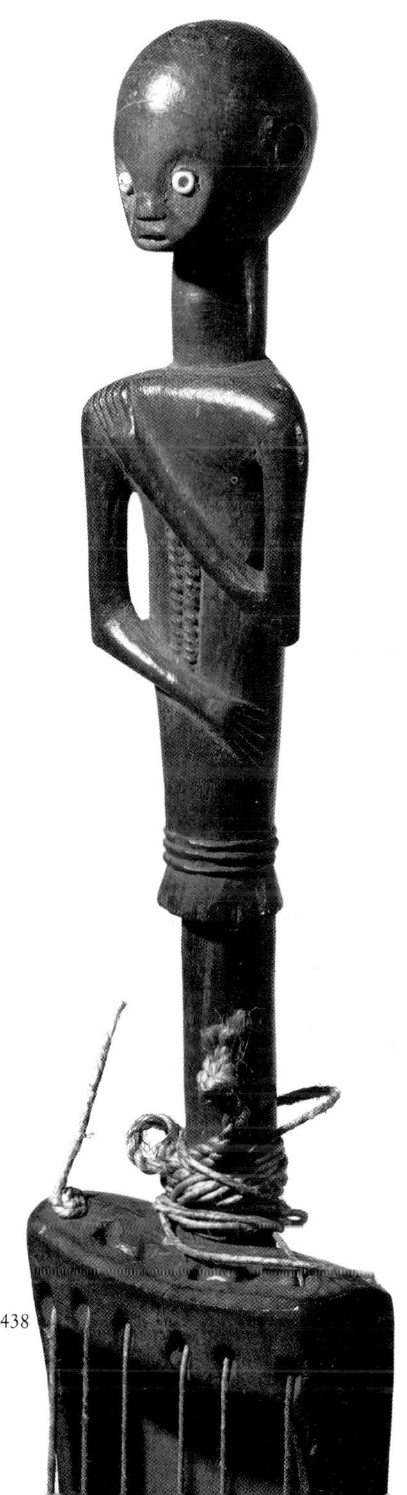

438

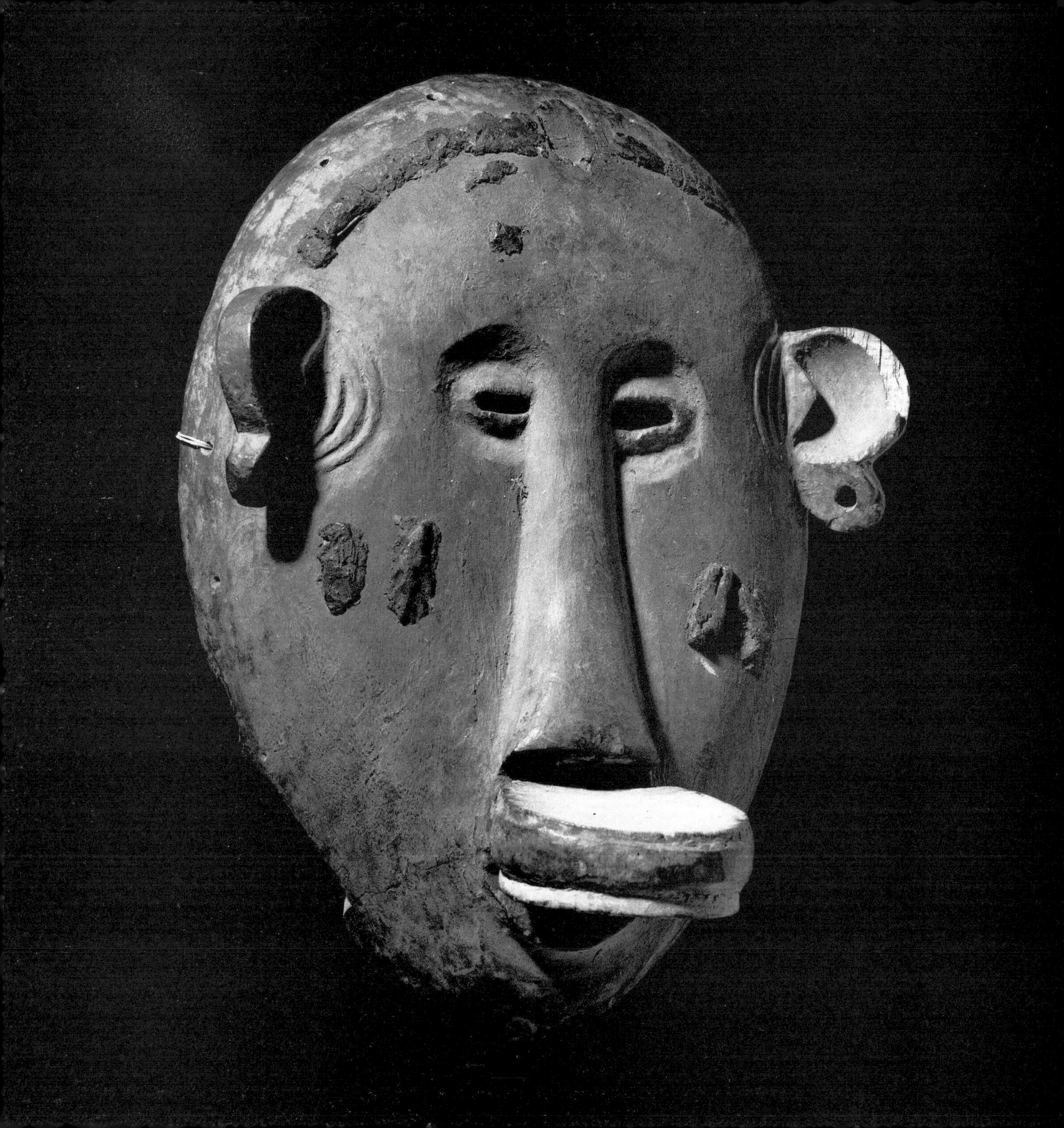

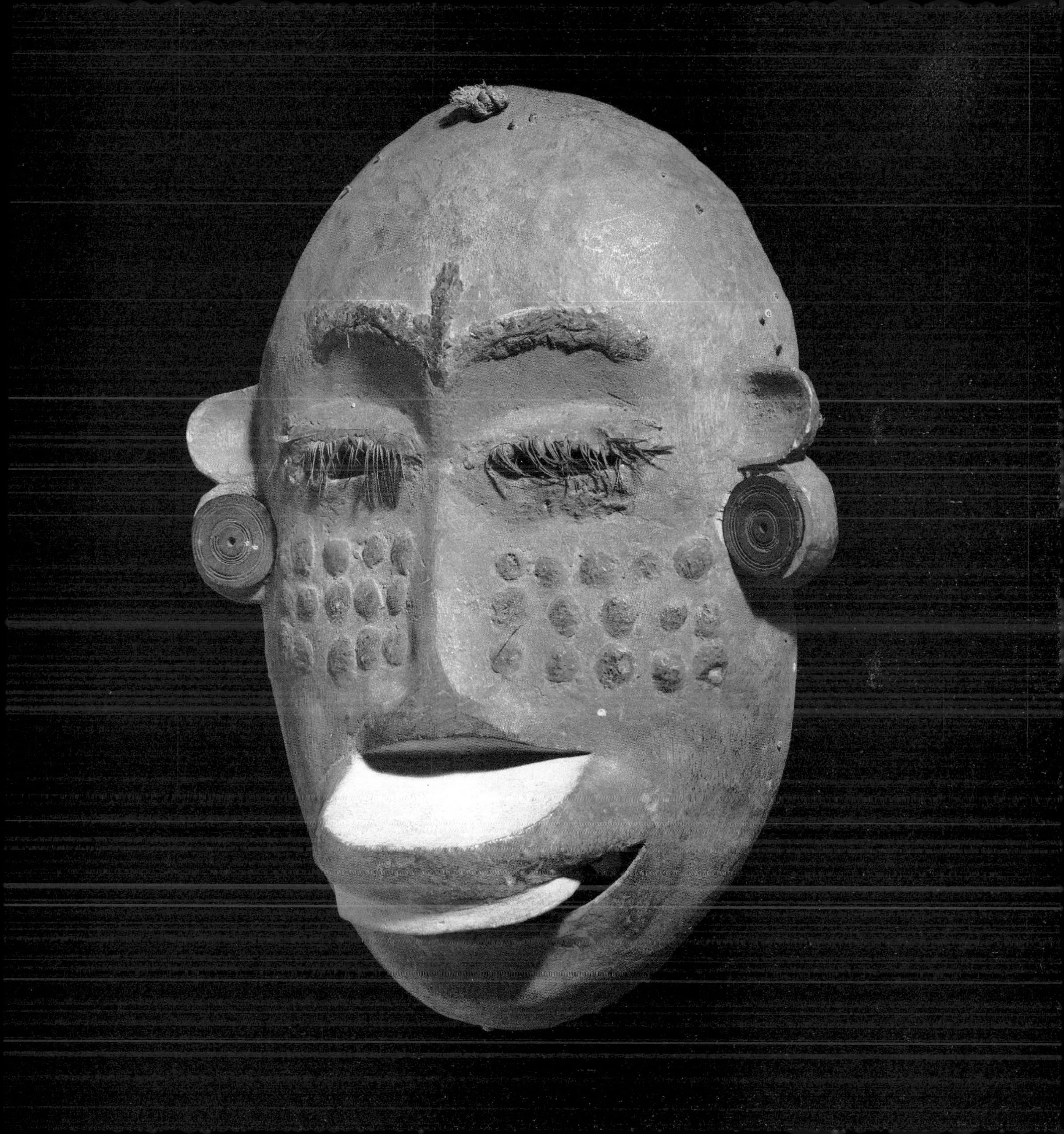

Makonde Masks (439-441)

Little is known of mask usage among the Makonde of Tanzania. The only certainty is that masks were used at the joint closing ceremonies of the boys' and girls' initiations. The masks—including animals as well as humans—represent spirits (*midimu*). Like Makonde women, the female masks shown are adorned with a large flat disk in the upper lip and with scarification (indicated by applied lumps of wax). No. 441 is an atypical male mask.

Lit.: L. Harris 1944, pp. 22, 38; L. Holy 1967, p. 30; W. Lang 1960, p. 33, 34; J. A. R. Wembach-Rashid 1971, pp. 38, 42-44; K. Weule 1908, pp. 112ff.

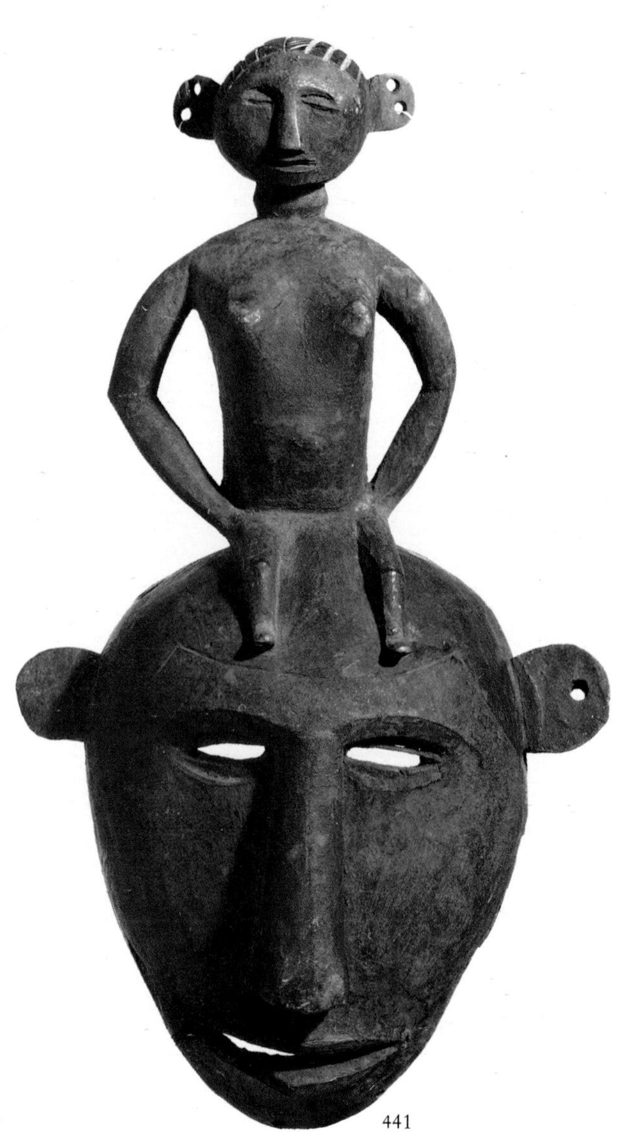

441

439,440 Two masks, wood, beeswax, animal hair, gourd pips.
Tanzania, Makonde.

Both these masks are of very light wood stained red. They represent a common type of Makonde mask whose characteristics are a flat oval face with small stylized ears, highly placed and protruding; small eyes, with and without eyelashes, set close to the bridge of the narrow but strong nose; and large white lip disk, the sign of a mature woman. Beeswax, an important commercial product in colonial times, is used to simulate tattoos. No. 439 displays ear ornaments typical of coastal people and has gourd pips as teeth.

Height 20.5 cm., 21 cm. 17-18-1,19-13-11
Acquired from A. Schroder 1917, W. Schimmer 1919

441 Mask with female figure, wood, animal hair.
Tanzania, Makonde.

This mask with typically male features has narrow close-set eyes, a prominent nose, and a smooth coiffure shaved into corners on the forehead. The holes at the ends of the protruding mouth hold beard hair.

The composition is not typical, however, for a small sculptured female figure sits on the crown of the mask. Her face corresponds to that of the mask though it is somewhat finer and rounder. The girl or young woman represented has undergone initiation, as may be seen by her pierced nose and ears. Presumably, the composition shows the initiates' ritual piggyback or shoulder ride during initiation, when magical powers produce the exceptional physical condition of puberty and the young people are forbidden to come in contact with the earth (see also No. 423). Both masks and figure are stained dark gray.

Height 32 cm. 28-1-128
Acquired from M. Kusters 1928

Lit.: W. Gillon 1979, Illus. 206; M. Kecskesi 1982, pp. 52-55.

Makonde Medicine or Snuff Containers (442, 443)

Small medicine or snuff containers are a specialty of the southern Makonde, also called Mawia, and are among the most significant examples of east African miniature art. The receptacle itself is made of an unadorned piece of bamboo or wood tube. The lid, however, is always ornamented with stylized human or animal heads, and sometimes with a human torso.

Lit.: K. Weule 1908, p. 50.

442 Wooden medicine or snuff container (*mtete*), with animal head.
Tanzania, Makonde.

The lid of this container is adorned with the head and neck of a *litotwe,* a rabbitlike animal with a long snout. Among animal representations, those of the *litotwe* are the most carefully executed. Examples are usually in an idealized naturalistic style; here, however, the linear head is abstract.

Length 9 cm. 19-13-23
Acquired from W. Schimmer 1919 (Collection K. Schimmer)

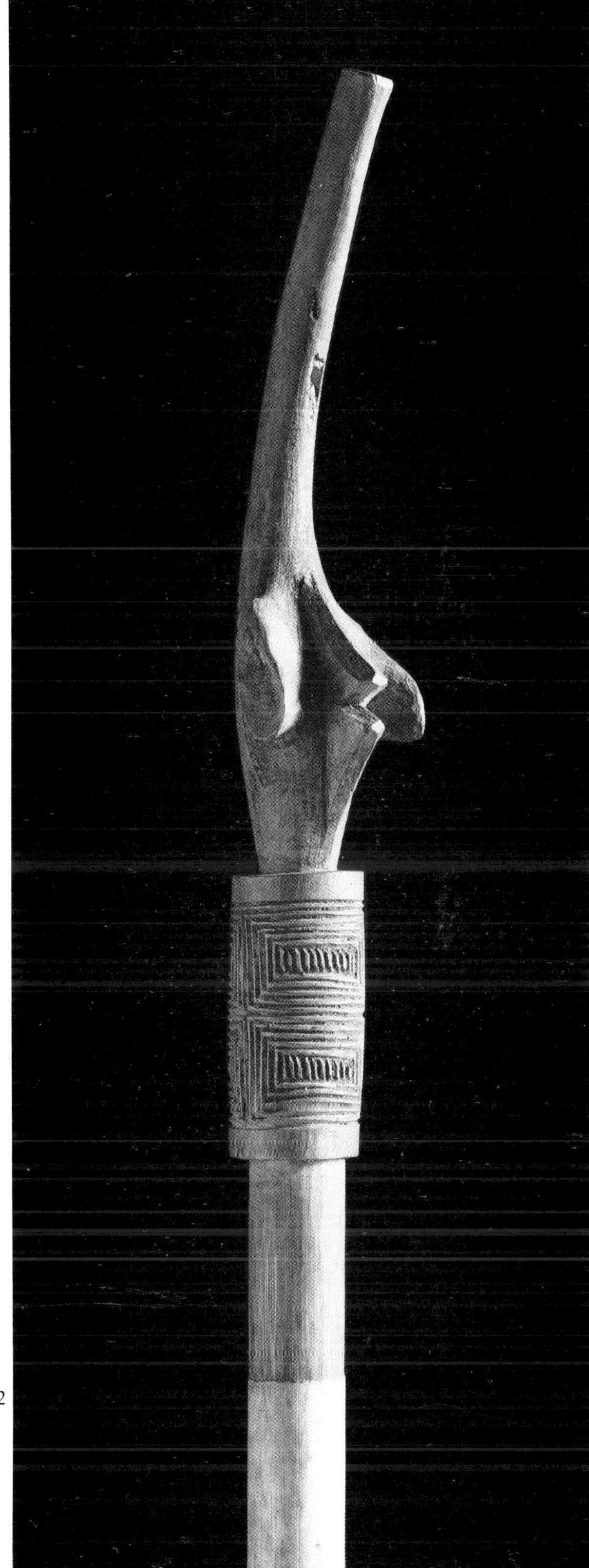
442

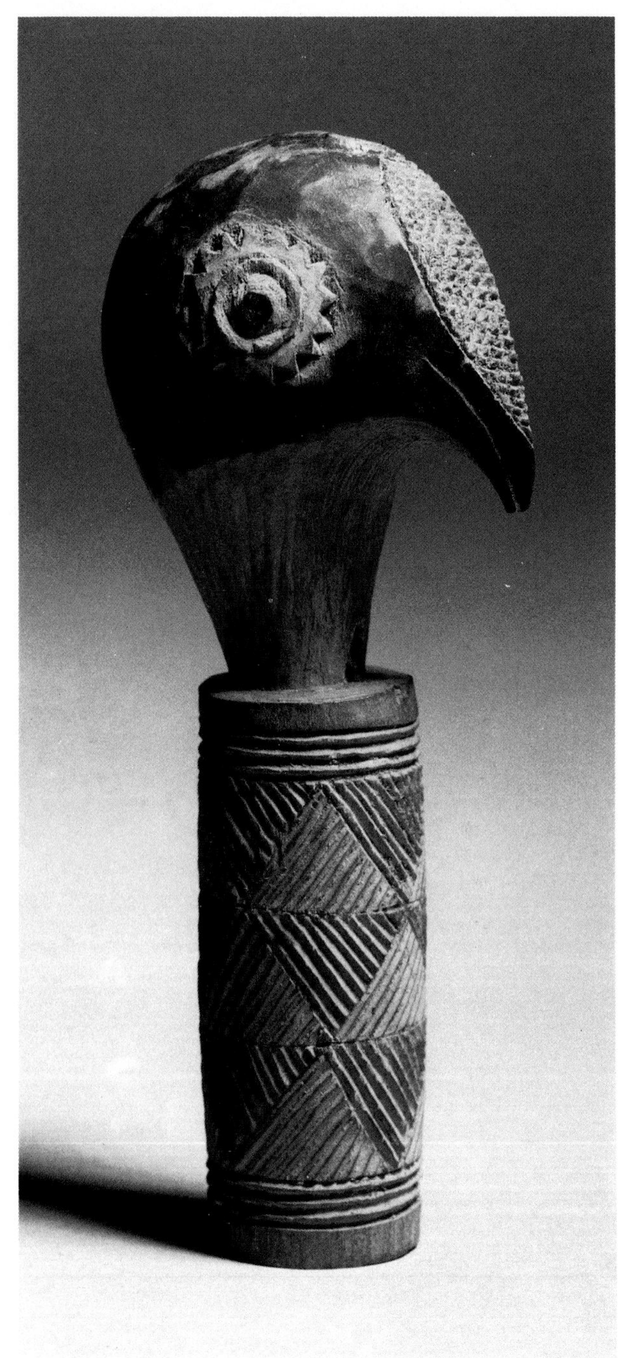
443

443 Lid of a wooden medicine or snuff container (*mtete*).
Tanzania, Makonde.

Only the lid of this piece, carved with the head of a parrot, is extant. Neck and beak are decorated with a low-relief geometric design. The piece was singed with a hot poker to produce its color.

Length 22 cm. 19-13-21
Acquired from W. Schimmer 1919 (Collection K. Schimmer)

444 Dance staff with carved tip, wood.
Tanzania, Pangwa (?).

In general, this male figure in European jacket and trousers is in the pole style. Its dished face in a globular head, strongly accentuated forehead and nose, and conspicuous mouth represent what Fagg has called the "concave-cubistic" trend. According to the collector, such staffs were "carried by men at dances to mark the rhythm. Not used at funeral dances." This piece's provenance, recorded as Pangwa, is uncertain, for neither similar staffs nor figurative wood carvings are found in their central area in the Livingstone Mountains. The piece was probably acquired at the missionary station of Lituhi on the Manda Plain near the Ruhuhu River. Other groups as well as Pangwa dwell in this area.

Length 75.8 cm. 28-1-30
Acquired from M. Kusters 1928

Lit.: W. Fagg 1964, p. 121; M. Kusters 1928/29 (unpublished manuscript); H. Stirnimann 1976, pp. 292, 93, 303ff.

Fertility Dolls (445, 446)

This curious type of small sculpture occurs only among the Bantu peoples of southern Africa. Both ends of the figure are shaped alike for perfect symmetry. In most cases representations of face, sexual characteristics, and extremities are omitted. The rich bead ornament imitates the traditional polychrome beadwork of the southern Bantu. Beads preferred by various groups outfit the dolls, which are both toys and fertility symbols. From the earliest years small girls are cautioned to carry the dolls with them constantly (see also No. 436).

Lit.: W. Foy 1909b, pp. 231-33; P. Germann 1929, p. 139; S. Paul 1970, pp. 10-12; A. Radcliffe-Brown 1925, p. 99.

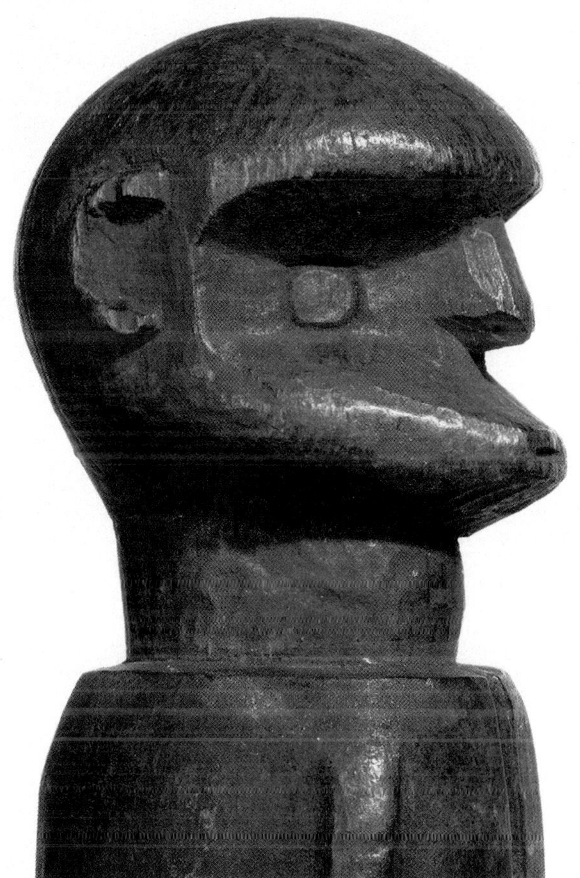

444

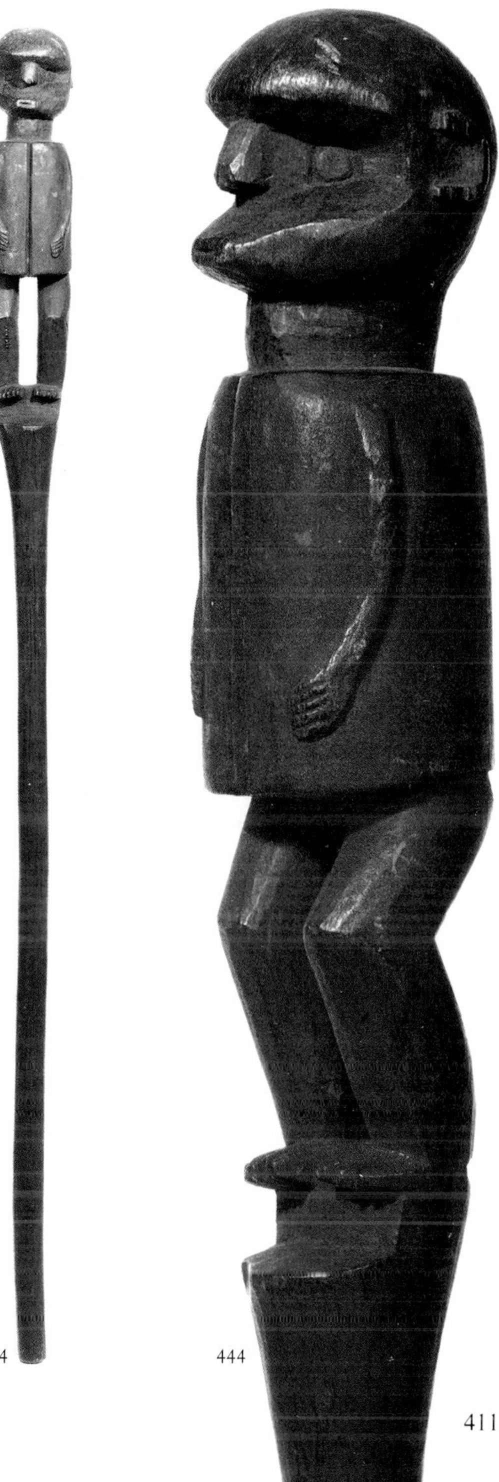

444

444

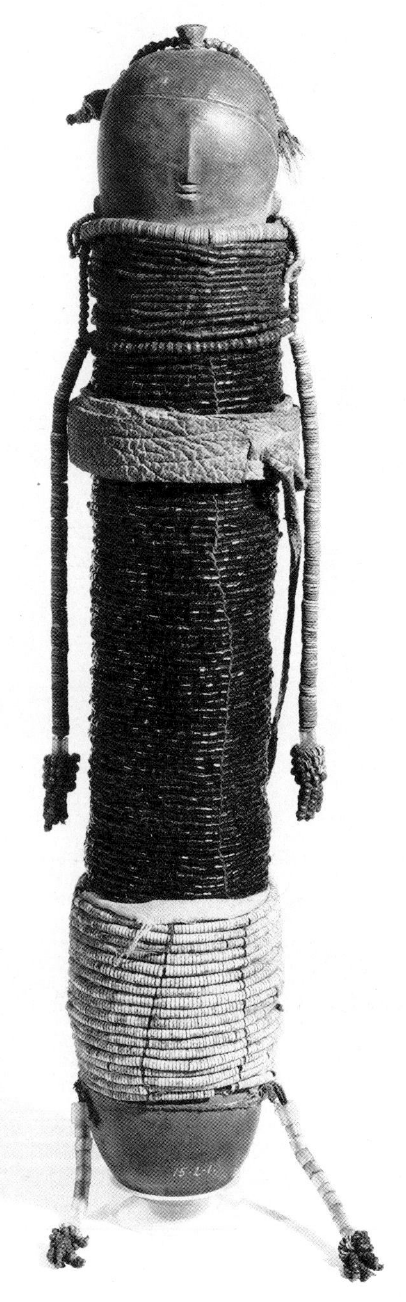

445

445 Fertility doll, wood, ostrich shell, glass and iron beads, plant-fiber strings.
Namibia, Ambo, Ondonga.

In contrast to most others, this doll has a head with sculptured nose, mouth, and coiffure. The extremities, usually missing, are also represented. Arm proportions are approximately correct, but the legs are shortened. Following the local custom the doll is wearing blue glass beads as well as strings of iron and ostrich-eggshell beads, the hip ornament of the women.

Height 43 cm. 15-2-1
Acquired from F. Schmetzger 1915

446 Fertility doll, wooden sticks, gourd skins, glass beads, brass, plant-fiber strings, leather strap.
Southern Africa, Mangwato.

The torso of this figure consists of a bundle of wooden sticks held together by gourds at top and bottom. The doll wears two shades of red glass beads corresponding to the hip ornament of the women. Allowance was made for arms, hands, and even fingers in this composition, but as is usually the case with fertility dolls, the legs were omitted. This doll was acquired by Emil Holub during his second journey throughout southern Africa, from 1883 to 1887.

Height 28 cm. 6139
Acquired from E. Holub 1883-87

Lit.: W. Foy 1909, pp. 232-34.

Southern African Leather Dolls (447-451)

While leather dolls similar to ours are in several European museums, those of the Munich collection are the earliest dated pieces. They somehow came into the possession of the French apothecary and traveler Lamare Piquot, who was in Mauritius and Madagascar between 1815 and 1830. In 1841 King Ludwig I of Bavaria ordered the purchase of Piquot's collection, which mainly comprised objects from Asia and Oceania. In the list of "royal household effects" there is this terse entry: "Human figures, Africa." A later official added the presumably correct, more precisely identified "Hottentot" or "Kaffer," formerly common designations of the southern African Bantu.

Imported European cloth dolls probably served as models for the leather dolls. The methods both of sewing pieces of leather together with minute stitches and of stuffing the dolls with cotton wool is similar to those that European doll makers employed. The function of these dolls is unknown. Probably they played no role in indigenous southern African customs but were manufactured as costumed dolls for sale to Europeans. Our pieces depict a Xhosa or Tswana couple and a Khoikhoi (Hottentot) family of three.

Lit.: L. Frobenius 1954, Table 107 a/b; P. Germann 1929, pp. 132-34; C. C. Muller 1980, p. 24; S. Paul 1970, p.14, Illus. 4/5; J. Vansina 1984, p. 61, and personal communication.

447,448 Pair of costumed dolls, leather, cotton wool, pins, glass beads.
Southern Africa, Xhosa, Tswana, or Khoikhoi.

These dolls' red leather costumes consist, for the male, of a cape with an apron suspended from the chest and, for the female, of a cape and a loincloth with leather strips. Their dress, including the man's headring and the woman's pointed cap, indicates that this is a Xhosa or Tswana couple. However, the characteristic leather cape *(kaross),* which reaches to the ground when worn (see No. 451), is too short here and was cut off in a straight line. The omission of the male leather and skin arm ornament is typical. These dolls have very little bead ornament: the man is wearing long earrings, a necklace, and a belt of

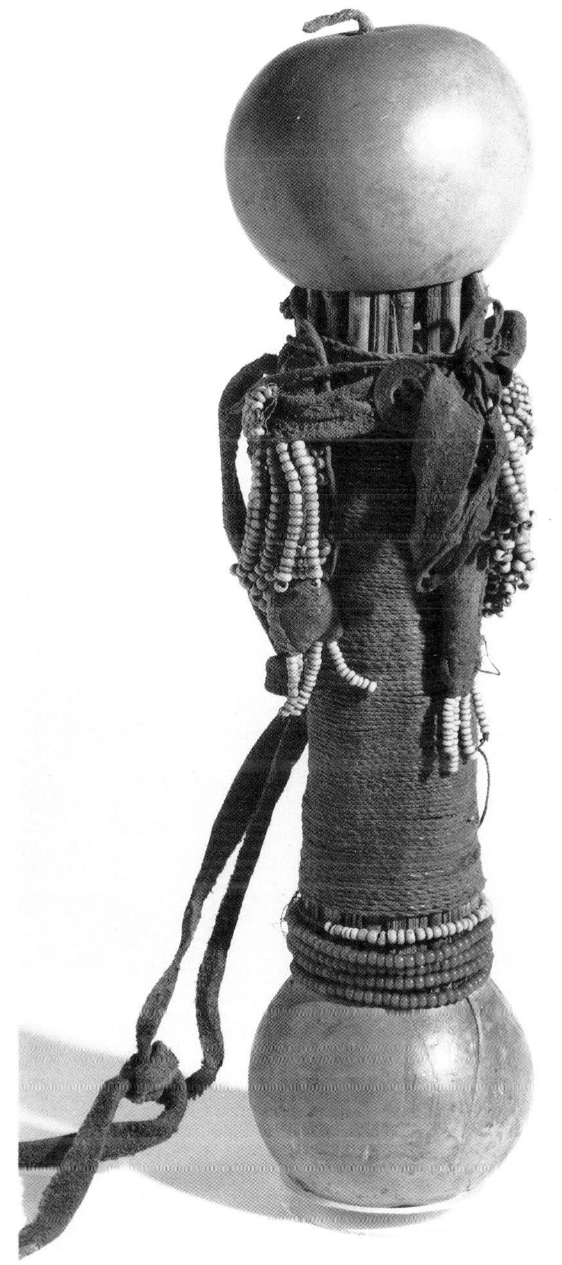

446

beads; the woman, apart from her hood and necklace, has no beaded accessories. The male figure's bent fingers indicate that he was originally holding weapons (a spear and shield or perhaps a club).

Height 36.5 cm., 35 cm. L.956, L.957
Acquired from Lamare Piquot 1815-30

449-451 Costumed dolls (man, woman, and child), leather, cotton wool, pins. Southern Africa, Khoikhoi.

Physical characteristics (shape of skull, peppercorn hair, steatopygia) and leather costume (shoulder cape, fringed apron, thong ornament on arms and legs) show beyond a doubt that these figures depict a Khoikhoi family. The length and manner of wearing the leather cape (*kaross*) are represented correctly only in the case of the child. Loincloth and cape are fixed to the dolls with European pins. Details of construction can be seen on the female figure, undressed for this purpose (No. 449a-c).

Height 32 cm., 30 cm., 23 cm. L.958-960
Acquired from Lamare Piquot 1815-30

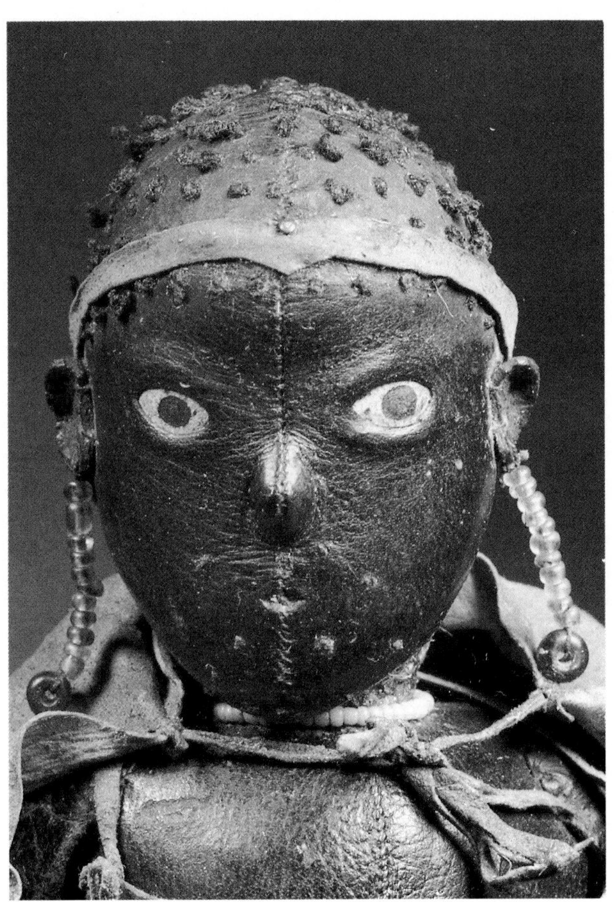

447

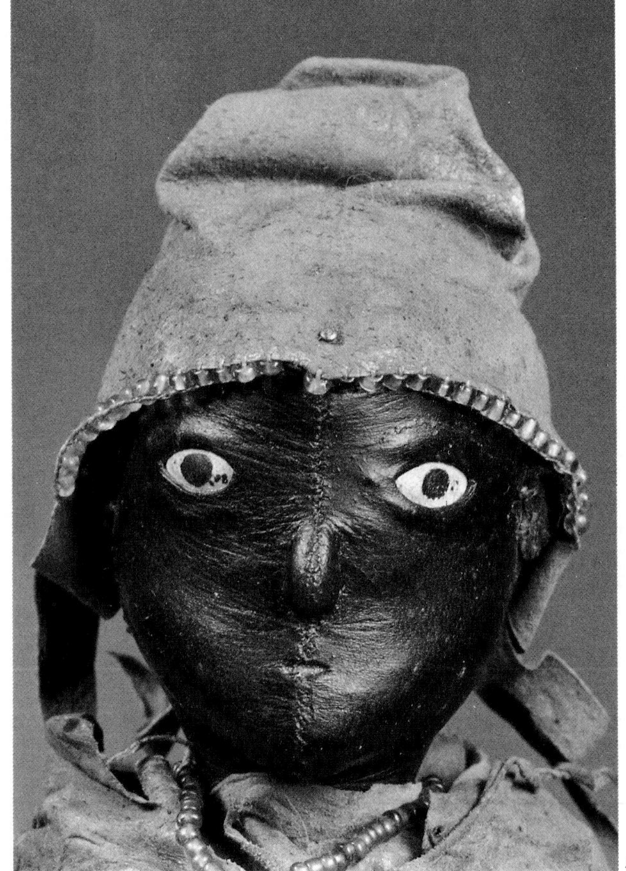

448

44

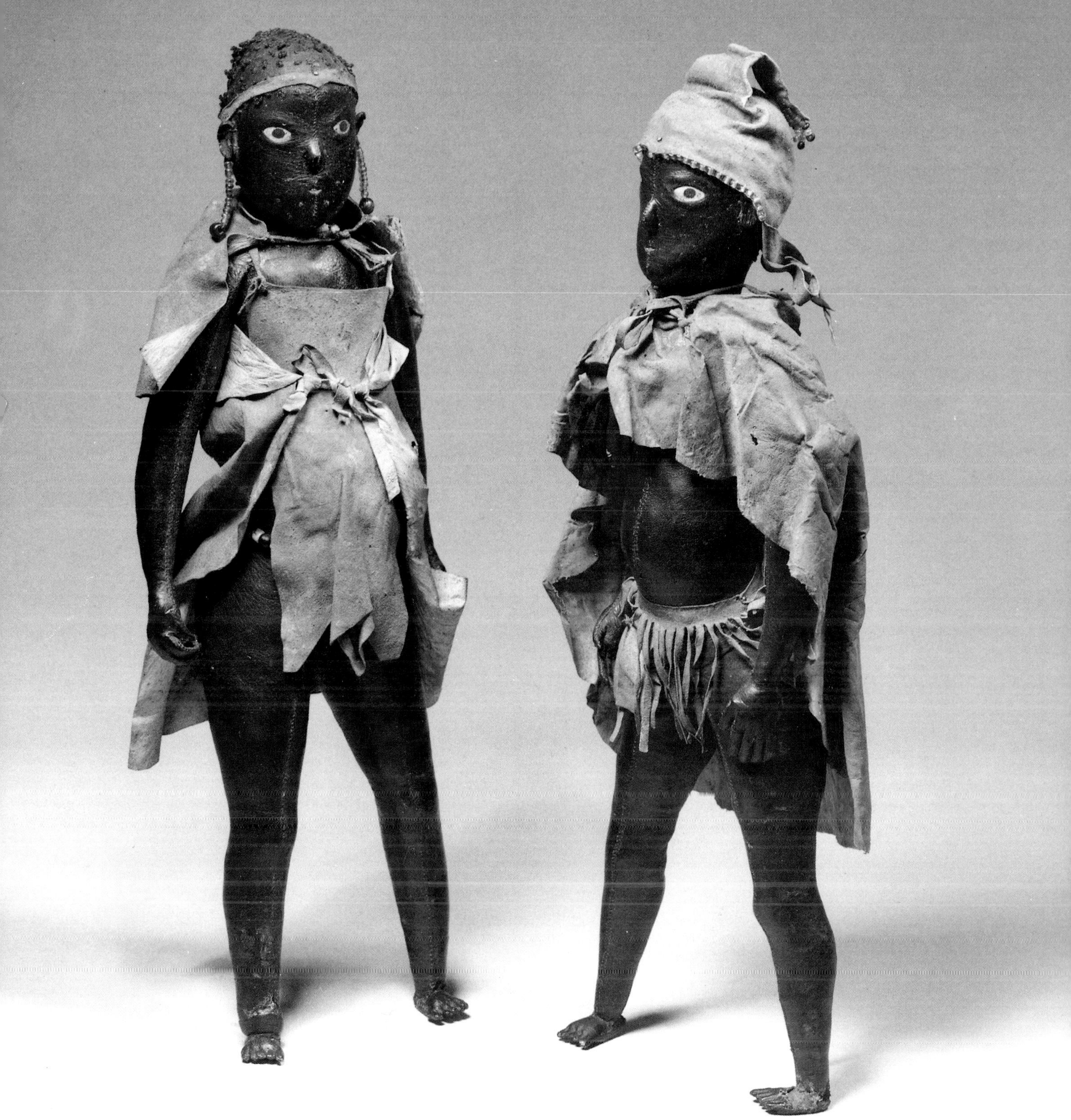

449

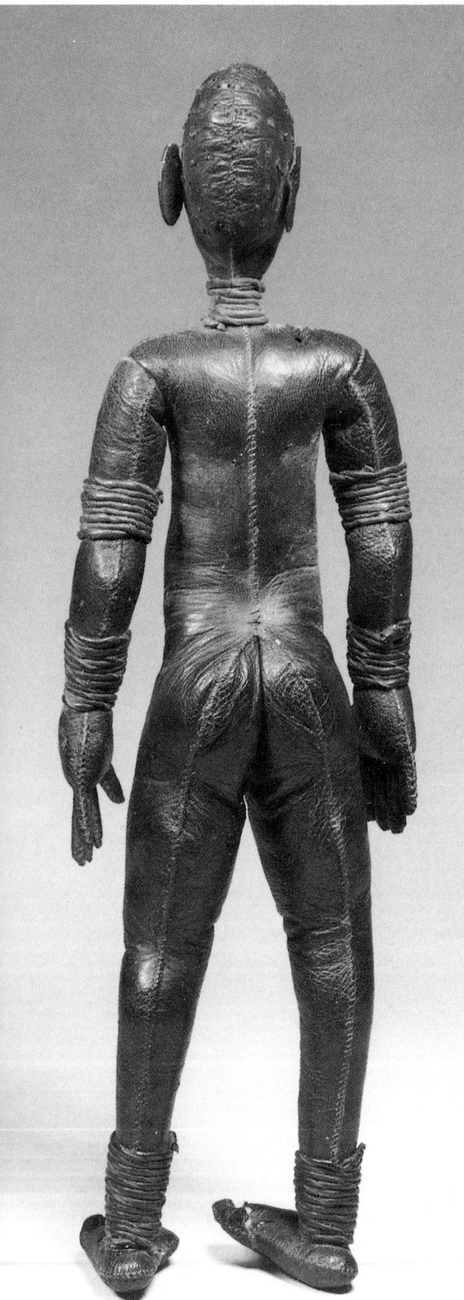

449

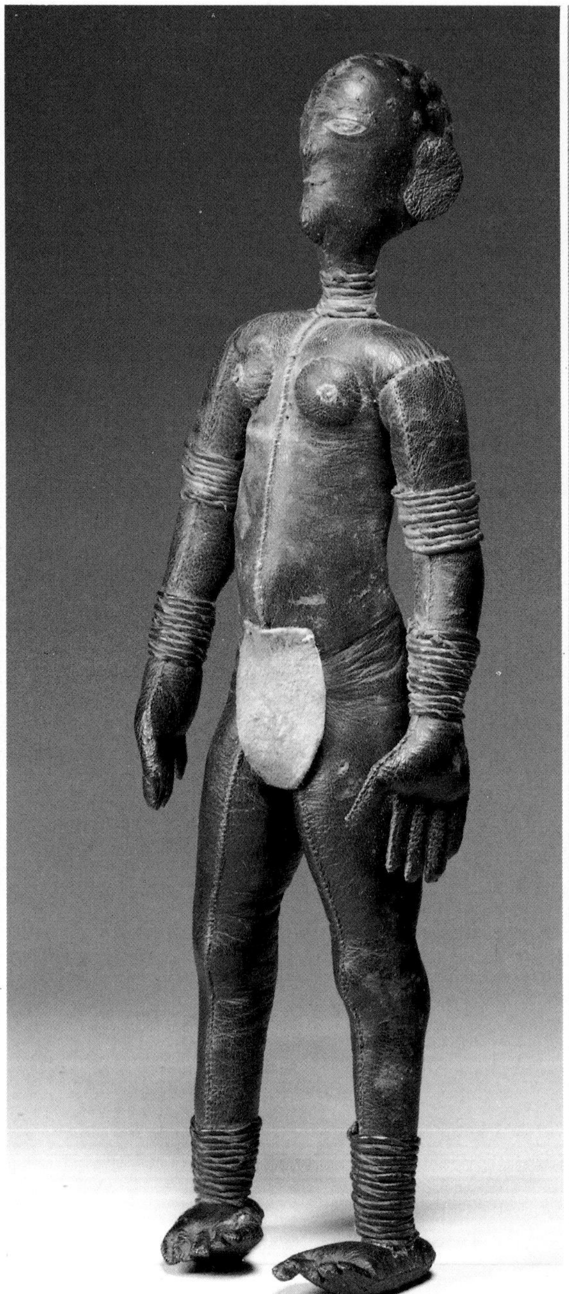

449

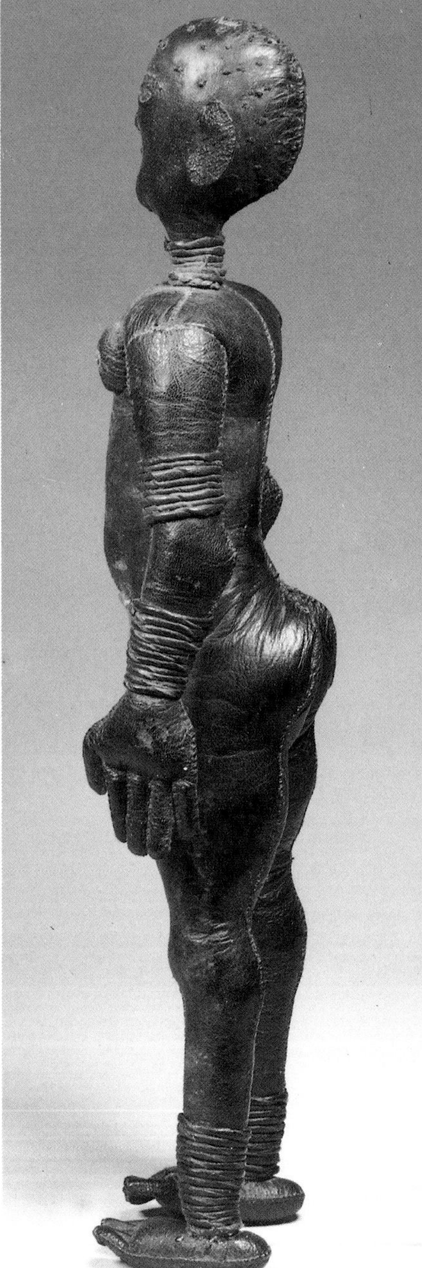

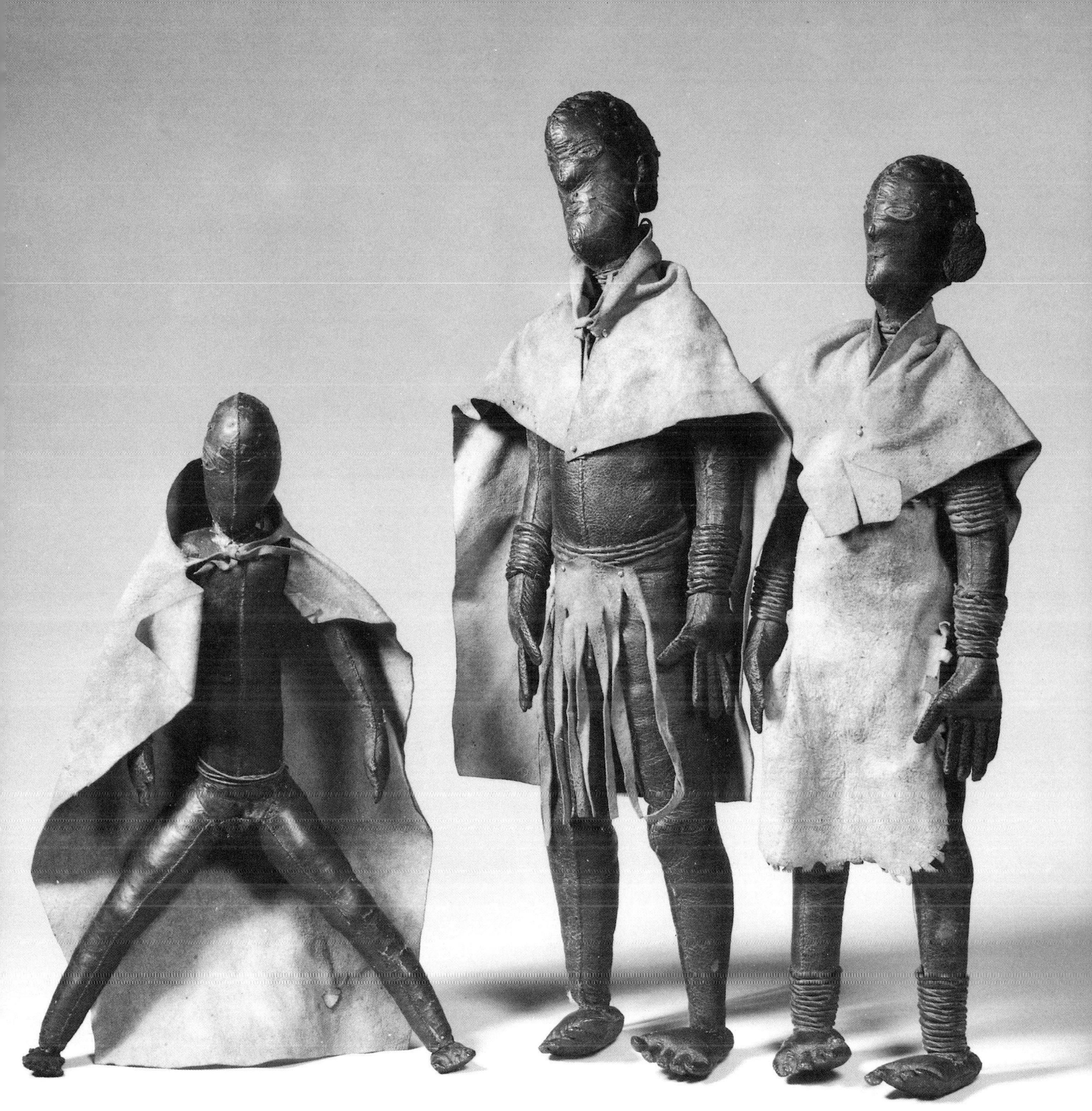

Bibliography

Adams, M. J., 1978: Kuba Embroidered Cloth. African Arts, vol. 12, no. 1, pp. 24-39, 106.

Adamson, J., 1975: The Peoples of Kenya. London (repr.).

Agthe, J., 1983: Luba Hemba—Werke unbekannter Meister. Afrika-Sammlung, vol. 1. Frankfurt am Main.

Alldridge, T. J., 1901: The Sherbro and its Hinterland. London.

Alldridge, T. J., 1910: A Transformed Colony—Sierra Leone. London.

Ankermann, B., 1901: Die afrikanischen Musikinstrumente. Ethnologisches Notizblatt, vol. 3, no. 1, pp. 1-134.

Appiah, P., 1979: Akan Symbolism. African Arts, vol. 13, no. 1, pp. 64-67.

Bachmann, Oberleutn., 1923/24: Mitteilungen über den Labi-Kult der Mandschiavölker. Baessler Archiv, vol. 8, pp. 54-59.

Bartsch, E., 1914: Landeskundlicher Bericht der Logone-Pama-Grenz- expedition. Mitteilungen aus den Deutschen Schutzgebieten, Ergänzungsheft Nr. 9a, pp. 117-125.

Bascom, W., 1969: Ifa Divination: Communication between Gods and Men in West Africa. Bloomington.

Bassani, E., 1977 a): Musei d'Italia—Meraviglie d'Italia. Bologna.

Bassani, E., 1977 b): Oggetti Africani in Antiche Collezioni Italiane, 1. Critica d'Arte, vol. 42, n.p., no. 151/153, pp. 151-182.

Bassani, E., 1977 c): Oggetti Africani in Antiche Collezioni Italiane, 2. Critica d'Arte, vol. 42, n.p., no. 154/156, pp. 187-202.

Bastian, A., 1874: Die deutsche Expedition an der Loango-Küste. Jena.

Bastin, M. L., 1961: Art décoratif Tshokwe. Lisboa.

Bastin, M. L., 1968: L'art d'un peuple d'Angola. Tshokwe. African Arts, vol. 2, no. 1, pp. 40-46, 60-64.

Bauer, W. P., 1975: Zusammensetzung und Gefügestruktur dreier Flachkappenköpfe aus Benin. Abhandlungen und Berichte aus dem Staatl. Museum für Völkerkunde zu Dresden, vol. 34, pp. 31-40.

Baumann, H., 1935: Lunda. Bei Bauern und Jägern in Inner-Angola. Berlin.

Baumann, H., Thurnwald, R., Westermann, D., 1940: Völkerkunde von Afrika. Essen.

Baumann, H., 1950: Nyama, die Rachemacht. Paideuma, vol. 4, pp. 191- 230.

Baumann, H., Vajda, L., 1959: Bernhard Ankermanns völkerkundliche Aufzeichnungen im Grasland von Kamerun 1907-1909, Baessler-Archiv, n.p., vol. 7, pp. 217-318.

Baumann, H., 1964: Die ethnologische Beurteilung einer vorgeschichtlichen Keramik in Mittelafrika. Festschrift für Adolf Jensen I, pp. 13-58. München.

Baumann, H., 1969: Afrikanische Plastik und sakrales Königtum. Bayerische Akademie der Wissenschaften, Sitzungsberichte, 1968, no. 5.

Baumann, H., 1975, 1979: Die Völker Afrikas und ihre traditionellen Kulturen, I-II. Wiesbaden.

Bay, E. G., 1975: The Heart-Shaped Face in African Art. In: African Images—Essays in African Iconology, edited by D. F. McCall and E. G. Bay, pp. 252-267. New York.

Béart, C., 1955: Jeux et jouets de l'Ouest africain. Mémoires de l'Institut Français d'Afrique Noire, no. 42, Dakar.

Beier, H. U., 1958: Gelede Masks. Odu, A Journal of Yoruba and Related Studies, no. 6, pp. 5-24.

Ben-Amos, P., 1976: Men and Animals in Benin Art. Man, n.p. vol. 11, pp. 243-252.

Ben-Amos, P., 1980: The Art of Benin. London.

Benzing, B., 1970: Die Fruchtbarkeitspuppen der Aschanti im National-Museum in Accra, Ghana. Tribus, vol. 19, pp. 71-78.

Bernatzik, H. A., 1947: Afrika. Handbuch der angewandten Völkerkunde. Innsbruck.

Biebuyck, D. P., 1981: Statuary from the pre-Bembe hunters. Tervuren.

Biebuyck, D. P., Van den Abbeele, 1984: The Power of Headdresses. Brussels.

Bodrogi, T., 1968: African Art. Budapest.

Böhning, W., Kalter, J., Sheikh-Dilthey, H., 1972: Ostrafrika. Geräte, Waffen, Schmuck. Ausstellungskatalog der Portheim-Stiftung, Herdelberg.

Bohner, H., 1898: Skizzen aus der Kameruner Mission. Evangelisches Missions-Magazin, pp. 372-385.

Bolz, J., 1966: Zur Kunst in Gabon. Ethnologica, vol. 3, pp. 85-221.

Boone, O., 1961: Carte ethnique du Congo, quart sud-est. Annales du Musée Royal de l'Afrique Centrale, Série in 8°, Sciences Humaines, no. 37.

Born, K., 1981: Skulpturen aus Kamerun. Sammlung Thorbecke 1911/12. Bildhefte des Städt. Reiss-Museums Mannheim, Völkerkundl. Sammlungen vol. 2.

Boser-Sarivaxévanis, R., 1972: Textilhandwerk in West-Afrika. Basel.

Boston, J. S., 1960: Some Northern Ibo Masquerades. Journal of the Royal Anthropological Institute, vol. 90, pt. 1, pp. 54-65.

Bourgeois, A. P., 1981: Masques Suku. Arts d'Afrique Noire 39, pp. 26-41.

Bowen, R. LeB., 1955: Maritime superstitions of the Arabs. The American Neptune, no. 15, pp. 5-48.

Brain, R., Pollock, A., 1971: Bangwa Funerary Sculpture. London.

Bravmann, R. A., 1973: Open Frontiers—The Mobility of Art in Black Africa. Washington.

Bravmann, R. A., 1974: Islam and Tribal Art in West Africa. African Studies Series, no. 11. Cambridge.

Buchner, M., 1887: Kamerun, Skizzen und Betrachtungen Leipzig.

Buchner, M., 1884: Vortrag über das südliche Congo-Becken. Verhandlungen der Gesellschaft für Erdkunde zu Berlin, vol. 11, no. 1, p. 79f.

Buchner, M., 1914: Aurora colonialis. München.

Bufe, E., 1913: Die Bakundu. Archiv für Anthropologie, vol. 12, pp. 228-239.

Burton, W. F. P., 1961: Luba Religion and Magic in Custom and Belief. Annales du Musée Royal de l' Afrique Centrale, Série in 8°, Sciences Humaines, no. 35.

Cameron, V. L., 1877: Quer durch Afrika, I-II. Leipzig.

Campbell, K. F., 1983: Nsibidi Update. Arts d'Afrique Noire, no. 47, pp. 33-46.

Capron, J., 1973: Communautés villageoises Bwa, Mali-Haute Volta. Mémoires de l'Institut d'Ethnologie, IX, t.1, fasc.1. Paris.
Carroll, K., 1967: Yoruba Religious Carvings. New York.
Celenko, T., 1981: The Harrison Eiteljorg Collection. African Arts, vol.14, no.3, pp. 32-42.
Césard, E., 1936: Le Muhaya (L'Afrique Orietale), Kapitel 8. Anthropos, vol. 31, pp. 489-508.
Chaffin, A. and F., 1973: Art Kota. Arts d'Afrique Noire, no. 5, pp. 12-43.
Chilver, E. M., Kaberry, P. M., 1967: The Kingdom of Kom in West Cameroon. In: West African Kingdoms in the Nineteenth Century, edited by D. Forde and P. M. Kaberry. London. pp. 123-151.
Clarke, J. D., 1944: Three Yoruba Fertility Ceremonies. Journal of the Royal Anthropological Institute, vol. 74, no. 1/2, pp. 91-96.
Cole, H. M., 1969: Art as a Verb in Iboland. African Arts, vol. 3, no. 1, pp. 34-41, 88.
Cole, H. M., Ross, D. H., 1977: The Arts of Ghana. Los Angeles.
Cole, H. M., Aniakor, C. C., 1984: Igbo Arts—Community and Cosmos. Los Angeles.
Colle, R. P., 1913: Les Baluba, vol. 1, 2. Collection des Monographies ethnographiques, X, XI. Bruxelles.
Cornet, J., 1971: Art of Africa. Treasures from the Congo. London.
Dam-Mikkelsen, B., Lundbaek, T.,(Ed.), 1980: Ethnographic Objects in the Royal Danish Kunstkammer, 1650-1800. Ethnographical Series of the National Museum of Denmark, vol. 17. Copenhagen.
Dark, P. J. C., Forman, W. and B., 1960: Benin Art. London.
Dark, P. J. C., 1973: An Introduction to Benin Art and Technology. Oxford.
Darkowska-Nidzgorska, O., Ndiaye, F., 1977: Marionettes et Marottes d'Afrique Noire. Le Courrier du Musée de l'Homme, pp. 1-6.
Dechamps, R., 1981: Comment et pourquoi utiliser les rayons X en ehnographie. Africa-Tervuren, vol. 24, no. 3, pp. 57-70.
Delachaux, T., 1946: Méthodes et instruments de divination en Angola. Acta Tropica, vol. 3, no. 1/2, pp. 47-71, 138-149.
Delafosse, M., 1900: Sur quelques traces probables de civilisation égyptienne et d'homme de race blanche à la Côte d'Ivoire. L'Anthropologie, vol. 11.
Deonna, W., 1949: Daniel, le Maître des Fauves. Artibus Asiae, vol. 12, pp. 119-140, 347-374.
Deonna, W., 1952: Ouroboros. Artibus Asiae, vol. 15, pp. 163-170.
Dieterlen, G., 1970: La Serrure et sa Clef (Dogon, Mali), In: Echanges et Communications, Mélanges offerts à Claude Lévi-Strauss, vol. 1. Paris, pp. 7-28.
Dittmer, K., 1961: Nuna, Westafrika (Obervolta)—Schnitzen und Bemalen von Tanzmasken. Encyclopaedia Cinematographica, E 176/1959. Göttingen.
Dittmer, K., 1967. Die "prähistorischen" Steinfiguren aus Sierra Leone und Guinée. Baessler Archiv, vol. 15, pp. 183-228.
Dominik, H., 1902: Sechs Kriegs und Friedensjahre in deutschen Tropen, Berlin.
Donner, E., 1940: Kunst und Handwerk in N.O. Liberia. Baessler Archiv, vol. 23, pp. 45-110.
Douglas, M., Kaberry, P. M., 1969: Man in Africa. London.
Drewal, H. J., 1974 a): Efe—Voiced Power and Pageantry. African Arts, vol. 7, no. 2, pp. 26-29, 58-66, 82-84.
Drewal, H. J., 1974 b): Gelede Masquerade—Imagery and Motif. African Arts, vol. 7, no. 4, pp. 8-19, 62-63, 95-96.
Drewal, H. J., 1978: The Arts of Egungun among the Yoruba. African Arts, vol. 11, no. 3, pp. 18-19.
Drewal, H. J., 1980: African Artistry—Technique and Aesthetics in Yoruba Sculpture. Atlanta.
Drewal, M. T. and H. J., 1975: Gelede Dance of the Western Yoruba. African Arts, vol. 8, no. 2, pp. 36-45, 78.
Drewal, M. T., 1977: Projections from the Top in Yoruba Art. African Arts, vol. 11, no. 1. pp. 43-49, 91.
Drost, D., 1975: Die Gelbgüsse des Ali Amonikoyi im Museum für Völkerkunde zu Leipzig. Abhandlungen und Berichte des Staatl. Museums für Völkerkunde zu Dresden, vol. 34, pp. 41-68.
Egharevba, J. U., 1934: A Short History of Benin. Ibadan.
Elisofon, E., Fagg, W. B., 1958: The Sculpture of Africa. New York.
Ellis, A. B., 1894: The Yoruba Speaking Peoples of the Slave Coast of West Africa. London.
Eyo, E., 1974: Abua Masquerades. African Arts. vol. 7, no. 2, pp. 52-55.
Eyo, E., 1977: Two Thousand Years Nigerian Art. Lagos.
Fagg, W., 1959: Afro-Portugese Ivories. London.
Fagg, W., 1961: Nigeria—2000 Jahre Plastik. München.
Fagg, W., 1963: Nigerian Images. New York.
Fagg, W., 1965: Tribes and Forms in African Art. London.
Fagg, W., Plass, M., 1964/66: African Sculpture—An Anthology (Rev. Ed.). London.
Fagg, W., 1968: African Tribal Images. Cleveland.
Fagg, W., 1970 a): Miniature Wood Carvings of Africa. Greenwich/ Connecticut.
Fagg, W., 1970 b): African Sculpture. Cat. National Gallery of Art. Washington.
Fagg, W., Pemberton, J., 1980: Yoruba Beadwork—Art of Nigeria. New York.
Fagg, W., 1981: African Majesty—From Grassland and Forest. Toronto.
Fagg, W., Pemberton, J. 3rd, Holcombe, B. (Ed.), 1982: Yoruba - Sculpture of West Africa. New York.
Farrow, S. S., 1926: Faith, Fancies and Fetish or Yoruba Paganism. London.
Fernandez, J. W., 1974: L. Perrois, La statuaire des Fang du Gabon (Buchbespr.). African Arts, vol. 8, no. 1, pp. 76, 77.
Finke-Kraft, J., 1980: Ere-Ibeji-Zwillingsfiguren aus Nigeria. Archiv für Völkerkunde, vol. 34, pp. 1-52.
Fischer, E., 1963: Künstler der Dan. Baessler Archiv, vol. 10, pp. 161-263.
Fischer, E., 1966: Die Gelbgussmaske des Ali Amonikoyi (aus Togo) im Museum für Völkerkunde in Basel. Tribus, vol. 15, pp. 78-95.

Fischer, E., Himmelheber, H., 1975: Das Gold in der Kunst Westafrikas. Zürich.
Fischer, E., Himmelheber, H., 1976: Die Kunst der Dan. Zürich.
Fischer, E., 1978: Dan Forest Spirits—Masks in Dan Villages. African Arts, vol. 11, no. 2, pp. 16-23, 94.
Fischer, E., 1980: Masks in A Non-Poro Area: The Dan. Ethnologische Zeitschrift Zürich, no. 1, pp. 81-88.
Fischer, E., Homberger, L., 1985: Die Kunst der Guro, Elfenbeinküste. Zürich.
Forde, C. D., 1951: The Yoruba-Speaking Peoples of South-Western Nigeria. Ethnographic Survey of Africa, Western Africa, pt. 4. London.
Foy, W., 1909 a): Zur Geschichte der Eisentechnik, insbesondere des Gelbgusses. Ethnologica, vol. 1, pp. 185-222.
Foy, W., 1909 b): Südafricanische Zauberpuppen. Ethnologica, vol. 1 pp. 231, 232.
Frank, B., 1965: Die Rolle des Hundes in afrikanischen Kulturen. Studien zur Kulturkunde, vol. 17.
Franz, L., 1967: Das Zeichen des heiligen Rindes. Archaelogica Austriaca, vol. 40, pp. 99-112.
Fraser, D., Cole, H. M. (Eds.), 1972 a): African Art and Leadership. Madison.
Fraser, D., 1972: The Fish-Legged Figure in Benin and Yoruba Art. In: African Art and Leadership, ed. by D. Fraser and H. M. Cole. Madison. pp. 261-294.
Frobenius, L., 1897: Der Kameruner Schiffschnabel und seine Motive. Halle.
Frobenius, L., 1912-1913: Und Afrika sprach, vol. I-III, Berlin.
Frobenius, L., 1926: Die atlantische Götterlehre. Jena.
Frobenius, L., 1954: Kulturgeschichte Afrikas. Zürich.
Froehlich, W., 1966: Die Benin-Sammlung des Rautenstrauch-Joest-Museums in Köln. Ethnologica. vol. 3, pp. 231-310.
Fry, J. (Ed.), 1978: Vingt cinq sculptures Africaines. Ottawa.
Ganslmayr, H., 1969: Das Krokodil in Kult und Mythos afrikanischer Stämme. Nürnberg.
Gardi, R., 1969: Unter afrikanishen Handwerken, Bern.
Garrard, T. F., 1979: Akan Metal Arts. African Arts, vol. 13, no. 1, pp. 36-43, 100.
Garrard, T. F., 1980: Akan Weights and the Gold Trade. London.
Geary, C., 1979: Traditional Societies and Associations in We (North West Province, Cameroon). Paideuma, vol. 5, pp. 53-72.
Geary, C., 1983: Things of the Palace. A Catalogue of the Bamum Palace Museum in Foumban (Cameroon).
Gebauer, P., 1964: Spider Divination in the Cameroons. Milwaukee Public Museum. Publications in Anthropology, vol. 10.
Gebauer, P. and C., 1968: A Guide to Cameroon Art from the Collection of Paul and Clara Gebauer.
Gebauer, P., 1971: Architecture of Cameroon. African Arts, vol. 5, no.1, pp. 40-49.
Gebauer, P., 1979: Art of Cameroon. Portland.
Germann, P., 1929: Afrikanische Puppen. In: In Memoriam Karl Weule. Leipzig, pp. 123-148.
Germann, P., 1958: Negerplastiken aus dem Museum für Völkerkunde zu Leipzig. In: Beiträge zur afrikanischen Kunst (Veröffentlichungen des Museums für Völkerkunde zu Leipzig, H. 9), pp. 31-60.
Gillon, W., 1979: Collecting African Art. London.
Gillon, W., 1984: A Short History of African Art. Harmondsworth.
Glaze, A. J., 1975: Woman Power and Art in a Senufo Village. African Arts, vol. 8, no. 3, pp. 24-29, 64-68, 90.
Glaze, A. J., 1978: Senufo Ornament and Decorative Arts. African Arts, vol. 12, no. 1, pp. 63-71, 107.
Göttlicher, A., 1972: Zur sakralen Bedeutung des Schiffs-Stevens-Eine maritim-ethnologische Studie. Ethnologische Zeitschrift Zürich, no. 2, pp. 53-73.
Goldwater, R., 1960: Bambara Sculpture from the Western Sudan. New York.
Goldwater, R., 1964: Senufo Sculpture from West Africa. New York.
Graebner, F., 1927: Kopfbänke. Ethnologica, vol. 3, pp. 1-13.
Griaule, M., 1938: Masques Dogons. Travaux et Mémoires de l'Institut d'Ethnologie, vol. 33. Paris.
Griaule, M., 1965: Conversations with Ogotemmêli. London.
Grottanelli, V. L., 1975: Discovery of A Masterpiece—A 16th Century Ivory Bowl from Sierra Leone. African Arts, vol. 8, no. 4, pp. 14-23, 83.
Grunne, B. de, 1980: Terres cuites anciennes de l'Ouest Africain. Publications d'Histoire de l'Art et d'Archéologie de l'Université Catholique de Louvain, vol. 22. Louvain.
Güssfeldt, P., 1875 a): Bericht über die von ihm geleitete Expedition an der Loango-Küste. Verhandlungen der Gesellschaft für Erdkunde zu Berlin, vol. 2, no. 1, pp. 195-218.
Güssfeldt, P., 1875 b): Bericht Dr. Paul Güssfeldt's über seine Reise an den Gesellschaft fur Erdkunde zu Berlin, Bd. 10, pp. 142-159, 161-181.
Güssfeldt, P., 1876: Zur Kenntnis der Loango-Neger. Zeitschrift für Ethnologie, vol. 8, pp. 202-216.
Guimont, C., 1978: Djenné. Arts d'Afrique Noire, no. 28, pp. 11-21.
Hall, H. U., 1924: The American Cups Embodying Human Forms, Museum Journal Nr. 7, p. 9.
Harding, J. R., 1961: "Mwali" Dolls of the Wazaramo. Man, vol. 61, pp. 72, 73.
Harley, G. W., 1950: Masks as Agents of Social Control in Northeast Liberia. Papers of the Peabody Museum of American Anthropology and Ethnology, vol. 32, no. 2. Cambridge/Mass.
Harries, L., 1944: The initiation rites of the Makonde tribe. Communications from the Rhodes-Livingstone-Institute, no. 3.
Harter, P., 1973: Les pipes cérémonielles de l'Ouest camérounais. Arts d'Afrique Noire, no. 8, pp. 18-42.
Hartwig, G. W., 1969: The Role of Plastic Art Tradition in Tanzania: The Northwestern Region. Baessler Archiv vol. 17, pp. 25- 52.
Hauenstein, A., 1961: La corbeille aux osselets divinatoires des Tchokwe (Angola). Anthropos, vol. 56, pp. 114-157.
Heger, F., 1899: Alte Elfenbeinarbeiten aus Afrika. Mitteilungen der Anthropologischen Gesellschaft in Wien, vol. 29, pp. 101-109.
Himmelheber, H., 1935: Negerkünstler. Stuttgart.
Himmelheber, H., 1960: Negerkunst und Negerkünstler. Braunschweig.
Himmelheber, H., 1965: Wunkirle, die gastliche Frau. In Festschrift für Alfred Bühler. Basel. pp. 171-181.

Himmelheber, H., 1966: Figuren und Schnitztechnik bei den Lobi, Elfenbeinküste. Tribus, vol. 15, pp. 63-87.

Himmelheber, H., 1967: Ringe und Anhänger der Senufo (Nördliche Elfenbeinküste). Baessler Archiv, vol. 15, pp. 247-270.

Himmelheber, H., 1968: Die Technik des Vergoldens bei den Baule der Elfenbeinküste. Abhandlungen und Berichte des Staatl. Museums für Völkerkunde zu Dresden, vol. 28, pp. 83-90.

Himmelheber, H., 1972 a): Masken, Tänzer und Musiker der Elfenbeinküste. Göttingen.

Himmelheber, H., 1972 b): Gold plated objects of Baule notables. In: African Art and Leadership, edited by D. Fraser and H. M. Cole. Madison.

Hirschberg, W., 1963: Der Gottesname Nyambi im Lichte alter westafrikanischer Reiseberichte. Zeitschrift für Ethnologie, vol. 88, pp. 163-179.

Hirschberg, W., 1972: Religionsethnologie und ethnohistorische Religionsforschung: eine Gegenüberstellung. Weiner Ethnohistorische Blätter, Beiheft 1.

Holas, B., 1948: Le Masque Do des Baoule-Aitou. Notes Africaines, no. 38, pp. 5, 6.

Holas, B., 1960: Cultures matérielles de la Côte d'Ivoire. Paris.

Holas, B., 1969: Art de la Côte d'Ivoire. Vevey.

Holý, L., 1967: Masks and Figures from Eastern and Southern Africa. London.

Houlberg, M. H., 1973: Ibedji Images of the Yoruba. African Arts, vol. 7, no. 1, pp. 20-27, 91.

Hutter, F., 1902: Kamerun. Berlin.

Imperato, P. J., 1970: The Dance of the Tyi Wara. African Arts, vol. 4, no. 1, pp. 8-13, 71-80.

Imperato, P. J., 1972: Door Locks of the Bamana of Mali. African Arts, vol. 5, no. 3, pp. 52-56, 84.

Imperato, P. J., 1974: Bamana and Maninka Covers and Blankets. African Arts, vol. 7, no. 3, pp. 56-67, 91.

Imperato, P. J., 1978: Dogon Door Locks. African Arts, vol. 11, no. 4, pp. 54-57, 96.

Imperato, P. J., 1981: Sogoni Koun. African Arts, vol. 14, no. 2, pp. 38-47, 72, 88.

Imperato, P. J., Shamir, M., 1970: Bokolanfini—Mud Cloth of the Bamana of Mali. African Arts, vol. 3, no. 4, pp. 32-41, 80.

Ittman, I., 1936: Kameruner Geheimbünde. Evangelisches Missionsmagazin, Jg. 80, H. 10, pp. 305-311; H.11, pp.332-343.

Jahn, J., ed. 1983: Colon. Das Schwarze Bild vom weissen Mann. München.

Janzen, J. M., MacGaffey, W., 1974: An Anthology of Kongo Religion: Primary Texts from Lower Zaire. University of Kansas Publications in Anthropology, no. 5, pp. 1-163.

Johnson, S. 1921: The History of the Yorubas. London.

Jongmans, D. G., 1962: Nail Fetish and Crucifix. Mededelingen van het Rijksmuseum voor Volkenkunde, Leiden, no. 15, pp. 50-62.

Kandert, J., 1984: Afrika. Prag.

Kandt, R., 1904: Gewerbe in Ruanda. Zeitschrift für Ethnologie, vol. 36, pp. 329-372, Tafeln 1-4.

Karutz, R., 1901: Die afrikanische Hörnermasken. Lübeck.

Kauenhoven-Janzen, R., 1981: Chowke thrones. African Arts, vol. 14, no. 3, pp. 69-74, 92.

Kecskési, M., 1976: Afrikanische Kunste. Herausg. Lommel, A., München.

Kecskési, M., 1982: The Pickaback Motif in the Art and Initiation of the Rowuma Area. African Arts, vol. XVI, no. 1.

Kjersmeier, C., 1935: Centres de Style de la Sculpture Nègre Africaine. Paris.

Köhler, O., 1954: Das "Pferd" in den Gur-Sprachen. Afrika und Übersee, vol. 38, pp. 93-109.

Kollmann, P., 1898: Der Nordwesten unserer ostafrikanischen Kolonie. Berlin.

Koloss, H. J., 1977: Kamerun. Könige—Masken—Feste. Ethnologische Forschungen im Grasland der Nordwest-Provinz von Kamerun. Stuttgart.

Koloss, H. J., 1984: Njom among the Ejagham. African Arts, vol. 18, no. 1, pp. 71-73, 90.

Krauss, H., 1907: Speilzeug der Suahelikinder. Globus vol. 92, pp. 359-375.

Krieg, K. H., 1980: Kunst und Kunsthandwerk aus Westafrika. Leverkusen.

Krieger, K., 1965-1969: Westafrikanische Plastik I-III. Veröffentlichungen des Museums für Völkerkunde Berlin N.F. 7, Abt. Afrika II.

Küsters, M., 1928: Unyago der Knaben. Das Mädchen-Unyago (Mwera). Unveröffentlichtes Manuskript im Benediktinerkloster St. Ottilien.

Kussmaul, F., 1981: Bericht über das Linden-Museum Stuttgart im Jahr 1980. Tribus, vol. 30, pp. 91-134.

Kun, N. de., 1979: L'art boyo. Africa—Tervuren, vol. 25, no. 2, pp. 29-44.

Labouret, H., 1931: Les Tribus du Rameau Lobi. Paris.

Lagercrantz, S., 1941: Über willkommene und unwillkommene Zwillinge in Afrika. Etnologiska Studier, vol. 12, 13, pp. 5-292.

Lagercrantz, S., 1950: Contributions to the Ethnography of Africa. Studia Ethnographica Upsaliensia, vol. 1. Uppsala.

Laman, K., 1962: The Kongo, vol. 3. Studia Ethnographica Upsaliensia, vol. 12. Uppsala.

Lang, W., 1960: Makondemasken in der völkerkundlichen Sammlung der Universität Göttingen. Zeitschrift für Ethnologie vol. 85.

Laude, J., 1973: African Art of the Dogon. New York.

Lawal, B., 1978: New Light on Gelede. African Arts, vol. 11, no. 2, pp. 65-70, 94.

Lecoq, R., 1953: Les Bamiléké. Présence Africaine. Paris.

Lehuard, R., 1980: Fétiches à clous du Bas-Zaire. Arnouville.

Leiris, M., Delange, J., 1974: The Art and Peoples of Black Africa. New York.

Lem, F. H., 1949: Sudanese Sculpture. Paris.

Le Moal, G., 1980: Les Bobo—Nature et Fonction des Masques. Travaux et Documents de l'ORSTOM, no. 121. Paris.

Leurquin-Tefnin, A., 1980: Eshu, l'insaisissable: le "trickster" dans la pensée religieuse des Yoruba du Nigeria. Arts d'Afrique Noire, no. 36, pp. 26-37.

Leuzinger, E., 1970: Die Kunst von Schwarz-Afrika. Zürich.
Levtzion, N., 1973: Ancient Ghana and Mali. Studies in African History, vol. 7. London.
Lignitz, H., 1919-22: Die künstlichen Zahnverstümmelungen in Afrika im Lichte der Kulturkreisforschung. Anthropos, vol. 14/15, pp. 891-943; vol. 16/17, pp. 247-264, 866-889.
Lindblom. K. G., 1928: The Use of the Hammock in Africa. Riksmuseets Etnografiska Avdelning Smärre Meddelanden Nr. 7, Stockholm.
Lips, J., 1937: The Savage Hits Back. London.
Lohse, W., 1980: Colonne, colon, kolo. Kat. Galerie Fred Jahn. München.
Lommel, A., 1953: Zwei grosse Panther aus Benin. Die Kunst und das schöne Heim. Jhg. 51. pp. 178, 179.
Lopasic, A., 1965: The "Bini" Pantheon seen through the Masks of the "Ekpo" cult. Réincarnation et vie mystique en Afrique Noire. Paris.
Luschan, F. von, 1916: Über Schlösser mit Fallriegeln. Zeitschrift für Ethnologie, vol. 48, pp. 406-429.
Luschan, F. von, 1919: Die Altertümer von Benin, vol. 1-3 Berlin/Leipzig.

McCall, D. F., 1975: The Hornbill and Analogous Forms in West African Sculpture. In: African Images—Essays in African Iconology, edited by D. F. McCall and E. G. Bay. N. Y., pp. 269-324.
McIntosh, R. J. and S. K., 1979: Terracotta Statuettes from Mali. African Arts, vol. 12, no. 2, pp. 51-53.
McLeod, M. D., 1981: The Asante. London.
Maes, J., 1924: Aniota Kifwebe,. Antwerpen.
Maes, J., 1929: Les appuis-tête du Congo Belge. Annales du Musée du Congo Belge, série 6, vol. 1, fasc. 1. Bruxelles.
Maes, J., 1930: Les figurines sculpturées du Bas-Congo. Africa, vol. 3, pp. 347-359.
Maes, J., 1935: Fetischen of Tooverbeelden uit Kongo. Annales du Musée du Congo Belge, série 6, vol. 2, fasc. 1. Bruxelles
Maes, J., 1938: Kabila—en Grafbeelden uit Kongo. Anneles du Musée du Congo Belge, série 6, vol. 2, fasc. 2. Tervuren
Maes, J., 1943: Die soziale und kulturelle Bedeutung der Kabila-Figuren aus Belgisch-Kongo. Paideuma, vol. 2, pp. 249-267.
Maesen, A., 1960 : Umbangu—Art du Congo au Musée du Congo Belge. Bruxelles.
Maesen, A., 1980: Preface. In: Terres cuîtes anciennes de l'ouest African by B. de Grunne. Louvain-la-Neuve. pp. V-VII.
Maesen, A., 1981: Vioka Vana Lumoni Lu Nkisi . . . zoeklicht op de West-Kongo. Kunst nit de verzameling van de K. U. Leuven.
Mansfeld, A. 1908: Urwald-Dokumente. Berlin.
Martin, F., 1893: Afrikanische Skizzen. München.
Massion, A., 1964: Les bâtons africains décorés du Musée de l'Homme. Objects et Mondes, vol 4., fasc. 3, pp. 157-186.
Mato, D., 1979: Weaver and Carver—An Exhibition of Heddle Pulleys and Textiles. Manitoba.
Mato, D., 1984: Terrakotta-Figuren vom Niger und aus dem Niger-Binnendelta. In: Afrikanische Keramik—Traditionelle Handwerkskunst südlich der Sahara von A. Stossel. Munchen. pp. 22-30
Maurer, E. M., Roberts, A. F. (Eds.), 1985: Tabwa—The Rising of a New Moon—A Century of Tabwa Art. Ann Arbor.
Melzian, H., 1955: Zum Festkalender von Benin. Afrikanistische Studien Diedrich Westermann zum 80. Geburtstag gewidmet, pp. 87-107. Berlin.
Menzel, B., 1968: Goldgewichte aus Ghana. Veröffentlichungen aus dem Museum für Völkerkunde, vol. 12. Berlin.
Menzel, B., 1972: Textilien aus Westafrika, vol. 1-3. Veröffentlichungen aus dem Museum für Völkerkunde, vol. 26. Berlin.
Meurer, L., Kafando, E., 1964: Kinderpuppen der Mossi in Obervolta. Tribus, vol. 13, pp. 25-30.
Meurer, L., 1980: Zur figürlichen Plastik der Baule, Elfenbeinküste. Archiv für Völkerkunde, vol. 34, pp. 53-60.
Meyer, P., 1981: Kunst und Religion der Lobi. Zürich.
Mobolade, T., 1971: Ibedji Custom in Yorubaland. African Arts, vol. 4, no. 3, pp. 14, 15.
Monard, A., 1930: Notes sur les collection ethnographiques de la Mission scientifique suisse en Angola. Bulletin de la Société. Neuchâteloise de Géographie, vol. 39, pp. 100-122.
Müller, C. C., 1980: 400 Jahre Sammeln und Reisen der Wittelsbacher. München.
Murdock, G. P., 1959: Africa—Its People and their Culture History. New York.
Nekes, H., 1913: Totemistische-manistische Anschauungen der Jaunde in ihren Kultfeiern und Geheimbünden. Koloniale Rundschau, vol. 13, no. 3, pp. 134-153; no. 4, pp. 207-221.
Neyt, F., 1977: La grande statuaire Hemba du Zaire. Publications d'Histoire de l'Art et d'Archéologie de l'Université Catholique de Louvain, vol. 12. Louvain.
Neyt, F., 1979: L'Art Eket—Collection Azar. Abeielle à Paris.
Neyt, F., 1981: Arts traditionnels et histoire au Zaire. Publications d'Histoire de l'Art Archéologie de l'Université Catholique de Louvain, vol. 29. Louvain.
Ngumu, P. C., 1977: Ein Beitrag zur Religion der ewondo-sprechen den Beti (Kamerun) auf Grund schriftlicher und mündlicher Quellen. Wien.
Nicklin, K., 1974: Nigerian Skin-Covered Masks. African Arts, vol.7, no. 3, pp. 8-15, 67, 68, 92.
Nicklin, K., Salmons, J., 1984: Cross River Art Styles. African Arts, vol. 18, no. 1, pp. 28-43, 93.
Northern, T., 1973: Royal Art of Cameroon. Cat. Dartmouth College, Hannover, New Hampshire.
Northern, T., 1975: The Sign of the Leopard—Beaded Art of Cameroon. Storrs, Connecticut.
Northern, T., 1984: The Art of Cameroon. Washington.
Nsugbe, P. O., 1961: Oron Ekpu Figures. Nigeria Magazine, no. 71, pp. 357-365.
Odugbesan, C., 1969: Femininity in Yoruba Religious Art. In: Man in Africa, edited by E. M. Douglas and P. M. Kaberry. London. pp. 199-211.
Ogunba, O., 1964: Crowns and Okute at Idowa. Nigeria Magazine, no. 83, pp. 249-261.
Ojo, G. J. A., 1966: Yoruba Culture. London.
Olbrechts, F. M., 1959: Les arts plastiques du Congo Belge. Bruxelles.

Pageard, R., 1962: Travestis et Marionnettes de la Région de Ségou. Notes Africaines, no. 93, pp. 17-20.

Palau Marti, M., 1957: Les Dogon. Paris.

Palme, H., 1977: Spiegelfetische im Kongoraum und ihre Beziehung zu christlichen Reliquiaren. Wiener Ethnohistorische Blätter, Beiheft 5.

Patton, S. F., 1979: The Stool and Asante Chieftaincy. African Arts, vol. 13, no. 1, pp. 74-98.

Paul, S., 1970: Afrikanische Puppen. Baessler Archiv, Beiheft 6.

Pechuël-Loesche, E., 1884: Congoforschung und die Congo-Frage. Verhandlunge der Gesellschaft für Erdkunde zu Berlin, vol. 11, pp. 184-211.

Pechuël-Loesche, E., 1907: Volkskunde von Loango. Stuttgart.

Pemberton, J., 1975: Eshu-Elegba—the Yoruba Trickster God. African Arts, vol. 9, no. 1, pp. 20-27, 66.

Perrois, L., 1972: La statuaire Fan du Gabon. Mémoires de l'ORSTOM, no. 59. Paris.

Perrois, L., 1973 a): Gabun gestern und heute. Zeitschrift des Museums zu Hildesheim, Heft 24.

Perrois, L., 1973 b): La statuaire des Fang du Gabon. Arts d'Afrique Noire, no. 7, pp. 22-42.

Pervés, M., 1948: Parmi les Fang de la forêt équatorial—le jeu de l'abbia. La Revue de Géographie Humaine et d'Ethnologie, vol. 3, pp. 26-41.

Picton, J., Mack, J., 1980: African Textiles—Looms, Weaving and Design. London.

Pitt-Rivers, L. F., 1900: Antique Works of Art from Benin. London.

Posansky, M., 1977: Brass Casting and its Antecedents in West Africa (Review Article). Journal of African History, vol. 13, no. 2, pp. 287-300.

Poynor, R., 1976: Edo Influence on the Arts of Owo. African Arts, vol. 9, no. 4, pp. 40-45.

Quinn, F., 1970: Abbia Stones. African Arts, vol. 4, no. 1, pp. 30-32.

Radcliffe-Brown, A., 1925: Native Dolls in the Transvaal Museum. Annals of the Transvaal Museum, vol. 11, no. 2, pp. 99-102.

Raponda-Walker, A., Sillans, R., 1962: Rites et Croyances des Peuples du Gabon. Paris.

Rattray, R. S., 1923: Ashanti. Oxford.

Rattray, R. S., 1927: Religion and Art in Ashanti. London.

Ratton, C., 1951: L'or fétiche. Présence Africaine, no. 10/11, pp. 136-155.

Reche, O., 1921. Das abia-Glückspiel der Yaunde und die Darstellungen auf den Spielmarken. Mitteilungen aus dem Museum für Völkerkunde, Hamburg, vol. 9.

Rehse, H., 1910: Kiziba—Land und Leute. Stuttgart.

Rein-Wuhrmann, A., 1925: Mein Bamumvolk im Grasland von Kamerun. Stuttgart.

Robbins, W. M., 1966: African Art in American Collections. New York.

Rodriguez de Areira, M. L., 1978: Le panier divinatoire des Tshokwe. Arts d'Afrique Noire, no. 26, pp. 30-44.

Rodrigues de Areia, M. L., 1985: Les symboles divinatoires. Coimbra.

Ross, D. H., 1974: Ghanaian Forowa. African Arts, vol. 8, no. 1, pp.40-49, 88.

Roy, D. D., 1981: Mossi Dolls. African Arts, vol. 14, no. 47-51, 88.

Rubin, W., 1984: Primitivism in 20th Century Art. 2 vols. New York.

Ruel, M., 1969: Leopards and Leaders. London.

Ryder, A. F. C., 1964: A Note on the Afro-Portuguese Ivories. Journal of African History, vol. 5, no. 3, pp. 87-107.

Savary, C., Harter, P., 1980: Cameroun—arts et cultures des peuples de l'ouest. Genève.

Schilde, W., 1930: Die afrikanischen Hoheitszeichen. Zeitschrift für Ethnologie vol. 61, pp. 45-152.

Schmalenbach, W., 1953: Die Kunst Afrikas. Basel.

Schmalenbach, W., 1961: Die Kunst der Primitiven als Anregungsquelle für die europaische Kunst bis 1900. Köln.

Schweeger-Hefel, A., 1966: Nioniosi-Kunst. Baessler Archiv, vol. 14, pp. 187-267.

Schweeger-Hefel, A., 1980: Masken und Mythen—Sozialstrukturen der Nyonyosi und Sikomse in Obervolta, vol. 1, 2. Wien.

Schweeger-Hefel, A., Staude, W., 1972: Die Kurumba von Lurum - Monographie eines Volkes aus Obervolta (Westafrika), Wien.

Segy, L., 1951/52: Bakuba Cups—An Essay on Style Classification. Midwest Journal, vol. 4, no. 1, pp. 26-49.

Segy, L., 1963: The Ashanti Akua'ba Statues as Archetypes, and the Egyptian Ankh—A Theory of Morphological Assumption. Anthropos, vol. 58, pp. 839-867.

Segy, L., 1970: The Yoruba Ibeji Statue. Acta Tropica, vol. 27, no.2, pp. 97-145.

Segy, L., 1972: The Mossi Doll—An Archetypal Fertility Figure. Tribus, vol. 21, pp. 36-68.

Segy, L., 1975: African Sculpture Speaks. 4 editions, enlarged. New York.

Seligman, T. K., 1980: Animism and Islam—A Mask from North-East Liberia. Apollo, vol. 111, no. 216, pp. 143-145.

Shaw, T., 1978: Nigeria—Its Archaeology and Early History. London.

Sieber, R., 1962: Masks as Agents of Social Control. African Studies Bulletin, vol. 5, no. 2, pp. 8-13.

Sieber, R. Rubin, A., 1968: Sculpture of Black Africa—The Paul Tishman Collection. Los Angeles.

Siegmann, W. C., 1980: Spirit Manifestation and the Poro Society. Ethnologische Zeitschrift Zürich, no. 1, pp. 89-95

Siroto, L., 1953: A Note on Guro Statues. Man, vol. 53, pp. 17-18.

Siroto, L., 1968: The Face of the Bwiiti. African Arts, vol. 1, no. 3, pp. 22-27, 86-89.

Siroto, L., 1977: Njom—The Magical Bridge of the Beti and Bulu of Southern Cameroon. African Arts, vol. 10, no. 2, pp. 38-51.

Siroto, L., 1978: A propos Postscript on Njom. African Arts, vol. 11, no. 3, pp. 86-87.

Söderberg, B., 1975. Les figures d'ancêtres chez les Babembé. Arts d'Afrique Noire, no. 14, pp. 14-37.

Spini, T. and S., 1976: Togu na. Casa della parola, struttura di socializzazione della comunità Dogon. Milano.

Stirnimann, H., 1976: Existenzgrundlagen und traditionelles Handwerk der Pangwa von S. W. Tansania. Studia Ethnographica Friburgensia Nr. 4.

Stössel, A., 1984: Afrikanische Keramik—Traditionelle Handwerkskunst südlich der Sahara. München.

Stoll, M. and G., 1980: Ibeji—Zwillsfiguren der Yoruba. München.

Sousberghe, L. de, 1959: L'Art Pende. Académie Royal de Belgique, C. d. Beaux-Arts, Mémoires, Coll. in 4°, Deuxième série, vol. 9, fasc. 2.

Straube, H., 1960: Gedanken zur Farbensymbolik in afrikanischen Eingeborenen-Kulturen. Studium Generale, vol. 13, no. 7, pp. 392- 418.

Straube, H., 1965: Die historischen Wurzeln der ostafrikanischen Bodendellen-Keramik. Kölner Ethnologische Mitteilungen, no. 4, pp. 231-286.

Stritzl, A., 1971: Raffiaplüsche aus dem Königreich Kongo. Wiener Ethnohistorische Blätter, no. 3, pp. 37-55.

Sweeney, J. J., 1935: African Negro Art. New York.

Sydow, E. v., 1932: The Image of Janus in African Sculpture. Africa, vol. 5, pp. 14-27.

Tagliaferri, A., Hammacher, A., 1974: Fabulous Ancestors—Stone Carvings from Sierra Leone and Guinea. Milano.

Talbot, P. A., 1912: In the Shadow of the Bush. London.

Talbot, P. A., 1923: Life in Southern Nigeria. London.

Tardy, Ed., 1977: Les Ivoires. Paris.

Tauxier, L., 1921: Le Noir de Bondoukou. Paris.

Tauxier, L., 1924: Nègres Gouro et Gagou. Paris.

Tessman, G., 1913: Die Pangwe, vol. 1, 2. Berlin.

Tessman, G., 1934: Die Baja, vol. 1, 2. Stuttgart.

Thiel, J. F., Helf, H., 1984: Christliche Kunst in Afrika. Berlin.

Thompson, R. F., 1971 a): Sons of Thunder—Twin Images among the Oyo and other Yoruba Groups. African Arts, vol. 4, no. 3, pp. 8-13, 77.

Thompson, R. F., 1971 b): Black Gods and Kings—Yoruba Art at UCLA. Los Angeles.

Thompson, R. F., 1972: The Sign of the Divine King—Yoruba Bead-Embroidered Crowns with Veil and Bird Decorations. In: African Art and Leadership, edited by D. Fraser and H. Cole. Madison. pp. 227-260.

Thompson, R. F., 1974: African Art in Motion. Los Angeles.

Thompson, R. F., 1978: The Grand Detroit N'Kondi. Bulletin of the Detroit Institute of Arts. Vol. 56, no. 4, pp. 207-221.

Thorbecke, F., 1919: Im Hochland von Mittel-Kamerun, vol. III. Abhandlungen des Hamburger Kolonialinstitutes, Reihe C/7, vol. 41.

Timmermans, P., 1966: Essai de Typologie de la Sculpture des Bena Luluwa du Kasai. Africa-Tervuren, vol. 12, no. 1, pp. 17-27.

Torday, E., Joyce, T. A., 1910: Notes ethnographiques sur les peuples communément appelés Bakuba, ainsi que sur les peuplades apparentées—Les Bushongo. Annales du Musée du Congo Belge, série 3, vol. 2, fasc. 1. Bruxelles.

Torday E., 1925: On the Trail of the Bushongo. London.

Tunis, A., 1984: Neue Untersuchungen zur Berliner Beninsammlung. Wiener Ethnohistorische Blätter, no. 27, pp. 99-116.

Tunis, A., 1985: Der Crossriver in Kameron, 1904-1909—Ein Beitrag zur Juju-Frage. Baessler-Archiv, vol. 33, pp. 497-519.

Tunis, I. L., 1979: Origins, Chronology and Metallurgy of the Benin Bas-Reliefs. Thesis for the degree of Ph.D.. Univ. London, School of Oriental and African Studies. London.

Tunis, I. L., 1983: A Note on Benin Plaque Termination Dates. Tribus, vol. 32, pp. 45-53.

Tunis, I. L., 1984: Benin Art Styles. Baessler-Archiv, vol. 32, pp. 23-68.

Valentin, P., 1972: Plastiken der Kundu (Kamerun) im Basler Missionsmuseum. Ethnologische Zeitschrift Zürich, no. 2, pp. 35-51.

Valentin, P., 1977: Geschnitzte Türrahmen der Fungom (Kamerun). Tribus, vol. 26, pp. 63-69.

Valentin, P., 1979: Ekongolo, eine Maskengestalt aus dem Kameruner Waldland. Ethnologische Zeitschrift Zurich no. 1, pp. 143-148.

Valentin, P., 1982: Do the "Kundu" Figures Originate from the Balong? unpubl. MS.

Van der Heyden, M., 1977: The Epa Mask and Ceremony. African Arts, vol. 10, no. 2, pp. 14-21, 91.

Vansina, J., 1965: Introduction à l'ethnographie du Congo. Kinshasa.

Vansina, J., 1978: The Children of Woot. Madison.

Vansina, J., 1984: Art History in Africa. London/New York.

Vogel, S. M., 1973: Peoples of Wood—Baule Figure Sculpture. Art Journal, vol. 33, no. 1, pp. 23-26.

Vogel, S. M., 1980: Beauty in the Eyes of the Baule—Aesthetics and Cultural Values. Working Papers in the Traditional Arts, no.5/6. Philadelphia.

Vogel, S. M., 1981: For Spirits and Kings—African Art from the Tishman Collection. Cat. Metropolitan Museum of Art. New York.

Vogel, S., N'Diaye, F., 1985: African Masterpieces from the Musée de l'Homme. New York.

Volavkova, Z., 1972: Nkisi Figures of the Lower Congo. African Arts, vol. 5, no. 2, pp. 52-59, 84.

Volavkova, Z., 1981: Insignia of the Divine Authority. African Arts, vol. 14, no. 3, pp. 43-51, 90.

Volprecht, K., Stöhr, W., Bolz-Augenstein, J., 1967: Exotische Kunst im Rautenstrauch-Joest-Museum, Köln.

Volprecht, K., 1972: Sammlung Clausmeyer—Afrika. Ethnologica, vol. 5. Köln.

Wassing, R. S., 1968: African Art—Its Background and Traditions. New York.

Weiss, P., 1982: Kandinsky in Munich, 1896-1914. New York.

Wembah-Rashid, J. A. R., 1970: Mwananyanhiti: Kwere Fertility. Review of Ethnology, vol. 3, no. 1, pp. 1-4, Wien.

Wembah-Rashid, J. A. R., 1971: Isinyago and Midimu. Masked Dancers of Tanzania and Mozambique. African Arts vol.4, no.2.

Werner, O., 1970: Metallurgische Untersuchungen der Benin-Bronzen des Museums für Völkerkunde, Berlin. Baessler Archiv, vol. 18, pp. 71-153.

Wescott, J., 1962; The Sculpture and Myths of Eshu-Elegba. Africa, vol. 32, no. 4, pp. 336-353.
Westermann, D., 1952: Geschichte Afrikas. Köln.
Weston, J., Johnson, M., 1975: Benin Bronze Preservation. African Arts, vol. 8, no. 4, pp. 50, 51, 60, 61, 84.
Weule, K., 1908: Wissenschaftliche Ergebnisse meiner ethnographischen Forschungsreise in den Südosten Deutsch- Ostafrikas. Mitteilungen aus den Deutschen Schutzgebiten, Ergänzungsheft No. 1.
Widstrand, C. G., 1958: African Axes. Studia Ethnographica Upsaliensia, vol. 15. Uppsala.
Willett, F., 1967: Ife in the History of West African Sculpture. London.
Willett, F., Picton, J., 1967: On the Identification of Individual Carvers—A Study of Ancestor Shrine Carvings from Owo, Nigeria. Man, vol. 1, pp. 62-70.
Willett, F., 1971: African Art—An Introduction. New York.
Williams, D., 1974: Icon and Image—A Study of Sacred and Secular Forms of African Classical Art. London.
Wingert, P. S., 1954: Anatomical Interpretations in African Masks. Man, vol. 54, pp. 69-71.
Wissmann, H. v., et al., 1891: Im Innern Afrikas. Berlin.
Witte, H., 1984: Ifa and Esu—Iconography of Order and Disorder. Soest.
Wittkower, R., 1938/9: Eagle and Serpent. A Study of Migration of Symbols. Journal of the Warburg Institute, vol. 2, pp. 293-325.
Wittmer, M. K., 1973: Images of Authority from Benin to Gabon. Miami.
Wittmer, M. K., Arnett, W., 1978: Three Rivers of Nigeria. Atlanta.
Wolf, S., 1963: Vogelgestaltiges Benin-Zeremonialgerät aus Elfenbein. Abhandlungen und Berichte des Staatl. Museums für Völkerkunde Dresden, vol. 22, pp. 135-141.
Wolf, S., 1968: Neue Analysen von Benin-Legierungen in vergleichender Betrachtung. Abhandlungen und Berichte des Staatl. Museums für Völkerkunde Dresden, vol. 28, pp. 91-161.
Wolf, S., 1970: Zum Problem der Frauendarstellungen in der Benin Kunst. Abhandlungen und Berichte des Staatl. Museums für Völkerkunde Dresden, vol. 31, pp. 197-235.
Wolf, S., 1972: Benin. Europäerdarstellungen der Hofkunst eines afrikanischen Reiches. Die Schatzkammer, vol. 28. Leipzig.
Zahan, D., 1950: L'habitation Mossi. Bulletin de l'Institut Français d'Afrique Noire, no. 12, pp. 223-229.
Zahan, D., 1960: Sociétés d'Initiation Bambara—Le Ndomo, le Koré. Paris.
Zahan, D., 1974: The Bambara. Iconography of Religions, vol. 7, no.2. Leiden.
Zahan, D., 1980: Antilopes du Soleil. Wien.
Zenker, G., 1895: Yaunde. Mitteilungen aus den deutschen Schutzgebieten, vol. 8, pp. 36-70.
Zwernemann, J., 1961: Spiegel-und Nagelplastiken vom unteren Kongo im Linden-Museum, Tribus vol. 10, pp. 14-32.
Zwernemann, J., 1978: Masken der Bobo-Ule und Nuna im Hamburgischen Museum für Völkerkunde. Mitteilungen aus dem Museum für Völkerkunde Hamburg, vol. 8, pp. 45-84.
Zwernemann, J., Lohse, W., 1985: Aus Afrika. Ahnen-Geister-Göller-Hamburg.